Heaven
and
Hell

Heaven
and Its Wonders
and Hell

From Things Heard and Seen

EMANUEL SWEDENBORG

Translated from the Original Latin by
John C. Ager

STANDARD EDITION

SWEDENBORG FOUNDATION
West Chester, Pennsylvania

First published in Latin, London, 1758
First English translation, London, 1778
First translation published in the United States, 1812
First edition translated by J. C. Ager, 1900
Second Ager edition, 1995
Printed in the United States of America

Library of Congress Cataloging-in-Publication Data

Swedenborg, Emanuel, 1688–1772.
    [De coelo et ejus mirabilibus et de inferno, ex auditis et visis. English]
    Heaven and its wonders and hell : from things heard and seen /
  by Emanuel Swedenborg ; translated from the original Latin by
  John C. Ager. — Standard edition
      p.   cm.
    Includes index.

    ISBN 0-87785-273-1 (casebound)
    ISBN 0-87785-276-6 (paper)
    ISBN 0-87785-282-0 (boxed set with *Divine Love and Wisdom*
      and *Divine Providence*)

    1. Heaven—Christianity. 2. Hell—Christianity. 3. Future life—
Christianity—Early work to 1800. I. Title. II. Title: Heaven and hell.
BX8712.H5 1995
  236'.24—dc20   95—22213
                                                CIP

Typeset in Garamond by William Ross Woofenden
Designed by Joanna V. Hill
Printed and bound by BookCrafters, Inc.

For information contact:
  Swedenborg Foundation
  320 North Church Street
  West Chester, PA 19380

Contents

Editor's Preface   ix

Author's Preface   1

Part I: Heaven

1. The God of Heaven Is the Lord   7
2. It Is the Divine of the Lord That Makes Heaven   11
3. In Heaven the Divine of the Lord Is Love to Him and Charity toward the Neighbor   15
4. Heaven Is Divided into Two Kingdoms   21
5. There Are Three Heavens   26
6. The Heavens Consist of Innumerable Societies   33
7. Each Society Is a Heaven in a Smaller Form, and Each Angel in the Smallest Form   38
8. All Heaven in the Aggregate Reflects a Single Man   44
9. Each Society in Heaven Reflects a Single Man   49
10. Therefore Every Angel Is in a Complete Human Form   52
11. It Is from the Lord's Divine Human That Heaven as a Whole and in Part Reflects Man   57
    Extracts from *Arcana Coelestia* relating to the Lord and His Divine Human   62

12. There Is a Correspondence of All Things
of Heaven with All Things of Man 68

13. There Is a Correspondence of Heaven with
All Things of the Earth 76

14. The Sun in Heaven 86

15. Light and Heat in Heaven 93

16. The Four Quarters in Heaven 105

17. Changes of State of the Angels in Heaven 113

18. Time in Heaven 118

19. Representatives and Appearances in Heaven 122

20. The Garments with Which Angels
Appear Clothed 126

21. The Places of Abode and Dwellings
of Angels 130

22. Space in Heaven 135

23. The Form of Heaven That Determines
Affiliations and Communications There 140

24. Governments in Heaven 149

25. Divine Worship in Heaven 154

26. The Power of the Angels of Heaven 158

27. The Speech of Angels 163

28. The Speech of Angels with Man 171

29. Writings in Heaven 180

30. The Wisdom of the Angels of Heaven 185

31. The State of Innocence of Angels in Heaven 197

32. The State of Peace in Heaven 205

33. The Conjunction of Heaven with the
Human Race 211

34. Conjunction of Heaven with Man
by Means of the Word 220

35. Heaven and Hell Are from the
Human Race 229

36. The Heathen, or Peoples outside of
    the Church, in Heaven   236
37. Little Children in Heaven   246
38. The Wise and the Simple in Heaven   257
    Extracts from *Arcana Coelestia*
    respecting Knowledges   269
39. The Rich and the Poor in Heaven   273
40. Marriages in Heaven   284
41. The Occupations of Angels in Heaven   300
42. Heavenly Joy and Happiness   306
43. The Immensity of Heaven   321

Part II: The World of Spirits
and Man's State after Death

44. What the World of Spirits Is   329
45. In Respect to His Interiors Every Man
    Is a Spirit   335
46. The Resuscitation of Man from the Dead
    and His Entrance into Eternal Life   341
47. Man after Death Is in a Complete
    Human Form   346
48. After Death Man Is Possessed of Every
    Sense, and of All the Memory, Thought,
    and Affection That He Had in the World,
    Leaving Nothing Behind except His
    Earthly Body   354
49. Man after Death Is Such as His Life
    Had Been in the World   368
50. The Delights of Everyone's Life
    Are Changed after Death into Things
    That Correspond   384
51. The First State of Man after Death   393

52. The Second State of Man after Death 398

53. The Third State of Man after Death,
Which Is a State of Instruction for
Those Who Enter Heaven 409

54. No One Enters Heaven by Mercy
apart from Means 418

55. It Is Not So Difficult to Live the Life
That Leads to Heaven as Is Believed 425

Part III: Hell

56. The Lord Rules the Hells 439

57. The Lord Casts No One into Hell;
This Is Done by the Spirit 444

58. All Who Are in Hell Are in Evils
and Related Falsities Derived from
the Loves of Self and the World 449

59. What Hell Fire Is and What the
Gnashing of Teeth Is 462

60. The Malice and Heinous Artifices
of Infernal Spirits 471

61. The Appearance, Situation, and
Number of the Hells 476

62. The Equilibrium between Heaven
and Hell 483

63. By Means of the Equilibrium between
Heaven and Hell Man Is in Freedom 490
Extracts from *Arcana Coelestia* Respecting
the Freedom of Man, Influx, and the Spirits
through Whom Communications Are Effected 495

Index of Scripture References 499
Index 503

Editor's Preface

First published in London in 1758, *Heaven and Hell* has become Emanuel Swedenborg's most popular work. In sixty-six brief chapters, this book contains descriptions of some of Swedenborg's most startling spiritual revelations. These include actual descriptions of life after death, a delcaration that the final judgment foretold in the Bible did not predict the destruction of this earth (but that it had already taken place in the spiritual world), accounts involving married partners in heaven, and details about the work and character of angels.

There have been at least nineteen distinct translations or revised translations of this work in English since the first English translation by Thomas Hartley in 1778. There have also been editions in German, Spanish, French, Japanese, Arabic, and Russian, to mention a few. The present translation, by John C. Ager, was first published by the Swedenborg Foundation in both an English version and a Latin-English edition in 1900.

The text of this current edition was electronically scanned from the Foundation's Standard Edition of Swedenborg's theological works. This process has allowed the book to be completely reset in a more readable typeface. Certain stylistic elements have also been modernized and the spelling updated to reflect contemporary usage. In a few cases, English words that have changed meaning significantly since the turn of the century have been replaced by words that more accurately reflect Swedenborg's Latin. A case in point is the word "intercourse," which appeared nine times in the earlier edition to translate several Latin words with a range of meanings. But this word is seldom used today in its earlier general meaning, and words such as "association, "discussion," etc., have been substituted. Arabic numbers have replaced roman numerals, and several of the running heads have been reworded to reflect more clearly the subject matter of the chapters. On the whole, however, the Ager translation has not been materially altered.

This is the only major published work of Swedenborg in which the author inserted copious references from an earlier publication (his *Arcana Coelestia*), both in the form of footnotes and also as grouped excerpts. As these extracts are an integral part of the work, they have been retained in this edition. (The popular paperback editions of this work have generally omitted both the author's footnotes and the three sections of grouped extracts from *Arcana Coelestia,* which appear on pages 62–67, 269–272, and 495–498 in this edition.)

As was the custom in his day, Swedenborg referred to the Psalms as the book of David. As with previous printings, the bold numerals in brackets, ([2], [3], etc.) indicate divisions of Swedenborg's long numbered sections, made for the convenience of the reader by John Faulkner Potts in his six-volume *Swedenborg Concordance* (London: Swedenborg Society, 1888–1902).

William Ross Woofenden
Sharon, Massachusetts

Heaven

and

Hell

Author's Preface

1. The Lord, speaking in the presence of his disciples of the consummation of the age, which is the final period of the church,[1] says, near the end of what he foretells about its successive states in respect to love and faith:[2]

> Immediately after the tribulation of those days the sun shall be darkened, and the moon shall not give her light, and the stars shall fall from heaven, and the powers of the heavens shall be shaken. And then shall appear the sign of the Son of man in heaven; and then shall all the tribes of the earth mourn; and they shall see the Son of man coming in the clouds of heaven with power and great glory. And he shall send forth his angels with a trumpet and a great sound; and they shall gather together his elect from the four winds, from the end to end of the heavens (Matt. 24:29–31).

Those who understand these words according to the sense of the letter have no other belief than that during that latest period, which is called the final judgment, all these things are to come to pass just as they are described in the literal sense, that is, that the sun and moon will be darkened and the stars will fall from the sky, that the sign of the Lord will appear in the sky, and he himself will be seen in the clouds, attended by angels with trumpets; and furthermore, as is foretold elsewhere, that the whole visible universe will be destroyed, and afterwards a new heaven with a new earth will come into being. Such is

---

1. [References in this edition, unless otherwise noted, are to Emanuel Swedenborg's *Arcana Coelestia* and were made by Swedenborg.] The consummation of the age is the final period of the church (n. 4535, 10622).

2. The Lord's predictions in Matthew (24 and 25), respecting the consummation of the age and His coming, and the consequent successive vastation of the church and the final judgment, are explained in the prefaces to chapters 26–40 of Genesis (n. 3353–3356, 3486–3489, 3650–3655, 3751–3757, 3897–3901, 4056–4060, 4229–4231, 4332–4335, 4422–4424, 4635–4638, 4661–4664, 4807–4810, 4954–4959, 5063–5071).

the opinion of most men in the church at the present day. But those who so believe are ignorant of the arcana that lie hidden in every particular of the Word. For in every particular of the Word there is an internal sense which treats of things spiritual and heavenly, not of things natural and worldly, such as are treated of in the sense of the letter. And this is true not only of the meaning of groups of words, it is true of each particular word.[3] For the Word is written solely by correspondences,[4] to the end that there may be an internal sense in every least particular of it. What that sense is can be seen from all that has been said and shown about it in *Arcana Coelestia* [published 1749–1756]; also from quotations gathered from that work in the explanation of the *White Horse* [*of the Apocalypse,* published 1758] spoken of in Revelation.

It is according to that sense that what the Lord says in the passage quoted above respecting his coming in the clouds of heaven is to be understood. The "sun" there that is to be darkened signifies the Lord in respect to love;[5] the "moon" the Lord in respect to faith;[6] "stars" knowledges of good and truth, or of love and faith;[7] "the sign of the Son of man in heaven" the manifestation of Divine truth; "the tribes of the earth" that shall mourn, all things relating to truth and good or to faith and love;[8] "the coming of the Lord in the clouds of heaven with power and

3. Both in the wholes and particulars of the Word there is an internal or spiritual sense (n. 1143, 1984, 2135, 2333, 2395, 2495, 4442, 9048, 9063, 9086).

4. The Word is written solely by correspondences, and for this reason each thing and all things in it have a spiritual meaning (n. 1404, 1408, 1409, 1540, 1619, 1659, 1709, 1783, 2900, 9086).

5. In the Word the "sun" signifies the Lord in respect to love, and in consequence love to the Lord (n. 1529, 1837, 2441, 2495, 4060, 4696, 7083, 10809).

6. In the Word the "moon" signifies the Lord in respect to faith, and in consequence faith in the Lord (n. 1529, 1530, 2495, 4060, 4696, 7083).

7. In the Word "stars" signify knowledges of good and truth (n. 2495, 2849, 4697).

8. "Tribes" signify all truths and goods in the complex, thus all things of faith and love (n. 3858, 3926, 4060, 6335).

glory" his presence in the Word, and revelation,[9] "clouds" signifying the sense of the letter of the Word,[10] and "glory" the internal sense of the Word;[11] "the angels with a trumpet and great voice" signify heaven as a source of Divine truth.[12] All this makes clear that these words of the Lord mean that at the end of the church, when there is no longer any love, and consequently no faith, the Lord will open the internal meaning of the Word and reveal arcana of heaven. The arcana revealed in the following pages relate to heaven and hell, and also to the life of man after death. The man of the church at this date knows scarcely anything about heaven and hell or about his life after death, although all these matters are set forth and described in the Word; and yet many of those born within the church refuse to believe in them, saying in their hearts, "Who has come from that world and told us?" Lest, therefore, such a spirit of denial, which especially prevails with those who have much worldly wisdom, should also infect and corrupt the simple in heart and the simple in faith, it has been granted me to associate with angels and to talk with them as man with man, also to see what is in the heavens and what is in the hells, and this for thirteen years; so now from what I have seen and heard it has been granted me to describe these, in the hope that ignorance may thus be enlightened and unbelief dissipated. Such immediate revelation is granted at this day because this is what is meant by the coming of the Lord.

9. The coming of the Lord signifies His presence in the Word, and revelation (n. 3900, 4060).

10. In the Word "clouds" signify the Word in the letter or the sense of its letter (n. 4060, 4391, 5922, 6343, 6752, 8106, 8781, 9430, 10551, 10574).

11. In the Word "glory" signifies Divine truth as it is in heaven and as it is in the internal sense of the Word (n. 4809, 5922, 8267, 8427, 9429, 10574).

12. A "trumpet" or "horn" signifies Divine truth in heaven, and revealed from heaven (n. 8158, 8823, 8915); and "voice" has a like signification (n. 6771, 9926).

Part 1

Heaven

1

The God of Heaven
Is the Lord

2. First of all it must be known who the God of heaven is, since upon that all the other things depend. Throughout all heaven no other than the Lord alone is acknowledged as the God of heaven. There it is said, as he himself taught,

> That he is one with the Father; that the Father is in him, and he in the Father; that he who sees him sees the Father; and that everything that is holy goes forth from him (John 10:30, 38; 14:9–11; 16:13–15).

I have often talked with angels on this subject, and they have invariably declared that in heaven they are unable to divide the Divine into three, because they know and perceive that the Divine is One and this One is in the Lord. They also said that those of the church who come from this world having an idea of three Divine beings cannot be admitted into heaven, since their thought wanders from one Divine being to another; and it is not allowable there to think three and say one,[1] because in heaven everyone speaks from his thought, since speech there is the immediate product of the thought, or the thought speaking. Consequently, those in this world who have divided the Divine into three, and have adopted a different idea of each, and have not made that idea one and centered it in the Lord, cannot be received into heaven, because in heaven there is a sharing of all

---

1. Christians were examined in the other life in regard to their idea of the one God and it was found that they held the idea of three Gods (n. 2329, 5256, 10736, 10738, 10821). A Divine trinity in the Lord is acknowledged in heaven (n. 14, 15, 1729, 2005, 5256, 9303).

thoughts, and therefore if anyone came thinking three and saying one, he would be at once found out and rejected. But let it be known that all those who have not separated what is true from what is good, or faith from love, accept in the other life, when they have been taught, the heavenly idea of the Lord, that he is the God of the universe. It is otherwise with those who have separated faith from life, that is, who have not lived according to the precepts of true faith.

3. Those within the church who have denied the Lord and have acknowledged the Father only, and have confirmed themselves in that belief, are not in heaven; and as they are unable to receive any influx from heaven, where the Lord alone is worshiped, they gradually lose the ability to think what is true about any subject whatever; and finally they become as if dumb, or they talk stupidly, and ramble about with their arms dangling and swinging as if weak in the joints. Again, those who, like the Socinians, have denied the Divinity of the Lord and have acknowledged his humanity only, are likewise outside of heaven; they are brought forward a little toward the right and are let down into the deep, and are thus wholly separated from the rest that come from the Christian world. Finally, those who profess to believe in an invisible Divine, which they call the soul of the universe *[ens universi]*, from which all things originated, and who reject all belief in the Lord, find out that they believe in no God; since this invisible Divine is to them a property of nature in her first principles, which cannot be an object of faith and love, because it is not an object of thought.[2] Such have their lot among those called nature worshipers. It is otherwise with those born outside the church, who are called the heathen; these will be treated of hereafter.

4. Infants, who form a third part of heaven, are all initiated into the acknowledgment and belief that the Lord is their

2. A Divine that cannot be perceived by any idea cannot be received by faith (n. 4733, 5110, 5663, 6982, 6996, 7004, 7211, 9356, 9359, 9972, 10067, 10267).

Father, and afterwards that he is the Lord of all, thus the God of heaven and earth. That children grow up in heaven and are perfected by means of knowledges, even to angelic intelligence and wisdom, will be seen in the following pages.

5. Those who are of the church cannot doubt that the Lord is the God of heaven, for he himself taught,

That all things of the Father are his (Matt. 11:27; John 16:15; 17:2).

And that he hath all power in heaven and on earth (Matt. 28:18).

He says "in heaven and on earth," because he that rules heaven rules the earth also, for the one depends upon the other.[3] "Ruling heaven and earth" means to receive from the Lord every good pertaining to love and every truth pertaining to faith, thus all intelligence and wisdom, and in consequence all happiness, in a word, eternal life. This also the Lord taught when he said:

He that believeth on the Son hath eternal life; but he that believeth not the Son shall not see life (John 3:36).

I am the resurrection and the life; he that believeth on Me, though he die yet shall he live; and whosoever liveth and believeth on Me shall never die (John 11:25, 26).

I am the way, the truth, and the life (John 14:6).

6. There were certain spirits who while living in the world had professed to believe in the Father; but of the Lord they had the same idea as of any other man, and therefore did not believe him to be the God of heaven. For this reason they were permitted to wander about and inquire wherever they wished whether there were any other heaven than the heaven of the Lord. They searched for several days, but nowhere found any. These were such as place the happiness of heaven in glory and dominion;

---

3. The entire heaven is the Lord's (n. 2751, 7086). He has all power in the heavens and on the earths (n. 1607, 10089, 10827). As the Lord rules heaven He rules also all things that depend thereon, thus all things in the world (n. 2026, 2027, 4523, 4524). The Lord alone has power to remove the hells, to withhold from evil and hold in good, and thus to save (n. 10019).

and as they were unable to get what they desired, and were told that heaven does not consist in such things, they became indignant, and wished for a heaven where they could lord it over others and be eminent in glory like that in the world.

2

It Is the Divine of the Lord
That Makes Heaven

7. The angels taken collectively are called heaven, for they constitute heaven; and yet that which makes heaven in general and in particular is the Divine that goes forth from the Lord and flows into the angels and is received by them. And as the Divine that goes forth from the Lord is the good of love and the truth of faith, the angels are angels and are heaven in the measure in which they receive good and truth from the Lord.

8. Everyone in the heavens knows and believes and even perceives that he wills and does nothing of good from himself, and that he thinks and believes nothing of truth from himself, but only from the Divine, thus from the Lord; also that good from himself is not good, and truth from himself is not truth, because these have in them no life from the Divine. Moreover, the angels of the inmost heaven clearly perceive and feel the influx, and the more of it they receive the more they seem to themselves to be in heaven, because the more are they in love and faith and in the light of intelligence and wisdom, and in heavenly joy therefrom; and since all these go forth from the Divine of the Lord, and in these the angels have their heaven, it is clear that it is the Divine of the Lord, and not the angels from anything properly their own that makes heaven.[1] This is

---

1. The angels of heaven acknowledge all good to be from the Lord, and nothing from themselves, and the Lord dwells in them in His own and not in their own (n. 9338, 10125, 10151, 10157). Therefore in the Word by "angels" something of the Lord is meant (n. 1925, 2821, 3039, 4085, 8192, 10528).

why heaven is called in the Word the "dwelling place" of the Lord and "his throne," and those who are there are said to be in the Lord.[2] But in what manner the Divine goes forth from the Lord and fills heaven will be told in what follows.

9. Angels from their wisdom go still further. They say that not only everything good and true is from the Lord, but everything of life as well. They confirm it by this, that nothing can spring from itself, but only from something prior to itself; therefore all things spring from a first, which they call the very being [esse] of the life of all things. And in like manner all things continue to exist, for continuous existence is a ceaseless springing forth, and whatever is not continually held by means of intermediates in connection with the first instantly disperses and is wholly dissipated. They say also that there is but one fountain of life, and that man's life is a rivulet therefrom, which if it did not unceasingly continue from its fountain would immediately flow away.

[2] Again, they say that from this one fountain of life, which is the Lord, nothing goes forth except Divine good and Divine truth, and that each one is affected by these in accordance with his reception of them—those who receive them in faith and life find heaven in them while those who reject them or stifle them change them into hell; for they change good into evil and truth into falsity, thus life into death. Again, that everything of life is from the Lord they confirm by this: that all things in the universe have relation to good and truth—the life of man's will, which is the life of his love, to good, and the life of his under-

---

Furthermore, angels are called "gods" from the reception of the Divine from the Lord (n. 4295, 4402, 7268, 7873, 8192, 8301).

Again, all good that is good, and all truth that is truth, consequently all peace, love, charity, and faith, are from the Lord (n. 1614, 2016, 2751, 2882, 2883, 2891, 2892, 2904).

Also all wisdom and intelligence (n. 109, 112, 121, 124).

2. Those who are in heaven are said to be in the Lord (n. 3637, 3638).

standing, which is the life of his faith, to truth; and since everything good and true comes from above it follows that everything of life must come from above.

[3] This being the belief of the angels they refuse all thanks for the good they do, and are displeased and withdraw if anyone attributes good to them. They wonder how anyone can believe that he is wise from himself or does anything good from himself. Doing good for one's own sake they do not call good, because it is done from self. But doing good for the sake of good they call good from the Divine; and this they say is the good that makes heaven, because this good is the Lord.[3]

10. Such spirits as have confirmed themselves during their life in the world in the belief that the good they do and the truth they believe is from themselves, or is appropriated to them as their own (which is the belief of all who place merit in good actions and claim righteousness to themselves) are not received into heaven. Angels avoid them. They look upon them as stupid and as thieves; as stupid because they continually have themselves in view and not the Divine; and as thieves because they steal from the Lord what is his. These are averse to the belief of heaven, that it is the Divine of the Lord in the angels that makes heaven.

11. The Lord teaches that those that are in heaven and in the church are in the Lord and the Lord is in them, when he says:

> Abide in Me and I in you. As the branch cannot bear fruit of itself except it abide in the vine, so neither can ye, except ye abide in Me. I am the Vine, ye are the branches. He that abideth in Me and I in him, the same beareth much fruit; for apart from Me ye can do nothing (John 15:4, 5).

12. From all this it can now be seen that the Lord dwells in the angels of heaven in what is his own, and thus that the Lord

---

3. Good from the Lord has the Lord inwardly in it, but good from one's own has not (n. 1802, 3951, 8480).

is the all in all things of heaven; and this for the reason that good from the Lord is the Lord in angels, for what is from the Lord is the Lord; consequently heaven to the angels is good from the Lord, and not anything of their own.

3

In Heaven the Divine
of the Lord Is Love to Him
and Charity toward the Neighbor

13. The Divine that goes forth from the Lord is called in heaven Divine truth, for a reason that will presently appear. This Divine truth flows into heaven from the Lord from his Divine love. The Divine love and the Divine truth therefrom are related to each other as the fire of the sun and the light therefrom in the world, love resembling the fire of the sun and truth therefrom light from the sun. Moreover, by correspondence fire signifies love, and light truth going forth from love.[1] From this it is clear what the Divine truth that goes forth from the Lord's Divine love is—that in its essence it is Divine good joined to Divine truth, and being so conjoined it vivifies all things of heaven; just as in the world when the sun's heat is joined to light it makes all things of the earth fruitful, which takes place in spring and summer. It is otherwise when the heat is not joined with the light, that is, when the light is cold; then all things become torpid and lie dead. With the angels this Divine good, which is compared to heat, is the good of love; and Divine truth, which is compared to light, is that through which and out of which good of love comes.

---

1. In the Word "fire" signifies heavenly love and infernal love (n. 934, 4906, 5215).

"Holy and heavenly fire" signifies Divine love, and every affection that belongs to that love (n. 934, 6314, 6832).

"Light" from fire signifies truth going forth from good of love; and light in heaven signifies Divine truth (n. 3195, 3485, 3636, 3643, 3993, 4302, 4413, 4415, 9548, 9684).

14. The Divine in heaven which makes heaven is love, because love is spiritual conjunction. It conjoins angels to the Lord and conjoins them to one another, so conjoining them that in the Lord's sight they are all as one. Moreover, love is the very being *[esse]* of everyone's life; consequently from love both angels and men have life. Everyone who reflects can know that the inmost vitality of man is from love, since he grows warm from the presence of love and cold from its absence, and when deprived of it he dies.[2] But it is to be remembered that the quality of his love is what determines the quality of each one's life.

15. In heaven there are two distinct loves, love to the Lord and love toward the neighbor, in the inmost or third heaven love to the Lord, in the second or middle heaven love toward the neighbor. They both go forth from the Lord, and they both make heaven. How these two loves are distinct and how they are conjoined is seen in heaven in clear light, but in the world only obscurely. In heaven loving the Lord does not mean loving him in respect to his person, but it means loving the good that is from him; and to love good is to will and do good from love; and to love the neighbor does not mean loving a companion in respect to his person, but loving the truth that is from the Word; and to love truth is to will and do it. This makes clear that these two loves are distinct as good and truth are distinct, and that they are conjoined as good is conjoined with truth.[3] But this can scarcely be comprehended by men unless it is known what love is, what good is, and what the neighbor is.[4]

2. Love is the fire of life, and life itself is actually therefrom (n. 4906, 5071, 6032, 6314).

3. To love the Lord and the neighbor is to live according to the Lord's commandments (n. 10143, 10153, 10310, 10578, 10648).

4. To love the neighbor is not to love the person, but to love that in him from which he is what he is, that is, his truth and good (n. 5028, 10336).

Those who love the person, and not that in him from which he is what he is, love evil and good alike (n. 3820).

16. I have repeatedly talked with angels about this matter. They were astonished, they said, that men of the church do not know that to love the Lord and to love the neighbor is to love what is good and true, and to do this from the will, when they ought to know that one evinces love by willing and doing what another wishes, and it is this that brings reciprocal love and conjunction, and not loving another without doing what he wishes, which in itself is not loving; also that men should know that the good that goes forth from the Lord is a likeness of him, since he is in it; and that those who make good and truth to belong to their life by willing them and doing them become likenesses of the Lord and are conjoined to him. Willing is loving to do. That this is so the Lord teaches in the Word, saying,

He that hath My commandments and doeth them, he it is that loveth Me; and I will love him and will make My abode with him (John 14:21, 23).

If ye do My commandments ye shall abide in My love (John 15:10, 12).

17. All experience in heaven attests that the Divine that goes forth from the Lord and that affects angels and makes heaven is love; for all who are in heaven are forms of love and charity, and appear in ineffable beauty, with love shining forth from their faces, and from their speech and from every particular of their life.[5] Moreover, there are spiritual spheres of life emanating from and surrounding every angel and every spirit, by which their quality in respect to the affections of their love is known, sometimes at a great distance. For with everyone these spheres flow forth from the life of his affection and consequent thought,

---

Charity is willing truths and being affected by truths for the sake of truths (n. 3876, 3877). Charity toward the neighbor is doing what is good, just, and right, in every work and in every function (n. 8120–8122).

5. Angels are forms of love and charity (n. 3804, 4735, 4797, 4985, 5199, 5530, 9879, 10177).

or from the life of his love and consequent faith. The spheres that go forth from angels are so full of love as to affect the inmosts of life of those who are with them. They have repeatedly been perceived by me and have thus affected me.[6] That it is love from which angels have their life is further evident from the fact that in the other life everyone turns himself in accordance with his love—those who are in love to the Lord and in love toward the neighbor turning themselves always to the Lord, while those who are in love of self turn themselves always away from the Lord. This is so, however their bodies may turn, since with those in the other life spaces conform to the states of their interiors, likewise quarters, which are not constant as they are in this world, but are determined in accordance with the direction of their faces. And yet it is not the angels that turn themselves to the Lord; but the Lord turns to himself those that love to do the things that are from him.[7] But more on this subject hereafter, where the quarters in the other life are treated of.

18. The Divine of the Lord in heaven is love, for the reason that love is receptive of all things of heaven, such as peace, intelligence, wisdom and happiness. For love is receptive of each and all things that are in harmony with it; it longs for them, seeks them, and drinks them in as it were spontaneously, for it desires unceasingly to be enriched and perfected by them.[8] This, too, man well knows, for with him love searches as it were the stores

6. A spiritual sphere, which is a sphere of the life, overflows and pours forth from every man, spirit, and angel, and encompasses them (n. 4464, 5179, 7454, 8630).

It flows from the life of their affection and consequent thought (n. 2489, 4464, 6206).

7. Spirits and angels turn themselves constantly to their loves, and those in the heavens turn themselves constantly to the Lord (n. 10130, 10189, 10420, 10702). Quarters in the other life are to each one in accordance with the direction of his face, and are thereby determined, otherwise than in the world (n. 10130, 10189, 10420, 10702).

8. Innumerable things are contained in love, and love gathers to itself all things that are in harmony with it (n. 2500, 2572, 3078, 3189, 6323, 7490, 7750).

of his memory and draws forth all things that are in accord with itself, collecting and arranging them in and under itself—in itself that they may be its own, and under itself that they may be its servants; but other things not in accord with it, it discards and expels.

That there is present in love every capacity for receiving truths in harmony with itself, and a longing to conjoin them to itself, has been made clear also by the fact that some who were simple-minded in the world were taken up into heaven, and yet when they were with the angels they came into angelic wisdom and heavenly blessedness, and for the reason that they had loved what is good and true for its own sake, and had implanted it in their life, and had thereby become capacities for receiving heaven with all that is ineffable there. But those who are in love of self and of the world have no capacity for receiving what is good and true; they loathe and reject it, and at its first touch and entrance they flee and associate themselves with those in hell who are in loves like their own.

There were spirits who had doubts about there being such capacities in heavenly love, and who wished to know whether it were true; whereupon they were let into a state of heavenly love, whatever opposed being for the time removed, and were brought forward some distance, where there was an angelic heaven, and from it they talked with me, saying that they perceived a more interior happiness than they could possibly express in words, and they lamented greatly that they must return into their former state. Others also were taken up into heaven; and the higher or more interiorly they were exalted the more of intelligence and wisdom were they admitted into, such as enabled them to perceive what had before been incomprehensible to them. From this it is clear that the love that goes forth from the Lord is receptive of heaven and all things therein.

19. That love to the Lord and love toward the neighbor include in themselves all Divine truths is made evident by what the Lord himself said of these two loves:

> Thou shalt love thy God with all thy heart and with all thy soul. This is the greatest and first commandment. And the second, like unto it, is, Thou shalt love thy neighbor as thyself. On these two commandments hang the law and the prophets (Matt. 22:37–40).

"The law and the prophets" are the whole Word, thus all Divine truth.

4

Heaven Is Divided
into Two Kingdoms

20. As there are infinite varieties in heaven, and no one society nor any one angel is exactly like any other,[1] there are in heaven general, specific, and particular divisions. The general division is into two kingdoms, the specific into three heavens, and the particular into innumerable societies. Each of these will be treated of in what follows. The general division is said to be into kingdoms, because heaven is called "the kingdom of God."

21. There are angels that receive more interiorly the Divine that goes forth from the Lord, and others that receive it less interiorly; the former are called celestial angels, and the latter spiritual angels. Because of this difference heaven is divided into two kingdoms, one called the celestial kingdom, the other the spiritual kingdom.[2]

22. As the angels that constitute the celestial kingdom receive the Divine of the Lord more interiorly they are called interior

---

1. There is infinite variety, and nowhere anything the same as another (n. 7236, 9002).
Also in the heavens there is infinite variety (n. 684, 690, 3744, 5598, 7236).
Varieties in heaven are varieties of good (n. 3744, 4005, 7236, 7833, 7836, 9002).
All societies in the heavens, and all angels in a society, are thereby distinguished from each other (n. 690, 3241, 3519, 3804, 3986, 4067, 4149, 4263, 7236, 7833, 7836).
Nevertheless they are all made one by love from the Lord (n. 457, 3986).
2. Heaven as a whole is divided into two kingdoms, a celestial kingdom and a spiritual kingdom (n. 3887, 4138).
The angels of the celestial kingdom receive the Divine of the Lord in their voluntary part, thus more interiorly than the spiritual angels, who receive it in their intellectual part (n. 5113, 6367, 8521, 9936, 9995, 10124).

and also higher angels; and for the same reason the heavens that they constitute are called interior and higher heavens.[3] They are called higher and lower, because these terms designate what is interior and what is exterior.[4]

23. The love in which those are who are in the celestial kingdom is called celestial love, and the love in which those are who are in the spiritual kingdom is called spiritual love. Celestial love is love to the Lord, and spiritual love is love toward the neighbor. And as all good pertains to love (for good to anyone is what he loves) the good also of the one kingdom is called celestial, and the good of the other spiritual. Evidently, then, the two kingdoms are distinguished from each other in the same way as good of love to the Lord is distinguished from good of love toward the neighbor.[5] And as the good of love to the Lord is an interior good, and that love is interior love, so the celestial angels are interior angels, and are called higher angels.

24. The celestial kingdom is called also the Lord's priestly kingdom, and in the Word "his dwelling place"; while the spiritual kingdom is called his royal kingdom, and in the Word "his throne." And from the celestial Divine the Lord in the world was called "Jesus," while from the spiritual Divine he was called "Christ."

25. The angels in the Lord's celestial kingdom, from their more interior reception of the Divine of the Lord, far excel in wisdom and glory the angels that are in his spiritual kingdom; for they are in love to the Lord, and consequently are nearer

3. The heavens that constitute the celestial kingdom are called higher while those that constitute the spiritual kingdom are called lower (n. 10068).

4. Interior things are portrayed by higher things, and higher things signify interior things (n. 2148, 3084, 4599, 5146, 8325).

5. The good of the celestial kingdom is good of love to the Lord, and the good of the spiritual kingdom is good of charity toward the neighbor (n. 3691, 6435, 9468, 9680, 9683, 9780).

and more closely conjoined to him.[6] These angels are such because they have received and continue to receive Divine truths at once in their life, and not first in memory and thought, as the spiritual angels do. Consequently they have Divine truths written in their hearts, and they perceive them, and as it were see them in themselves; nor do they ever reason about them whether they are true or not.[7] They are such as are described in Jeremiah:

> I will put my law in their mind, and will write it in their heart. They shall teach no more everyone his friend and everyone his brother, saying, Know ye Jehovah. They shall know Me, from the least of them even to the greatest of them (Jer. 31:33, 34).

And they are called in Isaiah:

> Taught of Jehovah (Isa. 54:13).

That the "taught of Jehovah" are those who are taught by the Lord he himself teaches in John 6:45, 46.

26. It has been said that these angels have wisdom and glory above others for the reason that they have received and continue to receive Divine truths at once in their life. For as soon as they hear Divine truths, they will and do them, instead of storing them up in the memory and afterwards considering whether they are true. They know at once by influx from the Lord whether the truth they hear is true; for the Lord flows directly into man's willing, but mediately through his willing into his thinking. Or what is the same, the Lord flows directly

---

6. The celestial angels immeasurably surpass in wisdom the spiritual angels (n. 2718, 9995).

The nature of the distinction between celestial angels and spiritual angels (n. 2088, 2669, 2708, 2715, 3235, 3240, 4788, 7068, 8521, 9277, 10295).

7. The celestial angels do not reason about truths of faith, because they perceive them in themselves; but the spiritual angels reason about them whether they are true or not (n. 202, 337, 597, 607, 784, 1121, 1384, 1898, 1919, 3246, 4448, 7680, 7877, 8780, 9277, 10786).

into good, but mediately through good into truth.[8] That is called good which belongs to the will and action therefrom, while that is called truth that belongs to the memory and to the thought therefrom. Moreover, every truth is turned into good and implanted in love as soon as it enters into the will; but so long as truth remains in the memory and in the thought therefrom it does not become good, nor does it live, nor is it appropriated to man, since man is a man from his will and understanding therefrom, and not from his understanding separated from his will.[9]

27. Because of this difference between the angels of the celestial kingdom and the angels of the spiritual kingdom they are not together, and have no association with each other. They are able to communicate only through intermediate angelic societies, which are called celestial-spiritual. Through these the celestial kingdom flows into the spiritual;[10] and from this it

8. The Lord's influx is into good and through good into truth, and not the reverse; thus into the will and through that into the understanding, and not the reverse (n. 5482, 5649, 6027, 8685, 8701, 10153).

9. The will of man is the very being *[esse]* of his life, and the receptacle of the good of love, while his understanding is the outgo *[existere]* of his life therefrom, and the receptacle of the truth and good of faith (n. 3619, 5002, 9282).

Thus the will's life is the chief life of man, and the life of the understanding goes forth therefrom (n. 585, 590, 3619, 7342, 8885, 9282, 10076, 10109, 10110).

Whatever is received by the will comes to be the life, and is appropriated to man (n. 3161, 9386, 9393). Man is a man from his will and his understanding therefrom (n. 8911, 9069, 9071, 10076, 10109, 10110). Moreover, everyone who wills and understands rightly is loved and valued by others, while he that understands rightly and does not will rightly is rejected and despised (n. 8911, 10076).

Also, after death man remains such as his will and his understanding therefrom have been, while the things that pertain to the understanding and not also to the will then vanish, because they are not in the man (n. 9069, 9071, 9282, 9386, 10153).

10. Between the two kingdoms there is communication and conjunction by means of angelic societies which are called celestial-spiritual (n. 4047, 6435, 8796, 8802).

The influx of the Lord through the celestial kingdom into the spiritual (n. 3969, 6366).

comes to pass that although heaven is divided into two kingdoms it nevertheless makes one. The Lord always provides such intermediate angels through whom there is communication and conjunction.

28. As the angels of these two kingdoms will be fully treated of in what follows, particulars are here omitted.

5

There Are Three Heavens

29. There are three heavens, entirely distinct from each other, an inmost or third, a middle or second, and an outmost or first. These have a like order and relation to each other as the highest part of man, or his head, the middle part, or body, and the lowest, or feet; or as the upper, the middle, and the lower stories of a house. In the same order is the Divine that goes forth and descends from the Lord; consequently heaven, from the necessity of order, is threefold.

30. The interiors of man, which belong to his mind and disposition, are also in like order. He has an inmost, a middle, and an outmost part; for when man was created all things of Divine order were brought together in him, so that he became Divine order in form, and consequently a heaven in miniature.[1] For this reason also man, as regards his interiors, has communication with the heavens and comes after death among the angels, either among those of the inmost, or of the middle, or of the outmost

1. All things of Divine order are brought together in man, and by creation man is Divine order in form (n. 3628, 4219, 4220, 4223, 4523, 4524, 5114, 5168, 6013, 6057, 6605, 6626, 9706, 10156, 10472).

In man the internal man was formed after the image of heaven, and the external after the image of the world, and this is why man was called by the ancients a microcosm (n. 3628, 4523, 5115, 6013, 6057, 9279, 9706, 10156, 10472).

Thus man in respect to his interiors is by creation a heaven in least form after the image of the greatest; and such also man becomes when he has been created anew or regenerated by the Lord (n. 911, 1900, 1928, 3624–3631, 3634, 3884, 4041, 4279, 4523, 4524, 4625, 6013, 6057, 9279, 9632).

heaven, in accordance with his reception of Divine good and truth from the Lord during his life in the world.

31. The Divine that flows in from the Lord and is received in the third or inmost heaven is called celestial, and in consequence the angels there are called celestial angels; the Divine that flows in from the Lord and is received in the second or middle heaven is called spiritual, and in consequence the angels there are called spiritual angels; while the Divine that flows in from the Lord and is received in the outmost or first heaven is called natural; but as the natural of that heaven is not like the natural of the world, but has the spiritual and the celestial within it, that heaven is called the spiritual-natural and the celestial-natural, and in consequence the angels there are called spiritual-natural and celestial-natural.[2] Those who receive influx from the middle or second heaven, which is the spiritual heaven, are called spiritual-natural; and those who receive influx from the third or inmost heaven, which is the celestial heaven, are called celestial-natural. The spiritual-natural angels and the celestial-natural angels are distinct from each other; nevertheless they constitute one heaven, because they are in one degree.

32. In each heaven there is an internal and an external; those in the internal are called there internal angels, while those in the external are called external angels. The internal and the external in the heavens, or in each heaven, hold the same relation as the voluntary and intellectual in man—the internal corresponding to the voluntary, and the external to the intellectual. Everything voluntary has its intellectual; one cannot exist without the

2. There are three heavens, inmost, middle, and outmost, or third, second, and first (n. 684, 9594, 10270).

Goods therein also follow in triple order (n. 4938, 4939, 9992, 10005, 10017).

The good of the inmost or third heaven is called celestial, the good of the middle or second is called spiritual, and the good of the outmost or first, spiritual-natural (n. 4279, 4286, 4938, 4939, 9992, 10005, 10017, 10068).

other. The voluntary may be compared to a flame and the intellectual to the light therefrom.

33. Let it be clearly understood that with the angels it is the interiors that cause them to be in one heaven or another; for as their interiors are more open to the Lord they are in a more interior heaven. There are three degrees of interiors in each angel and spirit, and also in man. Those in whom the third degree is opened are in the inmost heaven. Those in whom the second degree is opened, or only the first, are in the middle or in the outmost heaven. The interiors are opened by reception of Divine good and Divine truth. Those who are affected by Divine truths and admit them at once into the life, thus into the will and into action therefrom, are in the inmost or third heaven, and have their place there in accordance with their reception of good from affection for truth. Those who do not admit truths at once into the will but into the memory, and thence into the understanding, and from the understanding will and do them, are in the middle or second heaven. But those who live morally and who believe in a Divine, and who care very little about being taught, are in the outmost or first heaven.[3] From this it is clear that the states of the interiors are what make heaven, and that heaven is within everyone, and not outside of him; as the Lord teaches when he says:

> The kingdom of God cometh not with observation, neither shall they say, Lo here, or Lo there; for behold the kingdom of God ye have within you (Luke 17:20, 21).

34. Furthermore, all perfection increases toward interiors and decreases toward exteriors, since interiors are nearer to the Divine, and are in themselves pure, while exteriors are more

---

3. There are as many degrees of life in man as there are heavens, and these are opened after death in accordance with his life (n. 3747, 9594).

Heaven is in man (n. 3884).

Therefore he that has received heaven into himself in the world, comes into heaven after death (n. 10717).

remote from the Divine and are in themselves grosser.[4] Intelligence, wisdom, love, everything good and the resulting happiness, are what constitute angelic perfection; but not happiness apart from these, for such happiness is external and not internal. Because in the angels of the inmost heaven the interiors have been opened in the third degree, their perfection immeasurably surpasses the perfection of angels in the middle heaven, whose interiors have been opened in the second degree. So the perfection of these angels exceeds in like measure the perfection of angels of the outmost heaven.

35. Because of this distinction an angel of one heaven cannot go among the angels of another heaven, that is, no one can ascend from a lower heaven and no one can descend from a higher heaven. One ascending from a lower heaven is seized with a distress even to anguish, and is unable to see those who are there, still less to talk with them; while one descending from a higher heaven is deprived of his wisdom, stammers in his speech, and is in despair. There were some from the outmost heaven who had not yet been taught that the interiors of angels are what constitute heaven, and who believed that they might come into a higher heavenly happiness by simply gaining access to a heaven where higher angels are. These were permitted to enter among such angels. But when they were there they could see no one, however much they searched, although there was a great multitude present; for the interiors of the newcomers not having been opened in the same degree as the interiors of the angels there, their sight was not so opened. Presently they were seized with such anguish of heart that they scarcely knew whether they were alive or not. Therefore they hastily betook

4. Interiors are more perfect because nearer to the Divine (n. 3405, 5146, 5147).

In the internal there are thousands and thousands of things that appear in the external as one general thing (n. 5707). As far as man is raised from externals toward interiors, so far he comes into light and thus into intelligence; the elevation is like rising out of a cloud into clearness (n. 4598, 6183, 6313).

themselves to the heaven from which they came, glad to get back among their like, and pledging themselves that they would no longer covet higher things than were in agreement with their life. Again, I have seen some let down from a higher heaven; and these were deprived of their wisdom until they no longer knew what their own heaven was. It is otherwise when, as is often done, angels are raised up by the Lord out of a lower heaven into a higher that they may behold its glory; for then they are prepared beforehand, and are encompassed by intermediate angels, through whom they have communication with those they come among. From all this it is plain that the three heavens are entirely distinct from each other.

36. Those, however, who are in the same heaven can affiliate with any who are there; but the delights of such affiliation are measured by the kinships of good they have come into; of which more will be said in the following chapters.

37. But although the heavens are so distinct that there can be no companionship between the angels of one heaven and the angels of another, still the Lord joins all the heavens together by both direct and mediate influx—direct from himself into all the heavens, and mediate from one heaven into another.[5] He thus makes the three heavens to be one, and all to be in such connection from the first to the last that nothing unconnected is possible. Whatever is not connected through intermediates with the First can have no permanent existence, but is dissipated and becomes nothing.[6]

5. Influx from the Lord is direct from Himself and also mediate through one heaven into another, and in like manner into man's interiors (n. 6063, 6307, 6472, 9682, 9683).

Direct influx of the Divine from the Lord (n. 6058, 6474–6478, 8717, 8728).

Mediate influx through the spiritual world into the natural world (n. 4067, 6982, 6985, 6996).

6. All things spring from things prior to themselves, thus from a First, and in like manner subsist, because subsistence is a ceaseless springing forth; therefore nothing unconnected is possible (n. 3626–3628, 3648, 4523, 4524, 6040, 6056).

38. Only he who knows how degrees are related to Divine order can comprehend how the heavens are distinct, or even what is meant by the internal and the external man. Most men in the world have no other idea of what is interior and what is exterior, or of what is higher and what is lower, than as something continuous, or coherent by continuity, from purer to grosser. But the relation of what is interior to what is exterior is discrete, not continuous.

Degrees are of two kinds, those that are continuous and those that are not. Continuous degrees are related like the degrees of the waning of a light from its bright blaze to darkness, or like the degrees of the decrease of vision from objects in the light to those in the shade, or like degrees of purity in the atmosphere from bottom to top. These degrees are determined by distance.

[2] On the other hand, degrees that are not continuous, but discrete, are distinguished like prior and posterior, like cause and effect, and like what produces and what is produced. Whoever looks into the matter will see that in each thing and all things in the whole world, whatever they are, there are such degrees of producing and compounding, that is, from one a second, and from that a third, and so on.

[3] Until one has acquired for himself a perception of these degrees he cannot possibly understand the differences between the heavens, nor between the interior and exterior faculties of man, nor the differences between the spiritual world and the natural world, nor between the spirit of man and his body. So neither can he understand the nature and source of correspondences and representations, or the nature of influx. Sensual men do not apprehend these differences, for they make increase and decrease, even according to these degrees, to be continuous, and are therefore unable to conceive of what is spiritual otherwise

than as a purer natural. And in consequence they remain outside of and a great way off from intelligence.[7]

39. Finally, a certain arcanum respecting the angels of the three heavens, which has not hitherto come into anyone's mind, because degrees have not been understood, may be related. In every angel and also in every man there is an inmost or highest degree, or an inmost or highest something, into which the Divine of the Lord primarily or proximately flows, and from which it disposes the other interiors in him that follow in accordance with the degrees of order. This inmost or highest degree may be called the entrance of the Lord to the angel or man, and his veriest dwelling place in them. It is by virtue of this inmost or highest that a man is a man, and is distinguished from irrational animals, for these do not have it. From this it is that man, unlike the animals, is capable, in respect to all his interiors which pertain to his mind and disposition, of being raised up by the Lord to himself, of believing in the Lord, of being moved by love to the Lord, and thereby beholding him, and of receiving intelligence and wisdom, and speaking from reason. Also, it is by virtue of this that he lives to eternity. But what is arranged and provided by the Lord in this inmost does not distinctly flow into the perception of any angel, because it is above his thought and transcends his wisdom.

40. These now are the general truths respecting the three heavens; but in what follows each heaven will be particularly treated of.

---

7. Things interior and things exterior are not continuous but distinct and discrete according to degrees, and each degree has its bounds (n. 3691, 5114, 5145, 8603, 10099).

One thing is formed from another, and the things so formed are not continuously purer and grosser (n. 6326, 6465).

Until the difference between what is interior and what is exterior according to such degrees is perceived, neither the internal and external man nor the interior and exterior heavens can be clearly understood (n. 5146, 6465, 10099, 10181).

6

The Heavens Consist
of Innumerable Societies

41. The angels of each heaven are not together in one place, but are divided into larger and smaller societies in accordance with the differences of good of love and of faith in which they are, those who are in like good forming a single society. Goods in the heavens are in infinite variety, and each angel is as it were his own good.[1]

42. Moreover, the angelic societies in the heavens are at a distance from each other as their goods differ in general and in particular. For in the spiritual world the only ground of distance is difference in the state of interiors, thus in the heavens difference in the states of love, those who differ much being far apart, and those who differ but little being but little apart, and likeness causing them to be together.[2]

1. There is infinite variety, and never anything the same with any other (n. 7236, 9002).

So in the heavens there is infinite variety (n. 684, 690, 3744, 5598, 7236).

Varieties in the heavens, which are infinite, are varieties of good (n. 3744, 4005, 7236, 7833, 7836, 9002).

These varieties exist through truths that are manifold, from which is each one's good (n. 3470, 3804, 4149, 6917, 7236).

It is because of this that all the societies in the heavens, and all angels in a society, are distinct from each other (n. 690, 3241, 3519, 3804, 3986, 4067, 4149, 4263, 7236, 7833, 7836).

Nevertheless they all make one through love from the Lord (n. 457, 3986).

2. All the societies of heaven have a constant position in accordance with the differences of their state of life, thus in accordance with the differences of love and faith (n. 1274, 3638, 3639).

43. All who are in the same society are arranged in like manner in respect to each other; those who are more perfect, that is, who excel in good, thus in love, wisdom, and intelligence, being in the middle; those who are less preeminent being round about at a distance in accordance with the decrease of their perfection. The arrangement is like light diminishing from the middle to the circumference, those who are in the middle being in the greatest light, and those toward the circumference in less and less.

44. Like are drawn spontaneously as it were to their like; for with their like they are as if with their own and at home, but with others they are as if with strangers and abroad; also when with their like they are in their freedom, and consequently in every delight of life.

45. All this makes clear that all in the heavens are affiliated by good, and are distinguished according to the quality of the good. Nevertheless it is not the angels who thus affiliate themselves, but the Lord, from whom the good is. The Lord leads them, conjoins and separates them, and preserves them in freedom proportionate to their good. Thus he holds everyone in the life of his love and faith, of his intelligence and wisdom, and the resulting happiness.[3]

46. Again, all who are in like good, even though they have never seen each other before, know each other, just as men in the world do their kinsmen, near relations, and friends; and for the reason that in the other life there are none but spiritual kinships, relationships, and friendships, thus such as spring from love and

---

Wonderful things in the other life, that is, in the spiritual world, respecting distance, situation, place, space and time (n. 1273-1277).

3. All freedom pertains to love and affection, since what a man loves, that he does freely (n. 2870, 3158, 8987, 8990, 9585, 9591). Because freedom pertains to love, everyone's life and delight is therefrom (n. 2873). Nothing appears as one's own, except what is from his freedom (n. 2880). The veriest freedom is to be led by the Lord, because one is thus led by the love of good and truth (n. 892, 905, 2872, 2886, 2890-2892, 9096, 9586-9591).

faith.[4] This it has sometimes been granted me to see, when I have been in the spirit, and thus withdrawn from the body, and in the society of angels. Some of those I then saw seemed as if I had known them from childhood, but others as if not known at all. Those whom I seemed to have known from childhood were such as were in a state similar to that of my spirit; but those who seemed unknown were in a dissimilar state.

47. All who form the same angelic society resemble each other in countenance in a general way, but not in particulars. How these general resemblances are related to differences in particulars can in some measure be seen from like things in the world. It is well known that with every race there is a certain general resemblance of face and eyes, by which it is known and distinguished from all other races. This is still more true of different families. In the heavens this is much more fully the case, because there all the interior affections appear in and shine forth from the face, for there the face is the external and representative form of those affections. No one there can have any other face than that of his own affection. It was also shown how this general likeness is varied in particulars with individuals in the same society. A face like an angel's appeared to me, and this was varied in accordance with such affections for good and truth as are in those who belong to a single society. These changes went on for a long time, and I noticed that the same face in general continued as a ground work, all besides being what was derived and produced from that. Thus by means of this face the affections of the whole society were exhibited, whereby the faces of those in it are varied. For, as has been said above, the faces of angels are the forms of their interiors, thus of the affections that belong to their love and faith.

---

4. All nearness, relationships, connections, and as it were ties of blood in heaven are from good and in accordance with its agreements and differences (n. 685, 917, 1394, 2739, 3612, 3815, 4121).

48. From this it also comes to pass that an angel who excels in wisdom instantly sees the quality of another from his face. In heaven no one can conceal his interiors by his expression, or feign, or really deceive and mislead by craft or hypocrisy. There are hypocrites who are experts in disguising their interiors and fashioning their exteriors into the form of that good in which those are who belong to a society, and who thus make themselves appear angels of light; and these sometimes insinuate themselves into a society; but they cannot stay there long, for they begin to suffer inward pain and torture, to grow livid in the face, and to become as it were lifeless. These changes arise from the contrariety of the life that flows in and affects them. Therefore they quickly cast themselves down into hell where their like are, and no longer want to ascend. These are such as are meant by the man found among the invited guests at the feast not clothed with a wedding garment, who was cast out into outer darkness (Matt. 22:11 seq.).

49. All the societies of heaven have communication with one another, though not by open conversation; for few go out of their own society into another, since going out of their own society is like going away from themselves or from their own life, and passing into another life which is less congenial. But all the societies communicate by an extension of the sphere that goes forth from the life of each. This sphere of the life is the sphere of the affections of love and faith. This sphere extends itself far and wide into the surrounding societies, and farther and wider in proportion as the affections are the more interior and perfect.[5] In the measure of that extension do the angels have intelligence and wisdom. Those that are in the inmost heaven

---

5. A spiritual sphere, which is the sphere of life, flows out from every man, spirit, and angel, and encompasses them (n. 4464, 5179, 7454, 8630).

It flows forth from the life of their affection and thought (n. 2489, 4464, 6206). These spheres extend themselves far into angelic societies in accordance with the quality and quantity of their good (n. 6598–6612, 8063, 8794, 8797).

and in the middle of it have extension into the entire heavens; thus there is a sharing of all in heaven with each one, and of each one with all.[6] But this extension will be considered more fully hereafter, where the form of heaven in accord with which the angelic societies are arranged, and also the wisdom and intelligence of angels, will be treated of; for in accordance with that form all extension of affections and thoughts proceeds.

50. It has been said above that in the heavens there are larger and smaller societies. The larger consist of myriads of angels, the smaller of some thousands, and the least of some hundreds. There are also some that dwell apart, house by house as it were, and family by family. Although these live in this scattered way, they are arranged in order like those who live in societies, the wiser in the middle and the more simple in the borders. Such are more closely under the Divine auspices of the Lord, and are the best of the angels.

6. In the heavens a sharing of all goods is possible because heavenly love shares with another everything that is its own (n. 549, 550, 1390, 1391, 1399, 10130, 10723).

Each Society Is a Heaven
in a Smaller Form,
and Each Angel
in the Smallest Form

51. Each society is a heaven in a smaller form, and each angel in the smallest form, because it is the good of love and of faith that makes heaven, and this good is in each society of heaven and in each angel of a society. It does not matter that this good everywhere differs and varies, it is still the good of heaven; and there is no difference except that heaven has one quality here and another there. So when anyone is raised up into any society of heaven he is said to come into heaven; and those who are there are said to be in heaven, and each one in his own. This is known to all in the other life; consequently those standing outside of or beneath heaven, when they see at a distance companies of angels, say that heaven is in this or that place. It is comparatively like civil and military officers and attendants in a royal palace or castle, who, although dwelling apart in their own quarters or chambers above and below, are yet in the same palace or castle, each in his own position in the royal service. This makes evident the meaning of the Lord's words, that:

In his Father's house are many abiding places (John 14:2);

also what is meant by the dwelling places of heaven, and the heavens of heavens, in the prophets.

52. That each society is a heaven in a smaller form can be seen from this also, that each society there has a heavenly form like that of heaven as a whole. In the whole heavens those who are superior to the rest are in the middle, with the less excellent round about in a decreasing order even to the borders (as stated in a preceding chapter, n. 43). It can be seen also from this, that the Lord directs all in the whole heaven as if they were a single angel; and the same is true of all in each society; and as a consequence an entire angelic society sometimes appears in angelic form like a single angel, as I have been permitted by the Lord to see. Moreover, when the Lord appears in the midst of the angels he does not appear as one surrounded by many, but the appearance is as a one, in an angelic form. This is why the Lord is called "an angel" in the Word, and why an entire society is so called. "Michael," "Gabriel," and "Raphael" are no other than angelic societies so named from their function.[1]

53. As an entire society is a heaven in a smaller form, so an angel is a heaven in the smallest form. For heaven is not outside of the angel, but is within him, since the interior things which belong to his mind are arranged into the form of heaven, thus for the reception of all things of heaven that are outside of him. These also he receives according to the quality of the good that is in him from the Lord. It is from this that an angel is a heaven.

54. It can in no sense be said that heaven is outside of anyone; it is within him. For it is in accordance with the heaven that is within him that each angel receives the heaven that is outside of him. This makes clear how greatly misled is he who believes that to come into heaven is simply to be taken up among angels, without regard to what one's interior life may be, thus that heaven is granted to each one by mercy apart from means;[2]

---

1. In the Word the Lord is called an angel (n. 6280, 6831, 8192, 9303).

A whole angelic society is called an angel, and Michael and Raphael are angelic societies, so called from their functions (n. 8192).

The societies of heaven and the angels have no names, but are distinguished by the quality of their good, and by the idea of it (n. 1705, 1754).

2. Heaven is not granted from mercy apart from means, but in accordance with the

when, in fact, unless heaven is within one, nothing of the heaven that is outside can flow in and be received. There are many spirits who have this idea. Because of this belief they have been taken up into heaven; but when they came there, because their interior life was contrary to the angelic life, their intellectual faculties began to be blinded until they became like fools; and they began to be tortured in their voluntary faculties until they became like madmen. In a word, if those that have lived wickedly come into heaven they gasp for breath and writhe about, like fishes out of water in the air, or like animals in ether in an air pump when the air has been exhausted. From this it can be seen that heaven is not outside of a man, but within him.[3]

55. As everyone receives the heaven that is outside of him in accordance with the quality of the heaven that is within him, so in like manner does everyone receive the Lord, since it is the Divine of the Lord that makes heaven. And for this reason when the Lord becomes manifestly present in any society his appearance there is in accord with the quality of the good in which the society is, thus not the same in one society as in another. This diversity is not in the Lord; it is in the angels who behold him from their own good, and thus in accordance with their good. And they are affected by his appearance in accordance with the quality of their love, those who love him inmostly being inmostly affected, and those who love him less being less affected; while the evil who are outside of heaven are tortured by his presence. When the Lord is seen in any society he is seen as

---

life; yet everything of the life by which man is led to heaven by the Lord belongs to mercy; this is what is meant by mercy (n. 5057, 10659). If heaven were granted from mercy apart from means it would be granted to all (n. 2401).

About some evil spirits cast down from heaven who believed that heaven was granted to everyone from mercy apart from means (n. 4226).

3. Heaven is in man (n. 3884).

an angel, but is distinguished from others by the Divine that shines through.

56. Again, heaven is where the Lord is acknowledged, believed in, and loved. Variety in worship of the Lord from the variety of good in different societies is not harmful, but beneficial, for the perfection of heaven is therefrom. This can scarcely be made clear to the comprehension without employing terms that are in common use in the learned world, and showing by means of these how unity, that it may be perfect, must be formed from variety. Every whole exists from various parts, since a whole without constituents is not anything; it has no form, and therefore no quality. But when a whole exists from various parts, and the various parts are in a perfect form, in which each attaches itself like a congenial friend to another in series, then the quality is perfect. So heaven is a whole from various parts arranged in a most perfect form, for the heavenly form is the most perfect of all forms. That this is the ground of all perfection is evident from the nature of all beauty, agreeableness and delight, by which the senses and the mind are affected; for these qualities spring and flow from no other source than the concert and harmony of many concordant and congenial parts, either coexisting in order or following in order, and never from a whole without many parts. From this is the saying that variety gives delight; and the nature of variety, as is known, is what determines the delight. From all this it can be seen as in a mirror how perfection comes from variety even in heaven. For from the things that exist in the natural world the things of the spiritual world can be seen as in a mirror.[4]

---

4. Every whole is from the harmony and concert of many parts. Otherwise it has no quality (n. 457).

From this the entire heaven is a whole (n. 457).

And for the reason that all there have regard to one end, which is the Lord (n. 9828).

57. What has been said of heaven may be said also of the church, for the church is the Lord's heaven on earth. There are also many churches, each one of which is called a church, and so far as the good of love and faith reigns therein is a church. Here, too, the Lord out of various parts forms a unity, that is, one church out of many churches.[5] And the like may be said of the man of the church in particular that is said of the church in general, namely, that the church is within man and not outside of him; and that every man is a church in whom the Lord is present in the good of love and of faith.[6] Again, the same may be said of a man that has the church in him as of an angel that has heaven in him, namely, that he is a church in the smallest form, as an angel is a heaven in the smallest form; and furthermore that a man that has the church in him, equally with an angel, is a heaven. For man was created that he might come into heaven and become an angel; consequently he that has good from the Lord is a man-angel.[7] What man has in common with an angel and what he has in contrast with angels may be mentioned. It is granted to man, equally with the angel, to have his interiors conformed to the image of heaven, and to become, so far as he is in the good of love and faith, an image of heaven. But it is granted to man and not to angels to have his exteriors conform to the image of the world; and so far as he is in good to have the world in him subordinated to heaven and made to serve heaven.[8]

5. If good were the characteristic and essential of the church, and not truth apart from good, the church would be one (n. 1285, 1316, 2982, 3267, 3445, 3451, 3452).

From good all churches make one church before the Lord (n. 7396, 9276).

6. The church is in man, and not outside of him, and the church in general is made up of men that have the church in them (n. 3884, [6637]).

7. A man who is a church is a heaven in the smallest form after the image of the greatest, because his interiors, which belong to his mind, are arranged after the form of heaven, and consequently for reception of all things of heaven (n. 911, 1900, 1928, 3624–3631, 3634, 3884, 4041, 4279, 4523, 4524, 4625, 6013, 6057, 9279, 9632).

8. Man has an internal and an external; his internal is formed by creation after the image of heaven, and his external after the image of the world; and for this reason man

And then the Lord is present in him both in the world and in heaven just as if he were in his heaven. For the Lord is in his Divine order in both worlds, since God is order.[9]

58. Finally it should be said that he who has heaven in himself has it not only in the largest or most general things pertaining to him but also in every least or particular thing, and that these least things repeat in an image the greatest. This comes from the fact that everyone is his own love, and is such as his ruling love is. That which reigns flows into the particulars and arranges them, and everywhere induces a likeness of itself.[10] In the heavens love to the Lord is the ruling love, for there the Lord is loved above all things. Hence the Lord there is the All-in-all, flowing into all and each, arranging them, clothing them with a likeness of himself, and making it to be heaven wherever he is. This is what makes an angel to be a heaven in the smallest form, a society to be a heaven in a larger form, and all the societies taken together a heaven in the largest form. That the Divine of the Lord is what makes heaven, and that he is the All-in-all, may be seen above (n. 7–12).

---

was called by the ancients a microcosm (n. 3628, 4523, 4524, 5115, 5368, 6013, 6057, 9279, 9706, 10156, 10472). Therefore man was created to have the world in him serve heaven, and this takes place with the good; but it is the reverse with the evil, in whom heaven serves the world (n. 9278, 9283).

9. The Lord is order, since the Divine good and truth that go forth from the Lord make order (n. 1728, 1919, 2011, 2258, 5110, 5703, 8988, 10336, 10619).

Divine truths are laws of order (n. 2447, 7995).

So far as a man lives according to order, that is, so far as he lives in good in accordance with Divine truths, he is a man, and the church and heaven are in him (n. 4839, 6605, 8513, [8547]).

10. The ruling or dominant love with everyone is in each thing and all things of his life, thus in each thing and all things of his thought and will (n. 6159, 7648, 8067, 8853).

Man is such as is the ruling quality of his life (n. 987, 1040, 1568, 3570, 6571, 6935, 6938, 8853–8858, 10076, 10109, 10110, 10284).

When love and faith rule they are in all the particulars of man's life, although he does not know it (n. 8854, 8864, 8865).

8

All Heaven in the Aggregate
Reflects a Single Man

59. That heaven in its whole complex reflects a single man is an arcanum hitherto unknown in the world, but fully recognized in the heavens. To know this and the specific and particular things relating to it is the chief thing in the intelligence of the angels there, and on it many things depend which without it as their general principle would not enter distinctly and clearly into the ideas of their minds. Knowing that all the heavens with their societies reflect a single man they call heaven the greatest man and the Divine man[1]—Divine because it is the Divine of the Lord that makes heaven (see above, n. 7–12).

60. That into such a form and image celestial and spiritual things are arranged and joined cannot be seen by those who have no right idea of spiritual and heavenly things. Such think that the earthy and material things of which man's outmost nature is composed are what makes the man; and that apart from these man is not a man. But let them know that it is not from these that man is a man, but from his ability to understand what is true and to will what is good. Such understanding and willing are the spiritual and celestial things of which man is made. Moreover, it is known that everyone's quality is determined by the quality of his understanding and will; and it can also be known that his earthly body is formed to serve the understanding and

---

1. Heaven in the whole complex appears in form like a man, and for this reason heaven is called the Greatest Man (n. 2996, 2998, 3624–3649, 3741–3745, 4625).

the will in the world, and to skillfully accomplish their uses in the outmost sphere of nature. For this reason the body by itself can do nothing, but is moved always in entire subservience to the bidding of the understanding and will, even to the extent that whatever a man thinks he speaks with his tongue and lips, and whatever he wills he does with his body and limbs, and thus the understanding and the will are what act, while the body by itself does nothing. Evidently, then, the things of the understanding and will are what make man; and as these act into the minutest particulars of the body, as what is internal into what is external, they must be in a like form, and on this account man is called an internal or spiritual man. Heaven is such a man in its greatest and most perfect form.

61. Such being the angelic idea of man, the angels give no thought to what a man does with his body, but only to the will from which the body acts. This they call the man himself, and the understanding they call the man so far as it acts in unison with the will.[2]

62. The angels, it is true, do not see heaven in its whole complex in the human form, for heaven as a whole does not come within view of any angel; but remote societies, consisting of many thousands of angels, they sometimes see as a one in the human form; and from a society, as from a part, they draw their conclusion as to the general, which is heaven. For in the most perfect form generals are like the parts, and parts are like the generals, with simply such a difference as there is between like things of greater or less magnitude; consequently, the angels say that since the Divine from what is inmost or highest sees all

2. The will of man is the very being [esse] of his life, and his understanding is the outgo [existere] of his life therefrom (n. 3619, 5002, 9282).

The chief life of man is the life of his will, and from that the life of the understanding proceeds (n. 585, 590, 3619, 7342, 8885, 9282, 10076, 10109, 10110).

Man is man by virtue of his will and his understanding therefrom (n. 8911, 9069, 9071, 10076, 10109, 10110).

things, so in the Lord's sight heaven as a whole must be in the human form.

63. Heaven being such, it is ruled by the Lord as a single man is ruled, thus as a one. For although man, as we know, consists of an innumerable variety of parts, not only as a whole but also in each part—as a whole, of members, organs, and viscera; and in each part, of series of fibers, nerves, and blood vessels, thus of members within members, and of parts within parts— nevertheless, when he acts he acts as a single man. Such likewise is heaven under the auspices and direction of the Lord.

64. So many different things in man act as a one, because there is no least thing in him that does not do something for the general welfare and perform some use. The general performs a use for its parts, and the parts for the general, for the general is composed of the parts and the parts constitute the general; therefore they provide for each other, have regard for each other, and are joined together in such a form that each thing and all things have reference to the general and its good; thus it is that they act as one.

[2] In the heavens there are like affiliations. Those there are conjoined according to uses in a like form; and consequently those who do not perform uses for the common good are cast out of heaven as something heterogeneous. To perform use is to will well to others for the sake of the common good; but to will well to others not for the sake of the common good but for the sake of self is not to perform use. These latter are such as love themselves supremely, while the former are such as love the Lord supremely. Thence it is that those who are in heaven act as a one; and this they do from the Lord, not from themselves, for they look to him as the Only One, the source of all things, and they regard his kingdom as the general, the good of which is to be sought. This is what is meant by the Lord's words,

Seek ye first the kingdom of God and his righteousness, and all things shall be added unto you (Matt. 6:33).

"To seek his righteousness" means to seek his good.[3]

[3] Those who in the world love their country's good more than their own, and their neighbor's good as their own, are they who in the other life love and seek the Lord's kingdom; for there the Lord's kingdom takes the place of country; and those who love doing good to others, not with self as an end but with good as an end, love the neighbor; for in heaven good is the neighbor.[4] All such are in the greatest man, that is, heaven.

65. As the whole heaven reflects a single man, and is a Divine spiritual man in the largest form, even in figure, so heaven like a man is arranged into members and parts, and these are similarly named. Moreover, angels know in what member this or that society is. This society, they say, is in a certain part or province of the head, that in a certain part or province of the breast, that in a certain part or province of the loins, and so on. In general, the highest or third heaven forms the head down to the neck; the middle or second heaven forms the breast down to the loins and knees; the lowest or first heaven forms the feet down to the soles, and also the arms down to the fingers. For the arms and hands belong to the lowest parts of man, although at the sides. From this again it is plain why there are three heavens.

3. In the Word "righteousness" is predicated of good, and "judgment" of truth; therefore "to do righteousness and judgment" is to do what is good and true (n. 2235, 9857).

4. In the highest sense the Lord is the neighbor; consequently to love the Lord is to love that which is from Him, that is to love good and truth because the Lord is in everything that is from Him (n. 2425, 3419, 6706, 6711, 6819, 6823, 8123).

Therefore all good that is from the Lord is the neighbor, and to will and do that good is to love the neighbor (n. 5028, 10336).

66. The spirits that are beneath heaven are greatly astonished when they hear that heaven is not only above but below, for they have a like faith and opinion as men in the world, that heaven is nowhere but above, for they do not know that the arrangement of the heavens is like the arrangement of the members, organs, and viscera in man, some of which are above and some below; or like the arrangement of the parts in each of the members, organs, and viscera, some of which are within and some without. Hence their confused notions about heaven.

67. These things about heaven as the greatest man are set forth, because what follows in regard to heaven cannot be at all comprehended until these things are known, neither can there be any clear idea of the form of heaven, of the conjunction of the Lord with heaven, of the conjunction of heaven with man, of the influx of the spiritual world into the natural, or any idea at all of correspondence—subjects to be treated of in their proper order in what now follows. To throw some light on these subjects, therefore, the above has been premised.

9

Each Society in Heaven
Reflects a Single Man

68. I have frequently been permitted to see that each society of heaven reflects a single man, and is in the likeness of a man. There was a society into which several had insinuated themselves who knew how to counterfeit angels of light. These were hypocrites. When these were being separated from the angels I saw that the entire society appeared at first like a single indistinct body, then by degrees in a human form, but still indistinctly, and at last clearly as a man. Those that were in that man and made up the man were such as were in the good of that society; the others who were not in the man and did not make up the man were hypocrites; these were cast out and the former were retained; and thus a separation was effected. Hypocrites are such as talk well and also do well, but have regard to themselves in everything. They talk as angels do about the Lord, heaven, love, and heavenly life, and also act rightly, so that they may appear to be what they profess to be. But their thinking is different; they believe nothing; and they wish good to none but themselves. Their doing good is for the sake of self, or if for the sake of others it is only for the appearance, and thus still for the sake of self.

69. I have also been permitted to see that an entire angelic society, where the Lord is visibly present, appears as a one in the human form. There appeared on high toward the east something like a cloud, from glowing white becoming red, and with little stars round about, which was descending; and as it gradually descended it became brighter, and at last appeared in a perfect human form. The little stars round about the cloud were angels, who so appeared by virtue of light from the Lord.

70. It must be understood that although all in a heavenly society when seen together as one appear in the likeness of a man; yet no one society is just such a man as another. Societies differ from one another like the faces of different individuals of the same family, for the reason given above (n. 47), that is, they differ in accordance with the varieties of good in which they are and which determines their form. The societies of the inmost or highest heaven, and in the center there, are those that appear in the most perfect and beautiful human form.

71. It is worthy of mention that the greater the number in any society in heaven and the more these make a one, the more perfect is its human form, for variety arranged in a heavenly form is what constitutes perfection, as has been shown above (n. 56), and number gives variety. Moreover, every society of heaven increases in number daily, and as it increases it becomes more perfect. Thus not only the society becomes more perfect, but also heaven in general, because it is made up of societies. As heaven gains in perfection by increase of numbers, it is evident how mistaken those are who believe that heaven may be closed by becoming full; for the opposite is true, that it will never be closed, but is perfected by greater and greater fullness. Therefore, the angels desire nothing so much as to have new angel guests come to them.

72. Each society, when it appears as one whole, is in the form of a man, for the reason that heaven as a whole has that form (as has been shown in the preceding chapter); moreover, in the most perfect form, such as the form of heaven is, there is a likeness of the parts to the whole, and of lesser forms to the greatest. The lesser forms and parts of heaven are the societies of which it consists, which are also heavens in lesser form (see

51–58). This likeness is perpetual because in the heavens the goods of all are from a single love, that is, from a single origin. The single love, which is the origin of the good of all in heaven, is love to the Lord from the Lord. It is from this that the entire heaven in general, each society less generally, and each angel in particular, is a likeness of the Lord, as has been shown above (n. 58).

10

Therefore Every Angel Is
in a Complete Human Form

73. In the two preceding chapters it has been shown that heaven in its whole complex, and likewise each society in heaven, reflects a single man. From the sequence of reasons there set forth it follows that this is equally true of each angel. As heaven is a man in largest form, and a society of heaven in a less form, so is an angel in least. For in the most perfect form, such as the form of heaven is, there is a likeness of the whole in the part and of the part in the whole. This is so for the reason that heaven is a common sharing, for it shares all it has with each one, and each one receives all he has from that sharing. Because an angel is thus a recipient he is a heaven in least form, as shown above in its chapter; and a man also, so far as he receives heaven, is a recipient, a heaven, and an angel (see above, n. 57). This is thus described in Revelation:

> He measured the wall of the holy Jerusalem, a hundred and forty and four cubits, the measure of a man, which is that of an angel (Rev. 21:17).

"Jerusalem" means here the Lord's church, and in a more eminent sense, heaven;[1] the "wall" means truth, which is a defense against the assault of falsities and evils;[2] "a hundred and forty and four" means all goods and truths in the complex;[3] "measure"

---

1. "Jerusalem" means the church (n. 402, 3654, 9166).

2. The "wall" means truth defending against the assault of falsities and evils (n. 6419).

3. "Twelve" means all truths and goods in the complex (n. 577, 2089, 2129, 2130, 3272, 3858, 3913). Likewise "seventy-two," and "a hundred and forty-four," since this comes from twelve multiplied into itself (n. 7973).

means what a thing is,[4] a "man" means one in whom are goods and truths in general and in particular, thus in whom is heaven. And as it is from this that an angel is a man, it is said "the measure of a man, which is that of an angel." This is the spiritual meaning of these words. Without that meaning how could it be seen that "the wall of the holy Jerusalem" is "the measure of a man, which is that of an angel"?[5]

74. Let us now turn to experience. That angels are human forms, or men, has been seen by me a thousand times. I have talked with them as man with man, sometimes with one, sometimes with many together; and I have seen nothing whatever in their form different from the human form; and have occasionally been surprised to find them such. And that this might not be said to be a delusion or a vision of fancy, I have been permitted to see angels when fully awake or in possession of all my bodily senses, and in a state of clear perception.

And I have often told them that men in the Christian world are in such blind ignorance in regard to angels and spirits as to believe them to be minds without form, even pure thoughts, of which they have no idea except as something ethereal in which there is some vitality. And as they thus ascribe to angels nothing human except a thinking faculty, they believe that having no eyes they do not see, having no ears they do not hear, and having no mouth or tongue they do not speak.

All numbers in the Word signify things (n. 482, 487, 647, 648, 755, 813, 1963, 1988, 2075, 2252, 3252, 4264, 4495, 5265).

Multiplied numbers have a like signification as the simple numbers from which they arise by multiplication (n. 5291, 5335, 5708, 7973).

4. "Measure" in the Word signifies the quality of a thing in respect to truth and good (n. 3104, 9603).

5. In regard to the spiritual or internal sense of the Word see the explanation of the white horse in Revelation, and the appendix to the *New Jerusalem and Its Heavenly Doctrine.*

[2] To this the angels replied that they are aware that such a belief is held by many in the world, and is prevalent among the learned, and to their surprise, even among the clergy. The reason, they said, is that the learned, who were the leaders and who first concocted such an idea of angels and spirits, conceived of them from the sense conceptions of the external man; and those who think from these, and not from interior light and from the general idea implanted in everyone, must needs fabricate such notions, since the sense conceptions of the external man take in only what belongs to nature, and nothing above nature, thus nothing whatever of the spiritual world.[6] From these leaders as guides this falsity of thought about angels extended to others who did not think from themselves but adopted the thoughts of their leaders; and those who first take their thoughts from others and make that thought their belief, and then view it with their own understanding, cannot easily recede from it, and are therefore in most cases satisfied with confirming it.

[3] The angels said, furthermore, that the simple in faith and heart have no such idea about angels, but think of them as the men of heaven, and for the reason that they have not extinguished by learning what is implanted in them from heaven, and have no conception of anything apart from form. This is why angels in churches, whether sculptured or painted, are always depicted as men. In respect to this insight from heaven they said that it is the Divine flowing into such as are in the good of faith and life.

---

6. Unless man is raised above the sense conceptions of the external man he has very little wisdom (n. 5089).

The wise man thinks above these sense conceptions (n. 5089, 5094).

When man is raised above these, he comes into clearer light, and finally into heavenly light (n. 6183, 6313, 6315, 9407, 9730, 9922).

Elevation and withdrawal from these was known to the ancients (n. 6313).

75. From all my experience, which is now of many years, I am able to say and affirm that angels are wholly men in form, having faces, eyes, ears, bodies, arms, hands, and feet; that they see and hear one another, and talk together, and in a word lack nothing whatever that belongs to men except that they are not clothed in material bodies. I have seen them in their own light, which exceeds by many degrees the noonday light of the world, and in that light all their features could be seen more distinctly and clearly than the faces of men are seen on the earth. It has also been granted me to see an angel of the inmost heaven. He had a more radiant and resplendent face than the angels of the lower heavens. I observed him attentively, and he had a human form in all completeness.

76. But it must be remembered that a man cannot see angels with his bodily eyes, but only with the eyes of the spirit within him,[7] because his spirit is in the spiritual world, and all things of the body are in the natural world. Like sees like from being like. Moreover, as the bodily organ of sight, which is the eye, is too gross, as everyone knows, to see even the smaller things of nature except through magnifying glasses, still less can it see what is above the sphere of nature, as all things in the spiritual world are. Nevertheless these things can be seen by man when he has been withdrawn from the sight of the body, and the sight of his spirit has been opened; and this can be effected instantly whenever it is the pleasure of the Lord that man should see these things; and in that case man does not know but what he is seeing them with his bodily eyes. Thus were angels seen by Abraham, Lot, Manoah, and the prophets; and thus, too, the Lord was seen by the disciples after the resurrection; and in the same way angels have been seen by me. Because the

7. In respect to his interiors man is a spirit (n. 1594).
   And that spirit is the man himself, and it is from that spirit that the body lives (n. 447, 4622, 6054).

prophets saw in this way they were called "seers," and were said "to have their eyes opened" (1 Sam. 9:9; Num. 24:3); and enabling them to see thus was called "opening their eyes," as with Elisha's servant, of whom we read:

> Elisha prayed and said, Jehovah, I pray Thee open his eyes that he may see; and Jehovah opened the eyes of the young man and he saw, and behold the mountain was full of horses and chariots of fire round about Elisha (2 Kings 6:17).

77. Good spirits, with whom I have spoken about this matter, have been deeply grieved at such ignorance in the church about the condition of heaven and of spirits and angels; and in their displeasure they charged me to declare positively that they are not formless minds nor ethereal breaths, but are men in very form, and see, hear, and feel equally with those who are in this world.[8]

---

8. Inasmuch as each angel is a recipient of Divine order from the Lord, he is in a human form, perfect and beautiful in the measure of his reception (n. 322, 1880, 1881, 3633, 3804, 4622, 4735, 4797, 4985, 5199, 5530, 6054, 9879, 10177, 10594).

It is by means of Divine truth that order exists; and Divine good is the essential of order (n. 2451, 3166, 4390, 4409, 5232, 7256, 10122, 10555).

11

It Is from the Lord's Divine Human That Heaven as a Whole and in Part Reflects Man

78. That it is from the Lord's Divine human that heaven as a whole and in part reflects man, follows as a conclusion from all that has been stated and shown in the preceding chapters, namely: (1) That the God of heaven is the Lord. (2) It is the Divine of the Lord that makes heaven. (3) Heaven consists of innumerable societies; and each society is a heaven in a smaller form, and each angel in the smallest form. (4) All heaven in the aggregate reflects a single man. (5) Each society in the heavens reflects a single man. (6) Therefore every angel is in a complete human form. All this leads to the conclusion that as it is the Divine that makes heaven, heaven must be human in form. That this Divine is the Lord's Divine human can be seen still more clearly, because in a compendium, in what has been collected, brought together and collated from *Arcana Coelestia* and placed as a supplement at the end of this chapter. That the Lord's human is Divine, and that it is not true that his human is not Divine, as those within the church believe, may also be seen in the same extracts, also in the chapter on the Lord, in the *New Jerusalem and Its Heavenly Doctrine,* at the end.

79. That this is true has been proved to me by much experience, about which something shall now be said. No angel in the heavens ever perceives the Divine as being in any other than a human form; and what is remarkable, those in the higher heavens are unable to think of the Divine in any other way. The necessity of thinking in this way comes from the Divine itself that flows in, and also from the form of heaven in harmony with which their thoughts spread forth. For every thought of an angel spreads forth into heaven; and the angels have intelligence and wisdom in the measure of that extension. It is in consequence of this that all in heaven acknowledge the Lord, because only in him does the Divine human exist. Not only have I been told all this by angels, but when elevated into the inner sphere of heaven I have been able to perceive it.

From this it is evident that the wiser the angels are the more clearly they perceive this truth; and it is from this that the Lord is seen by them; for the Lord is seen in a Divine angelic form, which is the human form, by those who acknowledge and believe in a visible Divine being, but not by those who believe in an invisible Divine. For the former can see their Divine being, but the latter cannot.

80. Because the angels have no perception of an invisible Divine, which they call a Divine devoid of form, but perceive only a visible Divine in human form, they are accustomed to say that the Lord alone is man, and that it is from him that they are men, and that each one is a man in the measure of his reception of the Lord. By receiving the Lord they understand receiving good and truth which are from him, since the Lord is in his good and in his truth, and this they call wisdom and intelligence. Everyone knows, they say, that intelligence and wisdom make man, and not a face without these. The truth of this is made evident from the appearance of the angels of the interior heavens, for these, being in good and truth from the Lord and in consequent wisdom and intelligence, are in a most beautiful and most perfect human form; while the angels of the lower heavens are in human form of less perfection and beauty. On the other hand, those who are in hell appear in the light of heaven hardly as men, but rather as monsters, since they are not in good and truth but in evil and falsity, and consequently in the opposites of wisdom and intelligence. For this reason their life is not called life, but spiritual death.

81. Because heaven as a whole and in part, from the Lord's Divine human, reflects a man, the angels say that they are in the Lord; and some say that they are in his body, meaning that they are in the good of his love. And this the Lord himself teaches, saying,

Abide in Me and I in you. As the branch cannot bear fruit of itself except it abide in the vine, so neither can ye, except ye abide in Me. For apart from Me ye can do nothing. Abide in My love. If ye keep My commandments ye shall abide in My love (John 15:4–10).

82. Because such a perception of the Divine exists in the heavens, to think of God as in a human form is implanted in every man who receives any influx from heaven. Thus did the ancients think of him; and thus do the moderns think of him both outside of the church and within it. The simple see him in thought as the Ancient One in shining light. But this insight has been extinguished in all those that by self-intelligence and by a life of evil have rejected influx from heaven. Those that have extinguished it by self-intelligence prefer an invisible God; while those that have extinguished it by a life of evil prefer no God. Neither of these are aware that such an insight exists, because they do not have it; and yet it is the Divine heavenly itself that primarily flows into man out of heaven, because man is born for heaven, and no one without a conception of a Divine can enter heaven.

83. For this reason he that has no conception of heaven, that is, no conception of the Divine from which heaven is, cannot be raised up to the first threshold of heaven. As soon as such a one draws near to heaven a resistance and a strong repulsion are perceived; and for the reason that his interiors, which should be receptive of heaven, are closed up from their not being in the form of heaven, and the nearer he comes to heaven the more tightly are they closed up. Such is the lot of those

within the church who deny the Lord, and of those who, like
the Socinians, deny his Divinity. But the lot of those who are
born out of the church, and who are ignorant of the Lord
because they do not have the Word, will be described hereafter.

84. That the men of old time had an idea of the Divine as
human is evident from the manifestation of the Divine to Abraham, Lot, Joshua, Gideon, Manoah and his wife, and others.
These saw God as a man, but nevertheless adored him as the
God of the universe, calling him the God of heaven and earth,
and Jehovah. That it was the Lord who was seen by Abraham
he himself teaches in John 8:56; and that it was he who was
seen by the rest is evident from his words:

> No one hath seen the Father, nor heard his voice, nor seen his form
> (John 1:18; 5:37).

85. But that God is man can scarcely be comprehended by
those who judge all things from the sense conceptions of the
external man, for the sensual man must needs think of the
Divine from the world and what is therein, and thus of a Divine and spiritual man in the same way as of a corporeal and
natural man. From this he concludes that if God were a man he
would be as large as the universe; and if he ruled heaven and
earth it would be done through many others, after the manner
of kings in the world. If told that in heaven there is no extension of space as in the world, he would not in the least comprehend it. For he that thinks only from nature and its light must
needs think in accord with such extension as appears before his
eyes. But it is the greatest mistake to think in this way about
heaven. Extension there is not like extension in the world. In
the world extension is determinate, and thus measurable; but in
heaven it is not determinate, and thus not measurable. But
extension in heaven will be further treated of hereafter in connection with space and time in the spiritual world. Furthermore, everyone knows how far the sight of the eye extends,
namely, to the sun and to the stars, which are so remote; and

whoever thinks deeply knows that the internal sight, which is of thought, has a still wider extension, and that a yet more interior sight must extend more widely still. What then must be said of Divine sight, which is the inmost and highest of all? Because thoughts have such extension, all things of heaven are shared with everyone there, so, too, are all things of the Divine which makes heaven and fills it, as has been shown in the preceding chapters.

86. Those in heaven wonder that men can believe themselves to be intelligent who, in thinking of God, think about something invisible, that is, inconceivable under any form; and that they can call those who think differently unintelligent and simple, when the reverse is the truth. They add, "Let those who thus believe themselves to be intelligent examine themselves, whether they do not look upon nature as God, some the nature that is before their eyes, others the invisible side of nature; and whether they are not so blind as not to know what God is, what an angel is, what a spirit is, what their soul is which is to live after death, what the life of heaven in man is, and many other things that constitute intelligence; when yet those whom they call simple know all these things in their way, having an idea of their God that he is the Divine in a human form, of an angel that he is a heavenly man, of their soul that is to live after death that it is like an angel, and of the life of heaven in man that it is living in accord with the Divine commandments." Such the angels call intelligent and fitted for heaven; but the others, on the other hand, they call not intelligent.

Extracts from *Arcana Coelestia*
Relating to the Lord
and His Divine Human

[2] The Divine was in the Lord from very conception (n. 4641, 4963, 5041, 5157, 6716, 10125).

The Lord alone had a Divine seed (n. 1438).

His soul was Jehovah (n. 1999, 2004, 2005, 2018, 2025).

Thus the Lord's inmost was the Divine itself, while the clothing was from the mother (n. 5041).

The Divine itself was the being *[esse]* of the Lord's life, and from this the human afterwards went forth and became the outgo *[existere]* from that being *[esse]* (n. 3194, 3210, 10269, 10738).

[3] Within the church where the Word is and by it the Lord is known, the Lord's Divine ought not to be denied, nor the holy that goes forth from Him (n. 2359).

Those within the church who do not acknowledge the Lord have no conjunction with the Divine; but it is otherwise with those outside of the church (n. 10205).

The essential of the church is to acknowledge the Lord's Divine and His union with the Father (n. 10083, 10112, 10370, 10730, 10738, 10816–10820).

[4] The glorification of the Lord is treated of in the Word in many passages (n. 10828).

And in the internal sense of the Word everywhere (n. 2249, 2523, 3245).

The Lord glorified His human, but not the Divine, since this was glorified in itself (n. 10057).

The Lord came into the world to glorify his human (n. 3637, 4287, 9315).

The Lord glorified His human by means of the Divine love that was in Him from conception (n. 4727).

The Lord's life in the world was His love toward the whole human race (n. 2253).

The Lord's love transcends all human understanding (n. 2077).

The Lord saved the human race by glorifying His human (n. 4180, 10019, 10152, 10655, 10659, 10828).

Otherwise the whole human race would have perished in eternal death (n. 1676).

The state of the Lord's glorification and humiliation (n. 1785, 1999, 2159, 6866).

Glorification in respect to the Lord is the uniting of His human with the Divine; and to glorify is to make Divine (n. 1603, 10053, 10828).

When the Lord glorified his human he put off everything human that was from the mother, until at last he was not her son (n. 2159, 2574, 2649, 3036, 10830).

[5] The Son of God from eternity was the Divine truth in heaven (n. 2628, 2798, 2803, 3195, 3704).

When the Lord was in the world he made his human Divine truth from the Divine good that was in him (n. 2803, 3194, 3195, 3210, 6716, 6864, 7014, 7499, 8127, 8724, 9199).

The Lord then arranged all things in himself into a heavenly form, which is in accord with Divine truth (n. 1928, 3633).

For this reason the Lord was called the Word, which is Divine truth (n. 2533, 2813, 2859, 2894, 3393, 3712).

The Lord alone had perception and thought from himself, and this was above all angelic perception and thought (n. 1904, 1914, 1919).

The Divine truth which was himself, the Lord united with Divine good which was in himself (n. 10047, 10052, 10076). The union was reciprocal (n. 2004, 10067).

[6] In passing out of the world the Lord also made his human Divine good (n. 3194, 3210, 6864, 7499, 8724, 9199, 10076).

This is what is meant by his coming forth from the Father and returning to the Father (n. 3194, 3210).

Thus he became one with the Father (n. 2751, 3704, 4766).

Since that union Divine truth goes forth from the Lord (n. 3704, 3712, 3969, 4577, 5704, 7499, 8127, 8241, 9199, 9398). How Divine truth goes forth, illustrated (n. 7270, 9407).

It was from his own power that the Lord united the human with the Divine (n. 1616, 1749, 1752, 1813, 1921, 2025, 2026, 2523, 3141, 5005, 5045, 6716).

From this it is clear that the Lord's human was not like the human of any other man, in that it was conceived from the Divine itself (n. 10125, 10825, 10826).

His union with the Father, from whom was his soul, was not as between two persons, but as between soul and body (n. 3737, 10824).

[7] The most ancient people could not worship the Divine being *[esse]*, but could worship only the Divine outgo *[existere]*, which is the Divine human; therefore the Lord came into the world in order to become the Divine Existere from the Divine Esse (n. 4687, 5321).

The ancients acknowledged the Divine because he appeared to them in a human form, and this was the Divine human (n. 5110, 5663, 6845, 10737).

The infinite being *[esse]* could flow into heaven with the angels and with men only by means of the Divine human (n. 1676, 1990, 2016, 2034).

In heaven no other Divine than the Divine human is perceived (n. 6475, 9303, 10067, 10267).

The Divine human from eternity was the Divine truth in heaven and the Divine passing through heaven; thus it was the Divine outgo *[existere]* which afterwards in the Lord became the Divine being *[esse per se]*, from which is the Divine Existere in heaven (n. 3061, 6280, 6880, 10579).

What the state of heaven was before the Lord's coming (n. 6371–6373).

The Divine was not perceptible except when it passed through heaven (n. 6982, 6996, 7004).

[8] The inhabitants of all the earth worship the Divine under a human form, that is, the Lord (n. 6700, 8541–8547, 10736–10738).

They rejoice when they hear that God actually became Man (n. 9361).

All who are in good and who worship the Divine under the human form, are received by the Lord (n. 9359).

God cannot be thought of except in human form; and what is incomprehensible does not fall into any idea, so neither into belief (n. 9359, 9972).

Man is able to worship that of which he has some idea, but not that of which he has no idea (n. 4733, 5110, 5663, 7211, 9356, 10067, 10267).

Therefore the Divine is worshiped under a human form by most of the inhabitants of the entire globe, and this is the effect of influx from heaven (n. 10159).

All who are in good in regard to their life, when they think of the Lord, think of the Divine human, and not of the human separate from the Divine; it is otherwise with those who are not in good in regard to their life (n. 2326, 4724, 4731, 4766, 8878, 9193, 9198).

In the church at this day those that are in evil in regard to their life, and those that are in faith separate from charity, think of the human of the Lord apart from the Divine, and do not even comprehend what the Divine human is—why they do not (n. 3212, 3241, 4689, 4692, 4724, 4731, 5321, 6872, 8878, 9193, 9198).

The Lord's human is Divine because it is from the being *[esse]* of the Father, and this was his soul—illustrated by a father's likeness in children (n. 10269, 10372, 10823).

Also because it was from the Divine love, which was the very being *[esse]* of his life from conception (n. 6872).

Every man is such as his love is, and is his love (n. 6872, 10177, 10284). The Lord made all his human, both internal and external, Divine (n. 1603, 1815, 1902, 1926, 2083, 2093).

Therefore, differently from any man, he rose again as to his whole body (n. 1729, 2083, 5078, 10825).

[9] That the Lord's human is Divine is acknowledged from his omnipresence in the Holy Supper (n. 2343, 2359).

Also from his transfiguration before his three disciples (n. 3212).

Also from the Word of the Old Testament, in that he is called God (n. 10154); and is called Jehovah (n. 1603, 1736, 1815, 1902, 2921, 3035, 5110, 6281, 6303, 8864, 9194, 9315).

In the sense of the letter a distinction is made between the Father and the Son, that is, between Jehovah and the Lord, but not in the internal sense of the Word, in which the angels of heaven are (n. 3035).

In the Christian world the Lord's human has been declared not to be Divine; this was done in a council for the pope's sake, that he might be acknowledged as the Lord's vicar (n. 4738).

[10] Christians were examined in the other life in regard to their idea of one God, and it was found they held an idea of three gods (n. 2329, 5256, 10736–10738, 10821).

A Divine trinity or trine in one person, constituting one God, is conceivable, but not in three persons (n. 10738, 10821, 10824).

A Divine trine in the Lord is acknowledged in heaven (n. 14, 15, 1729, 2004, 5256, 9303).

The trine in the Lord is the Divine itself, called the Father, the Divine human, called the Son, and the Divine going forth, called the Holy Spirit, and this Divine trine is a One (n. 2149, 2156, 2288, 2319, 2329, 2447, 3704, 6993, 7182, 10738, 10822, 10823).

The Lord himself teaches that the Father and he are One (n. 1729, 2004, 2005, 2018, 2025, 2751, 3704, 3736, 4766); also that the holy Divine goes forth from him and is his (n. 3969, 4673, 6788, 6993, 7499, 8127, 8302, 9199, 9228, 9229, 9264, 9407, 9818, 9820, 10330).

[11] The Divine human flows into heaven and makes heaven (n. 3038). The Lord is the all in heaven and is the life of heaven (n. 7211, 9128). In the angels the Lord dwells in what is his own (n. 9338, 10125, 10151, 10157).

Consequently those who are in heaven are in the Lord (n. 3637, 3638).

The Lord's conjunction with angels is measured by their reception of the good of love and charity from him (n. 904, 4198, 4205, 4211, 4220, 6280, 6832, 7042, 8819, 9680, 9682, 9683, 10106, 10810).

The entire heaven has reference to the Lord (n. 551, 552). The Lord is the common center of heaven (n. 3633, 3641).

All in heaven turn themselves to the Lord, who is above the heavens (n. 9828, 10130, 10189).

Nevertheless angels do not turn themselves to the Lord, but the Lord turns them to himself (n. 10189).

It is not a presence of angels with the Lord, but the Lord's presence with angels (n. 9415).

In heaven there is no conjunction with the Divine itself, but conjunction with the Divine human (n. 4211, 4724, 5663).

[12] Heaven corresponds to the Divine human of the Lord; consequently heaven in general is as a single man, and for this reason heaven is called the greatest man (n. 2996, 2998, 3624–3649, 3741–3745, 4625).

The Lord is the Only Man, and those only are men who receive the Divine from him (n. 1894).

So far as they receive are they men and images of him (n. 8547).

Therefore angels are forms of love and charity in human form, and this from the Lord (n. 3804, 4735, 4797, 4985, 5199, 5530, 9879, 10177).

[13] The whole heaven is the Lord's (n. 2751, 7086).

He has all power in the heavens and on earth (n. 1607, 10089, 10827).

As the Lord rules the whole heaven he also rules all things depending thereon, thus all things in the world (n. 2025, 2026, 4523, 4524).

The Lord alone has the power to remove the hells, to withhold from evils, and to hold in good, thus to save (n. 10019).

12

There Is a Correspondence
of All Things of Heaven
with All Things of Man

87. What correspondence is, is not known at the present day, for several reasons, the chief of which is that man has withdrawn himself from heaven by the love of self and love of the world. For he that loves self and the world above all things gives heed only to worldly things, since these appeal to the external senses and gratify the natural longings; and he does not give heed to spiritual things, since these appeal to the internal senses and gratify the mind, therefore he casts them aside, saying that they are too high for his comprehension. This was not so with the ancient people. To them the knowledge of correspondences was the chief of knowledges. By means of it they acquired intelligence and wisdom; and by means of it those who were of the church had communication with heaven; for the knowledge of correspondences is angelic knowledge. The most ancient people, who were celestial men, thought from correspondence itself, as the angels do. And therefore they talked with angels, and the Lord frequently appeared to them, and they were taught by him. But at this day that knowledge has been so completely lost that no one knows what correspondence is.[1]

1. How far the knowledge of correspondences excels other knowledges (n. 4280).

The knowledge of correspondences was the chief knowledge of the ancient people; but at the present day it is wholly forgotten (n. 3021, 3419, 4280, 4749, 4844, 4964, 4966, 6004, 7729, 10252).

The knowledge of correspondences flourished among the Eastern nations and in Egypt (n. 5702, 6692, 7097, 7779, 9391, 10407).

88. Since, then, without a perception of what correspondence is there can be no clear knowledge of the spiritual world or of its inflow into the natural world, neither of what the spiritual is in its relation to the natural, nor any clear knowledge of the spirit of man, which is called the soul, and its operation into the body, neither of man's state after death, it is necessary to explain what correspondence is and the nature of it. This will prepare the way for what is to follow.

89. First, what correspondence is. The whole natural world corresponds to the spiritual world, and not merely the natural world in general, but also every particular of it; and as a consequence everything in the natural world that springs from the spiritual world is called a correspondent. It must be understood that the natural world springs from and has permanent existence from the spiritual world, precisely like an effect from its effecting cause. All that is spread out under the sun and that receives heat and light from the sun is what is called the natural world; and all things that derive their subsistence therefrom belong to that world. But the spiritual world is heaven; and all things in the heavens belong to that world.

90. Since man is both a heaven and a world in least form after the image of the greatest (see above, n. 57), there is in him both a spiritual and a natural world. The interior things that belong to his mind, and that have relation to understanding and will, constitute his spiritual world; while the exterior things that belong to his body, and that have relation to its senses and activities, constitute his natural world. Consequently, everything in his natural world (that is, in his body and its senses and activities), that has its existence from his spiritual world (that is, from his mind and its understanding and will) is called a correspondent.

91. From the human face it can be seen what correspondence is. In a face that has not been taught to dissemble, all the affections of the mind present themselves to view in a natural form, as in their type. This is why the face is called the index of the mind; that is, it is man's spiritual world presented in his natural world. So, too, what pertains to the understanding is presented in speech, and what pertains to the will is presented in the movements of the body. So whatever effects are produced in the body, whether in the face, in speech, or in bodily movements, are called correspondences.

92. All this shows also what the internal man is and what the external, namely, that the internal is what is called the spiritual man, and the external what is called the natural man; also that the one is distinct from the other as heaven is from the world; also that all things that take place and come forth in the external or natural man take place and come forth from the internal or spiritual man.

93. This much has been said about the correspondence of man's internal or spiritual with his external or natural; now the correspondence of the whole heaven with everything pertaining to man shall be treated of.

94. It has been shown that the entire heaven reflects a single man, and that it is in image a man and is therefore called the greatest man. It has also been shown that the angelic societies, of which heaven consists, are therefore arranged as the members, organs, and viscera are in man, that is, some are in the head, some in the breast, some in the arms, and some in each of their particulars (see above, n. 59–72); consequently the societies in any member there correspond to the like member in man; those in the head corresponding to the head in man, those in the breast to the breast in man, those in the arms to the arms in man; and so with all the rest. It is from this correspondence that man has permanent existence, for from heaven alone does man have permanent existence.

95. That heaven is divided into two kingdoms, one called the celestial kingdom and the other the spiritual kingdom, may be

seen above in its own chapter. The celestial kingdom corresponds in general to the heart and all things of the heart in the whole body, and the spiritual kingdom to the lungs and to all things of the lungs in the whole body. Likewise in man heart and lungs form two kingdoms, the heart ruling there through the arteries and veins, and the lungs through the tendinous and motor fibers, both together in every exertion and movement.

So in every man, in his spiritual world, which is called his spiritual man, there are two kingdoms, one of the will and the other of the understanding, the will ruling through affections for good, and the understanding through affections for truth; and these kingdoms correspond to the kingdoms of the heart and of the lungs in the body. It is the same in the heavens; the celestial kingdom is the voluntary part of heaven, and in it good of love reigns; the spiritual kingdom is the intellectual part of heaven, and in it truth reigns. These are what correspond to the functions of the heart and lungs in man. It is on account of this correspondence that in the Word the "heart" signifies the will and also good of love, and the "breath" of the lungs signifies the understanding and the truth of faith. For the same reason affections are ascribed to the heart, although they are neither in it nor from it.[2]

___

2. The correspondence of the heart and lungs with the Greatest Man, which is heaven, from experience (n. 3883–3896).

The heart corresponds to those in the celestial kingdom, and the lungs to those in the spiritual kingdom (n. 3885–3887).

There is in heaven a pulse like that of the heart, and a respiration like that of the lungs, but interior (n. 3884, 3885, 3887).

There the pulse of the heart varies in conformity to states of love, and the respiration in conformity to states of charity and faith (n. 3886, 3887, 3889).

In the Word the "heart" means the will, and "from the heart" means from the will (n. 2930, 7542, 8910, 9113, 10336).

In the Word the "heart" also signifies love, and "from the heart" means from love (n. 7542, 9050, 10336).

96. The correspondence of the two kingdoms of heaven with the heart and lungs is the general correspondence of heaven with man. There is a less general correspondence with each one of his members, organs, and viscera; and what this is shall also be explained. In the greatest man, which is heaven, those that are in the head excel all others in every good, being in love, peace, innocence, wisdom, intelligence, and consequent joy and happiness. These flow into the head of man and the things belonging to the head and corresponding thereto. In the greatest man, or heaven, those that are in the breast are in the good of charity and of faith, and these flow into the breast of man and correspond to it. In the greatest man, or heaven, those that are in the loins and the organs devoted to generation are in marriage love. Those in the feet are in the lowest good of heaven, which is called spiritual-natural good. Those in the arms and hands are in the power of truth from good. Those that are in the eyes are in understanding; those in the ears are in attention and obedience; those in the nostrils are in perception; those in the mouth and tongue are in the ability to converse from understanding and perception; those in the kidneys are in truths searching, separating, and correcting; those in the liver, pancreas, and spleen are in various purifications of good and truth; and so with the rest. All these flow into the like things of man and correspond to them. This inflow of heaven is into the functions and uses of the bodily members; and the uses, since they are from the spiritual world, take on a form by means of such things as are in the natural world, and thus present themselves in effect. From this is the correspondence.

97. For the same reason these same members, organs, and viscera have a like significance in the Word; for everything there has a meaning in accordance with correspondence. Thus the "head" signifies intelligence and wisdom; the "breast" charity; the "loins" marriage love; the "arms and hands" power of truth; the "feet" what is natural; the "eyes" understanding; the "nostrils" perception; the "ears" obedience, the "kidneys" the scrutiny of truth, and so on.[3] So, too, in the common speech of man it is said of one who is intelligent and wise that he has a good head; of one who is charitable that he is a bosom friend; of one who has clear perception that he is keen scented; of one who is intelligent that he is sharp sighted; of one who is powerful that he is long handed; of one who exercises his will from love that it is done from the heart. These and many other expressions in the speech of men are from correspondence, for they are from the spiritual world, although man is ignorant of it.

98. That there is such a correspondence of all things of heaven with all things of man has been made clear to me by much experience, by so much that I am as convinced of it as of any evident fact that admits of no doubt. But it is not necessary to describe all this experience here; nor would it be permissible on account of its abundance. It may be seen set forth in *Arcana Coelestia,* where correspondences, representations, the influx of the spiritual world into the natural world, and the interaction between soul and body, are treated of.[4]

3. In the Word the "breast" signifies charity (n. 3934, 10081, 10087). The "loins" and organs of generation signify marriage love (n. 3021, 4280, 4462, 5050–5052). The "arms" and "hands" signify the power of truth (n. 878, 3091, 4931–4937, 6947, 7205, 10019).

The "feet" signify the natural (n. 2162, 3147, 3761, 3986, 4280, 4938–4952). The "eye" signifies understanding (n. 2701, 4403–4421, 4523–4534, 6923, 9051, 10569). The "nostrils" signify perception (n. 3577, 4624, 4625, 4748, 5621, 8286, 10054, 10292). The "ears" signify obedience (n. 2542, 3869, 4523, 4653, 5017, 7216, 8361, 8990, 9311, 9397, 10061).

The "kidneys" signify the scrutiny and correction of truth (n. 5380–5386, 10032).

4. The correspondence of all the members of the body with the Greatest Man, or heaven, in general and in particular, from experience (n. 3021, 3624–3649, 3741–3750, 3883–3895, 4039–4054, 4218–4228, 4318–4331, 4403–4421, 4523–4533, 4622–4633, 4652–4660, 4791–4805, 4931–4953, 5050–5061, 5171–5189, 5377–5396, 5552–5573, 5711–5727, 10030).

The influx of the spiritual world into the natural world, or of heaven into the world, and the influx of the soul into all things of the body, from experience (n. 6053–6058, 6189–6215, 6307–6326, 6466–6495, 6598–6626).

The intercourse between soul and body, from experience (n. 6053–6058, 6189–6215, 6307–6327, 6466–6495, 6598–6626).

99. But notwithstanding that all things of man's body correspond to all things of heaven, it is not in respect to his external form that man is an image of heaven, but in respect to his internal form; for man's interiors are what receive heaven, while his exteriors receive the world. So far, therefore, as his interiors receive heaven, man is in respect to them a heaven in least form, after the image of the greatest. But so far as his interiors do not receive heaven he is not a heaven and an image of the greatest, although his exteriors, which receive the world, may be in a form in accordance with the order of the world, and thus variously beautiful. For the source of outward beauty which pertains to the body is in parents and formation in the womb, and it is preserved afterwards by general influx from the world. For this reason the form of one's natural man differs greatly from the form of his spiritual man. What the form of a man's spirit is I have been shown occasionally; and in some who were beautiful and charming in appearance the spirit was seen to be so deformed, black and monstrous that it might be called an image of hell, not of heaven; while in others not beautiful there was a spirit beautifully formed, pure, and angelic. Moreover, the spirit of man appears after death such as it has been in the body while it lived therein in the world.

100. But correspondence applies far more widely than to man; for there is a correspondence of the heavens with one another. To the third or inmost heaven the second or middle heaven corresponds, and to the second or middle heaven the first or outmost heaven corresponds, and this corresponds to the bodily forms in man called his members, organs, and viscera. Thus it is the bodily part of man in which heaven finally terminates, and upon which it stands as upon its base. But this arcanum will be more fully unfolded elsewhere.

101. Especially it must be understood that all correspondence with heaven is with the Lord's Divine human, because heaven is from him, and he is heaven, as has been shown in previous chapters. For if the Divine human did not flow into all things of heaven, and in accordance with correspondences into all things of the world, no angel or man could exist. From this again it is evident why the Lord became Man and clothed his Divine from first to last with a human. It was because the Divine human, from which heaven existed before the Lord's coming, was no longer sufficient to sustain all things, for the reason that man, who is the foundation of the heavens, had subverted and destroyed order. What the Divine human was before the Lord's coming, and what the condition of heaven was at that time may be seen in the extracts appended to the preceding chapter.

102. Angels are amazed when they hear that there are men who attribute all things to nature and nothing to the Divine, and who also believe that their body, into which so many wonders of heaven are gathered, is a product of nature. Still more are they amazed that the rational part of man is believed to be from nature, when, if men will but lift their minds a little, they can see that such effects are not from nature but from the Divine; and that nature has been created simply for clothing the spiritual and for presenting it in a correspondent form in the outmost of order. Such men they liken to owls, which see in darkness, but in light see nothing.

13

There Is a Correspondence
of Heaven with All Things
of the Earth

103. What correspondence is has been told in the preceding chapter, and it has there been shown that each thing and all things of the animal body are correspondences. The next step is to show that all things of the earth, and in general all things of the universe, are correspondences.

104. All things of the earth are distinguished into three kinds, called kingdoms, namely, the animal kingdom, the vegetable kingdom, and the mineral kingdom. The things of the animal kingdom are correspondences in the first degree, because they live; the things of the vegetable kingdom are correspondences in the second degree, because they merely grow; the things of the mineral kingdom are correspondences in the third degree, because they neither live nor grow. Correspondences in the animal kingdom are living creatures of various kinds, both those that walk and creep on the ground and those that fly in the air; these need not be specially named, as they are well known. Correspondences in the vegetable kingdom are all things that grow and abound in gardens, forests, fields, and meadows; these, too, need not be named, because they are well known. Correspondences in the mineral kingdom are metals more and less noble, stones precious and not precious, earths of various kinds, and also the waters. Besides these the things prepared from them by human activity for use are correspondences, as foods of every kind, clothing, dwellings and other buildings, with many other things.

105. Also the things above the earth, as the sun, moon, and stars, and those in the atmosphere, as clouds, mists, rain, lightning and thunder, are likewise correspondences. Things resulting from the presence and absence of the sun, as light and shade, heat and cold, are also correspondences, as well as those that follow in succession therefrom, as the seasons of the year, spring, summer, autumn, and winter; and the times of day, morning, noon, evening, and night.

106. In a word, all things that have existence in nature, from the least to the greatest thereof, are correspondences.[1] They are correspondences because the natural world with all things in it springs forth and subsists from the spiritual world, and both worlds from the Divine. They are said to subsist also, because everything subsists from that from which it springs forth, subsistence being a permanent springing forth; also because nothing can subsist from itself, but only from that which is prior to itself, thus from a First, and if separated from that it would utterly perish and vanish.

107. Everything in nature that springs forth and subsists in accordance with Divine order is a correspondence. Divine order is caused by the Divine good that flows forth from the Lord. It begins in him, goes forth from him through the heavens in succession into the world, and is terminated there in outmosts; and everything there that is in accordance with order is a correspondence. Everything there is in accordance with order that is good and perfect for use, because everything good is good in the measure of its use; while its form has relation to truth, truth

---

1. All things that are in the world and its three kingdoms correspond to the heavenly things that are in heaven, that is, the things in the natural world correspond to the things in the spiritual world (n. 1632, 1881, 2758, 2760–2763, 2987–3003, 3213–3227, 3483, 3624–3649, 4044, 4053, 4116, 4366, 4939, 5116, 5377, 5428, 5477, 9280).

By correspondences the natural world is conjoined to the spiritual world (n. 8615).

For this reason all nature is a theater representative of the Lord's kingdom (n. 2758, 2999, 3000, 3483, 4938, 4939, 8848, 9280).

being the form of good. And for this reason everything in the whole world and of the nature thereof that is in Divine order has reference to good and truth.[2]

108. That all things in the world spring from the Divine, and are clothed with such things in nature as enable them to exist there and perform use, and thus to correspond, is clearly evident from the various things seen in both the animal and vegetable kingdoms. In both there are things that anyone who thinks interiorly can see to be from heaven. For illustration a few things out of a countless number may be mentioned; and first some things from the animal kingdom. Many are aware what knowledge there is engrafted as it were in every animal. Bees know how to gather honey from flowers, to build cells out of wax in which to store their honey, and thus provide food for themselves and their families, even for a coming winter. That a new generation may be born their queen lays eggs, and the rest take care of them and cover them. They live under a sort of government which all know by instinct. They preserve the working bees and cast out the drones, depriving them of their wings; besides other wonderful things implanted in them from heaven for the sake of their use, their wax everywhere serving the human race for candles, their honey for adding sweetness to food.

[2] Again, what wonders do we see in worms, the meanest creatures in the animal kingdom! They know how to get food from the juice of the leaves suited to them, and afterward at the appointed time to invest themselves with a covering and enter as it were into a womb, and thus hatch offspring of their own kind. Some are first turned into nymphs and chrysalides, spinning threads about themselves; and this travail being over they

---

2. Everything in the universe, both in heaven and in the world, that is in accordance with order, has reference to good and truth (n. 2451, 3166, 4390, 4409, 5232, 7256, 10122); and to the conjunction of these, in order to be anything (n. 10555).

come forth clad with a different body, furnished with wings with which they fly in the air as in their heaven, and celebrate marriages and lay eggs and provide posterity for themselves.

[3] Besides these special instances all creatures in general that fly in the air know the proper food for their nourishment, not only what it is but where to find it; they know how to build nests for themselves, one kind in one way and another kind in another way; how to lay their eggs in the nests, how to sit upon them, how to hatch their young and feed them, and to turn them out of their home when they are able to shift for themselves. They know, too, their enemies that they must avoid and their friends with whom they may associate, and this from early infancy; not to mention the wonders in the eggs themselves, in which all things lie ready in their order for the formation and nourishment of the chicks; besides numberless other things.

[4] Who that thinks from any wisdom of reason will ever say that these instincts are from any other source than the spiritual world, which the natural serves in clothing what is from it with a body, or in presenting in effect what is spiritual in the cause? The beasts of the earth and the birds of the air are born into all this knowledge, while man, who is far superior to them, is not; for the reason that animals are in the order of their life, and have not been able to destroy what is in them from the spiritual world, because they have no rational faculty. Man, on the other hand, whose thought is from the spiritual world, having perverted what is in him from that world by a life contrary to order, which his rational faculty has favored, must needs be born into mere ignorance and afterwards be led back by Divine means into the order of heaven.

109. How the things in the vegetable kingdom correspond can be seen from many instances, as that little seeds grow into trees, put forth leaves, produce flowers, and then fruit, in which again they deposit seed, these things taking place in succession and existing together in an order so wonderful as to be indescribable

in a few words. Volumes might be filled, and yet there would be still deeper arcana, relating more closely to their uses, which science would be unable to exhaust. Since these things, too, are from the spiritual world, that is, from heaven, which is in the human form (as has been shown above in its own chapter), so all the particulars in this kingdom have a certain relation to such things as are in man, as some in the learned world know. That all things in this kingdom also are correspondences has been made clear to me by much experience. Often when I have been in gardens and have been looking at the trees, fruits, flowers, and plants there, I have recognized their correspondences in heaven, and have spoken with those with whom these were, and have been taught whence and what they were.

110. But at the present day no one can know the spiritual things in heaven to which the natural things in the world correspond except from heaven, since the knowledge of correspondences is now wholly lost. But the nature of the correspondence of spiritual things with natural I shall be glad to illustrate by some examples. The animals of the earth correspond in general to affection, mild and useful animals to good affections, fierce and useless ones to evil affections. In particular, cattle and their young correspond to the affections of the natural mind, sheep and lambs to the affections of the spiritual mind; while birds correspond, according to their species, to the intellectual things of the natural or the spiritual mind.[3] For this reason various

3. From correspondence animals signify affections; mild and useful animals good affections, fierce and useless ones evil affections (n. 41, 45, 46, 142, 143, 246, 714, 716, 719, 2179, 2180, 3519, 9280); illustrated by experience from the spiritual world (n. 3218, 5198, 9090). Influx of the spiritual world into the lives of animals (n. 1633, 3646).

Cattle and their young from correspondence signify affections of the natural mind (n. 2180, 2566, 9391, 10132, 10407). What sheep signify (n. 4169, 4809); and lambs (n. 3994, 10132).

Flying creatures signify intellectual things (n. 40, 745, 776, 778, 866, 988, 991, 5149, 7441); with a difference according to their genera and species, from experience in the spiritual world (n. 3219).

animals, as cattle and their young, rams, sheep, he-goats, and
she-goats, he-lambs and she-lambs, also pigeons and turtledoves,
were devoted to a sacred use in the Israelitish church, which
was a representative church, and sacrifices and burnt offerings
were made of them. For they correspond in that use to spiritual
things, and in heaven these were understood in accordance with
the correspondences. Moreover, animals according to their kinds
and species, because they have life, are affections; and the life
of each one is solely from affection and in accordance with
affection; consequently every animal has an innate knowledge
that is in accord with its life's affection. Man is like an animal
so far as his natural man is concerned, and is therefore likened
to animals in common speech; for example, if he is gentle he is
called a sheep or lamb, if fierce a bear or wolf, if cunning a fox
or serpent, and so on.

111. There is a like correspondence with things in the vegetable kingdom. In general, a garden corresponds to the intelligence and wisdom of heaven; and for this reason heaven is
called the Garden of God, and Paradise;[4] and men call it the
heavenly paradise. Trees, according to their species, correspond
to the perceptions and knowledges of good and truth which are
the source of intelligence and wisdom. For this reason the ancient people, who were acquainted with correspondences, held
their sacred worship in groves;[5] and for the same reason trees
are so often mentioned in the Word, and heaven, the church,
and man are compared to them; as the vine, the olive, the cedar,

---

4. From correspondence a garden and a paradise signify intelligence and wisdom (n.
100, 108); from experience (n. 3220).

All things that have a correspondence have in the Word the same significance (n.
2896, 2987, 2989–2991, 3002, 3225).

5. Trees signify perceptions and knowledges (n. 103, 2163, 2682, 2722, 2972, 7692).

For this reason the ancient people held Divine worship in groves under trees according to their correspondence (n. 2722, 4552). Influx of heaven into subjects of the
vegetable kingdom, as into trees and plants (n. 3648).

and others, and the good works done by men are compared to fruits. Also the food derived from trees, and more especially from the grain harvests of the field, corresponds to affections for good and truth, because these affections feed the spiritual life, as the food of the earth does the natural life;[6] and bread from grain, in a general sense, because it is the food that specially sustains life, and because it stands for all food, corresponds to an affection for all good. It is on account of this correspondence that the Lord calls himself the bread of life; and that loaves of bread had a holy use in the Israelitish church, being placed on the table in the tabernacle and called "the bread of faces"; also the Divine worship that was performed by sacrifices and burnt offerings was called "bread." Moreover, because of this correspondence the most holy act of worship in the Christian church is the Holy Supper, in which bread is given, and wine.[7] From these few examples the nature of correspondence can be seen.

112. How conjunction of heaven with the world is effected by means of correspondences shall also be told in a few words. The Lord's kingdom is a kingdom of ends, which are uses; or what is the same thing, a kingdom of uses which are ends. For this reason the universe has been so created and formed by the Divine that uses may be everywhere clothed in such a way as to be presented in act, or in effect, first in heaven and afterwards in the world, thus by degrees and successively, down to the outmost things of nature. Evidently, then, the correspondence of natural things with spiritual things, or of the world with heaven, is

6. From correspondence foods signify such things as nourish the spiritual life (n. 3114, 4459, 4792, 4976, 5147, 5293, 5340, 5342, 5410, 5426, 5576, 5582, 5588, 5655, 5915, 6277, 8562, 9003).

7. Bread signifies every good that nourishes the spiritual life of man (n. 2165, 2177, 3478, 3735, 3813, 4211, 4217, 4735, 4976, 9323, 9545, 10686). Such was the signification of the loaves that were on the table in the tabernacle (n. 3478, 9545). Sacrifices in general were called bread (n. 2165). Bread includes all food (n. 2165). Thus it signifies all heavenly and spiritual food (n. 276, 680, 2165, 2177, 3478, 6118, 8410).

through uses, and uses are what conjoin; and the form in which uses are clothed are correspondences and are conjunctions just to the extent that they are forms of uses. In the nature of the world in its threefold kingdom, all things that exist in accordance with order are forms of uses, or effects formed from use for use, and this is why the things in nature are correspondences. But in the case of man, so far as he is in accordance with Divine order, that is, so far as he is in love to the Lord and in charity toward the neighbor, are his acts uses in form, and correspondences, and through these he is conjoined to heaven. To love the Lord and the neighbor means in general to perform uses.[8] Furthermore, it must be understood that man is the means by which the natural world and the spiritual world are conjoined, that is, man is the medium of conjunction, because in him there is a natural world and there is a spiritual world (see above, n. 57); consequently to the extent that man is spiritual he is the medium of conjunction; but to the extent that a man is natural, and not spiritual, he is not a medium of conjunction. Nevertheless, apart from this mediumship of man, a Divine influx into the world and into the things pertaining to man that are of the world goes on, but not into man's rational faculty.

---

8. Every good has its delight as well as its quality from use and in accordance with use; therefore such as the use is, such is the good (n. 3049, 4984, 7038).

Angelic life consists in the goods of love and charity, that is, in performing uses (n. 454). The Lord, and consequently the angels, look only, in regard to man, to ends, which are uses (n. 1317, 1645, 5854).

The Lord's kingdom is a kingdom of uses, that is, of ends (n. 454, 696, 1103, 3645, 4054, 7038). Serving the Lord is performing uses (n. 7038).

Each thing and all things in man have been formed for use (n. 3626, 4104, 5189, 9297); also from use, that is, the use is prior to the organic forms in man through which the use is performed, because use is from the inflowing of the Lord through heaven (n. 4223, 4926). Moreover man's interiors, which constitute his mind, when he grows to maturity are formed from use and for use (n. 1964, 6815, 9297).

Consequently man is such as are the uses with him (n. 1568, 3570, 4054, 6571, 6935, 6938, 10284). Uses are the ends for the sake of which (n. 3565, 4054, 4104, 6815).

Use is the first and the last, thus the all of man (n. 1964).

113. As all things that are in accord with Divine order correspond to heaven, so all things contrary to Divine order correspond to hell. All things that correspond to heaven have relation to good and truth; but those that correspond to hell have relation to evil and falsity.

114. Something shall now be said about the knowledge of correspondences and its use. It has been said above that the spiritual world, which is heaven, is conjoined with the natural world by means of correspondences; therefore by means of correspondences communication with heaven is granted to man. For the angels of heaven do not think from natural things, as man does; but when man has acquired a knowledge of correspondences he is able, in respect to the thoughts of his mind, to be associated with the angels, and thus in respect to his spiritual or internal man to be conjoined with them. That there might be such a conjunction of heaven with man the Word was written wholly by correspondences, each thing and all things in it being correspondent.[9] If man, therefore, had a knowledge of correspondences he would understand the spiritual sense of the Word, and from that it would be given him to know arcana of which he sees nothing in the sense of the letter. For there is a literal sense and there is a spiritual sense in the Word, the literal sense made up of such things as are in the world, and the spiritual sense of such things as are in heaven. And such a Word, in which everything down to the least jot is a correspondence, was given to men because the conjunction of heaven with the world is effected by means of correspondences.[10]

115. I have been taught from heaven that the most ancient men on our earth, who were celestial men, thought from corre-

9. The Word was written wholly by correspondences (n. 8615).

By means of the Word man has conjunction with heaven (n. 2899, 6943, 9396, 9400, 9401, 10375, 10452).

10. Concerning the spiritual sense of the Word see the little work *White Horse* referred to in Revelation.

spondences themselves, the natural things of the world before their eyes serving them as means of thinking in this way; and that they could be in fellowship with angels and talk with them because they so thought, and that thus through them heaven was conjoined to the world. For this reason that period was called the Golden Age, of which it is said by ancient writers that the inhabitants of heaven dwelt with men and associated with them as friends with friends. But after this there followed a period when men thought, not from correspondences themselves, but from a knowledge of correspondences, and there was then also a conjunction of heaven with man, but less intimate. This period was called the Silver Age. After this there followed men who had a knowledge of correspondences but did not think from that knowledge, because they were in natural good, and not, like those before them, in spiritual good. This period was called the Copper Age. After this man gradually became external, and finally corporeal, and then the knowledge of correspondences was wholly lost, and with it a knowledge of heaven and of the many things pertaining to heaven. It was from correspondence that these ages were named from gold, silver, and copper,[11] and for the reason that from correspondence gold signifies celestial good in which were the most ancient people, silver spiritual good in which were the ancient people that followed, and copper natural good in which were the next posterity; while iron, from which the last age takes its name, signifies hard truth apart from good.

11. Gold from correspondence signifies celestial good (n. 113, 1551, 1552, 5658, 6914, 6917, 9510, 9874, 9881). Silver signifies spiritual good, that is, truth from a celestial origin (n. 1551, 1552, 2954, 5658). Copper signifies natural good (n. 425, 1551). Iron signifies truth in the outmost of order (n. 425, 426).

14

The Sun in Heaven

116. In heaven neither the sun of the world, nor anything from that sun, is seen, because it is wholly natural. For nature has its beginning from that sun, and whatever is produced by means of it is called natural. But the spiritual, to which heaven belongs, is above nature and wholly distinct from what is natural; and there is no communication between the two except by correspondences. What the distinction between them is may be understood from what has been already said about degrees (n. 38), and what the communication is from what has been said in the two preceding chapters about correspondences.

117. Although the sun of the world is not seen in heaven, nor anything from that sun, there is nevertheless a sun there, and light and heat, and all things that are in the world, with innumerable others, but not from a like origin; since the things in heaven are spiritual, and those in the world are natural. The sun of heaven is the Lord; the light there is the Divine truth and the heat the Divine good that go forth from the Lord as a sun. From this origin are all things that spring forth and are seen in the heavens. This light and heat and things existing therefrom in heaven will be treated of in the following chapters; in this chapter we will speak only of the sun there. In heaven the Lord is seen as a sun, for the reason that he is Divine love, from which all spiritual things, and by means of the sun of the world all natural things, have their existence. That love is what shines as a sun.

118. That the Lord is actually seen in heaven as a sun I have not only been told by angels, but it has occasionally been granted me to see it; and therefore what I have heard and seen respecting the Lord as a sun I shall be glad to tell in a few words. The Lord is seen as a sun, not in heaven, but high above the heavens; and not directly overhead or in the zenith, but before the faces of the angels at a middle height. He is seen at a considerable distance, in two places, one before the right eye and the other before the left eye. Before the right eye he is seen exactly like a sun, as it were, with a glow and size like that of the sun of the world. But before the left eye he is not seen as a sun, but as a moon, glowing white like the moon of our earth, and of like size, but more brilliant, and surrounded with many little moons, as it were, each of them of similar whiteness and splendor. The Lord is seen so differently in two places because every person sees the Lord in accordance with the quality of his reception of the Lord, thus he is seen in one way by those that receive him with the good of love, and in another by those that receive him with the good of faith. Those that receive him with the good of love see him as a sun, fiery and flaming, in accordance with their reception of him; these are in his celestial kingdom; while those that receive him with the good of faith see him as a moon, white and brilliant in accordance with their reception of him, and these are in his spiritual kingdom.[1]

This is so because the good of love corresponds to fire; therefore in the spiritual sense fire is love; and the good of faith corresponds to light, and in the spiritual sense light is faith.[2]

---

1. The Lord is seen in heaven as a sun, and is the sun of heaven (n. 1053, 3636, 3643, 4060). The Lord is seen as a sun by those who are in His celestial kingdom, where love to Him reigns, and as a moon by those who are in His spiritual kingdom, where charity to the neighbor and faith reign (n. 1521, 1529–1531, 1837, 4696).

The Lord is seen as a sun at a middle height before the right eye, and as a moon before the left eye (n. 1053, 1521, 1529–1531, 3636, 3643, 4321, 5097, 7078, 7083, 7173, 7270, 8812, 10809). The Lord is seen as a sun and as a moon (n. 1531, 7173).

The Lord's Divine itself is far above His Divine in heaven (n. 7270, 8760).

2. "Fire" in the Word signifies love, both in a good sense and in a bad sense (n. 934, 4906, 5215).

And the Lord appears before the eyes because the interiors, which belong to the mind, see through the eyes, from good of love through the right eye, and from good of faith through the left eye;[3] since with angels and also with men all things at the right correspond to good from which truth is derived, and all at the left to truth that is from good.[4] Good of faith is in its essence truth from good.

119. This is why in the Word the Lord in respect to love is likened to the sun, and in respect to faith to the moon; also that the "sun" signifies love from the Lord to the Lord, and the "moon" signifies faith from the Lord in the Lord, as in the following passages:

The light of the moon shall be as the light of the sun, and the light of the sun shall be sevenfold, as the light of seven days (Isa. 30:26).

And when I shall extinguish thee I will cover the heavens and make the stars thereof dark; I will cover the sun with a cloud, and the moon shall not make her light to shine. All luminaries of light in the heavens will I make dark over thee, and I will set darkness upon thy land (Ezek. 32:7, 8).

I will darken the sun in his going forth, and the moon shall not make her light to shine (Isa. 13:10).

The sun and the moon shall be darkened, and the stars shall withdraw their shining. The sun shall be turned into darkness and the moon into blood (Joel 2:2, 10, 31; 3:15).

The sun became black as sackcloth and hair, and the moon became as blood, and the stars fell unto the earth (Rev. 6:12, 13).

Holy or heavenly fire signifies the Divine Love (n. 934, 6314, 6832).

Infernal fire signifies love of self and of the world and every lust of those loves (n. 1861, 5071, 6314, 6832, 7575, 10747).

Love is the fire of life and life itself is really from it (n. 4906, 5071, 6032, 6314).

"Light" signifies the truth of faith (n. 3195, 3485, 3636, 3643, 3993, 4302, 4413, 4415, 9548, 9684).

3. The sight of the left eye corresponds to truths of faith, and the sight of the right eye to their goods (n. 4410, 6923).

4. The things on man's right have relation to good from which is truth, and those on his left to truth from good (n. 9495, 9604).

Immediately after the affliction of those days the sun shall be darkened, and the moon shall not give her light, and the stars shall fall from heaven (Matt. 24:29).

And elsewhere. In these passages the "sun" signifies love, and the "moon" faith, and the "stars" knowledges of good and truth.[5] These are said to be darkened, to lose their light, and to fall from heaven, when they are no more. That the Lord is seen as a sun in heaven is evident also from his appearance when transfigured before Peter, James, and John:

That his face did shine as the sun (Matt. 17:2).

These disciples thus saw the Lord when they were withdrawn from the body, and were in the light of heaven. It was because of this correspondence that the ancient people, with whom was a representative church, turned the face to the sun in the east when they were in Divine worship; and for the same reason they gave to their temples an eastern aspect.

120. How great the Divine love is and what it is can be seen by comparison with the sun of the world, that it is most ardent, if you will believe it, much more ardent than that sun. For this reason the Lord as a sun does not flow without mediums into the heavens, but the ardor of his love is gradually tempered on the way. These temperings appear as radiant belts about the sun; furthermore, the angels are veiled with a thin adapting cloud to prevent their being harmed by the influx.[6] For this reason the heavens are more or less near in accordance with reception. As

---

5. "Stars" and "constellations" in the Word signify knowledges of good and truth (n. 2495, 2849, 4697).

6. What the Lord's Divine love is, and how great it is, is illustrated by comparison with the fire of this world's sun (n. 6834, 6849, 8644).

The Lord's Divine love is love toward the whole human race to save it (n. 1820, 1865, 2253, 6872).

The love that first goes forth from the fire of the Lord's love does not enter heaven, but is seen as radiant belts about the sun (n. 7270).

The angels are veiled with a corresponding thin cloud, to prevent their being harmed by the inflow of burning love (n. 6849).

the higher heavens are in good of love they are nearest to the Lord as the sun; and as the lower heavens are in good of faith they are farther away from him. But those that are in no good, like those in hell, are farthest away, at different distances in accordance with their opposition to good.[7]

121. When, however, the Lord appears in heaven, which often occurs, he does not appear encompassed with a sun, but in the form of an angel, yet distinguished from angels by the Divine shining through from his face, since he is not there in person, for in person the Lord is constantly encompassed by the sun, but he is present by look. For it is a common occurrence in heaven for persons to appear to be present in a place where their look is fixed or is terminated, even when this place is far away from where they really are. This presence is called the presence of internal sight, which will be treated of further on. I have also seen the Lord out of the sun in an angelic form, at a height a little below the sun; also nearby in a like form, with shining face, and once in the midst of angels as a flamelike radiance.

122. To the angels the sun of the world appears like a dense darkness opposite to the sun of heaven, and the moon like a darkness opposite to the moon of heaven, and this constantly; and for the reason that the world's fieriness corresponds to the love of self, and the light from it corresponds to what is false from that love; and the love of self is the direct opposite of the

7. The Lord's presence with the angels is in proportion to their reception of good of love and faith from Him (n. 904, 4198, 4320, 6280, 6832, 7042, 8819, 9680, 9682, 9683, 10106, 10811).

The Lord appears to each one in accordance with what he is (n. 1861, 3235, 4198, 4206).

The hells are at a distance from the heavens because they cannot bear the presence of Divine love from the Lord (n. 4299, 7519, 7738, 7989, 8137, 8265, 9327).

For this reason the hells are very far away from the heavens, and this is the "great gulf" (n. 9346, 10187).

Divine love; and what is false from that love is the direct opposite of the Divine truth; and the opposite of the Divine love and the Divine truth is to the angels thick darkness. Therefore, in the Word, to worship the sun and moon of this world and bow down to them, signifies to love self and the falsities that spring from the love of self, and it is said that such would be cut off (Deut. 4:19; 16:3–5; Jer. 8:1, 2; Ezek. 8:15, 16, 18; Rev. 16:8; Matt. 13:6).[8]

123. As it is from the Divine love that is in and from him that the Lord appears in heaven like a sun, so all in the heavens are turned constantly to him—those in the celestial kingdom to him as a sun and those in the spiritual kingdom to him as a moon. But those that are in hell turn themselves to an opposite darkness and dense darkness, that is, they turn backwards, away from the Lord; and for the reason that all in the hells are in love of self and the world, thus antagonistic to the Lord.

Those who turn themselves to the dense darkness that is in the place where this world's sun is are in the hells behind, and are called genii; while those that turn themselves to the darkness that is in the place of the moon are in the hells more in front, and are called spirits. This is why those in the hells are said to be in darkness, and those in the heavens in light, "darkness" signifying falsity from evil, and "light" truth from good. They so turn themselves because all in the other life look toward what rules in their interiors, thus to their loves; and with angels and spirits the interiors determine the face; and in the spiritual world quarters are not fixed, as in the natural world, but are determined by the face. In respect

8. The sun of the world is not seen by the angels, but in its place something dark behind, opposite to the sun of heaven or the Lord (n. 7078, 9755).

In the opposite sense the "sun" signifies the love of self (n. 2441); and in this sense "to worship the sun" signifies to worship what is contrary to heavenly love or to the Lord (n. 2441, 10584).

To those in the hells the sun of heaven is thick darkness (n. 2441).

to his spirit man turns himself in like manner as a spirit does, backwards from the Lord if he is in love of self and the world, and toward the Lord if he is in love to the Lord and the neighbor. But of this man is ignorant, because he is in the natural world where quarters are determined by the rising and setting of the sun. But as this cannot be easily comprehended by men it will be elucidated hereafter when quarters, space, and time in heaven are treated of.

124. Because the Lord is the sun of heaven and everything that is from him looks to him, he is also the common center, the source of all direction and determination.[9] So, too, all things beneath are in his presence and under his auspices, both in the heavens and on the earths.

125. From all this what has been said and shown in previous chapters about the Lord may now be seen in clearer light, namely: That he is the God of heaven (n. 2–6). That it is his Divine that makes heaven (n. 7–12). That the Lord's Divine in heaven is love to him and charity toward the neighbor (n. 13–19). That there is a correspondence of all things of the world with heaven, and through heaven with the Lord (n. 87–115). Also that the sun and moon of the world are correspondences (n. 105).

---

9. The Lord is the common center to which all things of heaven turn (n. 3633, 3641).

15

Light and Heat in Heaven

126. That there is light in the heavens those who think from nature alone cannot comprehend; and yet such is the light in the heavens that it exceeds by many degrees the noonday light of the world. That light I have often seen, even during the evening and night. At first I wondered when I heard the angels say that the light of this world is little more than a shadow in comparison with the light of heaven; but having seen it I can testify that it is so. The brightness and splendor of the light of heaven are such as cannot be described. All things that I have seen in the heavens have been seen in that light, thus more clearly and distinctly than things in this world.

127. The light of heaven is not a natural light, like the light of the world, but a spiritual light, because it is from the Lord as a sun, and that sun is the Divine love (as has been shown in the foregoing chapter). That which goes forth from the Lord as a sun is called in the heavens Divine truth, but in its essence it is Divine good united to Divine truth. From this the angels have light and heat, light from Divine truth, and heat from Divine good. As the light of heaven, and the heat also, are from such a source, it is evident that they are spiritual and not natural.[1]

---

1. All light in the heavens is from the Lord as a sun (n. 1053, 1521, 3195, 3341, 3636, 3643, 4415, 9548, 9684, 10809).

The Divine truth that goes forth from the Lord appears in heaven as light, and furnishes all the light of heaven (n. 3195, 3222, 3223, 5400, 8644, 9399, 9548, 9684).

128. The Divine truth is light to the angels because the angels are spiritual and not natural. Spiritual beings see from their sun, and natural beings from theirs. It is from Divine truth that angels have understanding, and their understanding is their inner sight, which flows into and produces their outer sight; therefore in heaven whatever is seen from the Lord as the sun is seen in light.[2] This being the source of light in heaven the light is varied there in accordance with the reception of Divine truth from the Lord; or what is the same, in accordance with the intelligence and wisdom in which the angels are, thus differently in the celestial kingdom and in the spiritual kingdom, and differently in each society. In the celestial kingdom the light appears flaming because the angels there receive light from the Lord as a sun; but in the spiritual kingdom the light is shining white, because the angels there receive light from the Lord as a moon (see above, n. 118). So, too, the light differs in different societies, and again in each society, those that are at the center being in greater light and those in the circumference in less light (see n. 43). In a word, the angels have light in the same degree in which they are recipients of Divine truth, that is, are in intelligence and wisdom from the Lord;[3] and this is why the angels of heaven are called angels of light.

129. As the Lord in the heavens is Divine truth, and the Divine truth there is light, so in the Word he is called Light, likewise all truth is from him, as in the following passages:

Jesus said, I am the light of the world; he that followeth Me shall not walk in darkness, but shall have the light of life (John 8:12).

2. The light of heaven illumines both the sight and the understanding of angels and spirits (n. 2776, 3138).

3. The light in heaven is in harmony with the intelligence and wisdom of the angels (n. 1524, 1529, 1530, 3339).

Differences of light in the heavens are as many as there are angelic societies; and as there are in the heavens endless varieties of good and truth, so are there are of wisdom and intelligence (n. 684, 690, 3241, 3744, 3745, 4414, 5598, 7236, 7833, 7836).

As long as I am in the world I am the light of the world (John 9:5).

Jesus said, Yet a little while is the light with you. Walk while ye have the light, lest darkness overtake you. While ye have the light believe in the light, that ye may be sons of light. I have come a light into the world, that whosoever believeth in Me may not abide in darkness (John 12:35, 36, 46).

Light has come into the world, but men have loved the darkness rather than the light (John 3:19).

John says of the Lord:

This is the true light which lighteneth every man (John 1:9).

The people that sit in darkness have seen a great light, and to them that were sitting in the shadow of death light is sprung up (Matt. 4:16).

I will give thee for a covenant of the people, for a light of the Gentiles (Isa. 42:6).

I have established Thee for a light of the Gentiles that Thou mayest be my salvation unto the end of the earth (Isa. 49:6).

The nations of them that are saved shall walk in his light (Rev. 21:24).

Send out Thy light and Thy truth; let them lead me (Ps. 43:3).

In these and other passages the Lord is called light from Divine truth, which is from him; and the truth itself is likewise called light. As light in the heavens is from the Lord as a sun, so when he was transfigured before Peter, James, and John:

His face did shine as the sun, and his raiment was white as the light (Matt. 17:2).

And his garments became shining, exceeding white as snow, so as no fuller on earth can whiten them (Mark 9:3; Matt. 17:2).

The Lord's garments had this appearance because they represented Divine truth which is from him in the heavens, "garments" also in the Word signifying truths,[4] consequently it is said in David:

---

4. In the Word "garments" signify truths, because truths clothe good (n. 1073, 2576, 5248, 5319, 5954, 9216, 9952, 10536).

The Lord's garments when He was transfigured signified Divine truth going forth from His Divine love (n. 9212, 9216).

O Jehovah, Thou coverest Thyself with light as with a garment (Ps. 104:2).

130. That light in the heavens is spiritual and that this light is Divine truth may be inferred also from the fact that men as well as angels have spiritual light, and have enlightenment from that light so far as they are in intelligence and wisdom from Divine truth. Man's spiritual light is the light of his understanding, and the objects of that light are truths, which he arranges analytically into groups, forms into reason, and from them draws conclusions in series.[5] The natural man does not know that the light from which the understanding sees such things is a real light, for he neither sees it with his eyes nor perceives it by thought. And yet there are many who recognize this light, and distinguish it from the natural light in which those are who think naturally and not spiritually. Those think naturally who take account of the world only, and attribute all things to nature; while those think spiritually who take account of heaven and attribute all things to the Divine. It has often been granted me to perceive and also to see that there is a true light that enlightens the mind, wholly distinct from the light that is called natural light *[lumen]*. I have been raised up interiorly into that light by degrees; and as I was raised up my understanding became so enlightened as to enable me to perceive what I did not perceive before, and finally such things as I could not even comprehend by thought from natural light. Sometimes I felt indignant that I could not comprehend these things when they

5. Man is rational because his understanding is illumined by the light of heaven (n. 1524, 3138, 3167, 4408, 6608, 8707, 9128, 9399, 10569).

The understanding is enlightened because it is a recipient of truth (n. 6222, 6608, 10659). The understanding is enlightened to the extent that man receives truth in good from the lord (n. 3619). The understanding is such as are the truths from good by which it is formed (n. 10064). The understanding has light from heaven, as the sight has light from the world (n. 1524, 5114, 6608, 9128).

The light of heaven from the Lord is always present with man, but it flows in only in the degree that man is in truth from good (n. 4060, 4214).

were so clearly and plainly perceived in the light of heaven.[6] Because there is a light that belongs to the understanding, the same things are said of it as of the eye, as that it sees and is in light when it perceives, and is in obscurity and shade when it does not perceive, and so on.

131. As the light of heaven is Divine truth, that light is also Divine wisdom and intelligence; therefore to be raised up into the light of heaven means the same as to be raised up into intelligence and wisdom and enlightened. For this reason the angels have light in just the same degree as they have intelligence and wisdom. Because the light of heaven is Divine wisdom, in that light the character of everyone is recognized. The interiors of everyone lie open to view in his face just as they are, with not the least thing hidden. And interior angels love to have all things that pertain to them lying open, since they will nothing but good. It is otherwise with those beneath heaven, who do not will what is good, and for that reason fear greatly to be seen in the light of heaven. And wonderful to tell, while those in hell appear to one another as men, in the light of heaven they appear as monsters, with a horrid face and body, the exact form of their own evil.[7] In respect to his spirit man appears, when seen by angels, in a like way; if good as a man, beautiful in accord with his good; if evil as a monster, ugly in accord with his evil. From this it is clear that in the light of heaven all things are made manifest, and for the reason that the light of heaven is Divine truth.

---

6. When man is raised up from the sensual he comes into a milder light, and at length into heavenly light (n. 6313, 6315, 9407).

When man is raised up into intelligence there is an actual elevation into the light of heaven (n. 3190). How great a light was perceived when I was withdrawn from worldly ideas (n. 1526, 6608).

7. Those in the hells, in their own light, which is like the light from burning coals, appear to themselves as men; but in the light of heaven they appear as monsters (n. 4531, 4533, 4674, 5057, 5058, 6605, 6626).

132. As Divine truth is light in the heavens, so all truths wherever they are, whether within an angel or outside of him, or whether within the heavens or outside of them, emit light. Nevertheless, truths outside of the heavens do not shine as truths within the heavens do. Truths outside of the heavens shine coldly, like something snowy, without heat, because they do not draw their essence from good, as truths within the heavens do; therefore that cold light vanishes as soon as the light of heaven falls on it, and if there is evil underneath it, it is turned into darkness. This I have occasionally seen, with many other noteworthy things about the shining of truth, which must be omitted here.

133. Something shall now be said about the heat of heaven. That heat in its essence is love. It goes forth from the Lord as a sun, which is Divine love in the Lord and from the Lord, as has been shown in the preceding chapter. It is evident, therefore, that the heat of heaven, like the light of heaven, is spiritual, because from the same source.[8] There are two things that go forth from the Lord as a sun, Divine truth and Divine good; Divine truth is manifested in the heavens as light, and Divine good as heat; and yet Divine truth and Divine good are so united that they are not two, but one. Nevertheless, with angels they are separate, for there are angels that receive more of Divine good than of Divine truth, and there are those that receive more of Divine truth than of Divine good. Those who receive more of Divine good are in the Lord's celestial kingdom, and those who receive more of Divine truth are in his spiritual kingdom. Those that receive both in a like degree are the most perfect angels.

---

8. There are two sources of heat and also two sources of light, the sun of the world and the sun of heaven (n. 3338, 5215, 7324).

Heat from the Lord as a sun is affection of love (n. 3636, 3643).

Therefore spiritual heat in its essence is love (n. 2146, 3338, 3339, 6314).

134. The heat of heaven, like the light of heaven, is everywhere different. It is different in the celestial kingdom from what it is in the spiritual kingdom, and it is different in each society therein. It differs both in degree and in quality. It is more intense and more pure in the Lord's celestial kingdom, because the angels there receive more of Divine good; and it is less intense and pure in his spiritual kingdom, because the angels there receive more of Divine truth. Also in each society the heat differs in accordance with reception. There is heat in the hells, but it is unclean heat.[9] The heat in heaven is what is meant by holy and heavenly fire, and the heat of hell by profane and infernal fire. Both mean love—heavenly fire meaning love to the Lord and love to the neighbor and every affection of those loves, and infernal fire meaning love of self and love of the world and every lust of those loves. That love is heat from a spiritual source is shown from one's growing warm with love; for in accordance with the strength and nature of his love a man is inflamed and grows warm; and the heat of his love is made manifest when it is opposed. From this also it is customary to speak of being inflamed, growing hot, burning, boiling, being on fire, both in regard to the affections of the love of good and the lusts of the love of evil.

135. Love going forth from the Lord as a sun is felt in heaven as heat, because the interiors of the angels are in a state of love from the Divine good that is from the Lord; and in consequence their exteriors which grow warm therefrom are in a state of heat. For this reason heat and love so correspond to each other in heaven that everyone there is in heat such as his love is, according to what has been said just above. This world's heat does not enter heaven at all, because it is too gross, and is natural,

---

9. There is heat in the hells, but it is unclean (n. 1773, 2757, 3340).
    The odor from it is like the odor from dung and excrement in the world, and in the worst hells like the odor of dead bodies (n. 814, 815, 817, 819, 820, 943, 944, 5394).

and not spiritual; but with men it is otherwise, because they are in both the spiritual world and the natural world. As to their spirits they grow warm in exact accordance with their loves; but as to the body they grow warm both from the heat of their spirit and from the heat of the world. The former flows into the latter, because they correspond. The nature of the correspondence of the two kinds of heat can be seen from animal life, in that the love of animals—the chief of which is the love of propagating offspring of their kind—bursts forth and becomes active in accordance with the presence and influence of heat from the sun of the world, which is the heat of the spring and the summer seasons. Those who believe that the world's heat flows in and excites these loves are greatly mistaken, for there can be no influx from the natural into the spiritual, but only from the spiritual into the natural. This influx is of Divine order, but the other would be contrary to Divine order.[10]

136. Angels, like men, have understanding and will. The light of heaven constitutes the life of their understanding, because that light is Divine truth and Divine wisdom therefrom; and the heat of heaven constitutes the life of their will, because that heat is Divine good and Divine love therefrom. The veriest life of the angels is from heat, and from light only so far as heat is in it. That life is from heat is shown by the fact that when heat is taken away life perishes. The same is true of faith without love or of truth without good; since the truth that is called truth of faith is light, and the good that is called good of love is heat.[11] This is more clearly shown by the heat and light of the

10. There is spiritual influx, but not physical, that is, there is influx from the spiritual world into the natural, but not from the natural world into the spiritual (n. 3219, 5119, 5259, 5427, 5428, 5477, 6322, 9109, 9110, 9111).

11. Truths apart from good are not in themselves truths because they have no life; for truths have all their life from good (n. 9603). Thus truths apart from good are like a body without a soul (n. 3180, 9154). Truths apart from good are not accepted by the Lord (n. 4368).

world, to which the heat and light of heaven correspond. By the world's heat when conjoined with light, as in spring and summer, all things on the earth are quickened and grow, but by light separate from heat nothing is quickened or grows, but everything lies torpid and dies. They are not conjoined in winter, when heat is absent though light remains. From this correspondence heaven is called paradise, since truth is there joined with good, or faith with love, as light is with heat in springtime on the earth. All this makes more clear the truth set forth in its own chapter (n. 13–19), that the Divine of the Lord in Heaven is love to him and charity toward the neighbor.

137. It is said in John:

> In the beginning was the Word, and the Word was with God, and God was the Word. All things were made through him, and without him was not anything made that hath been made. In Him was life, and the life was the light of men. He was in the world, and the world was made through him. And the Word became flesh and dwelt among us, and we beheld his glory (John 1:1–14).

Evidently the Lord is here meant by "the Word," for it is said that "the Word became flesh." But what is specifically meant by "the Word" is not known and shall therefore be explained. Here "the Word" means the Divine truth which is in the Lord and from the Lord;[12] and this is why it is also called "the Light," which is the Divine truth, as has been already shown in this chapter. That it was by means of Divine truth that all things were created and made shall now be explained.

What truth apart from good, that is, what faith apart from love is, and what truth from good or faith from love is (n. 1949–1951, 1964, 5830, 5951). It amounts to the same thing whether you say truth or faith, or whether you say good or love, since truth is of faith and good is of love (n. 2839, 4352, 4353, 4997, 7178, 7623, 7624, 10367).

12. In the Sacred Scripture "word" signifies various things, namely, speech, thought of the mind, anything that really exists, also something, and in the highest sense Divine truth, and the Lord (n. 9987). "Word" signifies Divine truth (n. 2803, 2894, 4692, 5075, 5272, 9383, 9987). "Word" signifies the Lord (n. 2533, 2859).

[2] In heaven Divine truth has all power, and apart from it there is no power whatever.[13] From the Divine truth angels are called powers, and are powers to the extent that they are recipients or receptacles of it. By means of it they prevail over the hells and over all that oppose them. A thousand enemies there cannot stand against a single ray of the light of heaven, which is Divine truth. As angels are angels by their reception of Divine truth it follows that the entire heaven is from no other source, since heaven consists of angels.

[3] That there is such power in Divine truth those cannot believe that have no other idea of truth than that it is thought or speech, which has in it no power except as others do it from obedience. But Divine truth has power in itself, and such power that by means of it heaven was created and the world with all things therein. That there is such power in Divine truth may be shown by two comparisons—by the power of truth and good in man, and by the power of light and heat from the sun in the world. *By the power of good and truth in man,* in that everything that a man does he does from his understanding and will—from his will by means of good and from his understanding by means of truth; for all things in the will have relation to good and all things in the understanding have relation to truth.[14] Therefore it is from good and truth that man moves his whole body, and

13. Divine truth going forth from the Lord has all power (n. 6948, 8200).

Truth from good has all power in heaven (n. 3091, 3563, 6344, 6423, 8304, 9643, 10019, 10182).

Angels are called powers, and are powers by the reception of Divine truth from the Lord (n. 9639).

Angels are recipients of Divine truth from the Lord and therefore in the Word are sometimes called gods (n. 4295, 4402, 7873, 8192, 8301).

14. The understanding is a recipient of truth, and the will a recipient of good (n. 3623, 6125, 7503, 9300, 9930).

Therefore all things in the understanding have relation to truths, whether they are really truths or are believed by man to be truths, and all things in the will in like manner have relation to goods (n. 803, 10122).

a thousand things therein rush with one accord to do their will and pleasure. This makes clear that the whole body is formed for subservience to good and truth, consequently is formed by good and truth.

[4] *By the power of heat and light from the sun in the world,* in that all things that grow in the world, as trees, cereals, flowers, grasses, fruits, and seeds, come into existence wholly by means of the heat and light of the sun; which shows what power of producing there is in them. What, then, must be the power in Divine light, which is Divine truth, and in Divine heat, which is Divine good? Because heaven has its existence from these, so does the world have its existence therefrom, since the world has its existence by means of heaven, as has been already shown. From all this the meaning of these words can be seen that "all things were made through the Word, and without the Word was not anything made that has been made"; also that "the world was made through him," that is, through Divine truth from the Lord.[15] For the same reason, in the book of Genesis, light is first spoken of, and then the things that are from light (Gen. 1:3, 4). For this reason also all things in the universe, both in heaven and in the world, have relation to good and truth and to their conjunction, in order to be anything.

139.[16] It must be understood that the Divine good and the Divine truth that are from the Lord as a sun in the heavens are not in the Lord, but are from the Lord. In the Lord there is only Divine love, which is the being *[esse]* from which the Divine good and the Divine truth spring. Outgo *[existere]* from being *[esse]* is meant by going forth *[procedere]*. This, too, can be made clear by comparison with the world's sun. The heat

---

15. Divine truth going forth from the Lord is the only real thing (n. 6880, 7004, 8200). By means of Divine truth all things were created and made (n. 2803, 2884, 5272, 7678).

16. [There is no n. 138 in the original. —*Editor.*]

and light that are in the world are not in the sun, but are from the sun. In the sun there is fire only, and it is from this that heat and light spring and go forth.

140. Since the Lord as a sun is Divine love, and Divine love is Divine good itself, the Divine that goes forth from the Lord, which is his Divine in heaven, is called, for the sake of distinction, Divine truth, although it is in fact Divine good united to Divine truth. This Divine truth is what is called the holy that goes forth from him.

16

The Four Quarters in Heaven

141. Both in heaven and in the world there are four quarters, east, south, west, and north, determined in each world by its own sun; in heaven by the sun of heaven, which is the Lord, in the world by the sun of the world. And yet there are great differences between them. In the first place, in the world that is called the south where the sun is in its greatest altitude above the earth, north where it is in its opposite position beneath the earth, east where it rises at an equinox, and west where it then sets. Thus in the world it is from the south that all the quarters are determined. But in heaven that is called the east where the Lord is seen as a sun, opposite to this is the west, at the right is the south in heaven, and at the left the north; and this in whatever direction the face and the body are turned. Thus in heaven it is from the east that all the quarters are determined. That is called the east *[oriens]* where the Lord is seen as a sun, because all origin *[origo]* of life is from him as a sun; moreover, so far as angels receive heat and light or love and intelligence from the Lord he is said to arise *[exoriri]* upon them. For the same reason the Lord is called the east *[oriens]* in the Word.[1]

142. Another difference is that to the angels the east is always before the face, the west behind, the south to the right, and the north to the left. But since this cannot be easily comprehended in the world, for the reason that men turn the face to every quarter, it shall be explained. The entire heaven turns itself to

---

1. In the highest sense the Lord is the east *[oriens]*, because He is the sun of heaven, which is always rising and never setting (n. 101, 5097, 9668).

the Lord as to its common center; to that center do all the angels turn themselves. Also on the earth, as is well known, there is a directing of all things toward a common center; but there is this difference between this directing in the world and that in heaven, that in heaven the front parts are turned to the common center, but in the world the lower parts of the body. In the world this directing is called centripetal force, also gravitation. The interiors of angels are actually turned forwards; and since interiors manifest themselves in the face it is the face that determines the quarters.[2]

143. It is still more difficult to comprehend in the world that *in every turning of their face and body* the angels have the east before the face, since man according as he turns, has every quarter before his face. This shall also be explained. Although angels, like men, turn and direct their faces and bodies in every direction, they nevertheless have the east always before their eyes. But the turnings of angels are unlike the turnings of men, because they are from a different origin. They appear alike, but they are not. The origin of these turnings is their ruling love, and from this all directions with angels and spirits are determined, for, as just said, their interiors are actually turned toward their common center, which in heaven is the Lord as a sun; consequently their ruling love is always before their face, because their love is always before their interiors, and the face has existence from the interiors, for it is their outward form; and in the heavens this love is the Lord as a sun because it is from him that they have their love.[3] And as the Lord himself is in angels in his love, it is

2. In heaven all turn themselves to the Lord (n. 9828, 10130, 10189, 10420).

Nevertheless, it is not the angels that turn themselves to the Lord, but the Lord turns the angels to Himself (n. 10189). It is not that the angels are present with the Lord, but the Lord is present with the angels (n. 9415).

3. In the spiritual world all constantly turn themselves to their loves; and the quarters there have their beginning in the face and are determined by it (n. 10130, 10189, 10420, 10702). The face is formed to a correspondence with the interiors (n. 4791–4805, 5695). Therefore the interiors shine forth from the face (n. 3527, 4066, 4796). With angels the

the Lord who causes them to look to him whithersoever they turn. This cannot be explained any further now; but it will be made clearer to the understanding in subsequent chapters, especially where representations and appearances, and time and space in heaven, are treated of. That the angels have the Lord constantly before their faces it has been granted me to know and also to perceive from much experience; for whenever I have been in company with angels I have noticed the Lord's presence before my face, not actually seen, and yet perceptible in a light; and angels have often testified that this is so. As the Lord is constantly before the faces of the angels, so it is said in the world of those who believe in the Lord and love him that they have God before their eyes and their face, and that they look to God, and see God. These expressions have their origin in the spiritual world, from which are many things in human speech, although their source is unknown to men.

144. This turning to the Lord is among the wonderful things in heaven. There may be many together in one place, some turning the face and body one way and some another, and yet all see the Lord before them, and everyone has the south at his right, the north at his left, and the west behind him. Another wonderful thing is that, although the angels look only to the east they have also a look toward the other three quarters; but the look to these is from their interior sight, which pertains to their thought. And it is yet another wonderful thing that in heaven no one is ever permitted to stand behind another and look at the back of his head, for this would disturb the influx of good and truth from the Lord.

145. The Lord is seen by the angels, and the angels are seen by the Lord in another way. Angels see the Lord through their

---

face makes one with the interiors (n. 4796, 4797, 4799, 5695, 8250). The influx of the interiors into the face and its muscles (n. 3631, 4800).

eyes; but the Lord sees the angels in the forehead, and this for the reason that the forehead corresponds to love, and it is through love that the Lord flows into their will, while it is through the understanding, to which the eyes correspond, that he causes himself to be seen.[4]

146. The quarters in the heavens that give form to the Lord's celestial kingdom differ from the quarters in the heavens that give form to his spiritual kingdom, for the reason that he is seen by the angels in his celestial kingdom as a sun, but by the angels in his spiritual kingdom as a moon; and where the Lord is seen is the east. The distance there between the position of the sun and that of the moon is thirty degrees, and there is a like difference in the position of the quarters. That heaven is divided into two kingdoms, called the celestial kingdom and the spiritual kingdom, may be seen in its own chapter (n. 20–28); and that the Lord is seen in the celestial kingdom as a sun, and in the spiritual kingdom as a moon (n. 118). But it does not follow that the quarters of heaven become confused on this account, for neither can the spiritual angels ascend among the celestial angels, nor the celestial descend among the spiritual, as may be seen above (n. 35).

147. This makes clear the nature of the Lord's presence in the heavens, that he is everywhere and with everyone in the good and truth that go forth from him; consequently he is with angels in what is his own, as has been said above (n. 12). The perception of the Lord's presence is in their interiors; and it is from these that their eyes see, and it is by this continuity that they see the Lord outside of themselves. This shows what is

---

4. The forehead corresponds to heavenly love; therefore in the Word the "forehead" signifies that love (n. 9936).

The eye corresponds to the understanding, because the understanding is internal sight (n. 2701, 4410, 4526, 9051, 10569).

For this reason "to lift up the eyes" and "to see" signifies to understand, perceive, and observe (n. 2789, 2829, 3198, 3202, 4083, 4086, 4339, 5684).

meant by the Lord's being in them and they in him, according to his own words:

Abide in Me and I in you (John 15:4).

He that eateth My flesh and drinketh My blood abideth in Me and I in him (John 6:56).

"The Lord's flesh" signifies Divine good and "his blood" Divine truth.[5]

148. All in the heavens have their own places of abode in accordance with the quarters. Those who are in the good of love dwell toward the east and west, those who are in clear perception of it toward the east, and those who are in obscure perception of it toward the west. Those who are in wisdom from the good of love dwell toward the south and north—those who are in the clear light of wisdom toward the south, and those who are in obscure light of it toward the north. The angels of the Lord's spiritual kingdom and those of his celestial kingdom dwell in a like order, but differently as their good of love and light of truth from good differ; for in the celestial kingdom the love is love to the Lord, and the light of truth therefrom is wisdom; while in the spiritual kingdom there is love toward the neighbor, which is called charity, and the light of truth therefrom is intelligence, which is also called faith (see above, n. 23). The quarters differ also in the two kingdoms by thirty degrees, as has been said just above (n. 146).

149. In like order the angels in each society in heaven dwell in relation to one another—toward the east there those who are in greater degree of love and charity, toward the west those who are in less degree; toward the south those who are in greater light of wisdom and intelligence, and toward the north

---

5. In the Word "the Lord's flesh" signifies His Divine human, and the Divine good of His love (n. 3813, 7850, 9127, 10283).

And "the Lord's blood" signifies Divine truth and the holy of faith (n. 4735, 4978, 6978, 7317, 7326, 7846, 7850, 7877, 9127, 9393, 10026, 10033, 10152, 10210).

those who are in less. This arrangement prevails because each society represents heaven, and is a heaven in a smaller form (see above, n. 51–58). The same arrangement prevails in their assemblies. They are brought into this order by virtue of the form of heaven, from which everyone knows his own place. The Lord also provides that there be in each society those of every kind, for the reason that in form heaven is everywhere like itself; and yet the arrangement of the whole heaven differs from the arrangement of a society as what is general from its parts, since the societies toward the east surpass those toward the west, and those toward the south surpass those toward the north.

150. Because of this the quarters in the heavens signify such things as pertain to those that dwell in them—the east signifying love and its good clearly perceived, the west the same obscurely perceived, the south wisdom and intelligence in clear light, and the north the same in obscure light. And because of this signification of the quarters in heaven they have a like signification in the internal or spiritual sense of the Word,[6] since the internal or spiritual sense of the Word is in entire accord with what is in heaven.

151. The reverse is true of those in the hells. Those who are there do not look to the Lord as a sun nor as a moon; but they look backward away from the Lord to that dense darkness that is in the place of the sun of the world, and to the darkness that is in the place of the earth's moon. Those that are called genii look to that dense darkness that is in the place of the world's sun, and those called spirits look to the darkness that is in the place of the earth's moon.[7] It has been shown above (n. 122)

---

6. In the Word the "east" signifies love clearly perceived (n. 1250, 3708); the "west" love obscurely perceived (n. 3708, 9653); the "south" a state of light, that is, of wisdom and intelligence (n. 1458, 3708, 5672); and the "north" that state in obscurity (n. 3708).

7. Who and what those are who are called genii, and who and what those are who

that the world's sun and the earth's moon are not seen in the spiritual world, but in place of that sun a dense darkness over against the sun of heaven, and in place of that moon a darkness over against the moon of heaven. For this reason the quarters with those in the hells are opposite to the quarters of heaven. The east to them is where that dense darkness and darkness are, the west is where the sun of heaven is, the south is to their right, and the north to their left, and this also in every turning of their bodies. Nor can they face otherwise, because the whole bent and consequent determination of their interiors tends and strives that way. It has been shown above (n. 143) that the bent and consequent actual determination of the interiors of all in the other life are in harmony with their love. The love of those in the hells is the love of self and the world, and these loves are what are signified by the world's sun and the earth's moon (see n. 122); and these loves are opposite to love to the Lord and love toward the neighbor;[8] and this is the cause of their turning themselves backwards away from the Lord to this dense darkness. Moreover, those in the hells dwell likewise in accordance with their quarters, those who are in evil from love of self dwelling from their east to their west, and those who are in the falsities of evil from their south to their north. But more will be said about this below, where the hells are treated of.

152. When an evil spirit comes among good spirits the quarters are usually so confused that the good scarcely know where

---

are called spirits (n. 947, 5035, 5977, 8593, 8622, 8625).

8. Those that are in the loves of self and of the world turn themselves backwards from the Lord (n. 10130, 10189, 10420, 10702).

Love to the Lord and charity toward the neighbor make heaven, while love of self and love of the world make hell, because the two are opposite (n. 2041, 3610, 4225, 4776, 6210, 7366, 7369, 7490, 8232, 8678, 10455, 10741–10745).

their east is. This I have sometimes seen take place, and have also heard about it from spirits who complained of it.

153. Evil spirits are sometimes seen turned toward the quarters of heaven; and they then have intelligence and perception of truth, but no affection for good; but as soon as they turn back to their own quarters they have no intelligence or perception of truth; and then they declare that the truths they heard and perceived are falsities and not truths, and they wish falsities to be truths. In respect to this turning I have been told that with the evil the intellectual part of the mind can be so turned, but not the voluntary part; and that this is provided by the Lord to the end that everyone may have the ability to see and acknowledge truths, but that no one can receive truths unless he is in good, since it is good, and never evil, that receives them; also that man has a like ability to the end that he may be made better by means of truths. Nevertheless, he is made better only so far as he is in good; consequently a man can in like manner be turned to the Lord; but if his life is evil he immediately turns himself back and confirms in himself the falsities of his evil, which are contrary to the truths he had understood and seen; and this takes place when he thinks in himself from his interior states.

17

Changes of State
of the Angels in Heaven

154. By changes of state of angels their changes in respect to love and faith, and wisdom and intelligence therefrom, are meant, thus their changes in respect to states of life. States are predicated of life and of what belongs to life; and as angelic life is a life of love and faith, and of wisdom and intelligence therefrom, states are predicated of these and are called states of love and faith, and states of wisdom and intelligence. How with angels these states are changed shall now be told.

155. Angels are not constantly in the same state in respect to love, and in consequence in the same state in respect to wisdom; for all their wisdom is from their love and in accordance with their love. Sometimes they are in a state of intense love, sometimes in a state of love not so intense. The state decreases by degrees from its greatest degree to its least. When in their greatest degree of love they are in the light and warmth of their life, or in a clear and delightful state; but in their least degree they are in shade and cold, or in an obscure and undelightful state. From this last state they return again to the first, and so on, these alternations following one after another with variety. There is a sequence of these states like the varied states of light and shade, or of heat and cold, or like morning, noon, evening, and night, day after day in the world, with unceasing variety throughout the year. There is also a correspondence, morning corresponding to the state of their love in its clearness, noon to the state of their wisdom in its clearness, evening to the state of their wisdom in its obscurity, and night to a state of no love or wisdom. But it must be understood that there is no correspondence of night with the states of life of those in heaven, although there is what corresponds to the dawn that precedes morning; what corresponds to night is with those in hell.[1] From this correspondence "day" and "year" signify in the Word states of life in general; "heat" and "light" signify love and wisdom; "morning" the first and highest degree of love; "noon" wisdom in its light; "evening" wisdom in its shade; "dawn" the obscurity that precedes the morning; and "night" the absence of love and wisdom.[2]

156. Together with the state of the angels' interiors which pertain to their love and wisdom, the states of various things that are outside of them and that they see with their eyes are changed; for the things outside of them take on an appearance that is in accord with the things within them. But what things these are, and what kind of things they are, shall be told presently in the chapter on representatives and appearances in heaven.

157. Every angel undergoes and passes through such changes of state, and also every society in general, and yet each one differently, for the reason that they differ in love and wisdom, those in the middle being in a more perfect state than those round about even to the circumference (see above, n. 43, 128). But it would be tedious to specify the differences, since the

1. In heaven there is a state corresponding to the dawn that precedes morning, but no state corresponding to night (n. 6110).

The "dawn" signifies a middle state between the last and the first (n. 10134).

2. Alternations of state in respect to enlightenment and perception occur in heaven, like the times of day in the world (n. 5672, 5962, 6110, 8426, 9213, 10605).

In the Word "day" and "year" signify all states in general (n. 23, 487, 488, 493, 893, 2788, 3462, 4850, 10656).

"Morning" signifies the beginning of a new state, and a state of love (n. 7218, 8426, 8427, 10114, 10134).

"Evening" signifies a state of declining light and love (n. 10134, 10135).

"Night" signifies a state of no love or faith (n. 221, 709, 2353, 6000, 6110, 7870, 7947).

changes each one undergoes are in accord with the quality of his love and faith. From this it happens that while one may be in clearness and delight another may be in obscurity and lack of delight, and this at the same time within the same society. So, too, the state differs in different societies; it is different in the societies of the celestial kingdom from what it is in those of the spiritual kingdom. These differences in the changes of state are in general like the variations of the states of days in different climates on the earth, for with some it is morning when with others it is evening, and with some it is hot when with others it is cold.

158. I have been taught from heaven why there are such changes of state there. The angels said that there are many reasons—first, the delight of life and of heaven, which they have from love and wisdom from the Lord, would gradually lose its value if they were in it continually, as happens with those that are in allurements and pleasures without variety. A second reason is that angels, as well as men, have what is their own [proprium], which is loving self; and all that are in heaven are withheld from what is their own, and so far as they are withheld from it by the Lord are in love and wisdom; but so far as they are not withheld they are in the love of self; and because everyone loves what is his own and is drawn by it[3] they have changes of state or successive alternations. A third reason is that they are in this way perfected, for they thus become accustomed to being held in love to the Lord and withheld from love of self; also that by alternations between delight and lack of delight the perception and sense of good becomes more exquisite.[4] The

3. Man's own [proprium] is loving self (n. 694, 731, 4317, 5660). The Lord cannot be present unless what is man's own is set aside (n. 1023, 1044). It is actually set aside when one is held in good by the Lord (n. 9334–9336, 9447, 9452–9454, 9938).

4. The angels are being perfected to eternity (n. 4803, 6648).

In the heavens one state is never just like another, and from this there is an unceasing process of perfection (n. 10200).

angels added that their changes of state are not caused by the Lord, since the Lord as a sun is unceasingly flowing in with heat and light, that is, with love and wisdom; but the cause is in themselves, in that they love what is their own, and this continually leads them away. This was illustrated by comparison with the sun of the world, that the cause of the changes of state of heat and cold and of light and shade, year by year and day by day, is not in that sun, since it stands unchanged, but the cause is in the earth.

159. I have been shown how the Lord as a sun appears to the angels of the celestial kingdom in their first state, in their second state, and in their third state. I saw the Lord as a sun, at first glowing and brilliant with a splendor that cannot be described; and I was told that such is the appearance of the Lord as a sun to the angels in their first state. Afterwards there appeared a great obscure belt about the sun, and by this its first glow and brilliancy, which gave it such splendor, began to be dulled, and I was told that such is the appearance of the sun to them in their second state. Then the belt seemed by degrees to grow darker, and the sun to appear less glowing, and this by degrees until at length it took on a shining whiteness; and I was told that such is the appearance of the sun to them in their third state. After this, that shining whiteness was seen to move to the left toward the moon of heaven, and to add itself to her light; and in consequence the moon shone forth with unwonted splendor; and I was told that such is the fourth state of those in the celestial kingdom and the first state of those in the spiritual kingdom, and that in both kingdoms changes of state have such alternations; yet not in the whole kingdom at once, but in one society after another. Furthermore, I was told that these alternations are not fixed, but come upon them sooner or later without their knowledge. And it was added that the sun in itself is not thus changed or moved; but it takes on this appearance in accord with their successive progressions of state, since the

Lord appears to everyone in accord with what his state is, thus glowing when one is in intense love and less glowing and finally shining white as his love subsides; and the quality of each one's state was represented by the obscure belt that induced upon the sun these apparent variations in its glow and light.

160. When angels are in the last of these states, which is when they are in what is their own, they begin to be sad. I have talked with them when they were in that state and have seen their sadness; but they said that they hoped to return soon to their former state, and thus into heaven again, as it were; for to them it is heaven to be withheld from what is their own.

161. There are also changes of state in the hells, but these will be described later when hell is treated of.

18

Time in Heaven

162. Although there is a succession and a progression of all things in heaven, as in the world, yet angels have no notion or idea of time and space; and this so completely that they do not even know at all what time and space are. Time in heaven will here be considered, and space in its own chapter.

163. Angels do not know what time is, although with them there is a successive progression of all things, as there is in the world, and this so completely that there is no difference whatever; and the reason is that in heaven instead of years and days there are changes of state; and where there are years and days there are times, but where there are changes of state there are states.

164. In the world there are times because the sun of the world seemingly advances in succession from one degree to another, producing times that are called seasons of the year; and besides, it revolves about the earth, producing times that are called times of day; both of these by fixed alternations. With the sun of heaven it is different. This does not mark years and days by successive progressions and revolutions, but in its appearance it marks changes of state; and this, as has been shown in the preceding chapter, is not done by fixed alternations. Consequently no idea of time is possible to angels; but in its place they have an idea of state (see above n. 154).

165. As angels have no idea derived from time, such as men in the world have, so neither do they have any idea about time and what pertains to it. They do not even know what is meant by the terms of time, such as year, month, week, day, hour, today, tomorrow, yesterday. When angels hear these terms used by man (for angels are always associated with man by the Lord) in place of them they perceive state and what pertains to states. Thus the natural thought of man is turned into spiritual thought with angels. This is why times in the Word signify states, and the terms of time, as enumerated above, signify corresponding spiritual things.[1]

166. The like is true of all things that exist from time, as the four seasons of the year, called spring, summer, autumn, and winter; the four periods of the day, morning, noon, evening, and night; and the four ages of man, infancy, youth, manhood, and old age; and all other things that either exist from time or have a succession in accordance with time. In thinking of these a man thinks from time, but an angel from state; and in consequence what there is in them from time with man is with the angels turned into an idea of state. Spring and morning are turned into an idea of the state of love and wisdom such as they are in angels in their first state; summer and noon are turned into an idea of love and wisdom such as they are in the second state; autumn and evening such as they are in the third state; night and winter into an idea of such a state as exists in hell. This is why these periods have a like significance in the Word (see above, n. 155). This makes clear how natural things in the thought of man become spiritual with the angels who are with man.

---

1. Times in the Word signify states (n. 2788, 2837, 3254, 3356, 4814, 4901, 4916, 7218, 8070, 10133, 10605).

Angels think apart from the idea of time and space (n. 3404); the reasons why (n. 1274, 1382, 3356, 4882, 4901, 6110, 7218, 7381).

What a "year" signifies in the Word (n. 487, 488, 493, 893, 2906, 7828, 10209). What a "month" (n. 3814). What a "week" (n. 2044, 3845). What a "day" (n. 23, 487, 488, 6110, 7680, 8426, 9213, 10132, 10605). What "today" (n. 2838, 3998, 4304, 6165, 6984, 9939). What "tomorrow" (n. 3998, 10497). What "yesterday" (n. 6983, 7114, 7140).

167. As angels have no notion of time so they have an idea of eternity different from that which men on the earth have. Eternity means to the angels infinite state, not infinite time.[2] I was once thinking about eternity, and was able, with the idea of time, to perceive what "to eternity" means, namely, without end, but not what "from eternity" means, thus not what God did from eternity before creation. When anxiety on this account arose in my mind I was raised up into the sphere of heaven, and thus into the perception that angels have in respect to eternity; and it was then made clear to me that eternity must be thought of, not from time but from state; and then the meaning of "from eternity" can be seen. This then happened to me.

168. When angels speak with men they never express themselves in natural ideas proper to man, all of which are from time, space, matter, and things analogous thereto, but in spiritual ideas, all of which are from states and their various changes within the angels and outside of them. Nevertheless, when these angelic ideas, which are spiritual, flow into men, they are turned in a moment and of themselves into natural ideas proper to man, that correspond perfectly to the spiritual ideas. Neither angels nor men know that this takes place; but such is all influx of heaven into man. Certain angels were permitted to enter more nearly into my thoughts, even into the natural thoughts in which there were many things from time and space; but as they then understood nothing they suddenly withdrew; and after they had withdrawn I heard them talking, and saying that they had been in darkness.

[2] It has been granted me to know by experience how ignorant the angels are about time. There was a certain one from heaven who was able to enter into natural ideas, such as man has; and after he had done this I talked with him as man with man. At

---

2. Men have an idea of eternity associated with time, but angels apart from time (n. 1382, 3404, 8325).

first he did not know what it was that I called time, and I was therefore obliged to tell him all about it, how the sun appears to be carried about our earth, and to produce years and days, and how years are thereby divided into four seasons, and also into months and weeks, and days into twenty-four hours; and how these times recur by fixed alternations, and how this is the source of times. On hearing this he was surprised, saying that he knew nothing about such things, but only what states are.

[3] In speaking with him I added that it is known in the world, for men speak as if they knew that there is no time in heaven, saying of those who die that they "leave the things of time," and that they "pass out of time," meaning by this out of the world. I said also that some know that times in their origin are states, for they know that times are in exact accord with the states of their affections, short to those who are in pleasant and joyous states, long to those who are in unpleasant and sorrowful states, and various in a state of hope and expectation; and this therefore leads learned men to inquire what time and space are, and some know that time belongs to the natural man.

169. The natural man might think that he would be deprived of all thought if the ideas of time, space, and material things were taken away; for upon these all the thought of man rests.[3] But let him know that so far as thoughts partake of time, space, and matter they are limited and confined, but are unlimited and extended so far as they do not partake of these, since the mind is in that measure raised above bodily and worldly things. This is the source of wisdom to the angels; and such wisdom as is called incomprehensible, because it does not fall into ideas that are wholly made up of what is material.

3. Man does not think, as angels do, apart from the idea of time (n. 3404).

19

Representatives and Appearances
in Heaven

170. The man who thinks from natural light alone is unable to comprehend that there is anything in heaven like what is in the world; and for the reason that from natural light he has previously thought, and established himself in the idea, that angels are nothing but minds, and that minds are like ethereal breaths, having no senses like those of men, thus no eyes, and if no eyes no objects of sight; and yet the angels have every sense that a man has, and far more exquisite senses; and the light by which angels see is far brighter than the light by which man sees. That angels are men in the most complete form, and enjoy every sense, may be seen above (n. 73–77); and that the light in heaven is far brighter than the light in the world (n. 126–132).

171. The nature of the objects that are visible to angels in heaven cannot be described in a few words. For the most part they are like things on earth, but in form far more perfect, and in number more abundant. That such things exist in the heavens is evident from things seen by the prophets—as by Ezekiel in relation to the new temple and the new earth (as described from chap. 40 to 48); by Daniel (from chap. 7 to 12); by John (from the first chapter of Revelation to the last); and by others, as described both in the historic and the prophetic part of the Word. These things were seen by them when heaven was open to them, and heaven is said to be opened when the interior sight, which is the sight of man's spirit, is opened. For what is in the heavens cannot be seen by the eyes of a man's body, but are seen by the eyes of his spirit; and when it seems good to the

Lord these are opened, and man is then withdrawn from the natural light that he is in from the bodily senses and is raised up into spiritual light, which he is in from his spirit. In that light the things in heaven have been seen by me.

172. But although the things seen in heaven are in large part like those on the earth, in essence they are unlike them; for the things in heaven come forth from the sun of heaven, and those on the earth from the sun of the world. The things that come forth from the sun of heaven are called spiritual; those that come forth from the sun of the world are called natural.

173. The things that come forth in heaven do not come forth in the same manner as those on the earth. All things in heaven come forth from the Lord in correspondence with the interiors of the angels. For angels have both interiors and exteriors. All things in their interiors have relation to love and faith, thus to the will and understanding, since the will and understanding are their receptacles; while their exteriors correspond to their interiors. That exterior things correspond to interior things may be seen above (n. 87–115). This is illustrated by what has been said above about the heat and light of heaven—that angels have heat in accordance with the quality of their love, and light in accordance with the quality of their wisdom (n. 128–134). The like is true of all other things that present themselves to the senses of angels.

174. When I have been permitted to be in company with angels, the things there appeared precisely the same as those in the world; and so plainly that I would not have known that I was not in the world and in a king's palace. I also talked with the angels as man with man.

175. As all things that correspond to interiors also represent them they are called "representatives"; and as they differ in each case in accordance with the state of the interiors they are called "appearances." Nevertheless, the things that appear before the

eyes of angels in heaven and are perceived by their senses appear to their eyes and senses as fully living as things on earth appear to man, and even much more clearly, distinctly and perceptibly. Appearances from this source in heaven are called real appearances, because they have real existence. There are appearances also that are not real, which are things that become visible, but do not correspond to interiors.[1] These will be treated of further on.

176. To show what the things are that appear to the angels in accordance with correspondences, I will here mention one only for the sake of illustration. By those who are intelligent, gardens and parks full of trees and flowers of every kind are seen. The trees are planted in a most beautiful order, combined to form arbors with arched approaches and encircling walks, all more beautiful than words can describe. There the intelligent walk, and gather flowers and weave garlands with which they adorn little children. Moreover, there are kinds of trees and flowers there that are never seen and cannot exist on earth. The trees bear fruit that are in accordance with the good of love, in which the intelligent are. These things are seen by them because a

---

1. All things that are visible to the angels are representative (n. 1971, 3213–3226, 3342, 3457, 3475, 3485, 9457, 9481, 9576, 9577). The heavens are full of representatives (n. 1521, 1532, 1619). The representatives are more beautiful as they are more interior in the heavens (n. 3475). As the representatives there are from the light of heaven they are real appearances (n. 3485). The Divine influx is turned into representatives in the higher heavens, and therefrom in the lower heavens also (n. 2179, 3213, 9457, 9481, 9576, 9577). Those things are called representative that appear before the eyes of the angels in such form as are in nature, that is, such as are in the world (n. 9457).

Internal things are thus turned into external (n. 1632, 2987–3002).

What representatives in the heavens are; this made clear by various examples (n. 1521, 1532, 1619–1628, 1807, 1973, 1974, 1977, 1980, 1981, 2299, 2601, 2761, 2762, 3217, 3219, 3220, 3348, 3350, 5198, 9090, 10276).

All things seen in the heavens are in accordance with correspondences and are called representatives (n. 3213–3226, 3342, 3475, 3485, 9457, 9481, 9576, 9577). All things that correspond also represent and likewise signify what they correspond to (n. 2896, 2987, 2989–2991, 3002, 3225).

garden or park and fruit trees and flowers correspond to intelligence and wisdom.[2] That there are such things in heaven is known also on the earth, but only to those who are in good, and who have not extinguished in themselves the light of heaven by means of natural light and its fallacies; for when such think about heaven they think and say that there are such things there as ear hath not heard and eye hath not seen.

2. A "garden" or "park" signifies intelligence and wisdom (n. 100, 108, 3220). What is meant by "the garden of Eden" and "the garden of Jehovah" (n. 99, 100, 1588).

How magnificent the things seen in parks are in the other life (n. 1122, 1622, 2296, 4528, 4529).

"Trees" signify perceptions and knowledges, from which wisdom and intelligence are derived (n. 103, 2163, 2682, 2722, 2972, 7692).

"Fruits" signify goods of love and goods of charity (n. 3146, 7690, 9337).

20

The Garments with Which
Angels Appear Clothed

177. Since angels are men, and live among themselves as men do on the earth, they have garments and dwellings and other such things, with the difference, however, that as they are in a more perfect state all things with them are in greater perfection. For as angelic wisdom surpasses human wisdom to such a degree as to be called ineffable, so is it with all things that are perceived and seen by angels, inasmuch as all things perceived and seen by them correspond to their wisdom (see above, n. 173).

178. The garments with which angels are clothed, like all other things with them, correspond; and because they correspond they have real existence (see above, n. 175). Their garments correspond to their intelligence, and therefore all in the heavens appear clothed in accordance with their intelligence; and as one is more intelligent than another so the garments of one surpass those of another. The most intelligent have garments that blaze as if with flame, others have garments that glisten as if with light; the less intelligent have garments that are glistening white or white without the effulgence; and the still less intelligent have garments of various colors. But the angels of the inmost heaven are not clothed.

179. As the garments of angels correspond to their intelligence they correspond also to truth, since all intelligence is from Divine truth; and therefore it is the same thing whether you say that angels are clothed in accordance with intelligence or in accordance with Divine truth. The garments of some blaze as if with flame, and those of others glisten as if with light, because flame corresponds to good, and light corresponds to truth from good.[1] Some have garments that are glistening white and white without the effulgence, and others garments of various colors, because with the less intelligent the Divine good and truth are less effulgent, and are also received in various ways,[2] glistening white and white corresponding to truth,[3] and colors to its varieties.[4] Those in the inmost heaven are not clothed, because they are in innocence, and innocence corresponds to nakedness.[5]

180. As in heaven the angels are clothed with garments, so when seen in the world they have appeared clothed with garments, as those seen by the prophets and those seen at the Lord's sepulcher:

Whose appearance was as lightning, and their garments glistening and white (Matt. 28:3; Mark 16:5; Luke 24:4; John 20:12, 13).

1. From correspondence "garments" in the Word signify truths (n. 1073, 2576, 5319, 5954, 9212, 9216, 9952, 10536). For the reason that truths clothe good (n. 5248). A "covering" signifies something intellectual, because the intellect is the recipient of truth (n. 6378). "Shining garments of fine linen" signify truths from the Divine (n. 5319, 9469). "Flame" signifies spiritual good, and the light therefrom truth from that good (n. 3222, 6832).

2. Angels and spirits appear clothed with garments in accordance with their truths, thus in accordance with their intelligence (n. 165, 5248, 5954, 9212, 9216, 9814, 9952, 10536).

The garments of some angels are resplendent, others are not (n. 5248).

3. In the Word "glistening white" and "white" signify truth because they are from light in heaven (n. 3301, 3993, 4007).

4. Colors in heaven are variegations of the light there (n. 1042, 1043, 1053, 1624, 3993, 4530, 4742, 4922). Colors signify various things pertaining to intelligence and wisdom (n. 4530, 4677, 4922, 9466). The precious stones in the Urim and Thummim signified, in accordance with their colors, all things of truth from good in the heavens (n. 9865, 9868, 9905). So far as colors partake of red they signify good; so far as they partake of white they signify truth (n. 9466).

5. All in the inmost heavens are innocences, and in consequence appear naked (n. 154, 165, 297, 2736, 3887, 8375, 9960). Innocence is presented in heaven as nakedness (n. 165, 8375, 9960). To the innocent and the chaste nakedness is no shame, because without offense (n. 165, 213, 8375).

And those seen in heaven by John:

> Who had garments of fine linen and white (Rev. 4:4; 19:14).

And because intelligence is from Divine truth:

> The garments of the Lord, when he was transfigured, were radiant and glistening white like the light (Matt. 17:2; Mark 9:3; Luke 9:29).

As light is Divine truth going forth from the Lord (see above, n. 129), so in the Word garments signify truths and intelligence from truths, as in Revelation:

> Those that have not defiled their garments shall walk with Me in white, for they are worthy. He that overcometh shall be clothed in white garments (Rev. 3:4, 5);

> Blessed is he that is awake and keepeth his garments (Rev. 16:15).

And of Jerusalem, which means a church that is in truth,[6] it is written in Isaiah:

> Awake, put on thy strength, O Zion; put on the garments of thy beauty, O Jerusalem (Isa. 52:1).

And in Ezekiel:

> Jerusalem, I girded thee about with fine linen, and covered thee with silk. Thy garments were of fine linen and silk (Ezek. 16:10, 13).

Besides many other passages. But he who is not in truths is said "not to be clothed with a wedding garment," as in Matthew:

> When the king came in he saw a man that had not on a wedding garment; and he said unto him, Friend, how camest thou in hither not having a wedding garment? Wherefore he was cast out into the outer darkness (Matt. 22:11–13).

The house of the wedding feast means heaven and the church because of the conjunction of the Lord with heaven and the church by means of his Divine truth; and for this reason the Lord is called in the Word the bridegroom and husband; and heaven, with the church, is called the bride and the wife.

---

6. "Jerusalem" signifies a church in which there is genuine doctrine (n. 402, 3654, 9166).

181. That the garments of angels do not merely appear as garments, but are real garments, is evident from the fact that angels both see them and feel them, that they have many garments, and that they put them off and put them on, that they care for those that are not in use, and put them on again when they need them. That they are clothed with a variety of garments I have seen a thousand times. When I asked where they got their garments, they said from the Lord, and that they receive them as gifts, and sometimes they are clothed with them unconsciously. They said also that their garments are changed in accordance with their changes of state, that in the first and second state their garments are shining and glistening white, and in the third and fourth state a little less bright; and this likewise from correspondence, because their changes of state have respect to intelligence and wisdom (of which see above, n. 154–161).

182. As everyone in the spiritual world has garments in accordance with his intelligence, that is, in accordance with truths which are the source of intelligence, so those in the hells, because they have no truths, appear clothed in garments, but in ragged, squalid, and filthy garments, each one in accordance with his insanity; and they can be clothed in no others. It is granted them by the Lord to be clothed, lest they be seen naked.

21

The Places of Abode
and Dwellings of Angels

183. As there are societies in heaven and the angels live as men, they have also places of abode, and these differ in accordance with each one's state of life. They are magnificent for those in higher dignity, and less magnificent for those in lower condition. I have frequently talked with angels about the places of abode in heaven, saying that scarcely anyone will believe at the present day that they have places of abode and dwellings; some because they do not see them, some because they do not know that angels are men, and some because they believe that the angelic heaven is the heaven that they see with their eyes around them, and as this appears empty and they suppose that angels are ethereal forms, they conclude that they live in ether. Moreover, they do not comprehend how there can be such things in the spiritual world as there are in the natural world, because they know nothing about the spiritual.

[2] The angels replied that they are aware that such ignorance prevails at this day in the world, and to their astonishment, chiefly within the church, and more with the intelligent than with those whom they call simple. They said also that it might be known from the Word that angels are men, since those that have been seen have been seen as men; and the Lord, who took all his human with him, appeared in like manner. It might be known also that as angels are men they have dwellings and places of abode, and do not fly about in air, as some think in their ignorance, which the angels call insanity, and that although they are called spirits they are not winds.

This they said might be apprehended if men would only think independently of their acquired notions about angels and spirits, as they do when they are not bringing into question and submitting to direct thought whether it is so. For everyone has a general idea that angels are in the human form, and have homes which are called the mansions of heaven, which surpass in magnificence earthly dwellings; but this general idea, which flows in from heaven, at once falls to nothing when it is brought under direct scrutiny and inquiry whether it is so, as happens especially with the learned, who by their own intelligence have closed up heaven to themselves and the entrance of heavenly light.

[3] The like is true of the belief in the life of man after death. When one speaks of it, not thinking at the same time about the soul from the light of worldly learning or from the doctrine of its reunion with the body, he believes that after death he is to live a man, and among angels if he has lived well, and that he will then see magnificent things and perceive joys; but as soon as he turns his thoughts to the doctrine of reunion with the body, or to his theory about the soul, and the question arises whether the soul be such, and thus whether this can be true, his former idea is dissipated.

184. But it is better to present the evidence of experience. Whenever I have talked with angels face to face, I have been with them in their abodes. These abodes are precisely like abodes on the earth which we call houses, but more beautiful. In them there are chambers, parlors, and bedrooms in great number; there are also courts, and there are gardens and flower beds and lawns round about. Where they live together their houses are near each other, arranged one next to the other in the form of a city, with avenues, streets, and public squares, exactly like cities on the earth. I have been permitted to pass through them, looking about on every side, and sometimes entering the houses. This occurred when my inner sight was opened, and I was fully awake.[1]

185. I have seen palaces in heaven of such magnificence as cannot be described. Above they glittered as if made of pure gold, and below as if made of precious stones, some more splendid than others. It was the same within. Both words and knowledge are inadequate to describe the decorations that adorned the rooms. On the side looking to the south there were parks, where, too, everything shone, in some places the leaves glistening as if made of silver, and fruit as if made of gold; while the flowers in their beds formed rainbows with their colors. Beyond the borders, where the view terminated, were seen other palaces. Such is the architecture of heaven that you would say that art there is in its art; and no wonder, because the art itself is from heaven. The angels said that such things and innumerable others still more perfect are presented before their eyes by the Lord; and yet these things are more pleasing to their minds than to their eyes, because in every one of them they see a correspondence, and through the correspondences what is Divine.

186. As to these correspondences I have also been told that not only the palaces and houses, but all things and each thing, both inside and outside of them, correspond to the interior things which they have from the Lord, the house itself in general corresponding to their good, the particular things inside of a house to the various things of which their good consists,[2] and the things outside to truths derived from good, and also to their

---

1. Angels have cities, palaces, and houses (n. 940–942, 1116, 1626–1631, 4622).

2. "Houses," with their contents, signify the things in man that belong to his mind, thus his interiors (n. 710, 2233, 2331, 2559, 3128, 3538, 4973, 5023, 6639, 6690, 7353, 7848, 7910, 7929, 9150); consequently the things relating to good and truth (n. 2233, 2331, 2559, 4982, 7848, 7929). "Rooms" and "bed chambers" signify interior things there (n. 3900, 5694, 7353). The "roof of a house" signifies what is inmost (n. 3652, 10184).

A "house of wood" signifies what relates to good, and a "house of stone" what relates to truth (n. 3720).

perceptions and knowledges (see note, n. 176); and as these things correspond to the goods and truths they have from the Lord they correspond to their love, and to their wisdom and intelligence from love, since love belongs to good, wisdom to good and truth together, and intelligence to truth from good. These are what the angels perceive when they behold what is around them, and thus their minds are more delighted and moved by them than their eyes.

187. This makes clear why the Lord called himself the temple at Jerusalem (John 2:19, 21),[3] namely, because the temple represented his Divine human; also why the New Jerusalem was seen to be of pure gold, its gates of pearls, and its foundations of precious stones (Rev. 21), namely, because the New Jerusalem signifies the church which was afterwards to be established, the twelve gates its truths leading to good, and the foundations the truths on which the church is founded.[4]

188. The angels of whom the Lord's celestial kingdom consists dwell for the most part in elevated places that appear as mountains of soil; the angels of whom the Lord's spiritual kingdom consists dwell in less elevated places that appear like hills; while the angels in the lowest parts of heaven dwell in places that appear like ledges of stone. These things spring from correspondence, for interior things correspond to higher things, and exterior things to lower things;[5] and this is why in the Word

3. In the highest sense "the house of God" signifies the Lord's Divine human in respect to Divine good, and "the temple" the same in respect to Divine truth; and in a relative sense, heaven and the church in respect to good and truth (n. 3720).

4. "Jerusalem" signifies the church in which is genuine doctrine (n. 402, 3654, 9166). "Gates" signify introduction to the doctrine of the church, and through doctrine introduction into the church (n. 2943, 4477, 4478).

"Foundation" signifies the truth on which heaven, the church, and doctrine are founded (n. 9643).

5. In the Word what is interior is expressed by what is higher and what is higher signifies what is interior (n. 2148, 3084, 4599, 5146, 8325). What is "high" signifies what is internal, and likewise heaven (n. 1735, 2148, 4210, 4599, 8153).

"mountains" signify celestial love, "hills" spiritual love, and "rocks" faith.[6]

189. There are also angels who do not live associated together, but apart, house by house. These dwell in the midst of heaven, since they are the best of angels.

190. The houses in which angels dwell are not erected, as houses in the world are, but are given to them gratuitously by the Lord, to everyone in accordance with his reception of good and truth. They also change a little in accordance with changes of the state of interiors of the angels (of which above, n. 154–160). Everything whatsoever that the angels possess they hold as received from the Lord; and everything they have need of is given them.

---

6. In heaven, mountains, hills, rocks, valleys, and lands are seen exactly the same as in the world (n. 10608).

On the mountains angels who are in the good of love dwell, on the hills those who are in the good of charity, on the rocks those who are in the good of faith (n. 10438).

Therefore in the Word "mountains" signify the good of love (n. 795, 4210, 6435, 8327, 8758, 10438, 10608).

"Hills" signify the good of charity (n. 6435, 10438).

"Rocks" signify the good and truth of faith (n. 8581, 10580).

"Stone," of which rock consists, in like manner signifies the truth of faith (n. 114, 643, 1298, 3720, 6426, 8609, 10376).

This is why "mountains" signify heaven (n. 8327, 8805, 9420).

And "the summit of a mountain" signifies the highest part of heaven (n. 9422, 9434, 10608).

Also why the ancients had their holy worship on mountains (n. 796, 2722).

22

Space in Heaven

191. All things in heaven appear, just as in the world, to be in place and in space, and yet the angels have no notion or idea of place and space. As this must needs sounds like a paradox, I will endeavor to present the matter in a clear light, as it is of great importance.

192. All changes of place in the spiritual world are effected by changes of state of the interiors, which means that change of place is nothing else than change of state.[1] In this way I have been taken by the Lord into the heavens and also to the earths in the universe; and it was my spirit that so journeyed, while my body remained in the same place.[2] Such are all movements of the angels; and in consequence they have no distances, and having no distances they have no spaces, but in place of spaces they have states and their changes.

1. In the Word places and spaces signify states (n. 2625, 2837, 3356, 3387, 7381, 10580); from experience (n. 1274, 1277, 1376–1381, 4321, 4882, 10146, 10580).

Distance signifies difference of state of life (n. 9104, 9967).

In the spiritual world movements and changes of place are changes of the state of life, because they originate in these (n. 1273–1275, 1377, 3356, 9440).

The same is true of journeyings (n. 9440, 10734); illustrated by experience (n. 1273–1277, 5605). For this reason "to journey" signifies in the Word to live and progress in life; and "to sojourn" has a like meaning (n. 3335, 4554, 4585, 4882, 5493, 5605, 5996, 8345, 8397, 8417, 8420, 8557). To go with the Lord means to live with Him (n. 10567).

2. Man may be led a long distance in respect to his spirit by means of changes of state, while his body remains in its place, also from experience (n. 9440, 9967, 10734).

What it is to be "led by the spirit to another place" (n. 1884).

193. As changes of place are thus effected it is evident that approaches are likenesses of state of the interiors, and separations are unlikenesses; and for this reason those are near each other who are in like states, and those are at a distance who are in unlike states; and spaces in heaven are simply the external conditions corresponding to the internal states. For the same reason the heavens are distinct from each other, also the societies of each heaven and the individuals in each society; and this is also why the hells are entirely separated from the heavens, because they are in a contrary state.

194. For the same reason, again, anyone in the spiritual world who intensely desires the presence of another comes into his presence, for he thereby sees him in thought, and puts himself in his state; and conversely, one is separated from another so far as he is averse to him. And since all aversion comes from contrariety of affection and from disagreement of thought, whenever in that world several are together in one place they are visible [to one another] so long as they agree, but vanish as soon as they disagree.

195. Again, when anyone goes from one place to another, whether it be in his own city, or in courts or in gardens, or to others out of his own society, he arrives more quickly when he eagerly desires it, and less quickly when he does not, the way itself being lengthened and shortened in accordance with the desire, although it remains the same. This I have often seen to my surprise. All this again makes clear how distances, and consequently spaces, are wholly in accord with states of the interiors of the angels;[3] and this being so, no notion or idea of space can enter their thought, although there are spaces with them equally as in the world.

---

3. Places and spaces are presented to the sight in accordance with the states of the interiors of angels and spirits (n. 5605, 9440, 10146).

196. This can be illustrated by the thoughts of man, in that space does not pertain to thought, for whatever is thought of intently is set before one as present. Again, whoever reflects about it knows that his sight recognizes space only by intermediate objects on the earth that are seen at the same time, or by recalling what he already knows about the distance. This happens because of the continuity; and in what is continuous there is no appearance of distance except from things not continuous. This is even more true of the angels, because their sight acts as one with their thought, and their thought acts as one with their affection, and things appear near or remote, and also varied, in accordance with the states of their interiors, as has been said above.

197. It follows from this that in the Word places and spaces, and all things that in any way relate to space, signify such things as relate to states, such as distances, near, far off, ways, journeys, sojourning, miles and furlongs, plains, fields, gardens, cities and streets, motions, measures of various kinds, long, broad, high, and deep, and innumerable other things; for most things in man's thought from the world take on something from space and time.

[2] I will mention here only what is signified in the Word by length, breadth, and height. In this world, that is called long or broad which is long or broad in relation to space, and the same is true of height. But in heaven, where there is no thought from space, length means a state of good, breadth a state of truth, and height the distinction between them in accordance with degrees (see n. 38). Such is the meaning of these three dimensions, because length in heaven is from east to west, and those that dwell there are in good of love; while breadth in heaven is from south to north, and those that dwell there are in truth from good (see n. 148); while height in heaven applies to both of these in respect to degrees. This is why length, breadth, and height have these significations in

the Word, as in Ezekiel (from chap. 40 to 48), where the new temple and the new earth, with the courts, chambers, gates, doors, windows, and surroundings are described by measures giving the length, breadth, and height, by which a new church, and the goods and truths that are in it are signified. Otherwise to what purpose would be all those measures?

[3] In like manner the New Jerusalem is described in Revelation in these words:

> The city lieth foursquare, and the length thereof is as great as the breadth; and he measured the city with the reed, twelve thousand furlongs; the length, the breadth, and the height are equal (Rev. 21:16).

Because "the New Jerusalem" here signifies a new church these measures signify the things of the church, "length" its good of love, "breadth" truth from that good, "height" good and truth in respect to degrees, "twelve thousand furlongs" all good and truth in the complex. Otherwise, how could there be said to be a height of twelve thousand furlongs, the same as the length and the breadth? That "breadth" in the Word signifies truth is evident from David:

> Jehovah, Thou hast not shut me up into the hand of the enemy, Thou hast made my feet to stand in a broad place (Ps. 31:8).

> Out of straitness I called upon Jah; he answereth me in a broad place (Ps. 118:5).

Besides other passages (as in Isa. 8:8; and in Hab. 1:6). So in all other cases.

198. From all this it can be seen that although there are spaces in heaven as in the world, still nothing there is reckoned in accordance with spaces but in accordance with states; and in consequence spaces there cannot be measured as in the world, but can be seen only from the state and in accordance with the state of the interiors there.[4]

---

4. In the Word "length" signifies good (n. 1613, 9487).
"Breadth" signifies truth (n. 1613, 3433, 3434, 4482, 9487, 10179).

199. The primary and veriest cause of this is that the Lord is present with everyone in the measure of his love and faith,[5] and that it is in accordance with the Lord's presence that all things appear near or far away, for it is from this that all things in the heavens are determined. Also it is through this that angels have wisdom, for it is through this that they have extension of thought and through this a sharing of all things in the heavens; in a word, it is through this that they think spiritually, and not naturally like men.

"Height" signifies good and truth in respect to their degrees (n. 9489, 9773, 10181).

5. The conjunction and presence of the Lord with the angels is according to their reception of love and charity from Him (n. 290, 681, 1954, 2658, 2886, 2888, 2889, 3001, 3741–3743, 4318, 4319, 4524, 7211, 9128).

23

The Form of Heaven
That Determines Affiliations
and Communications There

200. What the form of heaven is can be seen in some measure from what has been shown in the preceding chapters; as that heaven is like itself both in its greatest and in its least divisions (n. 72); that consequently each society is a heaven in a lesser form, and each angel in the least form (n. 51–58); that as the entire heaven reflects a single man, so each society of heaven reflects a man in a lesser form, and each angel in the least form (n. 59–77); that the wisest are at the center, and the less wise are round about even to the borders, and the like is true of each society (n. 43); and that those who are in the good of love dwell from the east to the west in heaven, and those who are in truths from good from the south to the north; and the same is true of each society (n. 148, 149). All this is in accord with the form of heaven; consequently it may be concluded from this what this form is in general.[1]

201. It is important to know what the form of heaven is, because not only is all affiliation there in accordance with it, but also all mutual communication, and in consequence of this all extension of thoughts and affections, and thus all the intelligence and wisdom of angels. From this it follows that each one

1. The entire heaven in respect to all angelic societies, is arranged by the Lord in accordance with His Divine order, since it is the Divine of the Lord with the angels that makes heaven (n. 3038, 7211, 9128, 9338, 10125, 10151, 10157).
Concerning the heavenly form (n. 4040–4043, 6607, 9877).

there is wise just to the extent that he is in the form of heaven, and is thus a form of heaven. It makes no difference whether you say "in the form of heaven," or "in the order of heaven," since the form of anything is from its order and in accordance with its order.[2]

202. Let us consider first what is meant by being in the form of heaven. Man was created both in the image of heaven and in the image of the world; his internal in the image of heaven, and his external in the image of the world (see above, n. 57); and "in the image" means the same thing as in accordance with the form. But as man by the evils of his will and consequent falsities of thought has destroyed in himself the image of heaven, that is, the form of heaven, and in place of it has brought in the image and form of hell, his internal is closed up from his very birth; and this is why man is born into pure ignorance, while animals of every kind are not. And that man may have the image of heaven or form of heaven restored to him he must be taught the things that pertain to order; since form, as has been said, is in accord with order. The Word contains all the laws of Divine order, for its precepts are the laws of Divine order; therefore to the extent that man knows these and lives in accordance with them his internal is opened and the order or image of heaven is there formed anew. This makes clear what is meant by being in the form of heaven, namely, that it is to live in accordance with those things that are in the Word.[3]

2. The form of heaven is a form in accordance with the Divine order (n. 4040–4043, 6607, 9877).

3. Divine truths are the laws of order (n. 2447, 7995). Man is a man to the extent that he lives in accordance with order, that is, to the extent that he is in good in accordance with Divine truths (n. 4839, 6605, 6626).

All things of Divine order are gathered up in man and he is from creation Divine order in form (n. 4219, 4220, 4222, 4223, 4523, 4524, 5114, 6013, 6057, 6605, 6626, 9706, 10156, 10472). Man is not born into good and truth, but into evil and falsity, that is, into the opposite of Divine order, and consequently into pure ignorance; and for this reason he must needs be born anew, that is, be regenerated, which is effected by means of Divine

203. So far as anyone is in the form of heaven he is in heaven, and is, in fact, a heaven in the least form (n. 57); consequently he is to the same extent in intelligence and wisdom; for as has been said above, all the thought of his understanding and all the affection of his will extend themselves on every side into heaven in accord with its form, and wonderfully communicate with the societies there, and these in turn with him.[4]

[2] There are some who do not believe that thoughts and affections really extend themselves around about them, but believe that they are within them, because whatever they think they see within in themselves, and not as distant; but such are greatly mistaken. For as the sight of the eye has extension to remote objects, and is affected in accordance with the order of the things seen in that extension, so the interior sight, which is that of the understanding, has a like extension in the spiritual world, although not perceived by man, for the reason given above (n. 196). The only difference is that the sight of the eye is affected in a natural way, because it is affected by the things in the natural world, while the sight of the understanding is affected in a spiritual way, because by the things in the spiritual world, all of which have relation to good and truth; and man's ignorance of this is because of his not knowing that there is any light that enlightens the understanding; and yet without the light that enlightens the understanding man could not think at all (of which light see above, n. 126–132).

---

truths from the Lord, that he may be introduced into order (n. 1047, 2307, 2308, 3518, 3812, 8480, 8550, 10283, 10284, 10286, 10731). When the Lord forms man anew, that is, regenerates him, He arranges all things in him in accordance with order, which means, into the form of heaven (n. 5700, 6690, 9931, 10303).

4. Everyone in heaven has communication of life, which may be called its extension into angelic societies round about, according to the quantity and quality of his good (n. 8794, 8797).

Thoughts and affections have such extension (n. 2470, 6598–6613).

They are united and separated in accordance with the ruling affections (n. 4111).

[3] There was a certain spirit who believed that his thought was from himself, thus without any extension outside of himself and communication thereby with societies outside of him. That he might learn that this was not true his communication with neighboring societies was cut off, and in consequence, not only was he deprived of thought but he fell down as if lifeless, although tossing his arms about like a newborn infant. After a while the communication was restored to him, and then as it was gradually restored he returned into the state of his thought.

[4] When other spirits had seen this they confessed that all thought and affection, and in consequence everything of life, flow in in accordance with communication, since everything of man's life consists in his ability to think and be moved by affection, or what is the same, in his ability to understand and will.[5]

204. But let it be understood that intelligence and wisdom vary with everyone in accordance with this communication, those whose intelligence and wisdom are formed out of genuine truths and goods having communication with societies in accordance with the form of heaven; while those whose intelligence and wisdom are not formed out of genuine truths and goods, and yet out of what is in accord therewith, have a broken and variously

5. There is only one Life, from which all, both in heaven and in the world, live (n. 1954, 2021, 2536, 2658, 2886–2889, 3001, 3484, 3742, 5847, 6467).

That life is from the Lord above (n. 2886–2889, 3344, 3484, 4319, 4320, 4524, 4882, 5986, 6325, 6468–6470, 9276, 10196).

It flows into angels, spirits, and men, in a wonderful manner (n. 2886–2889, 3337, 3338, 3484, 3742).

The Lord flows in from His Divine love, which is such that what is its own it wills should be another's (n. 3472, 4320).

For this reason life appears to be in man, and not flowing in (n. 3742, 4320).

Of the joy of angels, perceived and confirmed by what they told me, because of their not living from themselves but from the Lord (n. 6469).

The evil are unwilling to be convinced that life flows in (n. 3743).

Life from the Lord flows in also with the evil (n. 2706, 3743, 4417, 10196).

But they turn good into evil, and truth into falsity; for such as man is such is his reception of life, illustrated (n. 4319, 4320, 4417).

coherent communication, since it is not with societies that are in a series in which there is a form of heaven. On the other hand, those that are not in intelligence and wisdom, because they are in falsities from evil, have communication with societies in hell; and their extension is determined by the degree of their confirmation. Let it also be known that this communication with societies is not such a communication with them as is clearly perceptible to those there, but is a communication with what they really are, which is in them and flows from them.[6]

205. There is an affiliation of all in heaven in accordance with spiritual relationships, that is, relationships of good and truth in their order. It is so in the whole heaven; so in each society, and so in each house. Because of this angels who are in like good and truth recognize each other, as relatives by blood and marriage do on the earth, precisely as if they had been acquainted from infancy. The good and truth in each angel, which constitute his wisdom and intelligence, are affiliated in like manner; they recognize each other in like manner, and as they recognize each other they join themselves together;[7] and in consequence those in whom truths and goods are thus joined in accordance with a form of heaven see things following one another in series, and how they cohere widely round about; but those in whom goods and truths are not conjoined in accordance with the form of heaven do not see this.

206. In each heaven there is such a form, and in accordance with it the angels have communication and extension of thoughts

6. Thought pours itself into societies of spirits and of angels round about (n. 6600–6605).

Still it does not move or disturb the thoughts of the societies (n. 6601, 6603).

7. Good recognizes its truth, and truth its good (n. 2429, 3101, 3102, 3161, 3179, 3180, 4358, 5704, 5835, 9637).

In this way good and truth are conjoined (n. 3834, 4096, 4097, 4301, 4345, 4353, 4364, 4368, 5365, 7623–7627, 7752–7762, 8530, 9258, 10555).

This is effected by influx from heaven (n. 9079).

and affections, and thus in accordance with it they have intelligence and wisdom. But the communication of one heaven with another is different, that is, of the third or inmost with the second or middle, and of this with the first or outmost. But the communication between the heavens should not be called communication but influx. About this something shall now be said. That there are three heavens distinct from each other can be seen above in its own chapter (n. 29–40).

207. That between one heaven and another there is influx but not communication can be seen from their relative position. The third or inmost heaven is above, the second or middle heaven is below, and the first or outmost heaven is still lower. There is a like arrangement in all the societies in each heaven, for example, some dwell on elevated places that appear like mountains (n. 188); on the top of which those of the inmost heaven dwell; below these are the societies of the second heaven, below these again the societies of the outmost heaven. The same is true everywhere, both in elevated places and in those not elevated. A society of a higher heaven has no communication with a society of a lower except by correspondences (see above, n. 100); and communication by correspondences is what is called influx.

208. One heaven is joined with another, or a society of one heaven with the society of another, by the Lord alone, both by direct and by mediate influx, directly from himself, and mediately through the higher heavens in order into the lower.[8]

As the conjunction of the heavens by this inflowing is from the Lord alone there is a most careful precaution against any angel of a higher heaven looking down into a society of a lower heaven and talking with anyone there; for the angel is thus

---

8. There is direct influx from the Lord and mediate influx through heaven (n. 6063, 6307, 6472, 9682, 9683). There is a direct influx of the Lord into the minutest parts of all things (n. 6058, 6474–6478, 8717, 8728).

Of the mediate influx of the Lord through the heavens (n. 4067, 6982, 6985, 6996).

immediately deprived of his intelligence and wisdom. The reason of this also shall be told. As there are three degrees of heaven, so each angel has three degrees of life, those in the inmost heaven having the third or inmost degree open, while the second and first degrees are closed; those in the middle heaven having the second degree opened and the first and third closed; and those in the lowest heaven having the first degree opened and the second and third closed. Consequently, as soon as an angel of the third heaven looks down into a society of the second heaven and talks with anyone there his third degree is at once closed; and as his wisdom resides in that degree, if that is closed he is deprived of his wisdom, for he has none in the second or first degree. This is what is meant by the words of the Lord in Matthew:

> He that is on the housetop, let him not go down to take what is in his house; and he that is in the field, let him not turn back to take his garment (Matt. 24:17, 18).

And in Luke:

> In that day he that shall be on the housetop and his goods in the house, let him not go down to take them away; and he that is in the field let him not turn back. Remember Lot's wife (Luke 17:31, 32).

209. No influx is possible from the lower heavens into the higher, because this is contrary to order; but there is influx from the higher heavens into the lower. Moreover, the wisdom of the angels of a higher heaven surpasses the wisdom of the angels of a lower heaven as a myriad to one; and this is another reason why the angels of a lower heaven cannot converse with those of a higher heaven; and in fact when they look toward them they do not see them, the higher heaven appearing like a cloudy something over their heads. But the angels of a higher heaven can see those in a lower heaven, although if permitted to talk with them they would lose their wisdom, as has been said above.

210. The thoughts and affections as well as the speech of the angels of the inmost heaven are never perceived in the middle heaven, because they so transcend what is there. But when it pleases the Lord there is seen in the lower heavens from that source something like a flame, and from the thoughts and affections in the middle heaven there is seen in the outmost heaven something luminous, and sometimes a cloud glowing white and variegated. From that cloud, its ascent, descent, and form, what is being said there is in some measure known.

211. From all this it can be seen what the form of heaven is, namely, that it is the most perfect of all in the inmost heaven; in the middle heaven it is also perfect, but in a lower degree, and in the outmost heaven in a degree still lower; also that the form of one heaven has its permanent existence from another by means of influx from the Lord. But what communication by influx is cannot be understood unless it is known what degrees of height are, and how they differ from degrees of length and breadth. What these different degrees are may be seen above (n. 38).

212. When it comes to the particulars of the form of heaven and how it proceeds and flows, this not even the angels can comprehend. Some conception of it can be gained from the form of all things in the human body, when this is scanned and investigated by an acute and wise man; for it has been shown above, in their respective chapters, that the entire heaven reflects a single man (see n. 59–72); and that all things in man correspond to the heavens (n. 87–102). How incomprehensible and inexplicable that form is, is evident only in a general way from the nervous fibers, by which each part and all parts of the body are woven together.

What these fibers are, and how they proceed and flow in the brain, the eye cannot at all perceive; for innumerable fibers are there so interwoven that taken together they appear like a soft continuous mass; and yet it is in accord with these that each thing and all things of the will and understanding flow with the utmost distinctness into acts. How again they interweave themselves in the body is clear from the various plexuses, such as those of the heart, the mesentery, and others; and also from the knots called ganglions, into which many fibers enter from every region and there intermingle, and when variously joined together go forth to their functions, and this again and again; besides like things in every viscus, member, organ, and muscle.

Whoever examines these fibers and their many wonders with the eye of wisdom will be utterly bewildered. And yet the things seen with the eye are few, and those not seen are still more wonderful because they belong to an inner realm of nature. It is clearly evident that this form corresponds to the form of heaven, because all the workings of the understanding and the will are within it and are in accordance with it; for it is in accordance with this form that whatever a man wills passes spontaneously into act, and whatever he thinks spreads through the fibers from their beginnings even to their terminations, which is the source of sensations; and inasmuch as it is the form of thought and will, it is the form of intelligence and wisdom. Such is the form that corresponds to the form of heaven. And from this it can be known that such is the form in accordance with which every affection and thought of angels extends itself, and that so far as the angels are in that form they are in intelligence and wisdom. That this form of heaven is from the Divine human of the Lord can be seen above (n. 78–86). All this has been said to make clear also that the heavenly form is such that even as to its generals it can never be completely known, thus that it is incomprehensible even to the angels, as has been said above.

24

Governments in Heaven

213. As heaven is divided into societies, and the larger societies consist of some hundreds of thousands of angels (n. 50), and all within a society, although in like good, are not in like wisdom (n. 43), it must needs follow that governments exist there, since order must be observed, and all things of order must be guarded. But the governments in the heavens differ; they are of one sort in societies that constitute the Lord's celestial kingdom, and of another sort in the societies that constitute his spiritual kingdom; they differ also in accordance with the functions of the several societies. Nevertheless, no other government than the government of mutual love is possible in the heavens, and the government of mutual love is heavenly government.

214. Government in the Lord's celestial kingdom is called righteousness because all in that kingdom are in the good of love to the Lord from the Lord, and whatever is from that good is called righteous. Government there belongs to the Lord alone. He leads them and teaches them in the affairs of life. The truths that are called truths of judgment are written on their hearts; everyone knows them, perceives them, and sees them;[1] and in

1. The celestial angels do not think and speak from truths, as the spiritual angels do, because they have from the Lord a perception of all things of truth (n. 202, 597, 607, 784, 1121, 1384, 1398, 1442, 1919, 7680, 7877, 8780, 9277, 10336).

In respect to truths the celestial angels say, Yea, yea, or Nay, nay; but the spiritual angels reason about them whether they are true or not (n. 2715, 3246, 4448, 9166, 10786, where the Lord's words, "Let your speech be Yea, yea, Nay, nay; what is beyond these is from evil" [Matt. 5:37] are explained).

consequence matters of judgment there never come into question, but only matters of righteousness, which belong to the life. About these matters the less wise consult the more wise, and these consult the Lord and receive answers. Their heaven, that is, their inmost joy, is to live rightly from the Lord.

215. In the Lord's spiritual kingdom the government is called judgment; because those in that kingdom are in spiritual good, which is the good of charity toward the neighbor, and that good in its essence is truth;[2] and truth pertains to judgment, as good pertains to righteousness.[3] These, too, are led by the Lord, but mediately (n. 208); and in consequence they have governors, few or many according to the need of the society in which they are. They also have laws according to which they live together. The governors administer all things in accordance with the laws, which they understand because they are wise, and in doubtful matters they are enlightened by the Lord.

216. As government from good, which is the kind of government that exists in the Lord's celestial kingdom, is called righteousness, and government from truth, which is the kind of government that exists in the Lord's spiritual kingdom, is called judgment, so the terms "righteousness and judgment" are used in the Word when heaven and the church are treated of, "righteousness" signifying celestial good, and "judgment" spiritual good, which good, as has been said above, is in its essence truth, as in the following passages:

2. Those in the spiritual kingdom are in truths, and those in the celestial kingdom are in good (n. 863, 875, 927, 1023, 1043, 1044, 1555, 2256, 4328, 4493, 5113, 9596).

The good of the spiritual kingdom is the good of charity toward the neighbor and this good in its essence is truth (n. 8042, 10296).

3. In the Word "righteousness" is predicated of good, and "judgment" of truth, therefore "to do righteousness and judgment" means good and truth (n. 2235, 9857).

"Great judgments" means the law of Divine order, thus Divine truths (n. 7206).

Of peace there shall be no end upon the throne of David and upon his kingdom, to establish it and to uphold it in judgment and in righteousness from henceforth and even to eternity (Isa. 9:7).

By "David" here the Lord is meant;[4] and by "his kingdom" heaven, as is evident from the following passage:

I will raise unto David a righteous Branch, and he shall reign as King, and shall deal intelligently and shall execute judgment and righteousness in the land (Jer. 23:5).

Jehovah is exalted, for he dwelleth on high; he hath filled Zion with judgment and righteousness (Isa. 33:5).

"Zion" also means heaven and the church.[5]

I, Jehovah, doing judgment and righteousness on the earth, for in these things I delight (Jer. 9:24).

I will betroth thee unto Me forever, and I will betroth thee unto Me in righteousness and judgment (Hos. 2:19).

O Jehovah, in the heavens Thy righteousness is like the mountains of God, and Thy judgments are like the great deep (Ps. 36:5, 6).

They ask of Me the judgments of righteousness, they long for an approach unto God (Isa. 58:2).

So in other places.

217. In the Lord's spiritual kingdom there are various forms of government, differing in different societies, the variety being in accord with the functions performed by the societies; and the functions of these are in accord with the functions of all things in man to which they correspond. That these are various is well known, the heart having one function, the lungs another, the liver another, the pancreas and spleen another, and each sensory organ another. As in the body these organs perform various services, so there are various services pertaining to the societies in the greatest man, which is heaven, for the societies there correspond to these organs. That there is a correspondence of all things

---

4. By "David" in the prophetic parts of the Word, the Lord is meant (n. 1888, 9954).

5. In the Word "Zion" means the church, and specifically the celestial church (n. 2362, 9055).

of heaven with all things of man may be seen in its own chapter above (n. 87–102). But all these forms of government agree in this, that they look to the public good as their end, and in that good to the good of the individual.[6] And this is so because everyone in the whole heaven is under the auspices of the Lord, who loves all, and from Divine love ordains that there shall be a common good, from which each individual shall receive his own good. Each one, moreover, receives good according as he loves the common good; for so far as he loves the common good he loves all and everyone; and as that love is love of the Lord he is to that extent loved by the Lord, and good comes to him.

218. From all this it can be seen what the governors there are, namely, that they are such as are preeminent in love and wisdom, and therefore desire the good of all, and from wisdom know how to provide for the realization of that good. Such governors do not domineer or dictate, but they minister and serve (to serve meaning to do good to others from a love of the good, and to minister meaning to see to it that the good is done); nor do they make themselves greater than others, but less, for they put the good of society and of the neighbor in the first place, and put their own good last; and whatever is in the first place is greater and what is last is less. Nevertheless, the rulers have honor and glory; they dwell in the midst of the society, in higher position than the rest, and also in magnificent palaces; and this glory and honor they

---

6. Every man and every community, also one's country and the church and in the universal sense the kingdom of the Lord, is a neighbor, and to do good to these from love of good in accordance with their state is to love the neighbor; that is, the neighbor is the good of these, which is the common good that must be consulted (n. 6818–6824, 8123).

Civil good also, which is justice, is a neighbor (n. 2915, 4730, 8120–8123).

Therefore charity toward the neighbor extends itself to all things and each thing of the life of man; and loving good and doing good from love of good and truth, and also doing what is just from a love of what is just in every function and in every work, is loving the neighbor (n. 2417, 8121–8124).

accept not for the sake of themselves but for the sake of obedience; for all there know that they have this honor and glory from the Lord, and on that account should be obeyed. This is what is meant by the Lord's words to his disciples:

> Whosoever would become great among you let him be your minister; and whosoever would be first among you let him be your servant; as the Son of man came not to be ministered unto but to minister (Matt. 20:27, 28).

> He that is greatest among you let him be as the least, and he that is chief as he that doth minister (Luke 22:26).

219. Also in each house there is a like government in a lesser form. In every house there is a master and there are servants; the master loves the servants and the servants love the master, consequently they serve each other from love. The master teaches how they ought to live, and tells what is to be done; the servants obey and perform their duties. To perform use is the delight of everyone's life. This shows that the Lord's kingdom is a kingdom of uses.

220. Also in the hells there are governments, for without governments they could not be kept in restraint; but the governments there are opposite to the governments in the heavens; they are governments of the love of self. Everyone there wishes to dictate to others and to be over others. They hate those that do not favor them, and make them objects of their vengeance and fury, for such is the nature of the love of self. Therefore the more malignant are set over them as governors, and these they obey from fear.[7] But of this below, where the hells are treated of.

---

7. There are two kinds of rule, one from love toward the neighbor, the other from love of self (n. 10814). From the rule that is from love toward the neighbor flow all goods and all happinesses (n. 10160, 10814). In heaven no one desires to rule from the love of self, but all desire to minister, which means to rule from love to the neighbor; this is the source of their great power (n. 5732). From rule from the love of self all evils flow in (n. 10038). When the loves of self and the world had begun to prevail men were compelled to subject themselves to governments as a means of security (n. 7364, 10160, 10814).

25

Divine Worship in Heaven

221. Divine worship in the heavens is not unlike in externals Divine worship on the earth, but in internals it is different. In the heavens, as on the earth, there are doctrines, preachings, and church edifices. In essentials the doctrines there are everywhere the same; but in the higher heavens they contain more interior wisdom than in the lower. The preachings are in harmony with the doctrines; and as they have houses and palaces (n. 183–190), so they have also church edifices, in which there is preaching. Such things exist in heaven, because the angels are being perfected continually in wisdom and love. For they possess, as men do, understanding and will; and both their understanding and their will are capable of being continually perfected, the understanding by means of truths of intelligence, and the will by means of the goods of love.[1]

222. But essential Divine worship in the heavens does not consist in going to church and hearing preaching, but in a life of love, charity, and faith, in accordance with doctrine; preachings in churches serve solely as means of instruction in matters of life. I have talked with angels on this subject, and have told them that it is believed in the world that Divine worship consists solely in attending church, listening to the

---

1. The understanding is receptive of truth, and the will of good (n. 3623, 6125, 7503, 9300, 9930). As all things have relation to truth and good, so everything of man's life has relation to understanding and will (n. 803, 10122).

Angels are perfected to eternity (n. 4803, 6648).

preaching, observing the sacrament of the Supper three or four times a year, and performing other acts of worship according to the requirements of the church; also devoting special times to prayers, and at such times, behaving devoutly. The angels said that these are outward acts that ought to be done, but are of no avail unless there is an internal from which they proceed, which is a life in accordance with the precepts that doctrine teaches.

223. That I might learn about their meeting in places of worship, I have been permitted at times to attend and to hear the preaching. The preacher stands in a pulpit at the east. Those who are in the light of wisdom more than others sit in front of him; those who are in less light sit to the right and left of these. There is a circular arrangement of the seats, so that all are in the preacher's view, no one so sitting at either side as to be out of his view. At the entrance, which is at the east of the building and on the left of the pulpit, those stand who are being initiated. No one is permitted to stand behind the pulpit; when there is anyone there the preacher becomes confused. It is the same if anyone in the congregation dissents; and for this reason the dissenter must needs turn away his face. The wisdom of the preachings is such as to be above all comparison with the preachings of this world, for those in the heavens are in interior light. The church edifices in the spiritual kingdom are apparently built of stone, and those in the celestial kingdom of wood; because stone corresponds to truth, and those who are in the spiritual kingdom are in truth, while wood corresponds to good, and those in the celestial kingdom are in good.[2] In that kingdom the sacred edifices are not called churches but houses of God.

2. "Stone" signifies truth (n. 114, 643, 1298, 3720, 6426, 8609, 10376).

"Wood" signifies good (n. 643, 3720, 8354).

For this reason the most ancient people, who were in celestial good, had sacred buildings of wood (n. 3720).

In that kingdom they are without magnificence; but in the spiritual kingdom they are more or less magnificent.

224. I have also talked with one of the preachers about the holy state in which those are who listen to the preaching in the churches. He said that everyone is pious, devout, and holy in harmony with his interiors, which pertain to love and faith, for holiness itself is in love and faith, because the Divine of the Lord is in them. He also said that he did not know what outward holiness is apart from love and faith; and when he thought about it he said that perhaps it is something counterfeiting holiness in outward appearance, either conventional or hypocritical; and that such holiness is kindled and sustained by spurious fire from the love of self and the world.

225. All the preachers are from the Lord's spiritual kingdom; none are from the celestial kingdom. They are from the spiritual kingdom because the angels there are in truths from good, and all preaching must be from truths. There are no preachers from the celestial kingdom because those who are there are in the good of love, and they see and perceive truths from good, but do not talk about them. But although the angels in the celestial kingdom perceive and see truths there are preachings there, since by means of preachings they are enlightened in the truths that they already know, and are perfected by many truths that they did not know before. As soon as they hear truths they acknowledge them and thus perceive them; and the truths they perceive they love, and by living in accordance with them they make them to be of their life, declaring that living in accordance with truths is loving the Lord.[3]

226. All preachers are appointed by the Lord, and have therefrom a gift for preaching. No others are permitted to preach in

3. Loving the Lord and the neighbor is living in accordance with the Lord's commandments (n. 10143, 10153, 10310, 10578, 10645, 10683).

the churches. They are not called priests, but preachers. They are not called priests because the celestial kingdom is the priesthood of heaven; for priesthood signifies the good of love to the Lord, and those in the celestial kingdom are in that good; while the spiritual kingdom is the kingship of heaven, for kingship signifies truth from good, and those in the spiritual kingdom are in that truth (see above, n. 24).[4]

227. The doctrines with which their preachings are in accord all look to life as their end, and none look to faith separate from the life. The doctrine of the inmost heaven is more full of wisdom than the doctrine of the middle heaven, and this more full of intelligence than the doctrine of the outmost heaven; for in each heaven the doctrines are adapted to the perceptions of the angels. The essential of all doctrines is acknowledging the Divine human of the Lord.

---

4. Priests represented the Lord in respect to the Divine good, kings in respect to Divine truth (n. 2015, 6148).

Therefore, in the Word a "priest" signifies those who are in the good of love to the Lord, and the priesthood signifies that good (n. 9806, 9809).

A "king" in the Word signifies those who are in Divine truth, and therefore kingship signifies truth from good (n. 1672, 2015, 2069, 4575, 4581, 4966, 5044).

26

The Power of the Angels
of Heaven

228. That the angels possess power cannot be comprehended by those who know nothing about the spiritual world and its influx into the natural world. Such think that angels can have no power because they are spiritual and are even so pure and unsubstantial that no eye can see them. But those who look more interiorly into the causes of things take a different view. Such know that all the power that a man has is from his understanding and will (for apart from these he is powerless to move a particle of his body), and his understanding and will are his spiritual man. This moves the body and its members at its pleasure; for whatever it thinks the mouth and tongue speak, and whatever it wills the body does; and it bestows its strength at pleasure. As man's will and understanding are ruled by the Lord through angels and spirits, so also are all things of his body, because these are from the will and understanding; and if you will believe it, without influx from heaven man cannot even move a step. That this is so has been shown me by much experience. Angels have been permitted to move my steps, my actions, and my tongue and speech, as they pleased, and this by influx into my will and thought; and I have learned thereby that of myself I could do nothing. I was afterwards told by them that every man is so ruled, and that he can know this from the doctrine of the church and from the Word, for he prays that God may send his angels to lead him, direct his steps, teach him, and inspire in him what to think and what to say, and other like things; although he says and believes otherwise when he is thinking by himself apart from doctrine. All this has been said to make known what power angels have with man.

229. But so great is the power of angels in the spiritual world that if I should make known all that I have witnessed in regard to it, it would exceed belief. Any obstruction there that ought to be removed because it is contrary to Divine order the angels cast down or overthrow merely by an effort of the will and a look. Thus I have seen mountains that were occupied by the evil cast down and overthrown, and sometimes shaken from end to end as in earthquakes; also rocks cleft asunder to their bottoms, and the evil who were upon them swallowed up. I have seen also hundreds of thousands of evil spirits dispersed by angels and cast down into hell. Numbers are of no avail against them; neither are devices, cunning, or combinations; for they see through them all, and disperse them in a moment. (But more may be seen on this subject in the account of the destruction of Babylon.) Such power do angels have in the spiritual world. It is evident from the Word that they have like power in the natural world also when it is permitted; for instance, that they have given to destruction entire armies; and that they brought on a pestilence from which seventy thousand men died. Of this angel it is said:

> The angel stretched out his hand against Jerusalem to destroy it but Jehovah repented him of the evil, and said to the angel that destroyed the people, It is enough, now stay thy hand. And David saw the angel that smote the people (2 Sam. 24:16, 17).

Besides other passages. Because the angels have such power they are called powers; as in David:

> Bless Jehovah, ye angels, mighty in power (Ps. 103:20).

230. But it must be understood that the angels have no power whatever from themselves, but that all their power is from the Lord; and that they are powers only so far as they acknowledge this. Whoever of them believes that he has power from himself instantly becomes so weak as not to be able to resist even a single evil spirit. For this reason angels ascribe no merit whatever to themselves, and are averse to all praise and glory on account of anything they do, ascribing all the praise and glory to the Lord.

231. It is the Divine truth that goes forth from the Lord that has all power in the heavens, for the Lord in heaven is Divine truth united to Divine good (see n. 126–140). To the extent that angels are receptions of this truth they are powers.[1] Moreover each one is his own truth and his own good because each one is such as his understanding and will are. The understanding pertains to truth because everything of it is from truths, and the will pertains to good because everything of it is from goods; for whatever anyone understands he calls truth, and whatever he wills he calls good. From this it is that everyone is his own truth and his own good.[2] Therefore so far as an angel is truth from the Divine and good from the Divine he is a power, because to that extent the Lord is in him. And as no one's good and truth are wholly like or the same as another's, since in heaven, as in the world, there is endless variety (n. 20), so the power of one angel is not like the power of another. Those who constitute the arms in the greatest man, or heaven, have the greatest power because such are more in truths than others, and into their truths good flows from the entire heaven. Moreover, the power of the whole man passes into the arms, and by means of these the whole body exercises its powers. It is for this reason

1. Angels are called powers and are powers from their reception of Divine truth from the Lord (n. 9639).

Angels are recipients of Divine truth from the Lord and on this account are sometimes called "gods" in the Word (n. 4295, 4402, 7268, 7873, 8192, 8301, 9160).

2. A man or an angel is his own good and his own truth, thus his own love and his own faith (n. 10298, 10367).

He is his own understanding and his own will, for everything of life is therefrom; the life of good is from the will, and the life of truth is from the understanding (n. 10076, 10177, 10264, 10284).

that in the Word "arms" and "hand" signify powers.[3] Sometimes
on this account a naked arm is seen in heaven so powerful as
to be able to break in pieces everything in its way, even though
it were a great rock on the earth. Once it was moved toward
me, and I perceived that it was able to crush my bones to at-
oms.

232. It has been shown above (n. 137) that the Divine truth
that goes forth from the Lord has all power, and that angels
have power to the extent that they are receptions of Divine
truth from the Lord. But angels are so far receptions of Divine
truth as they are receptions of Divine good, for truths have all
their power from good, and none apart from good. So, too,
good has all its power through truths, and none apart from
truths. Power springs from the conjunction of these two. The
same is true of faith and love; for it is the same whether you say
truth or faith, since everything of faith is truth; also it is the
same whether you say good or love, since everything of love is
good.[4] The great power that angels have by means of truths
from good is shown also from this, that when an evil spirit is
merely looked at by the angels he falls into a swoon, and does
not appear like a man, and this until the angel turns away his
eyes. Such an effect is produced by the look of the eyes of
angels, because the sight of angels is from the light of heaven,

3. The correspondence of the hands, arms, and shoulders, with the Greatest Man or
heaven (n. 4931–4937). In the Word, "arms" and "hands" signify power (n. 878, 3091,
4932, 4933, 6947, 10019).

4. All power in heaven is the power of truth from good, thus of faith from love (n.
3091, 3563, 6423, 8304, 9643, 10019, 10182).

All power is from the Lord, because from Him is every truth of faith and every good
of love (n. 9327, 9410).

This power is meant by the keys given to Peter (n. 6344).

It is Divine truth going forth from the Lord that has all power (n. 6948, 8200).

This power of the Lord is what is meant by "sitting at the right hand of Jehovah"
(n. 3387, 4592, 4933, 7518, 7673, 8281, 9133).

The right hand means power (n. 10019).

and the light of heaven is Divine truth (see above, n. 126–132). Moreover, the eyes correspond to truths from good.[5]

233. As truths from good have all power, so falsities from evil have no power at all;[6] and as all in hell are in falsities from evil they have no power against truth and good. But what power they have among themselves, and what power evil spirits have before they are cast into hell, will be told hereafter.

5. The eyes correspond to truths from good (n. 4403–4421, 4523–4534, 6923).

6. Falsity from evil has no power, because truth from good has all power (n. 6784, 10481).

27

The Speech of Angels

234. Angels talk with each other just as men do in the world, and on various subjects, as on domestic matters, and on matters of the civil state, and of moral and spiritual life. And there is no difference except that their talk is more intelligent than that of men, because it is from more interior thought. I have been permitted to associate with them frequently, and to talk with them as friend with friend, and sometimes as stranger with stranger; and as I was then in a state like theirs I knew no otherwise than that I was talking with men on the earth.

235. Angelic speech, like human speech, is distinguished into words; it is also audibly uttered and heard; for angels, like men, have mouth, tongue, and ears, and an atmosphere in which the sound of their speech is articulated, although it is a spiritual atmosphere adapted to angels, who are spiritual. In their atmosphere angels breathe and utter words by means of their breath, as men do in their atmosphere.[1]

236. In the entire heaven all have the same language, and they all understand one another, to whatever society, near or remote, they belong. Language there is not learned but is instinctive with

---

1. In the heavens there is respiration, but it is of an interior kind (n. 3884, 3845), from experience (n. 3884, 3885, 3891, 3893).

There are differing respirations there, varying in accordance with their states (n. 1119, 3886, 3887, 3889, 3892, 3893).

The evil are wholly unable to breathe in heaven, and they are suffocated if they go there (n. 3894).

everyone, for it flows from their very affection and thought, the tones of their speech corresponding to their affections, and the vocal articulations which are words corresponding to the ideas of thought that spring from the affections; and because of this correspondence the speech itself is spiritual, for it is affection sounding and thought speaking.

[2] Anyone who gives any thought to it can see that all thought is from affection which pertains to love, and that the ideas of thought are the various forms into which the general affection is distributed; for no thought or idea is possible apart from affection—the soul and life of thought is from affection. This enables angels to know, merely from another's speech, what he is—from the tone what his affection is, and from the vocal articulations or words what his mind is. The wiser angels know what the ruling affection is from a single series of words, for that affection is what they chiefly attend to.

[3] It is known that each individual has a variety of affections, one affection when in joy, another when in grief, another when in sympathy and compassion, another when in sincerity and truth, another when in love and charity, another when in zeal or in anger, another when in simulation and deceit, another when in quest of honor and glory, and so on. But the ruling affection or love is in all of these; and for this reason the wiser angels, because they perceive that love, know from the speech the whole state of another.

[4] This it has been granted me to know from much experience. I have heard angels disclosing the character of another's life merely from hearing him speak. They also said that from any ideas of another's thought they could know all things of his life, because from those ideas they know his ruling love, in which are all things in their order. They know also that man's book of life is nothing else.

237. Angelic language has nothing in common with human languages except certain words that are the sounds of a specific affection; yet this is true not of the words themselves but of their sounds; on which subject something will be said in what follows. That angelic language has nothing in common with human languages is evident from the fact that angels are unable to utter a single word of human language. This was tried but they could not do it, because they can utter nothing except what is in entire agreement with their affections; whatever is not in agreement is repugnant to their very life, for life belongs to affection, and their speech is from their life. I have been told that the first language of men on our earth coincided with angelic language because they had it from heaven; and that the Hebrew language coincides with it in some respects.

238. As the speech of angels corresponds to their affection, and their affection belongs to their love, and as the love of heaven is love to the Lord and love toward the neighbor (see above, n. 13–19), it is evident how choice and delightful their talk must be, affecting not the ears only but also the interiors of the mind of those who listen to it. There was a certain hardhearted spirit with whom an angel spoke. At length he was so affected by what was said that he shed tears, saying that he had never wept before, but he could not refrain, for it was love speaking.

239. The speech of angels is likewise full of wisdom because it proceeds from their interior thoughts, and their interior thought is wisdom, as their interior affection is love, and in their speech their love and wisdom unite. For this reason their speech is so full of wisdom that they can express in a single word what man cannot express in a thousand words; also the ideas of their thought include things that are beyond man's comprehension, and still more his power of expression. This is why the things that have been heard and seen in heaven are said to be ineffable, and such as ear hath never heard nor eye seen.

[2] That this is true I have also been permitted to learn by experience. At times I have entered into the state in which angels are, and in that state have talked with them, and I then understood everything. But when I was brought back into my former state, and thus into the natural thought proper to man, and wished to recall what I had heard I could not; for there were thousands of things unadapted to the ideas of natural thought, and therefore inexpressible except by variegations of heavenly light, and thus not at all by human words.

[3] Also the ideas of thought of the angels from which their words spring are modifications of the light of heaven, and the affections from which the tones of the words spring are variations of the heat of heaven, the light of heaven being Divine truth or wisdom, and the heat of heaven the Divine good or love (see above, n. 126–140); and the angels have their affection from the Divine love, and their thought from the Divine wisdom.[2]

240. Because the speech of angels proceeds directly from their affection, and the ideas of their thought are the various forms into which their general affection is distributed (see above, n. 236), angels can express in a moment what a man cannot express in half an hour; also they can set forth in a few words what has been expressed in writing on many pages; and this, too, has been proved to me by much experience.[3] Thus the angels' ideas of thought and the words of their speech make one, like effecting cause and effect; for what is in the ideas of thought as cause is presented in the words as effect, and this is why every word comprehends in itself so many things. Also all the particulars of angelic thought, and thus of angelic speech, appear when pre-

2. The ideas of angels, from which they speak, are expressed by wonderful variegations of the light of heaven (n. 1646, 3343, 3993).

3. Angels can express by their speech in a moment more than a man can express by his in half an hour; and they can also express things that do not fall into the expressions of human speech (n. 1641–1643, 1645, 4609, 7089).

sented to view like a thin wave or circumfluent atmosphere, in which are innumerable things in their order derived from angelic wisdom, and these enter another's thought and affect him. The ideas of thought of everyone, both angel and man, are presented to view in the light of heaven, whenever the Lord pleases.[4]

241. The speech of angels of the Lord's celestial kingdom resembles the speech of the angels of his spiritual kingdom, but it is from more interior thought. Celestial angels are in good of love to the Lord, and therefore speak from wisdom; while spiritual angels are in the good of charity toward the neighbor, which in its essence is truth (n. 215), and therefore speak from intelligence, for wisdom is from good, and intelligence is from truth. For this reason the speech of celestial angels is like a gentle stream, soft, and as it were continuous; but the speech of spiritual angels is slightly vibratory and divided. The speech of celestial angels has much of the tones of the vowels *u* and *o;* while the speech of spiritual angels has much of the tones of *e* and *i*,[5] for the vowels stand for tone, and in the tone there is affection, the tone of the speech of angels corresponding to their affection, as has been said above (n. 236); while the vocal articulations, which are words, correspond to the ideas of thought which spring from affection. As the vowels are not essential to a language, but serve by means of tones to elevate the words to the various affections according to each one's state, so in the Hebrew tongue the vowels are not expressed, and are also variously pronounced. From this a man's quality

4. The innumerable things contained in one idea of thought (n. 1008, 1869, 4946, 6613–6618). The ideas of man's thought are opened in the other life, and what they are is presented to view to the life (n. 1869, 3310, 5510). What their appearance is (n. 6601, 8885). The ideas of angels of the inmost heaven present an appearance of flamy light (n. 6615). The ideas of angels of the outmost heaven present an appearance of thin white clouds (n. 6614). An angelic idea seen, from which there was a radiation toward the Lord (n. 6620). Ideas of thought extend themselves widely into the societies of angels round about (n. 6598–6613).

5. [As these vowels are pronounced in European languages. —*Translator.*]

in respect to his affection and love is known to the angels. Also in the speech of celestial angels there are no hard consonants, and it rarely passes from one consonant to another without the interposition of a word beginning with a vowel. This is why in the Word the particle "and" is so often interposed, as can be seen by those who read the Word in the Hebrew, in which this particle is soft, beginning and ending with a vowel sound. Again, in the Word, in Hebrew, it can in some measure be seen from the words used whether they belong to the celestial class or the spiritual class, that is, whether they involve good or truth. Those involving good partake largely of the sounds of *u* and *o,* and also somewhat of *a,* while those involving truth partake of the sounds of *e* and *i.* Because it is especially in tones that affections express themselves, so in human speech, when great subjects are discussed, such as heaven *[caelum]* and God *[Deus],* those words are preferred that contain the vowels *u* and *o;* and musical tones, whenever such themes are to be expressed, rise to the same fullness; but not when less exalted themes are rendered. By such means musical art is able to express affections of various kinds.

242. In angelic speech there is a kind of symphony that cannot be described;[6] which comes from the pouring forth and diffusion of the thoughts and affections from which speech flows, in accordance with the form of heaven, and all affiliation and all communication in heaven is in accordance with that form. That angels are affiliated in accordance with the form of heaven, and that their thoughts and affections flow in accordance with it may be seen above (n. 200–212).

243. Speech like that in the spiritual world is inherent in every man in his interior intellectual part; but man does not

6. In angelic speech there is a symphony with harmonious cadence (n. 1648, 1649, 7191).

know this, because this speech does not with man, as with angels, fall into words analogous to affection; nevertheless this is what causes man, when he enters the other life, to come into the same speech as spirits and angels, and thus to know how to speak without instruction.[7] But more on this subject hereafter.

244. In heaven, as has been said above, all have one speech; but it is varied in this respect, that the speech of the wise is more interior and more full of variations of affections and ideas of thought, while the speech of the less wise is more external and less full; and the speech of the simple is still more external, consisting of words from which the meaning is to be gathered in the same way as when men are talking to one another. There is also speech by the face, terminating in something sonorous modified by ideas. Again, there is speech in which heavenly representatives are mingled with the ideas, and go forth from ideas to sight. There is also speech by gestures that correspond to affections, and represent things like those expressed by their words. There is speech by means of the generals of affections and the generals of thoughts. There is speech like thunder; besides other kinds.

245. The speech of evil and infernal spirits is likewise natural to them because it is from affections; but it is from evil affections and consequent filthy ideas, to which angels are utterly averse. Thus the modes of speaking in hell are opposite to those of heaven; and in consequence evil spirits cannot endure angelic speech, and angels cannot endure infernal speech. To the angels infernal speech is like a bad odor striking the nostrils. The

---

7. There is spiritual or angelic speech belonging to man, though he does not know it (n. 4104). The ideas of the internal man are spiritual, but during his life in the world man perceives them naturally, because he then thinks in what is natural (n. 10236, 10237, 10551).

Man comes after death into his interior ideas (n. 3226, 3342, 3343, 10568, 10604). Those ideas then form his speech (n. 2470–2479).

speech of hypocrites, who are such as are able to feign them-selves angels of light, resembles in respect to words the speech of angels, but in respect to affections and consequent ideas of thought it is the direct opposite. Consequently, when the inner nature of their speech is perceived as wise angels perceive it, it is heard as the gnashing of teeth, and strikes with horror.

28

The Speech of Angels with Man

246. Angels who talk with man do not talk in their own language, nor in any language unknown to man, but in the man's own language, or in some other language with which he is acquainted. This is so because when angels speak with man they turn themselves to him and conjoin themselves with him; and this conjunction of angel with man causes the two to be in like thought; and as man's thought coheres to his memory, and this is the source of his speech, the two have the same language. Moreover, when an angel or a spirit comes to a man, and by turning to him is conjoined to him, he so enters into the entire memory of the man that he is scarcely conscious that he does not himself know whatever the man knows, including his languages.

[2] I have talked with angels about this, and have said that perhaps they thought that they were addressing me in my mother tongue, since it is so perceived; and yet it was I and not they that spoke; and that this is evident from the fact that angels cannot utter a single word of human language (see n. 237); furthermore, human language is natural and they are spiritual, and spiritual beings cannot give expression to anything in a natural way. To this they replied that they are aware that their conjunction with the man with whom they are speaking is with his spiritual thought; but because his spiritual thought flows into his natural thought, and his natural thought coheres to his memory, the language of the man and all his knowledge appear to them to be their own; and that this is so for this

reason, that while it is the Lord's pleasure that there should be such a conjunction with and sort of insertion of man into heaven, yet the state of man is now such that there can no longer be such conjunction with angels, but only with spirits who are not in heaven.

[3] When I talked about this with spirits also they were unwilling to believe that it is the man that speaks, insisting that they spoke in man, also that man's knowledge is their knowledge and not the man's knowledge, consequently that everything that man knows is from them. I tried to convince them by many proofs that this is not true, but in vain. Who are meant by spirits and who are meant by angels will be told further on when the world of spirits is treated of.

247. There is another reason why angels and spirits conjoin themselves so closely with man as not to know but that what is man's is their own, namely, that there is such conjunction between the spiritual world and the natural world in man that the two are seemingly one. But inasmuch as man has separated himself from heaven the Lord has provided that there should be angels and spirits with each individual, and that man should be ruled by the Lord through these. This is the reason for such close conjunction. It would have been otherwise if man had not separated himself; for in that case he might have been ruled by the Lord through the general influx from heaven, without spirits and angels being adjoined to him. But this subject will be specially considered in what follows, when the conjunction of heaven with man is treated of.

248. The speech of an angel or spirit with man is heard by him as audibly as the speech of man with man, yet by himself only, and not by others who stand near; and for the reason that the speech of an angel or spirit flows first into a man's thought, and by an inner way into his organ of hearing, and thus moves it from within; while the speech of man with man flows first into the air and by an outward way into his organ of hearing,

and moves it from without. Evidently, then, the speech of an angel or spirit with man is heard within him; but as the organs of hearing are thus equally moved, the speech is equally audible. That the speech of an angel or a spirit flows down from within even into the ear has been made clear to me by the fact that it flows also into the tongue, causing a slight vibration, but without any such motion as when the man himself by means of the tongue forms the sound of speech into words.

249. But at the present day to talk with spirits is rarely granted because it is dangerous;[1] for then the spirits know, what otherwise they do not know, that they are with man; and evil spirits are such that they hold man in deadly hatred, and desire nothing so much as to destroy him both soul and body, and this they do in the case of those who have so indulged themselves in fantasies as to have separated from themselves the enjoyments proper to the natural man. Some also who lead a solitary life sometimes hear spirits talking with them, and without danger; but that the spirits with them may not know that they are with man they are at intervals removed by the Lord; for most spirits are not aware that there is any other world than that in which they live, and therefore are unaware that there are men anywhere else; and this is why man is not permitted to speak with them in return. If he did they would know. Again, those who meditate much on religious subjects, and are so intent upon them as to see them as it were inwardly within themselves, begin to hear spirits speaking with them; for religious persuasions, whatever they are, when man dwells upon them by himself and does not adapt them to the various things

---

1. Man is able to talk with spirits and angels; and the ancient people frequently talked with them (n. 67–69, 784, 1634, 1636, 7802).

In some earths angels and spirits appear in human form and talk with the inhabitants (n. 10751, 10752).

But on this earth at this day it is dangerous to talk with spirits, unless man is in true faith, and is led by the Lord (n. 784, 9438, 10751).

of use in the world, penetrate to the interiors and rest there, and occupy the whole spirit of the man, and even enter into the spiritual world and act upon the spirits there. But such persons are visionaries and enthusiasts; and whatever spirit they hear they believe to be the Holy Spirit, when, in fact, such spirits are enthusiastic spirits. Such spirits see falsities as truths, and so seeing them they induce not themselves only but also those they flow into to believe them. Such spirits, however, have been gradually removed, because they began to lure others into evil and to gain control over them. Enthusiastic spirits are distinguished from other spirits by their believing themselves to be the Holy Spirit, and believing what they say to be Divine. As man honors such spirits with Divine worship they do not attempt to harm him. I have sometimes talked with them, and the wicked things they infused into their worshipers were then disclosed. They dwell together toward the left, in a desert place.

250. But to speak with the angels of heaven is granted only to those who are in truths from good, especially to those who are in the acknowledgment of the Lord and of the Divine in his human, because this is the truth in which the heavens are. For, as it has been shown above, the Lord is the God of heaven (n. 2–6); it is the Divine of the Lord that makes heaven (n. 7–12); the Divine of the Lord in heaven is love to him and charity toward the neighbor from him (n. 13–19); the whole heaven in one complex reflects a single man; also every society of heaven; and every angel is in complete human form, and this from the Divine human of the Lord (n. 59–86). All of which makes evident that only those whose interiors are opened by Divine Truths, even to the Lord, are able to speak with the angels of heaven, since it is into these truths with man that the Lord flows, and when the Lord flows in, heaven also flows in. Divine truths open the interiors of man because man was so created as to be in respect to his internal man an image of heaven, and in respect to his external an image of the world (n. 57); and the

internal man is opened only by means of Divine truth going forth from the Lord, because that is the light of heaven and the life of heaven (n. 126–140).

251. The influx of the Lord himself into man is into his forehead, and from that into the whole face, because the forehead of man corresponds to love, and the face corresponds to all his interiors.[2] The influx of spiritual angels into man is into his head everywhere, from the forehead and temples to the whole part that contains the cerebrum, because that region of the head corresponds to intelligence; but the influx of celestial angels is into that part of the head that contains the cerebellum, and is called the occiput, from the ears all around even to the neck, for that region corresponds to wisdom. All the speech of angels with man enters by these ways into his thought; and by this means I have perceived what angels they were that spoke with me.

252. Those who talk with the angels of heaven also see the things that exist in heaven, because they are then seeing in the light of heaven, for their interiors are in that light; also the angels through them see the things that are on the earth,[3] because in them heaven is conjoined to the world and the world is conjoined to heaven. For (as has been said above, n. 246), when the angels turn themselves to man they so conjoin themselves to him as to be wholly unaware that what pertains to the man is not theirs—not only what pertains to his speech but also

---

2. The "forehead" corresponds to heavenly love, and consequently in the Word signifies that love (n. 9936).

The "face" corresponds to the interiors of man, which belong to thought and affection (n. 1568, 2988, 2989, 3631, 4796, 4797, 4800, 5165, 5168, 5695, 9306).

The face is formed to correspondence with the interiors (n. 4791–4805, 5695).

Consequently the "face," in the Word, signifies the interiors (n. 1999, 2434, 3527, 4066, 4796).

3. Spirits are unable to see through man any thing that is in this solar world, but they have seen through my eyes; the reason (n. 1880).

to his sight and hearing; while man, on the other hand, is wholly unaware that the things that flow in through the angels are not his. Such was the conjunction that existed between angels of heaven and the most ancient people on this earth, and for this reason their times were called the Golden Age. Because this race acknowledged the Divine under a human form, that is, the Lord, they talked with the angels of heaven as with their friends, and angels of heaven talked with them as with their friends; and in them heaven and the world made one. But after those times man gradually separated himself from heaven by loving himself more than the Lord and the world more than heaven, and in consequence began to feel the delights of the love of self and the world as separate from the delights of heaven, and finally to such an extent as to be ignorant of any other delight. Then his interiors that had been open into heaven were closed up, while his exteriors were open to the world; and when this takes place man is in light in regard to all things of the world, but in thick darkness in regard to all things of heaven.

253. Since those times it is only rarely that anyone has talked with the angels of heaven; but some have talked with spirits who are not in heaven. This is so because man's interior and exterior faculties are such that they are turned either toward the Lord as their common center (n. 124), or toward self, that is, backwards from the Lord. Those that are turned toward the Lord are also turned toward heaven. But those that are turned toward self, are turned also toward the world. And to elevate these is a difficult matter; nevertheless the Lord elevates them as much as is possible, by turning the love about; which is done by means of truths from the Word.

254. I have been told how the Lord spoke with the prophets through whom the Word was given. He did not speak with them as he did with the ancients, by an influx into their interiors, but through spirits who were sent to them, whom he filled

with his look, and thus inspired with the words which they dictated to the prophets; so that it was not influx but dictation. And as the words came forth directly from the Lord, each one of them was filled with the Divine and contains within it an internal sense, which is such that the angels of heaven understand the words in a heavenly and spiritual sense, while men understand them in a natural sense. Thus has the Lord conjoined heaven and the world by means of the Word. How the Lord fills spirits with the Divine by his look has also been made clear. A spirit that has been filled by the Lord with the Divine does not know otherwise than that he is the Lord, and that it is the Divine that is speaking; and this continues until he has finished speaking. After that he perceives and acknowledges that he is a spirit, and that he spoke from the Lord and not from himself. Because this was the state of the spirits who spoke with the prophets they said that it was Jehovah that spoke; the spirits even called themselves Jehovah, as can be seen both from the prophetical and historical parts of the Word.

255. That the nature of the conjunction of angels and spirits with man may be understood, I am permitted to mention some notable things by which it may be elucidated and verified. When angels and spirits turn themselves to man they do not know otherwise than that the man's language is their own and that they have no other language; and for the reason that they are there in the man's language, and not in their own, which they have forgotten. But as soon as they turn themselves away from the man they are in their own angelic and spiritual language, and know nothing about the man's language. I have had a like experience when in company with angels and in a state like theirs. I then talked with them in their language and knew nothing of my own, having forgotten it; but as soon as I ceased to be present with them I was in my own language.

[2] Another notable fact is that when angels and spirits turn themselves to a man they are able to talk with him at any

distance; they have talked with me at a considerable distance as audibly as when they were near. But when they turn themselves away from man and talk with each other man hears nothing at all of what they are saying, even if it be close to his ear. From this it was made clear that all conjunction in the spiritual world is determined by the way they turn.

[3] Another notable fact is that many spirits together can talk with a man, and the man with them; for they send one of their number to the man with whom they wish to speak, and the spirit sent turns himself to the man and the rest of them turn to their spirit and thus concentrate their thoughts, which the spirit utters; and the spirit then does not know otherwise than that he is speaking from himself, and they do not know otherwise than that they are speaking. Thus also is the conjunction of many with one effected by turning.[4] But of these emissary spirits, who are also called subjects, and of communication by means of them, more will be said hereafter.

256. An angel or spirit is not permitted to speak with a man from his own memory, but only from the man's memory; for angels and spirits have a memory as well as man. If a spirit were to speak from his own memory with a man the man would not know otherwise than that the thoughts then in his mind were his own, although they were the spirit's thoughts. This would be like the recollection of something which the man had never heard or seen. That this is so has been given me to know from experience. This is the source of the belief held by some of the ancients that after some thousands of years they were to return into their former life, and into everything they had done, and

4. Spirits sent from one society of spirits to other societies are called subjects (n. 4403, 5856).

Communications in the spiritual world are effected by such emissary spirits (n. 4403, 5856, 5983).

A spirit, when he is sent forth and serves as a subject, thinks from those by whom he is sent forth and not from himself (n. 5985–5987).

in fact, had returned. This they concluded because at times there came to them a sort of recollection of things that they had never seen or heard. This came from an influx from the memory of spirits into their ideas of thought.

257. There are also spirits called natural and corporeal spirits. When these come to a man they do not conjoin themselves with his thought, like other spirits, but enter into his body, and occupy all his senses, and speak through his mouth, and act through his members, believing at the time that all things of the man are theirs. These are the spirits that obsess man. But such spirits have been cast into hell by the Lord, and thus wholly removed; and in consequence such obsessions are not possible at the present time.[5]

---

5. External or bodily obsessions are not permitted at the present time, as they were formerly (n. 1983).

But at present internal obsessions, which pertain to the mind, are permitted more than formerly (n. 1983, 4793).

Man is inwardly obsessed when he has filthy and scandalous thoughts about God and the neighbor, and is withheld from making them known only by external considerations, which are fear of the loss of reputation, honor, gain and fear of the law and of loss of life (n. 5990).

Of the devilish spirits who chiefly obsess the interiors of man (n. 4793).

Of the devilish spirits who long to obsess the exteriors of man; that such are shut up in hell (n. 2752, 5990).

29

Writings in Heaven

258. As the angels have speech, and their speech consists of words, they also have writings; and by writing as well as by speech they give expression to what is in their minds. At times I have had papers sent to me, traced with written words precisely like manuscripts in the world, and others like printed sheets; and I was able to read them in a like way, but was allowed to get from them only an idea here and there; for the reason that it is not in accordance with Divine order for man to be taught by writings from heaven; but he must be taught by means of the Word only; for it is only by means of the Word that there is communication and conjunction of heaven with the world, thus of the Lord with man. That papers written in heaven were seen also by the prophets is shown in Ezekiel:

> When I looked, behold a hand was put forth by a spirit unto me, and a roll of a book was therein which he unrolled in my sight; it was written on the front and on the back (Ezek. 2:9, 10).

And in John:

> I saw upon the right hand of him that sat on the throne a book written within and on the back, sealed up with seven seals (Rev. 5:1).

259. The existence of writings in the heavens is a provision of the Lord for the sake of the Word; for the Word in its essence is Divine truth, and from it is all heavenly wisdom, both with men and with angels; for the Word was dictated by the Lord, and what is dictated by the Lord passes through all the heavens in order and terminates with man. Thereby it is adapted both to the wisdom of angels and the intelligence of men. Thereby, too, the angels have a Word, and read it the same as men do on the earth, and also draw from it their doctrinals, and preach from it (n. 221). It is the same Word; but its natural sense, which is the sense of the letter with us, does not exist in heaven, but only the spiritual sense, which is its internal sense. What this sense is can be seen in the small treatise *White Horse* (spoken of in Revelation).

260. A little paper was at one time sent to me from heaven, on which there were a few words only written in Hebrew letters, and I was told that every letter involved arcana of wisdom, and that these arcana were contained in the inflections and curvatures of the letters, and thus also in the sounds. This made clear to me what is signified by these words of the Lord:

Verily I say unto you, until heaven and earth pass away, one iota or one tittle shall not pass away from the law (Matt. 5:18).

That the Word in every tittle of it is Divine is known in the church; but just where the Divine lies hid in every tittle has not been known heretofore, and therefore shall be told. In the inmost heaven the writing consists of various inflected and circumflected forms, and the inflections and circumflections are in accordance with the forms of heaven. By means of these angels express the arcana of their wisdom, and also many things that they are unable to express in spoken words; and what is wonderful, the angels know this writing without training or a teacher, it being implanted in them like their speech (see n. 236); therefore this writing is heavenly writing. It is implanted because all extension of thoughts and affections and consequent communication of intelligence and wisdom of the angels proceeds in accordance with the form of heaven (n. 201); and for the same reason their writing flows into that form. I have been told that the most ancient people on this earth, before letters were invented, had such writing; and that it was transferred into the letters of the Hebrew language, and these letters in ancient times were all inflected, and none of them, as at present, were bounded by straight lines. Thus it is that in the Word Divine things and arcana of heaven are contained even in its iotas, points, and tittles.

261. This writing in characters of a heavenly form is in use in the inmost heaven, the angels of which surpass all others in wisdom. By means of these characters they express the affections, from which thoughts flow and follow in order in accordance with the subject treated of. Consequently these writings, which I have also been permitted to see, involve arcana which thought cannot exhaust. But such writings do not exist in the lower heavens. The writings there resemble the writings in the world, having like characters, and yet they are not intelligible to man, because they are in angelic language; and angelic language is such that it has nothing in common with human languages (n. 237), since by the vowels they express affections, and by the consonants the ideas of thought from the affections, and by the words from these the sense of the matter (see above, n. 236, 241). Moreover, in this writing, which I have also seen, more is involved in a few words than a man can express in several pages. In this way they have the Word written in the lower heavens; but in the inmost heaven in heavenly characters.

262. It is a notable fact that the writings in the heavens flow naturally from their very thoughts, and this so easily that the thought puts itself forth, as it were, and the hand never hesitates in the choice of a word, because both the words they speak and those they write correspond to the ideas of their thought; and all correspondence is natural and spontaneous. There are also writings in the heavens that exist without the aid of the hand, from mere correspondence with the thoughts; but these are not permanent.

263. I have also seen writings from heaven made up of mere numbers set down in order and in a series, just as in writings made up of letters and words; and I have been taught that this writing is from the inmost heaven, and that their heavenly writing (spoken of above, n. 260, 261), when the thought from it flows down, is set forth before the angels of the lower heavens in numbers, and that this numerical writing likewise involves arcana, some of which can neither be comprehended by thought nor expressed by words. For all numbers correspond, and have a meaning, the same as words do, in accordance with the correspondence;[1] yet with the difference that in numbers generals are involved, and in words particulars; and as one general involves innumerable particulars, so more arcana are involved in numerical writing than in literal writing. From this I could see that in the Word numbers as well as words signify things. What the simple numbers signify, as 2, 3, 4, 5, 6, 7, 8, 9, 10, 12, and what the compound numbers, as 20, 30, 50, 70, 100, 144, 1000, 10,000, 12,000, and others, may be seen in *Arcana Coelestia,* where they are treated of. In this writing in heaven, a number is always prefixed on which those following in a series depend as on their subject; for that number is as it were an index to the matter treated of, and from it is the determination of the numbers that follow to the particular point.

264. Those who know nothing about heaven, and who are unwilling to have any other idea of it than as of something purely atmospheric, in which the angels fly about as intellectual

---

1. All numbers in the Word signify things (n. 482, 487, 647, 648, 755, 813, 1963, 1988, 2075, 2252, 3252, 4264, 4670, 6175, 9488, 9659, 10217, 10253).

Shown from heaven (n. 4495, 5265).

Composite numbers have the same signification as the simple numbers from which they result by multiplication (n. 5291, 5335, 5708, 7973).

The most ancient people possessed heavenly arcana expressed in numbers, forming a kind of computation of states of the church (n. 575).

minds, having no sense of hearing or seeing, are unable to conceive that the angels have speech and writing; for they place the existence of everything real in what is material; and yet the writings in heaven have as real an existence as those in the world, and the angels there have everything that is useful for life and useful for wisdom.

30

The Wisdom of the Angels
of Heaven

265. The nature of angelic wisdom can scarcely be comprehended, because it so greatly transcends human wisdom that the two cannot be compared; and whatever is thus transcendent does not seem to be anything. Moreover, some truths that must enter into a description of it are as yet unknown, and until these become known they exist in the mind as shadows, and thus hide the thing as it is in itself. Nevertheless, these truths can be known, and when known be comprehended, provided the mind takes any interest in them; for interest carries light with it because it is from love; and upon those who love the things pertaining to Divine and heavenly wisdom light shines forth from heaven and gives enlightenment.

266. What the wisdom of the angels is can be inferred from the fact that they are in the light of heaven, and the light of heaven in its essence is Divine truth or Divine wisdom; and this light enlightens at the same time their inner sight, or sight of the mind, and their outer sight, or sight of the eyes. (That the light of heaven is Divine truth or Divine wisdom may be seen above, n. 126–133.) The angels are also in heavenly heat, which in its essence is Divine good or Divine love, and from that they have an affection and longing to become wise. (That the heat of heaven is Divine good or Divine love may be seen above, n. 133–140.) That the angels are in wisdom, even to the extent that they may be called wisdoms, follows from the fact that their thoughts and affections all flow in accordance with the heavenly form, and this form is the form of Divine wisdom; also that their interiors, which are recipients of wisdom, are arranged in that form. (That the thoughts and affections of angels flow in accordance with the form of heaven, and consequently their intelligence and wisdom, may be seen above, n. 201–212.)

[2] That the angels have supereminent wisdom is shown also by the fact that their speech is the speech of wisdom, for it flows directly and spontaneously from thought, and their thought from their affection, thus their speech is thought from affection in outward form; consequently there is nothing to withdraw them from the Divine influx, and nothing from without such as enters into the speech of man from other thoughts. (That the speech of angels is the speech of their thought and affection may be seen above, n. 234–245.) That the angels have such wisdom is in accord with the fact that all things that they behold with their eyes and perceive by their senses agree with their wisdom, since they are correspondences of it, and thus the objects perceived are representative forms of the things that constitute their wisdom. (That all things seen in the heavens are correspondences with the interiors of angels and representations of their wisdom may be seen above, n. 170–182.)

[3] Furthermore, the thoughts of angels are not limited and contracted by ideas from space and time, as human thoughts are, for spaces and times belong to nature, and the things that belong to nature withdraw the mind from spiritual things, and deprive intellectual sight of its proper range. (That the ideas of angels are apart from time and space, and thus less limited than human ideas, may be seen above, n. 162–169 and 191–199.) Again, the thoughts of angels are neither brought down to earthly and material things, nor interrupted by anxieties about the necessities of life; thus they are not withdrawn by such things from the delights of wisdom, as the thoughts of men in the world are; for all things come to them gratuitously from the Lord; they are clothed gratuitously, are fed gratuitously, are housed gratuitously (n. 181–190), and besides this they receive delights and pleasures in the degree of their reception of wisdom

from the Lord. These things have been said to make clear why it is that angels have so great wisdom.[1]

267. Angels are capable of receiving such wisdom because their interiors are open; and wisdom, like every other perfection, increases toward the interiors, thus to the extent that interiors are opened.[2] In every angel there are three degrees of life, corresponding to the three heavens (see n. 29–40)—those in whom the first degree has been opened are in the first or outmost heaven; those in whom the second degree has been opened are in the second or middle heaven; while those in whom the third degree has been opened are in the third or inmost heaven. The wisdom of angels in the heavens is in accordance with these degrees. Therefore the wisdom of the angels of the inmost heaven immeasurably surpasses the wisdom of angels of the middle heaven, and the wisdom of these immeasurably surpasses the wisdom of angels of the outmost heaven (see above, n. 209, 210; and what degrees are, n. 38). There are such differences because the things which are in the higher degree are particulars, and those in the lower degree are generals, and generals are containers of particulars. Particulars compared with generals are as thousands or myriads to one; and such is the wisdom of the angels of a higher heaven compared with the wisdom of the angels of a lower heaven. In like manner the wisdom of the latter surpasses the wisdom of man, for man is in

1. The wisdom of angels, that it is incomprehensible and ineffable (n. 2795, 2796, 2802, 3314, 3404, 3405, 9094, 9176).

2. So far as man is raised up from outward toward inward things he comes into light, that is, into intelligence (n. 6183, 6313). There is an actual elevation (n. 7816, 10330).

Elevation from outward to inward things is like elevation out of a mist into light (n. 4598). As outer things in man are farther removed from the Divine they are relatively obscure (n. 6451). Likewise relatively confused (n. 996, 3855).

Inner things are more perfect because they are nearer to the Divine (n. 5146, 5147).

In what is internal there are thousands and thousands of things that appear in what is external as one general thing (n. 5707). Consequently as thought and perception are more interior they are clearer (n. 5920).

a bodily state and in those things that belong to the bodily senses, and man's bodily sense belongs to the lowest degree. This makes clear what kind of wisdom those possess who think from things of sense, that is, who are called sensual men, namely, that they have no wisdom, but merely knowledge.[3] But it is otherwise with men whose thoughts are raised above the things of sense, and especially with those whose interiors have been opened even into the light of heaven.

268. It can be seen how great the wisdom of angels is from the fact that in the heavens there is a communication of all things; intelligence and wisdom are communicated from one to another, and heaven is a common sharing of all goods; and this for the reason that heavenly love is such that it wishes what is its own to be another's; consequently no one in heaven perceives his own good in himself to be good unless it is also in another; and this is the source of the happiness of heaven. This the angels derive from the Lord, for such is his Divine love. That there is such a communication of all things in the heavens it has been permitted me to know by experience. Certain simple spirits were at one time taken up into heaven, and when there they entered into angelic wisdom, and then understood things that they were never

3. The sensual is the outmost of man's life adhering to and inhering in his bodily part (n. 5077, 5767, 9212, 9216, 9331, 9730).

He is called a sensual man who judges all things and draws all his conclusions from the bodily senses, and believes nothing except what he sees with his eyes and touches with his hands (n. 5094, 7693). Such a man thinks in externals, and not interiorly in himself (n. 5089, 5094, 6564, 7693). His interiors are so closed up that he sees nothing of spiritual truth in them (n. 6564, 6844, 6845).

In a word, he is in gross natural light and thus perceives nothing that is from the light of heaven (n. 6201, 6310, 6564, 6598, 6612, 6614, 6622, 6624, 6844, 6845). Interiorly he is antagonistic to the things of heaven and the church (n. 6201, 6316, 6844, 6845, 6948, 6949). The learned who have confirmed themselves against the truths of the church come to be such (n. 6316). Sensual men are more cunning and malicious than others (n. 7693, 10236). They reason keenly and cunningly, but from the bodily memory, in which they place all intelligence (n. 195, 196, 5700, 10236). But they reason from the fallacies of the senses (n. 5084, 6948, 6949, 7693).

before able to comprehend, and spoke things that they were unable to utter in their former state.

269. The wisdom of the angels is indescribable in words; it can only be illustrated by some general things. Angels can express in a single word what a man cannot express in a thousand words. Again, a single angelic word contains innumerable things that cannot be expressed in the words of human language; for in each of the things uttered by angels there are arcana of wisdom in continuous connection that human knowledges never reach. Again, what the angels fail to express in the words of their speech they make up by the tone, in which there is an affection for the things in their order; for (as has been said above, n. 236, 241) tones express affections, as words express ideas of thought from the affections; and for this reason the things heard in heaven are said to be ineffable. So, too, the angels are able to express in a few words every least thing written in an entire volume, and give to every word meanings that elevate the mind to interior wisdom; for their speech is such as to be in accord with their affections, and each word is in accord with their ideas; and their words are varied in infinite ways in accord with the series of things which in complex are in the thought.

[2] Still again, the interior angels are able to perceive from the tone and from a few words the entire life of one speaking; for from the tone as varied by the ideas in the words they perceive his ruling love upon which, as it were, every particular of his life is inscribed.[4] All this makes clear the nature of angelic

4. That which universally rules or is dominant in man is in every particular of his life, thus in each thing and all things of his thought and affection (n. 4459, 5949, 6159, 6571, 7648, 8067, 8853–8858). A man is such as his ruling love is (n. 917, 1040, 8858); illustrated by examples (n. 8854, 8857). That which rules universally constitutes the life of the spirit of man (n. 7648). It is his very will, his very love, and the end of his life, since that which a man wills he loves, and that which he loves he has as an end

wisdom. In comparison with human wisdom it is as a myriad to one, or as the moving forces of the whole body, which are numberless, to the activities from them which appear to human sense as a single thing, or as the thousand particulars of an object seen under a perfect microscope to the one obscure thing seen by the naked eye.

[3] Let me illustrate the subject by an example. An angel from his wisdom was describing regeneration, and brought forward arcana respecting it in their order even to some hundreds, filling each of them with ideas in which there were interior arcana, and this from beginning to end; for he explained how the spiritual man is conceived anew, is carried as it were in the womb, is born, grows up and is gradually perfected. He said that the number of arcana could be increased even to thousands, and that those told were only about the regeneration of the external man, while there were numberless more about the regeneration of the internal man. From these and other like things heard from the angels it has been made clear to me how great is their wisdom, and how great in comparison is the ignorance of man, who scarcely knows what regeneration is, and is ignorant of every least step of the process when he is being regenerated.

270. The wisdom of the angels of the third or inmost heaven shall now be described, and also how far it surpasses the wisdom of the angels of the first or outmost heaven. The wisdom of the angels of the third or inmost heaven is incomprehensible even to those who are in the outmost heaven, for the reason that the interiors of the angels of the third heaven have been opened to the third degree, while the interiors of angels of the first heaven have been opened only to the first degree; and all

---

(n. 1317, 1568, 1571, 1909, 3796, 5949, 6936). Therefore man is such as his will is, or such as his ruling love is, or such as the end of his life is (n. 1568, 1571, 3570, 4054, 6571, 6935, 6938, 8856, 10076, 10109, 10110, 10284).

wisdom increases toward interiors and is perfected as these are opened (n. 208, 267).

[2] Because the interiors of the angels of the third or inmost heaven have been opened to the third degree, Divine truths are as it were inscribed on them; for the interiors of the third degree are more in the form of heaven than the interiors of the second and first degrees, and the form of heaven is from the Divine truth, thus in accord with the Divine wisdom, and this is why the truth is as it were inscribed on these angels, or are as it were instinctive or inborn in them. Therefore as soon as these angels hear genuine Divine truths they instantly acknowledge and perceive them, and afterwards see them as it were inwardly in themselves. As the angels of that heaven are such they never reason about Divine truths, still less do they dispute about any truth whether it is so or not; nor do they know what it is to believe or to have faith. They say, "What is faith? For I perceive and see that a thing is so." This they illustrate by comparisons; for example, that it would be as when anyone with a companion, seeing a house and the various things in it and around it, should say to his companion that he ought to believe that these things exist, and that they are such as he sees them to be; or seeing a garden and trees and fruit in it, should say to his companion that he ought to have faith that there is a garden and trees and fruits, when yet he is seeing them clearly with his eyes. For this reason these angels never mention faith, and have no idea what it is; neither do they reason about Divine truths, still less do they dispute about any truth whether it is so or not.[5]

---

5. The celestial angels know innumerable things, and are immeasurably wiser than the spiritual angels (n. 2718). The celestial angels do not think and talk from faith, as the spiritual angels do, for they have from the Lord a perception of all things that constitute faith (n. 202, 597, 607, 784, 1121, 1384, 1442, 1898, 1919, 7680, 7877, 8780, 9277, 10336). In regard to the truths of faith they say only "Yea, yea, or Nay, nay," while the spiritual angels reason about whether a thing is true (n. 2715, 3246, 4448, 9166, 10786, where the Lord's words, "Let your discourse be Yea, yea, Nay nay" (Matt. 5:37), are explained).

[3] But the angels of the first or outmost heaven do not have Divine truths thus inscribed on their interiors, because with them only the first degree of life is opened; therefore they reason about truths, and those who reason see almost nothing beyond the fact of the matter about which they are reasoning, or go no farther beyond the subject than to confirm it by certain considerations, and having confirmed it they say that it must be a matter of faith and must be believed.

[4] I have talked with angels about this, and they said that the difference between the wisdom of the angels of the third heaven and the wisdom of the angels of the first heaven is like that between what is clear and what is obscure; and the former they compared to a magnificent palace full of all things for use, surrounded on all sides by parks, with magnificent things of many kinds round about them; and as these angels are in the truths of wisdom they can enter into the palace and behold all things, and wander about in the parks in every direction and delight in it all. But it is not so with those who reason about truths, especially with those who dispute about them, as such do not see truths from the light of truth, but accept truths either from others or from the sense of the letter of the Word, which they do not interiorly understand, declaring that truths must be believed, or that one must have faith, and are not willing to have any interior sight admitted into these things. The angels said that such are unable to reach the first threshold of the palace of wisdom, still less to enter into it and wander about in its grounds, for they stop at the first step. It is not so with those that are in truths themselves; nothing impedes these from going on and progressing without limit, for the truths they see lead them wherever they go, and into wide fields, for every truth has infinite extension and is in conjunction with manifold others.

[5] They said still further that the wisdom of the angels of the inmost heaven consists principally in this, that they see Divine and heavenly things in every single object, and wonderful things

in a series of many objects; for everything that appears before their eyes is a correspondent; as when they see palaces and gardens their view does not dwell upon the things that are before their eyes, but they see the interior things from which they spring, that is, to which they correspond, and this with all variety in accordance with the aspect of the objects; thus they see innumerable things at the same time in their order and connection; and this so fills their minds with delight that they seem to be carried away from themselves. That all things that are seen in the heavens correspond to the Divine things that are in the angels from the Lord may be seen above (n. 170–176).

271. Such are the angels of the third heaven because they are in love to the Lord, and that love opens the interiors of the mind to the third degree, and is a receptacle of all things of wisdom. It must be understood also that the angels of the inmost heaven are still being continually perfected in wisdom, and this differently from the angels of the outmost heaven. The angels of the inmost heaven do not store up Divine truths in the memory and thus make out of them a kind of science; but as soon as they hear them they perceive them and apply them to the life. For this reason Divine truths are as permanent with them as if they were inscribed on them, for what is committed in such a way to the life is contained in it. But it is not so with the angels of the outmost heaven. These first store up Divine truths in the memory and stow them away with their knowledge, and draw them out therefrom to perfect their understanding by them, and will them and apply them to the life, but with no interior perception whether they are truths; and in consequence they are in comparative obscurity. It is a notable fact that the angels of the third heaven are perfected in wisdom by hearing and not by seeing. What they hear from preachings does not enter into their memory, but enters directly into their perception and will, and comes to be a matter of life; but what they see with their eyes enters into their memory, and they reason and talk about it; which shows that with them the way of hearing is the way of wisdom. This, too, is from correspondence, for the ear corresponds to obedience, and obedience belongs to the life; while the eye corresponds to intelligence, and intelligence is a matter of doctrine.[6] The state of these angels is described in different parts of the Word, as in Jeremiah:

> I will put my law in their mind, and write it on their heart. They shall teach no more everyone his friend and everyone his brother, saying, Know ye Jehovah; for they shall all know Me, from the least of them even unto the greatest of them (Jer. 31:33, 34).

And in Matthew:

> Let your speech be Yea, yea, Nay, nay; what is more than these is from evil (Matt. 5:37).

"What is more than these is from evil" because it is not from the Lord; and inasmuch as the angels of the third heaven are in love to the Lord the truths that are in them are from the Lord. In that heaven love to the Lord is willing and doing Divine truth, for Divine truth is the Lord in heaven.

272. There is a still further reason, and this is in heaven the primary reason, why the angels are able to receive so great wisdom, namely, that they are without the love of self; for to the extent that anyone is without the love of self he can become wise in Divine things. It is that love that closes up the interiors against the Lord and heaven, and opens the exteriors and turns them toward itself; and in consequence all in whom that love rules are in thick darkness in respect to the things of heaven,

---

6. Of the correspondence of the ear and of hearing (n. 4652–4660).

The ear corresponds to and therefore signifies perception and obedience (n. 2542, 3869, 4653, 5017, 7216, 8361, 9311, 9397, 10061).

The ear signifies the reception of truths (n. 5471, 5475, 9926).

The correspondence of the eye and its sight (n. 4403–4421, 4523–4534); from which the sight of the eye signifies the intelligence that belongs to faith, and also faith (n. 2701, 4410, 4526, 6923, 9051, 10569).

however much light they may have in worldly matters. The angels, on the other hand, are in the light of wisdom because they are without the love of self, for the heavenly loves in which they are, which are love to the Lord and love toward the neighbor, open the interiors, because these loves are from the Lord and the Lord himself is in them. (That these loves constitute heaven in general, and form heaven in each one in particular, may be seen above, n. 13–19.) As heavenly loves open the interiors to the Lord so all angels turn their faces toward the Lord (n. 142); because in the spiritual world the love turns the interiors of everyone to itself, and whichever way it turns the interiors, it also turns the face, since the face there makes one with the interiors, for it is their outward form. Because the love turns the interiors and the face to itself, it also conjoins itself to them (love being spiritual conjunction), and shares its own with them. From that turning and consequent conjunction and sharing the angels have their wisdom. That all conjunction and all turning in the spiritual world are in accord may be seen above (n. 255).

273. Although the angels are continually perfected in wisdom,[7] their wisdom, even to eternity, cannot become so perfect that there can be any ratio between it and the Lord's Divine wisdom; for the Lord's Divine wisdom is infinite and the wisdom of angels finite; and between what is infinite and what is finite no ratio is possible.

274. As it is wisdom that makes the angels perfect and constitutes their life, and as heaven with its goods flows into everyone in accordance with his wisdom, so all in heaven desire and hunger for wisdom, much as a hungry man hungers for food. So, too, knowledge, intelligence, and wisdom are spiritual

7. Angels are perfected to eternity (n. 4803, 6648).

nutriment, as food is natural nutriment; and the one corresponds to the other.

275. The angels in the same heaven, or in the same society of heaven, are not all in like wisdom; their wisdom differs. Those at the center are in the greatest wisdom, and those round about even to the borders are in less wisdom. The decrease of wisdom in accord with the distance from the center is like the decrease of light verging to shade (see n. 43 and 128). Their light is in the same degree as their wisdom, since the light of heaven is the Divine wisdom, and everyone is in light in the measure of his reception of wisdom. Respecting the light of heaven and the varying kinds of reception of it see above (n. 126–132).

31

The State of Innocence
of Angels in Heaven

276. What innocence is and its nature few in the world know, and those who are in evil know nothing about it. It is, indeed, visible to the eyes, as seen in the face, speech and movements, particularly of children; and yet what innocence is, and especially that it is that in which heaven is stored up in man is unknown. In making this known let us proceed in order, and consider first the innocence of childhood, then the innocence of wisdom, and lastly the state of heaven in regard to innocence.

277. The innocence of childhood or of children is not genuine innocence, for it is innocence not in internal form but only in external form. Nevertheless one may learn from it what innocence is, since it shines forth from the face of children and from some of their movements and from their first speech, and affects those about them. It can be seen that children have no internal thought, for they do not yet know what is good and what is evil, or what is true and what is false, of which such thought consists.

[2] Consequently they have no prudence from what is their own, no purpose or deliberation, thus no end that looks to evil; neither have they anything of their own acquired from love of self and the world; they do not attribute anything to themselves, regarding all that they have as received from their parents; they are content with the few and paltry things presented to them, and find delight in them; they have no solicitude about food and clothing, and none about the future; they do not look to the world and covet many things from it; they love their parents and nurses and their child companions with whom they

play in innocence; they suffer themselves to be led; they give heed and obey.

[3] And being in this state they receive everything as a matter of life; and therefore, without knowing why, they have becoming manners, and also learn to talk, and have the beginning of memory and thought, their state of innocence serving as a medium whereby these things are received and implanted. But this innocence, as has been said above, is external because it belongs to the body alone, and not to the mind;[1] for their minds are not yet formed, the mind being understanding and will and thought and affection therefrom.

[4] I have been told from heaven that children are specially under the Lord's auspices, and that they receive influx from the inmost heaven, where there is a state of innocence; that this influx passes through their interiors, and that in its passing through, their interiors are affected solely by the innocence; and for this reason innocence is shown in their faces and in some of their movements and becomes evident; and that it is this innocence by which parents are inmostly affected, and that gives rise to the love that is called *storge*.

278. The innocence of wisdom is genuine innocence, because it is internal, for it belongs to the mind itself, that is, to the will itself and from that to the understanding. And when there is innocence in these there is also wisdom, for wisdom belongs to the will and understanding. This is why it is said in heaven that innocence has its abode in wisdom, and that an angel has just so

---

1. The innocence of children is not true innocence, but true innocence has its abode in wisdom (n. 1616, 2305, 2306, 3494, 4563, 4797, 5608, 9301, 10021).

The good of childhood is not spiritual good, but it becomes such by the implantation of truth (n. 3504).

Nevertheless the good of childhood is a medium whereby intelligence is implanted (n. 1616, 3183, 9301, 10110).

Without the good of innocence in childhood man would be a wild man (n. 3494).

Whatever the mind is imbued with in childhood appears natural (n. 3494).

much of innocence as he has of wisdom. This is confirmed by the fact that those who are in a state of innocence attribute nothing of good to themselves, but regard all things as received and ascribe them to the Lord. They wish to be led by Him and not by themselves. They love everything that is good and find delight in everything that is true, because they know and perceive that loving what is good, that is, willing and doing it, is loving the Lord, and loving truth is loving the neighbor.

They live contented with their own, whether it is little or much, because they know that they receive just as much as is good for them— those receiving little for whom a little is useful, and those receiving much for whom much is useful; also they do not themselves know what is good for them, the Lord alone knowing this, who looks in all things that he provides to what is eternal.

[2] Neither are they anxious about the future; anxiety about the future they call care for the morrow, which they define as grief on account of losing or not receiving things that are not necessary for the uses of life. With companions they never act from an evil end but from what is good, just, and sincere. Acting from an evil end they call cunning, which they shun as the poison of a serpent, since it is wholly antagonistic to innocence. As they love nothing so much as to be led of the Lord, attributing all things they receive to him, they are kept apart from what is their own *[proprium]*; and to the extent that they are kept apart from what is their own the Lord flows into them; and in consequence of this whatever they hear from the Lord, whether through the Word or by means of preaching, they do not store up in the memory, but instantly obey it, that is, will it and do it, their will being itself their memory. These for the most part outwardly appear simple, but inwardly they are wise and prudent. These are meant by the Lord in the words,

Be ye prudent as serpents and simple as doves (Matt. 10:16).

Such is the innocence that is called the innocence of wisdom.

[3] Because innocence attributes nothing of good to itself, but ascribes all good to the Lord, and because it thus loves to be led by the Lord, and is the source of the reception of all good and truth, from which wisdom comes—because of this man is so created as to be during his childhood in external innocence, and when he becomes old in internal innocence, to the end that he may come by means of the former into the latter, and from the latter return into the former. For the same reason when a man becomes old he dwindles in body and becomes again like a child, but like a wise child, that is, an angel, for a wise child is in an eminent sense an angel. This is why in the Word, "a little child" signifies one who is innocent, and "an old man" signifies one who is wise in whom is innocence.[2]

279. The same is true of everyone who is being regenerated. Regeneration, as regards the spiritual man, is rebirth. Man is first introduced into the innocence of childhood, which is that one knows no truth and can do no good from himself, but only from the Lord, and desires and seeks truth only because it is truth, and good only because it is good. As man afterwards advances in age good and truth are given him by the Lord. At first he is led into a knowledge of them, then from knowledge into intelligence, and finally from intelligence into wisdom, innocence always accompanying, which consists, as has been said, in his knowing nothing of truth, and being unable to do anything good from himself, but only from the Lord. Without such a belief and such a perception of it no one can receive anything of heaven. Therein does the innocence of wisdom chiefly consist.

---

2. In the Word "little children" signify innocence (n. 5608); likewise "sucklings" (n. 3183). An "old man" signifies one who is wise, and in an abstract sense wisdom (n. 3183, 6524). Man is so created that in proportion as he verges toward old age he may become like a little child, and that innocence may then be in his wisdom, and in that state he may pass into heaven and become an angel (n. 3183, 5608).

280. As innocence consists in being led by the Lord and not by self, so all who are in heaven are in innocence; for all who are there love to be led by the Lord, knowing that to lead themselves is to be led by what is their own, and what is one's own is loving oneself, he that loves himself not permitting himself to be led by anyone else. Therefore, so far as an angel is in innocence he is in heaven, in other words, is in Divine good and Divine truth, for to be in these is to be in heaven. Consequently the heavens are distinguished by degrees of innocence—those who are in the outmost or first heaven are in innocence of the first or outmost degree; those who are in the middle or second heaven are in innocence of the second or middle degree; while those who are in the inmost or third heaven are in innocence of the third or inmost degree, and are therefore the veriest innocences of heaven, for more than all others they love to be led by the Lord as little children by their father; and for the same reason the Divine truth that they hear immediately from the Lord or mediately through the Word and preaching they take directly into their will and do it, thus committing it to life. And this is why their wisdom is so superior to that of the angels of the lower heavens (see n. 270, 271). These angels of the inmost heaven, being such, are nearest to the Lord from whom they receive innocence, and are so separated from what is their own that they live as it were in the Lord. Externally they appear simple, and before the eyes of the angels of the lower heavens they appear like children, that is, as very small, and not very wise, although they are the wisest of the angels of heaven; since they know that they have nothing of wisdom from themselves, and that acknowledging this is being wise. They know also that what they know is as nothing compared to what they do not know; and they say that knowing, acknowledging, and perceiving this is the first step toward wisdom. These angels have no clothing, because nakedness corresponds to innocence.[3]

3. All in the inmost heaven are innocences (n. 154, 2736, 3887). Therefore they appear

281. I have talked much with angels about innocence, and have been told that innocence is the being *[esse]* of all good, and that good is therefore so far good as it has innocence in it, consequently that wisdom is so far wisdom as it partakes of innocence; and the same is true of love, charity, and faith;[4] and therefore no one can enter heaven unless he possesses innocence; and this the Lord teaches when He says:

> Suffer little children to come unto Me, and forbid them not; for of such is the kingdom of the heavens. Verily I say unto you, Whoever shall not receive the kingdom of the heavens as a little child, he shall not enter into it (Mark 10:14, 15; Luke 18:16, 17).

Here as elsewhere in the Word "little children" mean those who are innocent. A state of innocence is also described by the Lord in Matthew 6:25–34, but by correspondences only. Good is good so far as it has innocence in it, for the reason that all good is from the Lord, and innocence is a willingness to be led by the Lord. I have also been told that truth can be conjoined to good and good to truth only by means of innocence, and therefore an angel is not an angel of heaven unless he has innocence in him; for heaven is not in anyone until good is conjoined to truth in him; and this is why the conjunction of truth and good is called the heavenly marriage, and the heavenly marriage is heaven. Again, I have been told that true marriage love derives its existence from innocence, because it derives its existence from the conjunction of good and truth, and the two minds of husband and wife are in that conjunction, and when that conjunction descends it presents the appearance of marriage love; for consorts

---

to others like children (n. 154). They are also naked (n. 165, 8375, 9960). Nakedness belongs to innocence (n. 165, 8375). Spirits have a custom of exhibiting innocence by laying aside their garments and presenting themselves naked (n. 165, 8375, 9960).

4. Every good of love and truth of faith, to be good and true must have innocence in it (n. 2526, 2780, 3111, 3994, 6013, 7840, 9262, 10134). Innocence is the essential of good and truth (n. 2780, 7840). No one is admitted into heaven unless he possesses something of innocence (n. 4797).

are in mutual love, as their minds are. This is why in marriage love there is a playfulness like that of childhood and like that of innocence.[5]

282. Because innocence with the angels of heaven is the very being of good, it is evident that the Divine good that goes forth from the Lord is innocence itself, for it is that good that flows into angels, and affects their inmosts, and arranges and fits them for receiving all the good of heaven. It is the same with children, whose interiors are not only formed by means of innocence flowing through them from the Lord, but also are continually being fitted and arranged for receiving the good of heavenly love, since the good of innocence acts from the inmost; for that good, as has been said, is the being of all good. From all this it can be seen that all innocence is from the Lord. For this reason the Lord is called in the Word a "lamb," a lamb signifying innocence.[6] Because innocence is the inmost in all the good of heaven, it so affects minds that when it is felt by anyone—as when an angel of the inmost heaven approaches—he seems to himself to be no longer his own master and is moved and as it were carried away by such a delight that no delight of the world seems to be anything in comparison with it. This I say from having perceived it.

283. Everyone who is in the good of innocence is affected by innocence, and is affected to the extent that he is in that good;

---

5. True marriage love is innocence (n. 2736). Marriage love consists in willing what the other wills, thus mutually and reciprocally (n. 2731).

They who are in marriage love dwell together in the inmosts of life (n. 2732).

There is a union of the two minds, and thus from love they are a one (n. 10168, 10169). True marriage love derives its origin and essence from the marriage of good and truth (n. 2728, 2729). About angelic spirits who have a perception from the idea of the conjunction of good and truth whether anything of marriage exists (n. 10756).

Marriage love is wholly like the conjunction of good and truth (n. 1904, 2173, 2508, 2729, 3103, 3132, 3155, 3179, 3180, 4358, 5807, 5835, 9206, 9207, 9495, 9637).

Therefore in the Word "marriage" means the marriage of good and truth, such as there is in heaven and such as there will be in the church (n. 3132, 4434, 4835).

6. In the Word a "lamb" signifies innocence and its good (n. 3994, 10132).

but those who are not in the good of innocence are not affected by innocence. For this reason all who are in hell are wholly antagonistic to innocence; they do not know what it is; their antagonism is such that so far as anyone is innocent they burn to do him mischief; therefore they cannot bear to see little children; and as soon as they see them they are inflamed with a cruel desire to do them harm. From this it is clear that what is man's own, and therefore the love of self, is antagonistic to innocence; for all who are in hell are in what is their own, and therefore in the love of self.[7]

7. What is man's own is loving self more than God, and the world more than heaven, and making one's neighbor of no account as compared with oneself; thus it is the love of self and of the world (n. 694, 731, 4317, 5660).

The evil are wholly antagonistic to innocence, even to the extent that they cannot endure its presence (n. 2126).

32

The State of Peace in Heaven

284. Only those that have experienced the peace of heaven can have any perception of the peace in which the angels are. As man is unable, as long as he is in the body, to receive the peace of heaven, so he can have no perception of it, because his perception is confined to what is natural. To perceive it he must be able, in respect to thought, to be raised up and withdrawn from the body and kept in the spirit, and at the same time be with angels. In this way has the peace of heaven been perceived by me; and for this reason I am able to describe it, yet not in words as that peace is in itself, because human words are inadequate, but only as it is in comparison with that rest of mind that those enjoy who are content in God.

285. There are two inmost things of heaven, namely, innocence and peace. These are said to be inmost things because they proceed directly from the Lord. From innocence comes every good of heaven, and from peace every delight of good. Every good has its delight; and both good and delight spring from love, for whatever is loved is called good, and is also perceived as delightful. From this it follows that these two inmost things, innocence and peace, go forth from the Lord's Divine love and move the angels from what is inmost. That innocence is the inmost of good may be seen in the preceding chapter, where the state of innocence of the angels of heaven is described. That peace is the inmost of delight from the good of innocence shall now be explained.

286. The origin of peace shall be first considered. Divine peace is in the Lord; it springs from the union of the Divine itself and the Divine human in him. The Divine of peace in heaven is from the Lord, springing from his conjunction with the angels of heaven, and in particular from the conjunction of good and truth in each angel. These are the origins of peace. From this it can be seen that peace in the heavens is the Divine inmostly affecting with blessedness everything good therefrom, and from this is every joy of heaven; also that it is in its essence the Divine joy of the Lord's Divine love, resulting from his conjunction with heaven and with everyone there. This joy, felt by the Lord in angels and by angels from the Lord, is peace. By derivation from this the angels have everything that is blessed, delightful, and happy, or that which is called heavenly joy.[1]

287. Because these are the origins of peace the Lord is called "the Prince of peace," and he declares that from him is peace and in him is peace; and the angels are called angels of peace, and heaven is called a habitation of peace, as in the following passages:

Unto us a Child is born, unto us a Son is given, and the government shall be upon his shoulder; and his name shall be called Wonderful, Counselor, God, Mighty, Father of eternity, Prince of peace. Of the increase of his government and peace there shall be no end (Isa. 9:6, 7).

Jesus said, Peace I leave with you, my peace I give unto you; not as the world giveth give I unto you (John 14:27).

These things have I spoken unto you that in Me ye may have peace (John 16:33).

Jehovah lift up his countenance upon thee and give thee peace (Num. 6:26).

---

1. By peace in the highest sense the Lord is meant, because peace is from Him, and in the internal sense heaven is meant, because those are in a state of peace (n. 3780, 4681).

Peace in the heavens is the Divine inmostly affecting with blessedness everything good and true there, and this peace is incomprehensible to man (n. 92, 3780, 5662, 8455, 8665). Divine peace is in good, but not in truth apart from good (n. 8722).

The angels of peace weep bitterly, the highways are wasted (Isa. 33:7, 8).

The work of righteousness shall be peace; and my people shall dwell in a habitation of peace (Isa. 32:17, 18).

[2] That it is Divine and heavenly peace that is meant in the Word by "peace" can be seen also from other passages where it is mentioned (as Isa. 52:7; 54:10; 59:8; Jer. 16:5; 25:37; 29:11; Hag. 2:9; Zech. 8:12; Ps. 37:37; and elsewhere). Because "peace" means the Lord and heaven, and also heavenly joy and the delight of good, "Peace be with you" was an ancient form of salutation that is still in use; and it was ratified by the Lord in his saying to the disciples whom he sent forth:

Into whatsoever house ye enter, first say, Peace be to this house; and if a son of peace be there, your peace shall rest upon it (Luke 10:5, 6).

And when the Lord himself appeared to the apostles, he said:

Peace be with you (John 20:19, 21, 26).

[3] A state of peace is also meant in the Word where it is said that:

Jehovah smelled an odor of rest (as Exod. 29:18, 25, 41; Lev. 1:9, 13, 17; 2:2, 9; 6:8, 14; 23:12, 13, 18; Num. 15:3, 7, 13; 28:6, 8, 13; 29:2, 6, 8, 13, 36).

"Odor of rest" in the heavenly sense signifies a perception of peace.[2] As peace signifies the union of the Divine itself and the Divine human in the Lord, also the conjunction of the Lord with heaven and with the church, and with all who are in heaven, and with all in the church who receive him, so the Sabbath was instituted as a reminder of these things, its name meaning "rest" or "peace," and was the most holy representative

---

2. In the word an "odor" signifies the perception of agreeableness or disagreeableness, according to the quality of the love and faith of which it is predicated (n. 3577, 4626, 4628, 4748, 5621, 10292). An "odor of rest," in reference to Jehovah, means a perception of peace (n. 925, 10054). This is why frankincense, incense, and odors in oils and ointments, became representative (n. 925, 4748, 5621, 10177).

of the church. For the same reason the Lord called himself "the Lord of the Sabbath" (Matt. 12:8; Mark 2:27, 28; Luke 6:5).[3]

288. Because the peace of heaven is the Divine inmostly affecting with blessedness the veriest good in angels, it can be clearly perceived by them only in the delight of their hearts when they are in the good of their life, in the pleasure with which they hear truth that agrees with their good, and in gladness of mind when they perceive the conjunction of good and truth. From this it flows into all the acts and thoughts of their life, and there presents itself as joy, even in outward appearance.

[2] But peace in the heavens differs in quality and quantity in agreement with the innocence of those who are there; since innocence and peace walk hand in hand; for every good of heaven, as said above, is from innocence, and every delight of that good is from peace. Evidently, then, the same that has been said in the foregoing chapter about the state of innocence in the heavens may be said here of the state of peace there, since innocence and peace are conjoined like good and its delight; for good is felt in its delight, and delight is known from its good. This being so, it is evident that angels of the inmost or third heaven are in the third or inmost degree of peace, because they are in the third or inmost degree of innocence; and that angels of the lower heavens are in a less degree of peace, because they are in a less degree of innocence (see above n. 280).

---

3. The "Sabbath" signifies in the highest sense the union of the Divine itself and the Divine human in the Lord; in the internal sense the conjunction of the Divine human of the Lord with heaven and with the church; in general, the conjunction of good and truth, thus the heavenly marriage (n. 8495, 10356, 10730).

Therefore "rest on the Sabbath day" signified the state of that union, because then the Lord had rest, and thereby there is peace and salvation in the heavens and on the earth; and in a relative sense it signified the conjunction of the Lord with man, because man then has peace and salvation (n. 8494, 8510, 10360, 10367, 10370, 10374, 10668, 10730).

[3] That innocence and peace go together like good and its delight can be seen in little children, who are in peace because they are in innocence, and because they are in peace are in their whole nature full of play. Yet the peace of little children is external peace; while internal peace, like internal innocence, is possible only in wisdom, and for this reason only in the conjunction of good and truth, since wisdom is from that conjunction. Heavenly or angelic peace is also possible in men who are in wisdom from the conjunction of good and truth, and who in consequence have a sense of content in God; nevertheless, while they live in the world this peace lies hidden in their interiors, but it is revealed when they leave the body and enter heaven, for their interiors are then opened.

289. As the Divine peace springs from the conjunction of the Lord with heaven, and specially from the conjunction of good and truth in each angel, so when the angels are in a state of love they are in a state of peace; for then good and truth are conjoined in them. (That the states of angels undergo successive changes may be seen above, n. 154–160.) The like is true also of a man who is being regenerated. As soon as good and truth come to be conjoined in him, which takes place especially after temptations, he comes into a state of delight from heavenly peace.[4] This peace may be likened to morning or dawn in springtime, when, the night being passed, with the rising of the sun all things of the earth begin to live anew, the fragrance of growing vegetation is spread abroad with the dew that descends from heaven, and the mild vernal temperature gives fertility to the ground and imparts pleasure to the minds of men, and this because morning or dawn in the time of spring corresponds to the state of peace of angels in heaven (see n. 155).[5]

---

4. The conjunction of good and truth in a man who is being regenerated is effected in a state of peace (n. 3696, 8517).

5. The state of peace in the heavens is like a state of dawn or springtime on the earth

290. I have talked with the angels about peace, saying that what is called peace in the world is when wars and hostilities cease between kingdoms, and when enmities or discord cease among men; also that internal peace is believed to consist in rest of mind when cares are removed, especially in tranquillity and enjoyment from success in affairs. But the angels said that rest of mind and tranquillity and enjoyment from the removal of cares and success in affairs seem to be constituents of peace, but are so only with those who are in heavenly good, for only in that good is peace possible. For peace flows in from the Lord into the inmost of such, and from their inmost descends and flows down into the lower faculties, producing a sense of rest in the mind, tranquillity of disposition, and joy therefrom. But to those who are in evil peace is impossible.[6] There is an appearance of rest, tranquillity, and delight when things succeed according to their wishes; but it is external peace and not at all internal, for inwardly they burn with enmity, hatred, revenge, cruelty, and many evil lusts, into which their disposition is carried whenever anyone is seen to be unfavorable to them, and which burst forth when they are not restrained by fear. Consequently the delight of such dwells in insanity, while the delight of those who are in good dwells in wisdom. The difference is like that between hell and heaven.

(n. 1726, 2780, 5662).

6. The lusts that originate in love of self and of the world wholly take away peace (n. 3170, 5662).

There are some who think to find peace in restlessness, and in such things as are contrary to peace (n. 5662).

Peace is possible only when the lusts of evil are removed (n. 5662).

33

The Conjunction of Heaven with
the Human Race

291. It is well known in the church that all good is from God, and that nothing of good is from man, consequently that no one ought to ascribe any good to himself as his own. It is also well known that evil is from the devil. Therefore those who speak from the doctrine of the church say of those who behave well, and of those who speak and preach piously, that they are led by God; but the opposite of those who do not behave well and who speak impiously. For this to be true man must have conjunction with heaven and with hell; and this conjunction must be with man's will and with his understanding; for it is from these that the body acts and the mouth speaks. What this conjunction is shall now be told.

292. With every individual there are good spirits and evil spirits. Through good spirits man has conjunction with heaven, and through evil spirits with hell. These spirits are in the world of spirits, which lies midway between heaven and hell. This world will be described particularly hereafter. When these spirits come to a man they enter into his entire memory, and thus into his entire thought, evil spirits into the evil things of his memory and thought, and good spirits into the good things of his memory and thought. These spirits have no knowledge whatever that they are with man; but when they are with him they believe that all things of his memory and thought are their own; neither do they see the man, because nothing that is in our solar

world falls into their sight.[1] The Lord exercises the greatest care that spirits may not know that they are with man; for if they knew it they would talk with him, and in that case evil spirits would destroy him; for evil spirits, being joined with hell, desire nothing so much as to destroy man, not alone his soul, that is, his faith and love, but also his body. It is otherwise when spirits do not talk with man, in which case they are not aware that what they are thinking and also what they are saying among themselves is from man; for although it is from man that they talk with one another, they believe that what they are thinking and saying is their own, and everyone esteems and loves what is his own. In this way spirits are constrained to love and esteem man, although they do not know it. That such is the conjunction of spirits with man has become so well known to me from a continual experience of many years that nothing is better known to me.

293. The reason why spirits that communicate with hell are also associated with man is that man is born into evils of every kind, consequently his whole life is wholly from evil; and therefore unless spirits like himself were associated with him he could not live, nor indeed could he be withdrawn from his evils and reformed. He is therefore both held in his own life by means of evil spirits and withheld from it by means of good spirits; and by the two he is kept in equilibrium; and being in equilibrium he is in freedom, and can be drawn away from evils and turned toward good, and thus good can be implanted in him, which would not be possible at all if he were not in free-

---

1. There are angels and spirits with every man, and by means of them man has communication with the spiritual world (n. 697, 2796, 2886, 2887, 4047, 4048, 5846–5866, 5976–5993). Man without spirits attending him cannot live (n. 5993).

Man is not seen by spirits, even as spirits are not seen by man (n. 5862). Spirits can see nothing in our solar world pertaining to any man except the one with whom they are speaking (n. 1880).

dom; and freedom is possible to man only when the spirits from hell act on one side and spirits from heaven on the other, and man is between the two. Again, it has been shown that so far as a man's life is from what he inherits, and thus from self, if he were not permitted to be in evil he would have no life; also if he were not in freedom he would have no life; also that he cannot be forced to what is good, and that what is forced does not abide; also that the good that man receives in freedom is implanted in his will and becomes as it were his own.[2] These are the reasons why man has communication with hell and communication with heaven.

294. What the communication of heaven is with good spirits, and what the communication of hell is with evil spirits, and the consequent conjunction of heaven and hell with man, shall also be told. All spirits who are in the world of spirits have communication with heaven or with hell, evil spirits with hell, and good spirits with heaven. Heaven is divided into societies, and hell also. Every spirit belongs to some society, and continues to exist by influx from it, thus acting as one with it. Consequently as man is conjoined with spirits so is he conjoined with heaven or with hell, even with the society there to which he is attached by his affection or his love; for the societies of heaven are all distinguished from each other in accordance with their affections for good and truth, and the societies of hell in accordance

---

2. All freedom pertains to love and affection, since what a man loves, that he does freely (n. 2870, 3158, 8987, 8990, 9585, 9591). As freedom belongs to man's love, so it belongs to man's life (n. 2873). Nothing appears as man's own except what is from freedom (n. 2880). Man must have freedom that he may be reformed (n. 1937, 1947, 2876, 2881, 3145, 3146, 3158, 4031, 8700).

Otherwise no love of good and truth can be implanted in man and be appropriated seemingly as his own (n. 2877, 2879, 2880, 2883, 8700).

Nothing that comes from compulsion is conjoined to man (n. 2875, 8700).

If man could be reformed by compulsion everyone would be reformed (n. 2881).

Compulsion in reformation is harmful (n. 4031).

What states of compulsion are (n. 8392).

with their affections for evil and falsity. (As to the societies of heaven see above, n. 41–45; also n. 148–151.)

295. The spirits associated with man are such as he himself is in respect to his affection or love; but the Lord associates good spirits with him, while evil spirits are invited by the man himself. The spirits with man, however, are changed in accordance with the changes of his affections; thus there are some spirits that are with him in early childhood, others in boyhood, others in youth and manhood, and others in old age. In early childhood those spirits are present who are in innocence and who thus communicate with the heaven of innocence, which is the inmost or third heaven; in boyhood those spirits are present who are in affection for knowing, and who thus communicate with the outmost or first heaven; in youth and manhood spirits are present who are in affection for what is true and good, and in consequent intelligence, and who thus communicate with the second or middle heaven; while in old age spirits are present who are in wisdom and innocence, and who thus communicate with the inmost or third heaven. But the Lord maintains this association with such as can be reformed and regenerated. It is otherwise with such as cannot be reformed or regenerated. While with these also good spirits are associated, that they may be thereby withheld from evil as much as possible, they are directly conjoined with evil spirits who communicate with hell, whereby they have such spirits with them as are like themselves. If they are lovers of self or lovers of gain, or lovers of revenge, or lovers of adultery, like spirits are present, and as it were dwell in their evil affections; and man is incited by these, except so far as he can be kept from evil by good spirits, and they cling to him, and do not withdraw, so far as the evil affection prevails. Thus it is that a bad man is conjoined to hell and a good man is conjoined to heaven.

296. Man is governed by the Lord through spirits because he is not in the order of heaven, for he is born into evils which are of hell, thus into the complete opposite of Divine order; consequently he needs to be brought back into order, and this can only be done mediately by means of spirits. It would be otherwise if man were born into the good that is in accord with the order of heaven; then he would be governed by the Lord not through spirits, but by means of the order itself, thus by means of general influx. By means of this influx man is governed in respect to whatever goes forth from his thought and will into act, that is, in respect to speech and acts; for both of these proceed in harmony with natural order, and therefore with these the spirits associated with man have nothing in common. Animals also are governed by means of this general influx from the spiritual world, because they are in the order of their life, and animals have not been able to pervert and destroy that order because they have no rational faculty.[3] What the difference between man and beasts is may be seen above (n. 39).

297. As to what further concerns the conjunction of heaven with the human race, let it be noted that the Lord himself flows into each man, in accord with the order of heaven, both into his inmosts and into his outmosts, and arranges him for receiving heaven, and governs his outmosts from his inmosts, and at the same time his inmosts from his outmosts, thus holding in connection each thing and all things in man. This influx of the Lord is called direct influx; while the other influx that is effected through spirits is called mediate influx.

---

3. The difference between men and beasts is that men are capable of being raised up by the Lord to Himself, of thinking about the Divine, loving it, and being thereby conjoined to the Lord, from which they have eternal life; but it is otherwise with beasts (n. 4525, 6323, 9231).

Beasts are in the order of their life, and are therefore born into things suitable to their nature, but man is not, and he must therefore be led into the order of his life by intellectual means (n. 637, 5850, 6323).

According to general influx, thought with man falls into speech and will into movements (n. 5862, 5990, 6192, 6211).

The general influx of the spiritual world into the lives of beasts (n. 1633, 3646).

The latter is maintained by means of the former. Direct influx, which is that of the Lord himself, is from his Divine human, and is into man's will and through his will into his understanding, and thus into his good and through his good into his truth, or what is the same thing, into his love and through his love into his faith, and not the reverse; still less is it into faith apart from love or into truth apart from good or into understanding that is not from will. This Divine influx is unceasing, and in the good is received in good, but not in the evil; for in them it is either rejected or suffocated or perverted; and in consequence they have an evil life which in a spiritual sense is death.[4]

298. The spirits who are with man, both those conjoined with heaven and those conjoined with hell, never flow into man from their own memory and its thought, for if they should flow in from their own thought, whatever belonged to them would seem to man to be his (see above, n. 256). Nevertheless there flows into man through them out of heaven an affection belonging to the love of good and truth, and out of hell an affection belonging to the love of evil and falsity. Therefore as far as man's affection agrees with the affection that flows in, so far that affection is received by him in his thought, since man's interior thought is wholly in accord with his affection or love;

4. There is direct influx from the Lord, and also mediate influx through the spiritual world (n. 6063, 6307, 6472, 9682, 9683).

The Lord's direct influx is into the least particulars of all things (n. 6058, 6474–6478, 8717, 8728). The Lord flows in into firsts and at the same time into lasts—in what manner (n. 5147, 5150, 6473, 7004, 7007, 7270).

The Lord's influx is into the good in man, and through the good into truth and not the reverse (n. 5482, 5649, 6027, 8685, 8701, 10153). The life that flows in from the Lord varies in accordance with the state of man and in accordance with reception (n. 2069, 5986, 6472, 7343). With the evil the good that flows in from the Lord is turned into evil and the truth into falsity; from experience (n. 3642, 4632). The good and the truth therefrom that continually flow in from the Lord are received just to the extent that evil and falsity therefrom do not obstruct (n. 2411, 3142, 3147, 5828).

but so far as man's affection does not agree with that affection it is not received. Evidently, then, since thought is not introduced into man through spirits, but only an affection for good and an affection for evil, man has choice, because he has freedom; and is thus able by his thought to receive good and reject evil, since he knows from the Word what is good and what is evil. Moreover, whatever he receives by thought from affection is appropriated to him; but whatever he does not receive by thought from affection is not appropriated to him. All this makes evident the nature of the influx of good out of heaven with man, and the nature of the influx of evil out of hell.

299. I have also been permitted to learn the source of human anxiety, grief of mind, and interior sadness, which is called melancholy. There are spirits not as yet in conjunction with hell, because they are in their first state; these will be described hereafter when treating of the world of spirits. Such spirits love things undigested and pernicious, such as pertain to food becoming foul in the stomach; consequently they are present with man in such things because they find delight in them; and they talk there with one another from their own evil affection. The affection that is in their speech flows in from this source into man; and when this affection is the opposite of man's affection there arises in him sadness and melancholy anxiety; but when it agrees with it, it becomes in him gladness and cheerfulness. These spirits appear near to the stomach, some to the left and some to the right of it, and some beneath and some above, also nearer and more remote, thus variously in accordance with their affections. That this is the source of anxiety of mind has been shown and proved to me by much experience. I have seen these spirits, I have heard them, I have felt the anxieties arising from them, and I have talked with them; when they have been driven away the anxiety ceased; when they returned the anxiety returned; and I have noted the increase and decrease of it according to their approach and removal. From this it has been made

clear to me why some who do not know what conscience is, because they have no conscience, ascribe its pangs to the stomach.[5]

300. The conjunction of heaven with man is not like the conjunction of one man with another, but the conjunction is with the interiors of man's mind, that is, with his spiritual or internal man; although there is a conjunction with his natural or external man by means of correspondences, which will be described in the next chapter where the conjunction of heaven with man by means of the Word will be treated of.

301. It will also be shown in the next chapter that the conjunction of heaven with the human race and of the human race with heaven is such that one has its permanent existence with the other.

302. I have talked with angels about the conjunction of heaven with the human race, saying that while the man of the church declares that all good is from God, and that angels are with man, yet few believe that angels are conjoined to man, still less that they are in his thought and affection. The angels replied that they knew that such a belief and such a mode of speaking still exist in the world, and especially, to their surprise, within the church, where the Word is present to teach men about heaven and its conjunction with man; nevertheless, there is such a conjunction that man is unable to think the least thing

5. Those who have no conscience do not know what conscience is (n. 7490, 9121). There are some who laugh at conscience when they hear what it is (n. 7217). Some believe that conscience is nothing; some that it is something natural that is sad and mournful, arising either from causes in the body or from causes in the world; some that it is something that the common people get from their religion (n. 206, 831, 950; [see *True Christian Religion*, n. 665]).

There is true conscience, spurious conscience, and false conscience (n. 1033). Pain of conscience is an anxiety of mind on account of what is unjust, insincere, or in any respect evil, which man believes to be against God and against the good of the neighbor (n. 7217). Those have conscience who are in love to God and in charity toward the neighbor, but those who are not so have no conscience (n. 831, 965, 2380, 7490).

unless spirits are associated with him, and on this his spiritual life depends. They said that the cause of ignorance in this matter is man's belief that he lives from himself, and that he has no connection with the first being *[esse]* of life; together with his not knowing that this connection exists by means of the heavens; and yet if that connection were broken man would instantly fall dead. If man only believed, as is really true, that all good is from the Lord and all evil from hell, he would neither make the good in him a matter of merit nor would evil be imputed to him; for he would then look to the Lord in all the good he thinks and does, and all the evil that flows in would be cast down to hell from which it comes. But because man does not believe that anything flows into him either from heaven or from hell, and therefore supposes that all things that he thinks and wills are in himself and therefore from himself, he appropriates the evil to himself, and the good that flows in he defiles with merit.

34

Conjunction of Heaven with Man
by Means of the Word

303. Those who think from interior reason can see that there is a connection of all things through intermediates with the First, and that whatever is not in connection is dissipated. For they know, when they think about it, that nothing can have permanent existence from itself, but only from what is prior to itself, thus all things from a First; also that the connection with what is prior is like the connection of an effect with its effecting cause; for when the effecting cause is taken away from its effect the effect is dissolved and dispersed. Because the learned thought thus they saw and said that permanent existence is a perpetual springing forth; thus that all things have permanent existence from a First; and as they sprang from that First so they perpetually spring forth, that is, have permanent existence from it. But what the connection of everything is with that which is prior to itself, thus with the First which is the source of all things, cannot be told in a few words, because it is various and diverse. It can only be said in general that there is a connection of the natural world with the spiritual world, and that in consequence there is a correspondence of all things in the natural world with all things in the spiritual (see n. 103–115); also that there is a connection and consequently a correspondence of all things of man with all things of heaven (see n. 87–102).

304. Man is so created as to have a conjunction and connection with the Lord, but with the angels of heaven only an affiliation. Man has affiliation with the angels, but not conjunction, because in respect to the interiors of his mind man is by creation like an angel, having a like will and a like understanding. Consequently if a man has lived in accordance with the Divine order he becomes after death an angel, with the same wisdom as an angel. Therefore when the conjunction of man with heaven is spoken of, his conjunction with the Lord and affiliation with the angels is meant; for heaven is heaven from the Lord's Divine, and not from what is strictly the angels' own [proprium]. That it is the Lord's Divine that makes heaven may be seen above (n. 7–12).

[2] But man has, beyond what the angels have, that he is not only in respect to his interiors in the spiritual world, but also at the same time in respect to his exteriors in the natural world. His exteriors which are in the natural world are all things of his natural or external memory and of his thought and imagination therefrom; in general, knowledges and sciences with their delights and pleasures so far as they savor of the world, also many pleasures belonging to the senses of the body, together with his senses themselves, his speech, and his actions. And all these are the outmosts in which the Lord's Divine influx terminates; for that influx does not stop midway, but goes on to its outmosts. All this shows that the outmost of Divine order is in man; and being the outmost it is also the base and foundation.

[3] As the Lord's Divine influx does not stop midway but goes on to its outmosts, as has been said, and as this middle part through which it passes is the angelic heaven, while the outmost is in man, and as nothing can exist unconnected, it follows that the connection and conjunction of heaven with the human race is such that one has its permanent existence from the other, and that the human race apart from heaven would be like a chain

without a hook; and heaven without the human race would be like a house without a foundation.[1]

305. But man has severed this connection with heaven by turning his exteriors away from heaven, and turning them to the world and to self by means of his love of self and of the world, thereby so withdrawing himself that he no longer serves as a basis and foundation for heaven; therefore the Lord has provided a medium to serve in place of this base and foundation for heaven, and also for the conjunction of heaven with man. This medium is the Word. How the Word serves as such a medium has been shown in many places in *Arcana Coelestia,* all of which may be seen gathered up in the little work *White Horse* (mentioned in Revelation); also in the appendix to the *New Jerusalem and Its Heavenly Doctrine,* from which some notes are here appended.[2]

1. Nothing springs from itself, but from what is prior to itself, thus all things from a First, and they also have permanent existence from Him from whom they spring forth, and permanent existence is a perpetual springing forth (n. 2886, 2888, 3627, 3628, 3648, 4523, 4524, 6040, 6056).

Divine order does not stop midway, but terminates in an outmost, and that outmost is man, thus Divine order terminates in man (n. 634, 2853, 3632, 5897, 6239, 6451, 6465, 9215, 9216, 9824, 9828, 9836, 9905, 10044, 10329, 10335, 10548). Interior things flow into external things, even into the extreme or outmost in successive order, and there they spring forth and have permanent existence (n. 634, 6239, 6465, 9215, 9216). Interior things spring forth and have permanent existence in what is outmost in simultaneous order (n. 5897, 6451, 8603, 10099).

Therefore all interior things are held together in connection from a First by means of a Last (n. 9828). Therefore "the First and the Last" signify all things and each thing, that is, the whole (n. 10044, 10329, 10335). Consequently in outmosts there is strength and power (n. 9836).

2. The Word in the sense of the letter is natural (n. 8783). For the reason that the natural is the outmost in which spiritual and heavenly things, which are interior things, terminate and on which they rest, like a house upon its foundation (n. 9430, 9433, 9824, 10044, 10436). That the Word may be such it is composed wholly of correspondences (n. 1404, 1408, 1409, 1540, 1619, 1659, 1709, 1783, 8615, 10687). Because the Word is such in the sense of the letter it is the containant of the spiritual and heavenly sense (n. 9407). And it is adapted both to men and to angels (n. 1769-1772, 1887, 2143, 2157, 2275, 2333, 2395, 2540, 2541, 2547, 2553, 7381, 8862, 10322).

306. I have been told from heaven that the most ancient people, because their interiors were turned heavenwards, had direct revelation, and by this means there was at that time a conjunction of the Lord with the human race. After their times, however, there was no such direct revelation, but there was a mediate revelation by means of correspondences, inasmuch as all their Divine worship then consisted of correspondences, and for this reason the churches of that time were called representative churches. For it was then known what correspondence is and what representation is, and that all things on the earth correspond to spiritual things in heaven and in the church, or what is the same, represent them; and therefore the natural things that constituted the externals of their worship served them as mediums for thinking spiritually, that is, thinking with the angels. When the knowledge of correspondences and representations had been blotted out of remembrance a Word was written, in which all the words and their meanings are correspondences, and thus contain a spiritual or internal sense, in which are the angels; and in consequence, when a man reads the Word and perceives it according to the sense of the letter or the outer sense, the angels perceive it according to the internal or spiritual sense; for all the thought of angels is spiritual while the

---

And it is what makes heaven and earth one (n. 2310, 2495, 9212, 9216, 9357, 9396, 10375). The conjunction of the Lord with man is through the Word, by means of the internal sense (n. 10375). There is conjunction by means of all things and each particular thing of the Word, and in consequence the Word is wonderful above all other writing (n. 10632–10634). Since the Word was written the Lord speaks with men by means of it (n. 10290). The church, where the Word is and the Lord is known by means of it, in relation to those who are out of the church where there is no Word and the Lord is unknown, is like the heart and lungs in man in comparison with the other parts of the body, which live from them as from the fountains of their life (n. 637, 931, 2054, 2853). Before the Lord the universal church on the earth is as a single man (n. 7396, 9276). Consequently unless there were on this earth a church where the Word is, and where the Lord is known by means of it, the human race here would perish (n. 468, 637, 931, 4545, 10452).

thought of man is natural. These two kinds of thought appear diverse; nevertheless they are one because they correspond. Thus it was that when man had separated himself from heaven and had severed the bond, the Lord provided a medium of conjunction of heaven with man by means of the Word.

307. How heaven is conjoined with man by means of the Word I will illustrate by some passages from it. "The New Jerusalem" is described in Revelation in these words:

I saw a new heaven and a new earth, and the first heaven and the first earth had passed away. And I saw the holy city New Jerusalem coming down from God out of heaven. The city was foursquare, its length as great as its breadth; and an angel measured the city with a reed, twelve thousand furlongs; the length, the breadth, and the height of it are equal. And he measured the wall thereof, an hundred and forty-four cubits, the measure of a man, that is, of an angel. The building of the wall was of jasper; but the city itself was pure gold, and like unto pure glass; and the foundations of the wall were adorned with every precious stone. The twelve gates were twelve pearls; and the street of the city was pure gold, as it were transparent glass (Rev. 21:1, 2, 16–19, 21).

When man reads these words he understands them merely in accordance with the sense of the letter, namely, that the visible heaven with the earth is to perish, and a new heaven is to come into existence; and upon the new earth the holy city Jerusalem is to descend, with all its dimensions as here described. But the angels that are with man understand these things in a wholly different way, that is, everything that man understands naturally they understand spiritually.

[2] By "the new heaven and the new earth" they understand a new church; by "the city Jerusalem coming down from God out of heaven" they understand its heavenly doctrine revealed by the Lord; by "its length, breadth, and height, which are equal," and "twelve thousand furlongs," they understand all the goods and truths of that doctrine in the complex; by its "wall" they understand the truths protecting it; by "the measure of the wall, a hundred and forty-four cubits, which is the measure of

a man, that is, of an angel," they understand all those protecting truths in the complex and their character; by its "twelve gates, which were of pearls," they understand introductory truths, "pearls" signifying such truths; by "the foundations of the wall, which were of precious stones," they understand the knowledge on which that doctrine is founded; by "the gold like unto pure glass," of which the city and its street were made, they understand the good of love which makes the doctrine and its truths transparent. Thus do the angels perceive all these things; and therefore not as man perceives them. The natural ideas of man thus pass into the spiritual ideas with the angels without their knowing anything of the sense of the letter of the Word, that is, about "a new heaven and a new earth," "a new city Jerusalem," its "wall, the foundations of the wall, and its dimensions." And yet the thoughts of angels make one with the thoughts of man, because they correspond; they make one almost the same as the words of a speaker make one with the understanding of them by a hearer who attends solely to the meaning and not to the words. All this shows how heaven is conjoined with man by means of the Word.

[3] Let us take another example from the Word:

In that day there shall be a highway from Egypt to Assyria, and Assyria shall come into Egypt and Egypt into Assyria; and the Egyptians shall serve Assyria. In that day shall Israel be a third to Egypt and to Assyria, a blessing in the midst of the land, which Jehovah of hosts shall bless, saying, Blessed be my people the Egyptian, and the Assyrian the work of my hands, and Israel mine inheritance (Isa. 19:23–25).

What man thinks when these words are read, and what the angels think, can be seen from the sense of the letter of the Word and from its internal sense. Man from the sense of the letter thinks that the Egyptians and Assyrians are to be converted to God and accepted, and are then to become one with the Israelitish nation; but angels in accordance with the internal sense think of the man of the spiritual church who is here described in that sense, whose spiritual is "Israel," whose natural is the "Egyptian," and whose rational, which is the middle, is the "Assyrian."[3] Nevertheless, these two senses are one because they correspond; and therefore when the angels thus think spiritually and man naturally they are conjoined almost as body and soul are; in fact, the internal sense of the Word is its soul and the sense of the letter is its body. Such is the Word throughout. This shows that it is a medium of conjunction of heaven with man, and that its literal sense serves as a base and foundation.

308. There is also a conjunction of heaven by means of the Word with those who are outside of the church where there is no Word; for the Lord's church is universal, and is with all who acknowledge the Divine and live in charity. Moreover, such are taught after death by the angels and receive Divine truths;[4] on which subject more may be seen below, in the chapter on the heathen. The universal church on the earth in the sight of the Lord resembles a single man, just as heaven does (see n. 59–72); but the church where the Word is and where the Lord is known by means of it is like the heart and lungs in that man. It is known that all the viscera and members of the entire body draw their life from the heart and lungs through various derivations; and it is thus that those of the human race live who are outside of the church where the Word is, and who constitute

3. In the Word "Egypt" and "Egyptian" signify the natural and its knowledge (n. 4967, 5079, 5080, 5095, 5160, 5460, 5799, 6015, 6147, 6252, 7355, 7648, 9340, 9391).

"Assyria" signifies the rational (n. 119, 1186). "Israel" signifies the spiritual (n. 5414, 5801, 5803, 5806, 5812, 5817, 5819, 5826, 5833, 5879, 5951, 6426, 6637, 6862, 6868, 7035 7062, 7198, 7201, 7215, 7223, 7957, 8234, 8805, 9340).

4. The church specifically is where the Word is and where the Lord is known by means of it, thus where Divine truths from heaven are revealed (n. 3857, 10761).

The Lord's church is with all in the whole globe who live in good in accordance with the principles of their religion (n. 3263, 6637, 10765).

All wherever they are who live in good in accordance with the principles of their religion and who acknowledge the Divine are accepted of the Lord (n. 2589–2604, 2861, 2863, 3263, 4190, 4197, 6700, 9256).

And besides these all children wheresoever they are born (n. 2289–2309, 4792).

the members of that man. Again, the conjunction of heaven
with those who are at a distance by means of the Word may be
compared to light radiating from a center all around. The Divine light is in the Word, and there the Lord with heaven is
present, and from that presence those at a distance are in light;
but it would be otherwise if there were no Word. This may be
more clearly seen from what has been shown above respecting
the form of heaven in accordance with which all who are in
heaven have affiliation and communication. But while this arcanum may be comprehended by those who are in spiritual
light, it cannot be comprehended by those who are only in
natural light; for innumerable things are clearly seen by those
who are in spiritual light that are not seen or are seen obscurely
as a single thing by those who are only in natural light.

309. Unless such a Word had been given on this earth the
man of this earth would have been separated from heaven; and
if separated from heaven he would have ceased to be rational,
for the human rational exists by an influx of the light of
heaven. Again, the man of this earth is such that he is not
capable of receiving direct revelation and of being taught about
Divine truths by such revelation, as the inhabitants of other
earths are, that have been especially described in another small
work. For the man of this earth is more in worldly things, that
is, in externals, than the men of other earths, and it is internal
things that are receptive of revelation; if it were received in
external things the truth would not be understood. That such
is the man of this earth is clearly evident from the state of those
who are within the church, which is such that while they know
from the Word about heaven, about hell, about the life after
death, still in heart they deny these things; although among
them there are some who have acquired a preeminent reputation
for learning, and who might for that reason be supposed to be
wiser than others.

310. I have at times talked with angels about the Word, saying that it is despised by some on account of its simple style; and that nothing whatever is known about its internal sense, and for this reason it is not believed that so much wisdom lies hid in it. The angels said that although the style of the Word seems simple in the sense of the letter, it is such that nothing can ever be compared to it in excellence, since Divine wisdom lies concealed not only in the meaning as a whole but also in each word; and that in heaven this wisdom shines forth. They wished to declare that this wisdom is the light of heaven, because it is Divine truth, for that which shines in heaven is the Divine truth (see n. 132). Again, they said that without such a Word there would be no light of heaven with the men of our earth, nor would there be any conjunction of heaven with them; for there is conjunction only so far as the light of heaven is present with man, and that light is present only so far as Divine truth is revealed to man by means of the Word. This conjunction by means of the correspondence of the spiritual sense of the Word with its natural sense is unknown to man, because the man of this earth knows nothing about the spiritual thought and speech of angels, and how it differs from the natural thought and speech of men; and until this is known it cannot in the least be known what the internal sense is, and that such conjunction is therefore possible by means of that sense. They said, furthermore, that if this sense were known to man, and if man in reading the Word were to think in accordance with some knowledge of it, he would come into interior wisdom, and would be still more conjoined with heaven, since by this means he would enter into ideas like the ideas of the angels.

35

Heaven and Hell Are
from the Human Race

311. In the Christian world it is wholly unknown that heaven and hell are from the human race, for it is believed that in the beginning angels were created and heaven was thus formed; also that the devil or satan was an angel of light, but having rebelled he was cast down with his crew, and thus hell was formed. The angels never cease to wonder at such a belief in the Christian world, and still more that nothing is really known about heaven, when in fact that is the primary principle of all doctrine in the church. But since such ignorance prevails they rejoice in heart that it has pleased the Lord to reveal to mankind at this time many things about heaven and about hell, thereby dispelling as far as possible the darkness that has been daily increasing because the church has come to its end.

[2] They wish for this reason that I should declare from their lips that in the entire heaven there is not a single angel who was created such from the beginning, nor in hell any devil who was created an angel of light and cast down; but that all, both in heaven and in hell, are from the human race; in heaven those who lived in the world in heavenly love and belief, in hell those who lived in infernal love and belief, also that it is hell taken as a whole that is called the devil and satan—the name devil being given to the hell that is behind, where those are that are called evil genii, and the name satan being given to the hell that is in front, where those are that

are called evil spirits.[1] The character of these hells will be described in the following pages.

[3] The angels said that the Christian world had gathered such a belief about those in heaven and those in hell from some passages in the Word understood according to the mere sense of the letter not illustrated and explained by genuine doctrine from the Word; yet the sense of the letter of the Word until illuminated by genuine doctrine, draws the mind in different directions, and this begets ignorance, heresies, and errors.[2]

312. The man of the church also derives this belief from his believing that no man comes into heaven or into hell until the time of the final judgment; and about that he has accepted the opinion that all visible things will perish at that time and new things will come into existence, and that the soul will then return into its body, and from that union man will again live as a man. This belief involves the other—that angels were created such from the beginning; for it is impossible to believe that heaven and hell are from the human race when it is believed that no man can go there until the end of the world.

[2] But that men might be convinced that this is not true it has been granted me to be in company with angels, and also to talk with those who are in hell, and this now for some years, sometimes continuously from morning until evening, and thus

---

1. The hells taken together, or the infernals taken together, are called the devil and satan (n. 694).

Those that have been devils in the world become devils after death (n. 968).

2. The doctrine of the church must be derived from the Word (n. 3464, 5402, 6822, 6832, 10763, 10765). Without doctrine the Word is not understood (n. 9025, 9409, 9424, 9430, 10324, 10431, 10582). True doctrine is a lamp to those who read the Word (n. 10400). Genuine doctrine must be from those who are enlightened by the Lord (n. 2510, 2516, 2519, 9424, 10105). Those who are in the sense of the letter without doctrine come into no understanding of Divine truths (n. 9409, 9410, 10582).

And they are led away into many errors (n. 10431). The difference between those who teach and learn from the doctrine of the church derived from the Word and those who teach and learn from the sense of the letter alone (n. 9025).

to be informed about heaven and hell. This has been permitted that the man of the church may no longer continue in his erroneous belief about the resurrection at the time of judgment, and about the state of the soul in the meanwhile, also about angels and the devil. As this belief is a belief in what is false it involves the mind in darkness, and with those who think about these things from their own intelligence it induces doubt and at length denial, for they say in heart, "How can so vast a heaven, with so many constellations and with the sun and moon, be destroyed and dissipated; and how can the stars which are larger than the earth fall from heaven to the earth; and can bodies eaten up by worms, consumed by corruption, and scattered to all the winds, be gathered together again to their souls; and where in the meantime is the soul, and what is it when deprived of the senses it had in the body?"

[3] And they say many other like things, which being incomprehensible cannot be believed, and which destroy the belief of many in the life of the soul after death, and their belief in heaven and hell, and with these other matters pertaining to the faith of the church. That this belief has been destroyed is evident from its being said, "Who has ever come to us from heaven and told us that there is a heaven? What is hell? Is there any? What is this about man's being tormented with fire to eternity? What is the day of judgment? Has it not been expected in vain for ages?" with other things that involve a denial of everything.

[4] Therefore lest those who think in this way—as many do who from their worldly wisdom are regarded as erudite and learned— should any longer confound and mislead the simple in faith and heart, and induce infernal darkness respecting God and heaven and eternal life, and all else that depends on these, the interiors of my spirit have been opened by the Lord, and I have thus been permitted to talk with all after their decease with whom I was ever acquainted in the life of the body—with some for days, with some for months, and with some for a year, and

also with so many others that I should not exaggerate if I should say a hundred thousand; many of whom were in heaven, and many in hell. I have also talked with some two days after their decease, and have told them that their funeral services and obsequies were then being held in preparation for their interment; to which they replied that it was well to cast aside that which had served them as a body and for bodily functions in the world; and they wished me to say that they were not dead, but were living as men the same as before, and had merely migrated from one world into the other, and were not aware of having lost anything, since they had a body and its senses just as before, also understanding and will just as before, with thoughts and affections, sensations and desires, like those they had in the world.

[5] Most of those who had recently died, when they saw themselves to be living men as before, and in a like state (for after death everyone's state of life is at first such as it was in the world, but there is a gradual change in it either into heaven or into hell), were moved by new joy at being alive, saying that they had not believed that it would be so. But they greatly wondered that they should have lived in such ignorance and blindness about the state of their life after death; and especially that the man of the church should be in such ignorance and blindness, when above all others in the whole world he might be clearly enlightened in regard to these things.[3] Then they

3. There are few in Christendom at this day who believe that man rises again immediately after death (preface to Genesis chap. 16 and n. 4622, 10758); but it is believed that he will rise again at the time of the final judgment, when the visible world will perish (n. 10595). The reason of this belief (n. 10595, 10758). Nevertheless man does rise again immediately after death, and then he is a man in all respects, and in every least respect (n. 4527, 5006, 5078, 8939, 8991, 10594, 10758). The soul that lives after death is the spirit of man, which in man is the man himself, and in the other life is in a complete human form (n. 322, 1880, 1881, 3633, 4622, 4735, 5883, 6054, 6605, 6626, 7021, 10594); from experience (n. 4527, 5006, 8939); from the Word (n. 10597). What is meant by the dead seen in the holy city (Matt. 27:53) explained (n. 9229). In what manner man is raised from the dead, from experience (n. 168–189). His state after his resurrection (n. 317–319, 2119, 5079, 10596). False opinions about the soul and its resurrection (n. 444, 445, 4527, 4622, 4658).

began to see the cause of that blindness and ignorance, which is, that external things, which are things relating to the world and the body, had so occupied and filled their minds that they could not be raised into the light of heaven and look into the things of the church beyond its doctrinals; for when matters relating to the body and the world are loved, as they are at the present day, nothing but darkness flows into the mind when men go beyond those doctrines.

313. Very many of the learned from the Christian world are astonished when they find themselves after death in a body, in garments, and in houses, as in the world. And when they recall what they had thought about the life after death, the soul, spirits, and heaven and hell, they are ashamed and confess that they thought foolishly, and that the simple in faith thought much more wisely than they. When the minds of learned men who had confirmed themselves in such ideas and had ascribed all things to nature were examined, it was found that their interiors were wholly closed up and their exteriors were opened, that they looked toward the world and thus toward hell and not toward heaven. For to the extent that man's interiors are opened he looks toward heaven, but to the extent that his interiors are closed and his exteriors opened he looks toward hell, because the interiors of man are formed for the reception of all things of heaven, but the exteriors for the reception of all things of the world; and those who receive the world, and not heaven also, receive hell.[4]

314. That heaven is from the human race can be seen also from the fact that angelic minds and human minds are alike, both enjoying the ability to understand, perceive and will, and both formed to receive heaven; for the human mind is just as capable

---

4. In man the spiritual world and the natural world are conjoined (n. 6057).

The internal of man is formed after the image of heaven, but the external after the image of the world (n. 3628, 4523, 4524, 6013, 6057, 9706, 10156, 10472).

of becoming wise as the angelic mind; and if it does not attain to such wisdom in the world it is because it is in an earthly body, and in that body its spiritual mind thinks naturally. But it is otherwise when the mind is loosed from the bonds of that body; then it no longer thinks naturally, but spiritually, and when it thinks spiritually its thoughts are incomprehensible and ineffable to the natural man; thus it becomes wise like an angel, all of which shows that the internal part of man, called his spirit, is in its essence an angel (see above, n. 57);[5] and when loosed from the earthly body is, equally with the angel, in the human form. (That an angel is in a complete human form may be seen above, n. 73–77.) When, however, the internal of man is not open above but only beneath, it is still, after it has been loosed from the body, in a human form, but a horrible and diabolical form, for it is able only to look downwards toward hell, and not upwards toward heaven.

315. Moreover, anyone who has been taught about Divine order can understand that man was created to become an angel, because the outmost of order is in him (n. 304), in which what pertains to heavenly and angelic wisdom can be brought into form and can be renewed and multiplied. Divine order never stops midway to form there a something apart from an outmost, for it is not in its fullness and completion there; but it goes on to the outmost; and when it is in its outmost it takes on its form, and by means there collected it renews itself and produces itself further, which is accomplished through procreations. Therefore the seed-ground of heaven is in the outmost.

---

5. There are as many degrees of life in man as there are heavens, and they are opened after death in accordance with his life (n. 3747, 9594).

Heaven is in man (n. 3884).

Men who are living a life of love and charity have in them angelic wisdom, although it is for the time hidden, but they come into that wisdom after death (n. 2494).

The man who receives from the Lord the good of love and of faith is called in the Word an angel (n. 10528).

316. The Lord rose again not as to his spirit alone but also as to his body, because when he was in the world he glorified his whole human, that is, made it Divine; for his soul which he had from the Father was of itself the very Divine, while his body became a likeness of the soul, that is, of the Father, thus also Divine. This is why he, differently from any man, rose again as to both;[6] and this he made manifest to the disciples (who when they saw him believed that they saw a spirit), by saying:

> See my hands and my feet, that it is I myself; handle Me and see, for a spirit hath not flesh and bones as ye behold Me having (Luke 24:36–39).

He indicated thereby that he was a man both in respect to his spirit and in respect to his body.

317. That it might be made clear that man lives after death and enters in accordance with his life in the world either into heaven or into hell, many things have been disclosed to me about the state of man after death, which will be presented in due order in the following pages, where the world of spirits is treated of.

---

6. Man rises again only as to his spirit (n. 10593, 10594). The Lord alone rose again in respect also to His body (n. 1729, 2083, 5078, 10825).

36

The Heathen, or Peoples outside
of the Church, in Heaven

318. There is a general opinion that those born outside of the church, who are called the nations, or heathen, cannot be saved, because not having the Word they know nothing about the Lord, and apart from the Lord there is no salvation. But that these also are saved this alone makes certain, that the mercy of the Lord is universal, that is, extends to every individual; that these equally with those within the church, who are few in comparison, are born men, and that their ignorance of the Lord is not their fault. Anyone who thinks from any enlightened reason can see that no man is born for hell, for the Lord is love itself and his love is to will the salvation of all. Therefore he has provided a religion for everyone, and by it acknowledgment of the Divine and interior life; for to live in accordance with one's religion is to live interiorly, since one then looks to the Divine, and so far as he looks to the Divine he does not look to the world but separates himself from the world, that is, from the life of the world, which is exterior life.[1]

---

1. The heathen equally with the Christians are saved (n. 932, 1032, 1059, 2284, 2589, 2590, 3778, 4190, 4197). The lot of the nations and peoples outside of the church in the other life (n. 2589–2604). The church is specifically where the Word is, and by it the Lord is known (n. 3857, 10761). Nevertheless, those born where the Word is and where the Lord is known are not on that account of the church, but only those who live a life of charity and of faith (n. 6637, 10143, 10153, 10578, 10645, 10829).

The Lord's church is with all in the whole world who live in good in accordance with their religion and acknowledge a Divine, and such are accepted of the Lord and come into heaven (n. 2589–2604, 2861, 2863, 3263, 4190, 4197, 6700, 9256).

319. That the heathen equally with Christians are saved any-one can see who knows what it is that makes heaven in man; for heaven is within man, and those that have heaven within them come into heaven. Heaven with man is acknowledging the Divine and being led by the Divine. The first and chief thing of every religion is to acknowledge the Divine. A religion that does not acknowledge the Divine is no religion. The precepts of every religion look to worship; thus to the way in which the Divine is to be worshiped that the worship may be acceptable to him; and when this has been settled in one's mind, that is, so far as one wills this or so far as he loves it, he is led by the Lord. Everyone knows that the heathen as well as Christians live a moral life, and many of them a better life than Christians. Moral life may be lived either out of regard to the Divine or out of regard to men in the world; and a moral life that is lived out of regard to the Divine is a spiritual life. In outward form the two appear alike, but in inward form they are wholly differ-ent; the one saves man, the other does not. For he who lives a moral life out of regard to the Divine is led by the Divine; while he who leads a moral life out of regard to men in the world is led by himself.

[2] But this may be illustrated by an example. He that refrains from doing evil to his neighbor because it is antagonistic to religion, that is, antagonistic to the Divine, refrains from doing evil from a spiritual motive; but he that refrains from doing evil to another merely from fear of the law, or the loss of reputa-tion, of honor, or gain, that is, from regard to self and the world, refrains from doing evil from a natural motive, and is led by himself. The life of the latter is natural, that of the former is spiritual. A man whose moral life is spiritual has heaven within him; but he whose moral life is merely natural does not have heaven within him; and for the reason that heaven flows in from above and opens man's interiors, and through his interi-ors flows into his exteriors; while the world flows in from

beneath and opens the exteriors but not the interiors. For there can be no flowing in from the natural world into the spiritual, but only from the spiritual world into the natural; therefore if heaven is not also received, the interiors remain closed. All this makes clear who those are that receive heaven within them, and who do not.

[3] And yet heaven is not the same in one as in another. It differs in each one in accordance with his affection for good and its truth. Those that are in an affection for good out of regard to the Divine, love Divine truth, since good and truth love each other and desire to be conjoined.[2] This explains why the heathen, although they are not in genuine truths in the world, yet because of their love receive truths in the other life.

320. A certain spirit from among the heathen who had lived in the world in good of charity in accordance with his religion, hearing Christian spirits reasoning about what must be believed (for spirits reason with each other far more thoroughly and acutely than men, especially about what is good and true), wondered at such contentions, and said that he did not care to listen to them, for they reasoned from appearances and fallacies; and he gave them this instruction: "If I am good I can know from the good itself what is true; and what I do not know I can receive."

321. I have been taught in many ways that the heathen who have led a moral life and have lived in obedience and subordination and mutual charity in accordance with their religion, and have thus received something of conscience, are accepted in the other life, and are there instructed with solicitous care by the

2. Between good and truth there is a kind of marriage (n. 1904, 2173, 2508).

Good and truth are in a perpetual endeavor to be conjoined, and good longs for truth and for conjunction with it (n. 9206, 9207, 9495).

How the conjunction of good and truth takes place, and in whom (n. 3834, 3843, 4096, 4097, 4301, 4345, 4353, 4364, 4368, 5365, 7623–7627, 9258).

angels in the goods and truths of faith; and that when they are
being taught they behave themselves modestly, intelligently, and
wisely, and readily accept truths and adopt them. They have not
worked out for themselves any principles of falsity antagonistic
to the truths of faith that will need to be shaken off, still less
cavils against the Lord, as many Christians have who cherish no
other idea of him than that he is an ordinary man. The heathen
on the contrary when they hear that God has become a Man,
and has thus manifested himself in the world, immediately
acknowledge it and worship the Lord, saying that because God
is the God of heaven and of earth, and because the human race
is his, he has fully disclosed himself to men.[3] It is a Divine truth
that apart from the Lord there is no salvation; but this is to be
understood to mean that there is no salvation except from the
Lord. There are many earths in the universe, and all of them
full of inhabitants, scarcely any of whom know that the Lord
took on the human on our earth. Yet because they worship the
Divine under a human form they are accepted and led by the
Lord. On this subject more may be seen in the little work
Earths in the Universe.

322. Among the heathen, as among Christians, there are both
wise and simple. That I might learn about them I have been

3. Difference between the good in which the heathen are and that in which
Christians are (n. 4189, 4197).

Truths with the heathen (n. 3263, 3778, 4190).

The interiors cannot be so closed up with the heathen as with Christians (n. 9256).
Neither can so thick a cloud exist with the heathen who live in mutual charity in
accordance with their religion as with Christians who live in no charity; the reasons
(n. 1059, 9256).

The heathen cannot profane the holy things of the church as the Christians do,
because they are ignorant of them (n. 1327, 1328, 2051).

They have a fear of Christians on account of their lives (n. 2596, 2597).

Those that have lived well in accordance with their religion are taught by angels and
readily accept the truths of faith and acknowledge the Lord (n. 2049, 2595, 2598, 2600,
2601, 2603, 2861, 2863, 3263).

permitted to speak with both, sometimes for hours and days. But there are no such wise men now as in ancient times, especially in the ancient church, which extended over a large part of the Asiatic world, and from which religion spread to many nations. That I might wholly know about them I have been permitted to have familiar conversation with some of these wise men. There was with me one who was among the wiser of his time, and consequently well known in the learned world, with whom I talked on various subjects, and had reason to believe that it was Cicero. Knowing that he was a wise man I talked with him about wisdom, intelligence, order, and the Word, and lastly about the Lord.

[2] Of wisdom he said that there is no other wisdom than the wisdom of life, and that wisdom can be predicated of nothing else; of intelligence that it is from wisdom; of order, that it is from the Supreme God, and that to live in that order is to be wise and intelligent. As to the Word, when I read to him something from the prophets he was greatly delighted, especially with this, that every name and every word signified interior things; and he wondered greatly that learned men at this day are not delighted with such study. I saw plainly that the interiors of his thought or mind had been opened. He said that he was unable to hear more, as he perceived something more holy than he could bear, being affected so interiorly.

[3] At length I spoke with him about the Lord, saying that while he was born a man he was conceived of God, and that he put off the maternal human and put on the Divine human, and that it is he that governs the universe. To this he replied that he knew some things concerning the Lord, and perceived in his way that if mankind were to be saved it could not have been done otherwise. In the meantime some bad Christians infused various cavils; but to these he gave no attention, remarking that this was not strange, since in the life of the body they had

imbibed unbecoming ideas on the subject, and until they got rid of these they could not admit ideas that confirmed the truth, as the ignorant can.

323. It has also been granted me to talk with others who lived in ancient times, and who were then among the more wise. At first they appeared in front at a distance, and were able then to perceive the interiors of my thoughts, thus many things fully. From one idea of thought they were able to discern the entire series and fill it with delightful things of wisdom combined with charming representations. From this they were perceived to be among the more wise, and I was told that they were some of the ancient people; and when they came nearer I read to them something from the Word, and they were delighted beyond measure. I perceived the essence of their delight and gratification, which arose chiefly from this, that all things and each thing they heard from the Word were representative and significative of heavenly and spiritual things. They said that in their time, when they lived in the world, their mode of thinking and speaking and also of writing was of this nature, and that this was their pursuit of wisdom.

324. But as regards the heathen of the present day, they are not so wise, but most of them are simple in heart. Nevertheless, those of them that have lived in mutual charity receive wisdom in the other life, and of these one or two examples may be cited. When I read the seventeenth and eighteenth chapters of Judges (about Micah, and how the sons of Dan carried away his graven image and teraphim and Levite), a heathen spirit was present who in the life of the body had worshiped a graven image. He listened attentively to the account of what was done to Micah, and his grief on account of his graven image which the Danites took away, and such grief came upon him and moved him that he scarcely knew, by reason of inward distress, what to think. Not only was this grief perceived, but also the innocence that was in all his affections. The Christian spirits

that were present watched him and wondered that a worshiper
of a graven image should have so great a feeling of sympathy
and innocence stirred in him. Afterwards some good spirits
talked with him, saying that graven images should not be worshiped, and that being a man he was capable of understanding
this; that he ought, apart from a graven image, to think of God
the Creator and Ruler of the whole heaven and the whole earth,
and that God is the Lord. When this was said I was permitted
to perceive the interior nature of his adoration, which was
communicated to me; and it was much more holy than is the
case of Christians. This makes clear that at the present day the
heathen come into heaven with less difficulty than Christians,
according to the Lord's words in Luke:

> Then shall they come from the east and the west, and from the north
> and the south, and shall recline in the kingdom of God. And behold,
> there are last who shall be first, and there are first who shall be last (Luke
> 13:29, 30).

For in the state in which that spirit was he could be imbued
with all things of faith and receive them with interior affection;
there was in him the mercy of love, and in his ignorance there
was innocence; and when these are present all things of faith are
received as it were spontaneously and with joy. He was afterwards received among angels.

325. A choir at a distance was heard one morning, and from
the choir's representations I was permitted to know that they
were Chinese, for they exhibited a kind of woolly goat, then a
cake of millet, and an ivory spoon, also the idea of a floating
city. They desired to come nearer to me, and when they had
joined me they said that they wished to be alone with me, that
they might disclose their thoughts. But they were told that they
were not alone, and that some were displeased at their wishing
to be alone, although they were guests. When they perceived
this displeasure they began to think whether they had trans-
gressed against the neighbor, and whether they had claimed

anything to themselves that belonged to others. All thought in the other life being communicated, I was permitted to perceive the agitation of their minds. It consisted of a recognition that possibly they had injured those who were displeased, of shame on that account, together with other worthy affections; and it was thus known that they were endowed with charity. Soon after I spoke with them, and at last about the Lord. When I called him "Christ" I perceived a certain repugnance in them; but the reason was disclosed, namely, that they had brought this from the world, from their having learned that Christians lived worse lives than they did, and were destitute of charity. But when I called him simply "Lord" they were interiorly moved. Afterwards, they were taught by the angels that the Christian doctrine beyond every other in the world prescribes love and charity, but that there are few who live in accordance with it. There are heathen who have come to know while they lived in the world, both from conversation and report, that Christians lead bad lives, are addicted to adultery, hatred, quarreling, drunkenness, and the like, which they themselves abhor because such things are contrary to their religion. These in the other life are more timid than others about accepting the truths of faith; but they are taught by the angels that the Christian doctrine, as well as the faith itself, teaches a very different life, but that the lives of Christians are less in accord with their doctrine than the lives of heathen. When they recognize this they receive the truths of faith, and adore the Lord, but less readily than others.

326. It is a common thing for heathen that have worshiped any god under an image or statue, or any graven thing, to be introduced, when they come into the other life, to certain spirits in place of their gods or idols, in order that they may rid themselves of their fantasies. When they have been with these for some days, the fantasies are put away. Also those that have worshiped men are sometimes introduced to the men they have worshiped, or to others in their place—as many of the Jews to

Abraham, Jacob, Moses, and David—but when they come to see that they are human the same as others, and that they can give them no help, they become ashamed, and are carried to their own places in accordance with their lives. Among the heathen in heaven the Africans are most beloved, for they receive the goods and truths of heaven more readily than others. They especially wish to be called obedient, but not faithful. They say that as Christians possess the doctrine of faith they may be called faithful; but not they unless they accept that doctrine, or as they say, have the ability to accept it.

327. I have talked with some who were in the ancient church. That is called the ancient church that was established after the deluge, and extended through many kingdoms, namely, Assyria, Mesopotamia, Syria, Ethiopia, Arabia, Libya, Egypt, Philistia as far as Tyre and Sidon, and through the land of Canaan on both sides of the Jordan.[4] The men of this church knew about the Lord that he was to come, and were imbued with the goods of faith, and yet they fell away and became idolaters. These spirits were in front toward the left, in a dark place and in a miserable state. Their speech was like the sound of a pipe of one tone,

---

4. The first and most ancient church on this earth was that which is described in the first chapters of Genesis, and that church above all others was celestial (n. 607, 895, 920, 1121–1124, 2896, 4493, 8891, 9942, 10545).

What the celestial are in heaven (n. 1114–1125).

There were various churches after the flood which are called ancient churches (n. 1125–1127, 1327, 10355).

What the men of the ancient church were (n. 609, 895).

The ancient churches were representative churches (n. 519, 521, 2896).

In the ancient church there was a Word, but it has been lost (n. 2897).

The character of the ancient church when it began to decline (n. 1128).

The difference between the most ancient church and the ancient church (n. 597, 607, 640, 641, 765, 784, 895, 4493).

The statutes, the judgments, and the laws, which were commanded in the Jewish church, were in part like those in the ancient church (n. 4288, 4449, 10149).

The God of the most ancient church and of the ancient church was the Lord, and He was called Jehovah (n. 1343, 6846).

almost without rational thought. They said they had been there for many centuries, and that they are sometimes taken out that they may serve others for certain uses of a low order. From this I was led to think about many Christians—who are inwardly though not outwardly idolaters, since they are worshipers of self and of the world, and in heart deny the Lord—what lot awaits such in the other life.

328. That the church of the Lord is spread over all the globe, and is thus universal; and that all those are in it who have lived in the good of charity in accordance with their religion; and that the church, where the Word is and by means of it the Lord is known, is in relation to those who are out of the church like the heart and lungs in man, from which all the viscera and members of the body have their life, variously according to their forms, positions, and conjunctions, may be seen above (n. 308).

37

Little Children in Heaven

329. It is a belief of some that only such children as are born within the church go to heaven, and that those born out of the church do not, and for the reason that the children within the church are baptized and by baptism are initiated into faith of the church. Such are not aware that no one receives heaven or faith through baptism; for baptism is merely for a sign and memorial that man should be regenerated, and that those born within the church can be regenerated because the Word is there, and in the Word are the Divine truths by means of which regeneration is effected, and there the Lord who regenerates is known.[1] Let them know therefore that every child, wherever he is born, whether within the church or outside of it, whether of pious parents or impious, is received when he dies by the Lord and trained up in heaven, and taught in accordance with Divine order, and imbued with affections for what is good, and through these with knowledges of what is true; and afterwards as he is perfected in intelligence and wisdom is introduced into heaven and becomes an angel. Everyone who thinks from reason can be sure that all are born for heaven and no one for hell, and if man comes into hell he himself is culpable; but little children cannot be held culpable.

---

1. Baptism signifies regeneration by the Lord by means of the truths of faith from the Word (n. 4255, 5120, 9088, 10239, 10386–10388, 10392).

Baptism is a sign that the man baptized is of the church in which the Lord, who regenerates, is acknowledged, and where the Word is from which are the truths of faith, by means of which regeneration is effected (n. 10386–10388).

Baptism confers neither faith nor salvation, but it is a witness that those who are being regenerated will receive faith and salvation (n. 10391).

330. When children die they are still children in the other life, having a like infantile mind, a like innocence in ignorance, and a like tenderness in all things. They are merely in the rudiments of a capacity to become angels, for children are not angels but become angels. For everyone passing out of this world enters the other in the same state of life, a little child in the state of a little child, a boy in the state of a boy, a youth, a man, an old man, in the state of a youth, a man, or an old man; but subsequently each one's state is changed. The state of little children surpasses the state of all others in that they are in innocence, and evil has not yet been rooted in them by actual life; and in innocence all things of heaven can be implanted, for it is a receptacle of the truth of faith and of the good of love.

331. The state of children in the other life far surpasses their state in the world, for they are not clothed with an earthly body, but with such a body as the angels have. The earthly body is in itself gross, and receives its first sensations and first motions not from the inner or spiritual world, but from the outer or natural world; and in consequence in this world children must be taught to walk, to guide their motions, and to speak; and even their senses, as seeing and hearing, must be opened by use. It is not so with children in the other life. As they are spirits they act at once in accordance with their interiors, walking without practice, and also talking, but at first from general affections not yet distinguished into ideas of thought; but they are quickly initiated into these also, for the reason that their exteriors are homogeneous with their interiors. The speech of angels (as may be seen above, n. 234–245) so flows forth from affection modified by ideas of thought that their speech completely conforms to their thoughts from affection.

332. As soon as little children are resuscitated, which takes place immediately after death, they are taken into heaven and confided to angel women who in the life of the body tenderly loved little children and at the same time loved God. Because these during their life in the world loved all children with a kind of motherly tenderness, they receive them as their own; while the children, from an implanted instinct, love them as their own mothers. There are as many children in each one's care as she desires from a spiritual parental affection. This heaven appears in front before the forehead, directly in the line or radius in which the angels look to the Lord. It is so situated because all little children are under the immediate auspices of the Lord; and the heaven of innocence, which is the third heaven, flows into them.

333. Little children have various dispositions, some that of the spiritual angels and some that of the celestial angels. Those who are of a celestial disposition are seen in that heaven to the right, and those of a spiritual disposition to the left. All children in the Greatest Man, which is heaven, are in the province of the eyes—those of a spiritual disposition in the province of the left eye, and those of a celestial disposition in the province of the right eye. This is because the angels who are in the spiritual kingdom see the Lord before the left eye, and those who are in the celestial kingdom before the right eye (see above, n. 118). This fact that in the greatest man or heaven children are in the province of the eyes is a proof that they are under the immediate sight and auspices of the Lord.

334. How children are taught in heaven shall also be briefly told. From their nurses they learn to talk. Their earliest speech is simply a sound of affection; this by degrees becomes more distinct as ideas of thought enter; for ideas of thought from affections constitute all angelic speech (as may be seen in its own chapter, n. 234–245). Into their affections, all of which proceed from innocence, such things as appear before their eyes and cause delight are first instilled; and as these things are from a spiritual origin the things of heaven at once flow into them, and by means of these heavenly things their interiors are opened, and they are thereby daily perfected. But when this first age is completed they are transferred to another heaven, where they are taught by masters; and so on.

335. Children are taught chiefly by representatives suited to their capacity. These are beautiful and full of wisdom from within, beyond all belief. In this way an intelligence that derives its soul from good is gradually instilled into them. I will here describe two representatives that I have been permitted to see, from which the nature of others may be inferred. First there was a representation of the Lord's rising from the sepulcher, and at the same time of the uniting of his human with the Divine. This was done in a manner so wise as to surpass all human wisdom, and at the same time in an innocent infantile manner. An idea of a sepulcher was presented, and with it an idea of the Lord, but in so remote a way that there was scarcely any perception of its being the Lord, except seemingly afar off; and for the reason that in the idea of a sepulcher there is something funereal, and this was thus removed; afterwards they cautiously admitted into the sepulcher something atmospheric, with an appearance of thin vapor, by which with proper remoteness they signified spiritual life in baptism. Afterwards I saw a representation by the angels of the Lord's descent to those that are "bound," and of his ascent with these into heaven, and this with incomparable prudence and gentleness. In adaptation to the infantile mind they let down little cords almost invisible, very soft and tender, by which they lightened the Lord's ascent, always with a holy solicitude that there should be nothing in the representation bordering upon anything that did not contain what is spiritual and heavenly. Other representations are there given, whereby, as by plays adapted to the minds of children, they are guided into knowledges of truth and affections for good.

336. It was also shown how tender their understanding is. When I was praying the Lord's Prayer, and from their understanding they flowed into the ideas of my thought, their influx

was perceived to be so tender and soft as to be almost solely a matter of affection; and at the same time it was observed that their understanding was open even from the Lord, for what flowed forth from them was as if it simply flowed through them. Moreover, the Lord flows into the ideas of little children chiefly from inmosts, for there is nothing, as with adults, to close up their ideas, no principles of falsity to close the way to the understanding of truth, nor any life of evil to close the way to the reception of good, and thereby to the reception of wisdom. All this makes clear that little children do not come at once after death into an angelic state, but are gradually brought into it by means of knowledges of good and truth, and in harmony with all heavenly order; for the least particulars of their nature are known to the Lord, and thus they are led, in accord with each and every movement of their inclination, to receive the truths of good and the goods of truth.

337. I have also been shown how all things are instilled into them by delightful and pleasant means suited to their genius. I have been permitted to see children most charmingly attired, having garlands of flowers resplendent with most beautiful and heavenly colors twined about their breasts and around their tender arms; and once to see them accompanied by those in charge of them and by maidens, in a park most beautifully adorned, not so much with trees, as with arbors and covered walks of laurel, with paths leading inward; and when the children entered attired as they were the flowers over the entrance shone forth most joyously. This indicates the nature of their delights, also how they are led by means of pleasant and delightful things into the goods of innocence and charity, which goods the Lord continually instilled into these delights and pleasures.

338. It was shown me, by a mode of communication common in the other life, what the ideas of children are when they see objects of any kind. Each and every object seemed to them to

be alive; and thus in every least idea of their thought there is life. And it was perceived that children on the earth have nearly the same ideas when they are at their little plays; for as yet they have no such reflection as adults have about what is inanimate.

339. It has been said above that children are of a genius either celestial or spiritual. Those of a celestial genius are easily distinguished from those of a spiritual genius. Their thought, speech, and action, is so gentle that hardly anything appears except what flows from a love of good to the Lord and from a love for other children. But those of a spiritual genius are not so gentle; but in everything with them there appears a sort of vibration, as of wings. The difference is seen also in their illfeeling and in other things.

340. Many may suppose that in heaven little children remain little children, and continue as such among the angels. Those who do not know what an angel is may have had this opinion confirmed by paintings and images in churches, in which angels are represented as children. But it is wholly otherwise. Intelligence and wisdom are what constitute an angel, and as long as children do not possess these they are not angels, although they are with the angels; but as soon as they become intelligent and wise they become angels; and what is wonderful, they do not then appear as children, but as adults, for they are no longer of an infantile genius, but of a more mature angelic genius. Intelligence and wisdom produce this effect. The reason why children appear more mature, thus as youths and young men, as they are perfected in intelligence and wisdom, is that intelligence and wisdom are essential spiritual nourishment;[2] and thus the things

2. Spiritual food is knowledge, intelligence, and wisdom, thus the good and truth from which these are (n. 3114, 4459, 4792, 5147, 5293, 5340, 5342, 5410, 5426, 5576, 5582, 5588, 5655, 8562, 9003). Therefore in a spiritual sense everything that comes forth from the mouth of the Lord is food (n. 681).

Because bread means all food in general it signifies every good, celestial and spiritual (n. 276, 680, 2165, 2177, 3478, 6118, 8410).

that nourish their minds also nourish their bodies, and this from correspondence; for the form of the body is simply the external form of the interiors. But it should be understood that in heaven children advance in age only to early manhood, and remain in this to eternity. That I might be assured that this is so I have been permitted to talk with some who had been educated as children in heaven, and had grown up there; with some also while they were children, and again with the same when they had become young men; and I have heard from them about the progress of their life from one age to another.

341. That innocence is a receptacle of all things of heaven, and thus the innocence of children is a plane for all affections for good and truth, can be seen from what has been shown above (n. 276-283) in regard to the innocence of angels in heaven, namely, that innocence is a willingness to be led by the Lord and not by oneself; consequently so far as a man is in innocence he is separated from what is his own, and so far as one is separated from what is his own he is in what is the Lord's own. The Lord's own is what is called his righteousness and merit. But the innocence of children is not genuine innocence, because as yet it is without wisdom. Genuine innocence is wisdom, since so far as anyone is wise he loves to be led by the Lord; or what is the same, so far as anyone is led by the Lord he is wise.

[2] Therefore children are led from the external innocence in which they are at the beginning, and which is called the innocence of childhood, to internal innocence, which is the innocence of wisdom. This innocence is the end that directs all their instruction and progress; and therefore when they have attained to the innocence of wisdom, the innocence of childhood, which in the meanwhile has served them as a plane, is joined to them.

And for the reason that these nourish the mind, which belongs to the internal man (n. 4459, 5293, 5576, 6277, 8410).

[3] The innocence of children has been represented to me as a wooden sort of thing, almost devoid of life, which becomes vivified as they are perfected by knowledges of truth and affections for good. Afterwards genuine innocence was represented by a most beautiful child, naked and full of life; for the really innocent, who are in the inmost heaven and thus nearest to the Lord, always appear before the eyes of other angels as little children, and some of them naked; for innocence is represented by nakedness unaccompanied by shame, as is said of the first man and his wife in Paradise (Gen. 2:25); so when their state of innocence perished they were ashamed of their nakedness, and hid themselves (Gen. 3:7, 10, 11). In a word, the wiser the angels are the more innocent they are, and the more innocent they are the more they appear to themselves as little children. This is why in the Word "childhood" signifies innocence (see above, n. 278).

342. I have talked with angels about little children, whether they are free from evils, inasmuch as they have no actual evil as adults have; and I was told that they are equally in evil, and in fact are nothing but evil;[3] but, like all angels, they are so withheld from evil and held in good by the Lord as to seem to themselves to be in good from themselves. For this reason when children have become adults in heaven, that they may not have

3. All kinds of men are born into evils of every kind, even to the extent that what is their own is nothing but evil (n. 210, 215, 731, 874–876, 987, 1047, 2307, 2308, 3518, 3701, 3812, 8480, 8550, 10283, 10284, 10286, 10731). Consequently man must needs be reborn, that is, regenerated (n. 3701). Man's inherited evil consists in his loving himself more than God, and the world more than heaven, and in making his neighbor, in comparison with himself, of no account, except for the sake of self, that is, himself alone, thus it consists in the love of self and of the world (n. 694, 731, 4317, 5660). All evils are from the love of self and of the world, when those loves rule (n. 1307, 1308, 1321, 1594, 1691, 3413, 7255, 7376, 7488, 7490, 8318, 9335, 9348, 10038, 10742).These evils are contempt of others, enmity, hatred, revenge, cruelty, deceit (n. 6667, 7370–7374, 9348, 10038, 10742). And from these evils comes all falsity (n. 1047, 10283, 10284, 10286). These loves, so far as the reins are given them, rush headlong; and the love of self aspires even to the throne of God (n. 7375, 8678).

the false idea about themselves that the good in them is from themselves and not from the Lord, they are now and then let down into their evils, which they inherited, and are left in them until they know, acknowledge and believe the truth of the matter.

[2] There was one, the son of a king, who died in childhood and grew up in heaven, who held this opinion. Therefore he was let down into that life of evils into which he was born, and he then perceived from the sphere of his life that he had a disposition to domineer over others, and regarded adulteries as of no account; these evils he had inherited from his parents; but after he had been brought to recognize his real character he was again received among the angels with whom he had before been associated.

[3] In the other life no one ever suffers punishment on account of his inherited evil, because it is not his evil, that is, it is not his fault that he is such; he suffers only on account of actual evil that is his, that is, only so far as he has appropriated to himself inherited evil by actual life. When, therefore, the children that have become adults are let down into the state of their inherited evil it is not that they may suffer punishment for it, but that they may learn that of themselves they are nothing but evil, and that it is by the mercy of the Lord that they are taken up into heaven from the hell in which they are, and that it is from the Lord that they are in heaven and not from any merit of their own; and therefore they may not boast before others of the good that is in them, since this is contrary to the good of mutual love, as it is contrary to the truth of faith.

343. Several times when a number of children that were in a purely infantile state have been with me in choirs, they were heard as a tender unarranged mass, that is, as not yet acting as one, as they do later when they have become more mature. To my surprise the spirits with me could not refrain from inducing

them to talk. This desire is innate in spirits. But I noticed, each time, that the children resisted, unwilling to talk in this way. This refusal and resistance, which were accompanied by a kind of indignation, I have often perceived; and when an opportunity to talk was given them they would say nothing except that "It is not so." I have been taught that little children are so tempted in order that they may get accustomed to resisting, and may begin to resist falsity and evil, and also that they may learn not to think, speak, and act from another, and in consequence may learn to permit themselves to be led by no one but the Lord.

344. From what has been said it can be seen what child education is in heaven, namely, that it is leading them by means of an understanding of truth and the wisdom of good into the angelic life, which is love to the Lord and mutual love, in which is innocence. But how different in many cases is the education of children on the earth can be seen from this example. I was in the street of a large city, and saw little boys fighting with each other; a crowd flocked around and looked on with much pleasure; and I was told that little boys are incited to such fights by their own parents. Good spirits and angels who saw this through my eyes so revolted at it that I felt their horror; and especially that parents should incite their children to such things, saying that in this way parents extinguish in the earliest age all the mutual love and all the innocence that children have from the Lord, and initiate them into the spirit of hatred and revenge; consequently by their own endeavors they shut their children out of heaven, where there is nothing but mutual love. Let parents therefore who wish well to their children beware of such things.

345. What the difference is between those who die in childhood and those who die in mature life shall also be told. Those dying in mature life have a plane acquired from the earthly and

material world, and this they carry with them. This plane is their memory and its bodily natural affection. This remains fixed and becomes quiescent, but still serves their thought after death as an outmost plane, since the thought flows into it. Consequently such as this plane is, and such as the correspondence is between the things that are in it and the rational faculty, such is the man after death. But the children who die in childhood and are educated in heaven have no such plane, since they derive nothing from the material world and the earthly body; but they have a spiritual-natural plane. For this reason they cannot be in such gross affections and consequent thoughts, since they derive all things from heaven. Moreover, these children do not know that they were born in the world, but believe that they were born in heaven. Neither do they know about any other than spiritual birth, which is effected through knowledges of good and truth and through intelligence and wisdom, from which man is a man; and as these are from the Lord they believe themselves to be the Lord's own, and love to be so. Nevertheless it is possible for the state of men who grow up on the earth to become as perfect as the state of children who grow up in heaven, provided they put away bodily and earthly loves, which are the loves of self and the world, and receive in their place spiritual loves.

38

The Wise and the Simple in Heaven

346. It is believed that in heaven the wise will have more glory and eminence than the simple, because it is said in Daniel:

> They that are intelligent shall shine as with the brightness of the firmament, and they that turn many to righteousness as the stars forever and ever (Dan. 12:3).

But few know who are meant by the "intelligent" and by those that "turn many to righteousness." The common belief is that they are such as are called the accomplished and learned, especially such as have taught in the church and have surpassed others in acquirements and in preaching, and still more such among them as have converted many to the faith. In the world all such are regarded as the intelligent; nevertheless such are not the intelligent in heaven that are spoken of in these words, unless their intelligence is heavenly intelligence. What this is will now be told.

347. Heavenly intelligence is interior intelligence, arising from a love for truth, not with any glory in the world nor any glory in heaven as an end, but with the truth itself as an end, by which they are inmostly affected and with which they are inmostly delighted. Those who are affected by and delighted with the truth itself are affected by and delighted with the light of heaven; and those who are affected by and delighted with the light of heaven are also affected by and delighted with Divine truth, and indeed with the Lord himself; for the light of heaven is Divine truth, and Divine truth is the Lord in heaven (see above, n. 126–140). This light enters only into the interiors of the mind; for the interiors of the mind are formed for the reception of that light, and are affected by and delighted with that light as it enters; for whatever flows in and is received from heaven has in it what is delightful and pleasant. From this comes a genuine affection for truth, which is an affection for truth for truth's sake. Those who are in this affection, or what is the same thing, in this love, are in heavenly intelligence, and "shine in heaven as with the brightness of the firmament." They so shine because Divine truth, wherever it is in heaven, is what gives light (see above, n. 132); and the "firmament" of heaven signifies from correspondence the intellectual faculty, both with angels and men, that is in the light of heaven.

[2] But those that love the truth, either with glory in the world or glory in heaven as an end, cannot shine in heaven, since they are delighted with and affected by the light of the world, and not with the very light of heaven; and the light of the world without the light of heaven is in heaven mere thick darkness.[1] For the glory of self is what rules, because it is the end in view; and when that glory is the end man puts himself in the first place, and such truths as can be made serviceable to his glory he looks upon simply as means to the end and as instruments of service. For he that loves Divine truths for the sake of his own glory regards himself and not the Lord in Divine truths, thereby turning the sight pertaining to his understanding and faith away from heaven to the world, and away from the Lord to himself. Such, therefore, are in the light of the world and not in the light of heaven.

1. The light of the world is for the external man, the light of heaven for the internal man (n. 3222–3224, 3337).

The light of heaven flows into the natural light, and so far as the natural man receives the light of heaven he becomes wise (n. 4302, 4408).

The things that are in the light of heaven can be seen in the light of heaven but not in the light of the world, which is called natural light (n. 9755).

Therefore those who are solely in the light of the world do not perceive those things that are in the light of heaven (n. 3108).

To the angels the light of the world is thick darkness (n. 1521, 1783, 1880).

[3] In outward form or in the sight of men they appear just as intelligent and learned as those who are in the light of heaven, because they speak in a like manner; and sometimes to outward appearance they even appear wiser, because they are moved by love of self, and are skilled in counterfeiting heavenly affections; but in their inward form in which they appear before the angels they are wholly different. All this shows in some degree who those are that are meant by "the intelligent that will shine in heaven as with the brightness of the firmament." Who are meant by those that "turn many to righteousness," who will shine as the stars, shall now be told.

348. By those who "turn many to righteousness" are meant those who are wise, and in heaven those are called wise who are in good, and those are in good that apply Divine truths at once to the life; for as soon as Divine truth comes to be of the life it becomes good, since it comes to be of will and love, and whatever is of will and love is called good; therefore such are called wise because wisdom is of the life. But those that do not commit Divine truths at once to the life, but first to the memory, from which they afterwards draw them and apply them to the life, are called the "intelligent." What and how great the difference is between the wise and the intelligent in the heavens can be seen in the chapter that treats of the two kingdoms of heaven, the celestial and the spiritual (n. 20–28), and in the chapter that treats of the three heavens (n. 29–40). Those who are in the Lord's celestial kingdom, and consequently in the third or inmost heaven, are called "the righteous" because they attribute all righteousness to the Lord and none to themselves. The Lord's righteousness in heaven is the good that is from the Lord.[2] Such, then,

---

2. The merit and righteousness of the Lord is the good that rules in heaven (n. 9486, 9983). He that is "righteous" or "made righteous" is one to whom the merit and righteousness of the Lord is ascribed; and he is "unrighteous" who holds to his own righteousness and merit (n. 5069, 9263). The quality of those in the other life who claim righteousness to themselves (n. 942, 2027).

are here meant by those that "turn to righteousness"; and such are meant also in the Lord's words,

> The righteous shall shine forth as the sun in the kingdom of their Father (Matt. 13:43).

Such "shine forth as the sun" because they are in love to the Lord from the Lord, and that love is meant by the "sun" (see above, n. 116–125). The light of such is flame colored; and the ideas of their thought are so tinged with what is flaming because they receive the good of love directly from the Lord as the sun in heaven.

349. All who have acquired intelligence and wisdom in the world are received in heaven and become angels, each in accordance with the quality and degree of his intelligence and wisdom. For whatever a man acquires in the world abides, and he takes it with him after death; and it is further increased and filled out, but within and not beyond the degree of his affection and desire for truth and its good, those with but little affection and desire receiving but little, and yet as much as they are capable of receiving within that degree; while those with much affection and desire receive much. The degree itself of affection and desire is like a measure that is filled to the full, he that has a large measure receiving more, and he that has a small measure receiving less. This is so because man's love, to which affection and desire belong, receives all that accords with itself; consequently reception is measured by the love. This is what is meant by the Lord's words,

> To him that hath it shall be given, that he may have more abundantly (Matt. 13:12; 25:29).

> Good measure, pressed down, shaken together, and running over, shall be given into your bosom (Luke 6:38).

In the Word "righteousness" is predicated of good and "judgment" of truth; therefore "doing righteousness and judgment" is doing good and truth (n. 2235, 9857).

350. All are received into heaven who have loved truth and good for the sake of truth and good; therefore those that have loved much are called the wise, and those that have loved little are called the simple. The wise in heaven are in much light, the simple in less light, everyone in accordance with the degree of his love for good and truth. To love truth and good for the sake of truth and good is to will and do them; for those love who will and do, while those who do not will and do, do not love. Such also love the Lord and are loved by the Lord, because good and truth are from the Lord. And inasmuch as good and truth are from the Lord the Lord is in good and truth; and he is in those who receive good and truth in their life by willing and doing. Moreover, when man is viewed in himself he is nothing but his own good and truth, because good is of his will and truth of his understanding, and man is such as his will and understanding are. Evidently, then, man is loved by the Lord just to the extent that his will is formed from good and his understanding from truth. Also to be loved by the Lord is to love the Lord, since love is reciprocal; for upon him who is loved the Lord bestows ability to love.

351. It is believed in the world that those who have much knowledge, whether it be knowledge of the teachings of the church and the Word or of the sciences, have a more interior and keen vision of truth than others, that is, are more intelligent and wise; and such have this opinion of themselves. But what true intelligence and wisdom are, and what spurious and false intelligence and wisdom are, shall be told in what now follows.

[2] True intelligence and wisdom is seeing and perceiving what is true and good, and thereby what is false and evil, and clearly distinguishing between them, and this from an interior intuition and perception. With every man there are interior faculties and exterior faculties; interior faculties belonging to the internal or spiritual man, and exterior faculties belonging to the exterior or

natural man. Accordingly as man's interiors are formed and made one with his exteriors man sees and perceives. His interiors can be formed only in heaven, his exteriors are formed in the world. When his interiors have been formed in heaven the things they contain flow into his exteriors which are from the world, and so form them that they correspond with, that is, act as one with, his interiors; and when this is done man sees and perceives from what is interior. The interiors can be formed only in one way, namely, by man's looking to the Divine and to heaven, since, as has been said, the interiors are formed in heaven; and man looks to the Divine when he believes in the Divine, and believes that all truth and good and consequently all intelligence and wisdom are from the Divine; and man believes in the Divine when he is willing to be led by the Divine. In this way and none other are the interiors of man opened.

[3] The man who is in that belief and in a life that is in accordance with his belief has the ability and capacity to understand and be wise; but to become intelligent and wise he must learn many things, both things pertaining to heaven and things pertaining to the world—things pertaining to heaven from the Word and from the church, and things pertaining to the world from the sciences. To the extent that man learns and applies to life he becomes intelligent and wise, for to that extent the interior sight belonging to his understanding and the interior affection belonging to his will are perfected. The simple of this class are those whose interiors have been opened, but not so enriched by spiritual, moral, civil and natural truths. Such perceive truths when they hear them, but do not see them in themselves. But the wise of this class are those whose interiors have been both opened and enriched. Such both see truths inwardly and perceive them. All this makes clear what true intelligence is and what true wisdom is.

352. Spurious intelligence and wisdom is failing to see and perceive from within what is true and what is good, and

thereby what is false and what is evil, but merely believing that to be true and good and that to be false and evil which is said by others to be so, and then confirming it. Because such see truth from someone else, and not from the truth itself, they can seize upon and believe what is false as readily as what is true, and can confirm it until it appears true; for whatever is confirmed puts on the appearance of truth; and there is nothing that cannot be confirmed. The interiors of such are opened only from beneath; but their exteriors are opened to the extent that they have confirmed themselves. For this reason the light from which they see is not the light of heaven but the light of the world, which is called natural light [lumen]; and in that light falsities can shine like truths; and when confirmed they can even appear resplendent, but not in the light of heaven. Of this class those are less intelligent and wise who have strongly confirmed themselves, and those are more intelligent and wise who have less strongly confirmed themselves. All this shows what spurious intelligence and wisdom are.

[2] But those are not included in this class who in childhood supposed what they heard from their masters to be true, if in a riper age, when they think from their own understanding, they do not continue to hold fast to it, but long for truth, and from that longing seek for it, and when they find it are interiorly moved by it. Because such are moved by the truth for the truth's sake they see the truth before they confirm it.[3]

[3] This may be illustrated by an example. There was a discussion among spirits why animals are born into all the

3. It is the part of the wise to see and perceive whether a thing is true before it is confirmed and not merely to confirm what is said by others (n. 1017, 4741, 7012, 7680, 7950). Only those can see and perceive whether a thing is true before it is confirmed who are affected by truth for the sake of truth and for the sake of life (n. 8521). The light of confirmation is not spiritual light but natural light, and is even sensual light which the wicked may have (n. 8780). All things, even falsities, may be so confirmed as to appear like truths (n. 2477, 2480, 5033, 6865, 8521).

knowledge suited to their nature, but man is not; and the reason was said to be that animals are in the order of their life, and man is not, consequently man must needs be led into order by means of what he learns of internal and external things. But if man were born into the order of his life, which is to love God above all things and his neighbor as himself, he would be born into intelligence and wisdom, and as knowledges are acquired would come into a belief in all truth. Good spirits saw this at once and perceived it to be true, and this merely from the light of truth; while the spirits who had confirmed themselves in faith alone, and had thereby set aside love and charity, were unable to understand it, because the light of falsity which they had confirmed had made obscure to them the light of truth.

353. False intelligence and wisdom is all intelligence and wisdom that is separated from the acknowledgment of the Divine; for all such as do not acknowledge the Divine, but acknowledge nature in the place of the Divine, think from the bodily-sensual, and are merely sensual, however highly they may be esteemed in the world for their accomplishments and learning.[4] For their learning does not ascend beyond such things as appear before their eyes in the world; these they hold in the memory and look at them in an almost material way, although the same knowledges serve the truly intelligent in forming their under-

---

4. The sensual is the outmost of man's life, clinging to and inhering in his bodily part (n. 5077, 5767, 9212, 9216, 9331, 9730). He is called a sensual man who forms all his judgments and conclusions from the bodily senses, and who believes nothing except what he sees with his eyes and touches with his hands (n. 5094, 7693).

Such a man thinks in things outermost and not interiorly in himself (n. 5089, 5094, 6564, 7693). His interiors are so closed up that he sees nothing of Divine truth (n. 6564, 6844, 6845). In a word, he is in gross natural light and thus perceives nothing that is from the light of heaven (n. 6201, 6310, 6564, 6598, 6612, 6614, 6622, 6624, 6844, 6845).

Therefore he is inwardly opposed to all things pertaining to heaven and the church (n. 6201, 6310, 6844, 6845, 6948, 6949). The learned that have confirmed themselves against the truths of the church are sensual (n. 6316).

A description of the sensual man (n. 10236).

standing. By sciences the various kinds of experimental knowledge are meant, such as physics, astronomy, chemistry, mechanics, geometry, anatomy, psychology, philosophy, the history of kingdoms and of the literary world, criticism, and languages.

[2] The clergy who deny the Divine do not raise their thoughts above the sensual things of the external man; and regard the things of the Word in the same way as others regard the sciences, not making them matters of thought or of any intuition by an enlightened rational mind; and for the reason that their interiors are closed up, together with those exteriors that are nearest to their interiors. These are closed up because they have turned themselves away from heaven, and have retroverted those faculties that were capable of looking heavenward, which are, as has been said above, the interiors of the human mind. For this reason they are incapable of seeing anything true or good, this being to them in thick darkness, while whatever is false and evil is in light.

[3] And yet sensual men can reason, some of them more cunningly and keenly than anyone else; but they reason from the fallacies of the senses confirmed by their knowledges; and because they are able to reason in this way they believe themselves to be wiser than others.[5] The fire that kindles with affection their reasonings is the fire of the love of self and the world. Such are those who are in false intelligence and wisdom, and who are meant by the Lord in Matthew:

Seeing they see not, and hearing they hear not, neither do they understand (Matt. 13:13–15).

These things are hid from the intelligent and wise, and revealed unto babes (Matt. 11:25, 26).

5. Sensual men reason keenly and cunningly, since they place all intelligence in speaking from the bodily memory (n. 195, 196, 5700, 10236). But they reason from the fallacies of the senses (n. 5084, 6948, 6949, 7693). Sensual men are more cunning and malicious than others (n. 7693, 10236). By the ancients such were called serpents of the tree of knowledge (n. 195–197, 6398, 6949, 10313).

354. It has been granted me to speak with many of the learned after their departure from the world; with some of distinguished reputation and celebrated in the literary world for their writings, and with some not so celebrated, although endowed with profound wisdom. Those that in heart had denied the Divine, whatever their professions may have been, had become so stupid as to have little comprehension even of anything truly civil, still less of anything spiritual. I perceived and also saw that the interiors of their minds were so closed up as to appear black (for in the spiritual world such things become visible), and in consequence they were unable to endure any heavenly light or admit any influx from heaven. This blackness which their interiors presented was more intense and extended with those that had confirmed themselves against the Divine by the knowledges they had acquired. In the other life such accept all falsity with delight, imbibing it as a sponge does water; and they repel all truth as an elastic bony substance repels what falls upon it. In fact, it is said that the interiors of those that have confirmed themselves against the Divine and in favor of nature become bony, and their heads down to the nose appear callous like ivory, which is a sign that they no longer have any perception. Those of this description are immersed in quagmires that appear like bogs; and there they are harassed by the fantasies into which their falsities are turned. Their infernal fire is a lust for glory and reputation, which prompts them to assail one another, and from an infernal ardor to torment those about them who do not worship them as deities; and this they do one to another in turns. Into such things is all the learning of the world changed that has not received into itself light from heaven through acknowledgment of the Divine.

355. That these are such in the spiritual world when they come into it after death may be inferred from this alone, that all things that are in the natural memory and are in immediate conjunction with the things of bodily sense (which is true of such knowledges as are mentioned above) then become quiescent; and only such rational principles as are drawn from these then serve for thought and speech. For man carries with him his entire natural memory, but its contents are not then under his view, and do not come into his thought as when he lived in the world. He can take nothing from that memory and bring it forth into spiritual light because its contents are not objects of that light. But those things of the reason and understanding that man has acquired from knowledges while living in the body are in accord with the light of the spiritual world; consequently so far as the spirit of man has been made rational in the world through knowledge and science it is to the same extent rational after being loosed from the body; for man is then a spirit, and it is the spirit that thinks in the body.[6]

356. But in respect to those that have acquired intelligence and wisdom through knowledge and science, who are such as have applied all things to the use of life, and have also acknowledged the Divine, loved the Word, and lived a spiritual moral life (of which above, n. 319), to such the sciences have served as a means of becoming wise, and also of corroborating the things pertaining to faith. The interiors of the mind of such have been perceived by me, and were seen as transparent from light of a glistening white, flamy, or blue color, like that of translucent diamonds, rubies, and sapphires; and this in accordance with confirmations in favor of the Divine and Divine truths drawn from science. Such is the appearance of true intelligence and wisdom when they are presented to view in the spiritual world. This appearance is derived from the light of heaven; and that light is Divine truth going forth from the Lord, which is the source of all intelligence and wisdom (see above, n. 126–133).

[2] The planes of that light, in which variegations like those of colors exist, are the interiors of the mind; and these variegations are produced by confirmations of Divine truths by

6. Knowledges belong to the natural memory that man has while he is in the body (n. 5212, 9922). Man carries with him after death his whole natural memory (n. 2475) from experience (n. 2481–2486). But he is not able, as he was in the world, to draw anything out of that memory, for several reasons (n. 2476, 2477, 2479).

means of such things as are in nature, that is, in the sciences.[7]
For the interior mind of man looks into the things of the natural memory, and the things there that will serve as proofs it sublimates as it were by the fire of heavenly love, and withdraws and purifies them even into spiritual ideas. This is unknown to man as long as he lives in the body, because there he thinks both spiritually and naturally, and he has no perception of the things he then thinks spiritually, but only of those he thinks naturally. But when he has come into the spiritual world he has no perception of what he thought naturally in the world, but only of what he thought spiritually. Thus is his state changed.

[3] All this makes clear that it is by means of knowledges and sciences that man is made spiritual, also that these are the means of becoming wise, but only with those who have acknowledged the Divine in faith and life. Such also before others are accepted in heaven, and are among those there who are at the center (n. 43), because they are in light more than others. These are the intelligent and wise in heaven, who "shine as with the brightness of the firmament" and who "shine as the stars," while the simple there are those that have acknowledged the Divine, have loved the Word, and have lived a spiritual and moral life, but the interiors of their minds have not been so enriched by knowledges and sciences. The human mind is like soil which is such as it is made by cultivation.

7. Most beautiful colors are seen in heaven (n. 1053, 1624).

Colors in heaven are from the light there, and are modifications or variegations of that light (n. 1042, 1043, 1053, 1624, 3993, 4530, 4742, 4922).

Thus they are manifestations of truth from good, and they signify such things as pertain to intelligence and wisdom (n. 4530, 4677, 4922, 9466).

Extracts from *Arcana Coelestia*
Respecting Knowledges

Man ought to be fully instructed in knowledges and cognitions, since by means of them he learns to think, afterwards to understand what is true and good, and finally to be wise (n. 129, 1450, 1451, 1453, 1548, 1802).

Knowledges are the first things on which the life of man, civil, moral, and spiritual, is built and founded, and they are to be learned for the sake of use as an end (n. 1489, 3310).

Cognitions open the way to the internal man, and afterwards conjoin that man with the external in accordance with uses (n. 1563, 1616).

The rational faculty has its birth by means of knowledges and cognitions (n. 1895, 1900, 3086).

But not by means of cognitions themselves, but by means of affection for the uses derived from them (n. 1895).

[2] There are knowledges that give entrance to Divine truths, and knowledges that do not (n. 5213).

Empty knowledges are to be destroyed (n. 1489, 1492, 1499, 1581).

Empty knowledges are such as have the loves of self and of the world as an end, and sustain those loves, and withdraw from love to God and love toward the neighbor, because such knowledges close up the internal man, even to the extent that man becomes unable to receive anything from heaven (n. 1563, 1600).

Knowledges are means to becoming wise and means to becoming insane and by them the internal man is either opened or closed, and thus the rational is either enriched or destroyed (n. 4156, 8628, 9922).

[3] The internal man is opened and gradually perfected by means of knowledges if man has good use as an end, especially use that looks to external life (n. 3086).

Then knowledges, which are in the natural man, are met by spiritual and heavenly things from the spiritual man, and these adopt such of them as are suitable (n. 1495).

Then the uses of heavenly life are drawn forth by the Lord and perfected and raised up out of the knowledges in the natural man by means of the internal man (n. 1895, 1896, 1900–1902, 5871, 5874, 5901).

While incongruous and opposing knowledges are rejected to the sides and banished (n. 5871, 5886, 5889).

[4] The sight of the internal man calls forth from the knowledges of the external man only such things as are in accord with its love (n. 9394).

As seen by the internal man what pertains to the love is at the center and in brightness, but what is not of the love is at the sides and in obscurity (n. 6068, 6084).

Suitable knowledges are gradually implanted in man's loves and as it were dwell in them (n. 6325).

If man were born into love toward the neighbor he would be born into intelligence, but because he is born into the loves of self and of the world he is born into total ignorance (n. 6323, 6325).

Knowledge, intelligence, and wisdom are sons of love to God and of love toward the neighbor (n. 1226, 2049, 2116).

[5] It is one thing to be wise, another thing to understand, another to know, and another to do; nevertheless, in those that possess spiritual life these follow in order, and exist together in doing or deeds (n. 10331).

Also it is one thing to know, another to acknowledge, and another to have faith (n. 896).

[6] Knowledges, which pertain to the external or natural man, are in the light of the world, but truths that have been made truths of faith and of love, and have thus acquired life, are in the light of heaven (n. 5212).

The truths that have acquired spiritual life are comprehended by means of natural ideas (n. 5510).

Spiritual influx is from the internal or spiritual man into the knowledges that are in the external or natural man (n. 1940, 8005).

Knowledges are receptacles, and as it were vessels, for the truth and good that belong to the internal man (n. 1469, 1496, 3068, 5489, 6004, 6023, 6052, 6071, 6077, 7770, 9922).

Knowledges are like mirrors in which the truths and goods of the internal man appear as an image (n. 5201).

There they are together as in their outmost (n. 5373, 5874, 5886, 5901, 6004, 6023, 6052, 6071).

[7] Influx is not physical but spiritual, that is, influx is from the internal man into the external, thus into the knowledges of the external; and not from the external into the internal, thus not from the knowledges of the external into truths of faith (n. 3219, 5119, 5259, 5427, 5428, 5478, 6322, 9110).

A beginning must be made from the truths of doctrine of the church, which are from the Word, and those truths must first be acknowledged, and then it is permissible to consult knowledges (n. 6047).

Thus it is permissible for those who are in an affirmative state in regard to truths of faith to confirm them intellectually by means of knowledges, but not for those who are in a negative state (n. 2568, 2588, 4760, 6047).

He that will not believe Divine truths until he is convinced by means of knowledges will never believe (n. 2094, 2832).

To enter from knowledge into the truths of faith is contrary to order (n. 10236).

Those who do so become demented respecting the things of heaven and the church (n. 128–130).

They fall into the falsities of evil (n. 232, 233, 6047).

In the other life when they think about spiritual matters they become as it were drunken (n. 1072).

More respecting the character of such (n. 196).

Examples showing that things spiritual cannot be comprehended when entered into through knowledges (n. 233, 2094, 2196, 2203, 2209).

In spiritual things many of the learned are more demented than the simple, for the reason that they are in a negative state, which they confirm by means of the knowledges which they have continually and in abundance before their sight (n. 4760, 8629).

[8] Those who reason from knowledges against the truths of faith reason keenly because they reason from the fallacies of the senses, which are engaging and convincing, because they cannot easily be dispelled (n. 5700).

What things are fallacies of the senses, and what they are (n. 5084, 5094, 6400, 6948).

Those that have no understanding of truth, and also those that are in evil, are able to reason about the truths and goods of faith, but are not able to understand them (n. 4214).

Intelligence does not consist in merely confirming dogma but in seeing whether it is true or not before it is confirmed (n. 4741, 6047).

[9] Knowledges are of no avail after death, but only that which man has imbibed in his understanding and life by means of knowledges (n. 2480).

Still all knowledge remains after death, although it is quiescent (n. 2476–2479, 2481–2486).

[10] Knowledges with the evil are falsities, because they are adapted to evils, but with the good the same knowledges are truths, because applied to what is good (n. 6917).

True knowledges with the evil are not true, however much they may appear to be true when uttered, because there is evil within them (n. 10331).

[11] An example of the desire to know, which spirits have (n. 1974).

Angels have an illimitable longing to know and to become wise, since learning, intelligence, and wisdom are spiritual food (n. 3114, 4459, 4792, 4976, 5147, 5293, 5340, 5342, 5410, 5426, 5576, 5582, 5588, 5655, 6277, 8562, 9003).

The knowledge of the ancients was the knowledge of correspondences and representations, by which they gained entrance into the cognition of spiritual things; but that knowledge at this day is wholly lost (n. 4749, 4844, 4964, 4965).

[12] For spiritual truths to be comprehended the following universals must be known. (1) All things in the universe have relation to good and truth and to their conjunction that they may be anything, thus to love and faith and their conjunction. (2) Man has understanding and will; and the understanding is the receptacle of truth and the will of good; and all things in man have relation to these two and to their conjunction, as all things have relation to truth and good and their conjunction. (3) There is an internal man and an external man, which are as distinct from each other as heaven and the world are, and yet for a man to be truly a man, these must make one. (4) The internal man is in the light of heaven, and the external man is in the light of the world; and the light of heaven is Divine truth itself, from which is all intelligence. (5) Between the things in the internal man and those in the external there is a correspondence, therefore the different aspect they present is such that they can be distinguished only by means of a knowledge of correspondences. Unless these and many other things are known, nothing but incongruous ideas of spiritual and heavenly truths can be conceived and formed; therefore without these universals the knowledges and cognitions of the natural man can be of but little service to the rational man for understanding and growth. This makes clear how necessary knowledges are.

39

The Rich and the Poor in Heaven

357. There are various opinions about reception into heaven. Some are of the opinion that the poor are received and the rich are not; some that the rich and the poor are equally received; some that the rich can be received only by giving up their wealth and becoming like the poor; and proofs are found in the Word for all of these opinions. But those who make a distinction in regard to heaven between the rich and the poor do not understand the Word. In its interiors the Word is spiritual, but in the letter it is natural; consequently those who understand the Word only in accordance with its literal sense, and not according to any spiritual sense, err in many respects, especially about the rich and the poor; for example, that it is as difficult for the rich to enter into heaven as for a camel to pass through the eye of a needle; and that it is easy for the poor because they are poor, since it is said,

Blessed are the poor, for theirs is the kingdom of the heavens (Matt. 5:3; Luke 6:20, 21).

But those who know anything of the spiritual sense of the Word think otherwise; they know that heaven is for all who live a life of faith and love, whether rich or poor. But who are meant in the Word by "the rich" and who by "the poor" will be told in what follows. From much conversation and living with angels it has been granted me to know with certainty that the rich enter heaven just as easily as the poor, and that no man is shut out of heaven on account of his wealth, or received into heaven on account of his poverty. Both the rich and the poor are in heaven, and many of the rich in greater glory and happiness than the poor.

358. It should be said to begin with that a man may acquire riches and accumulate wealth as far as opportunity is given, if it is not done by craft or fraud; that he may enjoy the delicacies of food and drink if he does not place his life therein; that he may have a palatial dwelling in accord with his condition, associate with others in like condition, frequent places of amusement, talk about the affairs of the world, and need not go about like a devotee with a sad and sorrowful countenance and drooping head, but may be joyful and cheerful; nor need he give his goods to the poor except so far as affection leads him; in a word, he may live outwardly precisely like a man of the world; and all this will be no obstacle to his entering heaven, provided that inwardly in himself he thinks about God as he ought, and acts sincerely and justly in respect to his neighbor. For a man is such as his affection and thought are, or such as his love and faith are, and from these all his outward acts derive their life; since acting is willing, and speaking is thinking, acting being from the will, and speaking from the thought. So where it is said in the Word that man will be judged according to his deeds, and will be rewarded according to his works, it is meant that he will be judged and rewarded in accordance with his thought and affection, which are the source of his deeds, or which are in his deeds; for deeds are nothing apart from these, and are precisely such as these are.[1] All this shows

---

1. It is frequently said in the Word that man will be judged and will be rewarded according to his deeds and works (n. 3934). By "deeds and works" deeds and works in their internal form are meant, not in their external form, since good works in external form are likewise done by the wicked, but in internal and external form together only by the good (n. 3934, 6073). Works, like all activities, have their being and outgo [esse et existere] and their quality from the interiors of man, which pertain to his thought and will, since they proceed from these; therefore such as the interiors are such are the works (n. 3934, 8911, 10331). That is, such as the interiors are in regard to love and faith (n. 3934, 6073, 10331, 10332). Thus works contain love and faith, and are love and faith in effect (n. 10331). Therefore to be judged and rewarded in accordance with deeds and works, means in accordance with love and faith (n. 3147, 3934, 6073, 8911, 10331, 10332). So far as works look to self and the world they are not good, but they are good so far as they look to the Lord and the neighbor (n. 3147).

that the man's external accomplishes nothing, but only his internal, which is the source of the external. For example: if a man acts honestly and refrains from fraud solely because he fears the laws and the loss of reputation and thereby of honor or gain, and if that fear did not restrain him would defraud others whenever he could; although such a man's deeds outwardly appear honest, his thought and will are fraud; and because he is inwardly dishonest and fraudulent he has hell in himself. But he who acts honestly and refrains from fraud because it is against God and against the neighbor would have no wish to defraud another if he could; his thought and will are conscience, and he has heaven in himself. The deeds of these two appear alike in outward form, but inwardly they are wholly unlike.

359. Since a man can live outwardly as others do, can grow rich, keep a plentiful table, dwell in an elegant house and wear fine clothing according to his condition and function, can enjoy delights and gratifications, and engage in worldly affairs for the sake of his occupation and business and for the life both of the mind and body, provided he inwardly acknowledges the Divine and wishes well to the neighbor, it is evident that to enter upon the way to heaven is not so difficult as many believe. The sole difficulty lies in being able to resist the love of self and the world, and to prevent their becoming dominant; for this is the source of all evils.[2] That this is not so difficult as is believed is meant by these words of the Lord:

> Learn of Me, for I am meek and lowly of heart, and ye shall find rest to your souls; for my yoke is easy and my burden is light (Matt. 11:29, 30).

---

2. All evils are from the love of self and of the world (n. 1307, 1308, 1321, 1594, 1691, 3413, 7255, 7376, 7488, 7490, 8318, 9335, 9348, 10038, 10742).

These are contempt of others, enmities, hatred, revenge, cruelty, deceit (n. 6667, 7370–7374, 9348, 10038, 10742).

Into such loves man is born, thus in them are his inherited evils (n. 694, 4317, 5660).

The Lord's yoke is easy and his burden light because a man is led by the Lord and not by self just to the extent that he resists the evils that flow forth from love of self and of the world; and because the Lord then resists these evils in man and removes them.

360. I have spoken with some after death who, while they lived in the world, renounced the world and gave themselves up to an almost solitary life, so that by an abstraction of the thoughts from worldly things they might have opportunity for pious meditations, believing that thus they might enter the way to heaven. But these in the other life are of a sad disposition; they despise others who are not like themselves; they are indignant that they do not have a happier lot than others, believing that they have merited it; they have no interest in others, and turn away from the duties of charity by which there is conjunction with heaven. They desire heaven more than others; but when they are taken up among the angels they induce anxieties that disturb the happiness of the angels; and in consequence they are sent away; and when sent away they betake themselves to desert places, where they lead a life like that which they lived in the world.

[2] Man can be formed for heaven only by means of the world. In the world are the outmost effects in which everyone's affection must be terminated; for unless affection puts itself forth or flows out into acts, which is done in association with others, it is suffocated to such a degree finally that man has no longer any regard for the neighbor, but only for himself. All this makes clear that a life of charity toward the neighbor, which is doing what is just and right in every work and in every employment, is what leads to heaven, and not a life of piety apart from charity;[3] and from this it follows that only to the extent that man is

3. Charity toward the neighbor is doing what is good, just, and right, in every work and every employment (n. 8120–8122).

Thus charity toward the neighbor extends to all things and each thing that a man thinks, wills, and does (n. 8124).

engaged in the employments of life can charity be exercised and the life of charity grow; and this is impossible to the extent that man separates himself from those employments.

[3] On this subject I will speak now from experience. Of those who while in the world were employed in trade and commerce and became rich through these pursuits there are many in heaven, but not so many of those who were in stations of honor and became rich through those employments; and for the reason that these latter by the gains and honors that resulted from their dispensing justice and equity, and also by the lucrative and honorable positions bestowed on them were led into loving themselves and the world, and thereby separating their thoughts and affections from heaven and turning them to themselves. For to the extent that a man loves self and the world and looks to self and the world in everything, he alienates himself from the Divine and separates himself from heaven.

361. As to the lot of the rich in heaven, they live more splendidly than others. Some of them dwell in palaces within which everything is resplendent as if with gold and silver. They have an abundance of all things for the uses of life, but they do not in the least set their heart on these things, but only on uses. Uses are clearly seen as if they were in light, but the gold and silver are seen obscurely, and comparatively as if in shade. This is because while they were in the world they loved uses, and loved gold and silver only as means and instruments. It is the uses that are thus resplendent in heaven, the good of use like gold and the truth of use like silver.[4] Therefore their wealth in

---

A life of piety apart from a life of charity is of no avail, but together they are profitable for all things (n. 8252, 8253).

4. Every good has its delight from use and in accordance with use (n. 3049, 4984, 7038); also its quality; and in consequence such as the use is such is the good (n. 3049).

heaven is such as their uses were in the world, and such, too, are their delight and happiness. Good uses are providing oneself and one's own with the necessaries of life; also desiring wealth for the sake of one's country and for the sake of one's neighbor, whom a rich man can in many ways benefit more than a poor man. These are good uses because one is able thereby to withdraw his mind from an indolent life which is harmful, since in such a life man's thoughts run to evil because of the evil inherent in him. These uses are good to the extent that they have the Divine in them, that is, to the extent that man looks to the Divine and to heaven, and finds his good in these, and sees in wealth only a subservient good.

362. But the lot of the rich that have not believed in the Divine, and have cast out of their minds the things pertaining to heaven and the church, is the opposite of this. Such are in hell, where filth, misery, and want exist; and into these riches that are loved as an end are changed; and not only riches, but also their very uses, which are either a wish to live as they like and indulge in pleasures, and to have opportunity to give the mind more fully and freely to shameful practices, or a wish to rise above others whom they despise.

Such riches and such uses, because they have nothing spiritual, but only what is earthly in them, become filthy; for a spiritual purpose in riches and their uses is like a soul in the body, or like the light of heaven in moist ground; and such riches and uses become putrid as a body does without a soul, or as moist

---

All happiness and delight of life is from uses (n. 997).

In general, life is a life of uses (n. 1964). Angelic life consists in the goods of love and charity, thus in performing uses (n. 454). The ends that man has in view, which are uses, are the only things that the Lord, and thus the angels, consider (n. 1317, 1645, 5844). The kingdom of the Lord is a kingdom of uses (n. 454, 696, 1103, 3645, 4054, 7038). Performing uses is serving the Lord (n. 7038). Everyone's character is such as are the uses he performs (n. 4054, 6815); illustrated (n. 7038).

ground does without the light of heaven. Such are those that have been led and drawn away from heaven by riches.

363. Every man's ruling affection or love remains with him after death, nor is it rooted out to eternity, since a man's spirit is wholly what his love is, and what is unknown, the body of every spirit and angel is the outward form of his love, exactly corresponding to his inward form, which is the form of his disposition and mind; consequently the quality of his spirit is known from his face, movements, and speech. While a man is living in the world the quality of the spirit would be known if he had not learned to counterfeit in his face, movements, and speech what is not his own. All this shows that man remains to eternity such as his ruling affection or love is.

It has been granted me to talk with some who lived seventeen hundred years ago, and whose lives are well known from writings of that time, and it was found that the same love still rules them as when they were on the earth. This makes clear also that the love of riches, and of uses from riches, remains with everyone to eternity, and that it is exactly the same as the love acquired in the world, yet with the difference that in the case of those who devoted their riches to good uses riches are changed in the other world into delights which are in accord with the uses performed; while in the case of those who devoted their riches to evil uses riches are turned into mere filth, in which they then take the same delight as they did in the world in their riches devoted to evil uses.

Such then take delight in filth because filthy pleasures and shameful acts, which had been the uses to which they had devoted their riches, and also avarice, which is a love of riches without regard to use, correspond to filth. Spiritual filth is nothing else.

364. The poor come into heaven not on account of their poverty but because of their life. Everyone's life follows him, whether he be rich or poor. There is no peculiar mercy for one in preference to another;[5] he that has lived well is received, while he that has not lived well is rejected.

Moreover, poverty leads and draws man away from heaven just as much as wealth does. There are many among the poor who are not content with their lot, who strive after many things, and believe riches to be blessings;[6] and when they do not gain them are much provoked, and harbor ill thoughts about the Divine providence; they also envy others the good things they possess, and are as ready as anyone to defraud others whenever they have opportunity, and to indulge in filthy pleasures. But this is not true of the poor who are content with their lot, and are careful and diligent in their work, who love labor better than idleness, and act sincerely and faithfully, and at the same time live a Christian life. I have now and then talked with those belonging to the peasantry and common people, who while living in the world believed in God and did what was just and right in their occupations. Since they had an affection for knowing truth they inquired about charity and about faith, having heard in this world much about faith and in the other life much about charity. They were therefore told that charity is everything that pertains to life, and faith everything that pertains to doctrine; consequently charity is willing and doing what is just and right in every work, and faith is thinking justly and rightly; and faith and charity are conjoined, the same as doctrine and a life in accordance with it, or the same as thought

5. There can be no mercy apart from means, but only mercy through means, that is, to those who live in accordance with the commandments of the Lord; such the Lord by His mercy leads continually in the world, and afterwards to eternity (n. 8700, 10659).

6. Dignities and riches are not real blessings, therefore they are granted both to the wicked and to the good (n. 8939, 10775, 10776).

The real blessing is reception of love and faith from the Lord, and conjunction thereby, for this is the source of eternal happiness (n. 1420, 1422, 2846, 3017, 3406, 3504, 3514, 3530, 3565, 3584, 4216, 4981, 8939, 10495).

and will; and faith becomes charity when that which a man thinks justly and rightly he also wills and does, and then they are not two but one. This they well understood, and rejoiced, saying that in the world they did not understand believing to be anything else but living.

365. All this makes clear that the rich and the poor alike come into heaven, the one as easily as the other. The belief that the poor enter heaven easily and the rich with difficulty comes from not understanding the Word where the rich and the poor are mentioned. In the Word those that have an abundance of knowledges of good and truth, thus who are within the church where the Word is, are meant in the spiritual sense by the "rich"; while those who lack these knowledges, and yet desire them, thus who are outside of the church and where there is no Word, are meant by the "poor."

[2] The rich man clothed in purple and fine linen, and cast into hell, means the Jewish nation, which is called rich because it had the Word and had an abundance of knowledges of good and truth therefrom, "garments of purple" signifying knowledges of good, and "garments of fine linen" knowledges of truth.[7] But the poor man who lay at the rich man's gate and longed to be fed with the crumbs that fell from the rich man's table, and who was carried by angels into heaven, means the nations that have no knowledges of good and truth and yet desired them (Luke 16:19–31). Also the rich that were called to a great supper and excused themselves mean the Jewish nation, and the poor brought in in their place mean the nations outside of the church (Luke 14:16–24).

[3] By the rich man of whom the Lord says:

---

7. "Garments" signify truths, thus knowledges (n. 1073, 2576, 5319, 5954, 9212, 9216, 9952, 10536). "Purple" signifies celestial good (n. 9467). "Fine linen" signifies truth from a celestial origin (n. 5319, 9469, 9744).

It is easier for a camel to go through a needle's eye than for a rich man
to enter into the kingdom of God (Matt. 19:24);

the rich in both the natural sense and the spiritual sense are
meant. In the natural sense the rich are those that have an
abundance of riches and set their heart upon them; but in the
spiritual sense they are those that have an abundance of
knowledges and learning, which are spiritual riches, and who
desire by means of these to introduce themselves into the things
of heaven and the church from their own intelligence. And
because this is contrary to Divine order it is said to be "easier
for a camel to go through a needle's eye," a "camel" signifying
in general in the spiritual sense the knowing faculty and things
known, and a "needle's eye" signifying spiritual truth.[8] That
such is the meaning of a "camel" and a "needle's eye" is not at
present known, because the knowledge that teaches what is
signified in the spiritual sense by the things said in the literal
sense of the Word has not up to this time been disclosed. In
every particular of the Word there is a spiritual sense and also
a natural sense; for the Word was made to consist wholly of
correspondences between natural and spiritual things in order
that conjunction of heaven with the world, or of angels with
men might thereby be effected, direct conjunction having

8. A "camel" signifies in the Word the knowing faculty and knowledge in general (n.
3048, 3071, 3143, 3145).

What is meant by "needlework, working with a needle," and therefore by a "needle"
(n. 9688). To enter from knowledge into the truths of faith is contrary to Divine order
(n. 10236). Those that do this become demented in respect to the things of heaven and
the church (n. 128–130, 232, 233, 6047). And in the other life, when they think about
spiritual things they become as it were drunken (n. 1072). Further about such (n. 196).

Examples showing that when spiritual things are entered into through knowledges
they cannot be comprehended (n. 233, 2094, 2196, 2203, 2209).

It is permissible to enter from spiritual truth into knowledges which pertain to the
natural man, but not the reverse, because there can be spiritual influx into the natural,
but not natural influx into the spiritual (n. 3219, 5119, 5259, 5427, 5428, 5478, 6322,
9110). The truths of the word and of the church must first be acknowledged, after
which it is permissible to consider knowledges, but not before (n. 6047).

ceased. This makes clear who in particular are meant in the Word by the "rich man."

[4] That the "rich" in the Word mean in the spiritual sense those who are in knowledges of truth and good, and "riches" the knowledges themselves, which are spiritual riches, can be seen from various passages (as in Isa. 10:12–14; 30:6, 7; 45:3; Jer. 17:3; 48:7; 50:36, 37; 51:13; Dan. 5:2–4; Ezek. 26:7, 12; 27:1 to the end; Zech. 9:3, 4; Ps. 45:12; Hos. 12:9; Rev. 3:17, 18; Luke 14:33; and elsewhere). Also that the "poor" in the spiritual sense signify those who do not possess knowledges of good and of truth, and yet desire them (Matt. 11:5; Luke 6:20, 21; 14:21; Isa. 14:30; 29:19; 41:17, 18; Zeph. 3:12, 13). All these passages may be seen explained in accordance with the spiritual sense in *Arcana Coelestia* (n. 10227).

40

Marriages in Heaven

366. As heaven is from the human race, and angels therefore are of both sexes, and from creation woman is for man and man is for woman, thus the one belongs to the other, and this love is innate in both, it follows that there are marriages in heaven as well as on the earth. But marriages in heaven differ widely from marriages on the earth. Therefore what marriages in heaven are, and how they differ from marriages on the earth and wherein they are like them, shall now be told.

367. Marriage in heaven is a conjunction of two into one mind. It must first be explained what this conjunction is. The mind consists of two parts, one called the understanding and the other the will. When these two parts act as one they are called one mind. In heaven the husband acts the part called the understanding and the wife acts the part called the will. When this conjunction, which belongs to man's interiors, descends into the lower parts pertaining to the body, it is perceived and felt as love, and this love is marriage love. This shows that marriage love has its origin in the conjunction of two into one mind. This in heaven is called cohabitation; and the two are not called two but one. So in heaven a married pair is spoken of, not as two, but as one angel.[1]

---

1. It is not known at this day what marriage love is, or whence it is (n. 2727).

Marriage love is willing what another wills, thus willing mutually and reciprocally (n. 2731). Those that are in marriage love dwell together in the inmosts of life (n. 2732).

It is such a union of two minds that from love they are one (n. 10168, 10169).

For the love of minds, which is spiritual love, is a union (n. 1594, 2057, 3939, 4018, 5807, 6195, 7081–7086, 7501, 10130).

368. Moreover, such a conjunction of husband and wife in the inmosts of their minds comes from their very creation; for man is born to be intellectual, that is, to think from the understanding, while woman is born to be affectional, that is, to think from her will; and this is evident from the inclination or natural disposition of each, also from their form; from the disposition, in that man acts from reason and woman from affection; from the form in that man has a rougher and less beautiful face, a deeper voice and a harder body; while woman has a smoother and more beautiful face, a softer voice, and a more tender body. There is a like difference between understanding and will, or between thought and affection; so, too, between truth and good and between faith and love; for truth and faith belong to the understanding, and good and love to the will. From this it is that in the Word "youth" or "man" means in the spiritual sense the understanding of truth, and "virgin" or "woman" affection for good; also that the church, on account of its affection for good and truth, is called a "woman" and a "virgin"; also that all those that are in affection for good are called "virgins" (as in Rev. 14:4).[2]

369. Everyone, whether man or woman, possesses understanding and will; but with the man the understanding predominates, and with the woman the will predominates, and the character is determined by that which predominates. Yet in heavenly marriages there is no predominance; for the will of the wife is

2. In the Word "young men" signify understanding of truth, or the intelligent (n. 7668).

"Men" have the same signification (n. 158, 265, 749, 915, 1007, 2517, 3134, 3236, 4823, 9007). "Woman" signifies affection for good and truth (n. 568, 3160, 6014, 7337, 8994); likewise the church (n. 252, 253, 749, 770); "wife" has the same signification (n. 252, 253, 409, 749, 770); with what difference (n. 915, 2517, 3236, 4510, 4823).

In the highest sense "husband and wife" are predicated of the Lord and of His conjunction with heaven and the church (n. 7022).

A "virgin" signifies affection for good (n. 3067, 3110, 3179, 3189, 6729, 6742); likewise the church (n. 2362, 3081, 3963, 4638, 6729, 6775, 6788).

also the husband's will, and the understanding of the husband is also the wife's understanding, since each loves to will and to think like the other, that is mutually and reciprocally. Thus are they conjoined into one. This conjunction is actual conjunction, for the will of the wife enters into the understanding of the husband, and the understanding of the husband into the will of the wife, and this especially when they look into one another's faces; for, as has been repeatedly said above, there is in the heavens a sharing of thoughts and affections, more especially with husband and wife, because they reciprocally love each other. This makes clear what the conjunction of minds is that makes marriage and produces marriage love in the heavens, namely, that one wishes what is his own to be the other's, and this reciprocally.

370. I have been told by angels that so far as a married pair are so conjoined they are in marriage love, and also to the same extent in intelligence, wisdom and happiness, because Divine truth and Divine good, which are the source of all intelligence, wisdom, and happiness, flow chiefly into marriage love; consequently marriage love, since it is also the marriage of good and truth, is the very plane of Divine influx. For that love, as it is a conjunction of the understanding and will, is also a conjunction of truth and good, since the understanding receives Divine truth and is formed out of truths, and the will receives Divine good and is formed out of goods. For what a man wills is good to him, and what he understands is truth to him; therefore it is the same whether you say conjunction of understanding and will or conjunction of truth and good. Conjunction of truth and good is what makes an angel; it makes his intelligence, wisdom, and happiness; for an angel is an angel accordingly as good in him is conjoined with truth and truth with good; or what is the same, accordingly as love in him is conjoined with faith and faith with love.

371. The Divine that goes forth from the Lord flows chiefly into marriage love because marriage love descends from a conjunction of good and truth; for it is the same thing as has been said above, whether you say conjunction of understanding and will or conjunction of good and truth. Conjunction of good and truth has its origin in the Lord's Divine love toward all who are in heaven and on earth. From Divine love Divine good goes forth, and Divine good is received by angels and men in Divine truths. As truth is the sole receptacle of good nothing can be received from the Lord and from heaven by anyone who is not in truths; therefore just to the extent that the truths in man are conjoined to good is man conjoined to the Lord and to heaven. This, then, is the very origin of marriage love, and for this reason that love is the very plane of Divine influx. This shows why the conjunction of good and truth in heaven is called the heavenly marriage, and heaven is likened in the Word to a marriage, and is called a marriage; and the Lord is called the "bridegroom" and "Husband," and heaven and also the church are called the "bride" and the "wife."[3]

372. Good and truth conjoined in an angel or a man are not two but one, since good is then good of truth and truth is truth of good. This conjunction may be likened to a man's thinking what he wills and willing what he thinks, when the thought

---

3. The origin, cause, and essence of true marriage love is the marriage of good and truth; thus it is from heaven (n. 2728, 2729).

Respecting angelic spirits, who have a perception whether there is anything of marriage from the idea of a conjunction of good and truth (n. 10756).

It is with marriage love in every respect the same as it is with the conjunction of good and truth (n. 1904, 2173, 2429, 2508, 3101, 3102, 3155, 3179, 3180, 4358, 5807, 5835, 9206, 9495, 9637). How and with whom the conjunction of good and truth is effected (n. 3834, 4096, 4097, 4301, 4345, 4353, 4364, 4368, 5365, 7623–7627, 9258).

Only those that are in good and truth from the Lord know what true marriage love is (n. 10171). In the Word "marriage" signifies the marriage of good and truth (n. 3132, 4434, 4835). The kingdom of the Lord and heaven are in true marriage love (n. 2737).

and will make one, that is, one mind; for thought forms, that is, presents in form that which the will wills, and the will gives delight to it; and this is why a married pair in heaven are not called two, but one angel. This also is what is meant by the Lord's words:

> Have ye not read that he who made them from the beginning made them male and female, and said, For this cause shall a man leave father and mother and shall cleave to his wife, and they twain shall become one flesh? Therefore, they are no more twain, but one flesh. What, therefore, God hath joined together let not man put asunder. Not all can receive this word but they to whom it is given (Matt. 19:4–6, 11; Mark 10:6–9; Gen. 2:24).

This is a description both of the heavenly marriage in which the angels are and of the marriage of good and truth, "man's not putting asunder what God has joined together" meaning that good is not to be separated from truth.

373. From all this the origin of true marriage love is made clear, namely, that it is formed first in the minds of those who are in marriage, and descends therefrom and is derived into the body, where it is perceived and felt as love; for whatever is felt and perceived in the body has its origin in the spiritual, because it is from the understanding and the will. The understanding and the will constitute the spiritual man. Whatever descends from the spiritual man into the body presents itself there under another aspect, although it is similar and accordant, like soul and body, and like cause and effect; as can be seen from what has been said and shown in the two chapters on correspondences.

374. I heard an angel describing true marriage love and its heavenly delights in this manner: That it is the Lord's Divine in the heavens, which is Divine good and Divine truth so united

in two persons, that they are not as two but as one. He said that in heaven the two consorts are marriage love, since everyone is his own good and his own truth in respect both to mind and to body, the body being an image of the mind because it is formed after its likeness. From this he drew the conclusion that the Divine is imaged in the two that are in true marriage love; and as the Divine is so imaged so is heaven, because the entire heaven is Divine good and Divine truth going forth from the Lord; and this is why all things of heaven are inscribed on marriage love with more blessings and delights than it is possible to number.

He expressed the number by a term that involved myriads of myriads. He wondered that the man of the church should know nothing about this, seeing that the church is the Lord's heaven on the earth, and heaven is a marriage of good and truth. He said he was astounded to think that within the church, even more than outside of it, adulteries are committed and even justified; the delight of which in itself is nothing else in a spiritual sense, and consequently in the spiritual world, than the delight of the love of falsity conjoined to evil, which delight is infernal delight, because it is the direct opposite of the delight of heaven, which is the delight of the love of truth conjoined with good.

375. Everyone knows that a married pair who love each other are interiorly united, and that the essential of marriage is the union of dispositions and minds. And from this it can be seen that such as their essential dispositions or minds are, such is their union and such their love for each other. The mind is formed solely out of truths and goods, for all things in the universe have relation to good and truth and to their conjunction; consequently such as the truths and goods are out of which the minds are formed, exactly such is the union of minds; and consequently the most perfect union is the union of minds that are formed out of genuine truths and goods. Let it be known that no two things mutually love each other more than truth and good do; and therefore it is from that love that true marriage love descends.[4] Falsity and evil also love each other, but this love is afterwards changed into hell.

376. From what has now been said about the origin of marriage love one may conclude who are in that love and who are not; namely, that those are in marriage love who are in Divine good from Divine truths; and that marriage love is genuine just to the extent that the truths are genuine with which the good is conjoined. And as all the good that is conjoined with truths is from the Lord, it follows that no one can be in true marriage love unless he acknowledges the Lord and his Divine; for without that acknowledgment the Lord cannot flow in and be conjoined with the truths that are in man.

377. Evidently, then, those that are in falsities, and especially those that are in falsities from evil, are not in marriage love. Moreover, those that are in evil and in falsities therefrom have the interiors of their minds closed up; and in such, therefore, there can be no source of marriage love; but below those interiors, in the external or natural man separated from the internal, there can be a conjunction of falsity and evil, which is called infernal marriage. I have been permitted to see what this marriage is between those that are in the falsities of evil,

---

4. All things in the universe, both in heaven and in the world, have relation to good and truth (n. 2452, 3166, 4390, 4409, 5232, 7256, 10122). And to the conjunction of these (n. 10555). Between good and truth there is marriage (n. 1904, 2173, 2508).

Good loves truth, and from love longs for truth and for the conjunction of truth with itself, and from this they are in a perpetual endeavor to be conjoined (n. 9206, 9207, 9495). The life of truth is from good (n. 1589, 1997, 2572, 4070, 4096, 4097, 4736, 4757, 4884, 5147, 9667). Truth is the form of good (n. 3049, 3180, 4574, 9154).

Truth is to good as water is to bread (n. 4976).

which is called infernal marriage. Such converse together, and are united by a lustful desire, but inwardly they burn with a deadly hatred toward each other, too intense to be described.

378. Nor can marriage love exist between two partners belonging to different religions, because the truth of the one does not agree with the good of the other; and two unlike and discordant kinds of good and truth cannot make one mind out of two; and in consequence the love of such does not have its origin in anything spiritual. If they live together in harmony it is solely on natural grounds.[5] And this is why in the heavens marriages are found only with those who are in the same society, because such are in like good and truth and not with those outside of the society. It may be seen above (n. 41 seq.) that all there in a society are in like good and truth, and differ from those outside the society. This was represented in the Israelitish nation by marriages being contracted within tribes, and particularly within families, and not outside of them.

379. Nor is true marriage love possible between one husband and several wives; for its spiritual origin, which is the formation of one mind out of two, is thus destroyed; and in consequence interior conjunction, which is the conjunction of good and truth, from which is the very essence of that love, is also destroyed. Marriage with more than one is like an understanding divided among several wills; or it is like a man attached not to one but to several churches, since his faith is so distracted thereby as to come to naught. The angels declare that marrying several wives is wholly contrary to Divine order, and that they know this from several reasons, one of which is that as soon as they think of marriage with more than one

5. Marriages between those of different religions are not permissible, because there can be no conjunction of like good and truth in the interiors (n. 8998).

they are alienated from internal blessedness and heavenly happiness, and become like drunken men, because good is separated from its truth in them. And as the interiors of their mind are brought into such a state merely by thinking about it with some intention, they see clearly that marriage with more than one would close up their internal mind, and cause marriage to be displaced by lustful love, which love withdraws from heaven.[6]

[2] They declare further that this is not easily comprehended by men because there are few who are in genuine marriage love, and those who are not in it know nothing whatever of the interior delight that is in that love, knowing only the delight of lust, and this delight is changed into what is undelightful after living together a short time; while the delight of true marriage love not only endures to old age in the world, but after death becomes the delight of heaven and is there filled with an interior delight that grows more and more perfect to eternity. They said also that the varieties of blessedness of true marriage love could be enumerated even to many thousands, not even one of which is known to man, or could enter into the comprehension of anyone who is not in the marriage of good and truth from the Lord.

6. As husband and wife should be one, and should live together in the inmost of life, and as they together make one angel in heaven, so true marriage love is impossible between one husband and several wives (n. 1907, 2740).

To marry several wives at the same time is contrary to Divine order (n. 10837).

That there is no marriage except between one husband and one wife is clearly perceived by those who are in the Lord's celestial kingdom (n. 865, 3246, 9002, 10172).

For the reason that the angels there are in the marriage of good and truth (n. 3246).

The Israelitish nation were permitted to marry several wives, and to add concubines to wives, but not Christians, for the reason that that nation was in externals separate from internals, while Christians are able to enter into internals, thus into the marriage of good and truth (n. 3246, 4837, 8809).

380. The love of dominion of one over the other entirely takes away marriage love and its heavenly delight, for as has been said above, marriage love and its delight consists in the will of one being that of the other, and this mutually and reciprocally. This is destroyed by love of dominion in marriage, since he that domineers wishes his will alone to be in the other, and nothing of the other's will to be reciprocally in himself, which destroys all mutuality, and thus all sharing of any love and its delight one with the other. And yet this sharing and consequent conjunction are the interior delight itself that is called blessedness in marriage. This blessedness, with everything that is heavenly and spiritual in marriage love, is so completely extinguished by love of dominion as to destroy even all knowledge of it; and if that love were referred to it would be held in such contempt that any mention of blessedness from that source would excite either laughter or anger.

[2] When one wills or loves what the other wills or loves each has freedom, since all freedom is from love; but where there is dominion no one has freedom; one is a servant, and the other who rules is also a servant, for he is led as a servant by the lust of ruling. But all this is wholly beyond the comprehension of one who does not know what the freedom of heavenly love is. Nevertheless from what has been said above about the origin and essence of marriage love it can be seen that so far as dominion enters, minds are not united but divided. Dominion subjugates, and a subjugated mind has either no will or an opposing will. If it has no will it has also no love; and if it has an opposing will there is hatred in place of love.

[3] The interiors of those who live in such marriage are in mutual collision and strife, as two opposites are wont to be, however their exteriors may be restrained and kept quiet for

the sake of tranquillity. The collision and antagonism of the interiors of such are disclosed after their death, when commonly they come together and fight like enemies and tear each other; for they then act in accordance with the state of the interiors. Frequently I have been permitted to see them fighting and tearing one another, sometimes with great vengeance and cruelty. For in the other life everyone's interiors are set at liberty; and they are no longer restrained by outward bounds or by worldly considerations, everyone then being just such as he is interiorly.

381. To some a likeness of marriage love is granted. Yet unless they are in the love of good and truth there is no marriage love, but only a love which from several causes appears like marriage love, namely, that they may secure good service at home; that they may be free from care, or at peace, or at ease; that they may be cared for in sickness or in old age; or that the children whom they love may be attended to. Some are constrained by fear of the other consort, or by fear of the loss of reputation, or other evil consequences, and some by a controlling lust. Moreover, in the two consorts marriage love may differ; in one there may be more or less of it, in the other little or none; and because of this difference heaven may be the portion of one and hell the portion of the other.

382a. In the inmost heaven there is genuine marriage love because the angels there are in the marriage of good and truth, and also in innocence. The angels of the lower heavens are also in marriage love, but only so far as they are in innocence; for marriage love viewed in itself is a state of innocence; and this is why consorts who are in the marriage love enjoy heavenly delights together, which appear before their minds almost like the sports of innocence, as between little children; for everything delights their minds, since heaven with its joy flows into every particular of their lives. For the same reason marriage love is represented in heaven by the most beautiful objects. I have seen it represented by a maiden of indescribable beauty encompassed with a bright white cloud. It is said that the angels in heaven have all their beauty from marriage love. Affections and thought flowing from that love are represented by diamondlike auras with scintillations as if from carbuncles and rubies, which are attended by delights that affect the interiors of the mind. In a word, heaven itself is represented in marriage love, because heaven with the angels is the conjunction of good and truth, and it is this conjunction that makes marriage love.

382b. Marriages in heaven differ from marriages on the earth in that the procreation of offspring is another purpose of marriages on the earth, but not of marriages in heaven, since in heaven the procreation of good and truth takes the place of procreation of offspring. The former takes the place of the latter because marriage in heaven is a marriage of good and truth (as has been shown above); and as in that marriage good and truth and their conjunction are loved above all things so these are what are propagated by marriages in heaven. And because of this, in the Word births and generations signify spiritual births and generations, which are births and generations of good and truth; mother and father signify truth conjoined to good, which is what procreates; sons and daughters signify the truths and goods that are procreated; and sons-in-law and daughters-in-law conjunction of these, and so on.[7] All this makes clear that marriages in heaven are not like

---

7. Conceptions, pregnancies, births, and generations signify those that are spiritual, that is, such as pertain to good and truth, or to love and faith (n. 613, 1145, 1255, 2020, 2584, 3860, 3868, 4070, 4668, 6239, 8042, 9325, 10249). Therefore generation and birth signify regeneration and rebirth through faith and love (n. 5160, 5598, 9042, 9845). Mother signifies the church in respect to truth, and thus the truth of the church; father the church in respect to good, and thus the good of the church (n. 2691, 2717, 3703, 5581, 8897). Sons signify affections for truth, and thus truths (n. 489, 491, 533, 2623, 3373, 4257, 8649, 9807). Daughters signify affections for good, and

marriages on earth. In heaven marryings are spiritual, and cannot properly be called marryings, but conjunctions of minds from the conjunction of good and truth. But on earth there are marryings, because these are not of the spirit alone but also of the flesh. And as there are no marryings in heaven, consorts there are not called husband and wife; but from the angelic idea of the joining of two minds into one, each consort designates the other by a name signifying one's own, mutually and reciprocally. This shows how the Lord's words in regard to marrying and giving in marriage (Luke 20:35, 36), are to be understood.

383. I have also been permitted to see how marriages are contracted in the heavens. As everywhere in heaven those who are alike are united and those who are unlike are separated, so every society in heaven consists of those who are alike. Like are brought to like not by themselves but by the Lord (see above, n. 41, 43, 44 seq.); and equally consort to consort whose minds can be joined into one are drawn together; and consequently at first sight they inmostly love each other, and see themselves to be consorts, and enter into marriage. For this reason all marriages in heaven are from the Lord alone. They have also marriage feasts; and these are attended by many; but the festivities differ in different societies.

384. Marriages on the earth are most holy in the sight of the angels of heaven because they are seminaries of the human race, and also of the angels of heaven (heaven being from the human race, as already shown under that head), also because these marriages are from a spiritual origin, namely, from the marriage

---

thus goods (n. 489–491, 2362, 3963, 6729, 6775, 6778, 9055). Son-in-law signifies truth associated with affection for good (n. 2389). Daughter-in-law signifies good associated with its truth (n. 4843).

of good and truth, and because the Lord's Divine flows especially into marriage love. Adulteries on the other hand are regarded by the angels as profane because they are contrary to marriage love; for as in marriages the angels behold the marriage of good and truth, which is heaven, so in adulteries they behold the marriage of falsity and evil, which is hell. If, then, they but hear adulteries mentioned they turn away. And this is why heaven is closed up to man when he commits adultery from delight; and when heaven is closed man no longer acknowledges the Divine nor anything of the faith of church.[8] That all who are in hell are antagonistic to marriage love I have been permitted to perceive from the sphere exhaling from hell, which was like an unceasing endeavor to dissolve and violate marriages; which shows that the reigning delight in hell is the delight of adultery, and the delight of adultery is a delight in destroying the conjunction of good and truth, which conjunction makes heaven. From this it follows that the delight of adultery is an infernal delight directly opposed to the delight of marriage, which is a heavenly delight.

385. There were certain spirits who, from a practice acquired in the life of the body, infested me with peculiar craftiness, and this by a very gentle wavelike influx like the usual influx of well disposed spirits; but I perceived that there was craftiness and other like evils in them prompting them to ensnare and deceive. Finally, I talked with one of them who, I was told, had been when he lived in the world the leader of an army; and perceiving that there was a lustfulness in the ideas of his

---

8. Adulteries are profane (n. 9961, 10174). Heaven is closed to adulterers (n. 2750).

Those that have experienced delight in adulteries cannot come into heaven (n. 539, 2733, 2747–2749, 2751, 10175). Adulterers are unmerciful and destitute of religion (n. 824, 2747, 2748). The ideas of adulterers are filthy (n. 2747, 2748).

In the other life they love filth and are in filthy hells (n. 2755, 5394, 5722).

In the Word adulteries signify adulterations of good, and whoredoms perversions of truth (n. 2466, 2729, 3399, 4865, 8904, 10648).

thought I talked with him about marriage, using spiritual speech with representatives, which fully expresses all that is meant and many things in a moment. He said that in the life of the body he had regarded adulteries as of no account. But I was permitted to tell him that adulteries are heinous, although to those like himself they do not appear to be such, and even appear permissible, on account of their seductive and enticing delights. That they are heinous he might know from the fact that marriages are the seminaries of the human race, and thus also the seminaries of the heavenly kingdom; consequently they must on no account be violated, but must be esteemed holy. This he might know from the fact, which he ought to know because of his being in the other life and in a state of perception, that marriage love descends from the Lord through heaven, and from that love, as from a parent, mutual love, which is the foundation of heaven, is derived; and again from this, that if adulterers merely draw near to heavenly societies they perceive their own stench and cast themselves down therefrom toward hell. At least he must have known that to violate marriages is contrary to Divine laws, and contrary to the civil laws of all kingdoms, also contrary to the genuine light of reason, because it is contrary to both Divine and human order; not to mention other considerations. But he replied that he had not so thought in the life of the body. He wished to reason about whether it were so, but was told that truth does not admit of such reasonings; for reasonings defend what one delights in, and thus one's evils and falsities; that he ought first to think about the things that had been said because they are truths; or at least think about them from the principle well known in the world, that no one should do to another what he is unwilling that another should do to him; thus he should consider whether he himself would not have detested adulteries if anyone had in that way deceived his wife, whom he had loved as everyone loves in the first period of marriage, and if in his state of wrath he had expressed himself on the subject; also whether being a man of talent he would not in that case have confirmed himself more decidedly than others against adulteries, even condemning them to hell.

386. I have been shown how the delights of marriage love advance toward heaven, and the delights of adultery toward hell. The advance of the delights of marriage love toward heaven is into states of blessedness and happiness continually increasing until they become innumerable and ineffable, and the more interiorly they advance the more innumerable and more ineffable they become, until they reach the very states of blessedness and happiness of the inmost heaven, or of the heaven of innocence, and this through the most perfect freedom; for all freedom is from love, thus the most perfect freedom is from marriage love, which is heavenly love itself. On the other hand, the advance of adultery is toward hell, and by degrees to the lowest hell, where there is nothing but what is direful and horrible. Such a lot awaits adulterers after their life in the world, those being meant by adulterers who feel a delight in adulteries, and no delight in marriages.

41

The Occupations of Angels
in Heaven

387. It is impossible to enumerate the occupations in the heavens, still less to describe them in detail, but something may be said about them in a general way; for they are numberless, and vary in accordance with the functions of the societies. Each society has its peculiar function, for as societies are distinct in accordance with goods (see above, n. 41), so they are distinct in accordance with uses, because with all in the heavens goods are goods in act, which are uses. Everyone there performs a use, for the Lord's kingdom is a kingdom of uses.[1]

388. In the heavens as on the earth there are many forms of service, for there are ecclesiastical affairs, there are civil affairs, and there are domestic affairs. That there are ecclesiastical affairs is evident from what has been said and shown above, where Divine worship is treated of (n. 221–227); civil affairs, where governments in heaven are treated of (n. 213–220); and domestic affairs, where the dwellings and homes of angels are treated of (n. 183–190); and marriages in heaven (n. 366–368); all of which show that in every heavenly society there are many occupations and services.

---

1. The Lord's kingdom is a kingdom of uses (n. 454, 696, 1103, 3645, 4054, 7038). Performing uses is serving the Lord (n. 7038). In the other life all must perform uses (n. 1103); even the wicked and infernal, but in what manner (n. 696). All are such as are the uses they perform (n. 4054, 6815); illustrated (n. 7038). Angelic blessedness consists in the goods of charity, that is, in performing uses (n. 454).

389. All things in the heavens are organized in accordance with Divine order, which is everywhere guarded by the services performed by angels, those things that pertain to the general good or use by the wiser angels, those that pertain to particular uses by the less wise, and so on. They are subordinated just as uses are subordinated in the Divine order; and for this reason a dignity is connected with every function according to the dignity of the use. Nevertheless, an angel does not claim dignity to himself, but ascribes all dignity to the use; and as the use is the good that he accomplishes, and all good is from the Lord, so he ascribes all dignity to the Lord. Therefore he that thinks of honor for himself and subsequently for the use, and not for the use and subsequently for himself, can perform no function in heaven, because this is looking away backwards from the Lord, and putting self in the first place and use in the second. When use is spoken of the Lord also is meant, because, as has just been said, use is good, and good is from the Lord.

390. From this it may be inferred what subordinations in the heavens are, namely, that as anyone loves, esteems, and honors the use he also loves, esteems, and honors the person with whom the use is connected; also that the person is loved, esteemed and honored in the measure in which he ascribes the use to the Lord and not to himself; for to that extent he is wise, and the uses he performs he performs from good. Spiritual love, esteem, and honor are nothing else than the love, esteem, and honor of the use in the person, together with the honor to the person because of the use, and not honor to the use because of the person. This is the way, moreover, in which men are regarded when they are regarded from spiritual truth, for one man is then seen to be like another, whether he be in great or in little dignity, the only perceptible difference being a difference in wisdom; and wisdom is loving use, that is, loving the good of a fellow citizen, of society, of one's country, and of the church. It is this that constitutes love to the Lord, because every good that is a good of use is from the Lord; and it constitutes also love toward the neighbor, because the neighbor means the good that is to be loved in a fellow citizen, in society, in one's country, and in the church, and that is to be done in their behalf.[2]

391. As all the societies in the heavens are distinct in accordance with their goods (as said above, n. 41 seq.) so they are distinct in accordance with their uses, goods being goods in act, that is, goods of charity which are uses. Some societies are employed in taking care of little children; others in teaching and training them as they grow up; others in teaching and training in like manner the boys and girls that have acquired a good disposition from their education in the world, and in consequence have come into heaven. There are other societies that teach the simple good from the Christian world, and lead them into the way to heaven; there are others that in like manner teach and lead the various heathen nations.

There are some societies that defend from infestations by evil spirits the newly arrived spirits that have just come from the world; there are some that attend upon the spirits that are in the lower earth; also some that attend upon spirits that are in the hells, and restrain them from tormenting each other beyond prescribed limits; and there are some that attend upon those

2. Loving the neighbor is not loving the person, but loving that which is in him and which constitutes him (n. 5025, 10336).

Those who love the person, and not that which is in him, and which constitutes him, love equally an evil man and a good man (n. 3820); and do good alike to the evil and to the good; and yet to do good to the evil is to do evil to the good and that is not loving the neighbor (n. 3820, 6703, 8120).

The judge who punishes the evil that they may be reformed, and may not contaminate or injure the good, loves his neighbor (n. 3820, 8120, 8121). Every individual and every community, also one's country and the church, and in the most general sense the kingdom of the Lord, are the neighbor, and to do good to these from a love of good in accord with the quality of their state, is loving the neighbor; that is, the neighbor is their good, which is to be consulted (n. 6818–6824, 8123).

who are being raised from the dead. In general, angels from each society are sent to men to watch over them and to lead them away from evil affections and consequent thoughts, and to inspire them with good affections so far as they will receive them in freedom; and by means of these they also direct the deeds or works of men by removing as far as possible evil intentions.

When angels are with men they dwell as it were in their affections; and they are near to man just in the degree in which he is in good from truths, and are distant from him just in the degree in which his life is distant from good.[3] But all these occupations of angels are occupations of the Lord through the angels, for the angels perform them from the Lord and not from themselves. For this reason, in the Word in its internal sense "angels" mean, not angels, but something belonging to the Lord; and for the same reason angels are called "gods" in the Word.[4]

392. These occupations of the angels are their general occupations; but each one has his particular charge; for every general use is composed of innumerable uses which are called mediate, ministering, and subservient uses, all and each co-ordinated and subordinated in accordance with Divine order,

---

3. Of the angels that are with little children and afterwards with boys, and thus in succession (n. 2303). Man is raised from the dead by means of angels; from experience (n. 168–189). Angels are sent to those who are in hell to prevent their tormenting each other beyond measure (n. 967). Of the services rendered by the angels to men on their coming into the other life (n. 2131).

There are spirits and angels with all men and man is led by the Lord by means of spirits and angels (n. 50, 697, 2796, 2887, 2888, 5846–5866, 5976–5993, 6209).

Angels have dominion over evil spirits (n. 1755).

4. In the Word by angels something Divine from the Lord is signified (n. 1925, 2821, 3039, 4085, 6280, 8192).

In the Word angels are called "gods," because of their reception of Divine truth and good from the Lord (n. 4295, 4402, 8192, 8301).

and taken together constituting and perfecting the general use, which is the general good.

393. Those are concerned with ecclesiastical affairs in heaven who in the world loved the Word and eagerly sought in it for truths, not with honor or gain as an end, but uses of life both for themselves and for others. These in heaven are in enlightenment and in the light of wisdom in the measure of their love and desire for use; and this light of wisdom they receive from the Word in heaven, which is not a natural Word, as it is in the world, but a spiritual Word (see above, n. 259). These minister in the preaching office; and in accordance with Divine order those are in higher positions who from enlightenment excel others in wisdom.

[2] Those are concerned with civil affairs who in the world loved their country, and loved its general good more than their own, and did what is just and right from a love for what is just and right. So far as these from the eagerness of love have investigated the laws of justice and have thereby become intelligent, they have the ability to perform such functions in heaven, and they perform these in that position or degree that accords with their intelligence, their intelligence being in equal degree with their love of use for the general good.

[3] Furthermore, there are in heaven more functions and services and occupations than can be enumerated; while in the world there are few in comparison. But however many there may be that are so employed, they are all in the delight of their work and labor from a love of use, and no one from a love of self or of gain; and as all the necessaries of life are furnished them gratuitously they have no love of gain for the sake of a living. They are housed gratuitously, clothed gratuitously, and fed gratuitously. Evidently, then, those that have loved themselves and the world more than use have no lot in heaven; for his love or affection remains with everyone after his life in the world, and is not extirpated to eternity (see above, n. 563).

394. In heaven everyone comes into his own occupation in accordance with correspondence, and the correspondence is not with the occupation but with the use of each occupation (see above, n. 112); for there is a correspondence of all things (see n. 106). He that in heaven comes into the employment or occupation corresponding to his use is in much the same condition of life as when he was in the world; since what is spiritual and what is natural make one by correspondences; yet there is this difference, that he then comes into an interior delight, because into spiritual life, which is an interior life, and therefore more receptive of heavenly blessedness.

42

Heavenly Joy and Happiness

395. Hardly anyone at present knows what heaven is or what heavenly joy is. Those who have given any thought to these subjects have had so general and so gross an idea about them as scarcely to amount to anything. From spirits that have come from the world into the other life I have been able to learn fully what idea they had of heaven and heavenly joy; for when left to themselves, as they were in the world, they think as they then did. There is this ignorance about heavenly joy for the reason that those who have thought about it have formed their opinion from the outward joys pertaining to the natural man, and have not known what the inner and spiritual man is, nor in consequence the nature of his delight and blessedness; and therefore even if they had been told by those who are in spiritual or inward delight what heavenly joy is, would have had no comprehension of it, for it could have fallen only into an idea not yet recognized, thus into no perception; and would therefore have been among the things that the natural man rejects. Yet everyone can understand that when a man leaves his outer or natural man he comes into the inner or spiritual man, and consequently can see that heavenly delight is internal and spiritual, not external and natural; and being internal and spiritual, it is more pure and exquisite, and affects the interiors of man which pertain to his soul or spirit. From these things alone everyone may conclude that his delight is such as the delight of his spirit has previously been and that the delight of the body, which is called the delight of the flesh, is in comparison not heavenly; also that whatever is in the spirit of man when he leaves the body remains after death, since he then lives as a man-spirit.

396. All delights flow forth from love, for that which a man loves he feels to be delightful. No one has any delight from any other source. From this it follows that such as the love is such is the delight. The delights of the body or of the flesh all flow forth from the love of self and love of the world; consequently they are lusts and their pleasures; while the delights of the soul or spirit all flow forth from love to the Lord and love toward the neighbor, consequently they are affections for good and truth and interior satisfactions. These loves with their delights flow in out of heaven from the Lord by an inner way, that is, from above, and affect the interiors; while the former loves with their delights flow in from the flesh and from the world by an external way, that is, from beneath, and affect the exteriors. Therefore as far as the two loves of heaven are received and make themselves felt, the interiors of man, which belong to his soul or spirit and which look from the world heavenwards, are opened, while so far as the two loves of the world are received and make themselves felt, his exteriors, which belong to the body or flesh and look away from heaven toward the world, are opened. As loves flow in and are received their delights also flow in, the delights of heaven into the interiors and the delights of the world into the exteriors, since all delight, as has just been said above, belongs to love.

397. Heaven in itself is so full of delights that viewed in itself it is nothing else than blessedness and delight; for the Divine good that flows forth from the Lord's Divine love is what makes heaven in general and in particular with everyone there, and the Divine love is a longing for the salvation of all and the happiness of all from inmosts and in fullness. Thus whether you say heaven or heavenly joy it is the same thing.

398. The delights of heaven are both ineffable and innumerable; but he that is in the mere delight of the body or of the flesh can have no knowledge of or belief in a single one of these innumerable delights; for his interiors, as has just been said, look away from heaven toward the world, thus backwards. For he that is wholly in the delight of the body or of the flesh, or what is the same, in the love of self and of the world, has no sense of delight except in honor, in gain, and in the pleasures of the body and the senses; and these so extinguish and suffocate the interior delights that belong to heaven as to destroy all belief in them; consequently he would be greatly astonished if he were told that when the delights of honor and of gain are set aside other delights are given, and still more if he were told that the delights of heaven that take the place of these are innumerable, and are such as cannot be compared with the delights of the body and the flesh, which are chiefly the delights of honor and of gain. All this makes clear why it is not known what heavenly joy is.

399. One can see how great the delight of heaven must be from the fact that it is the delight of everyone in heaven to share his delights and blessings with others; and as such is the character of all that are in the heavens it is clear how immeasurable is the delight of heaven. It has been shown above (n. 268), that in the heavens there is a sharing of all with each and of each with all. Such sharing goes forth from the two loves of heaven, which are, as has been said, love to the Lord and love toward the neighbor; and to share their delights is the very nature of these loves. Love to the Lord is such because the Lord's love is a love of sharing everything it has with all, since it wills the happiness of all. There is a like love in every one of those who love the Lord, because the Lord is in them; and from this comes the mutual sharing of the delights of angels with one another. Love toward the neighbor is of such a nature, as will be seen in what follows. All this shows that it is the nature of these loves to share their delights. It is otherwise with the loves of self and of the world. The love of self takes away from others and robs others of all delight, and directs it to itself, for it wishes well to itself alone; while the love of the world wishes to have as its own what belongs to the neighbor. Therefore these loves are destructive of the delights of others; or if there is any disposition to share, it is for the sake of themselves and not for the sake of others. Thus in respect to others it is the nature of those loves not to share but to take away, except so far as the delights of others have some relation to self. That the loves of self and of the world, when they rule, are such I have often been permitted to perceive by living experience. Whenever the spirits that were in these loves during their life as men in the world drew near, my delight receded and vanished; and I was told that at the mere approach of such to any heavenly society the delight of those in the society diminished just in the degree of their proximity; and what is wonderful, the evil spirits are then in their delight. All this indicates the state of the spirit of such a man while he is in the body, since it is the same as it is after it is separated from the body, namely, that it longs for or lusts after the delights or goods of another, and finds delight so far as it secures them. All this makes clear that the loves of self and of the world tend to destroy the joys of heaven, and are thus direct opposites of heavenly loves, which desire to share.

400. But it must be understood that the delight of those who are in the loves of self and of the world, when they draw near to any heavenly society, is the delight of their lust, and thus is directly opposite to the delight of heaven. And such enter into this delight of their lust in consequence of their taking away and dispelling heavenly delight in those that are in such delight. When the heavenly delight is not taken away or dispelled it is different, for they are then unable to draw near; for so far as they draw near they bring upon themselves anguish and pain; and for this reason they do not often venture to come near.

This also I have been permitted to learn by repeated experience, something of which I would like to add.

[2] Spirits who go from this world into the other life desire more than anything else to get into heaven. Nearly all seek to enter, supposing that heaven consists solely in being admitted and received. Because of this desire they are brought to some society of the lowest heaven. But as soon as those who are in the love of self and of the world draw near the first threshold of that heaven they begin to be distressed and so tortured inwardly as to feel hell rather than heaven to be in them; and in consequence they cast themselves down headlong therefrom, and do not rest until they come into the hells among their like.

[3] It has also frequently occurred that such spirits have wished to know what heavenly joy is, and having heard that it is in the interiors of angels, they have wished to share in it. This therefore was granted; for whatever a spirit who is not yet in heaven or hell wishes is granted if it will benefit him. But as soon as that joy was communicated they began to be so tortured as not to know how to twist or turn because of the pain. I saw them thrust their heads down to their feet and cast themselves upon the ground, and there writhe into coils like serpents, and this in consequence of their interior agony. Such was the effect produced by heavenly delight upon those who are in the delights of the love of self and of the world; and for the reason that these loves are directly opposite to heavenly loves, and when opposite acts against opposite such pain results. And since heavenly delight enters by an inward way and flows into the contrary delight, the interiors which are in the contrary delight are twisted backwards, thus into the opposite direction, and the result is such tortures.

[4] They are opposite for the reason given above, that love to the Lord and love to the neighbor wish to share with others all that is their own, for this is their delight, while the loves of self and of the world wish to take away from others what they

have, and take it to themselves; and just to the extent that they are able to do this they are in their delight. From this, too, one can see what it is that separates hell from heaven; for all that are in hell were, while they were living in the world, in the mere delights of the body and of the flesh from the love of self and of the world; while all that are in the heavens were, while they lived in the world, in the delights of the soul and spirit from love to the Lord and love to the neighbor; and as these are opposite loves, so the hells and the heavens are entirely separated, and indeed so separated that a spirit in hell does not venture even to put forth a finger from it or raise the crown of his head, for if he does this in the least he is racked with pain and tormented. This, too, I have frequently seen.

401. One who is in the love of self and love of the world perceives while he lives in the body a sense of delight from these loves and also in the particular pleasures derived from these loves. But one who is in love to God and in love toward the neighbor does not perceive while he lives in the body any distinct sense of delight from these loves or from the good affections derived from them, but only a blessedness that is hardly perceptible, because it is hidden away in his interiors and veiled by the exteriors pertaining to the body and dulled by the cares of the world. But after death these states are entirely changed. The delights of love of self and of the world are then turned into what is painful and direful, because into such things as are called infernal fire, and by turns into things defiled and filthy corresponding to their unclean pleasures, and these, wonderful to tell, are then delightful to them. But the obscure delight and almost imperceptible blessedness of those that had been while in the world in love to God and in love to the neighbor are then turned into the delight of heaven, and become in every way perceived and felt, for the blessedness that lay hidden and unrecognized in their interiors while they lived in the world is then revealed and brought forth into evident sensation, because such had been the delight of their spirit, and they are then in the spirit.

402. In uses all the delights of heaven are brought together and are present, because uses are the goods of love and charity in which angels are; therefore everyone has delights that are in accord with his uses, and in the degree of his affection for use. That all the delights of heaven are delights of use can be seen by a comparison with the five bodily senses of man. There is given to each sense a delight in accordance with its use; to the sight, the hearing, the smell, the taste, and the touch, each its own delight; to the sight a delight from beauty and from forms, to the hearing from harmonious sounds, to the smell from pleasing odors, to taste from fine flavors. These uses which the senses severally perform are known to those who study them, and more fully to those who are acquainted with correspondences. Sight has such a delight because of the use it performs to the understanding, which is the inner sight; the hearing has such a delight because of the use it performs both to the understanding and to the will through giving attention; the smell has such a delight because of the use it performs to the brain, and also to the lungs; the taste has such a delight because of the use it performs to the stomach, and thus to the whole body by nourishing it. The delight of marriage, which is a purer and more exquisite delight of touch, transcends all the rest because of its use, which is the procreation of the human race and thereby of angels of heaven. These delights are in these sensories by an influx of heaven, where every delight pertains to use and is in accordance with use.

403. There were some spirits who believed from an opinion adopted in the world that heavenly happiness consists in an idle life in which they would be served by others; but they were told that happiness never consists in abstaining from work and getting satisfaction therefrom. This would mean everyone's desiring the happiness of others for himself, and what everyone

wished for no one would have. Such a life would be an idle not an active life, and would stupefy all the powers of life; and everyone ought to know that without activity of life there can be no happiness of life, and that rest from this activity should be only for the sake of recreation, that one may return with more vigor to the activity of his life. They were then shown by many evidences that angelic life consists in performing the good works of charity, which are uses, and that the angels find all their happiness in use, from use, and in accordance with use. To those that held the opinion that heavenly joy consists in living an idle life and drawing breaths of eternal joy in idleness, a perception was given of what such a life is, that they might become ashamed of the idea; and they saw that such a life is extremely sad, and that all joy thus perishing they would in a little while feel only loathing and disgust for it.

404. There were some spirits who thought themselves better instructed than others, and who said that they had believed in the world that heavenly joy would consist solely in praising and giving glory to God, and that this would be an active life. But these were told that praising and giving glory to God is not a proper active life, also that God has no need of praises and glorification, but it is his will that they should perform uses, and thus the good works that are called goods of charity. But they were unable to associate with goods of charity any idea of heavenly joy, but only of servitude, although the angels testified that this joy is most free because it comes from an interior affection and is conjoined with ineffable delight.

405. Almost all who enter the other life think that hell is the same to everyone, and heaven the same; and yet in both there are infinite varieties and diversities, and in no case is hell or heaven wholly the same to one as to another; as it is impossible that any one man, spirit, or angel should ever be wholly like another even as to the face. At my mere thought of two being just alike or equal the angels expressed horror, saying that every

one thing is formed out of the harmonious concurrence of many things, and that the one thing is such as that concurrence is; and that it is thus that a whole society in heaven becomes a one, and that all the societies of heaven together become a one, and this from the Lord alone by means of love.[1] Uses in the heavens are likewise in all variety and diversity, and in no case is the use of one wholly the same as and identical with the use of another; so neither is the happiness of one the same as and identical with the happiness of another. Furthermore, the delights of each use are innumerable, and these innumerable delights are likewise various, and yet conjoined in such order that they mutually regard each other, like the uses of each member, organ, and viscus, in the body, and still more like the uses of each vessel and fiber in each member, organ and viscus; each and all of which are so affiliated as to have regard to another's good in their own good, and thus each in all, and all in each. From this universal and individual aspect they act as one.

406. I have talked at times with spirits that had recently come from the world about the state of eternal life, saying that it is important to know who the Lord of the kingdom is, and what kind and what form of government it has. As nothing is more important for those entering another kingdom in the world than to know who and what the king is, and what the government is, and other particulars in regard to the kingdom, so is it of still greater consequence in regard to this kingdom in which they are to live to eternity. Therefore they should know

1. One thing consists of various things, and receives thereby its form and quality and perfection in accordance with the quality of the harmony and concurrence (n. 457, 3241, 8003). There is an infinite variety and never any one thing the same as another (n. 7236, 9002). It is the same in the heavens (n. 3744, 4005, 7236, 7833, 7836, 9002).

In consequence all the societies in the heavens and all the angels in a society are distinct from each other because they are in different goods and uses (n. 690, 3241, 3519, 3804, 3986, 4067, 4149, 4263, 7236, 7833).

The Lord's Divine love arranges all into a heavenly form, and so conjoins them that they are as a single man (n. 457, 3986, 5598).

that it is the Lord who governs both heaven and the universe, for he who governs the one governs the other; thus that the kingdom in which they now are is the Lord's; and that the laws of this kingdom are eternal truths, all of which rest upon the law that the Lord must be loved above all things and the neighbor as themselves; and even more than this, if they would be like the angels they must love the neighbor more than themselves. On hearing this they could make no reply, for the reason that although they had heard in the life of the body something like this they had not believed it, wondering how there could be such love in heaven, and how it could be possible for anyone to love his neighbor more than himself. But they were told that every good increases immeasurably in the other life, and that while they cannot go further in the life of the body than to love the neighbor as themselves, because they are immersed in what concerns the body, yet when this is set aside their love becomes more pure, and finally becomes angelic, which is to love the neighbor more than themselves. For in the heavens there is joy in doing good to another, but no joy in doing good to self unless with a view to its becoming another's, and thus for another's sake. This is loving the neighbor more than oneself. They were told that the possibility of such a love is shown in the world in the marriage love of some who have suffered death to protect a consort from injury, in the love of parents for their children, as in a mother's preferring to go hungry rather than see her child go hungry; in sincere friendship, in which one friend will expose himself to danger for another; and even in polite and pretended friendship that wishes to emulate sincere friendship, in offering the better things to those to whom it professes to wish well, and bearing such good will on the lips though not in the heart; finally, in the nature of love, which is such that its joy is to serve others, not for its own sake but for theirs. But all this was incomprehensible to those who loved themselves more than others, and in the life of the body had been greedy of gain; most of all to the avaricious.

407. There was one who in the life of the body had exercised power over others, and who had retained in the other life the desire to rule; but he was told that he was now in another kingdom, which is eternal, and that his rule on earth had perished, and that he was now where no one is esteemed except in accordance with his goodness and truth, and that measure of the Lord's mercy which he enjoyed by virtue of his life in the world; also that the same is true in this kingdom as on the earth, where men are esteemed for their wealth and for their favor with the prince, wealth here being good and truth, and favor with the prince the mercy bestowed on man by the Lord in accordance with his life in the world. Any wish to rule otherwise would make him a rebel, since he is in another's kingdom. On hearing these things he was ashamed.

408. I have talked with spirits who believed heaven and heavenly joy to consist in their being great; but such were told that in heaven he that is least is greatest, since he is called least who has, and wishes to have, no power or wisdom from himself, but only from the Lord, he that is least in that sense having the greatest happiness, and as he has the greatest happiness, it follows that he is greatest; for he has thereby from the Lord all power and excels all in wisdom. What is it to be the greatest unless to be the most happy? For to be the most happy is what the powerful seek through power and the rich through riches. It was further said that heaven does not consist in a desire to be least for the purpose of being greatest, for that would be aspiring and longing to be the greatest; but it consists in desiring from the heart the good of others more than one's own, and in serving others with a view to their happiness, not with recompense as an end, but from love.

409. Heavenly joy itself, such as it is in its essence, cannot be described, because it is in the inmost of the life of angels and therefrom in everything of their thought and affection, and from this in every particular of their speech and action. It is as if the interiors were fully opened and unloosed to receive delight and blessedness, which are distributed to every least fiber and thus through the whole. Thus the perception and sensation of this joy is so great as to be beyond description, for that which starts from the inmosts flows into every particular derived from the inmosts, propagating itself away with increase toward the exteriors. Good spirits who are not yet in that joy, because not yet raised up into heaven, when they perceive a sense of that joy from an angel from the sphere of his love, are filled with such delight that they come as it were into a delicious trance. This sometimes happens with those who desire to know what heavenly joy is.

410. When certain spirits wished to know what heavenly joy is they were allowed to feel it to such a degree that they could no longer bear it; and yet it was not angelic joy; it was scarcely in the least degree angelic, as I was permitted to perceive by sharing it, but was so slight as to be almost frigid; nevertheless they called it most heavenly, because to them it was an inmost joy. From this it was evident, not only that there are degrees of the joys of heaven, but also that the inmost joy of one scarcely reaches to the outmost or middle joy of another; also that when anyone receives his own inmost joy he is in his heavenly joy, and cannot endure what is still more interior, for such a joy becomes painful to him.

411. Certain spirits, not evil, sinking into a quiescence like sleep, were taken up into heaven in respect to the interiors of their minds; for before their interiors are opened spirits can be taken up into heaven and be taught about the happiness of those there. I saw them in the quiescent state for about half an hour, and afterwards they relapsed into their exteriors in which they were before, and also into a recollection of what they had seen. They said that they had been among the angels in heaven, and had there seen and perceived amazing things, all of which were resplendent as if made of gold, silver, and precious stones,

in exquisite forms and in wonderful variety; also that angels are not delighted with the outward things themselves, but with the things they represented, which were Divine, ineffable, and of infinite wisdom, and that these were their joy; with innumerable other things that could not be described in human language even as to a ten-thousandth part, or fall into ideas which partake of anything material.

412. Scarcely any who enter the other life know what heavenly blessedness and happiness are, because they do not know what internal joy is, deriving their perception of it solely from bodily and worldly gladness and joy; and in consequence what they are ignorant of they suppose to be nothing, when in fact bodily and worldly joys are of no account in comparison. In order, therefore, that the well disposed, who do not know what heavenly joy is, may know and realize what it is, they are taken first to paradisaical scenes that transcend every conception of the imagination. They then think that they have come into the heavenly paradise; but they are taught that this is not true heavenly happiness; and they are permitted to realize such interior states of joy as are perceptible to their inmost. They are then brought into a state of peace even to their inmost, when they confess that nothing of it is in the least expressible or conceivable. Finally they are brought into a state of innocence even to their inmost sense. Thus they are permitted to learn what true spiritual and heavenly good is.

413. But that I might learn the nature of heaven and heavenly joy I have frequently and for a long time been permitted by the Lord to perceive the delights of heavenly joys; but while I have been enabled to know by living experience what they are I am not at all able to describe them. Nevertheless, that some idea of them may be formed, something shall be said about them. Heavenly joy is an affection of innumerable delights and joys, which together present something general, and in this general, that is, this general affection, are harmonies of innumerable affections

that come to perception obscurely, and not distinctly, because the perception is most general. Nevertheless I was permitted to perceive that there are innumerable things in it, in such order as cannot be at all described, those innumerable things being such as flow from the order of heaven. The order in the particulars of the affection even to the least, is such that these particulars are presented and perceived only as a most general whole, in accordance with the capacity of him who is the subject. In a word, each general affection contains infinite affections arranged in a most orderly form, with nothing therein that is not alive, and that does not affect all of them from the inmosts; for heavenly joys go forth from inmosts. I perceived also that the joy and ecstasy came as from the heart, diffusing most softly through all the inmost fibers, and from these into the bundles of fibers, with such an inmost sense of delight that the fiber seemed to be nothing but joy and ecstasy, and everything perceptive and sensitive therefrom seemed in like manner to be alive with happiness. Compared with these joys the joy of bodily pleasures is like a gross and pungent dust compared with a pure and most gentle aura. I have noticed that when I wished to transfer all my delight to another, a more interior and fuller delight continually flowed in in its place, and the more I wished this, the more flowed in; and this was perceived to be from the Lord.

414. Those that are in heaven are continually advancing toward the spring of life, with a greater advance toward a more joyful and happy spring the more thousands of years they live; and this to eternity, with increase according to the growth and degree of their love, charity, and faith. Women who have died old and worn out with age, if they have lived in faith in the Lord, in charity to the neighbor, and in happy marriage love with a husband, advance with the succession of years more and more into the flower of youth and early womanhood, and into a beauty that transcends every conception of any such beauty

as is seen on the earth. Goodness and charity are what give this form and thus manifest their own likeness, causing the joy and beauty of charity to shine forth from every least particular of the face, and causing them to be the very forms of charity. Some who beheld this were struck with amazement. The form of charity that is seen in a living way in heaven, is such that it is charity itself that both forms and is formed; and this in such a manner that the whole angel is a charity, as it were, especially the face; and this is both clearly seen and felt. When this form is beheld it is beauty unspeakable, affecting with charity the very inmost life of the mind. In a word, to grow old in heaven is to grow young. Such forms or such beauties do those become in the other life who have lived in love to the Lord and in charity toward the neighbor. All angels are such forms in endless variety; and of these heaven is constituted.

43

The Immensity of Heaven

415. The immensity of the heaven of the Lord is evident from many things that have been said and shown in the foregoing chapters, especially from this, that heaven is from the human race (n. 311–317), both from those born within the church and from those born out of it (n. 318–328); thus it consists of all from the beginning of this earth that have lived a good life. How great a multitude of men there is in this entire world anyone who knows anything about the divisions, the regions, and kingdoms of the earth may conclude. Whoever goes into a calculation will find that several thousands of men die every day, that is, some myriads of millions every year; and this from the earliest times, since which several thousands of years have elapsed. All of these after death have gone into the other world, which is called the spiritual world, and they are constantly going into it. But how many of these have become or are becoming angels of heaven cannot be told. This I have been told, that in ancient times the number was very great, because men then thought more interiorly and spiritually, and from such thought were in heavenly affection; but in the following ages not so many, because in the process of time man became more external and began to think more naturally, and from such thought to be in earthly affection. All of this shows how great heaven is even from the inhabitants of this earth alone.

416. The immensity of the heaven of the Lord is shown also by this, that all children, whether born within the church or out of it, are adopted by the Lord and become angels; and the number of these amounts to a fourth or fifth part of the whole human race on the earth. That every child, wherever born, whether within the church or out of it, whether of pious or impious parents, is received by the Lord when it dies, and is brought up in heaven, and is taught and imbued with affections for good, and through these with knowledges of truth, in accordance with Divine order, and as he becomes perfected in intelligence and wisdom is brought into heaven and becomes an angel, can be seen above (n. 329–345). From all this a conclusion may be formed of the multitude of angels of heaven, derived from this source alone, from the first creation to the present time.

417. Again, how immense the heaven of the Lord is can be seen from this, that all the planets visible to the eye in our solar system are earths, and moreover, that in the whole universe there are innumerable earths, all of them full of inhabitants. These have been treated of particularly in a small work on those earths from which I will quote the following passage:

It is fully known in the other life that there are many earths inhabited by men from which spirits and angels come; for everyone there who desires from a love of truth and of use to do so is permitted to talk with spirits of other earths, and thus be assured that there is a plurality of worlds, and learn that the human race is not from one earth alone, but from innumerable earths. I have frequently talked about this with spirits of our earth, and was told that any intelligent person ought to know from many things that he does know that there are many earths inhabited by men; for it may be reasonably inferred that immense bodies like the planets, some of which exceed this earth in magnitude, are not empty masses created merely to be borne through space and to be carried around the sun, and to shine with their scanty light for the benefit of a single earth, but must have a more important use. He that believes, as everyone must believe, that the Divine created the universe for no other end than that the human race might exist, and heaven therefrom, for the human race is a seminary of heaven, must needs believe that wherever there is an earth there are men. That the planets visible to us because they are within the limits of our solar system are earths is evident from their being bodies of earthy matters, which is known from their reflecting the sun's light, and from their not appearing, when viewed through telescopes, like stars, sparkling with flame, but like earths varied with darker portions;

also from their passing like our earth around the sun and following in the path of the zodiac, thus making years and seasons of the year, spring, summer, autumn, and winter, also revolving on their axes like our earth, making days and times of the day, morning, midday, evening, and night; also from some of them having moons, called satellites, that revolve around their earth at stated times, as the moon does around ours; while the planet Saturn, being at a greater distance from the sun, has also a large luminous belt which gives much light, though reflected, to that earth. Who that knows all this and thinks rationally can ever say that the planets are empty bodies? Moreover, I have said to spirits that man might believe that there are more earths in the universe than one, from the fact that the starry heaven is so immense, and the stars there so innumerable, and each of them in its place or in its system a sun, resembling our sun, although of a varying magnitude. Anyone who duly weighs the subject must conclude that such an immense whole must needs be a means to an end that is the final end of creation; and this end is a heavenly kingdom in which the Divine may dwell with angels and men. For the visible universe or the heaven illumined by stars so numberless, which are so many suns, is simply a means for the existence of earths with men upon them from whom the heavenly kingdom is derived. From all this a rational man must needs conclude that so immense a means to so great an end could not have been provided merely for the human race on a single earth. What would this be for a Divine that is infinite, to which thousands and even myriads of earths, all of them full of inhabitants, would be little and scarcely anything? There are spirits whose sole pursuit is the acquisition of knowledges, because their delight is in this alone; and for this reason they are permitted to wander about, and even to pass out of our solar system into others, in acquiring knowledge. These spirits, who are from the planet Mercury, have told me that there are earths with men upon them not only in this solar system but also beyond it in the starry heaven in immense numbers. It was calculated that with a million earths in the universe, and on each earth three hundred millions of men, and two hundred generations in six thousand years, and a space of three cubic ells allowed to each man or spirit, the total number of so many men or spirits would not fill the space of this earth, and scarcely more than the space of one of the satellites about one of the planets—a space in the universe so small as to be almost invisible, since a satellite can scarcely be seen by the naked eye. What is this for the Creator of the universe, to whom it would not be sufficient if the whole universe were filled, since he is infinite? I have talked with angels about this, and they said that they had a similar idea of the fewness of the human race compared with the infinity of the Creator, although their thought is from states, not from spaces, and that in their thought earths amounting to as many myriads as could possibly be conceived of would still be nothing at all to the Lord. [*Earths in the Universe* n. 2–4, 6, and 126.2]

The earths in the universe, with their inhabitants, and the spirits and angels from them, are treated of in the above mentioned work. What is there related has been revealed and shown to me to the intent that it may be known that the heaven of the Lord is immense, and that it is all from the human race; also that our Lord is everywhere acknowledged as the God of heaven and earth.

418. Again, the immensity of the heaven of the Lord is shown in this, that heaven in its entire complex reflects a single man, and corresponds to all things and each thing in man, and that this correspondence can never be filled out, since it is a correspondence not only with each of the members, organs, and viscera of the body in general, but also with all and each of the little viscera and little organs contained in these in every minutest particular, and even with each vessel and fiber; and not only with these but also with the organic substances that receive interiorly the influx of heaven, from which come man's interior activities that are serviceable to the operations of his mind; since everything that exists interiorly in man exists in forms which are substances, for anything that does not exist in a substance as its subject is nothing. There is a correspondence of all these things with heaven, as can be seen from the chapter treating of the correspondence of all things of heaven with all things of man (n. 87–102). This correspondence can never be filled out because the more numerous the angelic affiliations are that correspond to each member the more perfect heaven becomes; for every perfection in the heavens increases with increase of number; and this for the reason that all there have the same end, and look with one accord to that end. That end is the common good; and when that reigns there is, from the common good, good to each individual, and from the good of each individual there is good to the whole community. This is so for the reason that the Lord turns all in heaven to himself (see above, n. 123), and thereby makes them to be one in himself. That the unanimity and concord of many, especially from such an origin and held together by such a bond, produces perfection, everyone with a reason at all enlightened can see clearly.

419. I have also been permitted to see the extent of the inhabited and also of the uninhabited heaven; and the extent of the uninhabited heaven was seen to be so great that it could not be filled to eternity even if there were many myriads of earths, and as great a multitude of men on each earth as on ours. (On this also see the treatise *Earths in the Universe*, n. 168.)

420. That heaven is not immense, but is of limited extent, is a conclusion that some have derived from certain passages in the Word understood according to the sense of its letter; for example, where it is said that only the poor are received into heaven, or only the elect, or only those within the church, and not those outside of it, or only those for whom the Lord intercedes; that heaven is closed when it is filled, and that this time is predetermined. But such are unaware that heaven is never closed, and that there is no time predetermined, or any limit of number; and that those are called the "elect" who are in a life of good and truth;[1] and those are called "poor" who are lacking in knowledges of good and truth and yet desire them; and such from that desire are also called hungry.[2] Those that have conceived an idea of the

1. Those are the elect who are in a life of good and truth (n. 3755, 3900).

Election and reception into heaven are not from mercy, as that term is understood, but are in accordance with the life (n. 5057, 5058).

There is no mercy of the Lord apart from means, but only through means, that is, to those that live in accordance with His precepts; such the Lord from His mercy leads continually in the world, and afterwards to eternity (n. 8700, 10659).

2. By the "poor," in the Word, those are meant who are spiritually poor, that is, who are ignorant of truth and yet wish to be taught (n. 9209, 9253, 10227).

small extent of heaven from the Word not understood believe it to be in one place, where all are gathered together; when, in fact, heaven consists of innumerable societies (see above, n. 41–50). Such also have no other idea than that heaven is granted to everyone from mercy apart from means, and thus that there is admission and reception from mere favor; and they fail to understand that the Lord from mercy leads everyone who accepts him, and that he accepts him who lives in accordance with the laws of divine order, which are the precepts of love and of faith, and that the mercy that is meant is to be thus led by the Lord from infancy to the last period of life in the world and afterwards to eternity. Let them know, therefore, that every man is born for heaven, and that he is received that receives heaven in himself in the world, and he that does not receive it is shut out.

Such are said to hunger and thirst, which is to desire knowledges of good and of truth, by which there is introduction into the church and into heaven (n. 4958, 10227).

Part 2

The World of Spirits
and Man's State after Death

44

What the World of Spirits Is

421. The world of spirits is not heaven, nor is it hell, but it is the intermediate place or state between the two; for it is the place that man first enters after death; and from which after a suitable time he is either raised up into heaven or cast down into hell in accord with his life in the world.

422. The world of spirits is an intermediate place between heaven and hell and also an intermediate state of the man after death. It has been shown to me not only that it is an intermediate place, having the hells below it and the heavens above it, but also that it is in an intermediate state, since so long as man is in it he is not yet either in heaven or in hell. The state of heaven in man is the conjunction of good and truth in him; and the state of hell is the conjunction of evil and falsity in him. Whenever good in a man-spirit is conjoined to truth he comes into heaven, because that conjunction, as just said, is heaven in him; but whenever evil in a man-spirit is conjoined with falsity he comes into hell, because that conjunction is hell in him. That conjunction is effected in the world of spirits, man then being in an intermediate state. It is the same thing whether you say the conjunction of the understanding and the will, or the conjunction of good and truth.

423. Let something first be said about the conjunction of the understanding and the will, and its being the same thing as the conjunction of good and truth, that being the conjunction that is effected in the world of spirits. Man has an understanding and a will. The understanding receives truths and is formed out of them, and the will receives goods and is formed out of them;

therefore whatever a man understands and thinks from his understanding he calls true, and whatever a man wills and thinks from his will he calls good. From his understanding man can think and thus perceive both what is true and what is good; and yet he thinks what is true and good from the will only when he wills it and does it. When he wills it and from willing does it, it is both in his understanding and in his will, consequently in the man. For neither the understanding alone nor the will alone makes the man, but the understanding and will together; therefore whatever is in both is in the man, and is appropriated to him. That which is in the understanding alone is in man, and yet not really in him; it is only a thing of his memory, or a matter of knowledge in his memory about which he can think when in company with others and outside of himself, but not in himself; that is, about which he can speak and reason, and can simulate affections and gestures that are in accord with it.

424. This ability to think from the understanding and not at the same time from the will is provided that man may be capable of being reformed; for reformation is effected by means of truths, and truths pertain to the understanding, as just said. For in respect to his will man is born into every evil, and therefore of himself wills good to no one but himself; and one who wills good to himself alone delights in the misfortunes that befall another, especially when they tend to his own advantage; for his wish is to divert to himself the goods of all others, whether honors or riches, and so far as he succeeds in this he inwardly rejoices. To the end that this will of man may be corrected and reformed, an ability to understand truths, and an ability to subdue by means of truths the affections of evil that spring from the will, are given to man. This is why man has this ability to think truths with his understanding, and to speak them and do them. But until man is such that he wills truths and does them from himself, that is, from the heart, he is not able to think truths from his will. When he becomes such, whatever he thinks from his understanding belongs to his faith, and whatever he thinks from his will belongs to his love; and in consequence his faith and his love, like his understanding and his will, are conjoined in him.

425. To the extent, therefore, that the truths of the understanding and the goods of the will are conjoined, that is, to the extent that a man wills truths and does them from his will, he has heaven in himself, since the conjunction of good and truth, as just said, is heaven. And on the other hand, just to the extent that the falsities of the understanding and the evils of the will are conjoined man has hell in himself, since the conjunction of falsity and evil is hell. But so long as the truths of the understanding and the goods of the will are not conjoined man is in an intermediate state. At the present time nearly everyone is in such a state that he has some knowledge of truths, and from his knowledge and understanding gives some thought to them, and conforms to them either much or little or not at all, or acts contrary to them from a love of evil and consequent false belief. In order, therefore, that man may have in him either heaven or hell, he is first brought after death into the world of spirits, and there with those who are to be raised up into heaven good and truth are conjoined, and with those who are to be cast down into hell evil and falsity are conjoined. For neither in heaven nor in hell is anyone permitted to have a divided mind, that is, to understand one thing and to will another; but everyone must understand what he wills, and will what he understands. Therefore in heaven he who wills good understands truth, while in hell he who wills evil understands falsity. So in the intermediate state the falsities that the good have are put away, and truths that agree and harmonize with their good are given them; while the truths that the evil have are put away, and falsities that agree and harmonize with their evil are given them. This shows what the world of spirits is.

426. In the world of spirits there are vast numbers, because the first meeting of all is there, and all are there explored and prepared. The time of their stay in that world is not fixed; some merely enter it, and are soon either taken into heaven or are cast down into hell; some remain only a few weeks, some several years, but not more than thirty. These differences in the time they remain depend on the correspondence or lack of correspondence of man's interiors with his exteriors. How man is led in that world from one state into another and prepared shall now be told.

427. As soon as men after death enter the world of spirits the Lord clearly discriminates between them; and the evil are at once attached to the infernal society in which they were, as to their ruling love while in the world; and the good are at once attached to the heavenly society in which they were as to their love, charity and faith while in the world. But although they are thus divided, all that have been friends and acquaintances in the life of the body, especially wives and husbands, and also brothers and sisters, meet and converse together whenever they so desire. I have seen a father talking with six sons, whom he recognized, and have seen many others with their relatives and friends; but having from their life in the world diverse dispositions, after a short time they separate. But those who have passed from the world of spirits into heaven or into hell, unless they have a like disposition from a like love, no longer see or know each other. The reason that they see each other in the world of spirits, but not in heaven or in hell, is that those who are in the world of spirits are brought into one state after another, like those they experienced in the life of the body; but afterwards all are brought into a permanent state in accord with their ruling love, and in that state one recognizes another only by similarity of love; for then similarity joins and dissimilarity disjoins (see above, n. 41–50).

428. As the world of spirits is an intermediate state between heaven and hell with man, so it is an intermediate place with the hells below and the heavens above. All the hells are shut toward that world, being open only through holes and clefts like those in rocks and through wide openings that are so guarded that no one can come out except by permission, which is granted in cases of urgent necessity (of which hereafter). Heaven, too, is enclosed on all sides; and there is no passage open to any heavenly society except by a narrow way, the entrance to which is also guarded. These outlets and entrances are what are called in the Word the gates and doors of hell and of heaven.

429. The world of spirits appears like a valley between mountains and rocks, with windings and elevations here and there. The gates and doors of the heavenly societies are visible to those only who are prepared for heaven; others cannot find them. There is one entrance from the world of spirits to each heavenly society, opening through a single path which branches out in its ascent into several. The gates and doors of the hells also are visible only to those who are about to enter, to whom they are then opened. When these are opened gloomy and seemingly sooty caverns are seen tending obliquely downwards to the abyss, where again there are many doors. Through these caverns nauseous and fetid stenches exhale, which good spirits flee from because they abominate them, but evil spirits seek for them because they delight in them. For as everyone in the world has been delighted with his own evil, so after death he is delighted with the stench to which his evil corresponds. In this respect the evil may be likened to rapacious birds and beasts, like ravens, wolves, and swine, which fly or run to carrion or dunghills when they scent their stench. I heard a certain spirit crying out loudly as if from inward torture when struck by a breath flowing forth from heaven; but he became tranquil and glad as soon as a breath flowing forth from hell reached him.

430. With every man there are two gates; one that leads to hell and that is open to evils and their falsities; while the other leads to heaven and is open to goods and their truths. Those that are in evil and its falsity have the gate to hell opened in them, and only through chinks from above does something of light from heaven flow into them, and by that inflowing they are able to think, to reason, and to speak; but the gate to heaven is opened in those that are in good and its truth. For there are two ways that lead to the rational mind of man; a higher or internal way through which good and truth from the Lord enter, and a lower or external way through which evil and falsity enter from hell. The rational mind itself is at the middle point to which the ways tend. Consequently, so far as light from heaven is admitted man is rational; but so far as it is not admitted he is not rational, however rational he may seem to himself to be. This has been said to make known the nature of the correspondence of man with heaven and with hell. While man's rational mind is being formed it corresponds to the world of spirits, what is above it corresponding to heaven and what is below to hell. With those preparing for heaven the regions above the rational mind are opened, but those below are closed to the influx of evil and falsity; while with those preparing for hell the parts below it are opened, and the parts above it are closed to the influx of good and truth. Thus the latter can look only to what is below themselves, that is, to hell; while the former can look only to what is above themselves, that is, to heaven. To look above themselves is to look to the Lord, because he is the common center to which all things of heaven look; while to look below themselves is to look backwards from the Lord to the opposite center, to which all things of hell look and tend (see above, n. 123, 124).

431. In the preceding pages whenever spirits are mentioned those that are in the world of spirits are meant; but when angels are mentioned those that are in heaven are meant.

45

In Respect to His Interiors
Every Man Is a Spirit

432. Whoever duly considers the subject can see that as the body is material it is not the body that thinks, but the soul, which is spiritual. The soul of man, upon the immortality of which many have written, is his spirit, for this as to everything belonging to it is immortal. This also is what thinks in the body, for it is spiritual, and what is spiritual receives what is spiritual and lives spiritually, which is to think and to will.

Therefore, all rational life that appears in the body belongs to the soul, and nothing of it to the body; for the body, as just said, is material, and the material, which is the property of the body, is added to and apparently almost joined to the spirit, in order that the spirit of man may be able to live and perform uses in the natural world, all things of which are material and in themselves devoid of life. And as it is the spiritual only that lives and not the material, it can be seen that whatever lives in man is his spirit, and that the body merely serves it, just as what is instrumental serves a moving living force. An instrument is said indeed to act, to move, or to strike; but to believe that these are acts of the instrument, and not of him who acts, moves, or strikes by means of the instrument, is a fallacy.

433. As everything in the body that lives, and that acts and feels from that life, belongs exclusively to the spirit, and nothing of it to the body, it follows that the spirit is the man himself; or what is the same thing, that a man viewed in himself is a spirit possessing a like form; for whatever lives and feels in man belongs to his spirit and everything in man, from his head to the sole of his foot, lives and feels; and in consequence when the body is separated from its spirit, which is what is called dying, man continues to be a man and to live. I have heard from heaven that some who die, while they are lying upon the bier, before they are resuscitated, continue to think even in their cold body, and do not know that they are not still alive, except that they are unable to move a particle of matter belonging to the body.

434. Unless man were a subject which is a substance that can serve a source and container he would be unable to think and will. Anything that is supposed to exist apart from a substantial subject is nothing. This can be seen from the fact that a man is unable to see without an organ which is the subject of his sight, or to hear without an organ which is the subject of his hearing. Apart from these organs, sight and hearing are nothing and have no existence. The same is true of thought, which is inner sight, and of perception, which is inner hearing; unless these were in substances and from substances which are organic forms and subjects, they would have no existence at all. All this shows that man's spirit as well as his body is in a form, and that it is in a human form, and enjoys sensories and senses when separated from the body the same as when it was in it, and that all the life of the eye and all the life of the ear, in a word, all the life of sense that man has, belongs not to his body but to his spirit, which dwells in these organs and in their minutest particulars. This is why spirits see, hear, and feel, as well as men. But when the spirit has been loosed from the body, these senses are exercised in the spiritual world, not in the natural world. The natural sensation that the spirit had when it was in the body it had by means of the material part that was added to it; but it then had also spiritual sensations in its thinking and willing.

435. All this has been said to convince the rational man that viewed in himself man is a spirit, and that the corporeal part that is added to the spirit to enable it to perform its functions in the natural and material world is not the man, but only an instrument of his spirit. But evidences from experience are preferable, because there are many that fail to comprehend rational deductions; and those that have established themselves in the opposite view turn such deductions into grounds of doubt by means of reasonings from the fallacies of the senses. Those that have established themselves in the opposite view are accustomed to think that beasts likewise have life and sensations and thus have a spiritual part, the same as man has, and yet that part dies with the body. But the spiritual of beasts is not the same as the spiritual of man is; for man has what beasts have not, an inmost, into which the Divine flows, raising man up to itself, and thereby conjoining man to itself. Because of this, man, in contrast with beasts, has the ability to think about God and about the Divine things of heaven and the church, and to love God from these and in these, and thus be conjoined to him; and whatever can be conjoined to the Divine cannot be dissipated, but whatever cannot be conjoined is dissipated. The inmost that man has, in contrast with beasts, has been treated of above (n. 39), and what was there said will here be repeated, since it is important to have the fallacies dispelled that have been engendered in the minds of many who from lack of knowledge and trained intellect are unable to form rational conclusions on the subject. The words are these:

I will mention a certain arcanum respecting the angels of the three heavens, which has not hitherto come into anyone's mind, because degrees have not been understood. In every angel and in every man there is an inmost or highest degree, or an inmost or highest something, into which the Divine of the Lord first or most directly flows, and from which it disposes the other interiors in him that succeed in accordance with the degrees of order. This inmost or highest degree may be called the entrance of the Lord to the angel or man, and his veriest dwelling place in them. It is by virtue of this inmost or highest that a man is a man, and distinguished from the animals, which do not have it. From this it is that man, unlike the animals, is capable, in respect to all his interiors which pertain to his mind and disposition, of being raised up by the Lord to himself, of believing in the Lord, of being moved by love to the Lord, and thereby beholding him, and of receiving intelligence and wisdom, and speaking from reason. Also it is by virtue of this that he lives to eternity. But what is arranged and provided by the Lord in this inmost does not distinctly fall into the perception of any angel, because it is above his thought and transcends his wisdom.

436. That in respect to his interiors man is a spirit I have been permitted to learn from much experience, which, to employ a common saying, would fill volumes if I were to describe it all. I have talked with spirits as a spirit, and I have talked with them as a man in the body; and when I talked with them as a spirit they knew no otherwise than that I myself was a spirit and in a human form as they were. Thus did my interiors appear before them, for when talking with them as a spirit my material body was not seen.

437. That in respect to his interiors man is a spirit can be seen from the fact that after his separation from the body, which takes place when he dies, man goes on living as a man just as before. That I might be convinced of this I have been permitted to talk with nearly everyone I had ever known in their life in the body; with some for hours, with some for weeks and months, and with some for years, and this chiefly that I might be sure of it and might testify to it.

438. To this may be added that every man in respect to his spirit, even while he is living in the body, is in some society with spirits, although he does not know it; if a good man he is by means of spirits in some angelic society; if an evil man in some infernal society; and after death he comes into that same society. This has been often told and shown to those who after death have come among spirits. Man, to be sure, does not appear in that society as a spirit while he is living in the world, for the reason that he then thinks naturally; but when one is thinking abstractly from the body, because he is then in the spirit, he sometimes appears in his society; and when seen he is

easily distinguished from the spirits there, for he goes about meditating and in silence, not looking at others, and apparently not seeing them; and as soon as any spirit speaks to him he vanishes.

439. To make clear that man in respect to his interiors is a spirit I will relate from experience what happens when man is withdrawn from the body, and what it is to be carried away by the spirit to another place.

440. First, as to withdrawal from the body, it happens thus. Man is brought into a certain state that is midway between sleeping and waking, and when in that state he seems to himself to be wide awake; all the senses are as perfectly awake as in the completest bodily wakefulness, not only the sight and the hearing, but what is wonderful, the sense of touch also, which is then more exquisite than is ever possible when the body is awake. In this state spirits and angels have been seen to the very life, and have been heard, and what is wonderful, have been touched, with almost nothing of the body intervening. This is the state that is called being withdrawn from the body, and not knowing whether one is in the body or out of it. I have been admitted into this state only three or four times, that I might learn what it is, and might know that spirits and angels enjoy every sense, and that man does also in respect to his spirit when he is withdrawn from the body.

441. As to being carried away by the spirit to another place, I have been shown by living experience what it is, and how it is done, but only two or three times. I will relate a single instance. Walking through the streets of a city and through fields, talking at the same time with spirits, I knew no otherwise than that I was fully awake, and in possession of my usual sight. Thus I walked on without going astray, and all the while with clear vision, seeing groves, rivers, palaces, houses, men, and other objects. But after walking thus for some hours, suddenly I saw with my bodily eyes, and noted that I was in another

place. Being greatly astonished I perceived that I had been in the same state as those who were said to have been led away by the spirit into another place. For in this state the distance, even though it be many miles, and the time, though it be many hours or days, are not thought of; neither is there any feeling of fatigue; and one is led unerringly through ways of which he himself is ignorant, even to the destined place.

442. But these two states of man, which are his states when he is in his interiors, or what is the same, when he is in the spirit, are extraordinary; but as they are states known about in the church, they were exhibited to me only that I might know what they are. But it has been granted to me now for many years to speak with spirits and to be with them as one of them, even in full wakefulness of the body.

443. That in respect to his interiors man is a spirit there are further evidences in what has been said and shown above (n. 311–317), where it is explained that heaven and hell are from the human race.

444. That man is a spirit in respect to his interiors means in respect to the things pertaining to his thought and will, for these are the interiors themselves that make man to be man, and such a man as he is in respect to these interiors.

46

The Resuscitation of Man
from the Dead and His Entrance
into Eternal Life

445. When the body is no longer able to perform the bodily functions in the natural world that correspond to the spirit's thoughts and affections, which the spirit has from the spiritual world, man is said to die. This takes place when the respiration of the lungs and the beatings of the heart cease. But the man does not die; he is merely separated from the bodily part that was of use to him in the world, while the man himself continues to live. It is said that the man himself continues to live since man is not a man because of his body but because of his spirit, for it is the spirit that thinks in man, and thought with affection is what constitutes man. Evidently, then, the death of man is merely his passing from one world into another. And this is why in the Word in its internal sense "death" signifies resurrection and continuation of life.[1]

446. There is an inmost communication of the spirit with the breathing and with the beating of the heart, the spirit's thought communicating with the breathing, and its affection, which is of love, with the heart,[2] consequently when these two motions

---

1. In the Word "death" signifies resurrection, for when man dies his life still goes on (n. 3498, 3505, 4618, 4621, 6036, 6221).

2. The heart corresponds to the will, thus to the affection which belongs to the love, while the respiration of the lungs corresponds to the understanding, thus to the thought (n. 3888). From this the "heart" in the Word signifies the will and love (n. 7542, 9050, 10336). The "soul" signifies understanding, faith, and truth; therefore "from the soul and from the heart" signifies what is from the understanding, faith, and truth, and what is from the will, love, and good (n. 2930, 9050). The correspondence of the heart and lungs with the Greatest Man, or heaven (n. 3883–3895).

cease in the body there is at once a separation. These two motions, the respiration of the lungs and the beating of heart, are the very bond on the sundering of which the spirit is left to itself; and the body being then deprived of the life of its spirit grows cold and begins to decay. This inmost communication of the spirit of man is with the respiration and with the heart, because on these all vital motions depend, not only in general but in every particular.[3]

447. After the separation the spirit of man continues in the body for a short time, but only until the heart's action has wholly ceased, which happens variously in accord with the diseased condition that causes death, with some the motion of the heart continuing for some time, with others not so long. As soon as this motion ceases the man is resuscitated; but this is done by the Lord alone. Resuscitation means the drawing forth of the spirit from the body, and its introduction into the spiritual world; this is commonly called the resurrection. The spirit is not separated from the body until the motion of the heart has ceased, for the reason that the heart corresponds to the affection of love, which is the very life of man, for it is from love that everyone has vital heat;[4] consequently as long as this conjunction continues correspondence continues, and thereby the life of the spirit in the body.

448. How this resuscitation is effected has both been told to me and shown to me in living experience. The actual experience was granted to me that I might have a complete knowledge of the process.

449. As to the senses of the body I was brought into a state of insensibility, thus nearly into the state of the dying; but with the interior life and thought remaining unimpaired, in order

3. The beating of the heart and the respiration of the lungs reign in the body throughout, and flow mutually into every part (n. 3887, 3889, 3890).

4. Love is the being [esse] of the life of man (n. 5002). Love is spiritual heat, and therefore the very vital itself of man (n. 1589, 2146, 3338, 4906, 7081–7086, 9954, 10740). Affection is a continuation of love (n. 3938).

that I might perceive and retain in the memory the things that happened to me, and that happen to those that are resuscitated from the dead. I perceived that the respiration of the body was almost wholly taken away; but the interior respiration of the spirit went on in connection with a slight and tacit respiration of the body. Then at first a communication of the pulse of the heart with the celestial kingdom was established, because that kingdom corresponds to the heart in man.[5] Angels from that kingdom were seen, some at a distance, and two sitting near my head. Thus all my own affection was taken away although thought and perception continued.

[2] I was in this state for some hours. Then the spirits that were around me withdrew, thinking that I was dead; and an aromatic odor like that of an embalmed body was perceived, for when the celestial angels are present everything pertaining to the corpse is perceived as aromatic, and when spirits perceive this they cannot approach; and in this way evil spirits are kept away from man's spirit when he is being introduced into eternal life. The angels seated at my head were silent, merely sharing their thoughts with mine; and when their thoughts are received the angels know that the spirit of man is in a state in which it can be drawn forth from the body. This sharing of their thoughts was effected by looking into my face, for in this way in heaven thoughts are shared.

[3] As my thought and perception continued, that I might know and remember how resuscitation is effected, I perceived the angels first tried to ascertain what my thought was, whether it was like the thought of those who are dying, which is usually about eternal life; also that they wished to keep my mind in that thought. Afterwards I was told that the spirit of man is held in its last thought when the body expires, until it returns to the thoughts that are from its general or ruling affection in

5. The heart corresponds to the Lord's celestial kingdom, the lungs to His spiritual kingdom (n. 3635, 3886, 3887).

the world. Especially was I permitted to see and feel that there was a pulling and drawing forth, as it were, of the interiors of my mind, thus of my spirit, from the body; and I was told that this is from the Lord, and that the resurrection is thus effected.

450. The celestial angels who are with the one that is resuscitated do not withdraw from him, because they love everyone; but when the spirit comes into such a state that he can no longer be affiliated with celestial angels, he longs to get away from them. When this takes place angels from the Lord's spiritual kingdom come, through whom is given the use of light; for before this he saw nothing, but merely thought. I was shown how this is done. The angels appeared to roll off, as it were, a coat from the left eye toward the bridge of the nose, that the eye might be opened and be enabled to see. This is only an appearance, but to the spirit it seemed to be really done. When the coat thus seems to have been rolled off there is a slight sense of light, but very dim, like what is seen through the eyelids on first awakening from sleep. To me this dim light took on a heavenly hue, but I was told afterwards that the color varies. Then something is felt to be gently rolled off from the face, and when this is done spiritual thought is awakened. This rolling off from the face is also an appearance, which represents the spirit's passing from natural thought into spiritual thought. The angels are extremely careful that only such ideas as savor of love shall proceed from the one resuscitated. They now tell him that he is a spirit. When he has come into the enjoyment of light the spiritual angels render to the new spirit every service he can possibly desire in that state; and teach him about the things of the other life so far as he can comprehend them. But if he has no wish to be taught, the spirit longs to get away from the company of the angels. Nevertheless, the angels do not withdraw from him, but he separates himself from them; for the angels love everyone, and desire nothing so much as to render service, to teach, and to lead into heaven; this constitutes their highest delight. When the spirit has thus withdrawn he is re-

ceived by good spirits, and as long as he continues in their company everything possible is done for him. But if he had lived such a life in the world as would prevent his enjoying the company of the good he longs to get away from the good, and this experience is repeated until he comes into association with such as are in entire harmony with his life in the world; and with such he finds his own life, and what is surprising, he then leads a life like that which he led in the world.

451. This opening state of man's life after death lasts only a few days. How he is afterwards led from one state to another, and finally either into heaven or into hell, will be told in what follows. This, too, I have been permitted to learn by much experience.

452. I have talked with some on the third day after their decease, when the process described above (n. 449, 450) had been completed, especially with three whom I had known in the world, to whom I mentioned that arrangements were now being made for burying their bodies; I said, for burying them; on hearing which they were smitten with a kind of surprise, saying that they were alive, and that the thing that had served them in the world was what was being buried. Afterwards they wondered greatly that they had not believed in such a life after death while they lived in the body, and especially that scarcely any within the church so believed. Those that have not believed in the world in any life of the soul after the life of the body are greatly ashamed when they find themselves to be alive. But those that have confirmed themselves in that disbelief seek affiliation with their like, and are separated from those that have had faith. Such are for the most part attached to some infernal society, because they have also denied the divine and have despised the truths of the church; for so far as anyone confirms himself against the eternal life of his soul he confirms himself also against whatever pertains to heaven and the church.

47

Man after Death
Is in a Complete Human Form

453. It has already been shown in several previous chapters that the form of the spirit of man is the human form, that is, that the spirit is a man even in form, especially where it is shown that every angel has a complete human form (n. 73–77); that in respect to his interiors every man is a spirit (n. 432–444); and that the angels in heaven are from the human race (n. 311–317).

[2] This can be seen still more clearly from the fact that it is by virtue of his spirit, and not by virtue of his body that man is a man, and that the bodily form is added to the spirit in accordance with the spirit's form, and not the reverse, for it is in accordance with its own form that the spirit is clothed with a body. Consequently the spirit of man acts into every part of the body, even the minutest, insomuch that if any part is not actuated by the spirit, or the spirit is not active in it, it does not live. Anyone can see that this is true from this fact alone, that thought and will actuate all things and each thing of the body with such entire command that everything concurs, and anything that does not concur is not a part of the body, but is cast out as something without life; and thought and will belong, not to the body, but to the spirit of man.

[3] A spirit that has been loosed from the body or the spirit in another man, is not visible in the human form to man, because the body's organ of sight, or its eye, so far as it sees in the world, is a material organ, and what is material can see only what is material, while what is spiritual sees what is spiritual. When, therefore, the material part of the eye becomes darkened and is

deprived of its cooperation with the spiritual, the eye sees spirits in their own form, which is the human form, not only the spirits that are in the spiritual world, but also the spirit of another man while it is yet in its body.

454. The form of the spirit is the human form because man is created in respect to his spirit in the form of heaven, for all things of heaven and of the order of heaven are brought together in the things that constitute the mind of man;[1] and from this comes his capacity to receive intelligence and wisdom. Whether you say the capacity to receive intelligence and wisdom or the capacity to receive heaven it is the same thing, as can be seen from what has been shown about the light and heat of heaven (n. 126–140); the form of heaven (n. 200–212); the wisdom of angels (n. 265–275); and in the chapter that the form of heaven as a whole and in part reflects a single man (n. 59–77); and this by virtue of the Divine human of the Lord, which is the source of heaven and its form (n. 78–86).

455. That which has now been said can be understood by the rational man, for he can see it from the connection of causes and from truths in their order; but it is not understood by a man who is not rational, and for several reasons, the chief of which is that he has no desire to understand it because it is opposed to the falsities that he has made his truths; and he that is unwilling to understand for this reason has closed to his rational faculty the way to heaven, although that way can still be opened whenever the will's resistance ceases (see above, n. 424). That man is able to understand truths and be rational whenever he so wishes has been made clear to me by much experience. Evil spirits that have become irrational in the world by rejecting the Divine and the truths of the church, and

---

1. Man is the being into whom are brought together all things of Divine order, and by creation he is Divine order in form (n. 4219, 4222, 4223, 4523, 4524, 5114, 6013, 6057, 6605, 6626, 9706, 10156, 10472).

So far as a man lives in accordance with Divine order he is seen in the other life as a man, complete and beautiful (n. 4839, 6605, 6626).

confirming themselves against them, have frequently been turned by Divine power toward those who were in the light of truth, and they then comprehended all things as the angels did, and acknowledged them to be true, and also that they comprehended them all. But the moment these spirits relapsed into themselves, and turned back to the love of their will, they had no comprehension of truths and affirmed the opposite.

[2] I have also heard certain dwellers in hell saying that they knew and perceived that which they did to be evil and that which they thought to be false; but that they were unable to resist the delight of their love, that is, their will, and that it is their will that drives their thought to see evil as good and falsity as truth. Evidently, then, those that are in falsity from evil have the ability to understand and be rational, but have no wish to; and they have no wish to for the reason that they have loved falsities more than truths, because these agree with the evils in which they are. To love and to will is the same thing, for what a man wills he loves, and what he loves he wills.

[3] Because the state of men is such that they are able to understand truths if they wish to, I have been permitted to confirm spiritual truths, which are truths of heaven and the church, even by reasonings, and this in order that the falsities by which the rational mind in many has been closed up may be dispersed by reasonings, and thus the eye may perhaps in some degree be opened; for to confirm spiritual goods by reasonings is permitted to all that are in truths. Who could ever understand the Word from the sense of its letter, unless he saw from an enlightened reason the truths it contains? Is not this the source of so many heresies from the same Word?[2]

---

2. The truths of doctrine of the church derived from the Word must be the starting point, and these must first be acknowledged, and afterwards it is permissible to consult knowledges (n. 6047). Thus it is permissible for those that are in an affirmative state toward the truths of faith to confirm them rationally by knowledges, but it is not permissible for those who are in a negative state (n. 2568, 2588, 4760, 6047).

It is in accordance with Divine order to enter rationally from spiritual truths into

456. That the spirit of man, when it has been loosed from the body, is still a man and in a like form, has been proved to me by the daily experience of many years; for I have seen such and have listened to them a thousand times, and have talked with them about this fact, that men in the world do not believe them to be men, and that those that do believe this are regarded by the learned as simple. Spirits are grieved at heart that such ignorance still continues in the world, and above all within the church.

[2] But this belief they said had emanated chiefly from the learned, who had thought about the soul from ideas derived from bodily sense; and from such ideas the only conception they formed of the soul was as being mere thought; and when this is regarded apart from any subject as its container and source it is merely a fleeting breath of pure ether that must needs be dissipated when the body dies. But as the church believes from the Word in the immortality of the soul they are compelled to ascribe to it something vital, such as pertains to thought, but they deny to it anything of sense, such as man possesses, until it has again been joined to the body. On this opinion the doctrine in regard to the resurrection is based, with the belief that the soul and body will be joined again at the time of the final judgment. For this reason when anyone thinks about the soul in accordance with this doctrine and these conjectures, he has no conception that it is a spirit, and in a human form. And still further, scarcely anyone at this day knows what the spiritual is, and still less that spiritual beings, as all spirits and angels are, have any human form.

[3] Consequently, nearly all that go from this world are greatly surprised to find that they are alive, and are as much men as before, that they see, hear, and speak, and that their

---

knowledges, which are natural truths, but not to enter from the latter into the former, because spiritual influx into natural things is possible, but not natural or physical influx into spiritual things (n. 3219, 5119, 5259, 5427, 5428, 5478, 6322, 9109, 9110).

body enjoys the sense of touch as before, with no difference whatever (see above, n. 74). And when they cease to be astonished at themselves they are astonished that the church should know nothing about this state of men after death, thus nothing about heaven or hell, when in fact all that have ever lived in the world are in the other life and live as men. And as they wondered also why this had not been disclosed to man by visions, being an essential of the faith of the church, they were told from heaven that although this might have been done, since nothing is easier when it is the Lord's good pleasure, yet those that have confirmed themselves in the opposite falsities would not believe even if they themselves should behold it; also that there is danger in confirming anything by visions when men are in falsities, for they would then first believe and afterwards deny, and thus would profane the truth itself, since to believe and afterwards deny is to profane; and those who profane truths are cast down into the lowest and most grievous of all the hells.[3]

[4] This danger is what is meant by the Lord's words:

He hath blinded their eyes and hardened their hearts lest they should see with their eyes, and understand with their heart, and should turn and I should heal them (John 12:40).

---

3. Profanation is the mixing of good and evil and of truth and falsity in man (n. 6348). Only those can profane truth and good, or the holy things of the Word and the church, who first acknowledge them, and still more who live according to them, and who afterwards recede from the belief and reject it, and live for themselves and the world (n. 593, 1008, 1010, 1059, 3398, 3399, 3898, 4289, 4601, 10284, 10287).

If man after repentance of heart relapses to former evils he profanes, and his latter state is then worse than his former (n. 8394). Those that have not acknowledged holy things, still less those that have no knowledge of them, cannot profane them (n. 1008, 1010, 1059, 9188, 10284). The heathen who are out of the church and do not have the Word cannot profane it (n. 1327, 1328, 2051, 2284).

On this account interior truths were not disclosed to the Jews, for if they had been disclosed and acknowledged that people would have profaned them (n. 3398, 4289, 6963). The lot of profaners in the other life is the worst of all, because not only the good and truth they have acknowledged, but also their evil and falsity remain, and as these cling together, the life is rent asunder (n. 571, 582, 6348). Consequently most careful provision is made by the Lord to prevent profanation (n. 2426, 10287).

And that those that are in falsities would not believe [even if visions were given] is meant by these words:

> Abraham said to the rich man in hell, They have Moses and the Prophets, let them hear them. But he said, Nay, father Abraham, but if one came to them from the dead they would be converted. But Abraham said to him, If they hear not Moses and the Prophets, neither will they believe though one should rise from the dead (Luke 16:29–31).

457. When the spirit of man first enters the world of spirits, which takes place shortly after his resuscitation, as described above, his face and his tone of voice resemble those he had in the world, because he is then in the state of his exteriors, and his interiors are not as yet uncovered. This is man's first state after death. But subsequently his face is changed, and becomes entirely different, resembling his ruling affection or ruling love, in conformity with which the interiors of his mind had been while he was in the world and his spirit while it was in the body. For the face of a man's spirit differs greatly from the face of his body. The face of his body is from his parents, but the face of his spirit is from his affection, and is an image of it. When the life of the spirit in the body is ended, and its exteriors are laid aside and its interiors disclosed, it comes into this affection. This is man's second state. I have seen some that have recently arrived from the world, and have recognized them from their face and speech; but seeing them afterwards I did not recognize them. Those that had been in good affections appeared with beautiful faces; but those that had been in evil affections with misshapen faces; for man's spirit, viewed in itself, is nothing but his affection; and the face is its outward form. Another reason why faces are changed is that in the other life no one is permitted to counterfeit affections that are not his own, and thus assume looks that are contrary to his love. All in the other life are brought into such a state as to speak as they think, and to manifest in their looks and gestures the inclinations of their will. And because of this the faces of all become forms and images of their affections; and in consequence all that have known each other in the world know each other in the world of spirits, but not in heaven nor in hell (as has been said above, n. 427).[4]

458. The faces of hypocrites are changed more slowly than those of others, because by practice they had formed a habit of so managing their interiors as to imitate good affections; consequently for a long time they appear not unbeautiful. But as that which they had assumed is gradually put off, and the interiors of the mind are brought into accord with the form of their affections, they become after awhile more misshapen than others. Hypocrites are such as have been accustomed to talk like angels, but interiorly have acknowledged nature alone and not the Divine, and have therefore denied what pertains to heaven and the church.

459. It should be known that everyone's human form after death is the more beautiful in proportion as he has more interiorly loved Divine truths and lived according to them; for everyone's interiors are opened and formed in accordance with his love and life; therefore the more interior the affection is the more like heaven it is, and in consequence the more beautiful the face is. This is why the angels in the inmost heaven are the most beautiful, for they are forms of celestial love. But those that have loved Divine truths more exteriorly, and thus have lived in accordance with them in a more external way, are less beautiful; for exterior affections only shine forth from their faces; and through these no interior heavenly love shines, consequently nothing of the form of heaven as it is in itself. There is seen in the faces of such something comparatively obscure,

---

4. The face is so formed as to correspond with the interiors (n. 4791–4805, 5695).

The correspondence of the face and its expressions with the affections of the mind (n. 1568, 2988, 2989, 3631, 4796, 4797, 4800, 5165, 5168, 5695, 9306).

With the angels of heaven the face makes one with the interiors that belong to the mind (n. 4796–4799, 5695, 8250). Therefore in the Word the face signifies the interiors that belong to the mind, that is, to the affection and thought (n. 1999, 2434, 3527, 4066, 4796, 5102, 9306, 9546). In what manner the influx from the brain into the face has been changed in process of time and with it the face itself as regards its correspondence with the interiors (n. 4326, 8250).

not vivified by anything of interior life shining through it. In a word, all perfection increases toward interiors and decreases toward exteriors, and as perfection increases and decreases so does beauty. I have seen angelic faces of the third heaven of such radiance that no painter with all his art could possibly give any such light to his colors as to equal a thousandth part of the brightness and life that shone forth from their countenances. But the faces of the angels of the lowest heaven may in some measure be equaled.

460. In conclusion I will mention a certain arcanum hitherto unknown to anyone, namely, that every good and truth that goes forth from the Lord and makes heaven is in the human form; and this not only as a whole and in what is greatest, but also in every part and what is least; also that this form affects everyone who receives good and truth from the Lord, and causes everyone who is in heaven to be in the human form in accordance with his reception of good and truth. It is in consequence of this that heaven is like itself in general and in particular, and that the human form is the form of the whole, of every society, and of every angel (as has been shown in the four chapters from n. 59 to 86); to which let it be added that it is the form of the least things of thought derived from heavenly love with the angels. No man, however, can easily comprehend this arcanum; but it is clearly comprehended by the angels, because they are in the light of heaven.

48

After Death Man Is Possessed of Every Sense, and of All the Memory, Thought, and Affection that He Had in the World, Leaving Nothing Behind except His Earthly Body

461. It has been proved to me by manifold experience that when man passes from the natural world into the spiritual, as he does when he dies, he carries with him all his possessions, that is, everything that belongs to him as a man, except his earthly body. For when man enters the spiritual world or the life after death, he is in a body as he was in the world, with no apparent difference, since he neither sees nor feels any difference. But his body is then spiritual, and thus separated or purified from all that is earthly; and when what is spiritual touches or sees what is spiritual, it is just the same as when what is natural touches or sees what is natural. So when a man has become a spirit he does not know otherwise than that he is in the same body that he had in the world and thus does not know that he has died.

[2] Moreover, a man's spirit enjoys every sense, both outer and inner, that he enjoyed in the world; he sees as before, he hears and speaks as before, smells and tastes, and when touched, he feels the touch as before; he also longs, desires, craves, thinks, reflects, is stirred, loves, wills, as before; and one who takes delight in studies, reads and writes as before. In a word, when a man passes from one life into the other, or from one world into the other, it is like passing from one place into another, carrying with him all things that he had possessed in

himself as a man; so that by death, which is only the death of the earthly body, man cannot be said to have lost anything really his own.

[3] Furthermore, he carries with him his natural memory, retaining everything that he has heard, seen, read, learned, or thought, in the world from earliest infancy even to the end of life; although the natural objects that are contained in the memory, since they cannot be reproduced in the spiritual world, are quiescent, just as they are when one is not thinking of them. Nevertheless, they are reproduced when the Lord so wills. But more will be said presently about this memory and its state after death. A sensual man finds it impossible to believe that such is the state of man after death, because he cannot comprehend it; for a sensual man must needs think naturally even about spiritual things; therefore, anything that does not appeal to his senses, that is, that he does not see with his bodily eyes and touch with his hands (as is said of Thomas in John 20:25, 27, 29) he denies the existence of. (What the sensual man is may be seen above, n. 267 and notes.)

462a. And yet there is a great difference between man's life in the spiritual world and his life in the natural world, in regard both to his outer senses and their affections and his inner senses and their affections. Those that are in heaven have more exquisite senses, that is, a keener sight and hearing, and also think more wisely than when they were in the world; for they see in the light of heaven, which surpasses by many degrees the light of the world (see above, n. 126); and they hear by means of a spiritual atmosphere, which likewise surpasses by many degrees the earthly atmosphere (n. 235). This difference in respect to the outward senses is like the difference between clear sunshine and dark cloudiness in the world, or between noonday light and evening shade. For the light of heaven, since it is Divine truth, enables the eyes of angels to perceive and distinguish most minute things.

[2] Moreover, their outer sight corresponds to their inner sight or understanding; for with angels one sight so flows into the other as to act as one with it; and this gives them their great keenness of vision. In like manner, their hearing corresponds to their perception, which pertains both to the understanding and to the will, and in consequence they perceive in the tone and words of one speaking the most minute things of his affection and thought; in the tone what pertains to his affection, and in the words what pertains to his thought (see above, n. 234–245).

But the rest of the senses with the angels are less exquisite than the senses of seeing and hearing, for the reason that seeing and hearing serve their intelligence and wisdom, and the rest do not; and if the other senses were equally exquisite they would detract from the light and joy of their wisdom, and would let in the delight of pleasures pertaining to various appetites and to the body; and so far as these prevail they obscure and weaken the understanding. This takes place in the world, where men become gross and stupid in regard to spiritual truths so far as they indulge the sense of taste and yield to the allurements of the sense of touch.

[3] From what has already been said and shown in the chapter on the wisdom of the angels of heaven (n. 265–275), it can be seen that the inner senses also of the angels of heaven, which pertain to their thought and affection, are more exquisite and perfect than the senses they had in the world. But as regards the state of those that are in hell as compared with the state of those in the world there is also a great difference, for as great as is the perfection and excellence of the outer and inner senses of the angels in heaven, with those who are in hell the imperfection is equally great. But the state of these will be treated of hereafter.

462b. That when a man leaves the world he takes with him all his memory has been shown to me in many ways, and many of the things I have seen and heard are worthy of mention, some of which I will relate in order. There were some who denied their crimes and villainies which they had perpetrated in the world; and in consequence, that they might not be believed innocent, all their deeds were disclosed and reviewed from their memory in order, from their earliest to their latest years; these were chiefly adulteries and whoredoms.

[2] There were some who had deceived others by wicked arts and had committed thefts. The deceits and thefts of these were also enumerated in detail, many of which were known to scarcely any in the world except themselves. These deeds they confessed, because they were plainly set forth, with every thought, intention, pleasure, and fear which occupied their minds at the time.

[3] There were others who had accepted bribes, and had rendered venal judgments, who were similarly explored from their memory and from it everything they had done from the beginning to the end of their office was reviewed. Every detail in regard to what and how much they had received, as well as the time, and their state of mind and intention, were brought to their recollection and made visibly clear to the number of many hundreds. This was done with several and what is wonderful, in some cases their memorandum books, in which they had recorded these things, were opened and read before them page by page.

[4] Others who had enticed maidens to shame or had violated chastity were called to a like judgment; and the details of their crimes were drawn forth from their memory and reviewed. The very faces of the maidens and women were also exhibited as if present, with the places, words, and intentions, and this as suddenly as when a scene is presented to the sight, the exhibitions continuing sometimes for hours.

[5] There was one who had made light of slandering others; and I heard his slanders recounted in order, and his defamations,

with the very words, and the persons about whom and before whom they were uttered; all of which were produced and presented to the very life, although while he lived in the world he had most carefully concealed everything.

[6] There was one who had deprived a relative of his inheritance under a fraudulent pretext; and he was in like manner convicted and judged; and what is wonderful, the letters and papers that passed between them were read in my hearing, and it was said that not a word was lacking.

[7] The same person shortly before his death had also secretly poisoned his neighbor. This was disclosed in this way. He appeared to be digging a trench under his feet, from which a man came forth as out of a grave, and cried out to him, "What have you done to me?" Then everything was revealed, how the poisoner had talked with him in a friendly manner, and had held out the cup, also what he thought beforehand, and what happened afterwards. When all this had been disclosed he was sentenced to hell.

[8] In a word, to each evil spirit all his evils, villainies, robberies, artifices, and deceits are made clear, and are brought forth from his very memory, and his guilt is fully established; nor is there any possible room for denial, because all the circumstances are exhibited together. Moreover, I have learned from a man's memory, when it was seen and inspected by angels, what his thoughts had been for a month, one day after another, and this without mistake, the thoughts being recalled just as they arose from day to day.

[9] From these examples it can be seen that man carries with him all of his memory, and that nothing can be so concealed in the world as not to be disclosed after death, which is done in the presence of many, according to the Lord's words:

> There is nothing concealed that shall not be uncovered, and nothing secret that shall not be known; therefore what ye have spoken in the dark

shall be heard in the light and what ye have spoken in the ear shall be proclaimed on the housetops (Luke 12:2, 3).

463. In disclosing his acts to a man after death, the angels to whom the office of searching is assigned look into his face, and their search extends through the whole body, beginning with the fingers of each hand, and thus proceeding through the whole. As I wondered at this the reason was given, namely, that as all things of the thought and will are inscribed on the brain, for their beginnings are there, so are they likewise inscribed on the whole body, since all things of thought and will extend from their beginnings into all things of the body and there terminate as in their outmosts; and this is why the things that are inscribed on the memory from the will and consequent thought are inscribed not only on the brain, but also upon the whole man, and there exist in order in accordance with the order of the parts of the body. It was thus made clear that man as a whole is such as he is in his will and its thought, even to the extent that an evil man is his own evil, and a good man his own good.[1] This shows what is meant by the book of man's life spoken of in the Word, namely, that all things that he has done and all things that he has thought are inscribed on the whole man, and when they are called forth from the memory they appear as if read in a book, and when the spirit is viewed in the light of heaven, they appear as in an image. To all this I would add something remarkable in regard to the continuance of the memory after death, by which I was assured that not only things in general but also the minutest particulars that have entered the memory remain and are never obliterated. I saw books there containing writings as in the world, and was told

---

1. A good man, spirit, or angel, is his own good and his own truth, that is, he is wholly such as his good and truth are (n. 10298, 10367). This is because good is what makes the will and truth the understanding; and the will and understanding make everything of life in man, spirit, or angel (n. 3332, 3623, 6065). It is the same thing to say that a man, spirit, or angel is his own love (n. 6872, 10177, 10284).

that they were from the memory of those who wrote, and that there was not a single word lacking in them that was in a book written by the same person in the world; and thus all the minutest particulars might be drawn from one's memory, even those that he had forgotten in the world. And the reason was given, namely, that man has an external and an internal memory, an external memory belonging to his natural man, and an internal memory belonging to his spiritual man; and that every least thing that a man has thought, willed, spoken, done or even heard and seen, is inscribed on his internal or spiritual memory;[2] and that what is there is never erased, since it is also inscribed on the spirit itself and on the members of its body, as has been said above; and that the spirit is thus formed in accordance with the thoughts and acts of its will. I know that this sounds like a paradox, and is therefore difficult to believe; but still it is true. Let no one believe, then, that there is anything that a man has ever thought in himself or done in secret that can be concealed after death; but let him believe that all things and each single thing are then laid open as clear as day.

464. Although the external or natural memory remains in man after death, the merely natural things in it are not reproduced

---

2. Man has two memories: an outer and an inner, or a natural and a spiritual memory (n. 2469–2494). Man does not know that he has an inner memory (n. 2470, 2471). How far the inner memory surpasses the outer (n. 2473). The things contained in the outer memory are in the light of the world, but the things contained in the inner are in the light of heaven (n. 5212). It is from the inner memory that man is able to think and speak intellectually and rationally (n. 9394). All things and each thing that a man has thought, spoken, and done, and that he has seen and heard, are inscribed on the inner memory (n. 2474, 7398). That memory is the book of his life (n. 2474, 9386, 9841, 10505). In the inner memory are the truths that have been made truths of faith, and the goods that have been made goods of love (n. 5212, 8067). Those things that have become matters of habit and have come to be things of the life, and have thus disappeared from the outer memory, are in the inner memory (n. 9394, 9723, 9841). Spirits and angels speak from the inner memory, and consequently have a universal language (n. 2472, 2476, 2490, 2493).

The languages of the world belong to the outer memory (n. 2472, 2476).

in the other life, but only the spiritual things adjoined to the natural by correspondences; but when these are present to the sight they appear in exactly the same form as they had in the natural world; for all things seen in the heavens have just the same appearance as in the world, although in their essence they are not natural but spiritual (as may be seen in the chapter on representatives and appearances in heaven, n. 170–176).

[2] But the external or natural memory in respect to the things in it that are derived from the material, and from time and space, and from other properties of nature, is not serviceable to the spirit in the way that it was serviceable to it in the world, for whenever man thinks in the world from his external sensual, and not at the same time from his internal or intellectual sensual, he thinks naturally and not spiritually; but in the other life when he is a spirit in the spiritual world he does not think naturally but spiritually, and to think spiritually is to think intellectually or rationally. For this reason the external or natural memory in respect to its material contents is then quiescent, and only those things that man has imbibed in the world by means of material things, and has made rational, come into use. The external memory becomes quiescent in respect to material things because these cannot then be brought forth, since spirits and angels speak from those affections and thoughts that are proper to their minds; and are therefore unable to give expression to anything that is not in accord with their affections and thoughts, as can be seen in what is said about the speech of angels in heaven and their speech with man (n. 234–257).

[3] Because of this man after death is rational, not in the degree that he was skilled in languages and sciences in the world, but in the degree in which he became rational by means of these. I have talked with many who were believed in the world to be learned because they were acquainted with ancient languages, such as the Hebrew, Greek, and Latin, but had not cultivated their rational faculty by what is written in those

languages. Some of them were seen to be just as simple as those who knew nothing of those languages, and some even stupid, and yet they retained the conceit of being wiser than others.

[4] I have talked with some who had believed in the world that man is wise in the measure of the contents of his memory, and who had stored up many things in their memory, speaking almost solely from the memory, and therefore not from themselves but from others, and their rationality had not been at all perfected by means of the things in their memory. Some of these were stupid and some sottish, not in the least comprehending whether a truth is true or not, and seizing upon all falsities that are passed off for truths by those who called themselves learned; for from themselves they are unable to see anything, whether it be true or not, and consequently are unable to see anything rationally when listening to others.

[5] I have also talked with some who had written much in the world on scientific subjects of every kind, and had thereby acquired a worldwide reputation for learning. Some of these, indeed, had the ability to reason about truths, whether they are true or not; and some, when they had turned to those who were in the light of truth, had some comprehension that truths are true, but still had no wish to comprehend them, and therefore when they were in their own falsities, and thus in themselves, denied them. Some had no more wisdom than the unlearned common people. Thus each differed from the other according as he had cultivated his rational faculty by means of the knowledges he had written about or collated. But those who were opposed to the truths of the church, and who thought from mere knowledges and confirmed themselves thereby in falsities, did not cultivate their rational faculty, but cultivated only an ability to reason, which in the world is believed to be rationality. But this ability is wholly different from rationality; it is an ability to prove anything it pleases, and from preconceived principles and from fallacies to see falsities and not

truths. Such persons can never be brought to acknowledge truths, since truths cannot be seen from falsities; but falsities may be seen from truths.

[6] The rational faculty of man is like a garden or shrubbery, or like fresh ground; the memory is the soil, truths known and knowledges are the seeds, the light and heat of heaven cause them to grow; without light and heat there is no germination; so is it with the mind when the light of heaven, which is Divine truth, and the heat of heaven, which is Divine love, are not admitted; rationality is solely from these. It is a great grief to the angels that learned men for the most part ascribe all things to nature, and have thereby so closed up the interiors of their minds as to be unable to see anything of truth from the light of truth, which is the light of heaven. In consequence of this such in the other life are deprived of their ability to reason that they may not disseminate falsities among the simple good and lead them astray; and are sent away into desert places.

465. A certain spirit was indignant because he was unable to remember many things that he knew in the life of the body, grieving over the lost pleasure which he had so much enjoyed, but he was told that he had lost nothing at all, that he still knew each and every thing that he had known, although in the world where he now was no one was permitted to call forth such things from the memory, and that he ought to be satisfied that he could now think and speak much better and more perfectly than before, and that his rational was not now immersed as before in gross, obscure, material, and corporeal things, which are of no use in the kingdom into which he had now come; also that he now possessed everything conducive to the uses of eternal life, and that this is the only way of becoming blessed and happy; and therefore it is the part of ignorance to believe that in this kingdom intelligence perishes with the removal or quiescence of the material things in the memory; for the real fact is that so far as the mind can be withdrawn from

things of sense pertaining to the external man or the body, so far it is elevated to things spiritual and heavenly.

466. What these two memories are is sometimes presented to view in the other life in forms not elsewhere seen; for many things which in man take the form of ideas are there presented as objects of sight. The external memory there presents the appearance of a callus, the internal the appearance of a medullary substance like that in the human brain; and from this what they are can be known. With those that have devoted themselves in the life of the body to the cultivation of the memory alone, and have not cultivated their rational faculty, the callosity appears hard and streaked within as with tendons. With those that have filled the memory with falsities it appears hairy and rough, because of the confused mass of things in it. With those that have cultivated the memory with the love of self and the world as an end it appears glued together and ossified. With those that have wished to penetrate into Divine arcana by means of learning, especially of a philosophical kind, with an unwillingness to believe until convinced by such proofs, the memory appears like a dark substance, of such a nature as to absorb the rays of light and turn them into darkness. With those that have practiced deceit and hypocrisy it appears hard and bony like ivory, which reflects the rays of light. But with those that have been in the good of love and the truths of faith there is no such callous appearance, because their inner memory transmits the rays of light into the outer; and in its objects or ideas as in their basis or their ground, the rays terminate and find delightful receptacles; for the outer memory is the outmost of order in which, when goods and truths are there, the spiritual and heavenly things are gently terminated and find their seat.

467. Men living in the world who are in love to the Lord and charity toward the neighbor have with them and in them angelic intelligence and wisdom, but it is then stored up in the

inmosts of the inner memory; and they are not at all conscious of it until they put off corporeal things. Then the natural memory is laid asleep and they awake into their inner memory, and then gradually into angelic memory itself.

468. How the rational faculty may be cultivated shall also be told in a few words. The genuine rational faculty consists of truths and not of falsities; whatever consists of falsities is not rational. There are three kinds of truths, civil, moral, and spiritual. Civil truths relate to matters of judgment and of government in kingdoms, and in general to what is just and equitable in them. Moral truths pertain to the matters of everyone's life which have regard to companionships and social relations, in general to what is honest and right, and in particular to virtues of every kind. But spiritual truths relate to matters of heaven and of the church, and in general to the good of love and the truth of faith.

[2] In every man there are three degrees of life (see above, n. 267). The rational faculty is opened to the first degree by civil truths, to the second degree by moral truths, and to the third degree by spiritual truths. But it must be understood that the rational faculty that consists of these truths is not formed and opened by man's knowing them, but by his living according to them; and living according to them means loving them from spiritual affection; and to love truths from spiritual affection is to love what is just and equitable because it is just and equitable, what is honest and right because it is honest and right, and what is good and true because it is good and true; while living according to them and loving them from the bodily affection is loving them for the sake of self and for the sake of one's reputation, honor or gain. Consequently, so far as man loves these truths from a bodily affection he fails to become rational, for he loves, not them, but himself; and the truths are made to serve him as servants serve their Lord; and when truths become servants they do not enter the man and open any degree of life in him, not

even the first, but merely rest in the memory as knowledges under a material form, and there conjoin themselves with the love of self, which is a bodily love.

[3] All this shows how man becomes rational, namely, that he becomes rational to the third degree by a spiritual love of the good and truth which pertain to heaven and the church; he becomes rational to the second degree by a love of what is honest and right; and to the first degree by a love of what is just and equitable. These two latter loves also become spiritual from a spiritual love of good and truth, because that love flows into them and conjoins itself to them and forms in them as it were its own semblance.

469. Spirits and angels, equally with men, have a memory, whatever they hear, see, think, will, and do, remaining with them, and thereby their rational faculty is continually cultivated even to eternity. Thus spirits and angels, equally with men, are perfected in intelligence and wisdom by means of knowledges of truth and good. That spirits and angels have a memory I have been permitted to learn by much experience, having seen everything that they have thought and done, both in public and in private, called forth from their memories when they were with other spirits; and I have seen those that were in some truth from simple good imbued with knowledges, and thereby with intelligence, and afterwards raised up into heaven. But it must be understood that such are not imbued with knowledges and thereby with intelligence beyond the degree of affection for good and for truth that they have attained to while in the world; for such and so much of affection as any spirit or angel had in the world remains with him; and this affection is afterwards perfected by being filled out, which goes on to eternity. For everything is capable of being filled out to eternity, since everything is capable of infinite variation, thus of enrichment by various things, and consequently of multiplication and fructification. To anything good there is no limit because it is from the Infinite. That spirits and angels are being perfected unceasingly in intelligence and wisdom by means of knowledges of truth and good may be seen above, in the chapters on the wisdom of the angels of heaven (n. 265–275); on the heathen or people outside the church in heaven (n. 318–328); and on little children in heaven (n. 329–345); and that this is done to that degree of affection for good and for truth in which they had been in the world, and not beyond it, may be seen in n. 349.

49

Man after Death Is Such
as His Life Had Been in the World

470. Every Christian knows from the Word that one's own life awaits him after death; for it is there said in many passages that man will be judged and rewarded according to his deeds and works; and no one who thinks from good and from real truth can help seeing that he who lives well goes to heaven and that he who lives wickedly goes to hell. But the evil man is unwilling to believe that his state after death is according to his life in the world; he thinks, especially when he is sick, that heaven is granted to everyone out of pure mercy, whatever his life may have been, and that this is done in accordance with his faith, which he separates from life.

471. That man will be judged and rewarded according to his deeds and works is declared in many passages in the Word, some of which I will here quote:

The Son of man shall come in the glory of his Father with his angels, and then he will render unto everyone according to his works (Matt. 16:27).

Blessed are the dead that die in the Lord; yea, saith the Spirit, that they may rest from their labors, for their works follow them (Rev. 14:13).

I will give to everyone according to his works (Rev. 2:23).

I saw the dead, small and great, standing before God; and the books were opened and the dead were judged out of the things that were written in the books according to their works. The sea gave up the dead that were in it, and death and hell gave up those that were in them, and they were judged everyone according to their works (Rev. 20:12, 13).

Behold I come, and my reward is with me, to give to everyone according to his works (Rev. 22:12).

Everyone that heareth my words and doeth them I will liken to a prudent man; but everyone that heareth my words and doeth them not is likened to a foolish man (Matt. 7:24, 26).

Not everyone that saith unto me, Lord, Lord, shall enter into the kingdom of the heavens; but he that doeth the will of my Father who is in the heavens. Many will say unto me in that day, Lord, Lord, have we not prophesied in Thy name, and through Thy name cast out demons, and in Thy name done many mighty works? But then will I confess to them, I know you not; depart from me, ye workers of iniquity (Matt. 7:21–23).

Then shall ye begin to say, We have eaten and drunk before Thee; Thou hast taught in our streets. But he will say, I tell you I know you not, ye workers of iniquity (Luke 13:25–27).

I will recompense them according to their work and according to the doing of their hands (Jer. 25:14).

Jehovah, whose eyes are open upon all the ways of men, to give to everyone according to his ways and according to the fruit of his works (Jer. 32:19).

I will visit upon his ways and recompense to him his works (Hos. 4:9).

Jehovah doeth with us according to our ways and according to our works (Zech. 1:6).

In foretelling the last judgment the Lord recounts nothing but works, teaching that those that have done good works will enter into eternal life, and those that have done evil works will enter into damnation, as in Matthew 25:32–46, and in many other passages that treat of the salvation and condemnation of man. It is clear that works and deeds constitute the outward life of man, and that the quality of his inward life is made evident in them.

472. But by deeds and works, what they are inwardly is here meant, and not the way they outwardly appear; for everyone knows that every deed and work goes forth from the man's will and thought; otherwise it would be nothing but a movement like that of an automaton or image. Consequently, a deed or work viewed in itself is merely an effect that derives its soul and life from will and thought, even to the extent that it is nothing but will and thought in effect, and thus is will and thought in outward form. From this it follows that a deed or work is in quality such as are the will and thought that produce it. If the thought and will are good the deeds and works are good; but if the thought and will are evil the deeds and works are evil, although in outward form they appear alike. A thousand men may act alike, that is, may do like deeds, so alike in outward form as to be almost indistinguishable, and yet each one regarded in itself be different, because from an unlike will.

[2] For example, when one acts honestly and justly with a companion, one person may do it for the purpose of appearing to be honest and just out of regard to himself and his own honor; another out of regard to the world and gain; a third out of regard to reward and merit; a fourth out of regard to friendship; a fifth from fear of the law and the loss of reputation or employment; a sixth that he may draw someone to his own side, even when he is in the wrong; a seventh that he may deceive; and others from other motives. In all these instances although the deeds are good in appearance, since it is a good thing to act honestly and justly with a companion, they are nevertheless evil, because they are done, not out of regard to honesty and justice and for the love of these, but out of regard to love of self and the world which are loved; and honesty and justice are made to serve that love as servants serve a lord, whom the lord despises and dismisses when they fail to serve him.

[3] In outward form those act in a like way who act honestly and justly with a companion because they love what is honest and just. Some of these act from the truth of faith or from obedience, because the Word so commands; some from the good of faith or from conscience, because from a religious motive; some from good of charity toward the neighbor because his good should be regarded; some from the good of love to the Lord because good should be done for the sake of good, as also what is honest and just should be done for the sake of honesty

and justice; and this they love because it is from the Lord, and because the Divine that goes forth from the Lord is in it, and consequently regarded in its very essence it is Divine. The deeds or works of such are inwardly good, and therefore are outwardly good also; for, as has been said above, deeds or works are precisely such in quality as the thought and will from which they proceed, and apart from thought and will they are not deeds and works, but only inanimate movements. All this explains what is meant in the Word by works and deeds.

473. As deeds and works are from the will and thought, so are they from the love and faith, consequently they are such as the love and faith are; for it is the same thing whether you say one's love or his will, and it is the same thing whether you say one's faith or his established thought; for that which a man loves he wills, and that which a man believes he thinks; and when a man loves what he believes he also wills it and as far as possible does it. Everyone may know that love and faith are within man's will and thought, and not outside of them, for love is what kindles the will, and the thought is what it enlightens in matters of faith; therefore only those that are able to think wisely are enlightened, and in the measure of their enlightenment they think what is true and will it, or what is the same, they believe what is true and love it.[1]

1. As all things that exist according to order in the universe have relation to good and truth, so in man all things have relation to will and understanding (n. 803, 10122).

For the reason that the will is a recipient of good and the understanding a recipient of truth (n. 3332, 3623, 5232, 6065, 6125, 7503, 9300, 9995).

It amounts to the same whether you say truth or faith, for faith belongs to truth and truth belongs to faith; and it amounts to the same whether you say good or love, for love belongs to good and good belongs to love (n. 4353, 4997, 7179, 10122, 10367).

From this it follows that the understanding is a recipient of faith, and the will a recipient of love (n. 7179, 10122, 10367). And since the understanding of man is capable of receiving faith in God and the will is capable of receiving love to God, man is capable of being conjoined with God in faith and love, and he that is capable of being conjoined with God in love and faith can never die (n. 4525, 6323, 9231).

474. But it must be understood that it is the will that makes the man, while thought makes the man only so far as it goes forth from the will; and deeds and works go forth from both; or what is the same, it is love that makes the man, and faith only so far as it goes forth from love; and deeds or works go forth from both. Consequently, the will or love is the man himself, for whatever goes forth belongs to that from which it goes forth. To go forth is to be brought forth and presented in suitable form for being perceived and seen.[2] All this makes clear what faith is when separated from love, namely, that it is no faith, but mere knowledge, which has no spiritual life in it; likewise what a deed or work is apart from love, namely, that it is not a deed or work of life, but a deed or work of death, which possesses an appearance of life from an evil love and a belief in what is false. This appearance of life is what is called spiritual death.

475. Again, it must be understood that in deeds or works the whole man is exhibited, and that his will and thought or his love and faith, which are his interiors, are not complete until they exist in deeds or works, which are his exteriors, for these are the outmosts in which the will and thought terminate, and without such terminations they are interminate, and have as yet

2. The will of man is the very being [esse] of his life, because it is the receptacle of love or good, and the understanding is the outgo [existere] of life therefrom, because it is the receptacle of faith or truth (n. 3619, 5002, 9282). Thus the life of the will is the chief life of man, and the life of the understanding proceeds therefrom (n. 585, 590, 3619, 7342, 8885, 9282, 10076, 10109, 10110). In the same way as light proceeds from fire or flame (n. 6032, 6314). From this it follows that man is man by virtue of his will and his understanding therefrom (n. 8911, 9069, 9071, 10076, 10109, 10110).

Every man is loved and esteemed by others in accordance with the good of his will and of his understanding therefrom, for he that wills well and understands well is loved and esteemed; and he that understands well and does not will well is set aside and despised (n. 8911, 10076). After death man continues to be such as his will is, and his understanding therefrom (n. 9069, 9071, 9386, 10153).

Consequently after death man continues to be such as his love is, and his faith therefrom; and whatever belongs to his faith and not also to his love then vanishes, because it is not in the man, thus not of the man (n. 553, 2364, 10153).

no existence, that is, are not yet in the man. To think and to will without doing, when there is opportunity, is like a flame that is enclosed in a vessel and goes out; also like seed cast upon the sand, which fails to grow, and so perishes with its power of germination. But to think and will and from that to do is like a flame that gives heat and light all around, or like a seed in the ground that grows up into a tree or flower and continues to live. Everyone can know that willing and not doing, when there is opportunity, is not willing; also that loving and not doing good, when there is opportunity, is not loving, but mere thought that one wills and loves; and this is thought separate, which vanishes and is dissipated. Love and will constitute the soul itself of a deed or work, and give form to its body in the honest and just things that the man does. This is the sole source of man's spiritual body, or the body of his spirit; that is, it is formed solely out of the things that the man does from his love or will (see above, n. 463). In a word, all things of man and his spirit are contained in his deeds or works.[3]

476. All this makes clear what the life is that awaits man after death, namely, that it is his love and his faith therefrom, not only in potency, but also in act; thus that it is his deeds or works, because in these all things of man's love and faith are contained.

477. It is man's ruling love that awaits him after death, and this is in no way changed to eternity. Everyone has many loves;

---

3. Interior things flow in successively into exterior things even down to the extreme or outmost, and there they come forth and have permanent existence (n. 634, 6451, 6465, 9215, 9216). They not only flow in, but in the outmost they form the simultaneous, in what order (n. 5897, 6451, 8603, 10099). Thereby all interior things are held together in connection, and have permanent existence (n. 9828). Deeds or works are the outmosts which contain the interiors (n. 10331). Therefore being recompensed and judged according to deeds and works is being recompensed and judged in accordance with all things of one's love and faith, or of his will and thought, because these are the interiors contained in deeds and works (n. 3147, 3934, 6073, 8911, 10331, 10332).

but they are all related to his ruling love, and make one with it or together compose it. All things of the will that are in harmony with the ruling love are called loves, because they are loved. These loves are both inner and outer; some directly connected and some mediately; some nearer and some more remote; they are subservient in various ways. Taken together they constitute a kingdom, as it were, such being the order in which they are arranged in man, although man knows nothing whatever about that arrangement. And yet something of it is made manifest to him in the other life, for the spread of his thought and affection there is in accordance with the arrangement of his loves, his thought and affection extending into heavenly societies when the ruling love is made up of the loves of heaven, but into infernal societies when it is made up of the loves of hell. That all the thought and affection of spirits and of angels has extension into societies may be seen above, in the chapters on the wisdom of the angels of heaven, and on the form of heaven which determines affiliations and communications there.

478. But what has been said thus far appeals only to the thought of the rational man. That it may also be presented to the perception derived from the senses, I will add some experiences by which it may be illustrated and confirmed. First, man after death is his own love or his own will. Second, man continues to eternity such as his will or ruling love is. Third, the man who has heavenly and spiritual love goes to heaven, while the man who has corporeal and worldly love, and no heavenly and spiritual love, goes to hell. Fourth, unless faith is from heavenly love it does not endure in man. Fifth, love in act, that is, the life of man, is what endures.

479. (1) *Man after death is his own love or his own will.* This has been proved to me by manifold experience. The entire heaven is divided into societies according to differences of good of love; and every spirit who is taken up into heaven and be-

comes an angel is taken to the society where his love is; and
when he arrives there he is, as it were, at home, and in the
house where he was born; this the angel perceives, and is affiliated with those there that are like himself. When he goes away
to another place he feels constantly a kind of resistance, and a
longing to return to his like, thus to his ruling love. Thus are
affiliations brought about in heaven; and in a like manner in
hell, where all are affiliated in accordance with loves that are the
opposites of heavenly loves. It has been shown above (n. 41–50
and 200–212) that both heaven and hell are composed of societies, and that they are all distinguished according to differences
of love.

[2] That man after death is his own love might also be seen
from the fact that whatever does not make one with his ruling
love is then separated and as it were taken away from him.
From one who is good everything discordant or inharmonious
is separated and as it were taken away, and he is thus let into
his own love. It is the same with an evil spirit, with the difference that from the evil truths are taken away, and from the
good falsities are taken away, and this goes on until each becomes his own love. This is effected when the man-spirit is
brought into the third state, which will be described hereafter.
When this has been done he turns his face constantly to his
own love, and this he has continually before his eyes, in whatever direction he turns (see above, n. 123, 124).

[3] All spirits, provided they are kept in their ruling love, can
be led wherever one pleases, and are incapable of resistance,
however clearly they may see that this is being done, and however much they may think that they will resist. They have often
been permitted to try whether they could do anything contrary
to their ruling love, but in vain. Their love is like a bond or a
rope tied around them, by which they may be led and from
which they cannot loose themselves. It is the same with men in
the world who are also led by their love, or are led by others

by means of their love; but this is more the case when they have become spirits, because they are not then permitted to make a display of any other love, or to counterfeit what is not their own.

[4] All interaction in the other life proves that the spirit of man is his ruling love, for so far as anyone is acting or speaking in accord with the love of another, to the same extent is the other plainly present, with full, joyous, and lively countenance; but when one is speaking or acting contrary to another's love, to that extent the other's countenance begins to be changed, to be obscured and indiscernible, until at length he wholly disappears as if he had not been there. I have often wondered how this could be, for nothing of the kind can occur in the world; but I have been told that it is the same with the spirit in man, which when it turns itself away from another ceases to be within his view.

[5] Another proof that a spirit is his ruling love is that every spirit seizes and appropriates all things that are in harmony with his love, and rejects and repudiates all that are not. Everyone's love is like a spongy or porous wood, which imbibes such fluids as promote its growth, and repels others. It is also like animals of every kind, which know their proper food and seek the things that agree with their nature, and avoid what disagrees; for every love wishes to be nourished on what belongs to it, evil love by falsities and good love by truths. I have sometimes been permitted to see certain simple good spirits desiring to instruct the evil in truths and goods; but when the instruction was offered them they fled far away, and when they came to their own they seized with great pleasure upon the falsities that were in agreement with their love. I have also seen good spirits talking together about truths, and the good who were present listened eagerly to the conversation, but the evil who were present paid no attention to it, as if they did not hear it. In the world of spirits ways are seen, some leading to heaven, some to hell,

and each to some particular society. Good spirits go only in the ways that lead to heaven, and to the society there that is in the good of their love; and do not see the ways that lead elsewhere; while evil spirits go only in the ways that lead to hell, and to the society there that is in the evil of their love; and do not see the ways that lead elsewhere; or if they see them have no wish to enter them. In the spiritual world these ways are real appearances, which correspond to truths or falsities; and this is why ways have this signification in the Word.[4] By this evidence from experience what has previously been affirmed on the ground of reason is made more certain, namely, that every man after death is his own love and his own will. It is said one's own will because everyone's will is his love.

480. (2) *Man after death continues to eternity such as his will or ruling love is.* This, too, has been confirmed by abundant experience. I have been permitted to talk with some who lived two thousand years ago, and whose lives are described in history, and thus known; and I found that they continued to be just the same as they were described, that is, in respect to the love out of which and according to which their lives were formed. There were others known to history, that had lived seventeen centuries ago, others that had lived four centuries ago, and three, and so on, with whom I was permitted to talk; and I found that the same affection still ruled in them, with no other difference than that the delights of their love were turned into such things as correspond. The angels declare that the life of the ruling love is never changed in anyone even to eternity, since everyone is his love; consequently to change that love in a spirit is to take away or extinguish his life; and for the reason that man after death is no longer capable of being reformed by instruction, as

---

4. A "way," a "path," a "road," a "street," and a "broad street," signify truths leading to good, or falsities leading to evil (n. 627, 2333, 10422). "To sweep [or prepare] a way" means to prepare for the reception of truths (n. 3142). "To make known the way" means, in respect to the Lord, to instruct in truths that lead to good (n. 10565).

in the world, because the outmost plane, which consists of natural knowledges and affections, is then quiescent and not being spiritual cannot be opened (see above, n. 464); and upon that plane the interiors pertaining to the mind and disposition rest as a house rests on its foundation; and on this account such as the life of one's love had been in the world such he continues to be to eternity. The angels are greatly surprised that man does not know that everyone is such as his ruling love is, and that many believe that they may be saved by mercy apart from means, or by faith alone, whatever their life may be; also that they do not know that Divine mercy works by means, and that it consists in man's being led by the Lord, both in the world and afterwards to eternity, and that those who do not live in evils are led by the Divine mercy; and finally that faith is affection for truth going forth from heavenly love, which is from the Lord.

481. (3) *The man who has heavenly and spiritual love goes to heaven; while the man who has corporeal and worldly love and no heavenly and spiritual love goes to hell.* This has been made evident to me from all whom I have seen taken up into heaven or cast into hell. The life of those taken up into heaven had been derived from a heavenly and spiritual love, while the life of those cast into hell had been derived from a corporeal and worldly love. Heavenly love consists in loving what is good, honest, and just, because it is good, honest, and just, and in doing this from love; and those that have this love have a life of goodness, honesty, and justice, which is the heavenly life. Those that love what is good, honest, and just, for its own sake, and who do this or live it, love the Lord above all things, because this is from him; they also love the neighbor, because this is the neighbor who is to be loved.[5] But corporeal love is loving

5. In the highest sense, the Lord is the neighbor, because he is to be loved above all things; but loving the Lord is loving what is from him, because he himself is in every

what is good, honest, and just, not for its own sake but for the sake of self, because reputation, honor, and gain can thus be acquired. Such, in what is good, honest, and just, do not look to the Lord and to the neighbor, but to self and the world, and find delight in fraud; and the goodness, honesty, and justice that spring forth from fraud are evil, dishonesty, and injustice, and these are what are loved by such in their practice of goodness, honesty, and justice.

[2] As the life of everyone is determined by these different kinds of love, as soon as men after death enter the world of spirits they are examined to discover their quality, and are joined to those that are in a like love; those that are in heavenly love to those that are in heaven, and those that are in corporeal love to those that are in hell; and after they have passed through the first and second state they are so separated as to no longer see or know each other; for each one becomes his own love, both in respect to his interiors pertaining to his mind, and in respect to his exteriors pertaining to his face, body, and speech; for everyone becomes an image of his own love, even in externals. Those that are corporeal loves appear gross, dusky,

---

thing that is from Him, thus it is loving what is good and true (n. 2425, 3419, 6706, 6711, 6819, 6823, 8123).

Loving what is good and true which is from the Lord is living in accordance with good and truth, and this is loving the Lord (n. 10143, 10153, 10310, 10336, 10578, 10645). Every man and every society, also one's country and the church, and in a universal sense the Lord's kingdom, are the neighbor, and doing good to these from a love of good in accord with their state is loving the neighbor; that is, their good that should be consulted is the neighbor (n. 6818–6824, 8123).

Moral good also, which is honesty, and civil good, which is justice, are the neighbor; and to act honestly and justly from the love of honesty and justice is loving the neighbor (n. 2915, 4730, 8120–8123). Thus charity toward the neighbor extends to all things of the life of man, and loving the neighbor is doing what is good and just, and acting honestly from the heart, in every function and in every work (n. 2417, 8121, 8124).

The doctrine in the ancient church was the doctrine of charity, and from that they had wisdom (n. 2385, 2417, 3419, 3420, 4844, 6628).

black and misshapen; while those that are heavenly loves appear fresh, bright, fair and beautiful. Also in their minds and thoughts they are wholly unlike, those that are heavenly loves being intelligent and wise, while those that are corporeal loves are stupid and as it were silly.

[3] When it is granted to behold the interiors and exteriors of thought and affection of those that are in heavenly love, their interiors appear like light, and some like a flamy light, while their exteriors appear in various beautiful colors like rainbows. But the interiors of those that are in corporeal love appear as if black, because they are closed up; and the interiors of some who were interiorly in malignant deceit appear like a dusky fire. But their exteriors appear of a dirty color, and disagreeable to the sight. (The interiors and exteriors of the mind and disposition are made visible in the spiritual world whenever the Lord pleases.)

[4] Those that are in corporeal love see nothing in the light of heaven; to them the light of heaven is thick darkness; but the light of hell, which is like light from burning coals, is to them as clear light. Moreover, in the light of heaven their inward sight is so darkened that they become insane; consequently they shun that light and hide themselves in dens and caverns, more or less deeply in accordance with the falsities in them derived from their evils. On the other hand those who are in heavenly love, the more interiorly and deeply they enter into the light of heaven, see all things more clearly and all things appear more beautiful to them, and they perceive truths more intelligently and wisely.

[5] Again, it is impossible for those who are in corporeal love to live at all in the heat of heaven, for the heat of heaven is heavenly love; but they can live in the heat of hell, which is the love of raging against others that do not favor them. The delights of that love are contempt of others, en-

mity, hatred, and revenge; and when they are in these delights they are in their life, and have no idea what it is to do good to others from good itself and for the sake of good itself, knowing only what it is to do good from evil and for the sake of evil.

[6] Those who are in corporeal love are unable to breathe in heaven. When any evil spirit is brought into heaven he draws his breath like one struggling in a contest; while those that are in heavenly love have a freer respiration and a fuller life the more interiorly they are in heaven. All this shows that heaven with man is heavenly and spiritual love, because on that love all things of heaven are inscribed; also that hell in man is corporeal and worldly love apart from heavenly and spiritual love, because on such loves all things of hell are inscribed. Evidently, then, he whose love is heavenly and spiritual enters heaven, and he whose love is corporeal and worldly apart from heavenly and spiritual love enters hell.

482. (4) *Unless faith is from heavenly love it does not endure in man.* This has been made clear to me by so much experience that if everything I have seen and heard respecting it were collected, it would fill a volume. This I can testify, that those who are in corporeal and worldly love apart from heavenly and spiritual love have no faith whatever, and are incapable of having any; they have nothing but knowledge or a persuasion that a thing is true because it serves their love. Some of those who claimed that they had faith were brought to those who had faith, and when they communicated with them they perceived that they had no faith at all; and afterwards they confessed that merely believing what is true and believing the Word is not faith, but that faith is loving truth from heavenly love, and willing and doing it from interior affection. Moreover, they were shown that their persuasion which they called faith was merely like the light of winter, in which light, because it has no

heat in it, all things on the earth are bound up in frost, become torpid, and lie buried under the snow. As soon, therefore, as the light of persuasive faith in them is touched by the rays of the light of heaven it is not only extinguished but is turned into a dense darkness, in which no one can see himself; and at the same time their interiors are so obscured that they can understand nothing at all, and at length become insane from falsities. Consequently with such, all the truths that they have known from the Word and from the doctrine of the church, and have called the truths of their faith, are taken away; and they imbibe in their place every falsity that is in accord with the evil of their life. For they are all let down into their loves and into the falsities agreeing with them; and they then hate and abhor and therefore reject truths, because they are repugnant to the falsities of evil in which they are. From all my experience in what pertains to heaven and hell I can bear witness that all those who from their doctrine have professed faith alone, and whose life has been evil, are in hell. I have seen many thousands of them cast down to hell. (Respecting these see the treatise *Last Judgment and the Destruction of Babylon.*)

483. (5) *Love in act, that is, the life of man, is what endures.* This follows as a conclusion from what has just been shown from experience, and from what has been said about deeds and works. Love in act is work and deed.

484. It must be understood that all works and deeds pertain to moral and civil life, and therefore have regard to what is honest and right, and what is just and equitable, what is honest and right pertaining to moral life, and what is just and equitable to civil life. The love from which deeds are done is either heavenly or infernal. Works and deeds of moral and civil life, when they are done from heavenly love, are heavenly; for what is done from heavenly love is done from the Lord, and everything done from the Lord is good. But the deeds and works of moral and civil life

when done from infernal love are infernal; for what is done from this love, which is the love of self and of the world, is done from man himself, and everything that is done from man himself is in itself evil; for man regarded in himself, that is, in regard to what is his own, is nothing but evil.[6]

6. Man's own consists in loving himself more than God, and the world more than heaven, and in making nothing of his neighbor in comparison with himself, thus it consists in the love of self and of the world (n. 694, 731, 4317).

Man is born into this own, and it is dense evil (n. 210, 215, 731, 874–876, 987, 1047, 2307, 2308, 3518, 3701, 3812, 8480, 8550, 10283, 10284, 10286, 10732).

From what is man's own not only every evil but also every falsity is derived (n. 1047, 10283, 10284, 10286). The evils that are from what is man's own are contempt for others, enmity, hatred, revenge, cruelty, deceit (n. 6667, 7370, 7373, 7374, 9348, 10038, 10742). So far as what is man's own rules, the good of love and the truth of faith are either rejected or suffocated or perverted (n. 2041, 7491, 7492, 7643, 8487, 10455, 10742).

What is man's own is hell in him (n. 694, 8480). The good that man does from what is his own is not good, but in itself is evil (n. 8480).

50

The Delights of Everyone's Life
Are Changed after Death
into Things That Correspond

485. It has been shown in the preceding chapter that the ruling affection or dominant love in everyone continues to eternity. It shall now be explained how the delights of that affection or love are changed into things that correspond. Being changed into corresponding things means into things spiritual that correspond to the natural. That they are changed into things spiritual can be seen from this, that so long as man is in his earthly body he is in the natural world, but when he leaves that body he enters the spiritual world and is clothed with a spiritual body. It has already been shown that angels, and men after death, are in a complete human form, and that the bodies with which they are clothed are spiritual bodies (n. 73–77 and 453–460); also what the correspondence is of spiritual things with natural (n. 87–115).

486. All the delights that a man has are the delights of his ruling love, for he feels nothing to be delightful except what he loves, thus especially that which he loves above all things. It means the same whether you say the ruling love or that which is loved above all things. These delights are various. In general, there are as many as there are ruling loves; consequently as many as there are men, spirits, and angels; for no one's ruling love is in every respect like that of another. For this reason no one has a face exactly like that of any other; for each one's face is an image of his mind; and in the spiritual world it is an image of his ruling love. In particular, everyone's delights are of infinite variety. It is impossible for any one delight to be exactly like another, or the same as another, either those that follow one after another or those that exist together at the same time, no one ever being the same as another. Nevertheless, the particular delights in everyone have reference to his one love, which is his ruling love, for they compose it and thus make one with it. Likewise all delights in general have reference to one universally ruling love, which in heaven is love to the Lord, and in hell is the love of self.

487. Only from a knowledge of correspondences can it be known what spiritual delights everyone's natural delights are changed into after death, and what kind of delights they are. In general, this knowledge teaches that nothing natural can exist without something spiritual corresponding to it. In particular it teaches what it is that corresponds, and what kind of a thing it is. Therefore, anyone that has this knowledge can ascertain and know what his own state after death will be, if he only knows what his love is, and what its relation is to the universally ruling loves spoken of above, to which all loves have relation. But it is impossible for those who are in the love of self to know what their ruling love is, because they love what is their own, and call their evils goods; and the falsities that they incline to and by which they confirm their evils they call truths. And yet if they were willing they might know it from others who are wise, and who see what they themselves do not see. This, however, is impossible with those who are so enticed by the love of self that they spurn all teaching of the wise.

[2] On the other hand, those who are in heavenly love accept instruction, and as soon as they are brought into the evils into which they were born, they see them from truths, for truths make evils manifest. From truth which is from good anyone can see evil and its falsity; but from evil none can see what is good and true; and for the reason that falsities of evil are darkness and correspond to darkness; consequently those that are in falsities from evil are like the blind, not seeing the things that

are in light, but shunning them instead like birds of night.[1] But as truths from good are light, and correspond to light (see above, n. 126–134), so those that are in truths from good have sight and open eyes, and discern the things that pertain to light and shade.

[3] This, too, has been proved to me by experience. The angels in heaven both see and perceive the evils and falsities that sometimes arise in themselves, also the evils and falsities in spirits in the world of spirits that are connected with the hells, although the spirits themselves are unable to see their own evils and falsities. Such spirits have no comprehension of the good of heavenly love, of conscience, of honesty and justice, except such as is done for the sake of self; neither what it is to be led by the Lord. They say that such things do not exist, and thus are of no account. All this has been said to the intent that man may examine himself and may recognize his love by his delights; and thus so far as he can make it out from a knowledge of correspondences may know the state of his life after death.

488. How the delights of everyone's life are changed after death into things that correspond can be known from a knowledge of correspondences; but as that knowledge is not as yet generally known I will try to throw some light on the subject by certain examples from experience. All who are in evil and who have established themselves in falsities in opposition to the truths of the church, especially those that have rejected the Word, flee from the light of heaven and take refuge in caves that appear at their openings to be densely dark, also in clefts of rocks, and there they hide themselves; and this because they have loved falsities and hated truths; for such caves and clefts

---

1. From correspondence "darkness" in the Word signifies falsities, and "thick darkness" the falsities of evil (n. 1839, 1860, 7688, 7711). To the evil the light of heaven is thick darkness (n. 1861, 6832, 8197). Those that are in the hells are said to be in darkness because they are in falsities of evil; of such (n. 3340, 4418, 4531). In the Word "the blind" signify those that are in falsities and are not willing to be taught (n. 2383, 6990).

of rocks,[2] as well as darkness, correspond to falsities, as light corresponds to truths. It is their delight to dwell in such places, and undelightful to dwell in the open country.

[2] Those that have taken delight in insidious and secret plots and in treacherous machinations do the same thing. They are also in such caves; and they frequent rooms so dark that they are even unable to see one another; and they whisper together in the ears in corners. Into this is the delight of their love changed. Those that have devoted themselves to the sciences with no other end than to acquire a reputation for learning, and have not cultivated their rational faculty by their learning, but have taken delight in the things of memory from a pride in such things, love sandy places, which they choose in preference to fields and gardens, because sandy places correspond to such studies.

[3] Those that are skilled in the doctrines of their own and other churches, but have not applied their knowledge to life, choose for themselves rocky places, and dwell among heaps of stones, shunning cultivated places because they dislike them. Those that have ascribed all things to nature, as well as those that have ascribed all things to their own prudence, and by various arts have raised themselves to honors and have acquired wealth, in the other life devote themselves to the study of magic arts, which are abuses of Divine order, and find in these the chief delight of life.

[4] Those that have adapted Divine truths to their own loves, and thereby have falsified them, love urinous things because these correspond to the delights of such loves.[3] Those that have been sordidly avaricious dwell in cells, and love swinish filth

---

2. In the word a "hole" or "the cleft of a rock" signifies obscurity and falsity of faith (n. 10582). Because a "rock" signifies faith from the Lord (n. 8581, 10580); and a "stone" the truth of faith (n. 114, 643, 1298, 3720, 6426, 8609, 10376).

3. The defilements of truth correspond to urine (n. 5390).

and such stenches as are exhaled from undigested food in the stomach.

[5] Those that have spent their life in mere pleasures and have lived delicately and indulged their palate and stomach, loving such things as the highest good that life affords, love in the other life excremental things and privies, in which they find their delight, for the reason that such pleasures are spiritual filth. Places that are clean and free from filth they shun, finding them undelightful.

[6] Those that have taken delight in adulteries pass their time in brothels, where all things are vile and filthy; these they love, and chaste homes they shun, falling into a swoon as soon as they enter them. Nothing is more delightful to them than to break up marriages. Those that have cherished a spirit of revenge, and have thereby contracted a savage and cruel nature, love cadaverous substances, and are in hells of that nature; and so on.

489. But the delights of life of those that have lived in the world in heavenly love are changed into such corresponding things as exist in the heavens, which spring from the sun of heaven and its light, that light presenting to view such things as have what is Divine inwardly concealed in them. The things that appear in that light affect the interiors of the minds of the angels, and at the same time the exteriors pertaining to their bodies; and as the Divine light, which is Divine truth going forth from the Lord, flows into their minds opened by heavenly love, it presents outwardly such things as correspond to the delights of their love. It has already been shown, in the chapter on representatives and appearances in heaven (n. 170–176), and in the chapter on the wisdom of the angels (n. 265–275), that the things that appear to the sight in the heavens correspond to the interiors of angels, or to the things pertaining to their faith and love and thus to their intelligence and wisdom.

[2] Having already begun to establish this point by examples from experience, to make clearer what has been previously said on the ground of causes of things I will state briefly some particulars respecting the heavenly delightful things into which the natural delights of those that have lived in heavenly love in the world are changed. Those that have loved Divine truths and the Word from an interior affection, or from an affection for truth itself, dwell in the other life in light, in elevated places that appear like mountains, where they are continually in the light of heaven. They do not know what darkness is, like that of night in the world; they live also in a vernal temperature; there are presented to their view fields filled with grain and vineyards; in their houses everything glows as if from precious stones; and looking through the windows is like looking through pure crystal. Such are the delights of their vision; but these same things are interiorly delightful because of their being correspondences of Divine heavenly things, for the truths from the Word which they have loved correspond to fields of grain, vineyards, precious stones, windows, and crystals.[4]

[3] Those that have applied the doctrinals of the church which are from the Word immediately to life, are in the inmost heaven, and surpass all others in their delights of wisdom. In every object they see what is Divine; the objects they see indeed with their eyes; but the corresponding Divine things flow in immediately into their minds and fill them with a blessedness that affects all their sensations. Thus before their eyes all things seem to laugh, to play, and to live (see above, n. 270).

---

4. In the Word a "field of corn" signifies a state of the reception and growth of truth from good (n. 9294). "Standing corn" signifies truth in conception (n. 9146).

"Vineyards" signify the spiritual church and the truths of that church (n. 1069, 9139).

"Precious stones" signify the truths of heaven and of the church transparent from good (n. 114, 9863, 9865, 9868, 9873, 9905). A "window" signifies the intellectual faculty which pertains to the internal sight (n. 655, 658, 3391).

[4] Those that have loved knowledges and have thereby cultivated their rational faculty and acquired intelligence, and at the
same time have acknowledged the Divine—these in the other life
have their pleasure in knowledges, and their rational delight
changed into spiritual delight, which is delight in knowing good
and truth. They dwell in gardens where flower beds and grass
plots are seen beautifully arranged, with rows of trees round
about, and arbors and walks, the trees and flowers changing
from day to day. The entire view imparts delight to their minds
in a general way, and the variations in detail continually renew
the delight; and as everything there corresponds to something
Divine, and they are skilled in the knowledge of correspondences, they are constantly filled with new knowledges, and by
these their spiritual rational faculty is perfected. Their delights
are such because gardens, flower beds, grass plots, and trees
correspond to sciences, knowledges, and the resulting intelligence.[5]

[5] Those that have ascribed all things to the Divine, regarding
nature as relatively dead and merely subservient to things spiritual, and have confirmed themselves in this view, are in heavenly light; and all things that appear before their eyes are made
by that light transparent, and in their transparency exhibit
innumerable variegations of light, which their internal sight
takes in as it were directly, and from this they perceive interior
delights. The things seen within their houses are as if made of
diamonds, with similar variegations of light. The walls of their
houses, as already said, are like crystal, and thus also transparent; and in them seemingly flowing forms representative of
heavenly things are seen also with unceasing variety, and this

---

5. A "garden," a "grove," and a "park," signify intelligence (n. 100, 108, 3220).
This is why the ancients celebrated holy worship in groves (n. 2722, 4552).
"Flowers" and "flower beds" signify truths learned and knowledges (n. 9553).
"Herbs," "grasses," and "grass plots" signify truths learned (n. 7571).
"Trees" signify perceptions and knowledges (n. 103, 2163, 2682, 2722, 2972, 7692).

because such transparency corresponds to the understanding when it has been enlightened by the Lord and when the shadows that arise from a belief in and love for natural things have been removed. With reference to such things and infinite others, it is said by those that have been in heaven that they have seen what eye has never seen; and from a perception of Divine things communicated to them by those who are there, that they have heard what ear has never heard.

[6] Those that have not acted in secret ways, but have been willing to have all that they have thought made known so far as civil life would permit, because their thoughts have all been in accord with what is honest and just from the Divine—these in heaven have faces full of light; and in that light every least affection and thought is seen in the face as in its form, and in their speech and actions they are like images of their affections. Such, therefore, are more loved than others. While they are speaking the face becomes a little obscured; but as soon as they have spoken, the things they have said become plainly manifest all at once in the face. And as all the objects that exist round about them correspond to their interiors, these assume such an appearance that others can clearly perceive what they represent and signify. Spirits that have found delight in clandestine acts, when they see such at a distance flee from them, and appear to themselves to creep away from them like serpents.

[7] Those that have regarded adulteries as abominable, and have lived in a chaste love of marriage, are more than all others in the order and form of heaven, and therefore in all beauty, and continue unceasingly in the flower of youth. The delights of their love are ineffable, and increase to eternity; for all the delights and joys of heaven flow into that love, because that love descends from the conjunction of the Lord with heaven and with the church, and in general from the conjunction of good and truth, which conjunction is heaven itself in general, and with each angel in particular (see above, n. 366–386). What

their outward delights are it is impossible to describe in human words. These are only a few of the things that have been told me about the correspondences of the delights of those that are in heavenly love.

490. All this makes evident that everyone's delights are changed after death into their correspondences, while the love itself continues to eternity. This is true of marriage love, of the love of justice, honesty, goodness and truth, the love of sciences and of knowledges, the love of intelligence and wisdom, and the rest. From these loves delights flow like streams from their fountain; and these continue; but when raised from natural to spiritual delights they are exalted to a higher degree.

51

The First State of Man after Death

491. There are three states that man passes through after death before he enters either heaven or hell. The first state is the state of his exteriors, the second state the state of his interiors, and the third his state of preparation. These states man passes through in the world of spirits. There are some, however, that do not pass through them; but immediately after death are either taken up into heaven or cast into hell. Those that are immediately taken up into heaven are those that have been regenerated in the world and thereby prepared for heaven. Those that have been so regenerated and prepared that they need simply to cast off natural impurities with the body are at once taken up by the angels into heaven. I have seen them so taken up soon after the hour of death. On the other hand, those that have been inwardly wicked while maintaining an outward appearance of goodness, and have thus filled up the measure of their wickedness by artifices, using goodness as a means of deceiving—these are at once cast into hell. I have seen some such cast into hell immediately after death, one of the most deceitful with his head downward and feet upward, and others in other ways. There are some that immediately after death are cast into caverns and are thus separated from those that are in the world of spirits, and are taken out from these and put back again by turns. They are such as have dealt wickedly with the neighbor under civil pretenses. But all these are few in comparison with those that are retained in the world of spirits, and are there prepared in accordance with Divine order for heaven or for hell.

492. In regard to the first state, which is the state of the exteriors, it is that which man comes into immediately after death. Every man, as regards his spirit, has exteriors and interiors. The exteriors of the spirit are the means by which it adapts the man's body in the world, especially the face, speech, and movements, to fellowship with others; while the interiors of the spirit are what belong to its own will and consequent thought; and these are rarely manifested in face, speech, and movement. For man is accustomed from childhood to maintain a semblance of friendship, benevolence, and sincerity, and to conceal the thoughts of his own will, thereby living from habit a moral and civil life in externals, whatever he may be internally. As a result of this habit man scarcely knows what his interiors are, and gives little thought to them.

493. The first state of man after death resembles his state in the world, for he is then likewise in externals, having a like face, like speech, and a like disposition, thus a like moral and civil life; and in consequence he is made aware that he is not still in the world only by giving attention to what he encounters, and from his having been told by the angels when he was resuscitated that he had become a spirit (n. 450). Thus is one life continued into the other, and death is merely transition.

494. The state of man's spirit that immediately follows his life in the world being such, he is then recognized by his friends and by those he had known in the world; for this is something that spirits perceive not only from one's face and speech but also from the sphere of his life when they draw near. Whenever anyone in the other life thinks about another he brings his face before him in thought, and at the same time many things of his life; and when he does this the other becomes present, as if he had been sent for or called. This is so in the spiritual world because thoughts there are shared, and there is no such space there as in the natural world (see above, n. 191–199). So all, as soon as they enter the other life, are recognized by their friends, their relatives, and those in any way known to them; and they talk with one another, and afterward associate in accordance with their friendships in the world. I have often heard that those that have come from the world were rejoiced at seeing their friends again, and that their friends in turn were rejoiced that they had come. Very commonly husband and wife come together and congratulate each other, and continue together, and this for a longer or shorter time according to their delight in living together in the world. But if they had not been united by a true marriage love, which is a conjunction of minds by heavenly love, after remaining together for a while they separate. Or if their minds had been discordant and were inwardly adverse, they break forth into open enmity, and sometimes into combat; nevertheless they are not separated until they enter the second state, which will be treated of presently.

495. As the life of spirits recently from the world is not unlike their life in the natural world, and as they know nothing about their state of life after death and nothing about heaven and hell except what they have learned from the sense of the letter of the Word and preaching from it, they are at first surprised to find themselves in a body and in every sense that they had in the world, and seeing like things; and they become eager to know what heaven is, what hell is, and where they are. Therefore their friends tell them about the conditions of eternal life, and take them about to various places and into various companies, and sometimes into cities, and into gardens and parks, showing them chiefly such magnificent things as delight the externals in which they are. They are then brought in turn into those notions about the state of their soul after death, and about heaven and hell, that they had entertained in the life of the body, even until they feel indignant at their total ignorance of such things, and at the ignorance of the church also. Nearly all are anxious to know whether they will get to heaven. Most of them believe that they will, because of their having lived in

the world a moral and civil life, never considering that the bad and the good live a like life outwardly, alike doing good to others, attending public worship, hearing sermons, and praying; and wholly ignorant that external deeds and external acts of worship are of no avail, but only the internals from which the externals proceed. There is hardly one out of thousands who knows what internals are, and that it is in them that man must find heaven and the church. Still less is it known that outward acts are such as the intentions and thoughts are, and the love and faith in these from which they spring. And even when taught they fail to comprehend that thinking and willing are of any avail, but only speaking and acting. Such for the most part are those that go at this day from the Christian world into the other life.

496. Such, however, are explored by good spirits to discover what they are, and this in various ways; since in this the first state the evil equally with the good utter truths and do good acts, and for the reason mentioned above, that like the good they have lived morally in outward respects, since they have lived under governments, and subject to laws, and have thereby acquired a reputation for justice and honesty, and have gained favor, and thus been raised to honors, and have acquired wealth. But evil spirits are distinguished from good spirits chiefly by this, that the evil give eager attention to whatever is said about external things, and but little attention to what is said about internal things, which are the truths and goods of the church and of heaven. These they listen to, but not with attention and joy. The two classes are also distinguished by their turning repeatedly in specific directions, and following, when left to themselves, the paths that lead in those directions. From such turning to certain quarters and going in certain ways it is known by what love they are led.

497. All spirits that arrive from the world are connected with some society in heaven or some society in hell, and yet only as

regards their interiors; and so long as they are in exteriors their interiors are manifested to no one, for externals cover and conceal internals, especially in the case of those who are in interior evil. But afterwards, when they come into the second state, their evils become manifest, because their interiors are then opened and their exteriors laid asleep.

498. This first state of man after death continues with some for days, with some for months, and with some for a year; but seldom with anyone beyond a year; for a shorter or longer time with each one according to the agreement or disagreement of his interiors with his exteriors. For with everyone the exteriors and interiors must make one and correspond. In the spiritual world no one is permitted to think and will in one way and speak and act in another. Everyone there must be an image of his own affection or his own love, and therefore such as he is inwardly such he must be outwardly; and for this reason a spirit's exteriors are first disclosed and reduced to order that they may serve the interiors as a corresponding plane.

52

The Second State of Man after Death

499. The second state of man after death is called the state of his interiors, because he is then let into the interiors of his mind, that is, of his will and thought; while his exteriors, which he has been in during his first state, are laid asleep. Whoever gives any thought to man's life and speech and action can see that everyone has exteriors and interiors, that is, exterior and interior thoughts and intentions. This is shown by the fact that in civil life one thinks about others in accordance with what he has heard and learned of them by report or conversation; but he does not talk with them in accordance with his thought; and if they are evil he nevertheless treats them with civility. That this is so is seen especially in the case of pretenders and flatterers, who speak and act in one way and think and will in a wholly different way; also in the case of hypocrites, who talk about God and heaven and the salvation of souls and the truths of the church and their country's good and their neighbor as if from faith and love, although in heart they believe otherwise and love themselves alone.

[2] All this makes clear that there are two kinds of thought, one exterior and the other interior; and that there are those who speak from exterior thought, while from their interior thought they have other sentiments, and that these two kinds of thought are kept separate, since the interior is carefully prevented from flowing into the exterior and becoming manifest in any way. By creation man is so formed as to have his interior and exterior thought make one by correspondence; and these

do make one in those that are in good, for such both think and
speak what is good only. But in those that are in evil interior
and exterior thought do not make one, for such think what is
evil and say what is good. With such there is an inversion of
order, for good with them is on the outside and evil within; and
in consequence evil has dominion over good, and subjects it to
itself as a servant, that it may serve it as a means for gaining its
ends, which are of the same nature as their love. With such an
end contained in the good that they seek and do, their good is
evidently not good, but is infected with evil, however good it
may appear in outward form to those not acquainted with their
interiors.

[3] It is not so with those that are in good. With such order
is not inverted; but good from interior thought flows into
exterior thought, and thus into word and act. Into this order
man was created; and in heaven, and in the light of heaven, his
interiors are in this order. And as the light of heaven is the
Divine truth that goes forth from the Lord, and consequently
is the Lord in heaven (n. 126–140), therefore such are led by the
Lord. All this has been said to make known that every man has
interior thought and exterior thought, and that these are distinct
from each other. The term thought includes also the will, for
thought is from the will, and thought apart from willing is
impossible. All this makes clear what is meant by the state of
man's exteriors and the state of his interiors.

500. When will and thought are mentioned will includes
affection and love, and all the delight and pleasure that spring
from affection and love, since all these relate to the will as to
their subject; for what a man wills he loves and feels to be
delightful or pleasurable; and on the other hand, what a man
loves and feels to be delightful or pleasurable, that he wills. But
by thought is then meant everything by which affection or love
is confirmed, for thought is simply the will's form, or that
whereby what is willed may appear in light. This form is made

apparent through various rational analyses, which have their origin in the spiritual world and belong properly to the spirit of man.

501. Let it be understood that man is wholly such as his interiors are, and not such as his exteriors are separate from his interiors. This is because his interiors belong to his spirit, and the life of his spirit is the life of man, for from it his body lives; and because of this such as a man's interiors are such he continues to be to eternity. But as the exteriors pertain to the body they are separated after death, and those of them that adhere to the spirit are laid asleep, and serve purely as a plane for the interiors, as has been shown above in treating of the memory of man which continues after death. This makes evident what is man's own and what is not his own, namely, that with the evil man nothing that belongs to his exterior thought from which he speaks, or to the exterior will from which he acts, is his own, but only that which belongs to his interior thought and will.

502. When the first state, which is the state of the exteriors treated of in the preceding chapter, has been passed through, the man-spirit is let into the state of his interiors, or into the state of his interior will and its thought, in which he had been in the world when left to himself to think freely and without restraint. Into this state he unconsciously glides, just as when in the world he withdraws the thought nearest to his speech, that is, from which he speaks, toward his interior thought and abides in the latter. Therefore in this state of his interiors the man-spirit is in himself and in his very life; for to think freely from his own affection is the very life of man, and is himself.

503. In this state the spirit thinks from his very will, thus from his very affection, or from his very love; and thought and will then make one, and one in such a manner that he seems scarcely to think but only to will. It is nearly the same when he speaks, yet with the difference that he speaks with a kind of fear that the thoughts of the will may go forth naked, since by his social life in the world this has come to be a part of his will.

504. All men without exception are let into this state after death, because it is their spirit's own state. The former state is such as the man was in regard to his spirit when in company; and that is not his own state. That this state, namely, the state of the exteriors into which man first comes after death (as shown in the preceding chapter) is not his own state, many things show, for example, that spirits not only think but also speak from their affection, since their speech is from their affection (as has been said and shown in the chapter on the speech of angels, n. 234–245). It was in this way that man had thought while in the world when he was thinking within himself, for at such times his thought was not from his bodily words, but he [mentally] saw the things, and in a minute of time saw more than he could afterwards utter in half an hour. Again that the state of the exteriors is not man's own state or the state of his spirit is evident from the fact that when he is in company in the world he speaks in accord with the laws of moral and civil life, and at such times interior thought rules the exterior thought, as one person rules another, to keep him from transgressing the limits of decorum and good manners. It is evident also from the fact that when a man thinks within himself, he thinks how he must speak and act in order to please and to secure friendship, good will, and favor, and this in extraneous ways, that is, otherwise than he would do if he acted in accordance with his own will. All this shows that the state of the interiors that the spirit is let into is his own state, and was his own state when he was living in the world as a man.

505. When the spirit is in the state of his interiors it becomes clearly evident what the man was in himself when he was in the world, for at such times he acts from what is his own. He that had been in the world interiorly in good then acts rationally and wisely, and even more wisely than in the world, because he

is released from connection with the body, and thus from those earthly things that caused obscurity and interposed as it were a cloud. But he that was in evil in the world then acts foolishly and insanely, and even more insanely than in the world, because he is free and under no restraint. For while he lived in the world he was sane in outward appearance, since by means of externals he made himself appear to be a rational man; but when he has been stripped of his externals his insanities are revealed. An evil man who in externals takes on the semblance of a good man may be likened to a vessel shining and polished on the outside and covered with a lid, within which filth of all kinds is hidden, in accordance with the Lord's saying:

> Ye are like unto whited sepulchers, which outwardly appear beautiful, but inwardly are full of dead men's bones and of all uncleanness (Matt. 23:27).

506. All that have lived a good life in the world and have acted from conscience, who are such as have acknowledged the Divine and have loved Divine truths, especially such as have applied those truths to life, seem to themselves, when let into the state of their interiors, like one aroused from sleep into full wakefulness, or like one passing from darkness into light. They then think from the light of heaven, thus from an interior wisdom, and they act from good, thus from an interior affection. Heaven flows into their thoughts and affections with an interior blessedness and delight that they had previously had no knowledge of; for they have communication with the angels of heaven. They then acknowledge the Lord and worship him from their very life, for being in the state of their interiors they are in their proper life (as has been said just above, n. 505); and as freedom pertains to interior affection they then acknowledge and worship the Lord from freedom. Thus, too, they withdraw from external sanctity and come into that internal sanctity in which worship itself truly consists. Such is the state of those that have lived a Christian life in accordance with the commandments in the Word.

[2] But the state of those that have lived an evil life in the world and who have had no conscience, and have in consequence denied the Divine, is the direct opposite of this. For everyone who lives an evil life, inwardly in himself denies the Divine, however much he may suppose when in external thought that he acknowledges the Lord and does not deny him; for acknowledging the Divine and living an evil life are opposites. When such in the other life enter into the state of their interiors, and are heard speaking and seen acting, they appear foolish; for from their evil lusts they burst forth into all sorts of abominations, into contempt of others, ridicule and blasphemy, hatred and revenge; they plot intrigues, some with a cunning and malice that can scarcely be believed to be possible in any man. For they are then in a state of freedom to act in harmony with the thoughts of their will, since they are separated from the outward conditions that restrained and checked them in the world. In a word, they are deprived of their rationality, because their reason while they were in the world did not have its seat in their interiors, but in their exteriors; and yet they seemed to themselves to be wiser than others.

[3] This being their character, while in the second state they are let down by short intervals into the state of their exteriors, and into a recollection of their actions when they were in the state of their interiors; and some of them then feel ashamed, and confess that they have been insane; some do not feel ashamed; and some are angry because they are not permitted to remain permanently in the state of their exteriors. But these are shown what they would be if they were to continue in that state, namely, that they would attempt to accomplish in secret ways the same evil ends, and by semblances of goodness, honesty, and justice, would mislead the simple in heart and faith, and would utterly destroy themselves; for their exteriors would at length burn with the same fire as their interiors, and their whole life would be consumed.

507. When in this second state spirits become visibly just what they had been in themselves while in the world, what they then did and said secretly being now made manifest; for they are now restrained by no outward considerations, and therefore what they have said and done secretly they now say and endeavor to do openly, having no longer any fear of loss of reputation, such as they had in the world. They are also brought into many states of their evils, that what they are may be evident to angels and good spirits. Thus are hidden things laid open and secret things uncovered, in accordance with the Lord's words:

> There is nothing covered up that shall not be revealed, and hid that shall not be known. Whatsoever ye have said in the darkness shall be heard in the light, and what ye have spoken in the ear in the inner chambers shall be proclaimed on the housetops (Luke 12:2, 3).

> I say unto you, that every idle word that men shall speak they shall give account thereof in the day of judgment (Matt. 12:36).

508. The nature of the wicked in this state cannot be described in a few words, for each one is insane in accord with his own lusts, and these are various; therefore I will merely mention some special instances from which conclusions may be formed respecting the rest. Those that have loved themselves above everything, and in their occupations and employments have looked to their own honor, and have performed uses and found delight in them not for the use's sake but for the sake of reputation, that they might because of them be esteemed more worthy than others, and have thus been fascinated by their reputation for honor, are more stupid in this second state than others; for so far as one loves himself he is separated from heaven, and so far as he is separated from heaven he is separated from wisdom.

[2] But those that have not only been in self-love but have been crafty also, and have raised themselves to honors by means of crafty practices, affiliate themselves with the worst of spirits, and learn magic arts, which are abuses of Divine order, and by

means of these they assail and infest all who do not honor them, laying snares, fomenting hatred, burning with revenge, and are eager to vent their rage on all who do not yield to them; and they rush into all these enormities so far as their fiendish companions favor them; and at length they meditate upon how they can climb up into heaven to destroy it, or be worshiped there as gods. To such length does their madness carry them.

[3] Papists of this character are more insane than the rest, for they cherish the notion that heaven and hell are subject to their power, and that they can remit sins at pleasure, claiming to themselves all that is Divine, and calling themselves Christ. This persuasion is such with them that wherever it flows in it disturbs the mind and induces darkness even to pain. Such are nearly the same in both the first and the second state; but in the second they are without rationality. Of their insanities and their lot after this state some particulars will be given in the treatise *Last Judgment and the Destruction of Babylon.*

[4] Those that have attributed creation to nature, and have therefore in heart if not with the lips denied the Divine, and thus all things of the church and of heaven, affiliate with their like in this second state, and call everyone a god who excels in craftiness, worshiping him even with Divine honors. I have seen such in an assembly adoring a magician, debating about nature, and behaving like fools, as if they were beasts under a human form, while among them there were some who in the world had been in stations of dignity, and some who had been esteemed learned and wise. So with others in other states.

[5] From these few instances it may be inferred what those are who have the interiors of their minds closed heavenwards, as is the case with all who have received no influx out of heaven through acknowledgment of the Divine and a life of faith. Everyone can judge from himself how he would act if, being such, he were left free to act with no fear of the law and no fear

in regard to his life, and with no outward restraints, such as fear of injury to one's reputation or of loss of honor and gain and consequent pleasures.

[6] Nevertheless, the insanity of such is restrained by the Lord that it may not rush beyond the limits of use; for even such spirits perform some use. In them good spirits see what evil is and its nature, and what man is when he is not led by the Lord. Another of their uses is their collecting together evil spirits like themselves and separating them from the good; and another, that the truths and goods that the evil had outwardly professed and feigned are taken away from them, and they are brought into the evils of their life and the falsities of their evil, and are thus prepared for hell.

[7] For no one enters hell until he is in his own evil and the falsities of evil, since no one is permitted there to have a divided mind, that is, to think and speak one thing and to will another. Every evil spirit there must think what is false from evil, and speak from the falsity of evil, in both respects from the will, thus from his own essential love and its delight and pleasure, in the same way that he thought while in the world when he was in his spirit, that is, in the same way as he thought in himself when he thought from interior affection. The reason is that the will is the man himself, and not the thought except so far as it partakes of the will, the will being the very nature itself or disposition of the man. Therefore man's being let into his will is being let into his nature or disposition, and likewise into his life; for by his life man puts on a nature; and after death he continues to be such as the nature is that he has acquired by his life in the world; and with the evil this nature can no longer be amended and changed by means of the thought or by the understanding of truth.

509. When evil spirits are in this second state, as they rush into evils of every kind they are subjected to frequent and

grievous punishments. In the world of spirits there are many kinds of punishment; and there is no regard for person, whether one had been in the world a king or a servant. Every evil carries its punishment with it, the two making one; therefore whoever is in evil is also in the punishment of evil. And yet no one in the other world suffers punishment on account of the evils that he had done in this world, but only on account of the evils that he then does; although it amounts to the same and is the same thing whether it be said that men suffer punishment on account of their evils in the world or that they suffer punishment on account of the evils they do in the other life, since everyone after death returns into his own life and thus into like evils; and the man continues the same as he had been in the life of the body (n. 470–484). Men are punished for the reason that the fear of punishment is the sole means of subduing evils in this state. Exhortation is no longer of any avail, neither is instruction or fear of the law and of the loss of reputation, since everyone then acts from his nature; and that nature can be restrained and broken only by punishments. But good spirits, although they had done evils in the world, are never punished, because their evils do not return. Moreover, I have learned that the evils they did were of a different kind or nature, not being done purposely in opposition to the truth, or from any other badness of heart than that which they received by inheritance from their parents, and that they were borne into this by a blind delight when they were in externals separate from internals.

510. Everyone goes to his own society in which his spirit had been in the world; for every man, as regards his spirit, is conjoined to some society, either infernal or heavenly, the evil man to an infernal society and the good man to a heavenly society, and to that society he is brought after death (see n. 438). The spirit is led to his society gradually, and at length enters it. When an evil spirit is in the state of his interiors he is turned by degrees toward his own society, and at length, before that

state is ended, directly to it; and when that state is ended he himself casts himself into the hell where those are who are like himself. This act of casting down appears to the sight like one falling headlong with the head downwards and the feet upwards. The cause of this appearance is that the spirit himself is in an inverted order, having loved infernal things and rejected heavenly things. In this second state some evil spirits enter the hells and come out again by turns; but these do not appear to fall headlong as those do that are fully vastated. Moreover, the society itself in which they had been as regards their spirit while in the world is shown to them when they are in the state of their exteriors, that they may thus learn that even while in the life of the body they were in hell, although not in the same state as those that are in hell itself, but in the same state as those who are in the world of spirits. Of this state, as compared with those that are in hell, more will be said hereafter.

511. In this second state the separation of evil spirits from good spirits takes place. For in the first state they are together, since while a spirit is in his exteriors he is as he was in the world, thus the evil with the good and the good with the evil; but it is otherwise when he has been brought into his interiors and left to his own nature or will. The separation of evil spirits from good spirits is effected by various means; in general by their being taken about to those societies with which in their first state they had communication by means of their good thoughts and affections, thus to those societies that they had induced to believe by outward appearances that they were not evil. Usually they are led about through a wide circle, and everywhere what they really are is made manifest to good spirits. At the sight of them the good spirits turn away; and at the same time the evil spirits who are being led about turn their faces away from the good toward that quarter where their infernal society is, into which they are about to come. Other methods of separation, which are many, will not now be mentioned.

53

The Third State of Man after Death,
Which Is a State of Instruction
for Those Who Enter Heaven

512. The third state of man after death, that is, of his spirit, is a state of instruction. This state is for those who enter heaven and become angels. It is not for those who enter hell, because such are incapable of being taught, and therefore their second state is also their third, ending in this, that they are wholly turned to their own love, thus to that infernal society which is in a like love. When this has been done they will and think from that love; and as that love is infernal they will nothing but what is evil and think nothing but what is false; and in such thinking and willing they find their delights, because these belong to their love; and in consequence of this they reject everything good and true which they had previously adopted as serviceable to their love as means.

[2] Good spirits, on the other hand, are led from the second state into the third, which is the state of their preparation for heaven by means of instruction. For one can be prepared for heaven only by means of knowledges of good and truth, that is, only by means of instruction, since one can know what spiritual good and truth are, and what evil and falsity are, which are their opposites, only by being taught. One can learn in the world what civil and moral good and truth are, which are called justice and honesty, because there are civil laws in the world that teach what is just, and there is association with others whereby man learns to live in accordance with moral laws, all of which have relation to what is honest and right. But spiritual

good and truth are learned from heaven, not from the world. They can be learned from the Word and from the doctrine of the church that is drawn from the Word; and yet unless man in respect to his interiors which belong to his mind is in heaven, spiritual good and truth cannot flow into his life; and man is in heaven when he both acknowledges the Divine and acts justly and honestly for the reason that he ought so to act because it is commanded in the Word. This is living justly and honestly for the sake of the Divine, and not for the sake of self and the world, as ends.

[3] But no one can so act until he has been taught, for example, that there is a God, that there is a heaven and a hell, that there is a life after death, that God ought to be loved supremely, and the neighbor as oneself, and that what is taught in the Word ought to be believed because the Word is Divine. Without a knowledge and acknowledgment of these things man is unable to think spiritually; and if he has no thought about them he does not will them; for what a man does not know he cannot think, and what he does not think he cannot will. So it is when man wills these things that heaven flows into his life, that is, the Lord through heaven, for the Lord flows into the will and through the will into the thought, and through both into the life, and the whole life of man is from these. All this makes clear that spiritual good and truth are learned not from the world but from heaven, and that one can be prepared for heaven only by means of instruction.

[4] Moreover, so far as the Lord flows into the life of anyone he instructs him, for so far he kindles the will with the love of knowing truths and enlightens the thought to know them; and so far as this is done the interiors of man are opened and heaven is implanted in them; and furthermore, what is Divine and heavenly flows into the honest things pertaining to moral life and into the just things pertaining to civil life in man, and makes them spiritual, since man then does these things from the

Divine, which is doing them for the sake of the Divine. For the things honest and just pertaining to moral and civil life which a man does from that source are the essential effects of spiritual life; and the effect derives its all from the effecting cause, since such as the cause is such is the effect.

513. Instruction is given by the angels of many societies, especially those in the northern and southern quarters, because those angelic societies are in intelligence and wisdom from a knowledge of good and truth. The places of instruction are toward the north and are various, arranged and distinguished according to the kinds and varieties of heavenly goods, that all and each may be instructed there according to their disposition and ability to receive; the places extending round about to a great distance. The good spirits who are to be instructed are brought by the Lord to these places when they have completed their second state in the world of spirits, and yet not all; for there are some that have been instructed in the world, and have been prepared there by the Lord for heaven, and these are taken up into heaven by another way—some immediately after death, some after a short stay with good spirits, where the grosser things of their thoughts and affections which they had contracted from honors and riches in the world are removed, and in that way they are purified. Some first endure vastations, which is effected in places under the soles of the feet, called the lower earth, where some suffer severely. These are such as had confirmed themselves in falsities and yet had led good lives, for when falsities have been confirmed they inhere with much force, and until they have been dispersed truths cannot be seen, and thus cannot be accepted. But vastations and how they are effected have been treated of in *Arcana Coelestia,* from which the notes below have been collected.[1]

---

1. Vastations are effected in the other life, that is, those that pass into the other life from the world are vastated (n. 698, 7122, 7474, 9763). The well-disposed are vastated

514. All who are in places of instruction dwell apart; for each one is connected in regard to his interiors with that society of heaven which he is about to enter; thus as the societies of heaven are arranged in accord with the heavenly form (see above, n. 200–212), so are the places there where instruction is given; and for this reason when those places are viewed from heaven something like a heaven in a smaller form is seen. They are spread out in length from east to west, and in breadth from south to north; but the breadth appears to be less than the length. The arrangement in general is as follows. In front are those who died in childhood and have been brought up in

---

in respect to falsities, while the evil are vastated in respect to truths (n. 7474, 7541, 7542). The well-disposed undergo vastations that they also may be divested of what pertains to the earth and the world, which they had contracted while living in the world (n. 7186, 9763). Also that evils and falsities may be removed, and thus there may be room for the influx of goods and truths out of heaven from the Lord, and ability to accept these (n. 7122, 9330). Elevation into heaven is impossible until such things have been removed, because they obstruct heavenly things and are not in harmony with them (n. 6928, 7122, 7186, 7541, 7542, 9763).

Those who are to be raised up into heaven are thus prepared for it (n. 4728, 7090). It is dangerous to come into heaven before being prepared (n. 537, 538).

The state of enlightenment and the joy of those who come out of vastation and are raised up into heaven, and their reception there (n. 2699, 2701, 2704). The region where those vastations are effected is called the lower earth (n. 4728, 7090).

That region is under the soles of the feet surrounded by the hells; its nature described (n. 4940–4951, 7090); from experience (n. 699). What the hells are which more than others infest and vastate (n. 7317, 7502, 7545). Those that have infested and vastated the well-disposed are afterwards afraid of them, shun them, and turn away from them (n. 7768). These infestations and vastations are effected in different ways in accordance with the adhesion of evils and falsities, and they continue in accordance with their quality and quantity (n. 1106–1113). Some are quite willing to be vastated (n. 1107). Some are vastated by fears (n. 4942). Some by being infested with the evils they have done in the world, and with the falsities they have thought in the world, from which they have anxieties and pangs of conscience (n. 1106). Some by spiritual captivity, which is ignorance of truth and interception of truth, combined with a longing to know truths (n. 1109, 2694). Some by sleep; some by a middle state between wakefulness and sleep (n. 1108). Those that have placed merit in works seem to themselves to be cutting wood (n. 1110). Others in other ways, with great variety (n. 699).

heaven to the age of early youth; these after passing the state of their infancy with those having charge of them, are brought hither by the Lord and instructed. Behind these are the places where those are taught who died in adult age, and who in the world had an affection for truth derived from good of life. Again, behind these are those who in the world were connected with the Mohammedan religion, and lived a moral life and acknowledged one Divine, and the Lord as the very Prophet. When these withdraw from Mohammed, because he can give them no help, they approach the Lord and worship him and acknowledge his Divinity, and they are then instructed in the Christian religion. Behind these more to the north are the places of instruction of various heathen nations who in the world have lived a good life in conformity with their religion, and have thereby acquired a kind of conscience, and have done what is just and right not so much from a regard to the laws of their government, as from a regard to the laws of religion, which they believed ought to be sacredly observed, and in no way violated by their doings. When these have been taught they are all easily led to acknowledge the Lord, because it is impressed on their hearts that God is not invisible, but is visible under a human form. These in number exceed all the rest, and the best of them are from Africa.

515. But all are not taught in the same way, nor by the same societies of heaven. Those that have been brought up from childhood in heaven, not having imbibed falsities from the falsities of religion or defiled their spiritual life with the dregs pertaining to honors and riches in the world, receive instruction from the angels of the interior heavens; while those that have died in adult age receive instruction mainly from angels of the lowest heaven, because these angels are better suited to them than the angels of the interior heavens, who are in interior wisdom which is not yet acceptable to them. But the Mohammedans receive instruction from angels who had been

previously in the same religion and had been converted to Christianity. The heathen, too, are taught by their angels.

516. All teaching there is from doctrine drawn from the Word, and not from the Word apart from doctrine. Christians are taught from heavenly doctrine, which is in entire agreement with the internal sense of the Word. All others, as the Mohammedans and heathen, are taught from doctrines suited to their apprehension, which differ from heavenly doctrine only in this, that spiritual life is taught by means of moral life in harmony with the good tenets of their religion from which they had derived their life in the world.

517. Instruction in the heavens differs from instruction on earth in that knowledges are not committed to memory, but to life; for the memory of spirits is in their life, for they receive and imbibe everything that is in harmony with their life, and do not receive, still less imbibe, what is not in harmony with it; for spirits are affections, and are therefore in a human form that is similar to their affections.

[2] Being such they are constantly animated by an affection for truth that looks to the uses of life; for the Lord provides for everyone's loving the uses suited to his genius; and that love is exalted by the hope of becoming an angel. And as all the uses of heaven have relation to the general use, which is the good of the Lord's kingdom, which in heaven is the fatherland, and as all special and particular uses are to be valued in proportion as they more closely and fully have regard to that general use, so all of these special and particular uses, which are innumerable, are good and heavenly; therefore in everyone an affection for truth is so conjoined with an affection for use that the two make one; and thereby truth is so implanted in use that the truths they acquire are truths of use. In this way are angelic spirits taught and prepared for heaven.

[3] An affection for truth that is suited to the use is insinuated by various means, most of which are unknown in the world; chiefly by representatives of uses which in the spiritual world are exhibited in a thousand ways, and with such delights and pleasures that they permeate the spirit from the interiors of its mind to the exteriors of its body, and thus affect the whole; and in consequence the spirit becomes as it were his use; and therefore when he comes into his society, into which he is initiated by instruction, he is in his life by being in his use.[2] From all this it is clear that knowledges, which are external truths, do not bring anyone into heaven; but the life itself, which is a life of uses implanted by means of knowledges.

518. There were some spirits who had convinced themselves, by thinking about it in the world, that they would go to heaven and be received before others because of their learning and their great knowledge of the Word and of the doctrines of their churches, believing that they were wise in consequence, and were such as are meant by those of whom it is said that:

> They shall shine as the brightness of the firmament, and as the stars (Dan. 12:3).

But these were examined to see whether their knowledges resided in the memory or in the life. Such of them as had a genuine affection of truth, that is, who had uses separated from what pertains to the body and the world as their end, which are essentially spiritual uses—these, when they had been instructed, were received into heaven; and it was then given them to know what it is that shines in heaven, namely, Divine truth (which

---

2. Every good has both its delight and its quality from uses and in accordance with uses; therefore such as the good is such the use is (n. 3049, 4984, 7038).

Angelic life consists in the goods of love and charity, thus in performing uses (n. 454).

The Lord, and therefore the angels, has regard to nothing in man but ends which are uses (n. 1317, 1645, 5854). The kingdom of the Lord is a kingdom of uses (n. 454, 696, 1103, 3645, 4054, 7038). Serving the lord is performing uses (n. 7038).

What man is, such are his uses (n. 1568, 3570, 4054, 6571, 6935, 6938, 10284).

is the light of heaven) in use, which is a plane that receives the rays of that light and turns them into various splendors. But those in whom knowledges resided merely in the memory, and who had acquired therefrom an ability to reason about truths and to prove what they had already accepted as principles, seeing such principles, after they had confirmed them, as truths, although they were falsities—these, as they were in no heavenly light, and yet were in a belief derived from the conceit that usually adheres to such intelligence that they were more learned than others, and would for that reason enter heaven and be served by the angels, in order that they might be withdrawn from their delusive faith, were taken up to the first or outmost heaven to be introduced into an angelic society. But at the very threshold their eyes began to be darkened by the inflowing of the light of heaven, and their understanding to be disturbed, and at length they began to gasp as if at the point of death; and as soon as they felt the heat of heaven, which is heavenly love, they began to be inwardly tormented. They were therefore cast down, and afterwards were taught that knowledges do not make an angel, but the life itself, which is gained by means of knowledges, for knowledges regarded in themselves are outside of heaven; but life acquired by means of knowledges is within heaven.

519. When spirits have been prepared for heaven by instruction in the places above described, which is effected in a short time on account of their being in spiritual ideas that comprehend many particulars together, they are clothed with angelic garments, which are mostly glowing white as if made of fine linen; and they are thus brought to the way that leads upwards toward heaven, and are delivered there to angel guards, and afterwards are received by other angels and introduced into societies and into many blessednesses there. After this each one is led by the Lord into his own society, which is also effected by various ways, sometimes by winding paths. The ways by which they are led are not known to any angel, but are known to the Lord alone. When they come to their own society their interiors are opened; and as these are in conformity with the interiors of the angels who are in that society they are immediately recognized and received with joy.

520. To this I will add a memorable fact respecting the ways that lead from these places to heaven, by which the newly arrived angels are introduced. There are eight ways, two from each place of instruction, one going up in an eastern direction, the other toward the west. Those that enter the Lord's celestial kingdom are introduced by the eastern way, while those that enter the spiritual kingdom are introduced by the western way. The four ways that lead to the Lord's celestial kingdom appear adorned with olive trees and fruit trees of various kinds; but those that lead to the Lord's spiritual kingdom appear adorned with vines and laurels. This is from correspondence, because vines and laurels correspond to affection for truth and its uses, while olives and fruits correspond to affection for good and its uses.

54

No One Enters Heaven by Mercy
apart from Means

521. Those that have not been instructed about heaven and the way to heaven, and about the life of heaven in man, suppose that being received into heaven is a mere matter of mercy, and is granted to those that have faith, and for whom the Lord intercedes; thus that it is an admission from mere favor; consequently that all men without exception might be saved if the Lord so pleased, and some even believe that all in hell might be so saved. But those who so think know nothing about man, that he is just such as his life is, and that his life is such as his love is, both in respect to the interiors pertaining to his will and understanding and in respect to the exteriors pertaining to his body; also that his bodily form is merely the external form in which the interiors exhibit themselves in effect; consequently that one's love is the whole man (see above, n. 363). Nor do they know that the body lives not from itself, but from its spirit, and that a man's spirit is his essential affection, and his spiritual body is nothing else than his affection in human form, and in such a form it appears after death (see above, n. 453–460). So long as man remains ignorant of all this he may be induced to believe that salvation involves nothing but the Divine good pleasure, which is called mercy and grace.

522. But first let us consider what the Divine mercy is. The divine mercy is pure mercy toward the whole human race, to save it; and it is also unceasing toward every man, and is never withdrawn from anyone; so that everyone is saved who can be saved. And yet no one can be saved except by Divine means, which means the Lord reveals in the Word. The Divine means are what are called Divine truths, which teach how man must live in order to be saved. By these truths the Lord leads man to heaven, and by them he implants in man the life of heaven. This the Lord does for all. But the life of heaven can be implanted in no one unless he abstains from evil, for evil obstructs. So far, therefore, as man abstains from evil he is led by the Lord out of pure mercy by his Divine means, and this from infancy to the end of his life in the world and afterwards to eternity. This is what is meant by the Divine mercy. And from this it is evident that the mercy of the Lord is pure mercy, but not apart from means, that is, it does not look to saving all out of mere good pleasure, however they may have lived.

523. The Lord never does anything contrary to order, because he himself is order. The Divine truth that goes forth from the Lord is what constitutes order; and Divine truths are the laws of order. It is in accord with these laws that the Lord leads man. Consequently to save man by mercy apart from means would be contrary to Divine order, and what is contrary to Divine order is contrary to the Divine. Divine order is heaven in man, and man has perverted this in himself by a life contrary to the laws of order, which are Divine truths. Into this order man is brought back by the Lord out of pure mercy by means of the laws of order; and so far as he is brought back into this order he receives heaven in himself; and he that receives heaven in himself enters heaven. This again makes evident that the Lord's Divine mercy is pure mercy, and not mercy apart from means.[1]

1. Divine truth going forth from the Lord is the source of order, and Divine good is the essential of order (n. 1728, 2258, 8700, 8988). Thus the Lord is order (n. 1919, 2011, 5110, 5703, 10336, 10619). Divine truths are the laws of order (n. 2447, 7995).

The whole heaven is arranged by the Lord in accordance with His Divine order (n. 3038, 7211, 9128, 9338, 10125, 10151, 10157). Therefore the form of heaven is a form in accord with the Divine order (n. 4040–4043, 6607, 9877).

So far as a man is living in accordance with order, that is, so far as he is living in good in accordance with Divine truths, he is receiving heaven in himself (n. 4839).

524. If men could be saved by mercy apart from means all would be saved, even those in hell; in fact, there would be no hell, because the Lord is mercy itself, love itself, and goodness itself. Therefore it is inconsistent with his Divine to say that he is able to save all apart from means and does not save them. It is known from the Word that the Lord wills the salvation of all, and the damnation of no one.

525. Most of those who enter the other life from the Christian world bring with them this belief that they can be saved by mercy apart from means, and pray for that mercy; but when examined they are found to believe that entering heaven is merely gaining admission, and that those who are let in are in heavenly joy. They are wholly ignorant of what heaven is and what heavenly joy is, and consequently are told that the Lord denies heaven to no one, and that they can be admitted and can stay there if they desire it. Those who so desired were admitted; but as soon as they reached the first threshold they were seized with such anguish of heart from a draft of heavenly heat, which is the love in which angels are, and from an inflow of heavenly light, which is Divine truth, that they felt in themselves infernal torment instead of heavenly joy, and struck with dismay they

---

Man is the being in whom are brought together all things of Divine order, and by creation he is Divine order in form, because he is a recipient of Divine order (n. 3628, 4219, 4220, 4223, 4523, 4524, 5214, 6013, 6057, 6605, 6626, 9706, 10156, 10472).

Man is not born into good and truth but into evil and falsity, thus not into Divine order but into the opposite of order, and for this reason he is born into pure ignorance; consequently it is necessary for him to be born anew, that is, to be regenerated, which is effected by the Lord by means of Divine truths, that he may be brought back into order (n. 1047, 2307, 2308, 3518, 8480, 8550, 10283, 10284, 10286, 10731).

When the Lord forms man anew, that is, regenerates him, He arranges all things in him in harmony with order, that is, in the form of heaven (n. 5700, 6690, 9931, 10303).

Evils and falsities are contrary to order; nevertheless those who are in them are ruled by the Lord not in accordance with order but from order (n. 4839, 7877, 10777).

It is impossible for a man who lives in evil to be saved by mercy alone, for that would be contrary to Divine order (n. 8700).

cast themselves down headlong. Thus they were taught by living experience that it is impossible to grant heaven to anyone from mercy apart from means.

526. I have occasionally talked with angels about this, and have told them that most of those in the world who live in evil, when they talk with others about heaven and eternal life, express no other idea than that entering heaven is merely being admitted from mercy alone. And this is believed by those especially who make faith the only medium of salvation. For such from the principles of their religion have no regard to the life and the deeds of love that make life, and thus to none of the other means by which the Lord implants heaven in man and renders him receptive of heavenly joy; and as they thus reject every actual mediation they conclude, as a necessary consequence of the principle, that man enters heaven from mercy alone, to which mercy God the Father is believed to be moved by the intercession of the Son.

[2] To all this the angels said that they knew such a tenet follows of necessity from the assumption that man is saved by faith alone, and since that tenet is the head of all the rest, and since into it, because it is not true, no light from heaven can flow, this is the source of the ignorance that prevails in the church at this day in regard to the Lord, heaven, the life after death, heavenly joy, the essence of love and charity, and in general, in regard to good and its conjunction with truth, consequently in regard to the life of man, whence it is and what it is; when it should be known that thought never constitutes anyone's life, but the will and the consequent deeds; and that the life is from the thought only to the extent that the thought is derived from the will; neither is life from the faith except so far as the faith is derived from love. Angels are grieved that these persons do not know that faith alone is impossible in anyone, since faith apart from its origin, which is love, is nothing but knowledge, and in some is merely a sort of persuasion

that has the semblance of faith (see above, n. 482). Such a persuasion is not in the life of man, but outside of it, since it is separated from man unless it coheres with his love.

[3] The angels said further that those who hold to this principle concerning the essential means of salvation in man must needs believe in mercy apart from means, for they perceive both from natural light and from the experience of sight that faith separate does not constitute the life of man, since those who lead an evil life are able to think and to be persuaded the same as others; and from this comes the belief that the evil as well as the good can be saved, provided that at the hour of death they talk with confidence about intercession, and about the mercy that is granted through that intercession. The angels declared that they had never yet seen anyone who had lived an evil life received into heaven from mercy apart from means, whatever trust or confidence (which is preeminently meant by faith) he had exhibited in his talk in the world.

[4] When asked about Abraham, Isaac, Jacob, David, and the apostles, whether they were not received into heaven from mercy apart from means, the angels replied that not one of them was so received, but each one in accordance with his life in the world; that they knew where these were, and that they were no more esteemed there than others. They said that these persons are mentioned with honor in the Word for the reason that in the internal sense the Lord is meant by them—by Abraham, Isaac, and Jacob, the Lord in respect to the Divine and the Divine human; by David the Lord in respect to the Divine royalty; and by the apostles the Lord in respect to Divine truths; also that when the Word is read by man the angels have no perception whatever of these men, for their names do not enter heaven; but they have instead a perception of the Lord as he has just been described; consequently in the Word that is in heaven (see above, n. 259) there are no such names mentioned,

since that Word is the internal sense of the Word that is in the world.[2]

527. I can testify from much experience that it is impossible to implant the life of heaven in those who in the world have lived a life opposite to the life of heaven. There were some who had believed that when after death they should hear Divine truths from the angels they would readily accept them and believe them, and consequently live a different life, and could thus be received into heaven. But this was tried with very many, although it was confined to those who held this belief, and was permitted in their case to teach them that repentance is not possible after death.

Some of those with whom the experiment was made understood truths and seemed to accept them; but as soon as they turned to the life of their love they rejected them, and even spoke against them. Others were unwilling to hear them, and at once rejected them. Others wished to have the life of love that they had contracted from the world taken away from them, and to have the angelic life, or the life of heaven, infused in its place. This, too, was permitted to be done; but as soon as the life of their love was taken away they lay as if dead, with their

2. In the internal sense of the Word by Abraham, Isaac, and Jacob, the Lord in respect to the Divine itself and the Divine Human is meant (n. 1893, 4615, 6098, 6185, 6276, 6804, 6847). In heaven Abraham is unknown (n. 1834, 1876, 3229).

By David the Lord in respect to the Divine royalty is meant (n. 1888, 9954).

The twelve apostles represented the Lord in respect to all things of the church, that is, all things pertaining to faith and love (n. 2129, 3354, 3488, 3858, 6397).

Peter represented the Lord in respect to faith, James in respect to charity, and John in respect to the works of charity (n. 3750, 10087). The twelve apostles sitting on twelve thrones and judging the twelve tribes of Israel, signified that the Lord will judge in accord with the truths and goods of faith and love (n. 2129, 6397).

The names of persons and of places in the Word do not enter heaven, but are changed into things and states; and in heaven these names cannot even be uttered (n. 1876, 5225, 6516, 10216, 10282, 10432). Moreover, the angels think abstractedly from persons (n. 8343, 8985, 9007).

powers gone. By these and other experiments the simple good were taught that no one's life can by any means be changed after death; and that an evil life can in no way be converted into a good life, or an infernal life into an angelic life, for every spirit from head to heel is such as his love is, and therefore such as his life is; and to convert his life into its opposite is to destroy the spirit completely. The angels declare that it would be easier to change a night owl into a dove, or a horned owl into a bird of paradise, than to change an infernal spirit into an angel of heaven. That man after death continues to be such as his life had been in the world can be seen above in its own chapter (n. 470–484). From all this it is evident that no one can be received into heaven from mercy apart from means.

55

It Is Not So Difficult to Live the Life That Leads to Heaven as Is Believed

528. There are some who believe that to live the life that leads to heaven, which is called the spiritual life, is difficult, because they have been told that man must renounce the world, must divest himself of the lusts called the lusts of the body and the flesh, and must live spiritually; and they understand this to mean that they must discard worldly things, which consist chiefly in riches and honors; that they must walk continually in pious meditation on God, salvation, and eternal life; and must spend their life in prayers and in reading the Word and pious books. Such is their idea of renouncing the world, and living in the spirit and not in the flesh. But that this is not at all true it has been given me to know by much experience and from conversation with the angels.

I have learned, in fact, that those who renounce the world and live in the spirit in this manner acquire a sorrowful life that is not receptive of heavenly joy, since everyone's life continues the same after death. On the contrary, to receive the life of heaven a man must needs live in the world and engage in its business and employments, and by means of a moral and civil life there receive the spiritual life. In no other way can the spiritual life be formed in man, or his spirit prepared for heaven; for to live an internal life and not at the same time an external life is like dwelling in a house that has no foundation, that gradually sinks or becomes cracked and rent asunder, or totters till it falls.

529. When the life of man is scanned and explored by rational insight it is found to be threefold, namely, spiritual, moral, and civil, with these three lives distinct from each other. For there are men who live a civil life and not as yet a moral and spiritual life; and there are men who live a moral life and not as yet a spiritual life; and there are those who live a civil life, a moral life, and a spiritual life at the same time. These live the life of heaven; but the former live the life of the world separated from the life of heaven. This shows, in the first place, that the spiritual life is not a life separated from natural life or the life of the world, but is joined with it as the soul is joined with its body, and if it were separated it would be, as was said, like living in a house that has no foundation. For moral and civil life is the active plane of the spiritual life, since to will well is the province of the spiritual life, and to act well of the moral and civil life, and if the latter is separated from the former the spiritual life consists solely of thought and speech, and the will, left with no support, recedes; and yet the will is the very spiritual part of man.

530. That it is not so difficult as some believe to live the life that leads to heaven will now be shown. Who cannot live a civil and moral life? For everyone from his childhood is initiated into that life, and learns what it is by living in the world. Moreover, everyone, whether evil or good, lives that life; for who does not wish to be called honest, and who does not wish to be called just? Almost everyone practices honesty and justice outwardly, so far as to seem to be honest and just at heart, or to seem to act from real honesty and justice. The spiritual man ought to live in like manner, and can do so as easily as the natural man can, with this difference only, that the spiritual man believes in the Divine, and acts honestly and justly, not solely because to so act is in accord with civil and moral laws, but also because it is in accord with Divine laws. As the spiritual man, in whatever he is doing, thinks about Divine things, he has communication with the angels of heaven; and so far as this takes place he is conjoined with them; and thereby his internal man, which regarded in itself is the spiritual man, is opened. When man comes into this state he is adopted and led by the Lord, although himself unconscious of it, and then whatever he does that is honest and just pertaining to moral and civil life, is done from a spiritual motive; and doing what is honest and just from a spiritual motive is doing it from honesty and justice itself, or doing it from the heart.

[2] His justice and honesty appear outwardly precisely the same as the justice and honesty of natural men and even of evil and infernal men; but in inward form they are wholly unlike. For evil men act justly and honestly solely for the sake of themselves and the world; and therefore if they had no fear of laws and penalties, or the loss of reputation, of honor, of gain, and of life, they would act in every respect dishonestly and unjustly, since they neither fear God nor any Divine law, and therefore are not restrained by any internal bond; consequently they would use every opportunity to defraud, plunder, and spoil others, and this from delight. That inwardly they are such can be clearly seen from those of the same character in the other life, while everyone's externals are taken away, and his internals in which he at last lives to eternity are opened (see above, n. 499–511). As such then act without external restraints, which are, as just said, fear of the law, of the loss of reputation, of honor, of gain, and of life, they act insanely, and laugh at honesty and justice.

[3] But those who have acted honestly and justly from regard to Divine laws, when their externals are taken away and

they are left to their internals, act wisely, because they are conjoined to the angels of heaven, from whom wisdom is communicated to them. From all this it can now be seen, in the first place, that when the internal man, that is, the will and thought, are conjoined to the Divine, the civil and moral life of the spiritual man may be wholly like the civil and moral life of the natural man (see above, n. 358–360).

531. Furthermore, the laws of spiritual life, the laws of civil life, and the laws of moral life are set forth in the ten commandments of the Decalogue; in the first three the laws of spiritual life, in the four that follow the laws of civil life, and in the last three the laws of moral life. Outwardly the merely natural man lives in accordance with the same commandments in the same way as the spiritual man does, for in like manner he worships the Divine, goes to church, listens to preachings, and assumes a devout countenance, refrains from committing murder, adultery, and theft, from bearing false witness, and from defrauding his companions of their goods. But all this he does merely for the sake of himself and the world, to keep up appearances; while inwardly such a person is the direct opposite of what he appears outwardly, since in heart he denies the Divine, in worship acts the hypocrite, and when left to himself and his own thoughts laughs at the holy things of the church, believing that they merely serve as a restraint for the simple multitude.

[2] Consequently he is wholly disjoined from heaven, and not being a spiritual man he is neither a moral man nor a civil man. For although he refrains from committing murder he hates everyone who opposes him, and from his hatred burns with revenge, and would therefore commit murder if he were not restrained by civil laws and external bonds, which he fears; and as he longs to do so it follows that he is continually committing murder. Although he does not commit

adultery, yet as he believes it to be allowable he is all the while an adulterer, since he commits adultery to the extent that he has the ability and as often as he has opportunity. Although he does not steal, yet as he covets the goods of others and does not regard fraud and wicked devices as opposed to what is lawful, in intent he is continually acting the thief. The same is true of the commandments relating to moral life, which forbid false witness and coveting the goods of others. Such is every man who denies the Divine, and who has no conscience derived from religion. That he is such is clearly evident from those of like character in the other life when their externals have been removed and they are let into their internals. As they are then separated from heaven they act in unity with hell, and in consequence are affiliated with those who are in hell.

[3] It is not so with those who in heart have acknowledged the Divine, and in the actions of their lives have had respect to Divine laws, and have lived as fully in accord with the first three commandments of the Decalogue as they have in accordance with the others. When the externals of such are removed and they are let into their internals they are wiser than they were in the world; for entering into their internals is like entering from darkness into light, from ignorance into wisdom, and from a sorrowful life into a happy life, because they are in the Divine, thus in heaven. This has been said to make known what the one kind of man is and what the other is, although they have both lived the same external life.

532. Everyone may know that thoughts are led or tend in accord with the intentions, that is, in the directions that one intends; for thought is man's internal sight, and resembles the external sight in this, that to whatever point it is directed or aimed, thither it turns and there it rests. Therefore when the internal sight or the thought is turned toward the world and rests there, the thought in consequence becomes worldly; when it turns to self and self-honor it becomes corporeal; but when it is turned heavenwards it becomes heavenly. So, too, when turned heavenwards it is elevated; but when turned selfward it is drawn down from heaven and immersed in what is corporeal; and when turned toward the world it is also turned downwards from heaven, and is spent upon those objects that are presented to the natural sight.

[2] Man's love is what constitutes his intention and determines his internal sight or thought to its objects; thus the love of self fixes it upon self and its objects, the love of the world upon worldly objects, and the love of heaven upon heavenly objects; and when the love is known the state of the interiors which constitute the mind can be known, that is, the interiors of one who loves heaven are raised toward heaven and are opened above; while the interiors of one who loves the world or who loves himself are closed above and are opened outwardly. From this the conclusion follows that when the higher regions of the mind are closed above, man can no longer see the objects pertaining to heaven and the church, but those objects are in thick darkness to him; and what is in thick darkness is either denied or not understood. And this is why those that love themselves and the world above all things, since the higher regions of their minds are closed, in heart deny Divine truths; and if from their memory they say anything about them they nevertheless do not understand them. Moreover, they regard them in the same way as they regard worldly and corporeal things. And being such they are able to direct the mind to those things only that enter through the senses of the body, and in these alone do they find delight. Among these are also many things that are filthy, obscene, profane and wicked; and these cannot be removed,

because into the minds of such no influx from heaven is possible, since their minds, as just now said, are closed above.

[3] Man's intention, by which his internal sight or thought is determined, is his will; for what a man wills he intends, and what he intends he thinks. Therefore when his intention is heavenward his thought is determined heavenward, and with it his whole mind, which is thus in heaven; and from heaven he beholds the things of the world beneath him like one looking down from the roof of a house. So the man that has the interiors of his mind open can see the evils and falsities that are in him, for these are beneath the spiritual mind. On the other hand, the man whose interiors are not open is unable to see his evils and falsities, because he is not above them but in them.

From all this one may conclude whence man has wisdom and whence insanity, also what a man will be after death when he is left to will and think and to act and speak in accordance with his interiors. All this also has been said in order to make clear what constitutes a man's interior character, however he may seem outwardly to resemble others.

533. That it is not so difficult to live the life of heaven as some believe can now be seen from this, that when anything presents itself to a man that he knows to be dishonest and unjust, but to which his mind is borne, it is simply necessary for him to think that it ought not to be done because it is opposed to the Divine precepts.

If a man accustoms himself so to think, and from so doing establishes a habit of so thinking, he is gradually conjoined to heaven; and so far as he is conjoined to heaven the higher regions of his mind are opened; and so far as these are opened he sees whatever is dishonest and unjust, and so far as he sees these evils they can be dispersed, for no evil can be dispersed until it is seen. Into this state man is able to enter because of his freedom, for is not anyone able from his freedom to so think? And when man has made a beginning the Lord quickens all that is good in him, and causes him not only to see evils to be evils, but also to refrain from willing them, and finally to turn away from them. This is meant by the Lord's words,

My yoke is easy and my burden is light (Matt. 11:30).

But it must be understood that the difficulty of so thinking and of resisting evils increases so far as man from his will does evils, for in the same measure he becomes accustomed to them until he no longer sees them, and at length loves them and from the delight of his love excuses them, and confirms them by every kind of fallacy, and declares them to be allowable and good. This is the fate of those who in early youth plunge into evils without restraint, and also reject Divine things from the heart.

534. The way that leads to heaven and the way that leads to hell were once represented to me. There was a broad way tending toward the left or the north, and many spirits were seen going in it; but at a distance a large stone was seen where the broad way came to an end. From that stone two ways branched off, one to the left and one in the opposite direction to the right. The way that went to the left was narrow or straitened, leading through the west to the south, and thus into the light of heaven; the way that went to the right was broad and spacious, leading obliquely downwards toward hell. All at first seemed to be going the same way until they came to the large stone at the head of the two ways. When they reached that point they divided; the good turned to the left and entered the straitened way that led to heaven; while the evil, not seeing the stone at the fork of the ways fell upon it and were hurt; and when they rose up they ran on in the broad way to the right which went toward hell.

[2] What all this meant was afterwards explained to me. The first way that was broad, wherein many, both good and evil, went together and talked with each other as friends, because there was no visible difference between them, represented those who externally live alike honestly and justly, and between whom seemingly there is no difference. The stone at the head of the two ways or at the corner, upon which the evil fell and from which they ran into the way leading to hell, represented the Divine truth, which is rejected by those who look toward hell; and in the highest sense this stone signified the Lord's Divine human. But those who acknowledged the Divine truth and also the Divine of the Lord went by the way that led to heaven. By this again it was shown that in externals the evil lead the same kind of life as the good, or go the same way, that is, one as readily as the other; and yet those who from the heart acknowledge the Divine, especially those within the church who acknowledge the Divine of the Lord, are led to heaven; while those who do not are led to hell.

[3] The thoughts of man that proceed from his intention or will are represented in the other life by ways; and ways are visibly presented there in exact accord with those thoughts of intention; and in accord with his thoughts that proceed from intention everyone walks. For this reason the character of spirits and their thoughts are known from their ways. This also makes clear what is meant by the Lord's words:

> Enter ye in through the narrow gate; for wide is the gate and broad is the way that leadeth to destruction, and many be they that enter in thereby; for straitened is the way and narrow the gate that leadeth to life, and few be they who find it (Matt. 7:13, 14).

The way that leads to life is straitened not because it is difficult but because there are few who find it, as is said here. The stone seen at the corner where the broad and common way ended, and from which two ways were seen to lead in opposite directions, illustrated what is signified by these words of the Lord:

> Have ye not read what is written? The stone which the builders rejected was made the head of the corner. Whosoever shall fall upon that stone shall be broken (Luke 20:17, 18).

"Stone" signifies Divine truth, and "the stone of Israel" the Lord in respect to his Divine human; the "builders" mean those who are of the church; "the head of the corner" is where the two ways are; "to fall" and "to be broken" is to deny and perish.[1]

535. I have been permitted to talk with some in the other life who had withdrawn from worldly affairs that they might live in a pious and holy manner, also with some who had afflicted themselves in various ways, believing that they were thereby renouncing the world and subduing the lusts of the flesh. But as most of these have thus acquired a sorrowful life and had withdrawn from the life of charity, which life can be lived only in the midst of the world, they are incapable of being affiliated with angels, because the life of angels is a life of joy resulting from a state of blessedness, and consists in performing good deeds, which are works of charity. Moreover, those who have lived a life withdrawn from worldly employments are inflamed with the idea of their own merit, and are continually desiring heaven on that account, and thinking of heavenly joy as a reward, utterly ignorant of what heavenly

---

1. "Stone" signifies truth (n. 114, 643, 1298, 3720, 6426, 8609, 10376). For this reason the law was inscribed on tables of stone (n. 10376). "The stone of Israel" means the Lord in respect to the Divine truth and His Divine Human (n. 6426).

joy is. When such are admitted into the company of angels and into their joy, which discards merit and consists in active labors and practical services, and in a blessedness resulting from the good thereby accomplished, they are astonished like one who has found out something quite foreign to his belief; and since they are not receptive of that joy they go away and ally themselves with spirits of their own kind that have lived in the world a life like their own.

[2] But those who have lived an outwardly holy life, constantly attending church and praying and afflicting their souls, and at the same time have thought constantly of themselves that they would be esteemed and honored for all this above others, and finally after death would be accounted saints—such in the other life are not in heaven because they have done all this for the sake of themselves. And as they have defiled Divine truths by the self-love in which they have immersed them, some of them are so insane as to think themselves gods; and are consequently in hell among those like themselves. Some are cunning and deceitful, and are in the hells of the deceitful. These are such as by means of cunning arts and devices have maintained such pious conduct as induced the common people to believe that they possessed a Divine sanctity.

[3] Of this character are many of the Roman Catholic saints. I have been permitted to talk with some of them, and their life was then plainly disclosed, such as it had been in the world and as it was afterwards. All this has been said to make known that the life that leads to heaven is not a life withdrawn from the world, but a life in the world; and that a life of piety separated from a life of charity, which is possible only in the world, does not lead to heaven; but a life of charity does; and a life of charity consists in acting honestly and justly in every employment, in every business, and in every work, from an interior, that is, from a heavenly, motive; and this motive is in that life

whenever man acts honestly and justly because doing so is in accord with the Divine laws. Such a life is not difficult. But a life of piety separate from a life of charity is difficult; and as much as such a life is believed to lead toward heaven so much it leads away from heaven.[2]

2. A life of piety separated from a life of charity is of no avail, but united with charity it is profitable for all things (n. 8252, 8253). Charity to the neighbor consists in doing what is good, just, and right in every work and in every employment (n. 8120–8122). Charity to the neighbor takes in all things and each thing that a man thinks, wills, and does (n. 8124). A life of charity is a life in accordance with the Lord's commandments (n. 3249). Living in accordance with the Lord's commandments is loving the Lord (n. 10143, 10153, 10310, 10578, 10645). Genuine charity claims no merit, because it is from interior affection and consequent delight (n. 2371, 2380, 2400, 3816, 3887, 6388–6393). Man continues to be after death such as was his life of charity in the world (n. 8256). Heavenly blessedness flows in from the Lord into a life of charity (n. 2363). Mere thinking admits no one into heaven; it must be accompanied by willing and doing good (n. 2401, 3459).

Unless doing good is joined with willing good and thinking good there is no salvation nor any conjunction of the internal man with the external (n. 3987).

Part 3

Hell

56

The Lord Rules the Hells

536. Above, in treating of heaven it has been everywhere shown (especially in n. 2–6) that the God of heaven is the Lord, thus that the whole government of the heavens is the Lord's government. And as the relation of heaven to hell and of hell to heaven is like the relation between two opposites which mutually act contrary to each other, and from the action and reaction of which an equilibrium results, which gives permanence to all things of their action and reaction, so in order that all things and each thing may be kept in equilibrium it is necessary that he who rules the one should rule the other; for unless the same Lord restrained the uprisings from the hells and checked insanities there, the equilibrium would perish and everything with it.

537. But something about that equilibrium shall first be told. It is acknowledged that when two things mutually act against each other, and as much as one reacts and resists, the other acts and impels, since there is equal power on either side, neither has any effect, and both can then be acted upon freely by a third. For when the force of the two is neutralized by equal opposition the force of a third has full effect, and acts as easily as if there were no opposition.

[2] Such is the equilibrium between heaven and hell. Yet it is not an equilibrium like that between two bodily combatants whose strength is equal; but it is a spiritual equilibrium, that is, an equilibrium of falsity against truth and of evil against good. From hell falsity from evil continually exhales, and from heaven

truth from good. It is this spiritual equilibrium that causes man to think and will in freedom; for whatever a man thinks and wills has reference either to evil and falsity therefrom or to good and truth therefrom.

[3] Therefore when he is in that equilibrium he is in freedom either to admit or accept evil and its falsity from hell or to admit or accept good and its truth from heaven. Every man is held in this equilibrium by the Lord, because the Lord rules both heaven and hell. But why man is held in this freedom by such an equilibrium, and why evil and falsity are not taken away from him and good and truth implanted in him by Divine power, will be told hereafter in its own chapter.

538. A perception of the sphere of falsity from evil that flows forth from hell has often been granted me. It was like a perpetual effort to destroy all that is good and true, combined with anger and a kind of fury at not being able to do so, especially an effort to annihilate and destroy the Divine of the Lord, and this because all good and truth are from him. But out of heaven a sphere of truth from good was perceived, whereby the fury of the effort ascending from hell was restrained. The result of this was an equilibrium. This sphere from heaven was perceived to come from the Lord alone, although it appeared to come from the angels in heaven. It is from the Lord alone, and not from the angels, because every angel in heaven acknowledges that nothing of good and of truth is from himself, but all is from the Lord.

539. In the spiritual world truth from good is the source of all power, and falsity from evil has no power whatever. This is because the Divine itself in heaven is Divine good and Divine truth, and all power belongs to the Divine. Falsity from evil is powerless because truth from good is the source of all power, and in falsity from evil there is nothing of truth from good. Consequently in heaven there is all power, and none in hell; for everyone in heaven is in truths from good, and everyone in hell is in falsities from evil. For no one is admitted into heaven until he is in truths from good, neither is anyone cast down into hell until he is in falsities from evil. (That this is so can be seen in the chapters treating of the first, second, and third states of man after death, n. 491–520; and that all power belongs to truth from good can be seen in the chapter on the power of angels in heaven, n. 228–233.)

540. Such, then, is the equilibrium between heaven and hell. Those who are in the world of spirits are in that equilibrium, for the world of spirits is midway between heaven and hell. From the same source all men in the world are kept in a like equilibrium, since men in the world are ruled by the Lord by means of spirits in the world of spirits, as will be shown hereafter in its own chapter. No such equilibrium would be possible unless the Lord ruled both heaven and hell and regulated both sides. Otherwise falsities from evil would preponderate, and would affect the simple good who are in the outmost regions of heaven, and who can be more easily perverted than the angels themselves; and thereby equilibrium would perish, and with it freedom in men.

541. Hell, like heaven, is divided into societies, and into as many societies as there are in heaven; for every society in heaven has a society opposite to it in hell, and this for the sake of equilibrium. But evils and falsities therefrom are what distinguish the societies in hell, as goods and truths therefrom are what distinguish the societies in heaven. That for every good there is an opposite evil, and for every truth an opposite falsity may be known from this, that nothing can exist without relation to its opposite, and what anything is in kind and degree can be known from its opposite, and from this all perception and sensation is derived. For this reason the Lord continually provides that every society in heaven shall have an opposite in some society of hell, and that there shall be an equilibrium between the two.

542. As hell is divided into the same number of societies as heaven, there are as many hells as there are societies of heaven; for as each society of heaven is a heaven in smaller form (see above, n. 51–58), so each society in hell is a hell in smaller form. As in general there are three heavens, so in general there are three hells, a lowest, which is opposite to the inmost or third heaven, a middle, which is opposite to the middle or second heaven, and a higher, which is opposite to the outmost or first heaven.

543. How the hells are ruled by the Lord shall be briefly explained. In general the hells are ruled by a general outflow from the heavens of Divine good and Divine truth whereby the general endeavor flowing forth from the hells is checked and restrained; also by a particular outflow from each heaven and from each society of heaven. The hells are ruled in particular by means of the angels, to whom it is granted to look into the hells and to restrain insanities and disturbances there; and sometimes angels are sent to them who moderate these insanities and disturbances by their presence. But in general all in the hells are ruled by means of their fears. Some are ruled by fears implanted in the world and still inherent in them; but as these fears are not sufficient, and gradually subside, they are ruled by fears of punishments; and it is especially by these that they are deterred from doing evil. The punishments in hell are manifold, lighter or more severe in accordance with the evils. For the most part the more wicked, who excel in cunning and in artifices, and who are able to hold the rest in subjection and servitude by means of punishments and consequent terror, are set over them; but these governors dare not pass beyond the limits prescribed to them. It must be understood that the sole means of restraining the violence and fury of those who are in the hells is the fear of punishment. There is no other way.

544. It has been believed heretofore in the world that there is one devil that presides over the hells; that he was created an angel of light; but having become rebellious he was cast down with his crew into hell. This belief has prevailed because the devil and satan, and also Lucifer, are mentioned by name in the Word, and the Word in those places has been understood according to the sense of the letter. But by "the devil" and "satan" there hell is meant, "devil" meaning the hell that is behind, where the worst dwell, who are called evil genii; and "satan" the hell that is in front, where the less wicked dwell, who are called evil spirits; and "Lucifer" those that belong to Babel, or Babylon, who would extend their dominion even into heaven. That there is no one devil to whom the hells are subject is evident also from this, that all who are in the hells, like all who are in the heavens, are from the human race (see n. 311–317); and that those who have gone there from the beginning of creation to this time amount to myriads of myriads, and every one of them is a devil in accord with his opposition to the Divine while he lived in the world (see above, n. 311, 312).

57

The Lord Casts No One into Hell;
This Is Done by the Spirit

545. An opinion has prevailed with some that God turns away his face from man, casts man away from himself, and casts him into hell, and is angry with him on account of his evil; and some believe also that God punishes man and does evil to him.

They establish themselves in this opinion by the sense of the letter of the Word, where such things are declared, not knowing that the spiritual sense of the Word, by which the sense of the letter is made clear, is wholly different; and consequently that the genuine doctrine of the church, which is from the spiritual sense of the Word, teaches otherwise, namely, that God never turns away his face from man, and never casts man away from himself, that he casts no one into hell and is angry with no one.[1] Everyone, moreover, whose mind is enlightened perceives this to be true when he reads the Word, from the simple truth that God is good itself, love itself, and mercy itself; and that good itself cannot do evil to anyone, and love itself and mercy itself cannot cast man away from itself, because this is contrary to the very essence of mercy and love, thus contrary to the

---

1. In the Word anger and wrath are attributed to the Lord, but they are in man, and it is so expressed because such is the appearance to man when he is punished and damned (n. 798, 5798, 6997, 8284, 8483, 8875, 9306, 10431).

Evil also is attributed to the Lord, although nothing but good is from Him (n. 2447, 6071, 6991, 6997, 7533, 7632, 7679, 7926, 8227, 8228, 8632, 9306).

Why it is so expressed in the Word (n. 6071, 6991, 6997, 7632, 7643, 7679, 7710, 7926, 8282, 9010, 9128). The Lord is pure mercy and clemency (n. 6997, 8875).

Divine itself. Therefore those who think from an enlightened mind clearly perceive, when they read the Word, that God never turns himself away from man; and as he never turns himself away from him he deals with him from goodness, love, and mercy, that is, wills good to him, loves him, and is merciful to him. And from this they see that the sense of the letter of the Word, in which such things are declared, has stored up within itself a spiritual sense, and that these expressions that are used in the sense of the letter in accommodation to man's apprehension and according to his first and general ideas are to be explained in accordance with the spiritual sense.

546. Those who are enlightened see further that good and evil are two opposites, and are therefore opposed as heaven and hell are, and that all good is from heaven and all evil from hell; and as it is the Divine of the Lord that makes heaven (n. 7–12), nothing but good flows into man from the Lord, and nothing but evil from hell; thus the Lord is continually withdrawing man from evil and leading him to good, while hell is continually leading man into evil. Unless man were between these two, he could have no thought nor any will, still less any freedom or any choice; for all these man has by virtue of the equilibrium between good and evil; consequently if the Lord should turn himself away, leaving man to evil alone, man would cease to be man. All this shows that the Lord flows into every man with good, into the evil man as well as the good; but with the difference that the Lord is continually withdrawing the evil man from evil and is continually leading the good man to good; and this difference lies in the man himself, because he is the recipient.

547. From this it is clear that it is from hell that man does evil, and from the Lord that he does good. But man believes that whatever he does he does from himself, and in consequence of this the evil that he does sticks to him as his own; and for this reason man is the cause of his own evil, and in no way the

Lord. Evil in man is hell in him, for it is the same thing whether you say evil or hell. And since man is the cause of his own evil he is led into hell, not by the Lord but by himself. For so far is the Lord from leading man into hell that it is he who delivers man from hell, and this he does so far as man does not will and love to be in his own evil. All of man's will and love continues with him after death (n. 470–484). He who wills and loves evil in the world wills and loves the same evil in the other life, but he no longer suffers himself to be withdrawn from it. If, therefore, a man is in evil he is tied to hell, and in respect to his spirit is actually there, and after death desires nothing so much as to be where his evil is; consequently it is man who casts himself into hell after death, and not the Lord.

548. How this comes about shall also be explained. When man enters the other life he is received first by angels, who perform for him all good offices, and talk with him about the Lord, heaven, and the angelic life, and instruct him in things that are true and good. But if the man, now a spirit, be one who knew about these things in the world, but in heart denied or despised them, after some conversation he desires and seeks to get away from these angels. As soon as the angels perceive this they leave him. After some association with others he at length unites himself with those who are in evil like his own (see above, n. 445–452). When this takes place he turns himself away from the Lord and turns his face toward the hell to which he had been joined in the world, in which those abide who are in a like love of evil. All this makes clear that the Lord draws every spirit to himself by means of angels and by means of influx from heaven; but those spirits that are in evil completely resist, and as it were tear themselves away from the Lord, and are drawn by their own evil, thus by hell, as if by a rope. And as they are so drawn, and by reason of their love of evil are eager to follow, it is evident that they themselves cast themselves into hell by their own free choice. Men in the world because of their idea of hell are unable to believe that this is so. In fact, in the other life before the eyes of those who are outside of hell it does not so appear; but only so to those who cast themselves into hell, for such enter of their own accord. Those who enter from a burning love of evil appear to be cast headlong, with the head downwards and the feet upwards. It is because of this appearance that they seem to be cast into hell by Divine power. (But about this more will be said below, n. 574.) From all this it can be seen that the Lord casts no one into hell, but everyone casts himself into hell, both while he is living in the world and also after death when he comes among spirits.

549. The Lord from his Divine essence, which is goodness, love, and mercy, is unable to deal in the same way with every man, because evils and their falsities prevent, and not only quench his Divine influx but even reject it. Evils and their falsities are like black clouds which interpose between the sun and the eye, and take away the sunshine and the serenity of its light; although the unceasing endeavor of the sun to dissipate the opposing clouds continues, for it is operating behind them; and in the meantime transmits something of obscure light into the eye of man by various roundabout ways. It is the same in the spiritual world. The sun there is the Lord and the Divine love (n. 116–140); and the light there is the Divine truth (n. 126–140); black clouds there are falsities from evil; the eye there is the understanding. So far as anyone in that world is in falsities from evil he is encompassed by such a cloud, which is black and dense according to the degree of his evil. From this comparison it can be seen that the Lord is unceasingly present with everyone, but that he is received variously.

550. Evil spirits are severely punished in the world of spirits in order that by means of punishments they may be deterred from doing evil. This also appears to be from the Lord; and yet nothing of punishment there is from the Lord, but is from the evil itself, since evil is so joined with its own punishment that

the two cannot be separated. For the infernal crew desire and love nothing so much as doing evil, especially inflicting punishments and torment upon others; and they maltreat and inflict punishments upon everyone who is not protected by the Lord. When, therefore, evil is done from an evil heart, because it thereby discards all protection from the Lord, infernal spirits rush upon the one who does the evil, and inflict punishment. This may be partly illustrated by evils and their punishments in the world, where the two are also joined. For laws in the world prescribe a penalty for every evil; therefore he that rushes into evil rushes also into the penalty of evil. The only difference is that in the world the evil may be concealed; but in the other life it cannot be concealed. All this makes clear that the Lord does evil to no one; and that it is the same as it is in the world, where it is not the king nor the judge nor the law that is the cause of punishment to the guilty, because these are not the cause of the evil in the evildoer.

58

All Who Are in Hell Are in Evils
and Related Falsities Derived
from Loves of Self and the World

551. All who are in the hells are in evils and in falsities therefrom, and no one there is in evils and at the same time in truths. In the world evil men for the most part have some knowledge of spiritual truths, which are the truths of the church, having been taught them from childhood and later by preaching and by reading the Word; and afterwards they have talked about them. Some have even led others to believe that they are Christians at heart because of their knowing how to talk with pretended affection in harmony with the truth, also how to act uprightly as if from spiritual faith. But those of this class whose interior thoughts have been hostile to these truths, and who have refrained from doing the evils that were in harmony with their thoughts only because of the civil laws, or with a view to reputation, honors, and gain, are all of them evil in heart, and are in truths and goods not in respect to their spirit but only in respect to their body; and consequently, when their externals are taken away from them in the other life, and their internals which pertain to their spirit are revealed, they are wholly in evils and falsities, and not at all in truths and goods; and it is thus made clear that truths and goods resided only in their memory merely as things known about, and that they brought them forth therefrom when talking, putting on a semblance of good seemingly from spiritual love and faith. When such are let into their internals and thus into their evils they are no longer able to speak what is true, but only what is false, since they speak from evils; for to speak what is true from evils is then impossible, since the spirit is nothing but his own evil, and from evil what is false goes forth. Every evil spirit is reduced to this state before he is cast into hell (see above, n. 499–512). This is called being vastated in respect to truths and goods.[1] Vastation is simply being let into one's internals, that is, into what is the spirit's own, or into the spirit itself (see above, n. 425).

552. When man after death comes into this state he is no longer a man-spirit, as he was in his first state (of which above, n. 491–498), but is truly a spirit; for he is truly a spirit who has a face and body that correspond to his internals which pertain to his mind, that is, has an external form that is a type or effigy of his internals. A spirit is such after he has passed through the first and second states spoken of above; consequently when he is looked upon, his character is at once known, not only from his face and from his body, but also from his speech and movements; and as he is then in himself he can be nowhere else than where his like are.

[2] For in the spiritual world there is a complete sharing of affections and their thoughts, and in consequence a spirit is conveyed to his like as if of himself, since it is done from his affection and its delight. In fact, he turns himself in that direction; for thus he inhales his own life or draws his breath freely, which he cannot do when he turns another way. It must be understood that this sharing with others in the spiritual world

---

1. Before the evil are cast down into hell they are devastated of truths and goods, and when these have been taken away they are of themselves carried into hell (n. 6977, 7039, 7795, 8210, 8232, 9330). The Lord does not devastate them, but they devastate themselves (n. 7643, 7926). Every evil has in it what is false; therefore those who are in evil are also in falsity, although some do not know it (n. 7577, 8094). Those who are in evil must needs think what is false when they think from themselves (n. 7437). All who are in hell speak falsities from evil (n. 1695, 7351, 7352, 7357, 7392, 7689).

is effected in accordance with the turning of the face, and that each one has constantly before his face those who are in a love like his own, and this in every turning of the body (see above, n. 151).

[3] In consequence of this all infernal spirits turn themselves away from the Lord toward the densely dark body and the dark body that are there in place of the sun and moon of this world, while all the angels of heaven turn themselves to the Lord as the sun of heaven and as the moon of heaven (see above, n. 123, 143, 144, 151). From all this it is clear that all who are in the hells are in evils and in falsities therefrom; also that they are turned to their own loves.

553. All spirits in the hells, when seen in any light of heaven, appear in the form of their evil; for everyone there is an image of his evil, since his interiors and his exteriors act as a one, the interiors making themselves visible in the exteriors, which are the face, body, speech and movements; thus the character of the spirit is known as soon as he is seen. In general evil spirits are forms of contempt of others and of menaces against those who do not pay them respect; they are forms of hatreds of various kinds, also of various kinds of revenge. Fierceness and cruelty from their interiors show through these forms. But when they are commended, venerated, and worshiped by others their faces are restrained and take on an expression of gladness from delight.

[2] It is impossible to describe in a few words how all these forms appear, for no one is like another, although there is a general likeness among those who are in the same evil, and thus in the same infernal society, from which, as from a plane of derivation, the faces of all are seen to have a certain resemblance. In general their faces are hideous, and void of life like those of corpses; the faces of some are black, others fiery like torches, others disfigured with pimples, warts, and ulcers; some seem to have no face, but in its stead something hairy or bony;

and with some only the teeth are seen; their bodies also are monstrous; and their speech is like the speech of anger or of hatred or of revenge; for what everyone speaks is from his falsity, while his tone is from his evil. In a word, they are all images of their own hell.

[3] I have not been permitted to see what the form of hell itself in general is; I have only been told that as the entire heaven in one complex reflects a single man (n. 59–67), so the entire hell in one complex reflects a single devil, and might be exhibited in an image of a single devil (see above, n. 544). But the forms of particular hells or infernal societies I have often been permitted to see; for at their entrances, which are called the gates of hell, a monster commonly appears that represents in a general way the form of those within. The fierce passions of those who dwell there are represented at the same time in horrible and hideous ways that I forbear to describe.

[4] But it must be understood that this is the way infernal spirits appear in the light of heaven, while among themselves they appear as men. This is of the Lord's mercy, that they may not appear as loathsome to one another as they appear before the angels. But this appearance is a fallacy, for as soon as any ray of light from heaven is let in, their human forms appear changed into monstrous forms, such as they are in themselves (as has been described above). For in the light of heaven everything appears as it is in itself. For this reason they shun the light of heaven and cast themselves down into their own light, which is like that from lighted coals, and in some cases like that from burning sulfur; but this light also is turned into mere thick darkness when any light from heaven flows in upon it. This is why the hells are said to be in thick darkness and in darkness; and why "thick darkness" and "darkness" signify falsities derived from evil, such as are in hell.

554. From an inspection of these monstrous forms of spirits in the hells (which, as I have said, are all forms of contempt of

others and of menaces against those who do not pay them honor and respect, also forms of hatred and revenge against those who do not favor them), it became evident that in general they were all forms of the love of self and the love of the world; and that the evils of which these are the specific forms have their origin in these two loves. Moreover, I have been told from heaven, and it has been proved to me by much experience, that these two loves, the love of self and the love of the world, rule in the hells and constitute the hells, as love to the Lord and love toward the neighbor rule in the heavens and constitute the heavens; also that the two loves that are the loves of hell and the two loves that are the loves of heaven are diametrically opposite to each other.

555. At first I wondered how it is that love of self and love of the world could be so diabolical, and how those who are in these loves could be such monsters in appearance; for in the world not much thought is given to love of self, but only to that elated state of mind in external matters which is called haughtiness, and that alone, being so apparent to the sight, is regarded as love of self. Furthermore, love of self, when it is not so displayed, is believed in the world to be the very fire of life by which man is stimulated to seek employment and to perform uses, and if he found no honor or glory in these his mind would grow torpid. It is asked, Who has ever done any worthy, useful, and distinguished deed except for the sake of being praised and honored by others, or regarded with esteem and honor by others? And can this be from any other source than the fire of love for glory and honor, consequently for self? For this reason, it is unknown in the world that love of self, regarded in itself, is the love that rules in hell and constitutes hell in man. This being so I will first describe what the love of self is, and then will show that all evils and their falsities spring from that love as their fountain.

556. The love of self is wishing well to oneself alone, and to others only for the sake of self, even to the church, one's country, or any human society. It consists also in doing good to all these solely for the sake of one's own reputation, honor, and glory; and unless these are seen in the uses he performs in behalf of others he says in his heart, How does it concern me? Why should I do this? What shall I get from it? and therefore he does not do it. Evidently, then, he who is in the love of self does not love the church or his country or society, nor any use, but himself alone. His delight is solely the delight of the love of self; and as the delight that comes forth from his love is what constitutes the life of man, his life is a life of self; and a life of self is a life from what is man's own, and what is man's own, regarded in itself, is nothing but evil. He who loves himself loves also those who belong to him, that is, in particular, his children and grandchildren, and in general, all who are at one with him, whom he calls his. To love these is to love himself, for he regards them as it were in himself, and himself in them. Among those whom he calls his are also all who commend, honor, and pay their court to him.

557. What love of self is can be seen by comparing it with heavenly love. Heavenly love consists in loving uses for the sake of uses, or goods for the sake of goods, which are done by man on behalf of the church, his country, human society, and a fellow citizen; for this is loving God and loving the neighbor, since all uses and all goods are from God, and are the neighbor who is to be loved. But he who loves these for the sake of himself loves them merely as servants, because they are serviceable to him; consequently it is the will of one who is in self-love that the church, his country, human societies, and his fellow citizens, should serve him, and not he them, for he places himself above them and places them beneath himself. Therefore so far as anyone is in love of self he separates himself from heaven, because he separates himself from heavenly love.

558a. Furthermore, so far as anyone is in heavenly love, which consists in loving uses and goods and being moved by delight of heart when doing them for the sake of the church, country, human society, and one's fellow citizens, he is so far led by the Lord, because that love is the love in which the Lord is, and which is from him. But so far as anyone is in the love of self, which consists in performing uses and goods for the sake of himself, so far he is led by himself; and so far as anyone is led by himself he is not led by the Lord. And from this it also follows that so far as anyone loves himself he separates himself from the Divine, thus also from heaven. To be led by oneself is to be led by what is one's own; and what is man's own is nothing but evil; for man's inherited evil consists in loving self more than God, and the world more than heaven.[2] Whenever man looks to himself in the good that he does he is let into what is his own, that is, into his inherited evils; for he then looks from good to himself and from himself to good, and therefore he presents an image of himself in his good, and not an image of the Divine. That this is so has also been proved to me by experience. There are evil spirits whose dwelling places are in the middle quarter between the north and the west, beneath the heavens, who are skilled in the art of leading well-disposed spirits into their nature *[proprium]* and thus into evils of various kinds. This they do by leading them into thoughts about themselves, either openly by praises and

2. Man's own, which he derives by inheritance from his parents, is nothing but dense evil (n. 210, 215, 731, 876, 987, 1047, 2307, 2308, 3518, 3701, 3812, 8480, 8550, 10283, 10284, 10286, 10731). Man's own is loving self more than God, and the world more than heaven, and making nothing of one's neighbor in comparison with oneself, except for the sake of self, that is one's own self; thus it consists in love of self and of the world (n. 694, 731, 4317, 5660). All evils flow from the love of self and the love of the world when these predominate (n. 1307, 1308, 1321, 1594, 1691, 3413, 7255, 7376, 7488, 7489, 8318, 9335, 9348, 10038, 10742). These evils are contempt of others, enmity, hatred, revenge, cruelty, deceit (n. 6667, 7370, 7374, 9348, 10038, 10742). From these evils all falsity flows (n. 1047, 10283, 10284, 10286).

honors, or secretly by directing their affections to themselves; and so far as this is done they turn the faces of the well-disposed spirits away from heaven, and to the same extent they obscure their understanding and call forth evils from what is their own.

558*b*. That the love of self is the opposite of love to the neighbor can be seen from the origin and essence of both. The love of the neighbor of one who is in the love of self begins with oneself, for he claims that everyone is neighbor to himself; and it goes forth from him as its center to all who make one with him, diminishing in accordance with the degree of their conjunction with him by love. All outside of this circle are regarded as of no account; and those who are opposed to those in the circle and to their evils are accounted as enemies, whatever their character may be, however wise, upright, honest, or just. But spiritual love to the neighbor begins with the Lord, and goes forth from him as its center to all who are conjoined to him by love and faith, going forth in accordance with the quality of their love and faith.[3] Evidently, then, the love of the

---

3. Those who do not know what it is to love the neighbor imagine every man to be a neighbor, and that good is to be done to everyone who is in need of help (n. 6704).

They also believe that everyone is neighbor to himself, and thus that love to the neighbor begins with self (n. 6933). Those who love themselves above all things, that is, with whom self-love prevails, also make their love to the neighbor begin with themselves (n. 6710). In what manner everyone is neighbor to himself, explained (n. 6933- 6938). But those who are Christians and who love God above all things make their love to the neighbor begin with the Lord, because He is to be loved above all things (n. 6706, 6711, 6819, 6824). The distinctions of neighbor are as many as the distinctions of good from the Lord, and there should be distinction in doing good to everyone in accordance with the quality of the person's state, and this is a matter of Christian prudence (n. 6707, 6709, 6711, 6818). These distinctions are innumerable, and for this reason the ancients, who knew what is meant by the neighbor, reduced the exercises of charity into classes, which they denoted by suitable names, and from this knew in what respect everyone was a neighbor, and in what manner good was to be done to everyone with prudence (n. 2417, 6628, 6705, 7259–7262). The doctrine in the ancient churches was the doctrine of charity toward the neighbor, and from this they had wisdom (n. 2417, 2385, 3419, 3420, 4844, 6628).

neighbor that has its beginning in man is the opposite of the love to the neighbor that has its beginning in the Lord; and the former proceeds from evil because it proceeds from what is man's own, while the latter proceeds from good because it proceeds from the Lord, who is good itself. Evidently, also, the love of the neighbor that proceeds from man and from what is his own is corporeal, while the love to the neighbor that proceeds from the Lord is heavenly. In a word, in the man in whom love of self prevails, that love constitutes the head, and heavenly love constitutes the feet. On that love he stands; and if it does not serve him he tramples it under foot. This is the cause of the appearance that those who are cast down into hell fall with the head downward toward hell, and with the feet upward toward heaven (see above, n. 548).

559. Again, love of self is such that so far as the reins are given it, that is, so far as external bonds are removed, which are fears of the law and its penalties, and of the loss of reputation, honor, gain, employment, and life, so far it rushes on until it finally longs to rule not only over the entire world but also over the entire heaven, and over the Divine himself, knowing no limit or end. This propensity lurks hidden in everyone who is in love of self, although it is not manifest to the world, where it is held in check by such bonds as have been mentioned.

Everyone can see examples of this in potentates and kings who are subject to no such restraints and bonds, but rush on and subjugate provinces and kingdoms so far as they are successful, and aspire to power and glory without limit; and still more strikingly in the Babylon of this day, which has extended its dominion into heaven, and has transferred to itself all the Divine power of the Lord, and continually lusts for more. That such men, when they have entered after death the other life, are directly opposed to the Divine and to heaven, and are on the side of hell, can be seen in the little work *Last Judgment and the Destruction of Babylon.*

560. Picture to yourself a society of such persons, all of whom love themselves alone and love others only so far as they make one with themselves, and you will see that their love is precisely like the love of thieves for each other, who embrace and call one another friends so long as they are acting together; but when they cease to act together and discard their subordination to one another, they rise up against and murder one another. When the interiors or the minds of such are explored they will be seen to be full of bitter hatred one against another, and at heart will laugh at all justice and honesty, and likewise at the Divine, which they reject as of no account. This is still more evident in the societies of such in the hells treated of below.

561. The interiors pertaining to the thoughts and affections of those who love themselves above all things are turned toward themselves and the world, and thus are turned away from the Lord and from heaven; and consequently they are obsessed with evils of every kind, and the Divine cannot flow in; for if it does flow in it is instantly submerged in thoughts of self, and is defiled, and is also mingled with the evils that flow from what is their own. This is why all such in the other life look backwards away from the Lord, and toward the densely dark body that is there in the place of the sun of the world, and is diametrically opposite to the sun of heaven, which is the Lord (see above, n. 123). "Thick darkness" signifies evil, and the "sun of the world" the love of self.[4]

562. The evils of those who are in the love of self are, in general, contempt of others, envy, enmity against all who do not favor them, and consequent hostility, hatred of various kinds, revenge, cunning, deceit, unmercifulness, and cruelty; and

4. "The sun of the world" signifies the love of self (n. 2441). In this sense "to worship the sun" signifies to worship those things that are antagonistic to heavenly love and to the Lord (n. 2441, 10584).

"The sun's growing hot" means an increasing lust of evil (n. 8487).

in respect to religious matters there is not merely a contempt for the Divine and for Divine things, which are the truths and goods of the church, but also hostility to them. When man becomes a spirit this hostility is turned into hatred; and then he not only cannot endure to hear these truths and goods mentioned, he even burns with hatred against all who acknowledge and worship the Divine. I once talked with a certain spirit who in the world had been a man in authority, and had loved self to an unusual degree; and when he simply heard someone mention the Divine, and especially when he heard him mention the Lord, he was so excited by hatred arising from anger as to burn with the desire to kill; and when the reins of his love were loosened he wished to be the devil himself, that from his love of self he might continually infest heaven. This is the desire also of some of the Papist religion when they perceive in the other life that the Lord has all power and they have none.

563. Certain spirits were seen by me in the western quarter toward the south, who said that they had been in positions of great dignity in the world, and that they deserved to be more highly esteemed than others and to rule over others. Their interior character was explored by angels, and it was found that in their offices in the world they had not looked to uses but to themselves, and thus that they had set themselves before uses. But as they were very eager and importunate to be set over others they were allowed to associate with those who were consulting about matters of great importance; but it was perceived that they were unable to give any thought to the business under discussion, or to see matters as they are in themselves, or to speak with reference to the use of the thing, but were able to speak only with reference to self, and that they wished to act from what is pleasing on the ground of favor. They were therefore dismissed from that duty, and left to seek employment for themselves elsewhere.

Therefore they went further into the western quarter, where they were received here and there, but everywhere were told that they thought only of themselves, and of no business except with reference to self, and for this reason were stupid and like merely sensual corporeal spirits. On this account wheresoever they went they were sent away. Some time afterwards they were seen reduced to a destitute state and asking alms. Thus it was made clear that those who are in the love of self, however from the fire of that love they may seem to speak in the world wisely, speak merely from the memory, and not from any rational light. Therefore in the other life, when they are no longer permitted to bring forth the things of the natural memory, they are more stupid than others, and for the reason that they are separated from the Divine.

564. There are two kinds of dominion, one of love toward the neighbor and the other of love of self. These two dominions in their essence are direct opposites. One who rules from love toward the neighbor wills good to all, and loves nothing so much as uses, that is, serving others; which is willing good to others and performing uses, either to the church, or to the country, or to society, or to a fellow citizen. This is his love and the delight of his heart. Moreover, so far as he is exalted to dignities above others he rejoices, not for the sake of the dignities but for the sake of the uses he is then able to perform in greater abundance and of a higher order. Such dominion exists in the heavens.

[2] But one who rules from the love of self wills good to no one except himself; the uses he performs are for the sake of his own honor and glory, which to him are the only uses; his end in serving others is that he may himself be served, honored, and permitted to rule; he seeks dignities not for the sake of the good offices he may render to his country and the church, but that he may gain eminence and glory and thereby the delight of his heart.

[3] Moreover this love of dominion continues with everyone after his life in the world. Those that have ruled from love toward the neighbor are entrusted with authority in the heavens; but then it is not they who rule, but the uses which they love; and when uses rule the Lord rules. But those who have ruled while in the world are in hell, and are there vile slaves. I have seen those who had power in the world, but who exercised dominion from love of self, cast out among the most vile, and some among those who are in excremental places.

565. But in respect to the love of the world: it is a love opposed to heavenly love in a less degree than love of self, because the evils hidden within it are lesser evils. The love of the world consists in one's desiring to secure to himself, by any kind of artifice, the wealth of others, and in setting his heart upon riches, and permitting the world to draw him and lead him away from spiritual love, which is love toward the neighbor, and thus from heaven and from the Divine.

But this love is manifold. There is a love of wealth for the sake of being exalted to honors, when these alone are loved. There is a love of honors and dignities with a view to the increase of wealth. There is a love of wealth for the sake of various uses that give delight in the world. There is a love of wealth merely for the sake of wealth, which is a miserly love; and so on. The end for the sake of which wealth is sought is called its use; and it is the end or use that gives to love its quality; for the love is such as is the end in view, and all other things merely serve it as means.

59

What Hell Fire Is and What the Gnashing of Teeth Is

566. What eternal fire is, and what the gnashing of teeth is, which are mentioned in the Word in reference to those who are in hell, scarcely anyone as yet has known, because the contents of the Word have been thought about only in a material way, and nothing has been known about its spiritual sense. So fire has been understood by some to mean material fire, by others to mean torment in general, by others remorse of conscience, and others have held that it is mentioned merely to excite terror in the wicked. Likewise some have supposed the gnashing of teeth to mean actual gnashing, and some only a horror, such as is excited when such a collision of teeth is heard. But anyone who is acquainted with the spiritual meaning of the Word may know what eternal fire is, and what the gnashing of teeth is; for every expression and every meaning of the expressions in the Word contains a spiritual meaning, since the Word in its bosom is spiritual; and what is spiritual can be set before man only in natural forms of expression, because man is in the natural world and thinks from the things of that world. Therefore it shall now be told what is meant by "eternal fire" and "the gnashing of teeth" into which the spirits of evil men enter after death, or which their spirits, then in the spiritual world, endure.

567. There are two origins of heat, one the sun of heaven which is the Lord, and the other the sun of the world. The heat that is from the sun of heaven, that is, the Lord, is spiritual heat; and this in its essence is love (see above, n. 126–140); but the heat from the sun of the world is natural heat, and this in its essence is not love, but serves spiritual heat or love as a receptacle. Evidently love in its essence is heat, since it is love, in accord with its degree and quality, that gives heat to the mind, and thence to the body; and this man experiences as well in the winter as in the summer. The heating of the blood is from the same source. That the natural heat that springs from the sun of the world serves spiritual heat as a receptacle is evident from the heat of the body, which is excited by the heat of its spirit, and is a kind of substitute for that heat in the body. It is especially evident from the spring and summer heat in animals of every kind which then annually renew their loves.

[2] It is not the natural heat that produces this effect, but it disposes their bodies to receive the heat that flows into them from the spiritual world; for the spiritual world flows into the natural as cause into effect. Whoever believes that natural heat produces these loves is much deceived, for influx is from the spiritual world into the natural world, and not from the natural world into the spiritual; and as all love belongs to the life itself it is spiritual.

[3] Again, he who believes that anything comes forth in the natural world without influx from the spiritual world is deceived, for what is natural comes forth and continues to exist only from what is spiritual. Furthermore, the subjects of the vegetable kingdom derive their germinations from influx out of the spiritual world. The natural heat of springtime and summer merely disposes the seeds into their natural forms by expanding and opening them so that influx from the spiritual world can there act as a cause. These things are mentioned to make clear that there are two kinds of heat, spiritual heat and natural heat; and that spiritual heat is from the sun of heaven and natural heat from the sun of the world, and that influx and consequent

cooperation produce the effects that appear before the eyes in the world.[1]

568. Spiritual heat in man is the heat of his life, because, as was said above, it is in its essence love. This heat is what is meant in the Word by "fire," love to the Lord and love toward the neighbor by "heavenly fire," and love of self and love of the world by "infernal fire."

569. Infernal fire or love springs from a like origin as heavenly fire or love, namely, the sun of heaven, or the Lord; but it is made infernal by those who receive it. For all influx from the spiritual world varies in accordance with reception, that is, in accordance with the forms into which it flows, just as it is with the heat and light from the sun of the world. The heat from that sun flowing into shrubberies and beds of flowers produces vegetation, and draws forth grateful and sweet odors; but the same heat flowing into excremental and decaying substances produces putrefactions, and draws forth rank and disgusting stenches. In like manner the light from the same sun produces in one subject beautiful and pleasing colors, in another unbeautiful and disagreeable colors. The same is true of the heat and light from the sun of heaven, which is love. When the heat, or love, from that sun flows into good, as it does in good men and angels, it makes their good fruitful; but when it flows into the evil it produces a contrary effect, for their evils either suffocate it or pervert it. In like manner when the light of heaven flows into the truths of good it imparts intelligence and wisdom; but when it flows into the falsities of evil it is turned into insanities and fantasies of various kinds. Thus in every instance the result is in accordance with reception.

1. There is an influx from the spiritual world into the natural world (n. 6053–6058, 6189–6215, 6307–6327, 6466–6495, 6598–6626). There is also an influx into the lives of animals (n. 5850). And into the subjects of the vegetable kingdom (n. 3648).

This influx is a continual endeavor to act in accordance with the Divine order (n. 6211 at the end).

570. As infernal fire is the love of self and of the world it is also every lust of these loves, since lust is love in its continuity, for what a man loves he continually lusts after. Infernal fire is also delight, since what a man loves and lusts after he perceives, when he obtains it, to be delightful. Man's delight of heart is from no other source. Infernal fire, therefore, is the lust and delight that spring from these two loves as their origins. The evils flowing from these loves are contempt of others, enmity, and hostility against those who do not favor them, envy, hatred, and revenge, and from these fierceness and cruelty; and in respect to the Divine they are denial and consequent contempt, derision, and detraction of the holy things of the church; and after death, when man becomes a spirit, these evils are changed to anger and hatred against these holy things (see above, n. 562). And as these evils breathe forth continually the destruction and murder of those whom they account as enemies, and against whom they burn with hatred and revenge, so it is the delight of their life to will to destroy and kill, and so far as they are unable to do this, to will to do mischief, to injure, and to exercise cruelty.

[2] Such is the meaning of "fire" in the Word, where the evil and the hells are treated of, some passages from which I will here quote in the way of proof:

> Everyone is a hypocrite and an evildoer, and every mouth speaketh folly. For wickedness burneth as the fire; it devoureth the briers and thorns, and kindleth in the thickets of the forests, and they roll upward in the rising of smoke; and the people is become like food for fire; no man spareth his brother (Isa. 9:17–19).

> I will show wonders in the heavens, and in the earth blood and fire, and pillars of smoke; the sun shall be turned into darkness (Joel 2:30, 31).

> The land shall become burning pitch; it shall not be quenched night nor day; the smoke thereof shall go up forever (Isa. 34:9, 10).

> Behold the day cometh burning as a furnace, and all the proud and every worker of wickedness shall be stubble; and the day that cometh shall set them on fire (Mal. 4:1).

Babylon is become a habitation of demons. They cried out as they saw the smoke of her burning. Her smoke goeth up unto the ages of the ages (Rev. 18:2, 18; 19:3).

He opened the pit of the abyss, and there went up a smoke out of the pit as the smoke of a great furnace; and the sun was darkened, and the air, by the smoke of the pit (Rev. 9:2).

Out of the mouth of the horses went forth fire and smoke and brimstone; by these was the third part of men killed, by the fire and by the smoke and by the brimstone (Rev. 9:17, 18).

If anyone adores the beast he shall drink of the wine of the wrath of God mixed with unmixed wine in the cup of his anger, and shall be tormented with fire and brimstone (Rev. 16:9, 10).

The fourth angel poured out his bowl upon the sun; and it was given unto it to scorch men with fire; therefore men were scorched with great heat (Rev. 16:8, 9).

They were cast into a lake burning with fire and brimstone (Rev. 19:20; 20:14, 15; 21:8).

Every tree that bringeth not forth good fruit shall be hewn down and cast into the fire (Matt. 3:10; Luke 3:9).

The Son of man shall send his angels, and they shall gather out of his kingdom all things that cause stumbling and them that do iniquity, and shall cast them into a furnace of fire (Matt. 13:41, 42, 50).

The King shall say to them that are on the left hand, Depart from me, ye cursed, into eternal fire, prepared for the devil and his angels (Matt. 25:41).

They shall be sent into everlasting fire, into the hell of fire, where their worm shall not die, and the fire shall not be quenched (Matt. 18:8, 9; Mark 9:43–49).

The rich man in hell said to Abraham that he was tormented in flame (Luke 16:24).

In these and in many other passages "fire" means the lust pertaining to love of self and love of the world, and the "smoke" therefrom means falsity from evil.

571. As the lust of doing the evils that are from the love of self and of the world is meant by "infernal fire," and as such is the lust of all in the hells (as shown in the foregoing chapter)

so when the hells are opened there is an appearance of fire with smoke, such as is seen in conflagrations, a dense fire from the hells where the love of self prevails, and a flaming fire from the hells where love of the world prevails. But when the hells are closed this fiery appearance is not seen, but in its place there is a kind of obscurity like a condensation of smoke; although the fire still rages within, as can be seen by the heat exhaling therefrom, which is like the heat from the burnt ruins after a fire, and in some places like the heat from a heated furnace, in others like the heat from a hot bath. When this heat flows into man it excites lusts in him, and in evil men hatred and revenge, and in the sick insanities.

Such is the fire or such the heat that affects those who are in the above-mentioned loves, because in respect to their spirit they are attached to those hells, even while living in the body. But it must be understood that those who are in the hells are not in fire; the fire is an appearance; those there are conscious of no burning, but only of a warmth like that which they had felt when in the world. This appearance of fire is from correspondence, since love corresponds to fire, and all things seen in the spiritual world are seen in accordance with correspondences.

572. It must be noted that this infernal fire or heat is changed into intense cold when heat from heaven flows in; and those who are in it then shiver like those seized with chills and fever, and are inwardly distressed; and for the reason that they are in direct opposition to the Divine; and the heat of heaven (which is Divine love) extinguishes the heat of hell (which is the love of self), and with it the fire of their life; and this is the cause of such cold and consequent shivering and distress. This is accompanied by thick darkness and by infatuation and mutual blindness therefrom. But this rarely happens, and only when outbreaks that have increased beyond measure need to be repressed.

573. Since infernal fire means every lust for doing evil that flows forth from the love of self, this fire means also such torment as exists in the hells. For the lust from that love is a lust for injuring others who do not honor, venerate, and worship oneself; and in proportion to the anger thereby excited, and the hatred and revenge from that anger, is there a lust for venting one's rage upon them. When such lust is active in everyone in a society, and is restrained by no external bond, such as the fear of the law, and of the loss of reputation, honor, gain, and life, everyone from the impulse of his own evil rushes upon another; and so far as he prevails subjugates the rest and subjects them to his dominion, and vents his rage with delight upon those who do not submit themselves. This delight is so intimately united with the delight of bearing rule that they exist in the same measure, since the delight of doing harm is contained in all enmity, envy, hatred, and revenge, which as said above, are the evils of that love. All the hells are such societies, and in consequence everyone there bears hatred in his heart against others, and from hatred bursts forth into cruelty so far as he has power. These cruelties and their torments are also meant by infernal fire, since they are the effects of lusts.

574. It has been shown above (n. 548) that an evil spirit casts himself into hell of his own accord. It shall now be told in a few words how this comes about, when yet there are in hell such torments. From every hell there exhales a sphere of the lusts of those who are in it. Whenever this sphere is perceived by one who is in a like lust he is affected at heart and filled with delight, for lust and its delight make one, since whatever one lusts after is delightful to him; and because of this a spirit turns himself hellward, and from delight of heart lusts to go thither, since he does not yet know that such torments exist there, although he who knows it still lusts to go there. For no one in the spiritual world can resist his lust, because his lust belongs to his love, and his love belongs to his will, and his will belongs to his nature, and everyone there acts from his nature.

[2] When, therefore, a spirit of his own accord and from his freedom drifts toward his hell and enters it, he is received at first in a friendly manner, which makes him believe that he has come among friends. But this continues for a few hours only. In the meanwhile he is explored in respect to his astuteness and consequent ability; and when this has been done they begin to infest him, and this by various methods, and with gradually greater severity and vehemence.

This is accomplished by introducing him more interiorly and deeply into hell; for the more interior and deeper the hell the more malignant are the spirits. After these infestations they begin to treat him cruelly by punishments, and this goes on until he is reduced to the condition of a slave.

[3] But rebellious movements are continually springing up there, since everyone wishes to be greatest, and burns with hatred against the others; and in consequence new uprisings occur, and thus one scene is changed into another, and those who are made slaves are delivered that they may assist some new devil to subjugate others; and again those who refuse to submit and render implicit obedience are tormented in various ways; and so on continually. Such torments are the torments of hell, which are called hell fire.

575. Gnashing of teeth is the continual contention and combat of falsities with each other, consequently of those who are in falsities, joined with contempt of others, with enmity, mockery, ridicule, blaspheming; and these evils burst forth into lacerations of various kinds; since everyone fights for his own falsity and calls it truth. These contentions and combats are heard outside of these hells like the gnashings of teeth; and are also turned into gnashings of teeth when truths from heaven flow in among them.

In these hells are all who have acknowledged nature and have denied the Divine. In the deeper of these hells are those that have confirmed themselves in such denials. As such are unable to receive anything of light from heaven, and are thus unable to see anything inwardly in themselves, they are for the most part corporeal sensual spirits, who believe nothing except what they see with their eyes and touch with their hands.

Therefore all the fallacies of the senses are truths to them; and it is from these that they dispute. This is why their contentions are heard as gnashings of teeth; for in the spiritual world all falsities give a grating sound, and the teeth correspond to the outmost things in nature and to the outmost things in man, which are corporeal sensual.[2] (That there is gnashing of teeth in the hells may be seen in Matt. 8:12; 13:42, 50; 22:13; 24:51; 25:30; Luke 13:28.)

---

2. The correspondence of the teeth (n. 5565–5568). Those who are purely sensual and have scarcely anything of spiritual light correspond to the teeth (n. 5565).

In the Word a "tooth" signifies the sensual, which is the outmost of the life of man (n. 9052, 9062). Gnashing of teeth in the other life comes from those who believe that nature is everything, and the Divine nothing (n. 5568).

60

The Malice and Heinous Artifices
of Infernal Spirits

576. In what way spirits are superior to men everyone can see and comprehend who thinks interiorly and knows anything of the operation of his own mind; for in his mind he can consider, evolve, and form conclusions upon more subjects in a single moment than he can utter or express in writing in half an hour.

This shows the superiority of man when he is in his spirit, and therefore when he becomes a spirit. For it is the spirit that thinks, and it is the body by which the spirit expresses its thoughts in speech or writing. In consequence of this, when man after death becomes an angel he is in intelligence and wisdom ineffable in comparison with his intelligence and wisdom while he lived in the world; for while he lived in the world his spirit was bound to his body, and was thereby in the natural world; and therefore whatever he thought spiritually flowed into natural ideas, which are comparatively general, gross, and obscure, and which are incapable of receiving innumerable things that pertain to spiritual thought; and which infold spiritual thought in the obscurities that arise from worldly cares.

It is otherwise when the spirit is released from the body and comes into its spiritual state, which takes place when it passes out of the natural world into the spiritual world to which it belongs. From what has already been said it is evident that the state of its thoughts and affections is then immeasurably superior to its former state. Because of this the thoughts of angels are ineffable and inexpressible, and are therefore incapable of entering into the natural thoughts of man; and yet every angel was born a man, and has lived as a man, and he then seemed to himself to be no wiser than any other like man.

577. In the same degree in which angels have wisdom and intelligence infernal spirits have malice and cunning; for the case is the same, since the spirit of man when released from the body is in his good or in his evil—if an angelic spirit in his good, and if an infernal spirit in his evil. Every spirit is his own good or his own evil because he is his own love, as has been often said and shown above. Therefore as an angelic spirit thinks, wills, speaks, and acts, from his good, an infernal spirit does this from his evil; and to think, will, speak, and act from evil itself, is to think, will, speak, and act from all things included in the evil.

[2] So long as man lived in the body it was different, since the evil of the spirit was then under the restraints that every man feels from the law, from hope of gain, from honor, from reputation, and from the fear of losing these; and therefore the evil of his spirit could not then burst forth and show what it was in itself. Moreover, the evil of the spirit of man then lay wrapped up and veiled in outward probity, honesty, justice, and affection for truth and good, which such a man professes and counterfeits for the sake of the world; and under these semblances the evil has lain so concealed and obscured that he himself scarcely knew that his spirit contained so much malice and craftiness, that is, that in himself he was such a devil as he becomes after death, when his spirit comes into itself and into its own nature.

[3] Such malice then manifests itself as exceeds all belief. There are thousands of evils that then burst forth from evil itself, among which are such as cannot be described in the words of any language. What they are has been granted me to know and also to perceive by much experience, since it has been granted me by the Lord to be in the spiritual world in respect to my spirit and at the same time in the natural world in respect to my body. This I can testify, that their malice is so great that it is hardly

possible to describe even a thousandth part of it; and so great that if man were not protected by the Lord he could never be rescued from hell; for with every man there are spirits from hell as well as angels from heaven (see above, n. 292, 293); and yet the Lord cannot protect man unless he acknowledges the Divine and lives a life of faith and charity; for otherwise man turns himself away from the Lord and turns himself to infernal spirits, and thus his spirit becomes imbued with a malice like theirs.

[4] Nevertheless, man is continually withdrawn by the Lord from the evils that he attaches and as it were attracts to himself by his affiliation with infernal spirits. If he is not withdrawn by the internal bonds of conscience, which he fails to receive if he denies a Divine, he is nevertheless withdrawn by external bonds, which are, as said above, fears in respect to the law and its penalties, and fears of the loss of gain and the deprivation of honor and reputation. In fact, such a man may be withdrawn from evils by means of the delights of his love and through fear of the loss or deprivation of those delights; but he cannot be led thereby into spiritual goods. For as soon as such a man is led into these he begins to give his thought to pretenses and devices by simulating or counterfeiting what is good, honest, and just, for the purpose of persuading and thus deceiving. Such cunning adjoins itself to the evil of his spirit and gives form to it, causing his evil to be of the same nature as itself.

578. Those are the worst of all who have been in evils from love of self and at the same time inwardly in themselves have acted from deceit; for deceit penetrates more deeply into the thoughts and intentions than other evils, and infects them with poison and thus wholly destroys the spiritual life of man. Most of these spirits are in the hells behind the back, and are called genii; and there they delight to make themselves invisible, and to flutter about others like phantoms secretly infusing evil into them, which they spread around like the poison of a viper. These are more direfully tormented than others. But those who are not deceitful, and who have not been so filled with malignant craftiness, and yet are in the evils derived from the love of self, are also in the hells behind, but in those less deep. On the other hand, those that have been in evils from the love of the world are in the hells in front, and are called spirits. These spirits are not such forms of evil, that is, of hatred and revenge, as those are who are in evils from the love of self; and therefore do not have such malice and cunning; and in consequence their hells are milder.

579. I have been permitted to learn by experience what kind of malice those possess who are called genii. Genii act upon and flow into the affections, and not the thoughts. They perceive and smell out the affections as dogs do wild beasts in the forest. Good affections, when they perceive them in another, they turn instantly into evil affections, leading and bending them in a wonderful manner by means of the other's delights; and this so secretly and with such malignant skill that the other knows nothing of it, for they most carefully guard against anything entering into the thought, as thereby they would be manifested. The seat of these in man is beneath the back part of the head. In the world they were such as deceitfully captivated the minds of others, leading and persuading them by the delights of their affections or lusts. But such spirits are not permitted by the Lord to come near to any man of whose reformation there is any hope; for they have the ability not only to destroy the conscience, but also to stir up in man his inherited evils, which otherwise lie hidden. Therefore to prevent man's being led into these evils, these hells, by the Lord's provision, are entirely closed up; and when any man of such a character comes after death into the other life, he is at once cast into their hell. When the deceit and craftiness of these spirits are clearly seen they appear as vipers.

580. The kind of malice infernal spirits possess is evident from their nefarious arts, which are so many that to enumerate them

would fill a volume, and to describe them would fill many volumes. These arts are mostly unknown in the world. One kind relates to abuses of correspondences; a second to abuses of the outmosts of Divine order; a third to the communication and influx of thoughts and affections by means of turning toward another, fixing the sight upon another, and by the instrumentality of other spirits apart from themselves, and spirits sent out by themselves; a fourth to operations by fantasies; a fifth to a kind of casting themselves out beyond themselves and consequent presence elsewhere than where they are in the body; a sixth to pretenses, persuasion, and lies. The spirit of an evil man enters of itself into these arts when he is released from his body, for they are inherent in the nature of the evil in which he then is. By these arts they torment each other in the hells. But as all of these arts, except those that are effected by pretenses, persuasions, and lies, are unknown in the world, I will not here describe them in detail, both because they would not be comprehended, and because they are too abominable to be told.

581. The Lord permits torments in the hells because in no other way can evils be restrained and subdued. The only means of restraining and subduing evils and of keeping the infernal crew in bonds is the fear of punishment. It can be done in no other way; for without the fear of punishment and torment evil would burst forth into madness, and everything would go to pieces, like a kingdom on earth where there is no law and there are no penalties.

61

The Appearance, Situation,
and Number of the Hells

582. In the spiritual world, that is, in the world where spirits and angels are, the same objects appear as in the natural world, that is, where men are. In external appearance there is no difference. In that world plains and mountains, hills and rocks, and valleys between them, are seen; also waters, and many other things that are seen on earth. And yet all these things are from a spiritual origin, and all are therefore seen by the eyes of spirits and angels, and not by the eyes of men, because men are in the natural world. Spiritual beings see such things as are from a spiritual origin, and natural beings such things as are from a natural origin. Consequently man with his eyes can in no way see the objects that are in the spiritual world unless he is permitted to be in the spirit, or after death when he becomes a spirit.

On the other hand, an angel or a spirit is unable to see anything at all in the natural world unless he is with a man who is permitted to speak with him. For the eyes of man are fitted to receive the light of the natural world, and the eyes of angels and spirits are fitted to receive the light of the spiritual world; although the eyes of the two are exactly alike in appearance.

That the spiritual world is such the natural man cannot comprehend, and least of all the sensual man, who believes nothing except what he sees with his bodily eyes and touches with his hands, and therefore takes in by sight and touch. As his thought is from such things it is material and not spiritual. Such being the likeness between the spiritual world and the natural world, man can hardly believe after death that he is not in the world where he was born, and from which he has departed. For this reason death is called simply a translation from one world into another like it. (That the two worlds are thus alike can be seen above, where representatives and appearances in heaven have been treated of, n. 170–176.)

583. The heavens are in the higher parts of the spiritual world, the world of spirits in the lower parts, and under both are the hells. The heavens are visible to spirits in the world of spirits only when their interior sight is opened; although they sometimes see them as mists or as bright clouds. This is because the angels of heaven are in an interior state in respect to intelligence and wisdom; and for this reason they are above the sight of those who are in the world of spirits. But spirits who dwell in the plains and valleys see one another; and yet when they are separated there, which takes place when they are let into their interiors, the evil spirits do not see the good spirits; but the good spirits can see the evil spirits. Nevertheless, the good spirits turn themselves away from the evil spirits; and when spirits turn themselves away they become invisible. But the hells are not seen because they are closed up. Only the entrances, which are called gates, are seen when they are opened to let in other like spirits. All the gates to the hells open from the world of spirits, and none of them from heaven.

584. The hells are everywhere, both under the mountains, hills, and rocks, and under the plains and valleys. The openings or gates to the hells that are under the mountains, hills, and rocks, appear to the sight like holes and clefts in the rocks, some extended and wide, and some straitened and narrow, and many of them rugged. They all, when looked into, appear dark and dusky; but the infernal spirits that are in them are in such a luminosity as arises from burning coals. Their eyes are adapted to the reception of that light, and for the reason that while they lived in the world they were in thick darkness in respect to

Divine truths, because of their denying them, and were in a sort of light in respect to falsities because of their affirming them. In this way did the sight of their eyes become so formed. And for the same reason the light of heaven is thick darkness to them, and therefore when they go out of their dens they see nothing. All this makes it abundantly clear that man comes into the light of heaven just to the extent that he acknowledges the Divine, and establishes in himself the things of heaven and the church; and that he comes into the thick darkness of hell just to the extent that he denies the Divine, and establishes in himself what is contrary to the truths of heaven and the church.

585. The openings or gates to the hells that are beneath the plains and valleys present to the sight different appearances. Some resemble those that are beneath the mountains, hills, and rocks; some resemble dens and caverns, some great chasms and whirlpools; some resemble bogs, and some standing water. They are all covered, and are opened only when evil spirits from the world of spirits are cast in; and when they are opened there bursts forth from them either something like the fire and smoke that is seen in the air from burning buildings, or like a flame without smoke, or like soot such as comes from a burning chimney, or like a mist and thick cloud. I have heard that the infernal spirits neither see nor feel these things, because when they are in them they are as in their own atmosphere, and thus in the delight of their life; and this for the reason that these things correspond to the evils and falsities in which they are, fire corresponding to hatred and revenge, smoke and soot to the falsities therefrom, flame to the evils of the love of self, and a mist or thick cloud to falsities from that love.

586. I have also been permitted to look into the hells and to see what they are within; for when the Lord wills, the sight of a spirit or angel from above may penetrate into the lowest depths beneath and explore their character, notwithstanding the coverings. In this way I have been permitted to look into them.

Some of the hells appeared to the view like caverns and dens in rocks extending inward and then downward into an abyss, either obliquely or vertically. Some of the hells appeared to the view like the dens and caves of wild beasts in forests; some like the hollow caverns and passages that are seen in mines, with caverns extending toward the lower regions. Most of the hells are threefold, the upper one appearing within to be in dense darkness, because inhabited by those who are in the falsities of evil; while the lower ones appear fiery, because inhabited by those who are in evils themselves, dense darkness corresponding to the falsities of evil, and fire to evils themselves.

Those that have acted interiorly from evil are in the deeper hells, and those that have acted exteriorly from evil, that is, from the falsities of evil, are in the hells that are less deep. Some hells present an appearance like the ruins of houses and cities after conflagrations, in which infernal spirits dwell and hide themselves. In the milder hells there is an appearance of rude huts, in some cases contiguous in the form of a city with lanes and streets, and within the houses are infernal spirits engaged in unceasing quarrels, enmities, fightings, and brutalities; while in the streets and lanes robberies and depredations are committed. In some of the hells there are nothing but brothels, disgusting to the sight and filled with every kind of filth and excrement. Again, there are dark forests, in which infernal spirits roam like wild beasts and where, too, there are underground dens into which those flee who are pursued by others.

There are also deserts, where all is barren and sandy, and where in some places there are ragged rocks in which there are caverns, and in some places huts. Into these desert places those are cast out from the hells who have suffered every extremity of punishment, especially those who in the world have been more cunning than others in undertaking and contriving intrigues and deceits. Such a life is their final lot.

587. As to the positions of the hells in detail, it is something wholly unknown even to the angels in heaven; it is known to the Lord alone. But their position in general is known from the quarters in which they are. For the hells, like the heavens, are distinguished by their quarters; and in the spiritual world quarters are determined in accordance with loves; for in heaven all the quarters begin from the Lord as the sun, who is the East; and as the hells are opposite to the heavens their quarters begin from the opposite point, that is, from the west. (On this see the chapter on the four quarters in heaven, n. 141–153.)

[2] For this reason the hells in the western quarter are the worst of all, and the most horrible, becoming gradually worse and more horrible by degrees the more remote they are from the east. In the western hells are those who in the world were in the love of self, and in consequent contempt of others, and in enmity against those who did not favor them, also in hatred and revenge against those who did not render them respect and homage. In the most remote hells in that quarter are those that had belonged to the Catholic religion, so called, and that had wished to be worshiped as gods, and consequently had burned with hatred and revenge against all who did not acknowledge their power over the souls of men and over heaven. These continue to have the same disposition, that is, the same hatred and revenge against those who oppose them, that they had in the world. Their greatest delight is to practice cruelties; but in the other life this delight is turned against themselves; for in their hells, with which the western quarter is filled, one rages against everyone who detracts from his Divine power. (But more will be said about this in the treatise *Last Judgment and the Destruction of Babylon.*)

[3] Nevertheless, no one can know how the hells in that quarter are arranged, except that the most dreadful hells of that kind are at the sides toward the northern quarter, and the less dreadful toward the southern quarter; thus the dreadfulness of

the hells decreases from the northern quarter to the southern, and likewise by degrees toward the east. Toward the east are the dwelling places of the haughty, who have not believed in the Divine, and yet have not been in such hatred and revenge, or in such deceit, as those have who are in a greater depth in the western quarter.

[4] In the eastern quarter there are at present no hells, those that were there having been transferred to the western quarter in front. In the northern and southern quarters there are many hells; and in them are those who while in the world were in love of the world, and in various kinds of evil therefrom, such as enmity, hostility, theft, robbery, cunning, avarice, and unmercifulness. The worst hells of this kind are in the northern quarter, the milder in the southern. Their dreadfulness increases as they are nearer to the western quarter, and also as they are farther away from the southern quarter, and decreases toward the eastern quarter and toward the southern quarter. Behind the hells that are in the western quarter there are dark forests, in which malignant spirits roam like wild beasts; and it is the same behind the hells in the northern quarter. But behind the hells in the southern quarter there are deserts, which have been described just above. This much respecting the situation of the hells.

588. In regard to the number of the hells, there are as many of them as there are angelic societies in the heavens, since there is for every heavenly society a corresponding infernal society as its opposite. That the heavenly societies are numberless, and are all distinguished in accordance with the goods of love, charity, and faith, may be seen in the chapter that treats of the societies of which the heavens consist (n. 41–50), and in the chapter on the immensity of heaven (n. 415–420). The like is true, therefore, of the infernal societies, which are distinguished in accordance with the evils that are the opposites of those goods.

[2] Every evil, as well as every good, is of infinite variety. That this is true is beyond the comprehension of those who have only a simple idea regarding every evil, such as contempt, enmity, hatred, revenge, deceit, and other like evils. But let them know that each one of these evils contains so many specific differences, and each of these again so many specific or particular differences, that a volume would not suffice to enumerate them. The hells are so distinctly arranged in order in accordance with the differences of every evil that nothing could be more perfectly ordered or more distinct. Evidently, then, the hells are innumerable, near to and remote from one another in accordance with the differences of evils generically, specifically, and particularly.

[3] There are likewise hells beneath hells. Some communicate with others by passages, and more by exhalations, and this in exact accordance with the affinities of one kind or one species of evil with others. How great the number is of the hells I have been permitted to realize from knowing that there are hells under every mountain, hill, and rock, and likewise under every plain and valley, and that they stretch out beneath these in length and in breadth and in depth. In a word, the entire heaven and the entire world of spirits are, as it were, excavated beneath, and under them is a continuous hell. Thus much regarding the number of the hells.

62

The Equilibrium between
Heaven and Hell

589. For anything to have existence there must be an equilibrium of all things. Without equilibrium is no action and reaction; for equilibrium is between two forces, one acting and the other reacting, and the state of rest resulting from like action and reaction is called equilibrium. In the natural world there is an equilibrium in all things and in each thing. It exists in a general way even in the atmosphere, wherein the lower parts react and resist in proportion as the higher parts act and press down. Again, in the natural world there is an equilibrium between heat and cold, between light and shade, and between dryness and moisture, the middle condition being the equilibrium. There is also an equilibrium in all the subjects of the three kingdoms of nature, the mineral, the vegetable, and the animal; for without equilibrium in them nothing can come forth and have permanent existence. Everywhere there is a sort of effort acting on the one side and reacting on the other.

[2] All existence or all effect is produced in equilibrium, that is, by one force acting and another suffering itself to be acted upon, or when one force by acting flows in, the other receives and harmoniously submits. In the natural world that which acts and reacts is called force, and also endeavor [or effort]; but in the spiritual world that which acts and reacts is called life and will. Life in that world is living force, and will is living effort; and the equilibrium itself is called freedom. Thus spiritual equilibrium or freedom has its outcome and permanence in the balance between good acting on the one side and evil reacting

on the other side; or between evil acting on the one side and good reacting on the other side.

[3] With the good the equilibrium is between good acting and evil reacting; but with the evil the equilibrium is between evil acting and good reacting. Spiritual equilibrium is between good and evil, because the whole life of man has reference to good and to evil, and the will is the receptacle. There is also an equilibrium between truth and falsity, but this depends on the equilibrium between good and evil. The equilibrium between truth and falsity is like that between light and shade, in that light and shade affect the objects of the vegetable kingdom only so far as heat and cold are in them. That light and shade themselves have no effect, but only the heat that acts through them, is evident from the fact that light and shade are the same in winter time and in spring time. This comparison of truth and falsity with light and shade is from correspondence, for truth corresponds to light, falsity to shade, and heat to the good of love; in fact, spiritual light is truth, spiritual shade is falsity, and spiritual heat is good of love (see the chapter where light and heat in heaven are treated of, n. 126–140).

590. There is a perpetual equilibrium between heaven and hell. From hell there continually breathes forth and ascends an endeavor to do evil, and from heaven there continually breathes forth and descends an endeavor to do good. In this equilibrium is the world of spirits; which world is intermediate between heaven and hell (see above, n. 421–431). The world of spirits is in this equilibrium because every man after death enters first the world of spirits, and is kept there in a state like that which he was in while in the world, and this would be impossible if there were not a perfect equilibrium there; for by means of this the character of everyone is explored, since they then remain in the same freedom as they had in the world. Spiritual equilibrium is freedom in man and spirit (as has been said just above, n. 589). What each one's freedom is the angels recognize by a communi-

cation of affections and thoughts therefrom; and it becomes visible to the sight of angelic spirits by the ways in which the spirits go. Good spirits there travel in the ways that go toward heaven, but evil spirits in the ways that go toward hell. Ways actually appear in that world; and that is the reason why ways in the Word signify the truths that lead to good, or in the opposite sense the falsities that lead to evil; and for the same reason going, walking, and journeying in the Word signify progressions of life.[1] Such ways I have often been permitted to see, also spirits going and walking in them freely, in accord with their affections and thoughts.

591. Evil continually breathes forth and ascends out of hell, and good continually breathes forth and descends out of heaven, because everyone is encompassed by a spiritual sphere; and that sphere flows forth and pours out from the life of the affections and the thoughts therefrom.[2] And as such a sphere flows forth from every individual, it flows forth also from every heavenly society and from every infernal society, consequently from all together, that is, from the entire heaven and from the entire hell. Good flows forth from heaven because all there are in good; and evil flows forth from hell because all there are in evil. The good that is from heaven is all from the Lord; for the angels in the heavens are all withheld from

1. In the word "to journey," as well as "to go," signifies progression of life (n. 3335, 4375, 4554, 4585, 4882, 5493, 5605, 5996, 8181, 8345, 8397, 8417, 8420, 8557).

"To go (and to walk) with the Lord" means to receive spiritual life, and to live with Him (n. 10567). "To walk" means to live (n. 519, 1794, 8417, 8420).

2. A spiritual sphere, which is a sphere of life, flows forth and pours forth from every man, spirit, and angel, and encompasses him (n. 4464, 5179, 7454, 8630).

It flows forth from the life of their affections and thoughts (n. 2489, 4464, 6206).

The quality of spirits is recognized at a distance from their spheres (n. 1048, 1053, 1316, 1504). Spheres from the evil are the opposites of spheres from the good (n. 1695, 10187, 10312). Such spheres extend far into angelic societies in accordance with the quality and quantity of good (n. 6598–6613, 8063, 8794, 8797). And into infernal societies in accordance with the quality and quantity of evil (n. 8794).

what is their own, and are kept in what is the Lord's own, which is good itself. But the spirits in the hells are all in what is their own, and everyone's own is nothing but evil; and because it is nothing but evil it is hell.[3] Evidently, then, the equilibrium in which angels are kept in the heavens and spirits in the hells is not like the equilibrium in the world of spirits. The equilibrium of angels in the heavens exists in the degree in which they have been willing to be in good, or in the degree in which they have lived in good in the world, and thus also in the degree in which they have held evil in aversion; but the equilibrium of spirits in hell exists in the degree in which they have been willing to be in evil, or have lived in evil in the world, and thus in heart and spirit have been opposed to good.

592. Unless the Lord ruled both the heavens and the hells there would be no equilibrium; and if there were no equilibrium there would be no heaven or hell; for all things and each thing in the universe, that is, both in the natural world and in the spiritual world, endure by means of equilibrium. Every rational man can see that this is true. If there were a preponderance on one part and no resistance on the other would not both perish? So would it be in the spiritual world if good did not react against evil and continually restrain its uprising; and unless this were done by the Divine itself both heaven and hell would perish, and with them the whole human race. It is said unless the Divine itself did this, because the self of everyone, whether angel, spirit, or man, is nothing but evil (see above, n. 591); consequently neither angels nor spirits are able in the least to resist the evils continually exhaling from the hells, since from self they all tend toward hell. It is evident, then, that unless the

---

3. Man's self is nothing but evil (n. 210, 215, 731, 874–876, 987, 1047, 2307, 2308, 3518, 3701, 3812, 8480, 8550, 10283, 10284, 10286, 10732). Man's self is hell in him (n. 694, 8480).

Lord alone ruled both the heavens and the hells no one could ever be saved. Moreover, all the hells act as one; for evils in the hells are connected as goods are in the heavens; and the Divine alone, which goes forth solely from the Lord, is able to resist all the hells, which are innumerable, and which act together against heaven and against all who are in heaven.

593. The equilibrium between the heavens and the hells is diminished or increased in accordance with the number of those who enter heaven and who enter hell; and this amounts to several thousands daily. The Lord alone, and no angel, can know and perceive this, and regulate and equalize it with precision; for the Divine that goes forth from the Lord is omnipresent, and sees everywhere whether there is any wavering, while an angel sees only what is near himself, and has no perception in himself of what is taking place even in his own society.

594. How all things are so arranged in the heavens and in the hells that each and all of those who are there may be in their equilibrium, can in some measure be seen from what has been said and shown above respecting the heavens and the hells, namely, that all the societies of heaven are distinctly arranged in accordance with goods and their kinds and varieties, and all the societies of hell in accordance with evils, and their kinds and varieties; and that beneath each society of heaven there is a society of hell corresponding to it from opposition, and from this opposing correspondence equilibrium results; and in consequence of this the Lord unceasingly provides that no infernal society beneath a heavenly society shall gain any preponderance, and as soon as it begins to do so it is restrained by various means, and is reduced to an exact measure of equilibrium. These means are many, only a few of which I will mention. Some of these means have reference to the stronger presence of the Lord; some to the closer communication and conjunction of one or more societies with others; some to the casting out of superabundant infernal spirits into deserts; some to the transference of certain spirits

from one hell to another; some to the reducing of those in the hells to order, and this also is effected in various ways; some to the screening of certain hells under denser and thicker coverings, also letting them down to greater depths; besides other means; and still others that are employed in the heavens above the hells. All this has been said that it may in some measure be perceived that the Lord alone provides that there shall be an equilibrium everywhere between good and evil, thus between heaven and hell; for on such equilibrium the safety of all in the heavens and of all on the earth rests.

595. It should be known that the hells are continually assaulting heaven and endeavoring to destroy it, and that the Lord continually protects the heavens by withholding those who are in it from the evils derived from their self, and by holding them in the good that is from himself. I have often been permitted to perceive the sphere that flows forth from the hells, which was wholly a sphere of effort to destroy the Divine of the Lord, and thus heaven. The ebullitions of some hells have also at times been perceived, which were efforts to break forth and to destroy. But on the other hand the heavens never assault the hells, for the Divine sphere that goes forth from the Lord is a perpetual effort to save all; and as those who are in the hells cannot be saved (since all who are there are in evil and are antagonistic to the Divine of the Lord), so as far as possible outrages in the hells are subdued and cruelties are restrained to prevent their breaking out beyond measure one against another. This also is effected by innumerable ways in which the Divine power is exercised.

596. There are two kingdoms into which the heavens are divided, the celestial kingdom and the spiritual kingdom (of which see above, n. 20–28). In like manner the hells are divided into two kingdoms, one of which is opposite to the celestial kingdom and the other opposite to the spiritual kingdom. That which is opposite to the celestial kingdom is in the western quarter, and those who are in it are called genii; and

that which is opposite to the spiritual kingdom is in the northern and southern quarters, and those which are in it are called spirits. All who are in the celestial kingdom are in love to the Lord, and all who are in the hells opposite to that kingdom are in the love of self; while all who are in the spiritual kingdom are in love toward the neighbor, and all who are in the hells opposite to that kingdom are in love of the world. Evidently, then, love to the Lord and the love of self are opposites; and in like manner love toward the neighbor and love of the world are opposites. The Lord continually provides that there shall be no outflowing from the hells that are opposite the Lord's celestial kingdom toward those who are in the spiritual kingdom; for if this were done the spiritual kingdom would perish (for the reason given above, n. 579, 678). These are the two general equilibriums that are unceasingly maintained by the Lord.

63

By Means of the Equilibrium between Heaven and Hell Man Is in Freedom

597. The equilibrium between heaven and hell has now been described, and it has been shown that it is an equilibrium between the good that is from heaven and the evil that is from hell, thus that it is a spiritual equilibrium, which in its essence is freedom. A spiritual equilibrium in its essence is freedom because it is an equilibrium between good and evil, and between truth and falsity, and these are spiritual. Therefore to be able to will either what is good or what is evil and to think either what is true or what is false, and to choose one in preference to the other, is the freedom which is here treated of. This freedom is given to every man by the Lord, and is never taken away; in fact, by virtue of its origin it is not man's but the Lord's, since it is from the Lord. Nevertheless, it is given to man with his life as if it were his; and this is done that man may have the ability to be reformed and saved; for without freedom there can be no reformation or salvation. With any rational intuition anyone can see that it is a part of man's freedom to be able to think wrongly or rightly, sincerely or insincerely, justly or unjustly; also that he is free to speak and act rightly, honestly, and justly; but not to speak and act wrongly, insincerely, and unjustly, because of the spiritual, moral, and civil laws whereby his external is held in restraint. Evidently, then, it is man's spirit, which thinks and wills, that is in freedom, and not his external which speaks and acts, except in agreement with the above mentioned laws.

598. Man cannot be reformed unless he has freedom, for the reason that he is born into evils of every kind; and these must be removed in order that he may be saved; and they cannot be removed unless he sees them in himself and acknowledges them, and afterwards ceases to will them, and finally holds them in aversion. Not until then are they removed. And this cannot be done unless man is in good as well as in evil, since it is from good that he is able to see evils, while from evil he cannot see good. The spiritual goods that man is capable of thinking he learns from childhood by reading the Word and from preaching; and he learns moral and civil good from his life in the world. This is the first reason why man ought to be in freedom.

[2] Another reason is that nothing is appropriated to man except what is done from an affection of his love. Other things may gain entrance, but no farther than the thought, not reaching the will; and whatever does not gain entrance into the will of man does not become his, for thought derives what pertains to it from memory, while the will derives what pertains to it from the life itself. Only what is from the will, or what is the same, from the affection of love, can be called free, for whatever a man wills or loves that he does freely; consequently man's freedom and the affection of his love or of his will are a one. It is for this reason that man has freedom, in order that he may be affected by truth and good or may love them, and that they may thus become as if they were his own.

[3] In a word, whatever does not enter into man's freedom has no permanence, because it does not belong to his love or will, and what does not belong to man's love or will does not belong to his spirit; for the very being *[esse]* of the spirit of man is love or will. It is said love or will, since a man wills what he loves. This, then, is why man can be reformed only in freedom. But more on the subject of man's freedom may be seen in *Arcana Coelestia* in the passages referred to below.

599. In order that man may be in freedom, to the end that he may be reformed, he is conjoined in respect to his spirit both with heaven and with hell. For with every man there are spirits from hell and angels from heaven. It is by means of hell that man is in his own evil, while it is by means of angels from heaven that man is in good from the Lord; thus is he in spiritual equilibrium, that is, in freedom. That angels from heaven and spirits from hell are joined to every man may be seen in the chapter on the conjunction of heaven with the human race (n. 291–302).

600. It must be understood that the conjunction of man with heaven and with hell is not a direct conjunction with them, but a mediate conjunction by means of spirits who are in the world of spirits. These spirits, and none from hell itself or from heaven itself, are with man. By means of evil spirits in the world of spirits man is conjoined with hell, and by means of good spirits there he is conjoined with heaven. Because of this the world of spirits is intermediate between heaven and hell, and in that world is equilibrium itself. (That the world of spirits is intermediate between heaven and hell may be seen in the chapter on the world of spirits, n. 421–431; and that the essential equilibrium between heaven and hell is there may be seen in the preceding chapter, n. 589–596.) From all this the source of man's freedom is evident.

601. Something more must be said about the spirits that are joined with man. An entire society can have communication with another society, or with an individual wherever he is; by means of a spirit sent forth from the society; this spirit is called the subject of the many. The same is true of man's conjunction with societies in heaven, and with societies in hell, by means of spirits from the world of spirits that are joined with man. (On this subject see also *Arcana Coelestia* in the passages referred to below.)

602. Finally something must be said respecting man's intuition in regard to his life after death which is derived from the influx of heaven into man. There were some of the simple common people who had lived in the world in the good of faith who were brought back into a state like that in which they had been in the world, which can be done with anyone when the Lord grants it; and it was then shown what opinion they had held about the state of man after death. They said that some intelligent persons had asked them in the world what they thought about their soul after the life on earth; and they replied that they did not know what the soul is. They were then asked what they believed about their state after death; and they said that they believed that they would live as spirits. Again they were asked what belief they had respecting a spirit; and they said that he is a man. They were asked how they knew this; and they said that they knew it because it is so. Those intelligent men were surprised that the simple had such a faith, which they themselves did not have. This is a proof that in every man who is in conjunction with heaven there is an intuition respecting his life after death. This intuition is from no other source than an influx out of heaven, that is, through heaven from the Lord by means of spirits from the world of spirits who are joined with man. This intuition those have who have not extinguished their freedom of thinking by notions previously adopted and confirmed by various arguments respecting the soul of man, which is held to be either pure thought, or some vital principle the seat of which is sought for in the body; and yet the soul is nothing but the life of man, while the spirit is the man himself; and the earthly body which he carries about with him in the world is merely an agent whereby the spirit, which is the man himself, is enabled to act fitly in the natural world.

603. What has been said in this work about heaven, the world of spirits, and hell, will be obscure to those who have no interest in learning about spiritual truths, but will be clear to those

who have such an interest, and especially to those who have an affection for truth for the sake of truth, that is, who love truth because it is truth; for whatever is then loved enters with light into the mind's thought, especially truth that is loved, because all truth is in light.

Extracts from *Arcana Coelestia* respecting the Freedom of Man, Influx, and the Spirits through Whom Communications Are Effected

FREEDOM

All freedom pertains to love or affection, since whatever a man loves he does freely (n. 2870, 3158, 8987, 8990, 9585, 9591).

Since freedom pertains to love it is the life of everyone (n. 2873).

Nothing appears to be man's own except what is from freedom (n. 2880).

There is heavenly freedom and infernal freedom (n. 2870, 2873, 2874, 9589, 9590).

[2] Heavenly freedom pertains to heavenly love, or the love of good and truth (n. 1947, 2870, 2872).

And as the love of good and truth is from the Lord freedom itself consists in being led by the Lord (n. 892, 905, 2872, 2886, 2890–2892, 9096, 9586, 9587, 9589–9591).

Man is led into heavenly freedom by the Lord through regeneration (n. 2874, 2875, 2882, 2892).

Man must have freedom in order to be regenerated (n. 1937, 1947, 2876, 2881, 3145, 3146, 3158, 4031, 8700).

In no other way can the love of good and truth be implanted in man, and appropriated by him seemingly as his own (n. 2877, 2879, 2880, 2888).

Nothing is conjoined to man in a state of compulsion (n. 2875, 8700).

If man could be reformed by compulsion all would be saved (n. 2881).

In reformation compulsion is harmful (n. 4031).

All worship from freedom is worship, but worship from compulsion is not worship (n. 1947, 2880, 7349, 10097).

Repentance must be effected in a free state, and repentance effected in a state of compulsion is of no avail (n. 8392).

States of compulsion, what they are (n. 8392).

[3] It is granted to man to act from the freedom of reason, to the end that good may be provided for him, and this is why man has the freedom to think and will even what is evil, and to do it so far as the laws do not forbid (n. 10777).

Man is kept by the Lord between heaven and hell, and thus in equilibrium, that he may be in freedom for the sake of reformation (n. 5982, 6477, 8209, 8987).

What is implanted in freedom endures, but not what is implanted under compulsion (n. 9588).

For this reason no one is ever deprived of his freedom (n. 2876, 2881).

The Lord compels no one (n. 1937, 1947).

Compelling oneself is from freedom, but not being compelled (n. 1937, 1947).

A man ought to compel himself to resist evil (n. 1937, 1947, 7914).

Also to do good as if from himself, and yet to acknowledge that it is from the Lord (n. 2883, 2891, 2892, 7914).

Man has a stronger freedom in the temptation combats in which he conquers, since he then compels himself more interiorly to resist, although it appears otherwise (n. 1937, 1947, 2881).

[4] Infernal freedom consists in being led by the loves of self and of the world and their lusts (n. 2870, 2873).

Those who are in hell know no other freedom (n. 2871).

Heavenly freedom is as far removed from infernal freedom as heaven is from hell (n. 2873, 2874).

Infernal freedom, which consists in being led by the loves of self and of the world, is not freedom but servitude (n. 2884, 2890).

For servitude is in being led by hell (n. 9586, 9589–9591).

INFLUX

[5] All things that man thinks and wills flow into him; from experience (n. 904, 2886–2888, 4151, 4319, 4320, 5846, 5848, 6189, 6191, 6194, 6197–6199, 6213, 7147, 10219).

Man's capacity to give attention to subjects, to think, and to draw conclusions analytically, is from influx (n. 4319, 4320, 5288).

Man could not live a single moment if influx from the spiritual world were taken away from him; from experience (n. 2887, 5849, 5854, 6321).

The life that flows in from the Lord varies in accordance with the state of man and in accordance with reception (n. 2069, 5986, 6472, 7343).

With those who are evil the good that flows in from the Lord is changed into evil, and the truth into falsity; from experience (n. 3642, 4632).

The good and truth that continually flow in from the Lord are received just to the extent that they are not hindered by evil and falsity (n. 2411, 3142, 3147, 5828).

[6] All good flows in from the Lord, and all evil from hell (n. 904, 4151).

At the present day man believes that all things are in himself and are from himself, when in fact they flow in; and this he might know from the doctrine of the church, which teaches that all good is from God, and all evil from the devil (n. 4249, 6193, 6206).

But if man's belief were in accord with this doctrine he would not appropriate evil to himself nor would he make good to be his own (n. 6206, 6324, 6325).

How happy man's state would be if he believed that all good flows in from the Lord and all evil from hell (n. 6325).

Those who deny heaven or who know nothing about it do not know that there is any influx from heaven (n. 4322, 5649, 6193, 6479).

What influx is, illustrated by comparisons (n. 6128, 6190, 9407).

[7] Everything of life flows in from the first fountain of life, because that is the source of it; and it continually flows in; thus everything of life is from the Lord (n. 3001, 3318, 3337, 3338, 3344, 3484, 3619, 3741–3743, 4318–4320, 4417, 4524, 4882, 5847, 5986, 6325, 6468–6470, 6479, 9276, 10196).

Influx is spiritual and not physical, that is, influx is from the spiritual world into the natural, and not from the natural into the spiritual (n. 3219, 5119, 5259, 5427, 5428, 5477, 6322, 9110).

Influx is through the internal man into the external, or through the spirit into the body, and not the reverse, because the spirit of man is in the spiritual world, and his body in the natural (n. 1702, 1707, 1940, 1954, 5119, 5259, 5779, 6322, 9380).

The internal man is in the spiritual world and the external in the natural world (n. 978, 1015, 3628, 4459, 4523, 4524, 6057, 6309, 9701–9709, 10156, 10472).

There is an appearance that there is an influx from the externals of man into internals, but this is a fallacy (n. 3721).

With man there is influx into things rational, and through these into knowledges, and not the reverse (n. 1495, 1707, 1940).

What the order of influx is (n. 775, 880, 1096, 1495, 7270).

There is direct influx from the Lord, and likewise mediate influx through the spiritual world or heaven (n. 6063, 6307, 6472, 9682, 9683).

The Lord's influx is into the good in man, and through good into truth, and not the reverse (n. 5482, 5649, 6027, 8685, 8701, 10153).

Good gives the capacity to receive influx from the Lord, but truth without good does not (n. 8321).

Nothing that flows into the thought is harmful, but only what flows into the will, since this is what is appropriated to man (n. 6308).

[8] There is a general influx (n. 5850).

This is a continual effort to act in accordance with order (n. 6211).

This influx is into the lives of animals (n. 5850).

Also into the subjects of the vegetable kingdom (n. 3648).

It is in accord with this general influx that thought falls into speech with man, and will into acts and movements (n. 5862, 5990, 6192, 6211).

SUBJECT SPIRITS

[9] Spirits sent forth from societies of spirits to other societies and to other spirits are called "subjects" (n. 4403, 5856).

Communications in the other life are effected by means of such emissary spirits (n. 4403, 5856, 5983).

A spirit sent forth to serve as a subject does not think from himself, but thinks from those by whom he is sent forth (n. 5985–5987).

Many particulars relating to such spirits (n. 5988, 5989).

Index of Scripture References

Bold figures designate verses fully quoted.
Italic figures designate verses given in substance.
Figures in parenthesis indicate verses merely referred to.

GENESIS			1 SAMUEL	
1 (3, 4)	¶ 137		9 (9)	¶ 76
2 *24*	372			
2 (25)	341		2 SAMUEL	
3 (7, 10, 11)	341		24 (15), **16, 17**	229
EXODUS			2 KINGS	
29 (18, 25, 41)	287		6 **17**	76
LEVITICUS			PSALMS	
1 (9, 13, 17)	287		31 **8**	197
2 (2, 9)	287		36 **5, 6**	216
6 (15, 21)	287		37 (37)	287
23 (1, 2, 13, 18)	287		43 **3**	129
			45 (12)	365
NUMBERS			103 **20**	229
6 **26**	287		104 **2**	129
15 (3, 7, 13)	287		118 **5**	197
24 (3)	76			
28 (6, 8, 13)	287		ISAIAH	
29 (2, 6, 8, 13, 36)	287		8 (8)	197
			9 **6, 7**	287
DEUTERONOMY			9 **7**	216
4 (19)	122		9 **17, 18, 19**	570
17 (3–5)	122		10 (12–14)	365
			13 **10**	119
JUDGES			14 (30)	365
17 *(Chap. cited)*	324		19 **23–25**	307
18 *(Chap. cited)*	324		29 (19)	365

ISAIAH (cont.)

30 (6, 7)	¶ 365
30 **26**	119
32 **17, 18**	287
32 **5**	216
32 **7, 8**	287
34 **9, 10**	570
41 (17, 18)	365
42 **6**	129
45 (3)	365
49 **6**	129
52 **1**	180
52 (7)	287
54 (10)	287
54 **13**	25
58 **2**	216
59 (8)	287

JEREMIAH

8 (1, 2)	122
9 **24**	216
16 (5)	287
17 (3)	365
23 **5**	216
25 **14**	471
25 (37)	287
29 (11)	287
31 **33, 34**	25, 271
32 **19**	471
48 (7)	365
50 (36, 37)	365
51 (13)	365

EZEKIEL

2 **9, 10**	258
8 (15, 16, 18)	122
16 **10, 13**	180
26 (7, 12)	365
27 *(Chap. cited)*	365

32 **7, 8**	¶ 119
40–48 *(Ch. cited)*	171, 197

DANIEL

5 (2–4)	65
7–12 *(Ch. cited)*	171
12 **3**	346
12 *3*	518

HOSEA

2 **19**	216
4 **9**	471
12 (9)	365

JOEL

2 (2), **10, 31**	119
2 **30,** (31)	570
3 **15**	119

HABAKKUK

1 (6)	197

ZEPHANIAH

3 (12, 13)	365

HAGGAI

2 (9)	287

ZECHARIAH

1 **6**	471
8 (12)	287
9 (3, 4)	365

MALACHI

4 **1**	570

MATTHEW

3 **10**	570
4 **16**	129

MATTHEW (cont.)

5 3	¶ 357
5 18	260
5 37	270 *note*
5 37	214 *note*, 271
6 (23–35)	281
6 33	64
7 13, 14	534

7 21–23	471
7 24, 26	471
10 16	278
11 (5)	365
11 25 (26)	353
11 27	5
11 29, 30	359
11 30	533
12 (8)	287
12 36	507
13 (6)	122
13 12	349
13 13 (14, 15)	353
13 41, 42 (50)	570
13 43	348
16 27	471
17 2	119, 129, 180
18 8, 9	570
19 4, 5, 6, 11	372
19 24	365
20 26, 27, 28	218
22 11, 12, *13*	180
22 (11 et seq.)	48
22 37, 38–40	19
23 27	505
24 17, 18	208
24 29	119
24 29–31	1
24 *(Chap. cited)*	1 *note*

25 29	¶ 349
25 (30)	575
25 (32, 46)	471
25 41	570
25 *(Chap. cited)*	1 *note*
27 (53)	312 *note*
28 3	180
28 8	5

MARK

2 (27, 28)	287
9 3	180
9 3	129
9 43–49	570
10 6–9	372
10 14, 15	281
16 (5)	180

LUKE

3 9	570
6 (5)	287
6 21, (22)	357
6 (20, 21)	365
6 38	349
9 29	180
10 5, 6	287
12 2, 3	462 [b], 507
13 26, 27	471
13 29, 30	324
14 16–24	365
14 (21)	365
14 (33)	365
16 (19, 31)	365
16 24	570
16 29–31	456
17 20, 21	33
17 31, 32	208
18 16, 17	281
20 17, 18	534

LUKE (cont.)

21 (35, 36)	¶ 382 [b]
22 26	218
24 (4)	180
24 (36–38), 39	316

JOHN

1 1, 3, 4, 10, 14	137
1 9	129
1 *18*	84
2 (19, 21)	187
3 19	129
3 36	5
5 *37*	84
6 (45, 46)	25
6 56	147
8 12	129
8 (56)	84
9 5	129
10 *30, 38*	2
11 25, 26	5
12 35, 36, 46	129
12 40	456
14 2	51
14 6	5
14 *9–11*	2
14 21, 23	16
14 27	287
15 4	147
15 4, 5	11
15 4, 5, 9, 10	81
15 10	16
16 *13–15*	2
16 *15*	5
16 33	287
17 *2*	5
20 (12)	180
20 19, 21, 26	287
20 (25, 27, 29)	461

REVELATION

1–22 *(Ch. cited)*	¶ 171
2 23	471
3 4, 5	180
3 (17, 18)	365
4 *4*	180
5 1	258
6 12, 13	119
9 2, 17, 18	570
14 (4)	368
14 9, 10	570
14 13	471
16 (8)	122
16 8, 9	570
16 15	180
18 2, 18	570
19 3	570
19 *14*	180
19 20	570
20 12, 13	471
20 (14, 15)	570
21 *(Chap. cited)*	187
21 1, 2, 16–19, 21	307
21 (8)	570
21 16	197
21 17	73
21 24	129
22 12	471

Index

Abodes of angels (Chap. 21, n. 183, 184); places of abode in heaven (n. 148, 149).

Abraham, why mentioned in the Word (n. 526); unknown in heaven (n. 526 note).

Action and reaction of heaven and hell (n. 537); *action* and reaction depend upon equilibrium (n. 589).

Acts, man's *acts* uses (n. 112); man's speech and *acts* governed by influx (n. 296); must be just if a man is to enter heaven (n. 358); affection must flow forth in *acts* (n. 360); *acts* of the body are those of an instrument merely (n. 432); love in *act* endures (n. 483); outward *acts* are such as are the intentions and thoughts (n. 495).

Administration of heavenly affairs (n. 388, 389).

Adoration of the Lord by an idolater (n. 324).

Adulterers are unmerciful and destitute of religion (n. 385 note); defined (n. 386); their delights in the other life (n. 488).

Adultery, a delight in falsity conjoined to evil (n. 374, 384); *adultery* is profane: a marriage of falsity and evil (n. 384, 385).

Adults, difference between those that die as infants and those that die as *adults* (n. 345); where and how those that die as *adults* are prepared for heaven (n. 514, 515).

Affairs of heaven (n. 388).

Affections expressed in angelic speech (n. 336, 244); expressed by tone (n. 269); expressed by written characters (n. 261); animals correspond to various *affections* (n. 110); vegetable foods correspond to *affection* for good and truth (n. 111); must terminate in the world in acts (n. 360); *affections* of the spirit communicate with the heart (n. 446); ascribed to the heart, although not in it or near it (n. 95); *affections* of marriage love represented in heaven (n. 382 [a]); everyone has many *affections,* but the ruling one is in them all (n. 236); the ruling *affection* determines the character of the face in the other life (n. 47, 48, 457); everyone in spiritual world an image of his *affection* or love (n. 498); are shared in world of spirits (n. 552); spirits are in human form corresponding to their *affections; affections* for truth insinuated into good spirits (n. 517); *affections* of children in heaven (n. 331, 334, 345); influx of children in heaven almost solely a matter of *affections* (n. 336); *affections* of evil spirits that cause melancholy (n. 299); genii act upon the *affections* (n. 579); *affections* of those in self-love (n. 561); *affections* of hypocrites render them misshapen (n. 458); extension of thought and *affections* (n. 203); man's thought and *affection* extended in heaven or hell according to his ruling love (n. 477); removed during resuscitation (n. 449); remain after death (Chap. 47); *affections* in heaven described (n. 413); genuine *affection* for truth (n. 347); *affections* for good and truth determine the degree of interior wisdom in heaven (n. 469); delights of the soul are *affections* for good and truth (n. 396); in heaven the more interior the *affection* the greater the beauty (n. 459); *affections* of a higher heaven never perceived in a lower (n. 210); contrariety of *affection* separates in heaven (n. 194); angels recognize the nature of a spirit's freedom by a communication of thought and *affections* (n. 590); spirits and angels speak from the thoughts and *affections* that are proper to their minds (n. 464); *affections* of the angels for wisdom (n. 266); angels can utter nothing not in agreement with their *affections* (n. 237); cannot be counterfeited in the other life (n. 457); quality of angels' *affections* known from their spheres (n. 17); when angels are with men they dwell in their *affections* (n. 391); the will rules in man through *affections* for good, the understanding through *affections* for truth (n. 95); everyone encompassed by a spiritual sphere flowing out from the life of his *affections* (n. 591); only what is done from the *affection* of his love is appropriated to man (n. 598); flow into man from spirits (n. 298); *affections* and thought determine the nature of a man (n. 358); to think freely from his own *affection* is the very life of man (n. 502); freedom pertains to *affections* (n. 389). (See Thought.)

Affiliations in heaven (Chap. 23, n. 36, 64, 304); angels *affiliated* not by themselves but by the Lord (n. 45,

205); in heaven or hell *affiliations* are through the ruling love (n. 479).

Africans are the most beloved of the heathen (n. 326); and the best (n. 514).

Age, consummation of (n. 1); golden, silver, copper, and iron *ages* (n. 115); golden *age* (n. 252); spirits associated with man in old *age* are in wisdom and innocence (n. 295); the good who die in old *age* rejuvenated (n. 414); *ages* in heaven (n. 340).

All-in-all, the Lord the *All-in-all* in heaven (n. 58).

Amusements of the world do not debar from heaven (n. 358).

Ancient One, the simple think of God as the *Ancient One* in shining light (n. 82).

Ancients, elevation above sense-conception known to the *ancients* (n. 74 note); their knowledge that of correspondences (n. 356 extract); more became angels than at present (n. 415); their understanding of love to the neighbor (n. 558 [b] note). (*See* People).

And, why so frequent in Hebrew (n. 241).

Angels, their understanding and will. (n. 136); activity of their senses (n. 462 [a]); natural man's idea of their senses (n. 170); their superiority over men (n. 576); their separation from self (n. 341); their appearance (n. 80); their veriest life (n. 136); their affiliations and relationships (n. 205); their garments (Chap. 20); their abodes (Chap. 21, n. 148, 184, 188); their numbers (n. 415, 416); their doctrines (n. 227); their writing (n. 258, 260); their inmosts (n. 435); their outer sight corresponds to their inner sight or understanding (n. 462 [a]); their reasoning about life (n. 9); their views of polygamy (n. 379); their horror at the idea of two individuals being just alike (n. 405); do not think from natural things (n. 114); how they look upon dignity and honor (n. 389); recognize the nature of a spirit's freedom (n. 590); their idea of eternity (n. 167); have no notion of time or space (n. 162–166); their life a life of joy (n. 555); how taught about heavenly joy (n. 412); all that is not in harmony with their ruling love is removed (n. 479); are being perfected to eternity (n. 158 note); turn themselves constantly to their loves (n. 17 note); their various employments (Chap. 41); heathen taught by *angels* (n. 325); each has his particular charge (n. 392); their administration of heavenly affairs (n. 389); those that care for little children in heaven (n. 332); *angels* who instruct good spirits (n. 513, 515); powers of *angels* (Chap. 26); called "powers" (n. 137, 231); examples of their power over evil (n. 229); if they look at an evil spirit he swoons (n. 232); may see into hell if the Lord wills (n. 586); hells ruled by their means (n. 543); could not resist the hells alone (n. 592); *angels* have no names, but are distinguished by the quality of their good and by the idea of it (n. 52 note); protected by clouds from the heavenly sun (n. 120); every *angel* in complete human form (Chap. 10, n. 73, 75, 77); those that become *angels* (n. 549); how children become *angels* (n. 329); not created such (n. 311); *angels* from other earths (n. 417 extract); spiritual-natural and celestial-natural (n. 31); difference between those that have died as children and

those that have died as adults (n. 345); appearance of those that have never concealed their thought and feelings (n. 489); *angels* called "gods" (n. 231 note); *angels* as charities (n. 414); appear as stars (n. 69, 356); *angels* in the goods of love and charity (n. 402); *angels* as receptions of Divine good and truth (n. 25, 133, 232); things that appear to them have real existence (n. 175); have all things useful (n. 264, 266); receive and hold all things that they possess from the Lord (n. 190); receive the things of heaven according to the quality of their good (n. 53); their reception into heaven (n. 519); a married pair not called two but one *angel* (n. 367, 372); *angels* and marriage love (n. 370, 371, 374); see correspondence in all things of heaven (n. 185); how affiliated (n. 36, 242); how they perceive truths (n. 270); their every thought spreads forth into heaven (n. 79); their division into societies (n. 41); cannot ascend or descend from one heaven to another (n. 35); *angels* of different heavens cannot communicate (n. 208); *angels* of a higher heaven can see those of a lower, but not vice versa (n. 209); internal and external *angels* in each heaven (n. 32); their interiors determine their heaven (n. 33); all in heaven are forms of love and charity (n. 17); those the *angels* call intelligent and fitted for heaven (n. 86); each a heaven in smallest form (Chap. 7); *angels* constitute heaven (n. 7); heaven within them (n. 53); *angels* of the inmost heaven appear as children (n. 280, 341); *angels* of the inmost heaven have had their interiors opened in the third degree (n. 34); *angels* of the inmost heaven have no clothing (n. 178, 280); not allowed to look at the back of the head of another (n. 144); can perceive falsities (n. 487); *angels* seen with the spiritual eyes only (n. 76); *angels* as depicted in churches (n. 74); the east always before their faces (n. 142, 143); wrong ideas of *angels* (n. 74). (See Affections, Delight, Divine, Heaven, Intelligence, Life, Lord, Love, Society, Speech, State, Swedenborg, Wisdom of Angels.)

Anger, why attributed to the Lord in the Word (n. 545 note).

Animals, their correspondence (n. 110); they are affections (n. 110); their knowledge (n. 108, 352); their loves (n. 135); are in the order of their life, therefore governed by influx (n. 296); difference between man and *animals* (n. 39, 108, 202, 296, 352, 435).

Anxiety, caused by certain spirits (n. 299).

Appearances of external things in heaven vary with angels' changes of state (n. 156); *appearances* and representatives in heaven (Chap. 19); real and unreal *appearances* in heaven (n. 175); *appearances* of the hells (Chap. 61); *appearance* of the Divine to man in human form (n. 82, 84, 86).

Appetites, their pleasures obscure and weaken the understanding (n. 462 [a]).

Apostles mean the Lord in respect to Divine truth (n. 526).

Arcana respecting the angels of the three heavens (n. 39); that heaven in the aggregate reflects a single man (n. 59); *arcana* in numbers (n. 263); *arcana* respecting regeneration (n. 269); *arcana* in regard to natural and spiritual light (n. 308); *arcana* of the form of truth (n. 460).

Arcana Coelestia, extracts (n. 86, 356, 603).

Architecture in heaven (n. 185).

Arms, correspondence of (n. 97, 231); *arms* of the Greatest Man (n. 96, 231).

Art in heaven: true *art* from heaven (n. 185).

Artifices of infernal spirits (Chap. 60).

Asia, religion spread from *Asia* (n. 322).

Assyria signifies the rational (n. 307).

Assemblies in heaven (n. 149).

Atmosphere of heaven (n. 235, 462 [a]); *atmosphere* of hell (n. 585).

Autumn, its correspondence (n. 166).

Avarice is spiritual filth (n. 363).

Aversion separates in heaven (n. 194).

Babel, Babylon, meaning of *"Babylon"* (n. 544); *Babylon* of the present day (n. 559).

Baptism only a sign and memorial (n. 329); what it signifies (n. 329 note).

Beasts, difference between man and *beasts* (n. 296 note, 435). (See Animal.)

Beauty of the body does not imply spiritual *beauty* (n. 99, 131); *beauty* of Angels (n. 382 [a]); personal *beauty* in heaven (n. 414); cause of internal *beauty* (n. 459).

Bed chamber signifies interior things (n. 186 note).

Bees, their instincts (n. 108).

Being, very *being* or *esse* (n. 9); belief in a Divine *Being* (n. 79, 80); Divine love the *being* (n. 139).

Belief, false *beliefs* in regard to the Lord (n. 3); false *beliefs* about heaven (n. 54, 420, 526); false *beliefs* about heavenly joy (n. 400–408); false *beliefs* about the spirit after death (n. 456); false *belief* that we ought to withdraw from the world (n. 535); those that take their *belief* from others (n. 74); *belief* does not come through knowledges (n. 356 extract); mere *belief* in what is true is not faith (n. 482); *belief* in life after death (n. 183); *belief* in the Divine (n. 351); *belief* of simple people in regard to life after death (n. 602); *belief* of those in good about heaven (n. 176).

Belts about the sun of heaven (n. 120, 159).

Birds, their instincts (n. 108); their correspondence (n. 110).

Birth, regeneration a *rebirth* (n. 279); how spiritual *birth* is effected (n. 345); correspondence of *birth* (n. 382 [b]).

Blessedness of marriage love (n. 379, 380); angelic *blessedness* consists in goods of charity (n. 387 note); *blessedness* of those in love to the Lord (n. 401).

Blessings, real and unreal (n. 364); *blessings* of true marriage love (n. 374).

Blind, correspondence of the *"blind"* in the Word (n. 487 note).

Blood of the Lord signifies Divine truth (n. 147); love the source of its heat (n. 567).

Body, its construction (n. 63); correspondences in the *body* (n. 91); it corresponds to the form of heaven (n. 212); is an image of the mind (n. 374); man's thought inscribed on the whole *body* (n. 463); merely as an instrument of the spirit (n. 432–435, 576, 602); the *body* merely the external form in which the internal exhibits itself (n. 521); the *body* formed to serve the will and understanding (n. 60); the *body* moved from good and truth (n. 137); the *body* is material, and does not think (n. 432); the *body* not a product of nature (n. 102);

whatever is felt in the *body* has its origin in the spiritual (n. 373); its heat excited by heat of the spirit (n. 567); man is man by virtue of his spirit, not of his *body* (n. 453); the natural and spiritual *bodies* have corresponding delights (n. 485); the spiritual *body* formed solely of the things done from the love or will (n. 475); the *body* the only thing left behind after death (Chap. 48); man dies when the *body* is no longer able to perform its functions (n. 445); what happens when a man is withdrawn from the *body* (n. 440); the *body* of a spirit (n. 363); the *body* of an evil spirit (n. 553); *bodies* of children in the other life (n. 331); form of an angel's *body* is the external of his interiors (n. 340); what is meant by an angel's being "in the Lord's *body*" (n. 181); the union of the Lord with the Father was as between soul and *body* (n. 86 extract).

Bogs in hell (n. 354).

Books brought forth from man's memory after death; *"book* of life" (n. 463).

Boys, spirits associated with *boys* are in an affection for knowing (n. 295); training of *boys* in heaven (n. 391).

Brain, the cerebrum and cerebellum (n. 251); all things of the thought and will inscribed on the *brain* (n. 463).

Bread, its correspondence and use in worship (n. 111); *"bread"* signifies every good (n. 340 note).

Breadth means a state of truth (n. 197, 307).

Breast signifies charity (n. 97); *breast* of the Greatest Man (n. 65).

Bride, why the church is called "the *bride*" (n. 371).

Bridegroom, why the Lord is called the

"Bridegroom" (n. 180, 371).

Builders signify those of the church (n. 534).

Camel, signification of *"camel* passing through the eye of a needle" (n. 365).

Catholics, their saints not all good (n. 535); situation in hell of evil *Catholics* (n. 587).

Cattle, their correspondence (n. 110).

Cause, the Lord's presence as a *cause* (n. 199); angel's ideas and words have the relation of *cause* and effect (n. 240); *cause* and effect (n. 303, 512); spiritual world flows into the natural as *cause* and effect (n. 567).

Center, the Lord the common *center* in heaven (n. 124, 142).

Cerebellum corresponds to wisdom (n. 251).

Cerebrum corresponds to intelligence (n. 251).

Chamber, correspondence of *bed chamber* to interiors (n. 186).

Character, determined by what predominates (n. 369); determined by interiors (n. 532); *character* of a spirit known as soon as he is looked upon (n. 552).

Charity, described and defined (n. 148, 360, 364, 481 note); life of *charity* described (n. 535); *charity* toward the neighbor (n. 13, 15 note, 23); life of *charity* leads to heaven (n. 360); life of *charity* can be lived only in the midst of the world (n. 535); those in heaven that have lived a life of *charity* (n. 489); heathen who have lived in *charity* (n. 324); *charity* of Chinese spirits (n. 325); the Lord's church in those who live in *charity* (n. 308); all in heaven are forms of love and *charity* (n. 17); life in heaven and *charity* (n. 403); heavenly joy result of *char-ity* (n. 404); heavenly beauty produced by goodness and *charity* (n. 414); those in the breast of the Greatest Man are in the good of *charity* (n. 96); angelic life consists in goods of love and *charity* (n. 112 note, 517 note); the good of spiritual kingdom is the good of *charity* (n. 215, 241); all who live in the good of *charity* according to their religion are in the Lord's church (n. 328); angelic blessedness consists in goods of *charity* (n. 387 note); good of *charity* as a motive (n. 472); how children in heaven are led into goods of *charity* (n. 337).

Childhood, innocence of *childhood* not genuine (n. 277); spirits associated with man in *childhood* (n. 295); falsities learned in *childhood* not necessarily confirmed (n. 352); all who die in *childhood* become angels (n. 416); when and how those dying in *childhood* are prepared for heaven (n. 514, 515).

Children signify innocence (n. 341); little *children* in heaven (Chap. 37); immediately after death confided to angel women (n. 332); how taught in heaven (n. 329, 334); states after death (n. 336); their manner of life in heaven (n. 337); never grow beyond early manhood in heaven (n. 340); in heaven sometimes let down into their inherited evil (n. 342); in heaven taught by temptation (n. 343); their education (n. 344); in heaven have no plane of the memory (n. 345); their innocence (n. 341); in the Greatest Man (n. 333); celestial and spiritual (n. 333, 339); described: specially under the Lord's auspices (n. 277); old men become like *children* (n. 278); how their interiors are formed (n. 282); their nature (n. 288); all belong to the Lord's church (n. 308 note); think of all things as alive (n. 338); societies in heaven employed in the care of *children* (n. 391); infants in heaven (n. 4).

Chinese in heaven (n. 325).

Choir, Chinese *choir* in heaven (n. 325)

Christ (See Jesus.)

Christians compared to heathen (n. 319); their false doctrines about the Lord (n. 321); Chinese and *Christians* (n. 325); all know of the future life (n. 470); their condition after death (n. 495).

Church, what it is (n. 57); final period of the *church* (n. 1, 311); the heathen or people outside the *church* in heaven (Chap. 36); the heathen cannot profane the holy things of the *church* (n. 322 note); why the *church* is called "bride" and "wife" (n. 371); why called a "woman" (n. 368); the essentials of the *church* (n. 86 extract); *church* where the Word is is as the heart and lungs of the Lord's universal *church* (n. 308); the *church* the Lord's heaven on earth (n. 57, 374); what and where the Lord's *church* is today (n. 328); Jerusalem means the Lord's *church* in heaven (n. 73); Jerusalem means a *church* that is in truth (n. 108); New Jerusalem means a *church* that is in truth (n. 108); New Jerusalem signifies the church to be established (n. 186, 197); "a new heaven and a new earth" means a new *church* (n. 307); "house of the wedding feast" means heaven and the *church* (n. 180); *church* in heaven (n. 221–223); hostility toward the *church* of those in self-love (n. 562); ignorance in the *church* (n. 77, 526); denial of truth by those within the *church* (n. 309); erroneous ideas in the

church in regard to conjunction (n. 302); those of the *church* who have an idea of the Divine as three (n. ?); condition after death of those in the *church* who acknowledge the Father only (n. 3, 6); representative *churches* (n. 306); *church* after the deluge (n. 327); sacrifices of the Israelitish *church* (n. 110); the wisdom of the ancient *church* (n. 322); most ancient and ancient *churches* (n. 327).

Cicero, Swedenborg talked with one who seemed to be *Cicero* (n. 322).

Cities in heaven (n. 184); in the hells (n. 586).

Civil affairs in heaven (n. 393).

Clergy who deny the Divine (n. 353).

Clothing, angels of the inmost heaven have none (n. 280); *clothing* of children in heaven (n. 337). (See Garments.)

Clouds signify the Word in the sense of the letter (n. 1); protect the angels (n. 120); *cloudy* belt about the sun of heaven (n. 159); black *clouds* of the other world are from evil (n. 549).

Colors, their significance (n. 179 note); how produced in heaven (n. 356).

Communication, man comes into *communication* with heaven through his interior (n. 30); man's *communication* with heaven is by means of correspondence (n. 114); man's *communication* with heaven depends upon his intelligence and wisdom (n. 204); the inmost *communication* of the spirit is with the respiration and the motion of the heart (n. 446); *communication* in heaven (Chap. 23); *communication* between the kingdoms of heaven is by intermediate societies (n. 27); *communication* between the heavens is really influx (n. 206); all heavenly societies have *communication* with one another through extension of sphere (n. 49); *communication* of all things in heaven (n. 206).

Comprehension of spiritual truths (n. 356 extract).

Compulsion, reformation cannot be by *compulsion* (n. 293).

Confirmation of truths (n. 352, 356 extract).

Conjunction, what it is in heaven (n. 369); angels have their wisdom through *conjunction* (n. 372); with the Lord (n. 16, 304, 473 note); of the Lord with angels (n. 86 extract); of the heavens (n. 208); of heaven with the world (n. 112, 252); of natural and spiritual worlds in man (n. 112, 247); of spirits and angels with man (n. 206, 255, 292, 365); *conjunction* in marriage love (n. 367, 370); of heaven with the human race (Chap. 33); of heaven with man by means of the Word (Chap. 34); of the spiritual man with heaven (n. 530); of man with heaven or hell (n. 292, 294); difference between *conjunction* of heaven with man and man with man (n. 300); erroneous ideas about *conjunction* of heaven with man (n. 302); of innocence and peace (n. 288); of good and truth (n. 286, 371, 422); of evil and falsity (n. 422).

Conscience as a motive (n. 358, 472); various views of it (n. 299); those that have obeyed it in the world (n. 506).

Consonants in angelic speech (n. 241); express ideas (n. 261).

Consorts in heaven (n. 383).

Consummation of the age (n. 1)

Contempt, one of the evils of self-love (n. 562).

Continuity, distance appears only when *continuity* is broken (n. 196)

Copper signifies natural good (n. 115).

Corporeal-sensual spirits (n. 575).

Corpse, its odor appears aromatic to spirits (n. 449).

Correspondence, what it is (n. 89); it is universal (n. 100); revelation only occurs now through *correspondences* (n. 306); the Word consists wholly of *correspondences* (n. 365); *correspondences* are the forms in which uses are clothed (n. 112); *correspondence* of all things (n. 303); degrees in *correspondence* in the kingdoms of nature (n. 104); all things of nature are *correspondences* (n. 106); things in the natural world are *correspondences* of things in the spiritual world (n. 89, 90); spiritual world is not understood without a knowledge of *correspondences* (n. 88); all nature is a theater representative of the Lord's kingdom (n. 106 note); a knowledge of *correspondences* is necessary to an understanding of the change of natural into spiritual delights (n. 487); Egyptians and other eastern nations had a knowledge of *correspondence* (n. 87 note); most ancient men thought from *correspondence* (n. 115); worship in the ancient times was through *correspondence* (n. 111, 306); the knowledge of the ancients was a knowledge of *correspondences* (n. 356 extract); those of the ancient church had communication with heaven by means of a knowledge of *correspondences* (n. 87, 114); conjunction of heaven with the world by means of *correspondences* (n. 112); *correspondences* are the only means of communication between societies of different heavens (n. 207); all knowledge of *correspondence* must come from heaven (n. 110); all *correspondence* with heaven is with the

Lord's Divine human (n. 101); all things that *correspond* to heaven have relation to good and truth (n. 113); as things in heaven *correspond* to goods and truths they *correspond* to love and wisdom (n. 186); *correspondence* of all things to the interiors of the angels (n. 173, 186); *correspondence* of all things of heaven to intelligence (n. 186); *correspondence* of all things of heaven with all things of man (Chap. 12, 13); *correspondence* of heavenly kingdoms in man (n. 95); man has permanent existence from his *correspondence* to heaven (n. 94); *correspondence* of heaven with man is never complete (n. 418); everything that appears before the eyes of angels of the inmost heaven is a *correspondence* (n. 270); things that become visible in heaven but do not *correspond* to interiors are not real appearances (n. 175); occupation in heaven is from *correspondence* (n. 394); there is nothing in heaven to *correspond* with night (n. 155); all things contrary to Divine order *correspond* to hell (n. 113); abuse of *correspondences* by evil spirits (n. 580); the Lord calls himself "the bread of life" from *correspondence* (n. 111). *Correspondence* of Abraham, Isaac, and Jacob to the Lord's Divine human (n. 526); of angels to something belonging to the Lord (n. 1, 391); of animals to affections (n. 110); of arms to power (n. 97, 231); of autumn to love in the third state of the angels (n. 166); of avarice to spiritual filth (n. 363). Baptism signifies regeneration (n. 329 note); *correspondence* of birds to intellectual things (n. 110 note); of birth to generation of truth (n. 382 [b]); of the blind to those in falsities who are unwilling to

be taught (n. 487 note); of the Lord's blood to Divine truth (n. 147); of various parts of the body (n. 91); the body *corresponds* to the form of heaven (n. 212); of bread to good (n. 111, 340 note); of breadth to a state of truth (n. 197); truth is to good as water is to bread (n. 375 note); of breast to charity (n. 97); of bride to heaven and the church (n. 180); of builders to those of the church (n. 534). Cattle signify affections (n. 110); *correspondence* of camel to the knowing faculty (n. 365); of cerebellum to wisdom (n. 251); of child and childhood to innocence (n. 278, 341); of clouds to the sense of the letter (n. 1); of color to things pertaining to intelligence and wisdom (n. 175 note); colors in heaven are manifestations of truths from good (n. 356 note); of copper to natural good (n. 115). Darkness signifies falsity from evil (n. 123, 553); daughters signify procreated truths and goods (n. 382 [b]); David means the Lord (n. 216, 526); Dawn signifies obscurity (n. 155); *correspondence* of various things to doctrine (n. 307); dove *corresponds* to affection (n. 110). Ears *correspond* to obedience (n. 97, 271); east signifies love and its good clearly perceived (n. 150); the Lord called the east (n. 141); Egyptian signifies the natural (n. 307); "the elect" are those in a life of good and truth (n. 420); evening signifies wisdom in its shade (n. 155); eyes signify understanding (n. 97, 145); eyes *correspond* to truths from good (n. 232 note). Face *corresponds* to interiors (n. 91, 251, 475 note); mother and father signify truth conjoined to good (n. 382 [b]); feet *correspond* to what is natural (n. 97);

the world's fieriness *corresponds* to love of self (n. 122); fire *corresponds* to love (n. 13), and to good of love (n. 118), and to the heat of man's life (n. 568), and to hatred and revenge (n. 585); holy and heavenly fire means the heat of heaven (n. 135); infernal fire is love of self (n. 566, 570); spiritual filth is avarice (n. 363); firmament signifies the intellectual faculty (n. 347); flame *corresponds* to good (n. 179), or to evils of love of self (n. 585); the Lord's flesh signifies Divine good (n. 147); food *corresponds* to affection for good (n. 111); the forehead to love (n. 145, 251); fruit *corresponds* to good works (n. 111), and to affections for good and its uses (n. 520); fruit in heaven *corresponds* to the good of love (n. 176). Garden *corresponds* to intelligence and wisdom (n. 111, 176); garments signify knowledges (n. 365); the Lord's garments represent the Divine truth (n. 129); garments of the angels are from *correspondence* (n. 177, 178); "the twelve gates of the New Jerusalem" signify truths of the church (n. 187); "glory" signifies the internal sense of the Word (n. 1); gold signifies celestial good (n. 115). Hands signify powers (n. 97, 231); head *corresponds* to intelligence and wisdom (n. 97, 251); heat to love (n. 135); heart to the will and the good of love (n. 95, 96); various *correspondences* of the heart (n. 446, 449); "a new heaven and a new earth" means a new church (n. 307); height means a distinction between good and truth according to degrees (n. 197); hills signify spiritual love (n. 188); "the house of the wedding feast" means heaven and the church (n. 180);

houses in heaven *correspond* to the good of the angels who dwell in them (n. 186); house of wood signifies what relates to good (n. 186 note, 223); hungry means those desirous of knowledges of good and truth (n. 420). Iron signifies truth apart from good (n. 115), or truth in the outmost of order (n. 115 note); Isaac *corresponds* to the Lord's Divine (n. 526); Israel signifies the spiritual (n. 307); "stone of Israel" signifies the Lord in respect to his Divine human (n. 534). Jacob *corresponds* to the Lord's Divine (n. 526); Jerusalem means the Lord's church in heaven (n. 73), or a church that is in truth (n. 180); journey signifies to live and to progress (n. 192 note, 590); judgment signifies spiritual good (n. 216). "Keys given to Peter" signify power (n. 232 note); kidneys signify the scrutiny of truth (n. 97); king signifies one in Divine truth (n. 226 note); knowledges are spiritual riches (n. 365). Lambs signify affections (n. 110), and innocence (n. 282); laurel *corresponds* to affections for truth (n. 520); left *corresponds* to truth from good (n. 118); length means a state of good (n. 197); light *corresponds* to truth going forth from love (n. 13), and to good of faith (n. 118), and to truth from good (n. 179); the light of the world's fieriness *corresponds* to what is false from love (n. 122); the Lord is called "the Light of the World" (n. 129); loins *correspond* to marriage love (n. 97); "Lucifer" means those that belong to Babylon (n. 544); lungs *correspond* to the spiritual kingdom (n. 95, 96). Man *corresponds* to understanding of truth (n. 368); *correspondence* of man with heaven (n.

94, 95); man means one who is in goods and truths (n 73); measurements of the New Jerusalem signify goods and truths of doctrine (n. 307); *correspondence* of the members of the body (n. 95, 96); *correspondence* of heaven to the substances of man's mind (n. 418); mist *corresponds* to falsities from love of self (n. 585); moon signifies faith (n. 1, 119); morning signifies the first and highest degrees of love (n. 155); mountain signifies celestial love (n. 188). Nakedness *corresponds* to innocence (n. 179, 280, 341); "New Jerusalem" signifies a church to be established (n. 187, 197); night signifies absence of love and wisdom (n. 155); noon *corresponds* to wisdom in its light (n. 155); nostrils to perceptions (n. 97); meaning and *correspondence* of numbers (n. 73 note, 263). Occiput *corresponds* to wisdom (n. 251); olives *correspond* to affections for good and its uses (n. 520); "one hundred and forty and four" means all goods and truths in the complex (n. 73); things in accordance with Divine order *correspond* to heaven, things contrary to Divine order to hell (n. 113). "Paradise" signifies intelligence and wisdom (n. 111); wisdom compared to a palace (n. 270); "path" signifies truth leading to good (n. 479 note); "the poor" signifies a nation that longs for truth (n. 375), or those desirous of but lacking in knowledges of good and truth (n. 420). Quarters in heaven signify such things as pertain to those that dwell in them (n. 150). Right *corresponds* to good from which truth is derived (n. 118); righteousness signifies celestial good (n. 216); rocks signify faith (n. 188); and clefts in rock falsities (n.

488); roof of a house signifies what is inmost (n. 186 note). Sabbath means rest and peace (n. 287); season *corresponds* to variations in love and wisdom (n. 155, 166); shade to falsity (n. 589); smoke to falsity from evil (n. 570, 585); space to states (n. 17, 197); soot to falsities from hatred and revenge (n. 585); stars to knowledges of good and truth (n. 1); the *correspondence* of the Lord's Divine human to "the stone at the dividing of the ways" (n. 534); sun signifies the Lord in respect to love (n. 1). Teeth *correspond* to outmosts in nature (n. 575); to thirst is to desire knowledge of good and truth (n. 420); *correspondence* between thought and writing in heaven (n. 262); times signify states (n. 165); trees *correspond* to knowledges of good and truth (n. 111); tribes signify all things of truth and good (n. 1). Vegetable foods *correspond* to affections for good and truth (n. 111); *correspondence* of various things of the vegetable kingdom (n. 109, 489). Walking *corresponds* to progressions of life (n. 590); wall signifies protecting truth (n. 73, 307); way means truth leading to good or falsity leading to evil (n. 479 note, 590); west signifies good obscurely perceived (n. 150); white signifies truth (n. 179); heaven and the church called the "wife" (n. 180, 371); wood *corresponds* to good (n. 223); woman to affections for good (n. 368); Word means Divine truth in the Lord from the Lord (n. 137). Youth *corresponds* to understanding of truth (n. 368). Zion means heaven and the church (n. 216).

Countenance, angels of the same society resemble each other (n. 47).

Covering signifies something intellectual (n. 179 note).

Creation, all things *created* by means of Divine truth: the book of Genesis (n. 137).

Creator, fewness of the human race compared with the infinity of the *Creator* (n. 417 extract).

Cruelty of evil spirits toward one another (n. 573).

Cunning, wholly antagonistic to innocence (n. 278).

Darkness signifies falsities from evil (n. 123, 553).

Daughters, sons and *daughters* signify procreated truths and goods (n. 382 [b]).

David signifies the Lord (n. 216, 526).

Dead, resurrection from the *dead* (Chap. 46); angels that attend man during resurrection from the *dead* (n. 391).

Death described (n. 445); man's resurrection from the *dead* (Chap. 46); man's rationality after *death* (n. 353, 464); man after *death* is such as his life has been in the world (Chap. 49, n. 535 note); man's denial or acknowledgment of the Divine determines his condition after *death* (n. 584); man cannot be reformed after *death* (n. 480); man's delights changed after *death* into corresponding delights (Chap. 50); by *death* man loses nothing that is really his own (n. 461); spiritual *death* (n. 80, 474); belief in life after *death* (n. 183); man's intuition in regard to life after *death* due to influx (n. 602); first state after *death* (Chap. 51); condition immediately after *death* (n. 433); after *death* man is in complete human form (Chap. 47); after *death* man is possessed of every sense, and the mem-

ory, thought, and affection (Chap. 48, n. 464); the ruling love remains with man after *death* (n. 363); what a man acquires in the world he takes with him after *death* (n. 349); whatever is in man's spirit in the body remains after *death* (n. 395); after *death* man continues to be such as is his will and his understanding therefrom (n. 474 note); after *death* man is his own love and his own will (n. 479); knowledge of no avail after *death* (n. 356 extract); repentance not possible after *death* (n. 527); those outside the church taught after *death* (n. 308); children after *death* (n. 332).

Decalogue, gives the laws for the three planes of life (n. 531).

Deceit, those that have been governed by *deceit* are the worst of all evil spirits (n. 578).

Deeds are nothing apart from thought and affection (n. 358); *deeds* of men influenced by angels (n. 391). (See Works.)

Degrees, discrete and continuous (n. 38, 211); *degrees* of interiors (n. 33, 34); *degrees* in correspondence (n. 104); in uses (n. 112); *degrees* of life in angels (n. 267, 270); *degrees* of life in man (n. 314 note); *degrees* of innocence (n. 280); *degrees* of intelligence in heaven (n. 469); in every angel and man there is an inmost or highest *degree* into which the Divine of the Lord first flows (n. 39); each angel has three *degrees* of life, but only one is open (n. 208).

Delights of the angels (n. 489); *delights* of angels of the inmost heaven (n. 270); *delights* of angels when in the good of life (n. 288); angels are in every *delight* of life when with their like (n. 44, 45); the *delight* of angels not in the outward things of heaven, but in what they represent (n. 411); *delight* of angels vanishes when evil spirits appear (n. 399). *Delights* of heaven (Chap. 42, n. 374); of heavenly peace (n. 285); of heavenly love (n. 558 [a]); *delights* of heaven are in accord with uses (n. 402); *delights* in labor and use in heaven (n. 393); *delights* of the rich in heaven (n. 361); examples of the *delights* of the good in heaven (n. 489, 506); *delights* of children in heaven (n. 337); in heaven to perform uses is the *delight* of everyone's life (n. 219); in heaven *delight* is internal and spiritual (n. 395); *delights* of heaven not distinctly felt in the world (n. 401); Swedenborg permitted to experience heavenly *delight* (n. 413); effect of heavenly *delight* on evil spirits (n. 400). *Delights* of love of self (n. 556); adultery the reigning *delight* of hell (n. 384); *delights* of the evil after death (n. 512); *delights* of corporeal love (n. 481); *delight* in infernal fire (n. 570); *delights* of the body turn away from heaven (n. 398); all man's *delights* are those of his ruling love (n. 396, 486); *delights* of man's life changed after death into corresponding spiritual *delights* (Chap. 50, n. 487, 488); *delights* of marriage love (n. 379, 382 [a], 386); *delights* of innocence (n. 282); alternative *delight* and lack of *delight* renders the perception of good more exquisite (n. 158).

Deluge, the church after the *deluge* (n. 327).

Deserts, in the hells (n. 586).

Desire, intensity of *desire* affects the rapidity of journeys in heaven (n. 195).

Devil, evil is from the *devil* (n. 291); meaning of term (n. 311, 544); none created angels and cast out (n. 311).

(See Lucifer, Satan.)

Dictation, the Lord spoke with the prophets by *dictation* through spirits (n. 254).

Dignity, angels' places of abode depend upon their *dignity* (n. 183); angels ascribe their *dignity* to their use (n. 389); *dignities* and riches not real blessings (n. 364 note); to be exalted to *dignities* (n. 564).

Direction in heaven (n. 142, 143, 151).

Dimensions, meaning of the three *dimensions* (n. 197).

Disposition of little children in heaven (n. 338).

Distance in heaven is a matter of states of life (n. 42, 192 note, 195).

Diversity, the basis of unity and perfection (n. 405).

Divine, angels cannot think of the *Divine* as three, because it is one (n. 2); a highest degree in all angels into which the *Divine* flows (n. 39); angels conceive of the *Divine* as in human form (n. 79); celestial angels receive the *Divine* more interiorly than spiritual angels (n. 21); angels see the *Divine* in all things of heaven through correspondence (n. 185, 270); the *Divine* flowing into the minds of angels (n. 489); divisions in heaven depend on the angels' reception of the *Divine* of the Lord (Chap. 4). The *Divine* that goes forth from the Lord has the same order as the three heavens (n. 29); the *Divine* that goes forth from the Lord flows chiefly into marriage love (n. 371); the *Divine* that goes forth from the Lord is love (n. 17); the Lord distinguished in heaven by the *Divine* shining through (n. 55); the *Divine* was in the Lord from very conception (n. 86 extract); the Lord's church is with all who acknowledge the *Divine* and live in charity (n. 308); what the *Divine* of the Lord is (n. 136); the Lord's *Divine* Itself is far above his *Divine* in heaven. (n. 118 note). The *Divine* in the heavens (Chap. 3, n. 31); the *Divine* of the Lord makes heaven (Chap. 2, n. 55, 59, 304); true insight in regard to heaven is the *Divine* flowing in (n. 74); no one without a conception of the *Divine* can enter heaven (n. 82); in heaven no other *Divine* than the Divine human is recognized (n. 86 extract). Condition after death of those that believe in an invisible *Divine* (n. 3); all intelligence and wisdom that are separated from an acknowledgment of the *Divine* are false (n. 353); men who deny the *Divine* (n. 353, 354, 508); hypocrites are those that have not acknowledged the *Divine* (n. 458); an evil life is a denial of the *Divine* (n. 506); the *Divine* can temporarily turn evil spirits to the comprehension of truth (n. 455); love of self separates from the *Divine* (n. 558 [a], 561); what is contrary to Divine order is contrary to the *Divine* (n. 523); hells in which are those that have denied the *Divine* (n. 575); infernal fire in respect to the *Divine* (n. 570); the *Divine* alone is able to resist the hells (n. 592); men of the olden time had an idea of the *Divine* as human (n. 84); to live a moral life out of regard for the *Divine* (n. 319); how man's interiors are formed from looking to the *Divine* (n. 351); confirmation of the *Divine* by the really wise (n. 356); man alienates himself from the *Divine* by self-love (n. 360); man has an inmost into which the *Divine* flows; beasts have not (n. 435); how the *Divine* flows into man

(n. 512); denial or acknowledgment of the *Divine* determines man's condition after death (n. 584); the *Divine* is worshiped in human form in other earths (n. 321); the *Divine* is in all good uses (n. 361); the *Divine* is charity toward the neighbor (n. 13), is love (n. 14), is the motive in spiritual life (n. 530); the first and chief thing of every religion is to acknowledge the *Divine* (n. 319); all things in the world spring from the *Divine* (n. 108); all power is from the *Divine* (n. 539); both worlds subsist from the *Divine* (n. 106); to glorify is to make *Divine* (n. 86 extract); peace springs from the union of the *Divine* with the Divine human (n. 286); looking to the *Divine* (n. 318); the *Divine* in the Word (n. 260); the *Divine* in marriage love (n. 371, 374, 384); the *Divine* created the universe for the human race (n. 417 extract).

Divisions in heaven (Chap. 4).

Doctrine, the essence of all *doctrine* is acknowledging the Divine human of the Lord (n. 227); the nature of true *doctrine* (n. 311 note); intelligence a matter of *doctrine* (n. 271); correspondence of various things to *doctrine* (n. 307); worship in heaven is in accordance with *doctrine* (n. 222); *doctrines* in the different heavens (n. 221, 227); mere knowledge of *doctrine* does not lead to heaven (n. 518); truths of *doctrine* (n. 455 note); Jerusalem signifies the church in which is genuine *doctrine* (n. 180 note, 188 note); a principle must be drawn from truths of *doctrine* (n. 356 extract); *doctrine* of the resurrection (n. 456); good spirits taught from *doctrine* (n. 516).

Dominion, heaven does not consist of glory and *dominion* (n. 6); love of

dominion takes away marriage love
(n. 380); two kinds of *dominion* (n.
564); *dominion* in the hells (n. 573).
Dwellings of angels (Chap. 21, n. 177);
dwellings in heaven (n. 148, 149);
dwellings in the hells (n. 151, 586);
dwellings of those being prepared for
heaven (n. 514).

Earth, its three kingdoms (n. 104);
meaning of the Lord's ruling (n. 5);
the church the Lord's heaven on *earth*
(n. 57); the Lord's church on *earth*
resembles a man (n. 308); correspondence of heaven with all things of the
earth (Chap. 13, n. 103); difference
between marriages in heaven and on
the *earth* (n. 382 [b]); inhabitants of
all *earths* worship the Divine under a
human form (n. 86 extract, 321); on
some *earths* angels and spirits appear
and talk with man (n. 249 note); men
of this *earth* more in exteriors than
those of others (n. 309); all *earths*
inhabited (n. 417); *Earths in the Universe* quoted (n. 417).
East, in heaven is where the Lord is
(n. 141); signifies love and its good
clearly perceived (n. 150); those who
dwell in the *east* in heaven (n. 148);
in hell (n. 151).
Ecclesiastical, those that administer *ecclesiastical* affairs in heaven (n. 393).
Edifices, church *edifices* in heaven
(n. 223).
Education of children in heaven
(n. 344).
Effect, uses take on form in the natural
world and present themselves in *effect*
(n. 96); *effects* of uses (n. 112); cause
and *effect* (n. 303). (See Cause.)
Egypt signifies the natural (n. 307);
Egyptians had a knowledge of correspondences (n. 87 note).

Elect, are those that are in the life of
good and truth (n. 420).
Employment of angels (Chap. 41); *employment* in heaven is a delight from
love of use (n. 393).
Ends, good as an *end* (n. 64); the Lord
in regard to man looks only to *ends,*
which are uses (n. 112 note); truth
itself is the only *end* of heavenly intelligence (n. 347); knowledges are to
be learned for the sake of use as an
end (n. 356 extract). (*See* Uses.)
Enlightenment of those who love Divine wisdom (n. 265); is due to wisdom of thought (n. 473).
Envy, one of the evils of those in self-
love (n. 562).
Equilibrium, man's *equilibrium* between
good and evil (n. 293); between
heaven and hell (Chap. 62, n. 536,
537); difference between *equilibrium*
in heaven and in hell (n. 591); its universal necessity (n. 589); what spiritual freedom or *equilibrium* is
(n. 597); man is in freedom by means
of the *equilibrium* between heaven
and hell (Chap. 63).
Esse, the first or very being (n. 9); innocence of the being *[esse]* of all good
(n. 281).
Essence, the Lord's Divine *essence*
(n. 549).
Eternity means infinite state, not infinite time, to the angels (n. 167); development of angels to *eternity*
(n. 469).
Evils, Evil, man born into *evils* (n. 293,
393, 424); are from love of self and
the world (n. 342 note, 359, 555);
evils of those in self-love (n. 562); are
removed by the Lord (n. 359); how
man may get rid of his *evils* (n. 598);
becomes harder for man to resist *evils*
if he wills them (n. 553); *evils* and

falsities open many gates to hell (n. 430); all in the hells are in *evils* and falsities therefrom (Chap. 58); infernal societies distinguished by the nature of their *evils* (n. 588); are disclosed in the other life (n. 462 [b]); are made manifest during second state after death (n. 497). *Evil* is from the devil (n. 291); flows into man from hell (n. 546); continually ascends out of hell (n. 591); *evil* spirits appear in the form of their own *evil* (n. 131, 553); to be led by what is one's own is to be led by *evil* (n. 558 [a]); everything done from man himself is in itself *evil* (n. 484); man the cause of his own *evil* (n. 547); how man appropriates *evil* to himself (n. 302); influx of *evil* (n. 603 extract); hereditary *evil* (n. 341); equilibrium between good and *evil* (n. 537, 589); those that are in *evil* are not in marriage love (n. 377); peace impossible to those in *evil* (n. 290); *evil* carries its own punishment with it (n. 509, 550); he that has been in *evil* in the world is foolish and insane in the other life (n. 505); black clouds in the other world are from *evil* (n. 549). With the *evil* knowledges become falsities (n. 356 extract); truths that the *evil* have are put away in the world of spirits (n. 425); the good and *evil* are separated at the dividing of the ways (n. 534); their condition after death (n. 506, 512); their motives (n. 530); their belief about heaven and hell (n. 470, 526); their delight in darkness in the other life (n. 488); their delight after death in the stench that corresponds to their own evil (n. 429); they are restrained in the world by outward circumstances (n. 577); to do good to the

evil is to do *evil* to the good (n. 390 note). (See Falsity.)

Existence, what it is (n. 9); depends upon connection with the First (n. 37); impossible apart from a substantial subject (n. 434); depends upon equilibrium (n. 589).

Existere, the Divine human was the Divine outgo *(existere)* (n. 86 extract).

Extension of spheres (n. 49); is not determinate in heaven (n. 85).

Exteriors, what man's *exteriors* are (n. 304); appearance of the *exteriors* of the good and evil (n. 481); *exteriors* of man's spirit (n. 492); are separated after death (n. 501); first state after death is one of *exteriors* (n. 491); are laid asleep in man's second state after death (n. 499). (See Interiors.)

Externals, men of this earth more in *externals* than men of the other earths (n. 309); interest of evil spirits in *externals* (n. 496). (See Internals.)

Eyes correspond to understanding (n. 97, 155); correspond to truths from good (n. 232 note); natural and spiritual *eyes* (n. 171); angels can be seen with the *eyes* of the spirit only (n. 76); angels' *eyes* see from interiors (n. 157); children in the Greatest Man are in the province of the *eyes* (n. 333); sensation of rolling off a coat from the *eye* during resuscitation (n. 450).

Face, correspondence shown in the *face* (n. 91); in the heavens the interior affections shine forth from the *face* (n. 47, 48, 123); is the outward form of the interiors (n. 143, 251, 272); all *faces* differ because all ruling loves differ (n. 486); in the world of spirits the *face* is changed to correspond with the ruling affection (n. 457); beauty of *face* in heaven (n. 414); in the spiritual world each one has before his *face* those in like love with himself (n. 552); *faces* of evil spirits (n. 553); *faces* of hypocrites (n. 458); the direction of the *face* in the hells (n. 151); angels speak by the *face* (n. 244); sensation of something being rolled off from the *face* during resuscitation (n. 450); representative *face* that appeared to Swedenborg (n. 47).

Faculty, firmament signifies the intellectual *faculty* (n. 347); perfecting the spiritual-rational *faculty* in heaven (n. 489); man has interior and exterior *faculties* (n. 351); the rational *faculty* has its birth by means of knowledges (n. 356 extract); the rational *faculty* like a garden (n. 461); how the rational *faculty* may be cultivated (n. 468).

Faith, what it is, and its relation to truth (n. 148, 364, 480, 482); rocks signify *faith* (n. 188); moon signifies *faith* (n. 119); good of *faith* corresponds to light: good of *faith* is truth from good (n. 118); truths of *faith* (n. 7); confirmation of truths of *faith* (n. 356 extract); everything of faith is truth (n. 232, 473 note); condition after death of those that enter from knowledges into truths of *faith* (n. 365 note); truths of *faith* as a motive (n. 472); celestial angels do not reason about truths of *faith*, spiritual angels do (n. 25 note, 270 note); angels of the inmost heaven do not know what it is to believe or to have *faith* (n. 270); its relation to life (n. 526); those who separate *faith* from life (n. 2); *faith* alone does not lead to heaven (n. 521); is not received through baptism (n. 329); *faith* of the heathen (n. 324); truths of *faith* received by the heathen (n. 325); Africans in heaven simply

accept the doctrine of *faith* (n. 326); those who have converted many to the *faith* not necessarily intelligent in the heavenly sense (n. 346); an invisible Divine cannot be an object of *faith* (n. 3). When *faith* and love rule they are in all the particulars of man's life (n. 58 note); *faith* without love perishes (n. 136); angelic changes of state mean changes in respect to love and *faith* (n. 154); all things in the interiors of the angels have relation to love and *faith* (n. 173); holiness is in love and *faith* (n. 224); influx into man's love and *faith* (n. 297); heaven is for all that live a life of *faith* and love (n. 357); conjunction of *faith* and love essential to reformation (n. 424); *faith* separated from love is not *faith* but mere knowledge (n. 474); *faith* and love in relation to works (n. 473); man's life after death is his love and his *faith* therefrom (n. 476); *faith* is affection for truth going forth from heavenly love (n. 480, 482); *faith* determines the quality of love to the neighbor (n. 558 [b]).

Fallacies of the senses cannot easily be dispelled (n. 356 extract).

Falsity, all things that correspond to hell have relation to evil and *falsity* (n. 113); darkness signifies *falsity* from evil (n. 123); confirmation of the *falsities* of evil (n. 153); *falsities* from evil have no power (n. 233); knowledges become *falsities* with the evil (n. 356 extract); evil and *falsity* in adultery (n. 374, 384); evil appears as good and *falsity* as truth to evil spirits (n. 455); man born into evil and *falsity* (n. 202 note, 523 note); smoke in the Word means *falsity* from evil (n. 570). *Falsity* in the teaching of enthusiastic spirits (n. 249); heathen in the other life not burdened with *falsities* of doctrine (n. 321); *falsities* may appear as truths in natural light (n. 352); eagerly accepted in the other life by those that have denied the Divine (n. 354); those in *falsities* are not in true marriage love (n. 377); the *falsities* of the good are put away in the world of spirits (n. 425, 513); *falsities* are all disclosed in the other life (n. 462 [b]); those without real faith are let down into *falsities* (n. 482); from truth anyone can perceive *falsities,* but not vice versa (n. 487); *falsity* is powerless (n. 539); "gnashing of teeth" in hell is the continual combat of *falsities* with one another (n. 575); equilibrium between truth and *falsity* (n. 589).

Father, condition after death of those in the church who acknowledge the *Father* only (n. 3, 6); the union of the Lord with the *Father* was as between soul and body (n. 86 extract); mother and *father* signify truth conjoined to good (n. 382 [b]).

Fear, *fear* of consequences and obsession (n. 257 note); hells ruled by means of *fear* (n. 543).

Feasts, marriage *feasts* in heaven (n. 383).

Feet, the first heaven forms the *feet* and arms of the Greatest Man (n. 65); their correspondence (n. 97).

Fibers, nerve *fibers* (n. 212); heart *fibers* (n. 413).

Fighting of children destroys their mutual love (n. 344).

Fire corresponds to love (n. 13, 118); in the Word *fire* means the heat of man's life (n. 568, 570); holy *fire* means the heat of heaven (n. 134); infernal *fire* of those that have denied the Divine (n. 354); corresponds to hatred and revenge (n. 585); what hell *fire* is (Chap. 59).

First or *esse,* or very being (n. 9); use is the *first* and the last (n. 112 note); all things must be connected through intermediates with the *First* (n. 37, 106, 303).

Flowers in heaven (n. 176, 185).

Food, correspondence of vegetable *foods* (n. 111); what constitutes spiritual *food* (n. 340 note).

Force is that which acts and reacts (n. 589).

Forehead, the Lord sees the angels in the *forehead* because it corresponds to love (n. 145); influx of the Lord is into the *forehead* (n. 251).

Forests in the hells (n. 585).

Form, *form* of anything is in accordance with its order (n. 201); correspondences are the *forms* in which uses are clothed (n. 112); uses take on *form* in the natural world (n. 96); Divine order takes on its form in outmosts (n. 315); the most perfect *forms* (n. 62); truth the *form* of good (n. 107); *form* of good and truth (n. 460); of spirits (n. 363, 454, 517); of evil spirits (n. 314, 553); every angel is in complete human *form* (Chap. 10, n. 73, 77); *form* of angelic thought (n. 266); *form* of heaven (Chap. 23, n. 60, 94, 99, 200, 211); angelic speech flows in the *form* of heaven (n. 242); some idea of the *form* of heaven can be gained by the study of the human body (n. 212); the *form* of the spirit (n. 434, 435, 453); a spirit's face is the outward *form* of his affection (n. 457); the face the outward *form* of the interiors (n. 143); written *forms* in heaven (n. 260); the simple have no conception of anything apart from *form* (n. 74); God cannot be thought of except in human *form* (n. 86 extract); the Divine in human *form* (n. 79); variety arranged in heavenly *form* constitutes perfection (n. 71); man an image of heaven in his internal *form* (n. 99); *form* of man after death (Chap. 47); man by creation is Divine order in *form* (n. 523 note); everything that exists interiorly in man exists in *forms* which are substances (n. 418).

Foundations signify truths on which the church is established (n. 187); the Word serves in place of man as a *foundation* for heaven (n. 305).

Freedom is from love (n. 380); pertains to love and affection (n. 45 note, 293 note); *freedom* and marriage love (n. 380); *freedom* of the angels (n. 44, 45); *freedom* in the world of spirits (n. 590); *freedom* of the evil in the other life (n. 506); man's *freedom* (n. 293, 298, 598); *freedom* of man due to equilibrium between heaven and hell (Chap. 63, n. 537, 599); *freedom* is equilibrium of the spiritual world (n. 589); what spiritual *freedom* or equilibrium is (n. 597). (See also extracts from *Arcana Coelestia* in n. 603.)

Friends, recognized in the world of spirits (n. 494, 495).

Friendship (See Relationship.)

Fruit, good works compared to *fruit* on account of correspondence (n. 111); *fruits* in heaven correspond to the good of love (n. 176, 185); correspond to affections for good and truth (n. 520).

Function, the government of heavenly societies depends on their *functions* (n. 213, 217); greater variety of *functions* in heaven than on earth (n. 393); *functions* cannot be performed in heaven by one who looks to self-honor (n. 389).

Gabriel is an angelic society (n. 52).

Gardens, their correspondence (n. 111); *gardens* in heaven (n. 184, 185).

Garments, signification of *garments* in the Word (n. 365); *garments* of angels (Chap. 20); *garments* in the hells (n. 182); *garments* of spirits entering heaven (n. 519); the Lord's *garments* represent the Divine truth (n. 129).

Gates, their correspondence (n. 187 note); *gates* of heaven and hell (n. 428, 430, 583, 585).

Generals, *generals* in the most perfect forms (n. 62); *generals* and their parts (n. 64); numbers involve *generals*, words particulars (n. 263); *generals* and particulars of angelic wisdom (n. 267); *generals* and particulars of heavenly affection (n. 413).

Generation, its signification (n. 382 [b]).

Genii, who they are (n. 123, 578); look toward darkness (n. 151); dwell in the hell that is behind (n. 311); the nature of their malice (n. 579); are in the western quarter (n. 596).

Girls, their training in heaven (n. 391).

Glorification of the Lord (n. 86 extract.)

Glory, its correspondence (n. 1); heaven does not consist of *glory* (n. 6); *glory* of angels (n. 25, 26); *glory* not the end of heavenly intelligence (n. 347).

God, the Lord the *God* of heaven (n. 2, 5); He is order (n. 57); how the simple think of *God* (n. 82); the sensual man cannot get a true idea of *God* as Man (n. 85, 86); He cannot be thought of except in human form (n. 86 extract); meaning of having *God* before the eyes (n. 143); peace of those that are content in *God* (n. 284); all good from *God* (n. 291); heathen readily accept the true ideas of *God* (n. 321); order is from the supreme *God* (n. 322); the *God* of the most ancient church (n. 327 note); spirits who thought that heavenly joy consisted in praising God (n. 404); everywhere in the universe the Lord acknowledged as God (n. 417); beasts cannot think about God (n. 435); God never turns from man or casts him into hell (n. 545).

Good, all good is from God (n. 291); influx of good (n. 603 extract); the common good (n. 64); good of love (n. 7); all good pertains to love (n. 23); to love good is to will it and do it (n. 15); its relation to love to the neighbor (n. 558 [b]); good belongs to the will (n. 26); alternate delight and lack of delight renders this perception of good more exquisite (n. 158); unless doing good is joined with willing good and thinking good there is no salvation (n. 535 note); those who separate faith and good (n. 2); good done from self is not good (n. 8, 556); when a man looks to himself in the good that he does (n. 558 [a]); in the hells none are in truths and goods (n. 551); man in equilibrium between good and evil (n. 293); to do good to the evil is to do evil to the good (n. 390 note); equilibrium between evil and good (n. 537, 589); for every good there is an opposite evil (n. 541); when a man's spirit is released it is either in his good or in his evil (n. 577); man must be in good to be able to see evils (n. 598); all good increases immeasurably in the other life (n. 406); good of others the desire of the angels (n. 408); angels are near to or far from man according as he is in good (n. 391); good of life of angels (n. 288); one angel's good differs from another's (n. 231); angels receive the things of heaven according to the

quality of the good that is in them from the Lord (n. 53); angels separated into societies according to the differences in their good of love and faith (n. 41, 42, 45); the good of love and faith makes heaven (n. 51); a church is a church insofar as the good of love and faith reigns therein (n. 57); good of love corresponds to fire and good of faith to light (n. 118); in heaven trees bear fruit in accordance with the good of love (n. 176); priesthood signifies good of love in the Lord (n. 226); those that "shine forth as the sun" receive the good of love directly from the Lord (n. 348); good that goes forth from the lord is a likeness of him (n. 16); how those in good think of the Lord (n. 86 extract); the belief of those in good in regard to heaven (n. 176); insofar as one ascribes the use he performs to the Lord he performs that use from good (n. 390); good of love to the Lord as a motive (n. 472); good flows into man from the Lord (n. 546); love to the Lord from the Lord is the origin of the good of all in heaven (n. 72); those in like good recognize each other in heaven (n. 46); in heaven good is the neighbor (n. 64); the good of the spiritual kingdom is the good of charity (n. 215, 241); all forms of government in heaven look to the public good (n. 217); the end in heaven is the common good (n. 217, 418); rational activity of the spirits who have been in good in the world (n. 505); good continually descends from heaven (n. 591); good of innocence (n. 283); those in a state of innocence do not attribute good to themselves (n. 218); innocence the being [esse] of all good (n. 281); conjunction of innocence and peace like that of *good* and its delight (n. 288); *good* in relation to the Greatest Man (n. 96); anything *good* is *good* in the measure of its use (n. 107); every *good* has its delight and quality from use (n. 112 note, 517 note); wisdom is loving use that is the *good* of others (n. 390); the general use the general *good* (n. 392); *good* used as a means is not *good* (n. 499); love of *good* and of use the basis of the dominion of love of the neighbor (n. 564). Gold, silver, and copper signify respectively celestial, spiritual, and natural *good* (n. 115); flames correspond to *good* (n. 179); length means a state of *good* (n. 197); in the Word righteousness signifies celestial *good,* and judgment spiritual *good* (n. 216); bread signifies every *good* (n. 340 note). Training of the simple *good* in heaven (n. 391, 527); their falsities removed in the world of spirits (n. 425); their internal and external thought make one by correspondence (n. 499). Divine *good* the heat of heaven (n. 117, 134); Divine order is caused by Divine *good* flowing forth from the Lord (n. 107, 523 note); Divine *good* that goes forth from the Lord is innocence itself (n. 282); Divine *good* is what makes heaven in general and particular (n. 397). *Goods* are in triple order (n. 31 note); *goods* in heaven in infinite variety (n. 41); sharing of all *goods* in heaven (n. 49 note, 268); heavenly societies vary according to *goods* (n. 387); heavenly love consists in loving *goods* for the sake of goods (n. 557).

Good and truth, truth is the form of good (n. 107); the form of *good and truth* (n. 460); truth the sole receptacle of good (n. 371); knowledges are receptacles for *good and truth* (n. 356 extract); the outer memory as a seat for *good and truth* (n. 466); spiritual truths relate to the good of love and truth of faith (n. 468); spiritual *goods and truths* are learned from heaven, not from the world (n. 512); what a man looks upon as *good and truth* (n. 423); all things in the universe have relation to *good and truth* (n. 137); all things that exist according to order have relation to *good and truth* (n. 473 note); power of *good and truth* (n. 137, 232); truths apart from good (n. 136 note); influx into man's *good and truth* (n. 297); *good and truth* conjoined in a man are not two but one (n. 372); *good and truth* can only be conjoined by means of innocence (n. 281); innocence a receptacle for *good and truth* (n. 329); those in the innocence of wisdom know no truth and do no good from themselves (n. 279); the innocence of children the plane for all affection for *good and truth* (n. 341); good of children not spiritual good, but becomes such by the implantation of truth (n. 277 note); children guided in heaven into knowledges of truth and affection for good (n. 334); reception of *good and truth* by children in heaven (n. 336, 344); spiritual life is fed by affection for *good and truth* (n. 111); angels are given houses according to their perception of *good and truth* (n. 190); angels affiliated according to the nature of their *good and truth* (n. 205); peace springs from the conjunction of *good and truth* in each angel (n. 286); Divine peace is in good, but not in truth apart from good (n. 287 note); true intelligence and wisdom is seeing and perceiving what is *true and good* (n. 351, 469); everyone can acknowledge truths, but only the good can perceive them (n. 153); reception of the Lord means reception of *good and truth* from him (n. 80); recognized in heaven that all *good and truth* are from the Lord (n. 8); every *good and truth* that goes forth from the Lord and makes heaven is in the human form (n. 460); every angel is in his own *truth and good* (n. 231); *good and truth* open man's gate to heaven (n. 430); spiritual birth effected through a knowledge of *good and truth* (n. 345); all received into heaven who have loved *truth and good* (n. 350); what a man receives in heaven depends upon the degree of his affection for *good and truth* (n. 349); delights of the soul are affections for *good and truth* (n. 396); delights that descend from the conjunction of *good and truth* (n. 489); their interest in *goods and truths* show the true nature of spirits in the first state after death (n. 496); Africans readily receive *goods and truths* in heaven (n. 326); man is man from his ability to understand what is true and to will what is good (n. 60); truth is changed into good as soon as it enters into the will (n. 26); the will relates to good, the understanding to truth (n. 137); the understanding and will of the angels are continually being perfected by means of truths of intelligence and goods of love (n. 221); what man understands he calls truth, and what he wills he calls good (n. 231); *good and truth* make the will and understanding (n. 463 note); man is loved by the Lord to the extent that his will is formed from good and his understanding from truth (n. 350); those in

the arms and hands of the Greatest Man are in the power of truth from good (n. 96); good of faith is in its essence truth from good (n. 118); only those in truths from good can speak with angels (n. 250); all spiritual power arises from truth from good (n. 538, 539); *good and truth* in relation to marriage (n. 374–382); no marriage love without the love of *good and truth* (n. 381); procreation of *good and truth* in heavenly marriages (n. 382 [b]); antagonism toward *goods and truths* of the church of those in self-love (n. 562); evil appears as good and falsity as truth to evil spirits (n. 455). Trees correspond to knowledges of *good and truth,* their fruit to affections for *good and truth* (n. 111); all things that correspond to heaven have relation to *good and truth* (n. 113); iron signifies truth apart from good (n. 115); light corresponds to truth from good (n. 179); in heaven houses correspond to the good of the angels, and the things outside to truths from good (n. 186); "the twelve gates of the New Jerusalem" signify the truths of the church leading to good (n. 187); measurements of the New Jerusalem signify *goods and truths* of doctrine (n. 307); in the Word righteousness is predicated of good and judgment of truth (n. 348 note); in heaven good of use looks like gold, and truth of use like silver (n. 361); signification of garments in relation to *good and truth* (n. 365); colors in heaven are manifestations of truth from good (n. 356 note); truth is to good as water is to bread (n. 375 note); the "elect" means those that are in a life of *good and truth* (n. 420); a "way" means truth leading to good

(n. 479 note, 590). Divine good and Divine truth go forth from the Lord, and man's reception of them determines his life (n. 9, 30); interiors are opened by the reception of Divine good and Divine truth (n. 33); order exists by means of them (n. 77 note); Divine truth, which was himself, the Lord united with Divine good which was in himself (n. 86 extract); that which goes forth from the Lord as a sun is in essence Divine good united to Divine truth (n. 127, 133); Divine good and Divine truth not in the Lord but from him (n. 139); the Lord's "flesh" signifies Divine good, his "blood" Divine truth (n. 147); angels as receptions of Divine good and Divine truth (n. 232); so far as an angel is in innocence he is in Divine good and Divine truth (n. 280); in heaven those are called wise that are in good, that is, those that apply Divine truth to the life (n. 348); Divine truth and Divine good flow chiefly into marriage love (n. 370); the hells are ruled by the outflow of Divine good and Divine truth from the heavens (n. 543).

Goodness and charity produce heavenly beauty (n. 414); what true goodness is (n. 481, 495).

Government in heaven (Chap. 24); it differs in the various societies and heavens (n. 213, 217); government in the spiritual kingdom is called judgment (n. 215); government in heaven is preeminent in love and wisdom (n. 218); government of heaven is by the Lord (n. 406); government of the hells (n. 220, 543).

Governors, in the spiritual kingdom (n. 215); in heaven they put the good of others first (n. 218); governors in the hells (n. 220).

Gravitation and the common center in heaven (n. 142).

Greatness in heaven (n. 408).

Habitation, heaven called a habitation of peace (n. 287). (See Abode and House.)

Hands signify power (n. 97, 231).

Happiness in heaven (Chap. 42, n. 6, 268); external happiness (n. 34); how the Lord holds men in happiness (n. 45); love to the Lord wills the happiness of all (n. 399); spirits that believed that heavenly happiness consists in idleness (n. 403); in heaven he that is least is happiest (n. 408); happiness permitted to those that enter the other life (n. 412).

Hatred in infernal marriages (n. 377); hatred of evil spirits for holy things (n. 570).

Head, its correspondence (n. 97, 251); head of the Greatest Man (n. 65); in heaven no one allowed to look at the back of the head of another (n. 144).

Hearing, organ of hearing affected from within by the speech of angels (n. 248); angels of inmost heaven taught by hearing (n. 271); use and delight of hearing (n. 402); hearing in the spiritual world (n. 462).

Heart, its correspondence (n. 95, 96); the church where the Word is is like the heart and lungs of a man (n. 308); the spirit remains in the body as long as the heart beats (n. 447); all vital motion depends upon the motion of the heart and lungs (n. 446).

Heat is from love (n. 14, 447); corresponds to love (n. 135); heat of heaven (Chap. 15, n. 117, 133, 134, 226); heat has two origins, the sun of heaven and the sun of the world

(n. 567); *heat* of man's life (n. 568); *heat* of heaven unendurable to those in corporeal love (n. 481); effect of heavenly *heat* in the hells (n. 572); *heat* in the hells (n. 134 note); *heat* from hell excites lusts in man (n. 571); the products of *heat* depend upon what it shines upon (n. 569).

Heaven, Heavens, *heaven* is a common sharing of all with each (n. 73); in *heaven* there is a sharing of thoughts and affections (n. 369); in *heaven* the interiors are not hidden (n. 131); the order of interiors in *heaven* (n. 499); speech and thought one in *heaven* (n. 2); its topography (n. 188); their situations (n. 207, 209, 583); their arrangement (n. 96); its form (Chap. 23, n. 200, 212); the three *heavens* (n. 20–29, 33); internal and external in each (n. 32); separated by differences of state (n. 193); those in the inmost *heaven* not clothed (n. 179); its two kingdoms (n. 20); the kingdoms united by intermediate societies (n. 27); societies in *heaven* (Chap. 6, 7); all conjoined by influx (n. 37, 208); how arranged to maintain an equilibrium (n. 594); the doctrines of the different *heavens* (n. 227); the extent of the uninhabited *heaven* (n. 419); the four quarters in *heaven* (Chap. 16); its immensity (Chap. 43); is a whole from various parts arranged in most perfect form (n. 56); all things in *heaven* organized according to Divine order (n. 389); it is perfected by greater and greater fullness (n. 71); it is in infinite variety (n. 405); all *heaven* in the aggregate reflects a single man (Chap. 8, n. 418); is in the form of a man (n. 62, 94, 99); the Greatest Man (n. 6, 86 extract); man a *heaven* in miniature (n. 30); man created in the form of *heav-*

en (n. 454); man an image of *heaven* in his internal form (n. 99); *heaven* terminates in and rests upon the bodily parts of man (n. 100); without the human race *heaven* would be like a house without a foundation (n. 304); man born for *heaven* (n. 82, 324); proof that *heaven* is from the human race (n. 314); the seed ground of *heaven* is in outmosts (n. 315); how man may live the life of *heaven* (n. 529); life that leads to *heaven* (Chap. 55); how the good are prepared for *heaven* (n. 512, 513); how spirits are introduced into *heaven* (n. 519); ways to *heaven* (n. 359, 520, 534); daily entrance into *heaven* (n. 593); conjunction of *heaven* with man and the human race (Chap. 33, 34); its conjunction with the world (n. 112, 252); there is a correspondence of *heaven* with all things of the earth (Chap. 13); correspondence of all things of *heaven* with all things of man (Chap. 12); all correspondence with *heaven* is with the Lord's Divine human (n. 101); from the Lord's Divine human *heaven* as a whole and in part reflects man (Chap. 11); the Divine human flows into *heaven* and makes *heaven* (n. 86 extract); man's communication with *heaven* (n. 204); when men talk with angels they also see the things of *heaven* (n. 252); *heaven* opened to interior sight (n. 171); those of the ancient church had communication with *heaven* by means of correspondences (n. 87); *heaven* not received through baptism (n. 329); no one without a conception of the Divine can enter *heaven* (n. 2, 82); the Lord the God of *heaven* (n. 2, 5); degrees in *heaven* (n. 34, 38 note, 39); *heaven* flows into the functions and uses of the bodily mem-

bers (n. 96); uses in *heaven* (n. 361);
renewed youth in *heaven* (n. 414);
employment in *heaven* (Chap. 41);
communication of all things in *heaven*
(n. 268); dominion in *heaven* (n. 564);
worship in *heaven* (Chap. 25); government in *heaven* (Chap. 24); those that
administer ecclesiastical affairs and
preach in *heaven* (n. 393); writing in
heaven (Chap. 29); writing varies in
the different *heavens* (n. 261); influx
from *heaven* to *heaven* (n. 206, 207);
light and heat in *heaven* (Chap. 15, n.
567); nothing in *heaven* to correspond
to night (n. 155); marriages and marriage love in *heaven* (Chap. 40); why
heaven is likened in the Word to marriage (n. 371); *heaven* a marriage of
good and truth (n. 374); advance of
marriage love toward *heaven* (n. 386);
the wise and simple in *heaven* (Chap.
37); simple-minded in *heaven* (n. 18);
rich and poor in *heaven* (Chap. 39);
the poor instructed in *heaven* (n. 364);
the heathen in *heaven* (Chap. 36);
Chinese, Jews, and Africans in *heaven*
(n. 326); conjunction of *heaven* with
those outside the church (n. 308); "a
new *heaven* and a new earth" means a
new church (n. 307); the church the
Lord's *heaven* on earth (n. 57); the
sun in *heaven* (Chap. 14); all things
seen in *heaven* originate from the
Lord as a sun (n. 117); in *heaven* all
things come from the Lord (n. 173);
the distances of the various *heavens*
from the Lord as a sun (n. 120); all in
heaven turned continually to the Lord
as a sun or as a moon (n. 123); all
things determined in *heaven* according
to the Lord's presence (n. 199); the
Lord often appears in *heaven* as an
angel, but not in person (n. 121);
heaven is *heaven* from the Lord's Divine (n. 304); the state of *heaven* before the Lord's coming (n. 86 extract);
life of *heaven* implanted in all by the
Lord (n. 522); the life that leads to
heaven a life in the world (n. 358,
360, 535); all are received into *heaven*
who have loved truth and good (n.
350); *heaven* consists of all from the
beginning of this earth that have lived
a good life (n. 415, 416); he who has
heaven in himself has it in all things
least and greatest (n. 58); *heaven* is
within one (n. 33, 319); is within the
angels (n. 53); *heaven* in each one differs (n. 319); space in *heaven* (Chap.
22); time in *heaven* (Chap. 18); no
time or space in *heaven*, but a progression of all things (n. 163); extension
in *heaven* is not determinate (n. 85);
the three dimensions in *heaven* (n.
197); representatives and appearances
in *heaven* (Chap. 19); appearances in
heaven illustrated (n. 176); in *heaven*
people often appear to be where their
look is fixed (n. 121); nature of objects in *heaven* (n. 171, 172); things
that appear to the angels have real
existence (n. 175); many objects in
heaven described (n. 189); houses, gardens, cities, palaces, etc., in *heaven* (n.
184, 185); appearance of external
things in *heaven* changes with the
changes of the angels' interiors (n.
156); appearances in *heaven* the same
as in the world (n. 464); delights of
the landscape, etc., in *heaven* (n. 489);
joy and happiness in *heaven* (Chap.
42); delights of *heaven* (n. 397, 399);
variety of uses and delights the basis
of *heaven* (n. 405); two distinct loves
in *heaven*, love to the Lord and love
toward the neighbor (n. 15); love to
the Lord the universal ruling love in
heaven (n. 486); love the foundation

of *heaven* (n. 386); all are conjoined
by love in *heaven* (n. 14); love of rule
not possible in *heaven* (n. 407); the
Word in *heaven* (n. 259); man would
have been separated from *heaven* if it
had not been for the Word (n. 309);
heaven is stored up in man's innocence (n. 276); all in *heaven* are in
innocence (n. 280); inmost in all the
good of *heaven* is innocence (n. 282);
peace and innocence the two inmost
things of *heaven* (n. 285); *heaven*
called a habitation of peace (n. 287);
heaven is for all who have lived a life
of love and peace (n. 357); life in
heaven (n. 506); so far as one is in the
form of *heaven* he is in *heaven* (n.
203); man has *heaven* within him to
the extent that he wills and does
truths (n. 425); those in *heaven* are in
the Lord and the Lord in them (n.
11); *heaven* is where the Lord is acknowledged and loved (n. 56); all in
heaven act as one from the Lord (n.
64); in *heaven* the Lord is the All-in-
all because he is the ruling love (n.
58); truths that are in the light of
heaven (n. 356 extract); little children
in *heaven* (Chap. 37, n. 4); mere admission into *heaven* does not give
heavenly joy (n. 525); no one enters
heaven by mercy apart from means
(Chap. 54, n. 54); self-love separates
from *heaven* (n. 357); those that do
not perform uses for the general good
are cast out of *heaven* (n. 64); spirits
that have confirmed themselves in a
belief in their own power not admitted to *heaven* (n. 10); experience in
heaven of those that do not belong
there (n. 40, 54); suffering of evil spirits in *heaven* (n. 400, 481); the sensual
man cannot get a true idea of *heaven*
(n. 85, 86); man's intention in regard

to life after death due to influx from
heaven (n. 607); good spirits grieved
at the ignorance in the church in regard to the things of *heaven* (n. 77);
man's erroneous ideas about his relations with *heaven* (n. 302); erroneous
ideas in regard to the extent of *heaven*
(n. 420). Erroneous beliefs in the
world in regard to *heaven* and hell (n.
311–313); man conjoined both to
heaven and to hell (n. 599); man's ruling love is *heaven* or hell (n. 477);
world of spirits the intermediate state
between *heaven* and hell (n. 421);
equilibrium between *heaven* and hell
(Chap. 62, n. 536); difference between
the equilibrium of *heaven* and that of
hell (n. 591); gates of *heaven* and hell
(n. 428); preparation for *heaven* and
hell (n. 430); *heaven* and hell are separated by a difference in state (n. 193,
400); *heaven* and hell are from the
human race (Chap. 35). (See Affection, Angel, Charity, Divine, Good,
Man, Marriage, Society, State, Wisdom.)

Hebrew, in some respects it coincides
with the language of heaven (n. 236);
vowels in *Hebrew* (n. 241); ancient
Hebrew (n. 260).

Height means a distinction between
good and truth according to degrees
(n. 197).

Hell, Hells, their appearance, situation,
and number (Chap. 61, n. 583, 584,
586, 588); societies in *hell* (n. 294, 542,
588); in general there are three *hells*
(n. 542); they are at different distances
according to their opposition to good
(n. 120); their position in detail
known to the Lord alone (n. 587);
ordered according to the varieties of
evil (n. 588); "satan," "Lucifer," etc.,
mean the different *hells* (n. 544); com-

munication between them (n. 588); two kingdoms in *hell* (n. 596); quarters, divisions, and limits of *hell* (n. 151, 587); *hell* in infinite variety (n. 405); how it is arranged to maintain an equilibrium (n. 594); the *hell* that is behind is called the "devil," the *hell* that is in front called "satan" (n. 311); *hells* of the genii entirely closed up (n. 579); the *hells* opposed to the celestial kingdom are not allowed to flow toward the spiritual kingdom (n. 596); how they are prevented from overcoming *heaven* (n. 594, 595); how they are ruled by the Lord (Chap. 56, n. 543); are restrained by certain angels (n. 391); are restrained by means of torment (n. 581); the government one of love of self and the world (n. 200, 554); love of self the universal ruling love in *hell* (n. 486); dominion from love of self leads to *hell* (n. 564); daily entrance into *hell* (n. 593); way to *hell* described (n. 534); its gates (n. 583, 585); how evil spirits turn from the Lord and cast themselves into *hell* (n. 548, 510); why evil spirits fall into *hell* head down (n. 588 [b]); no one cast into *hell* by the Lord (Chap. 57); how some are cast into *hell* (n. 491); those that profess faith alone are cast into *hell* (n. 482); spirits of obsession cast into *hell* (n. 257); those that profane truths are cast into the lowest *hell* (n. 456); the merely natural man is in *hell* (n. 531); the rich of the world who have denied the Divine are in *hell* (n. 362); *hell* of those that have been governed by deceit (n. 578); changes of state in *hell* (n. 161); first state of those entering hell (n. 462 [b]); all in the *hells* turned to their own loves (n. 552); those in *hell* look backward away from the Lord (n.

123, 151); all in the *hells* are in evils and falsities therefrom (Chap. 58); those in the *hells* appear to others as monsters (n. 80, 131); to those in the *hells* the sun of heaven is thick darkness (n. 122 note); those in the *hells* appear clothed in repulsive garments (n. 182); senses of those in the *hells* are very imperfect (n. 246); some in the *hells* know that what they believe is false but cannot resist the delights of their love (n. 455); those in *hell* cannot be saved (n. 595); speech in *hell* (n. 245, 553); lust in *hell* (n. 571); forms, voice, etc., of evil spirits (n. 553); torments in *hell* (n. 573, 574); gnashing of teeth in *hell* (n. 575); nature of the light (n. 584); what *hell* fire is (Chap. 59, n. 571, 572); heat in the *hells* (n. 134 note); its value and evil (n. 577); power in *hell* (n. 233); no power in hell (n. 539); life in *hell* called spiritual death (n. 80); exhalations of falsity and lusts from the *hells* (n. 538, 574); evil continually ascends out of *hell* (n. 591); *hell* in man (n. 425, 547); evil men's communication with *hell* (n. 204); we are saved by the Lord from the *hell* of our own evils (n. 342); there would be no *hell* if men could be saved by mercy apart from means (n. 524); advance of adultery toward *hell* (n. 386); all things contrary to Divine order correspond to *hell* (n. 113); vastation accomplished by means of the *hells* (n. 513 note); their antagonism toward innocence (n. 283). (See Heaven.)

Heresy, the sense of the letter may beget *heresies* (n. 311, 455).

Heredity, evil *heredity* (n. 509).

Hills signify spiritual love (n. 188).

Higher and lower designate interior and exterior (n. 22).

Holiness, true and counterfeit (n. 224).

Holy, Divine truth called the *holy* (n. 140).

Holy Supper (n. 111).

Honesty, motives of *honesty* (n. 358); love of *honesty* (n. 468); what true *honesty* is (n. 481); how it is made spiritual (n. 512).

Honor, how angels think about dignity and *honor* (n. 389).

Houses in heaven (n. 184, 489); signification of *houses* of wood and stone (n. 186 note); *houses* of angels (n. 180, 186); *house* of God (n. 223); in each *house* in heaven there is a government of servant and master (n. 219); the *house* of the wedding feast means heaven and the church (n. 180).

Human, why the Lord's *human* is Divine (n. 86 extract); the Lord glorified his *human* and made it Divine (n. 316); the Lord's Divine *human* (n. 86 extract); the Divine *human* exists only in the Lord (n. 79); heaven as a whole and in part reflects man from the Lord's Divine *human* (Chap. 11); all correspondence with heaven is with the Lord's Divine *human* (n. 101); in the Word the Lord's "flesh" signifies his Divine *human* (n. 147 note); the temple represents the Lord's Divine *human* (n. 187); the form of heaven is from the Lord's Divine *human* (n. 212); the essential of all doctrines is acknowledgment of the Lord's Divine *human* (n. 227); direct influx is from the Divine *human* (n. 297); correspondence of the Lord's Divine *human* (n. 534).

Hunger, Hungry, all angels *hunger* for wisdom (n. 274); means those desirous of knowledge of good and truth (n. 420).

Husband, why the Lord is called the *husband* (n. 80, 371); *husband* and wife after death (n. 368, 494); true marriage love not possible between one *husband* and several wives (n. 379).

Hypocrites in heaven (n. 48, 68); what they are (n. 458); their speech (n. 245); their external memory (n. 466); cast into hell (n. 491); the merely natural man a *hypocrite* (n. 531); *hypocrites* in the other life (n. 551), are the worst of all evil spirits (n. 578).

Idea, angelic *idea* converted into natural *ideas* for man's reception (n. 168); *ideas* about angels and heaven (n. 183); *ideas* of thought are the various forms into which the general affections are distributed (n. 236); *ideas* of angels are modifications of the light of heaven (n. 239); *ideas* of thought presented to view (n. 240); *ideas* of the internal man are spiritual (n. 243 note); words give expression to *ideas* of thought from the affections (n. 269); *ideas* of little children in heaven (n. 336, 338).

Idolaters in the other life (n. 324); how taught in the other life (n. 326); *idolaters* in the ancient church (n. 327).

Ignorance of those on earth in regard to heaven (n. 395); why man is born into *ignorance* (n. 108).

Image, man created in the *image* of both worlds (n. 202). (See Form.)

Immortality, man lives to eternity by virtue of his highest or inmost (n. 39); state after death of those that have not believed in *immortality* (n. 452).

Incarnation, reason for it (n. 101).

Infinite, the *Infinite* Being could flow into heaven only by means of the

Divine human (n. 86 extract); everything good is from the *Infinite* (n. 469).

Infinity, the heavens compared with the *infinity* of the creator (n. 417).

Influx, defined (n. 168); order of *influx* (n. 455 note); is into good and through good into truth, not the reverse (n. 26 note); is from higher into lower, not the reverse (n. 209); is from the spiritual into the natural, not the reverse (n. 135); is from the internal to the external, not the reverse (n. 356 extract); is of two kinds, direct and mediate (n. 37, 208, 297, 603 extract); there is a Divine *influx* into the world apart from man (n. 112); *influx* into the world apart from man (n. 112); *influx* into the vegetable kingdom (n. 567, 603 note); Divine *influx* terminates in man's outmosts (n. 304); Divine *influx* is turned into representatives in heaven (n. 175 note); *influx* in the heavens (n. 31, 37); from heaven to heaven (n.206, 207); *influx* of children in heaven (n. 336); children receive *influx* from the inmost heaven (n. 277); angels of the inmost heaven clearly perceive *influx* (n. 8); celestial angels know the truth by *influx* (n. 26); belief in reincarnation due to *influx* (n. 256); no one in heaven allowed to look at the back of the head of another because it would disturb *influx* (n. 144); the human rational exists by *influx* of light from heaven (n. 309); where *influx* into man occurs (n. 251); man can do nothing without *influx* from heaven (n. 228); why man is no longer ruled by *influx* (n. 247, 296); *influx* varies in accordance with its reception (n. 569); it is made possible by vastation (n. 513 note); those who have extinguished it (n. 82); it cannot enter if the higher regions of the mind are closed (n. 532); man's intuition in regard to the life after death is from *influx* (n. 602); the true idea of God as in human form is from *influx* (n. 82, 86 extract); the Lord draws all to himself by means of *influx* (n. 548); delight of the senses is from *influx* (n. 402); marriage love is the very plane of Divine *influx* (n. 370); *influx* from the brain to the face, how changed in process of time (n. 457 note). (See extracts from *Arcana Coelestia* in n. 603.) (See Interiors.)

Inheritance of evil (n. 558 [a]).

Inmost, the uses of man's *inmost* (n. 39); man has an *inmost* into which the Divine flows; beasts have not (n. 435); heavenly joy starts from *inmosts* (n. 409, 413); true peace flows from *inmosts* into the lower faculties (n. 290); innocence is the *inmost* in all the good of heaven (n. 282); the Lord flows into and governs man's *inmosts* and outmosts (n. 297); ideas of children in heaven flow chiefly from *inmosts* (n. 336).

Innocence, corresponds to nakedness (n. 179, 280); children signify *innocence* (n. 341); true nature of *innocence* is unknown to most (n. 276); it is willingness to be led by the Lord (n. 281); it is a receptacle for good and truth (n. 329); it is a receptacle for all things of heaven (n. 341); the Divine good that goes forth from the Lord is *innocence* itself (n. 282); genuine *innocence* is the *innocence* of wisdom (n. 278, 279); the delight of *innocence* (n. 282); the good of *innocence* (n. 283); all in heaven are in *innocence* (n. 280); the third heaven is the heaven of *innocence* (n. 332); *innocence* in

marriage love in heaven (n. 382 [a]);
state of *innocence* of the angels (Chap.
31); *innocence* of the heathen (n. 324);
innocence and peace the two inmost
things of heaven (n. 285); peace differs in agreement with the state of
innocence (n. 288).

Insanity, those in the hells clothed according to their *insanity* (n. 182); *insanity* of the evil (n. 290); *insanity* of
the wicked in the other life (n. 508).

Instincts of animals are from the spiritual world (n. 108).

Instruction of those entering the other
life (Chap. 53).

Instrument, the body merely the *instrument* of the spirit (n. 432, 435).

Intellectual and voluntary (n. 32); the
spiritual kingdom is the *intellectual*
part of heaven (n. 95).

Intelligence, defined (n. 148); in what it
consists (n. 356 extract); it is a matter
of doctrine (n. 271); is from Divine
truth (n. 80); what heavenly or interior *intelligence* is (n. 347, 348); *intelligence* in the doctrines of heaven (n.
227); *intelligence* of little children in
heaven (n. 334); chief thing in the
intelligence of angels (n. 59); *intelligence* of angels perfected by means of
knowledges of truth and good
(n. 469); angelic *intelligence* of those
in love to the Lord (n. 467); garments
of angels correspond to and vary with
their *intelligence* (n. 178); correspondence of things in heaven to *intelligence* (n. 186); cerebellum corresponds
to *intelligence* (n. 251); *intelligence* of
those that administer the civil affairs
of heaven (n. 393); those the angels
call *intelligent* (n. 86); why man is not
born into *intelligence* (n. 356 extract);
man is born to be *intelligent* (n. 368);
false beliefs in the world about the

intelligent (n. 346); sensual men remain outside of *intelligence* (n. 38);
temporary *intelligence* of evil spirits
(n. 153). Wisdom and *intelligence*
make man (n. 80); were acquired
among ancient people through a
knowledge of correspondence (n. 87);
heaven in relation to man's *intelligence* and wisdom (n. 203, 204); true
and false *intelligence* and wisdom
(n. 351–353); man's capacity to receive *intelligence* and wisdom (n. 454);
a garden corresponds to *intelligence*
and wisdom of heaven (n. 111); garden, park, fruit trees, and flowers correspond to *intelligence* and wisdom
(n. 176); colors signify various things
pertaining to *intelligence* and wisdom
(n. 179 note); angels have *intelligence*
and wisdom in proportion as their
affections are interior and perfect (n.
49); and in proportion to the extension of their thought throughout
heaven (n. 79); light of angels varies
as they are in *intelligence* and wisdom
from the Lord (n. 128); change of
state of angels is a change in respect
to love and faith, and wisdom and
intelligence therefrom (n. 154); *intelligence* and wisdom are what constitute an angel (n. 340); wisdom and
intelligence of angels immeasurably
superior to that of man (n. 576).

Intention of man described (n. 532).

Interaction in the other life (n. 479).

Interiors, the face corresponds to *interiors* (n. 251); all things in heaven
correspond to the *interiors* of the angels (n. 173, 186); things visible in
heaven that do not correspond to
interiors are not real appearances
(n. 175); in heaven spaces correspond
to *interiors* (n. 217); in heaven distances and spaces depend upon *interi-*

ors (n. 193, 195, 196); the states of the *interiors* are what make heaven (n. 33, 35); delight in heaven affects the *interiors* (n. 395); in heaven the *interiors* of the really wise appear brilliant and shining (n. 356); *interiors* not hidden in heaven (n. 131); *interiors* of those listening to preaching in heaven (n. 224); in the other life the *interiors* determine the face (n. 123); the *interiors* of the most ancient people were turned heavenward (n. 306); man has turned his *interiors* away from heaven (n. 305); the *interiors* of men who talk with angels (n. 250, 252); conjunction of heaven with man is with his *interiors* (n. 300); the *interiors* of those without true faith are obscured by the light of heaven (n. 482); the *interiors* of those who have no conception of the Divine are closed, therefore they cannot enter heaven (n. 82); the *interiors* of man are closed when he separates himself from heaven (n. 252); man must be in heaven in respect to his *interiors* to learn spiritual good and truth; how the Lord opens man's *interiors* (n. 512); man is wholly such as are his *interiors* (n. 501); *interiors* and exteriors of man's spirit (n. 492); wisdom of men whose *interiors* are opened (n. 267); man's *interiors* are elevated by truths from the Word (n. 253); man's *interiors* which constitute his mind are formed from use and for use (n. 112 note); man has three degrees of *interiors* (n. 33); the order of man's *interiors* (n. 30); love to the Lord opens the *interiors* of the mind to the third degree (n. 271); delights of the soul affect the *interiors* (n. 396); every man a spirit in respect to his *interiors* (Chap. 45, n. 436); *interiors* of men

who have denied the Divine (n. 353, 354); man is wholly such as are his *interiors* (n. 501); *interiors* of the learned closed (n. 513); love of self closes the *interiors* (n. 272); degrees in *interiors* and exteriors (n. 38); *interiors* and exteriors are signified higher and lower (n. 22); *interiors* not complete till they exist in works which are exteriors (n. 475); *interiors* are formed by looking to the Divine and heaven (n. 351); *interiors* of the mind are formed for the reception of Divine truth (n. 347); the perception of the Lord's presence is in the *interiors* (n. 147); *interiors* cannot be concealed in heaven (n. 48); are concealed during the first state after death (n. 497, 498); changes in the state of the *interiors* (n. 156); the correspondence between man's *interiors* and exteriors determines the length of his stay in the world of spirits (n. 426); the state of the *interiors* show the spirit as he was in the world (n. 505); man's second state after death called the state of the *interiors* (n. 270); wisdom increases toward *interiors* (n. 499); perfection increases toward *interiors* (n. 34); their nature may be known by the nature of man's love (n. 532); works have their being, outgo, and quality from the *interiors* (n. 358 note); the *interiors* see differently with the right and left eye (n. 118); *interiors* are not complete till they exist in works which are exteriors (n. 475); they exhibit themselves in the effect in the body (n. 521); *interiors* of children (n. 282); influx into the *interiors* of children (n. 277); how the *interiors* of little children in heaven are opened (n. 334); children in the other life act in accordance with their *interiors*

(n. 331); *interiors* of angels arranged in the form of Divine order (n. 266); an angel's ruling love is always before his *interiors* (n. 193); his *interiors* determine an angel's heaven (n. 33); the form of an angel's body is the external of his *interiors* (n. 340); the *interiors* not immediately opened on entrance into the world of spirits (n. 457); are opened when an angel reaches his society (n. 519); angels receive wisdom because their *interiors* are opened (n. 267); after death the *interiors* are formed and opened in accordance with the love and the life (n. 459); the appearance of the *interiors* of the good and the evil in the spiritual world (n. 481); *interiors* of hypocrites (n. 458); of those in false marriage love (n. 380); of those in self-love (n. 560); of those in the hells (n. 151); in the hells the *interiors* and the exteriors are as one (n. 553); *interiors* of evil spirits tortured by heavenly delight (n. 400).

Internal, man's *internal* is formed by creation after the image of heaven (n. 57 note); in the internal there are thousands of things that appear in the external as one general thing (n. 34 note); man's *internal* corresponds to the voluntary and his external to the intellectual (n. 32); man is *internal* or spiritual, or external or natural (n. 92); man's *internal* is now closed from birth (n. 202); influx is through the *internal* man (n. 603 extract); the *internal* and external of Divine worship (n. 221); the diabolical form of spirits whose *internal* is not open to heaven (n. 314); spiritual influx is from *internal* to external (n. 356 extract); it is man's *internal* that accomplishes, not his external (n. 358); good

spirits in first state after death are more interested in *internals* than in externals (n. 496); vastation is simply being let into one's *internals* (n. 551).

Isaac, correspondence (n. 526).

Israel signifies the spiritual (n. 370); "the stone of *Israel*" signifies the Lord in respect to his Divine human (n. 534).

Israelites, their marriage explained (n. 378, 379 note).

Jehovah was the soul of the Lord (n. 86 extract); *Jehovah* spoke through spirits (n. 254); he was the God of the most ancient and ancient churches (n. 327).

Jerusalem means the Lord's church in heaven (n. 73); means the church that is in truth (n. 180).

Jerusalem (the new), what it and its parts signify (n. 187, 307); signifies a new church (n. 197).

Jesus Christ, the Lord called *Jesus* from the celestial Divine, *Christ* from the spiritual Divine (n. 24).

Jews in the other life (n. 326).

Jewish nation, is meant by the rich man cast into hell (n. 365).

Journey signifies to live and to progress in life (n. 190 [a], 590); *journeys* in heaven (n. 195).

Joy in heaven (Chap. 42); what heavenly *joy* is (n. 525); the source of *joy* in heaven (n. 281); heavenly *joy* described from experience (n. 413); permitted to certain spirits (n. 410); heaven and heavenly *joy* the same thing (n. 397); in the celestial kingdom the inmost *joy* is to live rightly from the lord (n. 214); peace means *joy* and delight (n. 287, 288).

Judgment, government in the spiritual kingdom is called *judgment* (n. 215); in the celestial kingdom truths of *judgment* do not come into question

(n. 214); signifies spiritual good in the Word (n. 216); civil truths relate to matters of *judgment* (n. 468); *judgment* after death is according to works (n. 470, 471); erroneous views about the last *judgment* (n. 1, 603 extract). (See Righteousness.)

Justice, love of *justice* (n. 468); what true *justice* is (n. 481); how it is made spiritual (n. 512).

Keys, given to Peter signify power (n. 232 note).

Kidneys, their correspondence (n. 97); the *kidneys* in the Greatest Man (n. 96).

Kingdom, the three *kingdoms* on earth (n. 105); influx into the vegetable *kingdom* (n. 603 extract); equilibrium in the natural *kingdom* (n. 589); man's loves arranged to form a *kingdom* (n. 477); all in heaven look upon the Lord's *kingdom* as the general, the good of which is to be sought (n. 64); the Lord's *kingdom* a *kingdom* of ends or uses (n. 112, 219, 387); the celestial *kingdom* called the Lord's priestly *kingdom*, the spiritual his royal *kingdom* (n. 24, 226); the government of the Lord's *kingdom* (n. 406), the heavenly *kingdom* the end for which the universe was created (n. 417 extract); *kingdoms* in heaven (Chap. 4); correspondences of the heavenly *kingdoms* in man (n. 95); quarters differ in the different *kingdoms* of heaven (n. 146); topography of the *kingdom* of heaven (n. 188); ways to the different *kingdoms* (n. 520); variations in light in the different *kingdoms* (n. 128); difference in speech (n. 241); how the Lord appears as a sun in the different *kingdoms* (n. 118, 159); government in the spiritual *kingdom* (n. 215, 217); all

preachers in heaven are from the spiritual *kingdom* (n. 225); form of government in the celestial *kingdom* (n. 214); during resuscitation there is a communication between the pulse and the celestial *kingdom* (n. 449).

Kinship (See Relationship).

Knowledges as riches; signify garments (n. 365); trees correspond to *knowledges* of good and truth (n. 111); all *knowledge* of correspondence must come from heaven (n. 110); they do not bring anyone into heaven (n. 517, 518); their use in heaven (n. 464); are acquired in heaven (n. 489); are not committed to memory in heaven, but to life (n. 517); condition in the other life of those that enter from *knowledges* into truths of faith (n. 365 note); the outmost plane consists of *knowledges* and affections (n. 480); angels of the inmost heaven store up truths as *knowledges* (n. 271); intelligence and wisdom of angels perfected by means of *knowledges* of good and truth (n. 469); their use to man (n. 356 extract); they serve to make man rational (n. 355); faith separated from love is mere *knowledge* (n. 474); mere *knowledge* not wisdom (n. 351); those in corporeal love have mere *knowledge* (n. 482); *knowledge* of heavenly joy impossible to those in the mere delights of the body (n. 398); *knowledges* of the ancients (n. 356 extract); of inhabitants of other earths (n. 417 extract); of man (n. 352); of animals (n. 108, 110, 352).

Lamb corresponds to affections (n. 110), and to innocence (n. 282).

Landscape in heaven (n. 489).

Language, differences between angelic and human *language* (n. 237); all in

heaven have the same *languages*
(n. 236, 463 note); *language* in the
communication between men and
angels (n. 255).

Last, use in the first and the *last* (n. 112
note).

Law, the Word contains all the *laws* of
Divine order (n. 202); Divine truths
are *laws* of order (n. 57 note); *laws* of
the Lord's kingdom (n. 406); the *laws*
of the three planes of life are in the
Decalogue (n. 531); to violate marriage is contrary to Divine *law*
(n. 385); "the *law* and the prophets"
mean the whole Word (n. 19).

Learned, their erroneous ideas about
heaven, angels, etc. (n. 74, 183, 267,
312, 354); their state after death
(n. 464, 488); who the really *learned*
are (n. 347).

Learning of sensual men (n. 353).

Letter, wisdom in Hebrew *letters*
(n. 260).

Life, its three planes (n. 529–531); laws
of *life* in the Decalogue (n. 531);
man's first *life* wholly evil (n. 293);
externally the *lives* of the evil and of
the good are alike (n. 534); *life* from
love of self (n. 556); an evil *life* is a
denial of the Divine (n. 506); *life* in
the world governed by external laws
(n. 504); spiritual heat the heat of
man's *life* (n. 568); *life* in the world
should be one of activity (n. 528); *life*
of charity can be lived only in the
midst of the world (n. 535); man's *life*
depends upon knowledges (n. 356
extract); interior and exterior *life*
(n. 318); the civil and moral *life*
(n. 530); moral and spiritual *life*
(n. 319); all works and deeds pertain
to the moral and civil *life* (n. 484);
deeds designate the quality of the
outmost *life* (n. 471); moral truths

relate to matters of individual *life*
(n. 468); *life* according to order (n.
322); man is such as is his *life* (n.
521); *life* is from love (n. 14, 17, 118
note); those that separate faith from
life (n. 2); the ruling love with everyone is in each thing of his *life* (n. 58
note); *life* is from the thought only to
the extent that the thought is from
the will (n. 526); all rational *life* belongs to the soul (n. 432); man's spiritual *life* depends upon his conjunction
with spirits (n. 302); all *life* is in the
spirit, which is man (n. 433, 501); the
will and understanding in relation to
life (n. 61 note); all things of man's
life depend upon ability to understand
and to will (n. 203); freedom is the
life of everyone (n. 603 extract); those
who apply Divine truth to the *life*
(n. 348); obedience belongs to *life*
(n. 271); *life* of the poor (n. 364);
things of the natural world are in
themselves devoid of *life* (n. 432); all
life is from the Lord (n. 9, 203 note);
those in whose *life* the Lord is
(n. 350); how and where the Lord
flows into the *life* (n. 512); *life* in accordance with truths is loving the
Lord (n. 225); the Lord's *life* in the
world was his love toward the race
(n. 86 extract); development of those
who possess spiritual *life* (n. 356 extract); *life* of love and faith leads to
heaven (n. 357); *life* of heaven implanted in all by the Lord (n. 522);
life that leads to heaven not difficult
(Chap. 55, n. 533); intuition regarding
life after death due to influx (n. 602);
man's entrance into eternal *life*
(Chap. 46); the passage from one *life*
to the other (n. 461); man's reception
into the other *life* (n. 548); *life* in the
world continued into *life* in the spirit

in the first state after death (n. 493); difference between *life* in the spiritual world and *life* in the natural world (n. 462 [a]); what heavenly *life* is (n. 403, 450, 481, 506); *life* after death such as it has been in the world (Chap. 49); heavenly *life* cannot be implanted after death (n. 527); *life* after death is man's love and his faith therefrom (n. 476); the delights of everyone's *life* are changed after death into corresponding delights (Chap. 50); in heaven to perform uses is the delight of everyone's *life* (n. 219); essential Divine worship in heaven consists in a *life* of love, etc. (n. 222); kinship in the other *life* (n. 46); spiritual *life* is fed by affections for good and truth (n. 111); the love and the *life* determine the interiors and consequently beauty in heaven (n. 459); the uses of heavenly *life* derived from knowledges (n. 356 extract); those in the other *life* who have renounced the world in this (n. 360); communication in the other *life* is effected through subject spirits (n. 603 extract); heathen instructed in the other *life* (n. 321, 324, 516); *life* is the force of the spiritual world (n. 589); the memory of spirits is their *life* (n. 517); *life* of children in heaven (n. 337, 344); an idea of *life* in all the thoughts of children (n. 338); angelic *life* consists in the goods of love and charity (n. 517 note); states of *life* of angels (n. 154, 183); *life*, not knowledge, makes an angel (n. 518); the *life* of angels in heaven (n. 136); wisdom constitutes the *life* of the angels; degrees of *life* in angels (n. 267); goods of *life* of angels (n. 288); angelic *life* consists in goods of love and charity, that is, in performing uses (n. 112 note); angels of

the inmost heaven apply truths to the *life* as soon as they hear them (n. 271); interior angels recognize the entire *life* of one speaking from his tone (n. 269); the *life* of animals is solely from affections (n. 110); animals are in the order of their *life*, men are not (n. 352); walking and journeying correspond to progression of *life* (n. 590).

Light corresponds to truths from good (n. 179); the *light* of the world's fieriness corresponds to what is false from love (n. 122); *light* corresponds to truths going forth from love (n. 13); its effect depends upon the nature of its reception (n. 569); mere belief is like winter *light*, which is without heat (n. 482); thought from natural *light* cannot comprehend the things of heaven (n. 170), contents of the natural memory not objects of spiritual *light* (n. 355); natural and spiritual *light* (n. 352); man's spiritual *light* (n. 130); all truths emit *light* (n. 132); man is rational insofar as he receives *light* from heaven (n. 430); *light* in heaven (Chap. 15); Divine truth the *light* of heaven (n. 117, 126–128, 232, 347, 462 [a], 518, 549); the *light* of heaven is Divine wisdom and intelligence (n. 131); the *light* of heaven is spiritual because it is from the Lord as a sun (n. 127, 128); *light* in heaven differs according to the reception of Divine truth (n. 128); *light* of heaven compared to *light* in the world (n. 126, 347); the pleasures of heavenly *light* (n. 489); *light* of heaven enlightens both the eye and the mind (n. 266); in heaven the wise are in much *light*, the simple are in less (n. 350); planes of heavenly *light* (n. 353); the ideas of angels are modifications of the *light* of heaven (n. 239); the *light* of the angels (n. 75, 128, 275); the Divine *light* radiates from the Word (n. 308); *light* of heaven is thick darkness to those in corporeal love (n. 481); why evil spirits shun the *light* of heaven (n. 553); *light* in hell (n. 131 note).

Lord, correspondence of sun and moon (n. 1, 119); calls himself the "bread of life" from correspondence (n. 101); the *Lord* the Only Man (n. 80, 86 extract); his body, soul, and resurrection (n. 86 extract, 316); why called "Bridegroom" and "husband" (n. 180, 371); called "Prince of Peace" (n. 287); called the "East" (n. 191); called "Light" (n. 129); his Divine Essence (n. 546); what is from the *Lord* is the *Lord* (n. 12); he is the fountain of all life (n. 9); life flows in from the *Lord* (n. 203 note); when use is spoken of the *Lord* is meant (n. 389); serving the *Lord* is performing uses (n. 112 note); false doctrines about the *Lord* (n. 321); Divine mercy consists in man's being led by the *Lord* (n. 480); so far as one is in heavenly mercy he is led by the *Lord* (n. 558 [a]); the *Lord* leads those whose interiors are in heavenly order (n. 499); as regards man, the *Lord* looks only to ends, which are uses (n. 112 note); how and where the *Lord* flows into the life (n. 512); he turns to himself those that love to do the things that are from him (n. 17); man turns himself to or away from the *Lord* (n. 123, 545); why he does not instruct man by visions (n. 456); good from heaven is from the *Lord* (n. 591); what is done from heavenly love is done from the *Lord* (n. 484); how man is protected by the *Lord* from evil spirits (n. 577);

spiritual freedom is the *Lord's* (n. 597); his "righteousness" (n. 348); his "yoke" and "burden" (n. 359); his coming (n. 1); he is the "neighbor" in the highest sense (n. 64 note, 481 note); spiritual love to the neighbor begins with the *Lord* (n. 558 [b]); he never does anything contrary to order (n. 523); he is in his Divine order in both worlds (n. 857); he receives all who live in accordance with the laws of Divine order (n. 420); innocence is willingness to be led by the *Lord* (n. 281); innocence and peace are from the *Lord* (n. 282, 285); those in a state of innocence ascribe all things to the *Lord* (n. 278); how those in good think of him (n. 86 extract); everyone receives the *Lord* in the same manner that he receives heaven (n. 55); the *Lord* flows directly into man's willing, but mediately into his thinking (n. 26); his love for the race (n. 86 extract); man's spiritual sight is opened whenever the *Lord* pleases (n. 76); how he spoke with the prophets (n. 254); he leads the spiritual man (n. 530); draws all to himself by means of influx (n. 548); his influence on man's interiors (n. 253); he rules man through angels and spirits (n. 247); he flows into each man (n. 297); he flows into Divine truths in man (n. 250); how he regenerates man (n. 329); looking to the *Lord* (n. 430); everywhere in the universe he is acknowledged as the God of heaven and earth (n. 417); no one can be in true marriage unless he acknowledges the *Lord* (n. 376); he is mercy itself, and love itself, and goodness itself (n. 524); the form of good and truth from the *Lord* (n. 460); Divine good and Divine truth are not in the *Lord*, but from him; in him is only Divine love (n. 139); the Word means Divine truth in the Lord from the Lord (n. 137); the Divine goes forth from the Lord as the good of love and the truth of faith (n. 7); the Divine was in the Lord from conception (n. 86 extract); he forms one church out of many according as the good of love and faith reigns in them (n. 57); he is continually withdrawing the evil man from evil and leading the good man into good (n. 54); he holds every man in an equilibrium between evil and good (n. 537); those in self-love look backward away from the Lord (n. 561); his love receptive of heaven and all things therein (n. 18); he provided the Word as a medium of conjunction between heaven and man (n. 304, 306); he prevents spirits knowing that they are with man (n. 292); the Lord alone is Man (n. 80); how he governs heaven and earth (n. 406); the lot of those that deny the Lord (n. 3, 6, 83); he rules the hells (Chap. 56); no one is cast into hell by the Lord (Chap. 57); the punishment of evil spirits is not from the Lord, but from the evil itself (n. 550); unless he ruled heaven and hell there would be no equilibrium (n. 592); he alone knows the position of the hells in detail (n. 587); in the Word "angels" mean something belonging to the Lord (n. 391); the Lord conjoins or separates the angels according to their good (n. 45, 383); all the power of the angels is from the Lord (n. 230); he gives houses to the angels according to their perception of good and truth (n. 190); employments of the angels are really employments of the Lord (n. 391); what is arranged by the Lord is above

the thought and transcends the wisdom of the angels (n. 39); he sees the angels in the forehead (n. 145); he turns the angels to himself (n. 143 note); his appearance to the angels (n. 55, 118); when he appears in the midst of the angels they appear as one angelic form (n. 52); he appears in heaven as an angel, but not in person (n. 121); angels say that they are in the Lord's body (n. 81); the angels of the inmost heaven live as it were in the Lord (n. 280); angels of the inmost heaven are in love to the Lord (n. 271); those in heaven are in the Lord and the Lord is in them (n. 8, 11); the Lord is the sun of heaven (n. 117, 120, 159, 549); the Lord seen as a moon (n. 118); the Lord the common center in heaven (n. 124); in heaven the Lord is the All-in-all (n. 58); worship of the Lord in heaven (n. 506); the Lord the God of heaven (n. 2, 5); his presence in heaven (n. 147); heaven is where the Lord is acknowledged, believed in, and loved (n. 56); those in heaven are in the Lord (n. 86 extract); heaven in the Lord's sight is in human form (n. 62); he directs all the heavens as if they were one angel (n. 52); he withholds those in heaven from what is their own (n. 158); each heaven, society, and angel is a likeness of the Lord (n. 72); he conjoins all in heaven by means of influx, direct or mediate (n. 37); in the spiritual kingdom the Lord governs mediately through governors (n. 215); government in the celestial kingdom belongs to the Lord alone (n. 214); he receives and teaches all who die in childhood (n. 416); children are under his immediate auspices (n. 277, 332); he flows into the ideas of little children chiefly from inmosts (n. 336); his resurrection taught to children in heaven (n. 334). (See Divine, human, Love.)

Love, heat corresponds to *love* (n. 135); forehead corresponds to *love* (n. 145); mountains signify celestial *love,* hills spiritual *love* (n. 188); as things in heaven correspond to goods and truths they correspond to *love* and wisdom (n. 155, 166); good of *love* corresponds to fire (n. 118); angels are in the good of the Lord's *love* (n. 81); the celestial kingdom is the voluntary part of heaven and in it the good of *love* reigns (n. 95); *love* kindles the will (n. 473); what a man *loves* that he wills (n. 500); after death man is his own *love* and his own will (n. 479, 547); spiritual heat is the essence of *love* (n. 133, 567); vital heat is from *love* (n. 447); all life and heat are from *love* (n. 14, 17); the quality of the *love* determines the quality of the life (n. 14); the quality of *love* is determined by the end or use (n. 565); wisdom is *loving* use (n. 390); *love* of use in heaven (n. 393, 394); *love* of serving is the basis of heavenly happiness (n. 408); all delight flows from *love* (n. 396); *love* is reciprocal (n. 350); *love* in act endures (n. 483); genuine *love* of truth defined (n. 468); *love* in animals (n. 135); celestial and spiritual *love* (n. 33); everything of *love* is good (n. 232); the *love* of doing good (n. 64); the effect of *love* depends upon the nature of that into which it flows (n. 569); *love* is receptive of all things in harmony with itself, and discards all else (n. 18, 349); true and false *love* to the neighbor (n. 558 [b]); *love* from which deeds are done is either heavenly or infernal (n. 484); states in the world of those in

selfish and unselfish *love* (n. 401); in what heavenly *love* consists (n. 481); it is the nature of heavenly *love* to share all things (n. 399); delights of those in heavenly *love* (n. 489); *love* of family and friends an indication of heavenly *love* (n. 406). *Love* makes the man (n. 474); man's *love* is turned about (n. 253); man is warmed or inflamed by *love* (n. 134); the nature of a man's *love* determines the nature of his thought (n. 532); man's *loves* are arranged to form a kingdom (n. 477); man's spiritual body is formed solely out of the things that he does from his *love* and will (n. 475); knowledges in relation to man's *love* (n. 356 extract); spirits associated with man are such as is his affection or *love* (n. 295). Man's ruling *love* (n. 269 note); all man's delights are those of his ruling *love* (n. 486); the ruling *love* seizes upon what agrees with it, and rejects what does not (n. 479); a man's ruling *love* remains with him after death (n. 363, 477); a man may know of his future state from his ruling *love* (n. 487); after death man continues such as is his will or ruling *love* (n. 480, 481); the ruling *love* determines the future state (n. 427); how the ruling *love* of spirits is disclosed in the first state after death (n. 496); spirits can do nothing apart from their ruling *love* (n. 479); angels turn according to their ruling *love* (n. 143); everyone is his own *love,* and is such as is his reigning *love* (n. 58, 269 note). *Love* in the speech of angels (n. 238); intensity of the *love* of angels varies (n. 155); angels are continually being perfected in wisdom and *love* (n. 221); when angels are in a state of *love* they are in a state of peace (n. 289); angels have their affections from Divine *love* and their thought from Divine wisdom (n. 239); *love* and life determine the interiors and consequently beauty in heaven (n. 459); in heaven all are in light in the degree of their *love* for good and truth (n. 350); different kinds of *love* in the different kingdoms of heaven (n. 148); all the various forms of government in heaven are governments of mutual love (n. 213, 218); *love* of rule not possible in heaven (n. 407). Love to the Lord is willing and doing Divine truth (n. 271); love to the Lord is "heavenly fire" (n. 134, 568); *love* to the Lord opens the interiors of the mind to the third degree (n. 271); *love* to the Lord and the neighbor the law of heaven (n. 406, 486); the angelic life is *love* to the Lord and mutual *love* (n. 344); *love* to the Lord is the source of angelic wisdom and intelligence (n. 467); *love* to the Lord from the Lord is the origin of the good of all in heaven (n. 72); *love* to the Lord and the neighbor include in themselves all Divine truths (n. 19); *love* to the Lord and the neighbor include means in general to perform uses (n. 112); meaning of *love* to the Lord and *love* of the neighbor (n. 15, 16, 350, 399); *love* to the Lord and *love* of self are opposites, and love of the neighbor and *love* of the world are opposites (n. 596); good of *love* to the Lord as a motive (n. 472); the Lord's life in the world was his *love* toward the race (n. 86 extract); the Divine *love* of the Lord is what is seen as a sun in heaven (n. 117); the Divine that goes forth from the Lord is *love* (n. 17); in heaven the Lord is the reigning *love* (n. 58, 486); the Lord is

present with everyone according to the measure of his *love* and faith (n. 199); those that receive good of *love* directly from the Lord (n. 348); Divine *love* is the Being *[esse]* (n. 139); Divine *love* is a longing for the salvation and happiness of all (n. 397); the greatness of Divine *love;* it is tempered by flowing through mediums (n. 120). Love of self (n. 18, 87, 558 [b]); man is born into *love* of self and the world (n. 390 note); nature and source of *love* of self (n. 555, 556); *love* of self and its results (n. 559); dominion of *love* of self (n. 564); *love* of self as a motive to piety (n. 535); *love* of self separates from the Divine (n. 558 [a]); comparison of *love* of self and heavenly *love* (n. 557); the world's fieriness corresponds to *love* of self (n. 122); *love* of self is antagonistic to innocence (n. 283); appearance of the external memory in heaven of those that have cultivated it from *love* of self (n. 466); angels can receive wisdom because they are without the *love* of self (n. 272); knowledges that have *love* of self and the world as an end are empty knowledges (n. 356 extract); infernal fire means *love* of self and the world (n. 134, 568); *love* of the world (n. 565); results of *love* of the world not as bad as results of *love* of self (n. 578); man separated himself from heaven through *love* of self and the world (n. 252); *love* of self and the world cannot bring forth good works (n. 472); the forms of evil spirits are the forms of *love* of self and the world (n. 554); all in the hells are in evils and falsities therefrom derived from the *love* of self and the world (Chap. 58); *love* of those in the hells

(n. 151); *love* of evil is from hell (n. 571); lust is *love* in continuity (n. 570); light of heaven is thick darkness to those in corporeal *love* (n. 481); quarters in the hells are determined in accordance with their *loves* (n. 587). (See Affection, Faith and Love, Marriage.)

Lumen or natural light (n. 352).

Lungs, correspondence (n. 95, 96). (See Heart.)

Lust destroys true peace (n. 290); it is the source of torment in the hells (n. 571, 573); from every hell there exhales a sphere of its *lust* (n. 574); love is *lust* in continuity (n. 570); *lust* of those in love of self and the world (n. 400).

Magic, delight of evil spirits in *magic* arts (n. 488); *magic* in the other life (n. 508).

Malice of infernal spirits (Chap. 60); *malice* of genii (n. 579); the *malice* and cunning of evil spirits takes the place of the wisdom and intelligence of angels (n. 577).

Man, his two memories (n. 463 note); his method of reasoning (n. 130); the use of knowledges to *men* (n. 356 extract); thought and affection constitute the *man* (n. 358, 445); he is a subject that will serve as a source and container (n. 434); the first *man* (n. 341); *man* in the different Ages (n. 115, 252); his freedom (n. 598, 603 extract); he is such as is his life (n. 521); spiritual heat is the heat of *man's* life (n. 568); deeds designate the quality of his life (n. 471, 475); the degrees of his life (n. 314 note); the three planes of his life (n. 529, 530); his reception into the other life (n. 548); how he is reformed (n. 424);

why he becomes smaller in old age (n. 278); one *man* the same as another (n. 390); difference between *men* and beasts (n. 296 note); *man* is like an animal as concerns his natural (n. 110); natural *man's* ideas of heaven (n. 183); *man* in the body thinks both naturally and spiritually (n. 356); the forms of the spiritual and the natural *man* differ greatly (n. 99); the natural *man* a hypocrite (n. 531); how he becomes rational (n. 468); he is rational so far as he receives light from heaven (n. 430); his elevation into the light of heaven (n. 130 note); he cannot comprehend the things of heaven from natural light (n. 170); may be withdrawn from natural into spiritual light (n. 171); *men* are enlightened to a certain degree by spiritual light (n. 130); *man's* ignorance of spiritual things (n. 310); his ignorance of extension of thought and affection (n. 203); his ignorance about regeneration (n. 269); the sensual *man's* inability to get a true idea of God as *Man*, or of heaven (n. 85, 86); sensual *man* cannot comprehend the meaning of discrete degrees (n. 38); sensual *men* have knowledge but not wisdom (n. 267); sensual *men* described (n. 269 note, 353 note); all *man's* thought rests upon the idea of time and space (n. 169); the nature of his thought depends upon its direction (n. 532); his spiritual sight can be opened by the Lord (n. 76); he cannot see spiritual objects (n. 582); every *man* has two gates (n. 430); his state in the world (n. 504); he should not separate himself from the world (n. 528); he was created in the image of both worlds (n. 202); he is in both worlds (n. 135, 304); is the means by which the natural and spiritual worlds are conjoined (n. 112, 247), has within him both a natural and a spiritual world (n. 90); relation of things in the vegetable kingdom to things in *man* (n. 109); every part of *man* performs a use (n. 64); *man* can worship only that of which he has some idea (n. 86 extract); the highest degree in all, into which the Divine flows (n. 34); Divine influx apart from *man* (n. 112); *man's* inmost or highest (n. 39). The outmost of Divine order is in *man* (n. 304, 315); *man* by creation is Divine order in form (n. 30, 523 note); so far as *man* is in Divine order his acts are uses in form (n. 112); the incarnation became necessary because *man* had destroyed order (n. 101); *man* is born in ignorance because his life is contrary to order (n. 108); spiritual speech is inherent in the interior intellectual part of *man* (n. 243); the source of *man's* immortality (n. 39); no *man* is born for hell (n. 318); *man* is excited to lust by heat from hell (n. 571); the church is in *man*, not outside of him (n. 57); *men* and women (n. 366, 368, 369). Angels' speech with *man* (Chap. 28, n. 253); *men* who can speak with angels (n. 115, 249 note, 250); how angels talk with *man* (n. 246); angels and spirits present with every *man* (n. 165, 247); nature of conjunction with angels (n. 255, 307, 365); *man* communicates with heaven and angels by means of correspondence (n. 114); *men* were created to become angels (n. 57); great numbers that become angels (n. 415); angels say they are *men* (n. 183, 576); *men* are watched over by angels (n. 391); how *men* ought to think about angels (n. 183); angelic ideas are

converted into natural ideas for *man's* reception (n. 168); *man* cannot comprehend angelic peace (n. 284); neither *men* nor angels could exist if the Divine human did not flow into heaven and all things of the world (n. 101); as regards *man* angels think only of the will from which the body acts (n. 61); what angels say of *men* with wrong ideas of God and heaven (n. 86); angels are present while a *man* is being withdrawn from the body (n. 440, 449); angels first receive *man* into the other life (n. 548); angels inspect and search the memories of those entering the world of spirits (n. 462 [b]; 463); why *man* was called a microcosm (n. 57 note). Heaven reflects a single *man* (Chap. 8, 11, n. 59, 78); each society in heaven reflects a single *man* (Chap. 9, n. 68); *man* an image of heaven (n. 99); *man* is the base and termination of heaven (n. 100); correspondence of heaven to *man* (n. 418); correspondence of all things of heaven with all things of *man* (Chap. 12, n. 87); *man* has permanent existence from his correspondence with heaven (n. 94); *man's* interiors are arranged in the form of heaven (n. 57 note); Divine order is heaven in *man* (n. 523); heaven is stored up in *man's* innocence (n. 276); all *men* are born for heaven (n. 82, 420); how he may live the life of heaven (n. 529, 533); he is formed for heaven only by means of the world (n. 360); he has turned himself away from heaven (n. 305); his freedom is due to the equilibrium between heaven and hell (Chap. 63, n. 537); his communication with heaven or hell (n. 204); his looking to heaven or to hell (n. 313); he is conjoined both to heaven and to hell (n. 292, 599); difference between the conjunction of heaven with *man* and *man* with *man* (n. 300); the conjunction of heaven with *man* is by means of the Word (Chap. 34); *man* would have been separated from heaven but for the Word (n. 309); every *man* who is in conjunction with heaven has an intuition regarding life after death (n. 602); *man's* delight in heaven (n. 395). The "Greatest *Man*" means heaven (n. 59, 94, 96, 217); the parts of the Greatest *Man* (n. 59, 94, 96, 231, 333). (See Affection, Death, Evil, External, Internal, Lord, Love, Spirit, Understanding, Will, Wisdom.)

Man-spirit (n. 422, 456, 461, 552).

Manhood, children in heaven never grow beyond early *manhood* (n. 340).

Mansions in heaven (n. 183).

Marriage, *marriage* in its essential is the union of disposition or mind (n. 281, 375); various motives in *marriage* life (n. 381); the meaning of man's not putting asunder what God has joined together (n. 372); differences between *marriages* in heaven and on earth (n. 382 [b]); *marriage* in heaven (Chap. 40, n. 366–369, 383); what infernal *marriage* is (n. 377); *married* couples remain together during the first state after death (n. 494). True *marriage* love (n. 281, 367, 370); origin of *marriage* love (n. 373); there is no *marriage* love without the love of good and truth (n. 381); true *marriage* love continues after death (n. 494); it descends from the Lord through heaven (n. 385); delights of *marriage* love (n. 386); love in heavenly *marriages* (n. 369); how *marriage* love is represented in heaven (n. 382 [a]); true *marriage* love described by an

angel (n. 374); angels and *marriage* love (n. 370, 371); a *married* pair is not called two but one angel (n. 367, 372); those in the loins in the Greatest Man are in *marriage* love (n. 96); those that are in *marriage* love and those that are not (n. 376); true *marriage* love not possible in polygamy (n. 379); love of dominion takes away true *marriage* love (n. 370); those in evils and falsities are not in true *marriage* love (n. 377); condition after death of those that have lived in false *marriage* love (n. 380).

Masters in heaven (n. 219); children in heaven taught by *masters* (n. 334).

Means, no one enters heaven by mercy apart from *means* (Chap. 54); knowledges as *means* (n. 356 extract); *means* of salvation revealed in the Word (n. 522).

Measure, means what a thing is (n. 73).

Measurements of the New Jerusalem signify truths of doctrine (n. 307).

Melancholy caused by certain spirits (n. 299).

Members, heaven is arranged in parts or *members* like a man (n. 65); *members* of the body (n. 95, 96).

Memory, the internal and external *memory* (n. 463); the two are represented to the sight in heaven (n. 466); the inmost of the inner *memory* (n. 467); those who commit Divine truths to the *memory* (n. 348); man's interior mind weighs the things of the natural *memory* (n. 356); those in genuine innocence do not store up truths in the *memory* (n. 278); truths and goods merely in the *memory* are removed by vastation (n. 551); truths in the *memory* do not open the rational faculty (n. 468); that which is merely in the *memory* is not really in man (n. 423);

spirits enter into man's *memory* (n. 292); spirits do not flow into man from their own *memory* (n. 298); spirits are unable to call forth mere knowledges from the *memory* (n. 465); angels enter into man's *memory* (n. 246); angels cannot talk with man from their own *memory* (n. 256); angels of the inmost heaven do not store up truths in the *memory* (n. 271); knowledges are not committed to the *memory* in heaven, but to the life (n. 517); the *memory* of sensual men (n. 353); the *memory* of those that die in childhood (n. 345); the *memory* remains after death (Chap. 48); the natural *memory* is retained in the other life, but is useless (n. 355); the *memory* is retained and laid bare in the world of spirits (n. 462 [b], 463); the merely natural things of the *memory* do not remain after death (n. 464).

Mercury, spirits from the planet *Mercury* (n. 417 extract).

Mercy, Divine *mercy* defined (n. 522, 523); erroneous beliefs about *mercy* (n. 526); *mercy* is for all (n. 318, 364); reception into heaven is not my *mercy* apart from means (Chap. 54, n. 54, 420 note); all in heaven are there from the *mercy* of the Lord (n. 342); Divine *mercy* works by means, and consists in man's being led by the Lord (n. 480).

Merit, the *merit* of the Lord (n. 348 note); *merit* as a motive does not lead to heaven (n. 535).

Microcosm, why man was so called by the ancients (n. 57 note).

Mind, the body is an image of the *mind* (n. 374); the human *mind* is like the soil (n. 356); the *minds* of children (n. 277); the correspondence of

heaven to the substance of man's *mind* (n. 418); things of man's *mind* belong to the spiritual world (n. 90); truth that is lived enters with light into the *mind's* thought (n. 603); the *mind* has two entrances, one for truth and the other for falsity (n. 430); the two parts of the *mind* (n. 367); the result of closure of the higher regions of the *mind* (n. 532); in order to elevate the *mind* to things spiritual and heavenly it must be withdrawn from the things of the senses (n. 465); the *mind* may be raised above worldly things (n. 169); love to the Lord opens the interiors of the *mind* to the third degree (n. 271); man's interior *mind* weighs the thoughts of the natural memory (n. 356); its interiors are formed for the reception of Divine truth (n. 347); man's interiors which constitute his *mind* are formed from use and for use (n. 112 note); the interiors and dispositions of the *mind* are made visible in the spiritual world when the Lord pleases (n. 481); human and angelic *minds* the same (n. 314); the *mind* during resuscitation (n. 449); the exploration of the *minds* of those in self-love (n. 560); in the second state after death man is let into the interiors of his *mind* (n. 499); an angel knows another's *mind* by his articulation (n. 236); things of heaven are more pleasant to the *minds* of angels than to their eyes, because they see correspondences in them (n. 185); neither in heaven nor in hell is a man allowed to have a divided *mind* (n. 425); the conjunction of *minds* in true marriage (n. 281, 375).

Mirror, from the things that exist in the natural world the things that exist in the spiritual world can be seen as in a *mirror* (n. 56).

Mohammedans, where and how they are prepared for heaven (n. 514–516).

Moon, its correspondence (n. 1, 119); angels see the Lord as a *moon* with the left eye (n. 118); the natural *moon* appears to the angels as dense darkness (n. 122, 151).

Morality, true and false morality (n. 319).

Mother, the angels who act as *mothers* (n. 332); *mother* and father signifies truth conjoined to good (n. 382 [b]).

Motion, all vital *motions* depend upon the heart and lungs (n. 446).

Motive, the *motive* behind deeds and works determines their true character (n. 472); *motives* are the essentials of acts (n. 358); *motives* in the three planes of life (n. 530, 531); love of self as a *motive* (n. 555); true *motives* to a life of charity (n. 535); *motives* of a moral life (n. 319).

Mouth, those in the *mouth* of the Greatest Man (n. 96).

Music, its expression of affections (n. 241).

Nakedness, corresponds to innocence; *nakedness* in heaven (n. 179, 280, 341).

Names, societies and angels in heaven have no *names* (n. 52 note); no *names* in the Word in heaven (n. 520 note).

Nation, eastern *nations* had a knowledge of correspondences (n. 87 note); the "poor man" in the Word signifies the *nations* that long for truth (n. 365).

Natural, the *natural* Divine (n. 31); sensual men conceive of what is spiritual as merely a purer *natural* (n. 38); what comes forth from the sun of the world is called *natural* (n. 172); angels cannot give expression to things in a *natural* way (n. 246); the *natural* is

the outmost (n. 305 note); nothing *natural* exists without something spiritual corresponding to it (n. 487); *natural* beings see such things as are from a *natural* origin (n. 582).

Nature, all *nature* has its beginnings in the sun of the world (n. 116); all things of *nature* are correspondences (n. 101–107); all *nature* is a theater representative of the Lord's kingdom (n. 106 note); *nature* is relatively dead, and is subservient to things spiritual (n. 489); all things in *nature* are forms or effects of uses (n. 112); the body not a product of *nature* (n. 102); those that acknowledge *nature* in place of the Divine (n. 353); hells in which are those that have acknowledged *nature* and denied the Divine (n. 575); *nature* of the evil in the second state after death (n. 508); everyone in the spiritual world acts from his *nature* (n. 574).

Neighbor, what the *neighbor* is (n. 217 note, 290, 481 note, 558 [b] note); nature of love to the *neighbor* (n. 15, 16, 255 note, 399); true and false love to the *neighbor* (n. 558); in heaven good is the *neighbor* (n. 64); in the highest sense the Lord is the *neighbor* (n. 64 note); in heaven the *neighbor* is loved more than self (n. 406); delights of the soul flow from love to the Lord and the *neighbor* (n. 396).

Nervous System, described (n. 212).

Night signifies absence of love and wisdom; no *night* in heaven (n. 115).

Nostrils of the Greatest Man (n. 96).

Numbers, their correspondence (n. 263); all *numbers* in the Word signify things; their multiples have the same significance (n. 73 note); *number* of the hells (Chap. 61).

Nutriment, knowledge, intelligence, and

wisdom are spiritual *nutriment* (n. 274, 340).

Obedience, the ear corresponds to *obedience* (n. 271); those in the ears of the Greatest Man are in attention and *obedience* (n. 96); in heaven rulers accept honor for the sake of *obedience* (n. 218); *obedience* as a motive for work (n. 472).

Objects, nature of *objects* in heaven (n. 171, 172).

Obsession, how it was accomplished; it is no longer possible (n. 257); *obsession* of the mind of men still common (n. 257 note).

Occupation in heaven is from correspondence (n. 394).

Odor signifies what is agreeable or disagreeable (n. 287); foul *odors* from the hells (n. 134 note).

Offspring, of marriage (n. 382 [b]).

One, the Divine is *One* and that *One* is the Lord (n. 2).

Organs, societies correspond to *organs* (n. 217); are the subjects of the special senses (n. 434).

Order is from the supreme good (n. 322); the true *order* of man's life (n. 352); the Incarnation became necessary because man had destroyed *order* (n. 101); true and false *order* in thought and speech (n. 499); *order* of heaven in the mind of man (n. 454); man is born in ignorance because his life is contrary to *order,* animals are born with knowledge because they are in natural *order* (n. 108); all things that exist according to *order* have relation to good and truth (n. 473 note); *order* exists by means of Divine truth, and Divine good is the essential of *order* (n. 77 note); the Lord never does anything contrary to *order*

(n. 523); *order* in the vegetable kingdom (n. 109); iron signifies truth in the outmosts of *order* (n. 115 note) Divine *order* and its workings (n. 532); the cause of Divine *order* (n. 107, 304 note); activity of Divine *order* (n. 315); man is Divine *order* in form (n. 30); man is born into the complete opposite of Divine *order;* relation of degrees to divine *order* (n. 38); uses are coordinated according to Divine *order* (n. 392); all things in heaven are organized according to Divine *order* (n. 389); heaven is arranged according to Divine *order* (n. 200 note); everything that is in Divine *order* has relation to good and truth (n. 107); the Lord receives all who live in accordance with the laws of Divine *order* (n. 420); the Lord is in his Divine *order* in both worlds, since God is *order* (n. 57); all things in accordance with Divine *order* correspond to heaven; things contrary to it to hell (n. 113); violation of marriage is contrary to Divine *order* (n. 385); polygamy is contrary to Divine *order* (n. 379). (See Outmosts.)

Origin of marriage love (n. 371); *origin* of spiritual and natural things (n. 582); all *origin* of life is from the Lord as a sun (n. 141).

Outmosts, teeth correspond to *outmosts* in nature (n. 575); works are the *outmosts* in which the will and the thought terminate (n. 475); the *outmost* plane of knowledges and affections is quiescent in the other life (n. 480); the *outmosts* of Divine order are in man (n. 304); Divine order does not stop short of *outmosts* (n. 315); Divine order terminates in the world in *outmosts* (n. 107); abuse of the *outmosts* of Divine order by infernal spirits (n. 580).

Own, man's *own* defined (n. 484 note, 501, 558 [a] note); spirits in hell are in what is their own (n. 591).

Palaces in heaven (n. 184, 185, 218, 361); heaven compared to a *palace* (n. 51); wisdom compared to a *palace* (n. 270).

Pancreas of the Greatest Man (n. 96, 217).

Papists in the other life (n. 508, 562).

Paradise, signifies intelligence and wisdom (n. 111); innocence of *paradise* (n. 341); why heaven is called a *paradise* (n. 136).

Parents, their mistakes in the education of children (n. 344).

Parks in heaven (n. 176).

Particulars, Parts (See Generals.)

Paths in the world of spirits (n. 496).

Peace, what true *peace* is (n. 290); origin of *peace* (n. 286); *peace* is the inmost of delight from good of innocence (n. 285); different meanings of *peace* (n. 286 note); Sabbath means rest and *peace* (n. 287); *peace* of angels and heaven (Chap. 32, n. 284, 288); *peace* differs in quality and quantity in agreement with the state of innocence (n. 288); *peace* and innocence the two inmost things of heaven (n. 285).

People of the different ages (n. 115); the ancient *people* were celestial men (n. 87), and worshiped the Divine human (n. 86 extract); they possessed arcana expressed in numbers (n. 263 note); their interiors were turned heavenward, and they had direct revelation (n. 306). The ancient *people* worshiped in groves toward the east, on account of correspondences (n. 111, 119); they frequently talked with angels (n. 249 note); their writing (n. 260); their chief knowledge

was that of correspondences (n. 87); Swedenborg talked with spirits of the ancient *people* (n. 323).

Perception, those in the nostrils of the Greatest Man are in *perception* (n. 96; "odor of rest" signifies *perception* of peace (n. 287); *perception* in the light of heaven (n. 130); the doctrines of the different heavens are adapted to the *perception* of the angels (n. 227); *perception* of truth by the angels of the inmost heaven (n. 270); the angels are given houses according to their *perception* of good and truth (n. 190); the *perception* of good and truth (n. 190); the *perception* of the angels is very clear (n. 462 [a]); *perception* of heavenly joy impossible to a natural man (n. 395); Swedenborg's *perception* of heavenly joy (n. 413); man's *perception* of thought (n. 356); *perception* of truth (n. 352); *perception* of life after death (n. 478); the *perception* of the Lord's presence is in the interiors (n. 147); the Lord alone has *perception* and thought from himself (n. 86 extract).

Perfection is through diversity (n. 405); the ground of all *perfection* is unity of parts (n. 56); variety arranged in heavenly form constitutes *perfection* (n. 71); it increases toward interiors and decreases toward exteriors (n. 34, 459); how it is produced in heaven (n. 56, 418).

Person, loving the neighbor is not loving the *person* (n. 390 note).

Piety, true and false *piety* (n. 535); life of *piety* apart from charity is of no avail (n. 360, 505 note).

Place, in the spiritual world change of *place* is a change of state (n. 192).

Planes of the memory (n. 345).

Planets are all inhabited (n. 417).

Plays used to teach children in heaven (n. 334).

Pleasures of the world do not bar from heaven (n. 358, 359).

Polygamy (n. 379).

Poor, means those desirous of, but lacking in, knowledges of good and truth (n. 420); the temptations of the *poor* (n. 364); the *poor* in heaven (Chap. 39); the *poor* man at the rich man's gate (n. 365); they enter heaven on account of their life, not on account of their poverty (n. 364).

Pope, the divinity of the Lord's human denied in council for the *pope's* sake (n. 86 extract).

Power is from the conjunction of good and truth (n. 232); all a man's *power* is from his will and understanding (n. 228); all spiritual *power* is from truth from good (n. 539); Divine truth has all *power* in the heavens (n. 137, 231); angels are *powers* (n. 137, 231); *power* of the angels (Chap. 26); *power* in hell (n. 233); arms and hands signify *powers* (n. 231).

Prayer in heaven (n. 222); *prayer* is an acknowledgment of the power of God and his angels (n. 228).

Preachers in heaven are from the spiritual kingdom (n. 225), and are not called priests (n. 226).

Preaching in heaven (n. 221, 223, 393).

Presence, all things are in the Lord's *presence* (n. 124); the Lord's *presence* as a cause (n. 199); the Lord's *presence* in heaven (n. 147); in the spiritual world one comes into the *presence* of another by desiring to do so (n. 194); in heaven people often appear to be where their look is fixed (n. 121).

Priest (See Preachers.)

Priesthood signifies good of love to the Lord (n. 226).

Prince of Peace, the Lord called "the *Prince of peace*" (n. 287).

Principle, must be drawn from truths of doctrine (n. 356 extract).

Printing in heaven (n. 258).

Procreation in heaven and on earth (n. 382); Divine order renews itself in *procreation* (n. 315).

Profanation, those that *profane* truths are cast into the lowest hells (n. 456).

Progression of all things in heaven (n. 163).

Prophets, they saw angels with their spiritual eyes (n. 76); how the Lord spoke with the prophets (n. 254).

Proprium of angels (n. 158); those in genuine innocence are kept apart from their *proprium* (n. 278).

Providence, the poor may have ill thoughts about Divine *providence* (n. 364).

Prudence, children have no *prudence* (n. 277).

Pulse, during resuscitation (n. 449).

Punishment in hell (n. 543, 574, 581); there is no *punishment* in the other life for inherited evils (n. 342); *punishment* of the wicked in the second state after death (n. 509); *punishment* of spirits is not from the Lord, but from the evil itself (n. 550).

Quality, everyone's *quality* is determined by the *quality* of his understanding and will (n. 60); a man's *quality* is known to the angels from his use of vowels (n. 241); the *quality* of deeds and works is determined by the thought and will behind them (n. 472); the *quality* of love is determined by its end or use (n. 565).

Quarters in heaven (Chap. 16, n. 17); they signify such things as pertain to those that dwell in them (n. 150); they differ in the different heavenly kingdoms (n. 146); places of abode in heaven are in different *quarters* according to the qualities of the angels (n. 148); they are not fixed in the spiritual world (n. 123); they are determined in each world by its sun (n. 141).

Race, the human *race* is maintained by the Lord by equilibrium (n. 592); marriages are the seminaries of the *race* (n. 384); the universe was created for the *race* (n. 417 extract); those of the *race* outside the church where the Word is, draw their life from that church (n. 308); one-fifth to one-quarter of the *race* dies in childhood (n. 416); conjunction of heaven with the *race* (Chap. 32); heaven and hell are from the human *race* (Chap. 35, n. 311); the similarity of the human and angelic minds a proof that heaven is from the human *race* (n. 314).

Rational, the *rational* is either enriched or destroyed by knowledges (n. 356 extract); the *rational* in heaven is clearer (n. 465); cultivation of the *rational* faculty (n. 468, 489); beasts have no *rational* faculty (n. 108).

Rationality, true and false (n. 464); the evil are deprived of their *rationality* after death (n. 506).

Reason, the *reason* of sensual men (n. 267 note, 353); what those that think from interior *reason* can perceive (n. 303).

Reasoning of spirits about what is to be believed (n. 320); it may defend any delight, evil or good (n. 385); *reasoning* about truth and falsity (n. 455).

Receptacle, knowledges are *receptacles* for good and truth (n. 356 extract).

Reception is measured by the love (n. 349); *reception* of the Lord means *reception* of good and truth from him (n. 80); angels are *receptions* of Divine good and truth (n. 232); *reception* of rich and poor into heaven (n. 357).

Reformation, how it is effected (n. 424); is aided by evil spirits (n. 293).

Regeneration, depends upon freedom (n. 603 extract); how it is effected (n. 202 note, 523 note); of what it consists (n. 342 note); it is rebirth (n. 279); *regeneration* explained by an angel (n. 269); it is not accomplished by baptism (n. 329); *regeneration* before death (n. 491); state of peace of those being *regenerated* (n. 289).

Reincarnation, the cause of a belief in *reincarnation* (n. 256).

Relationships in the other life are such as spring from love and faith (n. 46).

Relatives in the world of spirits (n. 427, 494).

Religion spread from the Asiatic world (n. 322); everyone has a *religion* of some kind (n. 318); the chief thing of every *religion* is to acknowledge the Divine (n. 319); marriage love cannot exist between those of different *religions* (n. 378).

Repentance is not possible after death (n. 527); it must be from freedom (n. 603 extract).

Representatives and appearances in heaven (Chap. 19); what they are (n. 175); children in heaven are taught chiefly by *representatives* (n. 334); they are employed in teaching good spirits (n. 517).

Respiration during resuscitation (n. 449).

Rest, sabbath means *rest* and peace (n. 287); a mere state of *rest* not true peace (n. 290).

Resurrection, the Lord's *resurrection*

(n. 86 extract, 316, 334); true and false idea of the *resurrection* (n. 312, 456).

Resuscitation of man after death (Chap. 46, n. 447–450).

Revelation, direct *revelation* of Divine truth to man is not possible (n. 309); most ancient people had direct *revelation* (n. 306).

Rich in heaven (Chap. 39); they enter heaven just as easily as the poor (n. 357); signification of *riches* (n. 365); "*rich*" and "*poor*" in the Word (n. 365); *rich* in hell (n. 362); desire for *riches* (n. 365); *riches* not real blessings (n. 364).

Right, correspondence of *right* and left (n. 118).

Righteous, who they are (n. 348); the government in the celestial kingdom is called *righteous* (n. 214).

Righteousness, in the Word "*righteousness*" is predicated of good, and "judgment" of truth (n. 64 note); "*righteousness*" in the Word signifies celestial good (n. 216); the *righteousness* of the Lord and those that turn to it (n. 348).

Rock signifies faith (n. 188); clefts in the *rocks* correspond to falsities.

Rooms in angels' houses (n. 184).

Rule in heaven (n. 564); two kinds of *rule* (n. 220 note); love of *rule* not possible in heaven (n. 407); lust of *ruling* destroys marriage love (n. 380).

Rulers (See Governors.)

Sabbath means rest and peace (n. 287).

Sadness, the angels are *sad* in certain states (n. 159).

Saints, not all the Roman Catholic *saints* were really good (n. 535).

Sanctity, external and internal (n. 506).

Salvation is from the Lord (n. 321); it is not by mercy alone (n. 521); *salvation* of the heathen (n. 318, 319); those in hell cannot be saved (n. 595); Swedenborg talked with angels about *salvation* (n. 526).

Satan, a name given to the hell that is in front (n. 311); meaning of "*satan*" (n. 544).

Saturn, its belt gives it reflected light (n. 417 extract).

Sciences, the *sciences* enumerated (n. 353); they should serve as a means of becoming wise (n. 356); angels of the inmost heaven do not store up truths in the memory and make a *science* (n. 271); reasoning of *scientists* in the other world (n. 464); delights of *scientists* in heaven (n. 489).

Seasons, correspond to states in heaven (n. 166); *seasons* on other planets (n. 417 extract).

See, to *see* signifies to understand, perceive, and observe (n. 145 note).

Seers were those whose eyes were opened (n. 76).

Self, separation from *self* (n. 341); the glory of *self* makes truth merely an end (n. 347). (See Love.)

Seminaries, marriages on earth are the *seminaries* of the human race (n. 384).

Sense-conceptions are misleading (n. 74); spiritual sense of the Word (n. 259, 307).

Senses, the *senses* remain after death (Chap. 48); they are active when a man is being withdrawn from the body (n. 440); in heaven sight and hearing are more exquisite than the other *senses* (n. 462 [a]); ideas about the soul based on bodily *senses* are erroneous (n. 456); the organs are the subjects of the special *senses* (n. 434); the delights of the *senses* are from their use (n. 402); the delights of the *senses* turn away from heaven (n. 398).

Sensual, what the *sensual* man is (n. 267, 353 note, 461).

Series, things in heaven are seen in coherent *series* (n. 205).

Servants in heaven (n. 219).

Serve, to *serve* means to do good to others from a love of good (n. 218).

Service, forms of *service* in heaven (n. 388).

Sexes in heaven (n. 366).

Sharing of delights in heaven (n. 399).

Sight, *sight* of the left eye corresponds to truths of faith; of the right eye to their goods (n. 118 note); thought is internal *sight* (n. 532); interior *sight* has extension into the spiritual world (n. 171, 203); extension of natural and spiritual *sight* (n. 85); the outer and inner *sight* of angels (n. 128, 462 [a]); *sight* in heaven is enlightened by Divine truth (n. 266); angelic speech in *sight* (n. 244); the fullness of *sight* of angels in the inmost heaven (n. 270).

Similes are based on correspondences (n. 110).

Simple, who they are (n. 350, 356); the *simple* have a true idea of God, of heaven, and of the angels (n. 74, 86); they think of God as the Ancient One in shining light (n. 82); the belief of the *simple* in regard to life after death (n. 602); the genuinely innocent appear outwardly *simple* (n. 278); the *simple* in heaven (Chap. 38, n. 18).

Situation of the hells (Chap. 61).

Societies in heaven (Chap. 4); *societies* in heaven are in the form of a man (Chap. 9, n. 68, 94); celestial spiritual *societies* (n. 27); each is a heaven in smaller form (Chap. 7, n. 51, 72); their governments (n. 213); their employments (n. 391); each has its own sphere (n. 591); they are distant according to their uses (n. 393); worship in the different *societies* (n. 56); they communicate by extension of sphere (n. 49); there is no communication between *societies* of different heavens except by correspondence (n. 207); the ways to *societies* from the world of spirits (n. 479); order of abode in heavenly *societies* (n. 149); they differ according to their good (n. 70); their growth (n. 71); their arrangement (n. 43, 52); subject spirits are sent out by the different *societies* (n. 603 extract); all in the same *society* resemble each other (n. 47); a man enters the heavenly *society* where his love is (n. 479, 510); a man in respect to his spirit is in some angelic *society* and sometimes appears there (n. 438); *societies* are joined by influx from the Lord (n. 208); the appearance of the Lord as a sun in the different heavenly *societies* (n. 159); the appearance of a *society* where the Lord is visibly present (n. 69); for every heavenly *society* there is a corresponding infernal *society* (n. 542, 588, 594); men in the world of spirits are attached to the heavenly or infernal *society* to which their ruling love corresponds (n. 427); every spirit is connected with a heavenly or infernal *society* (n. 497); *societies* in hell (n. 541). Angels sometimes see *societies* in heaven as one man (n. 52, 62); arrangement of the angels in the different *societies* (n. 43, 52); employments of angels vary according to the functions of their *societies* (n. 387); how angels are brought to their own *society* (n. 519); few angels go out of their own *society* into another, but their spheres extend into other *societies* (n. 49); angels from the northern and southern *societies* instruct spirits in the third state after death (n.

513); the best angels live apart from *societies* and are more directly under the Divine auspices (n. 50, 189); the larger heavenly *societies* consist of hundreds of thousands of angels (n. 50).

Socinians, their condition after death (n. 3, 83).

Son of God from eternity was the Divine truth in heaven (n. 86 extract); the *Son* as a mediator (n. 526); *sons* and daughters signify procreated truths and goods (n. 382 [b]).

Soul, the *soul* and the resurrection (n. 456); beliefs about the *soul*, true and false (n. 183, 312, 456, 602); state after death of those that have not believed in immortality (n. 452); the *soul* can only be understood by a knowledge of correspondences (n. 88); the *soul* is spiritual and thinks, but the body does not (n. 432); the delights of the *soul* (n. 396); the *soul* of the Lord (n. 86 extract, 316).

Space does not pertain to thought (n. 196); *space* in heaven (Chap. 22); *space* in heaven conforms to the state of the interiors (n. 17); angels have no notion of time and *space* (n. 162); no idea of *space* enters into the thought of the angels, although there is an appearance of *space* with them (n. 191, 195).

Speech, things in human *speech* that are from correspondence (n. 97); man's *speech* is ordered to please others (n. 504); man's *speech* and acts are governed by influx, because they are in true order (n. 296); spiritual *speech* in man's interiors (n. 243); thought and *speech* among ancient people (n. 325). *Speech* of angels with men (Chap. 28); angels cannot speak human language (n. 237); but when

they talk with man they use his language by conjoining themselves with him (n. 246, 249, 250); the ideas of angels are converted into natural ideas when they converse with men (n. 168); subjects of *speech* in the other life (n. 234, 355); the *speech* of angels (Chap. 27; n. 266, 235, 331, 333); it is from interior thought (n. 234); its beauty (n. 238); its symphony (n. 242); its wisdom (n. 239); the letters of angelic *speech* (n. 241); its expressiveness (n. 240); varieties of *speech* among the angels and in the different kingdoms of heaven (n. 241, 244); the *speech* of a higher heaven is not understood in a lower (n. 210); *speech* in heaven (n. 2); *speech* of little children in the other life (n. 331, 333); the *speech* of spirits and angels is from thought and affection (n. 464); *speech* and thought coincide in the other life (n. 457); celestial angels do not think and speak from truths (n. 214 note). *Speech* in the hells (n. 245); *speech* of evil spirits (n. 553).

Spheres of angels (n. 17); *spheres* of heaven and hell (n. 538); extension of *sphere* from the heavenly societies (n. 49); the spiritual *sphere* or *sphere* of life encompasses every human being (n. 591, 49 note); the *sphere* of hell (n. 384, 574).

Spirit, the *spirit* the real man (Chap. 45, n. 76 note, 432, 433, 436, 602); the *spirit* freed from the body is still a man (n. 456); the body lives from the *spirit* (n. 521); the *spirit* is the real source of sense activity (n. 434, 435); after death it appears as it really was in the body (n. 99); the *spirit* remains in the body as long as the heart beats (n. 447); there is an inmost communication of the *spirit* with the breathing

(n. 446); man's *spirit* is what his life is (n. 363); the interiors and exteriors of man's *spirit* (n. 492); man's *spirit* is rational in the other life only so far as it becomes so in this (n. 355); delight in heaven is such as has been the delight of man's *spirit* (n. 395); man's *spirit* is in the spiritual world (n. 76, 438); man's spiritual life depends upon his conjunction with *spirits* (n. 302); man is man by virtue of his *spirit*, not his body (n. 453); why man is governed through *spirits* (n. 296); how man is led by *spirits* (n. 441); what happens when man is withdrawn from the body (n. 440); when man's *spirit* is released it is either in his good or in his evil (n. 577); when man becomes a *spirit* he does not know that he has died (n. 461). *Spirits* associated with man are such as is his affection or love (n. 245, 292, 295); *spirits* do not flow into man from his memory (n. 298); *spirits* are not aware of the existence of the world (n. 249, 292); they cannot see natural objects (n. 582); *spirits* from other earths (n. 417 extract); *spirits* who experience heavenly joy (n. 409, 410); erroneous ideas of *spirits* in regard to heavenly happiness (n. 403, 404); *spirits* taken into heaven to be taught (n. 411); they do not commit knowledges to memory but to life, which is their memory (n. 517); they can do nothing contrary to their ruling love, and what is not in harmony with it is removed (n. 479); their memory and its cultivation (n. 469); why they are invisible and in human form (n. 453, 454); they have three degrees of interiors (n. 33); their past evils are disclosed on entering the other life (n. 462 [b]); their character known

from their ways (n. 534); they soon choose congenial companions after death (n. 450); when in the state of interiors they show what they really were in the world (n. 505); state of a *spirit* whose communication with others was cut off (n. 203); their reasoning about what is to be believed (n. 320); they exhibit innocence by presenting themselves naked (n. 280 note); their discussion of the order of life of men and animals (n. 352); they cannot approach a corpse (n. 449); certain simple *spirits* taken up into heaven (n. 268); certain *spirits* were indignant because they were unable to remember (n. 465); how they lead men (n. 441); their superiority over men (n. 576); each goes to his own society after death (n. 510); how they are clothed to enter heaven (n. 519); the *spirits* who spoke with the prophets did not know but that they were Jehovah (n. 602); their grief at the ignorance in the church in regard to the things of heaven (n. 77); subject *spirits* (n. 601, 603 extract); emissary *spirits* (n. 255); enthusiastic *spirits* (n. 249); difference between a *spirit* and a man-*spirit* (n. 552); children in heaven tempted to speak by *spirits* (n. 343). Evil *spirits* dwell in the hell that is in front (n. 311); they are associated with man for his reformation (n. 293); evil *spirits* hate men (n. 249); the delights of evil *spirits* (n. 389, 574); they suffer in the presence of heavenly delight (n. 400); when an angel looks at an evil *spirit* he swoons (n. 232); they are tortured by a breath from heaven (n. 429, 572); their punishment (n. 509); their torment (n. 573); evil *spirits* admitted to heaven temporarily (n. 18, 525); the punishment of evil *spirits* is not from the Lord but from their evil (n. 550); how evil *spirits* cast themselves into hell (Chap. 57, n. 510, 558 [b], 573); the reception of evil *spirits* in hell (n. 574); their appearance in hell (n. 584); they hide in caverns to escape the light of heaven (n. 481); their abodes in the hells (n. 586, 587); *spirits* in hell are turned toward darkness (n. 123, 151); their irrationality (n. 455); vastation of evil *spirits* (n. 551); they sometimes turn temporarily toward the quarters of heaven and perceive truths (n. 153); evil *spirits* cannot perceive falsities (n. 487); evil *spirits* cannot see good *spirits,* but the good can see the evil (n. 583); evil *spirits* seen in the light of heaven appear in the form of their own evil (n. 553); their forms are the forms of love of self and the world (n. 554); the *spirits* beneath heaven have confused notions in regard to it (n. 66); confusion caused by evil *spirits* coming among good *spirits* (n. 152); *spirits* who lead others into what is their own (n. 558 [a]); *spirits* who cause melancholy and anxiety (n. 299); *spirits* who obsessed man were natural and corporeal (n. 257); *spirits* who had loved rule in the world (n. 563); the malice and artifices of infernal *spirits* (Chap. 60, 577, 580); *spirits* who believed that knowledges would give them entrance to heaven (n. 518); those that believed that they could change their life and accept Divine truths after death (n. 527); those that had rejected the world and afflicted themselves not happy in heaven (n. 535); those that have confirmed themselves in a belief in their own powers not received into heaven (n. 10). (See Angels, World of

Spirits, Swedenborg.)

Spiritual, the things that come forth from the sun of heaven are called *spiritual* (n. 172); the *spiritual* is above and wholly distinct from the natural (n. 116); nature was created to clothe the *spiritual* (n. 102); things *spiritual* cannot be comprehended through knowledges (n. 356 extract); the difference between celestial and *spiritual* children (n. 339); difference between the *spiritual* of man and the *spiritual* of beasts (n. 435); the *spiritual* Divine and the *spiritual* of angels (n. 31); the change of the natural into *spiritual* delights (n. 488).

States of little children after death (n. 336, 345); in the Word all things that relate to space signify such things as relate to *state* (n. 197); negative and affirmative *states* toward truth (n. 356 extract); *states* after death (n. 547); *states* before and after death are the same (n. 312); *state* of the well-disposed when they first enter the other life (n. 412); the opening *state* after death lasts a few days (n. 451); in the spiritual world change of place is a change of *state* (n. 192, 193); the first *state* after death (Chap. 51, n. 493, 496, 498); the second *state* after death (Chap. 52, n. 502, 503); the separation of the evil and the good takes place in the second *state* after death (n. 511); the second *state* of the wicked (n. 508); the third *state* of man after death (Chap. 53, n. 512); some do not pass through the three preliminary *states* after death (n. 491); *state* of man in the world of spirits (n. 481); change of *state* in the world of spirits (n. 427); the world of spirits is the intermediate *state* between heaven and hell (n. 421); a man may know of

his future *state* from his ruling love
(n. 487); *state* of heaven is one of
conjunction of good and truth; *state*
of hell is one of conjunction of evil
and falsity (n. 422). Angels' changes
of *states* correspond to changes of
time and seasons (n. 155); change of
state of the angels (Chap. 17,
n. 157–159); *states* of innocence and
peace of the angels and in heaven
(Chap. 31, 32, n. 284, 289); angels'
movements are changes of *state*
(n. 192); angels know each other's
states (n. 236); reasons for changes of
state in heaven (n. 158); the *states* of
the interiors are what make heaven
(n. 17, 33); in heaven there are
changes of *state* instead of years and
days (n. 163); eternity means *state,*
not time, to angels (n. 167); holy *state*
of those listening to preaching in
heaven (n. 224).

Stomach, the spirits that cause melancholy have relation to the *stomach*
(n. 299).

Stones signify truths of faith (n. 188
note); signify divine truth (n. 534);
houses of *stone* signify what relates to
truth (n. 186 note); churches in the
spiritual kingdom are built of *stone*
(n. 223); precious *stones* in heaven
(n. 489).

Storge, the love called *storge* (n. 277).

Subject, emissary spirits called *subjects*
(n. 255); man a *subject* that will serve
as a source and container; the organs
are *subjects* of the special senses
(n. 434).

Substance, all things that exist interiorly
in man exist in forms which are *substances* (n. 418); anything that is supposed to exist apart from a *substantial*
subject is nothing (n. 434).

Sun, its correspondence (n. 1, 119);

those "that shine forth as the *sun*"
(n. 348); everything spread out under
the *sun* and that receives heat and
light from it is what is called the natural world (n. 89); all nature has its
beginning in the *sun* of the world (n.
116); the power of its heat and light
(n. 137); the natural *sun* appears to
the angels as dense darkness (n. 122,
151); the world's *sun* used as a comparison to explain the Lord's activity
(n. 139); its changelessness represents
the changelessness of the Lord (n.
158); the natural *sun* produces times
and seasons in the world; the *sun* of
heaven by its appearance marks
changes of state in heaven (n. 164);
the four quarters are determined in
each world by its *sun* (n. 141); things
in heaven come forth from the *sun* of
heaven and those on earth from the
sun of earth (n. 172); the two *suns* the
origins of the two kinds of heat (n.
567); the *sun* of heaven (Chap. 14);
the Lord as the *sun* of heaven (n. 117,
549); appearance and position of the
sun of heaven (n. 118, 159); the difference in position of the *sun* and moon
in heaven is thirty degrees (n. 146).

Swedenborg, admitted into the state of
being withdrawn from the body
(n. 440, 441); permitted to experience
resuscitation (n. 449); why he was
permitted to see and hear spiritual
things (n. 312); how he talked with
angels (n. 246); his language in talking
with angels (n. 255); he was raised up
into light by degrees (n. 130); was
elevated to the inner sphere of heaven
(n. 79); was permitted to see the extent of the uninhabited heaven (n.
419); the appearance to him of objects
in heaven (n. 174); he journeyed
through space by change of state (n.

192); was given a heavenly perception of the meaning of eternity (n. 67); entered into the angelic state (n. 234); experienced the peace of heaven (n. 284); was permitted to experience heavenly joys and delights (n. 413); often saw that angels are human forms or men when he was in his bodily senses (n. 74, 75); saw the Lord in various ways (n. 118, 121); saw an angelic society with the Lord present (n. 69); was shown how the angels have the Lord continually before their faces (n. 143); saw a whole society as one angel (n. 52); was shown the power of the angels (n. 229, 231); saw the ways to heaven and hell (n. 534); saw the forms of certain hells (n. 553); was permitted to look into the hells (n. 586); witnessed the effect of heavenly delight on evil spirits (n. 400); was taught about the correspondences in the vegetable kingdom (n. 109); saw writing and printing in heaven (n. 258); received from heaven a paper written in Hebrew (n. 260); saw children in heaven and their happiness (n. 337). Angels were permitted to enter into *Swedenborg's* natural thoughts (n. 168); he was withdrawn from the body into the society of angels (n. 46, 47), and talked with them (n. 16, 234), about the conjunction of heaven with man (n. 302), about salvation (n. 526), about their places of abode (n. 183, 184), about their form (n. 77), about the Word (n. 310), about time (n. 168), about eternal life (n. 406), about true marriage love (n. 374), about adultery (n. 385); he was taught by angels in regard to the last judgment (n. 312), in regard to Divine worship in heaven (n. 222, 223), in regard to changes of

state in heaven (n. 158); he talked with spirits as a spirit and as a man in the body (n. 436); he talked with those who had lived at various times in the past (n. 363, 480), with those who had withdrawn themselves in the world and had lived apart (n. 359, 535), with learned men in the other world (n. 354, 464), with the poor in heaven (n. 364), with spirits on the third day after their death (n. 452), with Chinese spirits (n. 325), with saints (n. 535), with spirits from other earths (n. 417 extract), with one who seemed to be Cicero (n. 322).

Symphony of angelic speech (n. 242).

Talk, to *talk* with spirits is dangerous, and therefore rarely permitted (n. 249).

Taste, the five senses (n. 402, 462).

Teaching of little children in heaven (n. 334).

Teeth, what "the gnashing of *teeth*" is (Chap. 59, n. 575); *teeth* correspond to outmost things in nature (n. 575).

Temple, represents the Divine human of the Lord (n. 187); why the *temples* of the ancients were turned toward the east (n. 119).

Temptation, state of peace after *temptation* (n. 289); *temptation* of children in heaven (n. 343); *temptation* and freedom (n. 603 extract).

Thinking, the Lord flows mediately into man's *thinking* through his willing (n. 26).

Theater, nature a *theater* representing the Lord's kingdom (n. 106).

Thought, what the term "*thought*" means (n. 500); its relation to the life (n. 526); all *thought* is from affection (n. 236, 298); it is led in accordance with the intentions (n. 532); *thought* among ancient people (n. 323); many heavenly things are expressible in ideas of natural *thought* (n. 239); extension of *thought* and affection (n. 203, 477); source of *thought* in the good and in the evil (n. 577); all that man *thinks* is from influx (n. 603 extract); *thought* without action is nothing, and is dissipated (n. 475); all things of *thought* are inscribed not only on the brain but also on the whole body (n. 463); truth that is loved enters with light into the mind's *thought* (n. 603); an invisible Divine is not an object of *thought* (n. 3). Man's *thought* from natural light (n. 170); *thoughts* of those in self-love (n. 561); natural *thought* rests upon ideas of time and space (n. 169); space does not pertain to *thought* (n. 196); examples of internal and external *thought* (n. 496); internal and external *thought* should make one by correspondence (n. 499); children have no internal *thought* (n. 277); when a man is thinking abstractedly from the body he sometimes appears in his angelic society (n. 438); spirits enter into man's *thought* (n. 292); speech of angels flows first into man's *thought* (n. 248); the natural *thought* of man is changed by angels into spiritual *thought* (n. 165); in the body man *thinks* both naturally and spiritually (n. 356); *thought* of angels is spiritual, of men, natural (n. 306); difference between natural and spiritual *thought* (n. 130, 464); how spiritual *thought* is acquired (n. 512); angels permitted to enter into Swedenborg's natural *thought* (n. 168); proper *thought* about angels (n. 183); *thought* remains after death (Chap. 48; *thought* of the spirit communicates

with the breathing (n. 446); the sharing of *thought* with angels during resuscitation (n. 449); right *thought* about God essential to entering heaven (n. 358); *thought* is represented in the other life by ways (n. 534); *thought* of angels is immeasurably superior to that of men (n. 576); *thought* is wiser in heaven (n. 462 [a]); *thought* of angels (n. 266); why angels think spiritually (n. 199); the speech of angels enters into their *thought* (n. 251); *thought* derived from heavenly love with angels is in human form (n. 460); appearance of the particulars of angels' *thought* (n. 240); objects of *thought* in the other world (n. 355); angels recognize the nature of a spirit's freedom by a communication of affection and *thought* (n. 590); every *thought* of an angel spreads forth into heaven (n. 79); language in heaven flows from affection and *thought* (n. 236); speech and *thought* coincide in the other life (n. 2, 457); writing in heaven flows naturally from *thought* (n. 262); those in the spiritual world see in *thought* those whom they desire to see (n. 194, 494); *thought* of a higher heaven never perceived by a lower (n. 210); subject spirits do not think from themselves (n. 603 extract). *Thought* apart from willing is impossible (n. 199); how *thought* and will make one (n. 372); in the second state after death man's will and *thought* make one (n. 503); *thought* may be from the understanding alone without the will (n. 424); man is such as are his will and *thought* (n. 463); thought makes the man only so far as it goes forth from the will (n. 474); *thought* is the form of the will (n. 500); to live spiritually is to think and to will (n. 432); *thought* and will are the interiors (n. 444); *thought* and will control the body (n. 453); will and *thought* are completed in works (n. 475), will and *thought* behind deeds and works determine their character (n. 472). (See Life, Perception.)

Throne, the Lord's *throne* signifies his kingdom and heaven (n. 8, 24).

Time in heaven (Chap. 18, n. 411); correspondence of *times* and seasons in heaven (n. 155); angels have no notion of *time* and space (n. 162); to angels eternity means state and *time* (n. 167); *time* that spirits stay in the world of spirits (n. 426).

Tone, angels know each other's affections by their *tone* (n. 236); angels express much by *tone* (n. 269).

Tongue of the Greatest Man (n. 96); *tongue* is caused to vibrate by angelic speech (n. 248).

Torment in hell (n. 573, 574); *torment* is permitted in the hells for the purpose of restraint (n. 581).

Transparency of objects seen in heaven corresponds to an enlightened understanding (n. 489).

Trees, their correspondence (n. 111, 176, 489, 520); in heaven *trees* bear fruit in accordance with the good of love (n. 176).

Trinity, the true idea of the *Trinity* (n. 86 extract).

Truth, wall signifies *truth* as a defense (n. 73, 307); garments of angels correspond to *truth* (n. 179); breadth means a state of *truth* (n. 197); needle's eye signifies spiritual *truth* (n. 365); man corresponds to understanding of *truth,* woman to affection for *truth* (n. 368); man means one in whom are goods and *truths* (n. 73);

truth defiled corresponds to urine (n. 488); *truth* is represented by "the stone at the dividing of the ways" (n. 534); there are three kinds of *truth,* civil, moral, and spiritual (n. 468); those in the kidneys of the Greatest Man are in *truths* searching, separating, and correcting (n. 96); all *truths* emit light (n. 132); *truths* in the light of heaven (n. 356 extract); perception of *truth* in the light of heaven (n. 481); those in heavenly love accept instruction and perceive *truths* (n. 487); *truth* is implanted in use and makes one with it in heaven (n. 517); *truths* of doctrine of the church; the comprehension of spiritual *truths* (n. 356 extract); *truth* belongs to the memory and to thought therefrom (n. 26); man has ability to acknowledge *truth* without receiving it (n. 153); *truth* that is loved enters with light into the mind's thought (n. 603); *truths* that must be learned by man (n. 351); true intelligence arises from a love for *truth* (n. 347); indulging the senses of touch and taste renders a man stupid in regard to spiritual *truth* (n. 462 [a]); unrecognized *truths* (n. 265); every *truth* has infinite extension (n. 270); reformation is effected by means of *truths* (n. 424); man's interiors are elevated by means of *truths* from the Word (n. 253); *truths* are received from others by children; *truths* must be seen from within (n. 352); *truth* is not a matter of reasoning (n. 385); mere reasoning about *truth* is not an acceptance of it (n. 518); *truth* learned from the Word is removed from those without real faith (n. 482); *truth* from self is not *truth* (n. 8); *truths* that the evil have are put away in the world of spirits

(n. 425); evil spirits become irrational by rejecting the Divine and the *truths* of the church (n. 455); the genuine rational faculty consists of *truths* and not falsities (n. 468); from *truth* anyone can perceive falsity, but not vice versa (n. 487); the equilibrium between *truth* and falsity (n. 589); for every *truth* there is an opposite falsity (n. 541); those that profane *truths* are cast into the lowest hell (n. 456); angels of the inmost heaven do not store up *truths* in the memory (n. 271); celestial angels know by influx whether the *truths* they have are true (n. 26); celestial angels do not think and speak from *truths* (n. 214 note); celestial angels see *truths* but do not talk about them (n. 225); scientists in heaven reason about *truths* (n. 464). Divine *truths* are the laws of order (n. 523); they cannot be received after death by the angels (n. 527); all things are created by means of Divine *truth* (n. 137); Divine *truth* has all power (n. 231, 232); intelligence is from Divine *truth* (n. 180); direct revelation of Divine *truth* to man is not possible (n. 309); the Word in its essence is Divine *truth* (n. 259); some knowledges give entrance to Divine *truth,* some do not (n. 356 extract); the true and false love for Divine *truth* (n. 347); beauty after death depends upon the degree of love for Divine *truth* (n. 459); Divine means are Divine *truths* (n. 522); the Lord's garments represent Divine *truths* (n. 129); the reception of Divine *truths* by angels (n. 25); Divine *truths* are inscribed on the interiors of angels of the inmost heaven (n. 270); Divine *truth* is the light of heaven (n. 117, 266, 462 [a], 549); Divine *truth* as

Divine light in the minds of angels (n. 489); the Divine is called in heaven Divine *truth* (n. 13); the Son of God from eternity was the Divine *truth* in heaven (n. 86 extract). Love to the Lord is willing and doing Divine *truth* (n. 271); all Divine *truths* are included in love to the Lord and love to the neighbor (n. 19); the Word means Divine *truth* in the Lord from the Lord (n. 137). (See Faith, Good and Truth.)

Turning, angels *turn* according to their ruling love (n. 143); the great things about *turning* to the Lord (n. 144); *turning* of evil spirits toward the quarters of heaven (n. 153); conjunction effected by *turning* (n. 255).

Understanding, its enlightenment (n. 130 note); man's *understanding* is the outgo *[existere]* of his life (n. 26 note, 474 note); the life of man's *understanding* is the life of his faith (n. 9); it is obscured and weakened by the pleasures of the appetites (n. 462 [a]); it is obscured by looking to what is one's own (n. 558 [a]); the *understanding* of children in heaven (n. 336); the transparency of objects seen in heaven correspond to an enlightened *understanding* (n. 489); the light of heaven illuminates both the sight and *understanding* (n. 127 note); angels have *understanding* from Divine truth, and their *understanding* is their inner sight (n. 128); with angels the outer sight corresponds to the inner sight or *understanding* (n. 462 [a]); those in the eye of the Greatest Man are in the *understanding* (n. 96). (See Will.)

Union, the *union* of Divine good and truth in the Lord; the *union* of the

Lord with the Father (n. 86 extract); what true marriage *union* is (n. 375).

Unity, perfect *unity* is from diversity or variety (n. 56, 405).

Universe, its creation (n. 112); all things in it have relation to good and truth (n. 137); all the planets are inhabited (n. 417); the Lord the God of the *universe* (n. 2).

Use, *use* is the end for which; it is the first and last (n. 112 note); *use* as an end in the dominion of love of the neighbor (n. 564); *uses* are goods of love and charity (n. 402); what it is to perform *uses* (n. 64); those that perform *uses* (n. 390); every general *use* is composed of innumerable mediate *uses* (n. 392); the number of *uses* in the vegetable kingdom (n. 109); *uses* take on a form in the natural world and present themselves in effect (n. 96); *uses* are everywhere present in act or effect (n. 96); every good has its delight and quality from *use* (n. 112 note); the *use* of the senses causes their delights (n. 402); everything good is good in the measure of its *use* (n. 107); the body is furnished to the spirit in order that it may perform *uses* in the world (n. 432); every part of man performs some *use* (n. 64); wisdom is loving *use* (n. 390); knowledges with *use* as an end (n. 356 extract); the Lord's kingdom is a kingdom of ends or *uses* (n. 112); *uses* in heaven (n. 361 note, 405, 517); occupation in heaven is according to the correspondence of a man's *use* (n. 394); heavenly love consists in loving *uses* for the sake of *uses* (n. 557); in heaven to perform *uses* is the delight of everyone's life (n. 219); all delights of heaven are brought together in *uses* (n. 402); the rich in heaven set their hearts on *uses* only (n. 361); heavenly societies are distinct in accordance with *use* (n. 387, 391); those who do not perform *uses* for the general good are cast out of heaven (n. 64); *uses* performed from love of self (n. 556); those that have performed *uses* for their own advantage (n. 508); spirits who had in the world looked to themselves and not to *uses* (n. 563); good and evil *uses* in the other life (n. 363); perverted *uses* in hell (n. 362); all evil spirits perform a *use* (n. 508).

Variety in heaven (n. 20 note, 56, 71, 405); *variety* or goods (n. 41, 231).

Vastation of good and evil (n. 513); *vastation* of evil spirits (n. 551).

Vipers, genii appear as *vipers* (n. 579).

Visions, why *visions* are not used to instruct men about the future life (n. 456).

Voice signifies Divine truth (n. 1); *voices* of evil spirits (n. 553).

Voluntary and intellectual (n. 32).

Vowels of angelic speech (n. 241); they express affection (n. 261).

Ways signify truths that lead to good (n. 479 note, 590); *ways* to heaven and to hell (n. 479, 534); *ways* from places of instruction to heaven (n. 520).

Wealth does not debar from heaven (n. 357); various forms of love of *wealth* (n. 575).

West, the *west* in heaven (n. 148, 149), and in hell (n. 587).

Whole, every *whole* exists from the harmony of its parts (n. 56).

Wicked, how they are cast into hell (n. 491); the *wicked* after death (n. 508).

Wife, husband and *wife* after death

(n. 368, 494); heaven and the church called *"wife"* (n. 180, 371).

Wind, angels are not *winds* (n. 183).

Will, what the term *"will"* means (n. 500); it is the *will* that makes the man (n. 474); man is such as are his *will* and thought (n. 463); the *will* is the very spiritual part of man (n. 529); the *will* is the receptacle for good or evil (n. 589); man's intention is his *will* (n. 532); the life of man's *will* is the life of his love (n. 9); everyone's lust belongs to his love, and his love to his *will* (n. 574); all that man wills is from influx (n. 603 extract); only what gains entrance into man's *will* becomes his (n. 598); in respect to his *will* man is born into every evil (n. 424); the *will* of those in genuine innocence is their memory (n. 278); a subjugated mind has either no *will* or an opposing *will* (n. 380); the *will* is kindled by love (n. 473); all things of the *will* that are in harmony with the ruling love are called loves (n. 477); man has the same *will* and love after death as before (n. 547); after death man is his own love and his own *will* (n. 479); the *will* is manifested in the looks and gestures in the other life (n. 457); the celestial kingdom is the *voluntary* part of heaven (n. 95); the activity of the *will* of evil spirits (n. 508). *Will* and understanding together make the man (n. 423); man is such as are his *will* and understanding (n. 350); all things of man's life depend upon his ability to understand and to *will* (n. 203); the *will* and understanding constitute the spiritual man (n. 26, 373); all man's power is from his *will* and understanding (n. 137, 228); whatever is felt in the body has its origin in the *will*

and understanding (n. 373); the *will* relates to good and the understanding to truth (n. 137); man is loved in accordance with the good of his *will* and of his understanding therefrom (n. 474 note); the *will* of man is the very being *(esse)* of his life and his understanding is the outgo *(existere)* (n. 61 note); man is man from his ability to understand what is true and to *will* what is good (n. 60); the *will* and understanding are ruled by the Lord (n. 228); influx into the *will* and understanding (n. 247); true innocence is of the *will* and understanding (n. 278); *will* and understanding in relation to marriage (n. 369, 370); *will* and understanding in man and woman and as husband and wife (n. 367, 368); after death man continues to be such as are his *will* and understanding (n. 474 note); the conjunction of the *will* and understanding in the world of spirits (n. 423); angels have *will* and understanding (n. 136); every angel is such as are his *will* and understanding (n. 231); all things in the interiors of the angels have relation to the *will* and understanding (n. 173); the *will* and understanding of angels are continually being perfected (n. 221). (See Life, Thought and Will.)

Willing is loving to do (n. 16); the Lord flows directly into man's *willing,* but mediately into his thinking (n. 26).

Wisdom, the part of the head that contains the cerebellum corresponds to *wisdom* (n. 251); *wisdom* compared to a palace (n. 270); *wisdom* defined (n. 148); *wisdom* is of the life (n. 348); *wisdom* is loving use (n. 390); how true *wisdom* is acquired (n. 356); knowing, acknowledging, and perceiving how little one knows is the first step toward *wisdom* (n. 280); Divine *Wisdom* in the Word (n. 310); *wisdom* is not dependent upon what is stored up in the memory (n. 464); the possibilities of *wisdom* to the human mind (n. 314, 356); *wisdom* of men who are in love to the Lord (n. 467); the degrees of man's *wisdom* (n. 267 note); *wisdom* of the ancient church (n. 322); heavenly peace is possible in men who are in true *wisdom* (n. 288); the innocence of *wisdom* (n. 279); *wisdom* indicated by Hebrew letters (n. 260); sensual men have knowledge but not *wisdom* (n. 74 note, 267). Angels called *"wisdom"* (n. 266); *wisdom* of angels (Chap. 30); the *wisdom* of angels is due to their interiors being opened (n. 267); angels can receive *wisdom* because they are without the love of self (n. 272); their *wisdom* differs (n. 275); the source of their *wisdom* (n. 169); their *wisdom* depends upon the extent to which they are in the form of heaven (n. 201); the degree of their *wisdom* (n. 208, 267); *wisdom* of angels of the different heavens (n. 25, 26, 209, 270); the hunger of angels for *wisdom* (n. 274); angels long to know and to become wise (n. 356 extract); illustration of angelic *wisdom* (n. 269); *wisdom* in the speech of angels (n. 239); angels are continually being perfected in *wisdom* and love (n. 221, 271, 469); the *wisdom* of the angels is not comparable with that of the Lord (n. 273); an angel who excels in *wisdom* instantly sees the quality of another from his face (n. 48); all things seen by angels in heaven correspond to their *wisdom* (n. 177); *wisdom* in heaven of those that have acknowl-

edged the Divine (n. 531); *wisdom* of scientists in heaven (n. 464); the comprehension of heavenly *wisdom* (n. 265); communication of *wisdom* in heaven (n. 268); *wisdom* of those in heaven who have loved the Word (n. 393); *wisdom* in the doctrines of heaven (n. 227).

Wise, the *wise* in heaven (Chap. 38); who the really *wise* are (n. 348, 350); the *wise* and simple among the heathen (n. 322).

Woman, corresponds to affection for good; was born to be affectional, that is, to think from her will (n. 368); men and *women* (n. 366, 369).

Wood signifies good; churches in the celestial kingdom are built of *wood* (n. 223); houses of *wood* signify what relates to good (n. 186 note); those that have placed merit in works appear to themselves in the other life to be cutting *wood* (n. 513 note).

Word, the *Word* serves in place of man for a foundation for heaven (n. 305, 309); it teaches spiritual good and truth (n. 512); conjunction of heaven with man by means of the *Word* (Chap. 34); man must be taught by the *Word*, and not by writings from heaven (n. 258); its dictation to the prophets (n. 254, 259); it was written after the knowledge of correspondences had been lost (n. 306); it has a spiritual sense throughout (n. 114, 150, 365); the spiritual sense of various passages (n. 307); the glorification of the Lord is everywhere treated of in the internal sense of the *Word* (n. 86 extract); there is no distinction in the angelic sense of the *Word* between Jehovah and the Lord (n. 86 extract); the sense of the letter may beget heresies (n. 311); the church where the

Word is is like the heart and lungs of a man (n. 308); mere knowledge of the *Word* and doctrines does not bring anyone into heaven (n. 518); truth learned from the *Word* is removed from those without faith (n. 482); Divine wisdom in the *Word* (n. 310); it contains all laws of Divine order (n. 202); opinions drawn from the *Word* about the rich and poor in heaven (n. 357); Swedenborg read the *Word* to spirits (n. 322); angels say that the *Word* teaches that angels are men (n. 183); good spirits are taught from the doctrines drawn from the *Word* (n. 516); the *Word* in heaven (n. 261, 393, 526). Angelic *words* express far more than human *words* (n. 239, 269). (See Correspondence.)

Works, love in act is *works* (n. 48); *works* apart from love are of death, not of life (n. 474); their real character is determined by the will and thought behind them (n. 472); *works* and deeds go forth from the love and faith (n. 474); judgment is according to *works* (n. 470, 471); *works* have their being, outgo, and quality from the interiors (n. 358 note); *works* are the exteriors or outmosts (n. 475); all *works* and deeds pertain to moral and civil life (n. 484); good *works* compared to fruit (n. 111).

World, love of the *world* (n. 154, 565); correspondence of the *world's* fieriness (n. 122); force in the natural *world* (n. 589); ignorance and false beliefs in the *world* about heaven and hell (n. 311, 312, 357), about the truly intelligent (n. 346), about heavenly joy (n. 412); the *world* is conjoined to heaven in man (n. 252); conjunction of heaven with the *world* by means of correspondences (n. 112); life of the

world (n. 318); heat and light in the *world* (n. 136); the sun produces times and seasons in the *world* (n. 164); all things of the natural *world* are material, and devoid of life (n. 432); Divine influx into the *world* apart from man (n. 112); so far as man is in good the *world* in him is subordinated to heaven and made to serve heaven (n. 57); man is formed for heaven only by means of the *world* (n. 360). Spiritual *world* flows into the natural *world* as cause into effect (n. 567); conjunction of natural and spiritual *worlds* in man (n. 112, 247); natural *world* subsists from the spiritual *world* and both from the Divine (n. 106); there can be no flowing from the natural into the spiritual *world* (n. 319); everything in the natural *world* springs from and corresponds to something in the spiritual *world* (n. 89); from the things of the natural *world* the things of the spiritual *world* may be seen as in a mirror (n. 56); the spiritual *world* appears like the natural *world* (n. 582); the Lord is in his Divine order in both *worlds* (n. 57); man is in both *worlds* (n. 304); spiritual *world* is not understood without a knowledge of correspondences (n. 88); in the spiritual *world* distances are matters of difference (n. 42); quarters are not fixed in the spiritual *world* (n. 123); in the spiritual *world* there is a complete sharing of affections (n. 552); man's condition on entering the spiritual *world* (n. 330). *World* of spirits (n. 292); what the *world* of spirits is (Chap. 44); its use (n. 420); its numbers (n. 426); its appearance and exits (n. 429, 479); its situation (n. 423, 583); the *world* of spirits and those in it are kept in equilibrium between heaven and hell (n. 540, 590); men are kept in equilibrium by means of spirits in the *world* of spirits (n. 540); the *world* of spirits serves to conjoin man with heaven and hell (n. 600); the memory is retained and laid bare in the *world* of spirits (n. 462 [b]); the conjunction of the understanding and will in the *world* of spirits (n. 423); the conjunction of good and truth and evil and falsity in man takes place in the *world* of spirits (n. 422); condition of the spirit at entrance into the *world* of spirits (n. 457, 494); treatment in the *world* of spirits (n. 427); protection in the *world* of spirits (n. 391); reception of spirits into the *world* of spirits (n. 548); spirits are explored there (n. 496); their surprise at entrance (n. 495); everyone there must be an image of his own affection or love (n. 498); all in the *world* of spirits have communication with heaven or hell (n. 294); man in the *world* of spirits is in equilibrium (n. 590); time that spirits stay in the *world* of spirits (n. 426); their exit from the *world* of spirits (n. 429). (See State.)

Worms, their instincts (n. 108).

Worship in heaven (Chap. 25, n. 221, 222, 506); variety in *worship* in the different heavenly societies (n. 56); *worship* in ancient times (n. 306); the most ancient people *worshiped* the Divine human (n. 86 extract); *worship* of the Divine in other earths (n. 321); *worship* the basis of all religion (n. 319); *worship* must be from freedom (n. 603 extract); *worship* of sun and moon (n. 122); correspondence of *worship* (n. 111).

Wrath, why *wrath* is attributed to the Lord (n. 545).

Writing in heaven (Chap. 29); it varies in the different heavens (n. 261); *written* forms in heaven (n. 260); *writing* in numbers (n. 263); erroneous views of *writing* in heaven (n. 264).

Yoke, the Lord's *yoke* and burden (n. 359).

Youth corresponds to understanding of truth (n. 368); fate of those that plunge into evils in *youth* (n. 533); spirits associated with man in *youth* (n. 295); renewed *youth* in heaven (n. 414).